JOHN F. TANNER, JR. Dr. Tanner is the research director of Baylor University's Center for Professional Selling and associate professor of Marketing. He earned his PhD from the University of Georgia. Prior to entering academia, Dr. Tanner spent eight years in industry with Rockwell International and Xerox Corporation. His experience includes new product development, strategic planning, and marketing research, as well as sales and sales management. He earned Xerox's top sales honor, President's Club, twice, was named Region Sales Representative of the Year, and received the Eagle Award.

Dr. Tanner was the first Marketing Professor of the Year at Baylor's Hankamer School of Business and was also named Outstanding Young Researcher, the school's top research honor for non-tenured faculty. His sales teaching efforts have been recognized by *Sales & Marketing Management* and the Dallas *Morning News*. He has received research grants from the Trade Show Bureau, the Institute for the Study of Business Markets, University Research Council, the Wollongong Group, and others.

Dr. Tanner has published over 20 articles in journals such as the *Journal of Marketing, Journal of Business Research, Journal of Personal Selling and Sales Management*, international journals, and others. His research has also been published by the Trade Show Bureau, the Center for Professional Selling, the Institute for the Study of Business Markets, and the United States Army. He serves on the review boards of several journals, including the *Journal of Marketing Education, Journal of Personal Selling and Sales Management*, and the *Journal of Marketing Theory and Practice*, and is the book review editor for the *Journal of Personal Selling and Sales Management*. Dr. Tanner has also written for many trade publications, including *Business Marketing, Decisions, Sales Managers' Bulletin, American Salesman*, and *Potentials in Marketing*. A nationally recognized speaker and author on issues facing the trade show industry, Dr. Tanner has presented seminars at international conventions of several trade organizations, including the International Exhibitor's Association and the Canadian Association of Exposition Managers.

Second Edition

SELLING

BUILDING PARTNERSHIPS

BARTON A. WEITZ
University of Florida

STEPHEN B. CASTLEBERRY
University of Minnesota, Duluth

JOHN F. TANNER
Baylor University

IRWIN

Chicago • Bogota • Boston • Buenos Aires • Caracas
London • Madrid • Mexico City • Toronto

© RICHARD D. IRWIN, INC., 1992 and 1995

Senior sponsoring editor: Stephen M. Patterson
Senior developmental editor: Nancy Barbour
Marketing manager: Jim Lewis
Project editor: Susan Trentacosti
Production manager: Bob Lange
Designer: Mercedes Santos
Art coordinator: Heather Burbridge
Photo research coordinator: Patricia A. Seefelt
Photo researcher: Mike Hruby
Compositor: The Clarinda Co.
Typeface: 10/12 Sabon
Printer: Von Hoffmann Press, Inc.

Library of Congress Cataloging-in-Publication Data

Weitz, Barton A.
    Selling: building partnerships/Barton A. Weitz, Stephen B. Castleberry, John F. Tanner.
        p.   cm. — (The Irwin series in marketing)
    Includes index.
    ISBN 0-256-13675-0
    1. Selling.   I. Castleberry, Stephen Bryon.   II. Tanner, John F.
    III. Title.   IV. Series.
    HF5438.25.W2933   1995
    658.85—dc20   94–10545

Printed in the United States of America

1 2 3 4 5 6 7 8 9 0 VH 1 0 9 8 7 6 5 4

To Edward Weitz, a great father and salesman.

Bart Weitz

To the precious little unborn baby we lost and miss dearly; and to the latest "partner" in our family, Elijah David.

Steve Castleberry

To those most precious: My God, my wife, my children, and my parents.

Jeff Tanner

THE IRWIN SERIES IN MARKETING

Gilbert A. Churchill, Jr., Consulting Editor
University of Wisconsin, Madison

The last few years have been an exciting time, for us as individuals and for the world at large. The response to the first edition of *Selling: Building Partnerships* has been terrific. One wonderful by-product for us has been getting to know so many teachers of selling. We've learned and shared a great deal of information; it has been thrilling!

In the world at large, we've seen major changes, such as the fragmentation of the Soviet Union, passage of NAFTA, and many other changes. The global marketplace and the information highway are becoming realities. New alliances that once seemed impossible are now commonplace; old alliances that were thought unshakable are gone. In essence, the skills of partnering are more important now than ever before.

that will be useful no matter what their occupation may become.

Another objective is to integrate material from other "theory-driven" courses. While nothing may be more practical than a good theory, students sometimes say that this is the only class in which they learned something they could use. That is unfortunate. We have strengthened our efforts to integrate material from other courses and disciplines to illustrate the application of theories in the practice of selling. Several of you have told us that you have had the same experience and found this book to be useful in integrating material. We're glad that we have been successful and hope you find this edition to do an even better job.

Our Philosophy

The skills of partnering go well beyond the arena of selling a product. Strategic alliances are important to virtually all businesses and all aspects of business. That is why we are excited to see professional selling become a required course for marketing majors at many schools, and part of the core curriculum for all business majors at a few institutions.

Our assumption, then, is not that all students of sales will become salespeople. Students in this course should learn principles of selling so well that they would have enough confidence in themselves to begin making calls if provided no additional training by their employer, even if those calls occurred in a nonselling field (for example, an accountant soliciting new business). At the same time, more students than ever before are being exposed to selling who have no plans to enter the sales profession. One of our objectives in this course is to provide sound partnering and communication skills

Partnering and Sales Education

The importance of partnering to business and partnering skills to students has changed the way sales has been taught. Several unique features place this book at the cutting edge of sales technology and partnering research:

1. A revision of the traditional selling process—approach, opening, making a presentation, demonstrating benefits, overcoming objections, and closing—into the new partnering process. The new process includes strategically planning each sales call within a larger account strategy, making the sales call, strengthening communications, responding helpfully to objections, obtaining commitment, and building partnerships.

2. A thorough description of the partnering and buying processes used by business firms and the changes occurring in these

processes. Methods of internal and external partnering to deliver total quality.

3. An emphasis throughout the text on the need for salespeople to be flexible—to adapt their strategies to customer needs and buyer social styles.

4. A complete discussion of how effective selling and career growth are achieved through planning and continual learning.

These unique content features are presented in a highly readable format, supported with examples from current sales programs and salespeople, and illustrated with four-color exhibits and photographs.

Partnering: From the Field to the Classroom

Textbooks are generally developed, reviewed, and edited by academicians. In that respect, this book is no different. We have improved the text based on feedback from users and reviewers. What is different is that *Selling: Building Partnerships* was also reviewed by sales executives and field salespeople who are locked in the daily struggle of adapting to the new realities of selling. They have told us what the field is like now, where it is going, and what students must do to be prepared for the challenges that will face them in the next century.

Students have also reviewed chapters. They are, after all, the ones who must learn from the book. We asked for their input prior to and during the revision process. And judging by their comments and suggestions, this book is effectively delivering the content.

As you can see in About the Authors, we have spent considerable time in the field in a variety of sales positions. We continue to spend time in the field, observing and serving professional salespeople. We believe the book has benefited greatly because of such a never-ending development process.

Users of the first edition will find several improvements in this edition:

- **A complete chapter devoted to the partnering process.** Chapter 2 now discusses the importance of *the partnering*

process and describes the stages that organizations go through in developing partnerships. The book still gets to the selling process quickly.

- **Expanded telephone and direct mail prospecting.** The prospecting chapter has more material concerning *writing sales letters* and *using the telephone* to gain appointments.

- **Increased emphasis on proposal writing and presentation.** *Quantifying the solution* portion has been strengthened by combining information on writing proposals into the same section. New material concerning *presenting proposals to groups* has also been added in the chapter.

- **Stronger organization of objection-handling chapter.** While the objection-handling chapter (and the obtaining commitment chapter) *retains its "no-tricks" philosophy,* the *effective overall strategy* material is now introduced early in the chapter. Common objections were organized into useful categories to enhance student learning.

- **New information on revenue growth within accounts.** The after-sale service chapter has been rewritten to emphasize partnering activities after the initial sale. Topics concerning customer service were retained, but new material on topics such as *cross-selling, full-line selling, managing change, preferred supplier status,* and other current customer sales strategies are now discussed.

- **Revised chapter on selling to resellers.** This chapter, already a favorite with reviewers, includes a discussion on the latest partnering issues in selling to resellers. Attention is focused on strategies such as *category management, efficient consumer response,* and others.

- **Stronger internal partnering chapter.** The Managing within the Company chapter *emphasizes the internal partnerships that must be formed,* with particular attention to identifying and satisfying the needs of internal partners so that external customer and salesperson needs can also be satisfied.

- **Integrated ethics material.** The chapter on ethics and legal issues is still presented early in the text so that instructors can forestall any objections about teaching unethical behaviors. But more information is presented regarding *specific ethical topics throughout the chapters*. For example, students are presented an array of choices from which salespeople can select when faced with an unethical request from their manager (in Chapter 17).

Text Features and Supplement

AN INTEGRATED TEACHING AND TESTING SYSTEM Everything in this edition of *Selling: Building Partnerships* is designed to help teachers be more effective and to help students develop skills they can use every day and in the field. Several features help both students and teachers achieve their objectives.

Profiles of field salespeople set the stage for each chapter in the text. In each profile, the salesperson discusses his or her experiences and how they relate to the material that follows. This edition finds the number of profiles greatly increased and written specifically for this text. We used recent graduates as much as possible so that they could speak directly to your students.

Each chapter begins with a series of questions that will guide the student's reading experience. In each chapter, **Selling Scenarios** present the real-life experiences of professional salespeople. Most selling scenarios are new to this edition; many were written specifically for the text. The selling scenarios are tied to the material within each chapter, reinforcing the concepts and presenting applications of selling principles.

A feature called **Thinking It Through** will help students internalize key concepts. Thinking It Through is an involving exercise that could be the start of wonderful classroom dialogue or a short essay exam question. But most important for students, reading and using Thinking It Through is a method of experiencing the concepts as they read, which increases their comprehension and retention. Based in user feedback, we have expanded the number of Thinking It Throughs.

Expanded global references now marked with a global symbol. Most chapters have at least two global references that apply the material to other cultures or settings. A prime example is the negotiations chapter.

Key Terms at the end of each chapter are followed by page references so the student can look up the definitions. The list of key terms will help students prepare for exams; the chapter references will improve their retention because they will be more likely to read supporting material, and not just a definition. You'll find many new terms, such as category management, discussed in detail in this new edition.

The **Questions and Problems** at the end of each chapter are also designed to involve the student, but in a slightly different manner. The questions are designed to: (a) review concepts and definitions, (b) require the student to apply a concept to a selling situation, or (c) start discussion during class. Therefore students will want to review the questions to study for exams, while the teacher will use the questions to stimulate classroom discussion.

Cases are also available at the end of each chapter. We have found these cases to work well as daily assignments and as frameworks for lectures, discussion, or small group practices. Some cases are tied to the videotapes, for complete integration. Many of them have been tested in our classes and have been refined based on student feedback. User favorites have been revised and updated while we have also added many new cases, some of which were provided by users.

Roleplay scenarios are also provided in the text, with various buyer roles in the Instructor's Manual. These roleplays serve two functions. First, students practice their skills in a friendly environment. They can try out their partnering skills in an environment that will encourage personal growth. Second, and this is unique, the roleplays are written to serve as minicases. Student observers will see situations that call for applications of many of the concepts and principles from the book. Both vicarious and experiential learning are enhanced for the observers. New scenarios will be available each August for adopters so role plays will always be fresh. Simply write to Bart Weitz, College of Business Administration, The University of Florida, 200 Bryan, Gainesville, FL, 32611. These roleplay scenarios have been updated in the new edition and we've included in the text an essay for students on how to prepare for roleplays.

Instructor's manuals are available with any text, but the quality often varies. Because we teach the course every semester, as well as presenting and participating in basic sales seminars in industry, we feel that we have created an **Instructor's Manual** that can significantly assist the teacher. We've also asked instructors what they would like to see in a manual. In addition to suggested course outlines, chapter outlines, lecture suggestions, answers to questions and cases, and transparencies (many that are not from exhibits in the book), we include helpful suggestions on how to use the videotapes. We also include many of the in-class exercises we have developed over the years. These have been subjected to student critique and we are confident you will find them useful. You will also find a number of additional roleplay scenarios.

Students do need to practice their selling skills in a selling environment. And they need to do it in a way that is helpful. **Small group practice exercises,** complete with instructions for student evaluations, are provided in the Instructor's Manual. These sessions can be held as part of class but are also designed for out-of-class time for teachers who want to save class time for full-length role plays.

The **Test Bank** has been carefully and completely rewritten. Questions are directly tied to the learning goals presented at the beginning of each chapter and the material covered in the Questions and Problems. In addition, key terms will be covered in the test questions. Application questions are available so students can demonstrate their understanding of the key concepts by applying those selling principles.

Teachers and students alike have been thrilled with the **Videotapes** that have been created especially for this package. Corporate training videos, Learning International's Professional Selling Skills seminar, and customized videos developed expressly for this new edition have been carefully integrated with material from the text. For example, Chapter 15 discusses a brochure that Dial used when launching a new product. The video for that chapter shows an actual Dial salesperson using the brochure. Students not only read about the brochure, they see it in use.

Each segment is short, generally under 10 minutes, with opportunities for stopping and discussing what has been viewed. Or students can watch the videos outside of class and still learn. Video information, including in-class and homework exercises, is incorporated for the teacher in the Instructor's Manual so that all can make the most of the video.

Acknowledgments

Staying current with the rapidly changing field of professional selling is a challenge. Our work has been blessed with the excellent support of reviewers, users, editors, salespeople, and students.

Reviewers who contributed greatly to the second edition are:

Dr. Brett Boyle, DePaul University

Dr. David Burns, Youngstown State University

Dr. James Decconick, University of Dayton

Dr. Donald Gehris, Bloomsburg University

Dr. Ray Hagelman, Nassau Community College

Dr. Joan Hall, Macomb Community College

Professor Rita Mix, University of North Texas

Dr. James Munch, Kent State University

Dr. Jim Porterfield, Pennsylvania State University

Dr. Robert Thompson, Indiana State University

Readers will become familiar with many of the salespeople who contributed to the development of the second edition through various selling scenarios or profiles. But other salespeople and sales executives contributed in less obvious, but no less important, ways. For providing video material, reviewing chapters, updating cases, providing material for Selling Scenarios, or other support, we'd like to thank:

Bill Arend: branch sales manager, SOS Technologies

Caralee Bradbury: manager, George's Casual and Western Wear

Tracey Brill: medical sales specialist, Bristo-Meyers Squibb/Mead Johnson Laboratories Division

Jim Bruce: district manager, Messina-Zunich Realty, Inc.

Dick Crovisier: sales manager, Central Transportation Systems

Jeffrey Ducate: account executive, San Antonio Convention and Visitor's Bureau

Pat Lynch Eaton: national account manager, Freeman Exhibit Services

Raja Farah: territory sales manager, Campbell Soup Co.

C. David Fields: executive vice president, Zellerbach

Carrie Freeman: president, Freeman Exhibit Services

Sandra Garrett: branch manager, Personnel One Temporary and Permanent Personnel

Wade Hallisey: rental agent, Rollins Truck Leasing

Eloise Haverland: director of sales training, Wallace Computer Services Inc.

Ray Hanson: branch manager, Fastenal

Jim Hersma: vice president of sales, Baxter Healthcare Corp.

Greg Hoffman: realtor, Messina-Zunich Realty, Inc.

Tia Kallas: account executive, MetroVision Advertising

George Kiebala: account executive, Direct Marketing Technology, Inc.

Sheryl L. Koehler: healthcare representative, Wallace Computer Services

Richard Langlotz: branch sales manager, Minolta Business Systems

Michelle LeBlanc: representative, Richard D. Irwin, Inc.

E. Jane Lorimer: executive director, Trade Show Bureau

Sal LoSchiavo; account manager, Motorola

Van Martin: vice president of marketing, Tribble and Stephens

Tom McCarty: manager, national training department, Motorola Communications & Electronics Inc.

Terry Michels: sales manager, Enesco Corporation

Leon Montgomery: account executive, Goodyear Tire and Rubber Co.

Phil Neri: vice-president, Dial Corporation

Bob Newzell: Sales Talk

Michael Petry: marketing representative, XL/Datacomp Inc.

Neil Rackham: Huthwaite Inc.

Jerry Robison: institutional representative, Marion Merrell Dow Pharmaceuticals

Ray Schmitz: account manager, Data Comm Networking, Inc.

Chris Suffolk: director of training, Dial Corporation

Brian Vollmert: inside sales representative, Sauber Manufacturing Co.

Marvin Wagner: quality engineer, John Deere

Trent Weaver: account executive, Health Images Inc.

Wayne B. Wilhelm: president, Computermax

Ronald Williams: director of national accounts, Champion Apparel

Ron Woodyard: district manager, Pfizer Pharmaceuticals

In addition to the support of these individuals, many companies also provided us with material. We'd like to express our sincere grattitude for their support.

Arthur Andersen

Beckman Industrial

Conductor Software

The Dial Corporation

Huthwaite Inc.

Ideal Industries

Lanier Voice Products

Learning International

Motorola
National Cinema Network
Trade Show Bureau
Wallace Computer Services

The editorial and staff support from Richard D. Irwin, Inc., was again exceptional—we really appreciate the support provided by Steve Patterson and the wonderful staff assembled for this project. We'd particularly like to thank Nancy Barbour, who kept us on time, listened to and encouraged us, and served as a creative sounding board; Mike Hruby, who located and obtained most of the photographs; our project editor, Susan Trentacosti; and Bob Lange, who coordinated the production of this edition. Nick Childers, of Arthur Scott Productions, once again delivered an excellent video package.

Several people assisted in manuscript preparation, and we gratefully appreciate their help: Kathy Brown, Margaret Jones, and Karen Tanner.

Many students and teachers have made comments that have helped us strengthen the overall package. They deserve our thanks, as do others who prefer to remain anonymous.

Bart Weitz
Steve Castleberry
Jeff Tanner

CONTENTS IN BRIEF

CONTENTS

PROLOGUE

S elling: Building Partnerships is divided into five parts. In Part I you will learn about the field of selling. This includes topics such as the nature, role, and rewards of selling and what partnering really means, as well as the legal and ethical responsibilities of salespeople.

Part II describes the fundamental skills needed to be successful as a salesperson. You will learn about the buying process, the principles for communicating effectively, and methods for adapting to the unique styles and needs of each customer.

In Part III you will explore the activities to build partnerships between buyers and sellers. After completing this section, you should have enhanced skills and understanding about prospecting, planning, discovering needs, using visual aids and conducting demonstrations effectively, responding to objections, obtaining commitment, and providing excellent after-sale service.

Special applications are covered in Part IV. You will learn about the exciting and somewhat unique role of selling to resellers.

Part V discusses the important topic of how a salesperson can improve his or her effectiveness. This includes managing your time and territory, working with your company, and managing your career.

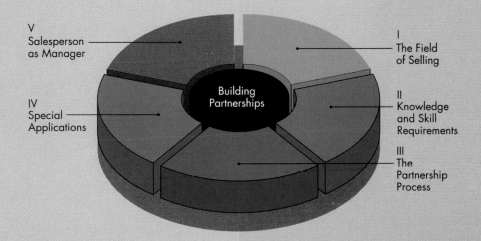

THE FIELD OF SELLING

*P*art I introduces the nature of personal selling. In Chapter 1 we define personal selling and illustrate how everyone can use skills associated with effective selling. Then the importance of selling and salespeople in business is discussed. A review of the evolution of personal selling illustrates how modern salespeople focus on developing long-term relationships—partnerships—between their firm and its customers. Finally, the activities performed by salespeople and the skills needed to be a successful salesperson are outlined.

Chapter 2 discusses the nature of the partnering relationships that salespeople build with their customers. We first examine the different types of relationships that arise between firms and their customers. Then, the evolution of these relationships over time is reviewed. Finally, we explore the role of the salesperson in this evolutionary process.

Chapter 3 focuses on ethical and legal responsibilities confronting salespeople. In the beginning of the chapter, we review some of the situations that require salespeople to make ethical choices. The development of a selling partnership is based on mutual trust and respect—both are more likely to exist when salespeople have a strong code of ethics and behave in accord with these ethical principles. After examining these ethical decisions, we discuss the laws that govern selling activities. Laws define the appropriate behavior in relationships; however, they only indicate a minimum acceptable level of conduct.

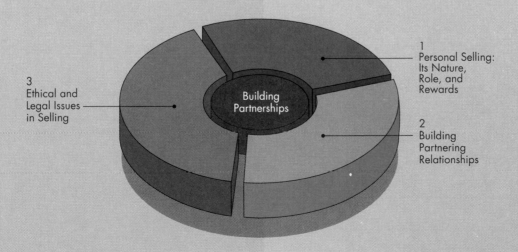

3
Ethical and
Legal Issues
in Selling

Building
Partnerships

1
Personal Selling:
Its Nature,
Role, and
Rewards

2
Building
Partnering
Relationships

Personal Selling
Its Nature, Role, and Rewards

*E*ach night Gillette merchandisers plug their palmtop computers into telephones, dial a host computer, and transmit information about retail conditions in the Pathmark supermarkets they visited during the day. Then they receive instructions about what they should do during tomorrow's store visits. The salesperson responsible for the Pathmark account reviews the information from the merchandisers to plan a presentation for the Pathmark headquarters' buyer for razors and blades. The salesperson also uses the information to provide instructions for merchandisers on future calls.[1] This scenario is not a vision of the future; it is a description of selling in today's business environment.

Businesses compete in global markets using sophisticated communication, transportation, and management information systems. In this dynamic business environment, salespeople play a vital role coordinating the resources of their firms to help customers solve problems.

This chapter discusses the importance of personal selling to business firms and discusses how the nature of selling is changing from persuading prospects to buy products to managing the firm's relationships with its customers. The chapter concludes with a description of the activities performed by salespeople, different types of selling jobs, the skills needed to be a successful salesperson, and the rewards of a sales career.

Some questions answered in this chapter are:

What is selling?

Why should you learn about selling even if you do not plan to be a salesperson?

What is the role of personal selling in a business firm?

How does selling today differ from selling in the past?

What are the different types of salespeople?

What are the rewards in a selling career?

Jane Lee began her career teaching special education in an elementary school. For the next 18 years selling was the last thing on her mind. "Sales? What did I know about sales?" she recalls thinking when an Apple representative approached her about a job selling computers to school districts. "I had never sold anything before in my life."

After a series of interviews, Lee left her job as director of technology for the Georgia Department of Education and joined Apple Computer. Although she was apprehensive about giving up her position, she was intrigued because of her experience with Apple computers. "I would never have considered leaving to sell textbooks, but I used Apples and knew what they could do for education."

She changed jobs because she felt selling would be both personally and financially rewarding. "I knew it would be a challenging job for me and that I could do a great deal for education. I even thought I could accomplish more because I'd be out of a big state bureaucracy."

Lee was confident about her ability to understand and work with computers, but she wasn't sure she could sell them. "I had been told I had people skills, and I knew the product because I used it. But I didn't know much about selling." She was so naive, in fact, that she was caught off guard when her manager asked her to estimate her next month's sales. The only reply she could make was, "How should I know?"

But Lee quickly learned how to sell. After only one year at Apple, she ranked third in sales at the company

J A N E   L E E

Apple Computer

and was earning three times more than in her previous job. Lee credits much of her success to her sales managers and the "Apple environment," which she says is short on red tape and long on trust. "There aren't a lot of restraints put on you here." Her background, of course, was another big plus. For the most part, she calls on administrators and school board members, most of whom have the same training in education that she does. "I was in their position, so I really know their needs."

There are, of course, drawbacks to the job. Lee often works nights and weekends, and she no longer has much one-on-one contact with students. Still, she says taking the job was a "great" decision. Along with the financial rewards, there is the satisfaction in knowing that she is making a difference.

Recently she was promoted to manager of special education in the marketing department, where she will help market computers designed to help disabled students. "I've seen what computers can do for people." Lee was talking about a young man with a severe muscle disorder who learned to operate a computer and communicate with the outside world for the first time. "A lot of people thought he was mentally disabled, but as it turned out, he is intellectually gifted. Now he's able to go to school and sit in class with other students. That's what this job is all about."

Source: Adapted from Bill Kelley, "Ideal Selling Jobs," *Sales and Marketing Management,* December 1988, p. 31.

WHY LEARN ABOUT PERSONAL SELLING?

Personal selling is defined as an *interpersonal communication process by which a seller uncovers and satisfies the needs of a buyer to the mutual, long-term benefit of both parties.* This definition stresses that selling is more than making a sale and getting an order. The objective is to build a relationship—a partnership—by providing long-term benefits to both the seller and the customer. Thus, selling involves helping customers identify problems, offering information about potential solutions, and providing after-the-sale service to ensure long-term satisfaction. Influence and persuasion are only one part of selling.

EVERYONE SELLS

This text discusses personal selling as a business activity undertaken by salespeople. But the principles of selling are useful to everyone in business and nonprofit organizations, not just those people with the title of *salesperson.* Influencing people and developing mutually beneficial, long-term relationships are vital to all of us. Thus, the principles of selling are useful even if you do not plan to work as a salesperson.

THINKING IT THROUGH	*T*hink of an instance during the last month when you tried to influence someone but you were unsuccessful. What was your objective? What approach did you use? Why did you fail in your influence attempt? How would you handle the situation differently if you had it to do over again?

As a college student, you might use selling techniques to convince your professor that your paper was not graded correctly. When you near graduation, you will confront a more important sales job: selling yourself to an employer.

To get a job after graduation, you will go through the same steps used in the sales process (discussed in Part III, Chapters 7 through 12). First, you will identify some potential employers. Based on an analysis of each employer's needs, you will develop a presentation to demonstrate your ability to satisfy those needs. During the interview, you will listen to what the recruiter says, ask and answer questions, and perhaps alter your presentation based on the new information you receive during the interview. At some point, you might negotiate with the employer over starting salary. Eventually, you will try to secure a commitment from the employer to hire you. This is selling at a very personal level.

Because of its importance to all areas of business and life, many people study selling even though they do not plan a career in sales. They realize that everyone in business uses selling principles every day. Accountants "sell" new cost-control programs to production managers to gain their co-operation; engineers "sell" research budgets to management; industrial relations executives use selling approaches when negotiating with unions; and aspiring management trainees sell themselves to associates, superiors, and subordinates.

People in nonbusiness situations also practice the art of selling. Presidents encourage politicians in Congress to support their programs, charities solicit contributions and volunteers to run their organizations, and doctors encourage their patients to adopt healthier lifestyles. People skilled at influencing others and developing long-term relationships are usually leaders in our society.

THE ROLE OF SALESPEOPLE IN BUSINESSES

IMPORTANCE OF SALESPEOPLE IN BUSINESSES

Even if you are not interested in becoming a salesperson, you need to know what salespeople do and how they do it, because salespeople play a critical role in the performance of businesses. Selling Scenario 1.1 describes how everyone sells at Kiwi International.

Salespeople are involved in many activities undertaken by firms. Marketing activities are classified into the four elements of the **marketing mix**— product, price, place (distribution), and promotion. These elements are shown in Exhibit 1.1.

E X H I B I T   1 . 1

SALESPEOPLE AND THE MARKETING MIX

Product

Place

Price

Promotion

SELLING SCENARIO

1.1

Everyone Sells at Kiwi International

The bankruptcy of Eastern, Pan Am, and Midway airlines left a lot of pilots and flight attendants out of work and a lot of planes available for lease. In 1992, Bob Iverson, a former Eastern and Pan Am pilot, formed Kiwi International by getting pilots and other workers to contribute $10 million. Naming the airline after a small, flightless bird once reminded the owner-operators that they, too, were unable to fly.

The company has only seven marketing and sales representatives to call on the 7,000 travel agents in the United States, so everyone associated with Kiwi has their job responsibility—and they have their sales responsibilities: "Selling is considered a point of honor here."

All employees are assigned 10 travel agents near their home. "Our business comes from the little guy on the corner," says Maxine Krill, director of sales administration, "so we want our employees to become friends with their local agents and give them whatever help they can."

Kiwi periodically launches "sales blitzes" in its key markets: Newark, Atlanta, Orlando, and Chicago. As many as 15 pairs of Kiwi employees—pilots, flight attendants, executives, and mechanics—fly into a target market and spend two or three days calling on agents. When Kiwi pilots walk into an agency, they really get the customer's attention: "Most travel agents have never met a pilot and they are really impressed."

Source: Adapted from Joe Brancatelli, "On a Wing and a Sale," *Selling*, November 1993, pp. 43–47.

Product

Product includes decisions about what products, features, accessories, warranties, and services to offer to customers in the firm's target market. These decisions are based on an analysis of customers' needs.

Salespeople contribute to the development of new products. They are in a unique position to observe what customers are doing with products and the problems they are having. As they interact with many different customers, salespeople can see when customers have similar problems and can provide this market research information to their companies. Selling Scenario 1.2 describes how Ballard Medical Products salespeople work with hospitals and engineers in their company to develop products for improving medical care.

Price

Price is the amount that customers are required to spend to acquire the product and services. Pricing decisions, including special discount and purchasing terms and conditions, are based on the value of the products and services to customers.

Salespeople are often involved in pricing decisions. They negotiate with customers about special design features that can be added to the product and the price the customer will pay.

Everyone can benefit from learning the principles of selling from young entrepreneurs starting a business to adults earning millions by playing a game.

 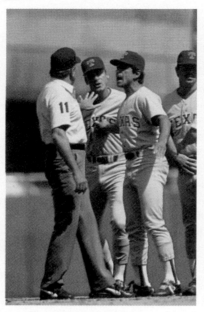 

Palmer-Kane/TSW.   Ronald C. Modra/Sports Illustrated.   Courtesy ARA Services.

Place

Place is the activities involved in making the firm's products available to customers. For example, customers are able to buy Gillette razors, blades, and toiletries in over 500,000 locations in the United States. In contrast, when Boeing is interested in buying Pratt & Whitney jet engines, it must contact Pratt & Whitney in Connecticut directly or through one of Pratt & Whitney's sales offices.

Salespeople are an important part of the firm's place or distribution programs. For example, Apple salespeople might select electronics retailers to sell Macintosh computers and help retailers decide on the number and models of computers to be stocked and how they will be displayed. Then an Apple salesperson trains the retailers' salespeople on the features of the computers and how these features provide benefits to computer users.

Promotion

Promotion is the firm's efforts to communicate with customers about the firm's products and where and how they can be bought, and to influence customers to buy the products. Messages are sent to customers through impersonal media such as television, radio, magazine, and newspaper advertising and through personal selling.

Many people think—incorrectly—that advertising is the most important part of the firm's promotion program. However, industrial companies place far more emphasis on personal selling than on advertising.[2] Even in consumer products firms such as Lever Brothers, which spends over $1 billion

SELLING SCENARIO

1.2

Better Health Care through Selling

Ballard Medical Products is a small manufacturer of medical products that are sold to hospitals. Ballard uses its 35 salespeople to gather market intelligence and provide ideas for new products. The salespeople find their work interesting and satisfying because they help create and improve the products they sell.

For example, Bob Meyer, a salesperson working for a Ballard distributor, was demonstrating Trach Care, a product used with patients on respirators. A surgeon participating in the demonstration commented that he could not tell if he was using the product correctly because of an opaque tube. Based on Meyer's call to the vice president of engineering at Ballard, the product was redesigned, substituting a clear tube for the opaque tube.

Most manufacturers of disposable products, such as Trach Care, give hospitals free samples. But Bal-lard makes hospitals buy a 30-day supply for evaluation and insists that the hospital let Ballard salespeople instruct every nurse on how to use the product. In addition to helping the nurses use the product correctly, the training sessions give Ballard salespeople an opportunity to establish an intelligence-gathering outpost inside the hospital. After completing the training, the salespeople know the names and faces of the hospital nurses. They can walk through the hospital, see how Trach Care is being used, and chat with the nurses. Problems and new ideas surface naturally during these casual conversations.

Source: Adapted from Tom Richards, "Seducing the Customer—Dale Ballard's Perfect Selling Machine," *Inc.*, April 1988, pp. 96–98. Copyright April 1990. Reprinted by permission.

annually on advertising, personal selling still plays a critical role. Although advertising informs customers about Lever Brothers' products, salespeople make sure the products are available and properly displayed in retail stores. All marketing people at Lever Brothers spend considerable time in the field with salespeople, learning about the needs of the retail stores as well as those of consumers.

Salespeople are a vital link between the company and its customers. As you can see from the discussion above, their participation in the firm's marketing activities goes beyond simply telling customers about the firm' products and services.

Salespeople are problem solvers in the business world. Consider their importance in improving the business efficiency of a railroad with problems in scheduling its operations. At the railroad's request, IBM assigned four salespeople to study the problem. They spent three years examining every operation of the railroad—riding the lines, working in the dispatcher's office, and inspecting the switch yards.

Based on their analysis, IBM designed and installed a $13.5 million computer-controlled communication system to run the train system. Then the salespeople trained the railroad staff to use the system. Before the system was installed, only 10 percent of the railroad's cars were in use at any time because dispatchers could not locate them. Now the dispatchers can tell where every car is.

A Lever Brothers salesperson works with retailers to make sure his products are properly displayed so both Lever Brothers and the retailer will be more profitable.

Courtesy Lever Brothers Company; photo by Harry O. Wilks.

EVOLUTION OF PERSONAL SELLING

Exhibit 1.2 illustrates how the nature of business and the role of salespeople have evolved through four stages over the last hundred years.[3]

Production Era

Prior to 1930, demand for products exceeded supply. Competition was limited. Manufacturers focused on making products. They had little concern for buyers' needs and developing products to satisfy those needs. For example, Henry Ford made one car, the Model T, in one color, black. The role of salespeople in this **production era** was relegated to taking orders.

Sales Era

After the stock market crash in 1929, the sellers' market shifted to a buyers' market. There were not enough customers to buy all of the products manufactured. Competition between manufacturers increased significantly.

During this **sales era,** the role of the salesperson was to create demand for products. To persuade customers that they needed a supplier's products, salespeople relied on aggressive selling techniques. The salesperson's job was to coax customers to buy their products even if the customers did not want or need them.

Marketing Era

During the late 1950s and the 1960s, the marketing concept emerged as a response to increased customer sophistication and competition. The **marketing concept** is a business philosophy emphasizing that the key to business success is satisfying customer needs. Under this philosophy, all employees, not just marketers, should orient themselves toward satisfying customer

EXHIBIT 1.2

EVOLUTION OF PERSONAL
SELLING

Era	Production	Sales	Marketing	Partnering
Time period	Before 1930	1930 to 1960	1960 to 1990	After 1990
Objective	Making sales	Making sales	Satisfying customer needs	Building relationships
Orientation	Short-term seller needs	Short-term seller needs	Short-term customer needs	Long-term customer and seller needs
Role of salesperson	Provider	Persuader	Problem solver	Value creator
Activities of salespeople	Taking orders, delivering goods	Aggressively convincing buyers to buy products	Matching available offerings to buyer needs	Creating new alternatives, matching buyer needs with seller capabilities

needs. During this **marketing era** engineers designed products customers wanted, not products that were challenging to design. Production built products that customers needed, not products that were easy to manufacture. Salespeople became problem solvers. They were responsible for identifying the customer's needs and demonstrating how their products would satisfy those needs.

Selling became much more complex. Salespeople had to develop greater product knowledge and better communication skills. Firms began to use specialized sales forces. For example, some computer manufacturers had separate sales forces calling on financial services, retailing, manufacturing, and government customers.

In the marketing era, salespeople often were responsible for employing all of their company's resources to solve a customer's problem. For example, an AT&T account executive managed a team of 80 people, including experts in accounting, finance, engineering, and marketing, to make sure that Merrill Lynch's needs for telecommunication services were being satisfied.

Partnering Era

In the early 1990s, both sellers and buyers recognized that they could develop strategic advantages over their competitors by working together. Rather than treating suppliers as interchangeable parts, manufacturers developed close, long-term relationships with a few suppliers. By freely exchanging sensitive information, the suppliers could develop products specifically tailored to the manufacturer's needs, which resulted in the ultimate need satisfaction.[4]

SELLING SCENARIO

1.3

The Evolution of a Sales Force

When Franklin Green became the sales manager for the Fiber Glass Reinforcement Division of PPG Industries, he described the sales force as "a group of order takers and goodwill ambassadors." The sales force was still in the production era. Green immediately moved the sales force into the sales era by developing a plan for scheduling sales calls on customers and teaching salespeople to use time-management techniques.

The transformation into problem solvers, associated with the marketing era, started when salespeople were trained to recognize how changing technology would create new needs for their customers. Salespeople were required to interview customers and develop work plans outlining these needs.

PPG entered the partnering stage when sales teams were developed to work with each customer. The teams worked with each customer's development staff to create and test products designed for the customer's applications. Green sums up the role of the salesperson as a value creator: "The pivotal function of the sales organization is to exercise leadership with, and on behalf of, the customer. If the overall organization was to be truly customer driven, the sales force had to assume this vital role."

Source: Kevin Sullivan, Richard Bobbe, and Martin Strasmore, "Transforming the Salesforce in a Mature Industry," *Management Review*, June 1988, pp. 46–49. Copyright June 1988. Reprinted by permission.

In the **partnering era,** the salesperson has become a value creator. Salespeople work with the customer and their company to develop solutions that enhance the profits of both firms. In this capacity, salespeople have two roles. First, they must develop an understanding of each customer's needs and convince the customer that their firm has the capabilities to satisfy those needs. Then, they must go back to their company and arrange for internal employees to create an offering tailored to the customer's needs.

Raymond Catledge, CEO of Union Camp, emphasizes this point. "Good salespeople do much more than talk with customers. One of the toughest jobs salespeople have is to sell their own company. It's their job to articulate their customers' needs in a way their company can satisfy them."[5] (In Chapter 17, we discuss internal selling in more detail.)

Selling in the partnering era is directed toward developing long-term relationships with customers. These relationships are similar to marriages. They involve commitments by both parties to work together in a mutually beneficial manner. The parties focus on long-term outcomes and do not quibble about short-term problems.

Although each of the eras in Exhibit 1.2 is associated with a time period, all of the various roles for salespeople still exist. For example, inbound telephone salespeople working for direct-mail catalog retailers like Lands End or Spiegel are providers. They answer an 800-number and simply take orders. Many outbound telephone, automobile, and insurance salespeople are persuaders. They use high-pressure selling techniques to get prospects to place orders. Selling Scenario 1.3 illustrates how one sales organization evolved through all four stages in 10 years.

The concept of developing partnering relationships is stressed throughout this textbook. However, Chapter 2 focuses on the nature and development of partnering relationships, and Chapter 13 reviews the activities of salespeople in growing these relationships.

WHAT DO SALESPEOPLE DO?

The activities of salespeople depend on the type of selling job they choose. The responsibilities of salespeople selling steam turbines for Westinghouse differ greatly from those of people selling pharmaceuticals for Upjohn or paper products for Scott Paper. But certain basic activities are common to all types of selling, regardless of the product or the company. In addition to face-to-face and telephone contact with customers, all salespeople have to undertake servicing, reporting, and internal selling activities.

SELLING

Sales jobs involve prospecting for new customers, increasing sales to existing customers, making sales presentations, demonstrating products, negotiating price and delivery terms, and writing orders. But these sales-generating activities (discussed in Chapters 7 through 12) are only part of the job. Exhibit 1.3 shows how salespeople spend their time. On average, they work over nine hours a day; many work through lunch. However, only 33 percent of their time is spent in face-to-face contact with existing customers. An additional 16 percent goes to prospecting for new customers and working with existing customers by phone. The rest of their time is spent in meetings selling internally, traveling, waiting for a sales interview, doing paperwork, and servicing customers.

A Parker salesperson discusses the performance of the valves he sold for use in an SIPA automated production system. By providing this after-the-sale customer service, the salesperson builds a partnering relationship with the production manager.

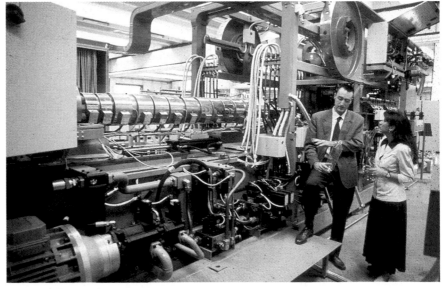

Courtesy Parker Hannifin Corporation.

EXHIBIT 1.3

HOW SALESPEOPLE SPEND THEIR TIME

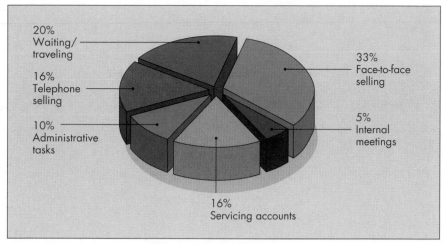

- 20% Waiting/traveling
- 16% Telephone selling
- 10% Administrative tasks
- 33% Face-to-face selling
- 5% Internal meetings
- 16% Servicing accounts

Source: William O'Connell and William Keenan, Jr., "The Shape of Things to Come," *Sales & Marketing Management,* January 1990, p. 39. Copyright January 1990. Reprinted by permission.

SERVICING CUSTOMERS

The salesperson's job does not end when the customer places an order. Sales representatives must make sure that customers get the benefits they are expecting from the product. Thus, salespeople work with other company employees to make sure that deliveries are made on time, equipment is properly installed, operators are trained to use the equipment, and questions or complaints are resolved quickly. Providing these services is critical to developing partnerships, the long-term objective of selling. (Chapter 13 focuses on developing partnerships through customer services.)

Selling and servicing customers can be very challenging in less developed countries where many customers are difficult to reach. For example, Sabritas, Mexico's largest snack-food company, has an extensive distribution system to reach customers in isolated mountain and jungle villages. Salespeople drive specially equipped vans to make weekly calls on these remote villages. They often sleep in their vans or in customers' stores. Salespeople reach villages in the lake region by canoe and ride donkeys into some mountain villages.[6]

INTERNAL SELLING

Salespeople also spend time in meetings, coordinating the activities of their firms to solve customer problems. Dick Holder, now the president of Reynolds Metal Company, spent five years "selling" Campbell Soup Company on using aluminum cans for its tomato juice products. He coordinated a team of graphic designers, marketing people, and engineers to educate Campbell about a packaging material it had never used before.[7] Approaches for improving your efficiency in performing these nonselling activities are discussed in Chapter 16.

REPORTING

In their reporting activities, salespeople provide information to their firms about expenses, calls made, future calls scheduled, sales forecasts, competitive activities, business conditions, and unsatisfied customer needs. For example, at Flexatard, a manufacturer of fitness bodywear, the sales force is the eyes and ears of the company. Salespeople provide information on customer reactions to changing fashions, new styles introduced by competitors, and designs the company is thinking about offering.[8]

The next section describes the basic types of sales positions. These positions differ in terms of the time spent on the various activities outlined above.

TYPES OF SALESPEOPLE

Almost everyone is familiar with people who sell products and services to consumers in retail outlets. Behind these **retail salespeople** is an army of salespeople working for commercial firms. Consider a VCR that you might purchase in a store. To make the VCR, the manufacturer bought processed material, such as plastic and electronic components, from salespeople. In addition, capital equipment was purchased from other salespeople to mold the plastic, assemble the components, and test the VCR. Finally, the VCR manufacturer bought services such as an employment agency to hire people and an accounting firm to audit the company's financial statements. The manufacturer's salespeople then sold the VCRs to a wholesaler. The wholesaler purchased transportation services and warehouse space from other salespeople. Then the wholesaler's salespeople sold the VCRs to a retailer.

SELLING AND DISTRIBUTION CHANNELS

As the VCR example shows, salespeople work for different types of firms and call on different types of customers. These differences in sales positions come from the many roles of salespeople in a firm's channel of distribution. A **distribution channel** is a set of people and organizations responsible for the flow of products and services from the producer to the ultimate user. Exhibit 1.4 shows the principal types of distribution channels used for business-to-business and consumer products. Looking at the exhibit, you can see the varied roles salespeople play.

Business-to-Business Products Channels

The two main channels for manufacturers of business-to-business, or industrial, products are (1) direct sales to a business customer and (2) sales through distributors. In the direct channel, salespeople working for the manufacturer call directly on other manufacturers. For example, USX salespeople sell steel directly to automobile manufacturers, and salespeople with Dow Chemical sell plastics directly to toy manufacturers.

In the distributor channel, the manufacturer employs salespeople to sell to distributors. These salespeople are referred to as **trade salespeople,** because they sell to firms that resell the products rather than using them within their firms. Distributor salespeople sell products made by a number of manufacturers to businesses. For example, some Motorola salespeople sell microprocessors to distributors such as Arrow Electronics, and Arrow salespeople then resell the microprocessors and other electronic components to

EXHIBIT 1.4

SALES JOBS AND THE
DISTRIBUTION CHANNEL

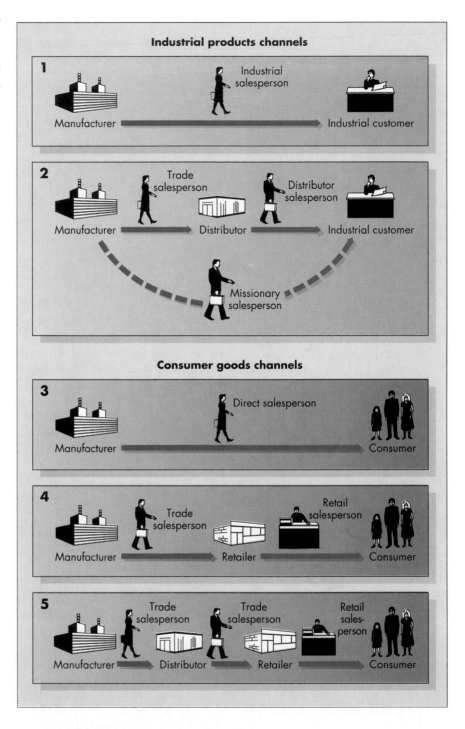

customers such as Digital Equipment. Chapter 15 focuses on the special issues confronting trade salespeople.

Many firms use more than one channel of distribution and, thus, employ several types of salespeople. For example, Motorola, USX, and Dow Chemical have trade salespeople calling on distributors and direct salespeople calling on large companies.

In the second business-to-business channel (see Exhibit 1.4), a missionary salesperson is shown. **Missionary salespeople** work for a manufacturer and promote the manufacturer's products to other firms. But those firms buy the products from distributors or other manufacturers, *not* directly from the salesperson's firm. For example, sales representatives for Driltech, a manufacturer of mining equipment, call on mine owners to promote their products. But the mines place orders for a drill with the local Driltech distributor, not Driltech directly. Normally, missionary and local distributor salespeople work together to build relationships with customers.

Frequently, missionary salespeople call on people who influence a buying decision but do not actually place the order. For example, Du Pont sales representatives call on clothing designers to encourage them to design garments made with nylon, and Syntex sales representatives call on physicians to encourage them to prescribe Syntex pharmaceutical products.

Consumer Products Channels

The remaining channels shown in Exhibit 1.4 are used by manufacturers of consumer products. The third channel shows a firm, such as State Farm Insurance, whose salespeople sell insurance directly to consumers. The fourth and fifth channels show manufacturers that employ trade salespeople to sell to either retailers or distributors. For example, Revlon uses the fourth channel when its salespeople sell directly to Wal-Mart. However, Revlon uses the fifth channel to sell to small owner-operated retailers through distributors.

Some of the salespeople shown in Exhibit 1.4 may be manufacturers' agents. **Manufacturers' agents** are independent businesspeople who are paid a commission by a manufacturer for all products or services sold. Unlike distributors and retailers, agents never own the products. They simply perform the selling activities and then transmit the orders to the manufacturers.

▌ DESCRIBING SALES JOBS

Descriptions of sales jobs focus on certain factors:

1. The customer's relationship to the salesperson's firm.
2. The salesperson's duties.
3. The importance of the purchase decision to the customer.
4. Where the salesperson contacts the customer.
5. The products/services sold.
6. The role the salesperson plays in securing a commitment from the customer.

Customer–Firm Relationship: New or Continuing?

Some sales jobs emphasize finding and selling to new customers. Selling to prospects requires different skills than selling to existing customers. To convince prospects to purchase a product they have never used before, salespeople need to be especially self-confident and aggressive. They must be able to deal with the inevitable rejections that occur when making initial contacts with potential customers. On the other hand, salespeople responsible for existing customers place more emphasis on building relationships and servicing customers than on selling to them.

Duties: Taking Orders or Creating Alternatives?

Some sales jobs focus primarily on taking orders. The salespeople are providers (see Exhibit 1.2). For example, most Frito-Lay salespeople go to grocery stores, check the stock, and prepare an order for the store manager to sign.

However, some Frito-Lay salespeople sell only to buyers in the headquarters of supermarket chains. These salespeople are value creators, and require a much higher level of skill and creativity to do their job effectively. They work with buyers to develop new systems and methods to increase the retailer's sales and profits.

The Buying Decision: How Crucial Is It to the Customer?

Consumers and businesses make many purchase decisions each year. Some are important to them, such as purchasing a home or a telephone system. Others are less crucial, such as buying candy or cleaning supplies.

Sales jobs involving important decisions for customers differ greatly from sales jobs involving minor decisions. Consider the company that needs a computer-controlled drill press. Buying the drill press is a big decision. The drill press sales representative needs to be knowledgeable about the customer's needs and the features of drill presses. The salesperson will have to interact with a number of different people involved in the purchase decision.

Contact Location: Field or Inside Sales?

Field salespeople spend considerable time in the customer's place of business, communicating with the customer face to face. **Inside salespeople** work at their employer's location and typically communicate with customers by telephone or letter.

Field selling typically is more demanding than is inside selling, because of the more intense interactions with customers. Field salespeople are more involved in problem solving with customers, whereas inside salespeople often respond to customer-initiated requests.

Products or Services: Tangible versus Intangible Benefits

The nature of the benefits provided by products and services affects the nature of the sales job. Products such as chemicals and trucks typically have tangible benefits—customers can objectively measure a chemical's purity and a truck's payload. The benefits of services, such as business insurance or investment opportunities, are typically intangible—customers cannot easily see how the insurance company handles claims, or objectively measure the riskiness of an investment.

Tangible benefits are easier to demonstrate and sell than intangible benefits. Customers can evaluate the benefits demonstrated by the Radio Shack computer salesperson on the left easier than the benefits of mutual funds sold by the stockbroker on the right.

Courtesy Tandy Corporation.

Bruce Ayers/TSW

Intangible benefits are harder to sell than are tangible benefits, because it is difficult to demonstrate intangible benefits to customers. It is much easier to show a customer the payload of a truck than the benefits of carrying insurance.[9]

Securing Customer Commitment: The Salesperson's Role

Sales jobs differ by the types of commitments sought and the manner in which they are obtained. For example, the Du Pont missionary salesperson encouraging clothing designers to use Du Pont synthetic fibers might ask the designer to make a commitment to use the fiber, but does not undertake the more difficult task of asking the designer to place an order. If the designer decides to use nylon fabric in a dress, the order for nylon will be secured by the salesperson calling on a company that makes the fabric.

THINKING IT THROUGH	Which of the selling activities just described do you think you would be good at doing? Why do you think you would be effective in those activities and not in others? Which would you like to do? Why?

EXHIBIT 1.5

THE CREATIVITY LEVEL OF
SALES JOBS

Factors in Sales Jobs	Lower Creativity	Higher Creativity
Nature of customer. Does the salesperson contact predominately:	Present customers?	New prospects?
Nature of salesperson's duties. Is the emphasis of the salesperson's duties on:	Servicing customers?	Persuading customers?
Importance of buying decision. To the customer, is the buying decision:	Not very important?	Very important?
Location of selling activity. Do the salesperson's selling activities take place:	Inside the company?	In the field?
Nature of salesperson's duties. Do the products or services sold by the salesperson have:	Tangible benefits?	Intangible benefits?
Closing skills. Is the level of skills required to gain commitment:	Low?	High?

THE SALES JOBS CONTINUUM

In Exhibit 1.5, the factors discussed above are used to illustrate the continuum of sales jobs in terms of creativity. Sales jobs described by the responses in the right-hand column require salespeople to go into the field and call on new customers who make important buying decisions. These selling assignments emphasize selling to new customers rather than building relations with old customers, promoting products or services with intangible benefits, and/or gaining commitments from customers. These types of sales jobs require the most creativity and skill and, consequently, offer the highest pay. In the next section, the responsibilities of specific types of salespeople are examined in more detail.

EXAMPLES OF SALES JOBS

JCPenney Retail Salesperson

JCPenney salespeople sell to customers who come into their store. In many cases, the customers know what they want; the salesperson just rings up the sale. However, JCPenney, like most department stores, is upgrading their salespeople from order takers to relationship builders. They are encouraging salespeople to keep customer books, notify customers of new merchandise, and make special appointments with key customers to present merchandise selected to meet their needs.

Carnation Packaged Goods Salesperson

Carnation salespeople increase the sales of their firm's products by influencing retailers and distributors to stock their brands and then by servicing them. Typically, most Carnation salespeople service existing customers rather than finding new ones. They typically make regularly scheduled calls on customers in an assigned territory. Some of the responsibilities of a Carnation trade salesperson are:

1. Convincing the retailer to buy and display all Carnation products in its stores.

2. Making sure that the retailer has enough stock displayed on shelves and stored in the back room so that an out-of-stock condition will not arise.
3. Counting stock and preparing orders for the store manager if inventories are low.
4. Checking to see that Carnation products are priced competitively.
5. Trying to get Carnation's products displayed on a shelf so that consumers can see them easily.
6. Encouraging managers to develop special displays for Carnation products and helping them build the display.
7. Convincing store managers to feature Carnation products in advertising and to place in-store ads and signs to promote the sale of Carnation products.

Smithkline Pharmaceutical Salesperson

Salespeople who represent the classic example of missionary sales work for pharmaceutical companies such as Smithkline. The Smithkline salespeople provide information on their products to physicians, pharmacists, and other people licensed to provide medical services in their territory. Typically, they make four to eight calls on doctors and three to six calls on pharmacists each day, usually without an appointment.

The salespeople spend 10 to 15 minutes with doctors on each call. Their presentations include accurate information about the symptoms for which a pharmaceutical is effective, how effective it is, and what side effects might occur. Doctors consider these presentations an important source of information about new products.

Colgate salesperson engages in missionary selling when presenting the benefits of a product to a Latin American dentist. The salesperson realizes the dentist will never place an order, but she attempts to get the dentist to recommend the product to his patients.

Courtesy Colgate-Palmolive Company.

Hewlett-Packard Computer Salesperson

Some of the most challenging sales jobs involve selling capital goods. Hewlett-Packard salespeople sell computers used to control manufacturing processes. Because these capital-equipment purchases are made infrequently, Hewlett-Packard salespeople often approach new customers. The selling task requires working with customers who are making a major investment and are involved in an important buying decision. Many people are involved in this sort of purchase decision. Hewlett-Packard salespeople need to demonstrate both immediate, tangible benefits and future, intangible benefits.

In the next section, the skills required to be effective in the sales positions discussed above are reviewed.

CHARACTERISTICS OF SUCCESSFUL SALESPEOPLE

For the last 75 years, many people have written books and articles about the determinants of success in sales. After all of this research, no one has identified the profile for the perfect salesperson because sales jobs are so different. As the job descriptions in the previous section show, the characteristics and skills needed for success when selling for Carnation differ from those needed for success when selling for Hewlett-Packard.

In addition, customers are all different. Some like to interact with an aggressive salesperson, whereas others are turned off by aggressive behavior. Some are all business and want formal relationships with salespeople, whereas others look forward to chatting with salespeople in an informal way. Thus, the stereotype of the hard-driving, back-slapping sales personality will not succeed with all customers.[10] No magic selling formula works in all sales jobs or with all customers.

Although no one personality profile exists for the ideal salesperson, successful salespeople are hard workers and smart workers. They are highly motivated, dependable, ethical, knowledgeable, good communicators, and flexible.

MOTIVATION

Most salespeople work in the field without direct supervision. Under these conditions, they may be tempted to get up late, take long lunch breaks, and stop work early. But successful salespeople do not succumb to these temptations. They are "self-starters" who do not need the fear inspired by a glaring supervisor to get them going in the morning or to keep them working hard all day.

Spending long hours on the job is not enough. Salespeople must use their time efficiently. They need to maximize the time spent in contacting customers and minimize the time spent in traveling and waiting for customers. To do this, salespeople must organize and plan their work (a subject discussed in more detail in Chapter 16).

Finally, successful salespeople are motivated to learn as well as work hard. They must continually work at improving their skills by analyzing their past performance and using their mistakes as learning opportunities.

S E L L I N G   S C E N A R I O

1.4

A Salesperson You Can Count On

Leo Kelly is a senior sales executive in Xerox's business systems group. In the 20 years he has worked for Xerox, he has been a member of the President's Club (the award given to top salespeople) 17 times.

Kelly takes an entrepreneurial approach to his sales territory. "Any assignment I'm given, whether it's [defined] by geography or by industry, I run as though it's my own business and try to maximize the potential."

After-sale support is key to Kelly's success. "I'll be there after the sale because if I've sold something to someone, I can sell them more . . . You see me as much after the sale as you do before the sale." His after-sale support keeps competitors out of his accounts. "I want to be sure that my competitor doesn't . . . get past the reception area, because I try to be a problem solver in every area. If something goes wrong with a Xerox machine, it affects everybody, and I value everybody in the company I'm doing business with. I try to eliminate their being negative toward me or my products."

Source: Adapted from Leslie Brennan, "Sales Secrets of Incentive Stars," *Sales & Marketing Management*, April 1990, pp. 88–98.

DEPENDABILITY

In some selling, such as used-car sales, the salesperson rarely deals with the same customer twice. However, this book deals with business-to-business selling situations in which the customer and salesperson have a continuing relationship—a partnership. Such salespeople are interested not just in what the customers will buy this time, but also in getting orders in the years to come. Selling Scenario 1.4 describes how a top Xerox salesperson builds long-term relationships by providing after-sales support for his customers.

Customers develop long-term relationships only with salespeople who are dependable and trustworthy. When salespeople say the equipment will perform in a certain way, they had better make sure the equipment performs that way! If it doesn't, the customer will never rely on them again. (Chapter 2 focuses on the development of long-term relationships with customers.)

ETHICAL SALES BEHAVIOR

Honesty and integrity are important parts of dependability. In the long run, customers will know whom they can trust. Good ethics is good business. (Ethical sales behavior is such an important topic that Chapter 3 is devoted to it.)

CUSTOMER AND PRODUCT KNOWLEDGE

Effective salespeople need to know how businesses make purchase decisions and how individuals evaluate product alternatives. In addition, they need product knowledge—how their products work and how the products' features are related to the benefits that customers are seeking. (Information about the buying process is reviewed in Chapter 4 and product knowledge is discussed in Chapter 6.)

Salesperson selling animal health products explains how a new product can help an Argentine cattle farmer treat his infected cows. Salespeople need to have excellent product knowledge to help customers solve their problems.

Courtesy PFIZER Inc.

COMMUNICATION SKILLS

The key to practicing the marketing concept is being responsive to a customer's needs. To do that, the salesperson needs to be a good communicator. But talking is not enough; you have to listen to what the customer says, ask questions that uncover problems and needs, and pay attention to the responses.

To compete in world markets, salespeople need to learn how to communicate in international markets. For example, business is conducted differently in Europe than in the United States. In the United States, business transactions generally proceed at a rapid pace, whereas Europeans take more time reaching decisions. European customers place more emphasis on the rapport developed with a salesperson, whereas US firms look more at the size and reputation of the salesperson's company. Because Europeans want to do business with salespeople they like and trust, they spend more time building a close personal relationship.[11] (Chapter 5 is devoted to developing communication skills, with considerable emphasis placed on communicating in other cultures.)

FLEXIBILITY

Adapt sales style to situation

The successful salesperson also realizes that the same sales approach does not work with all customers—it must be adapted to each selling situation. The salesperson must be sensitive to what is happening and flexible enough to make those adaptations during the sales presentation.[12]

Donald Trump, the real estate developer, emphasized the importance of flexibility: "Great salespeople truly understand the people they are dealing with. They know when to take a low-key approach, when to be more assertive, or when to sell with pizazz. Flexibility is the key. The biggest mistake you make is to sell the same way with all people."[13]

The importance of flexibility is illustrated by the costs and effects of personal selling versus impersonal communication modes, such as advertising. Personal selling is the most costly method for communicating with customers. It costs less than $\frac{1}{10}$ of a cent to communicate with a customer through a TV ad, about 1 cent through a print ad, $1 through direct mail, $10 through a telephone sales call, and more than $200 through a personal (face-to-face) sales call.

Why do companies spend money on personal selling when it is so expensive? The higher cost is justified by its greater effectiveness. Personal selling works better than any other communication vehicle because salespeople are able to develop a unique message for each customer. Salespeople can do "market research" on each customer by asking questions and listening carefully. They then use this information to develop and deliver a sales presentation tailored to the needs and beliefs of each customer. In addition, salespeople can observe verbal and nonverbal behaviors (body language) in their customers and, in response, adjust their presentation. If the customer is uninterested in the contents of the presentation or turned off by the salesperson's style, the salesperson can make changes quickly.

In contrast, advertising messages are tailored toward the typical customer in a segment, and thus are not ideally suited to many of the customers who may see the ad. Advertisers are also limited in how fast they can make adjustments. Salespeople can adjust on the spot, but it might takes months to determine that a advertisement is not working and then develop a new one.

Only personal selling provides the opportunity to be truly adaptive in making presentations. Consequently, selling effectiveness hinges on the salesperson's ability to practice adaptive selling and exploit this unique opportunity. (Adaptive selling is treated in detail in Chapter 6.)

ARE SALESPEOPLE BORN OR MADE?[14]

On the basis of the above discussion, you can see that the skills required to be a successful salesperson can be learned. People can learn to work hard, to plan their time, and to adapt their sales approach to their customers' needs. Research has shown that innate characteristics such as personality traits, gender, and height are largely unrelated to sales performance. In fact, companies show their faith in their ability to teach sales skills by spending over $10 billion each year on training programs. The next section discusses the rewards you can realize if you develop the skills required for sales success.

REWARDS IN SELLING

Personal selling offers interesting and rewarding career opportunities. Presently more than 7 million people in the United States work in sales positions. The US Department of Labor lists nontechnical sales as 1 of the 40 occupations with the highest anticipated growth rates in the 90s.[15] Sales positions are challenging, exciting, and financially rewarding. They can provide the base for promotion to management positions in a firm or for launching a new business.

EXHIBIT 1.6   AVERAGE ANNUAL COMPENSATION OF SALESPEOPLE

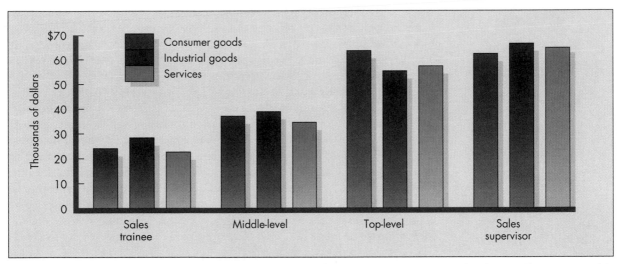

Source: "1991 Survey of Selling Cost," *Sales & Marketing Management*, February 26, 1991, p. 46. Copyright February 26, 1991. Reprinted by permission

INDEPENDENCE AND RESPONSIBILITY

Many people do not want to spend long hours behind a desk, doing the same thing every day. They prefer to be outside, moving around, meeting people, and working on different problems. Selling ideally suits people with these interests. The typical salesperson interacts with dozens of people daily. Most of these contacts involve challenging, new experiences.

Selling also offers unusual freedom and flexibility. It is not a nine-to-five job. Most salespeople decide how to spend their time; they do not have to report in. They have the freedom to determine what they do during a day, to decide what customers to call on and when to do paperwork. Long hours might be required on some days and other days may bring fewer demands.

Because of this freedom, salespeople are like independent entrepreneurs. They have a territory to manage and few restrictions on how to do it. They are responsible for the sales and profits generated by the territory. Thus, their success or failure rests largely on their own skills and efforts.

FINANCIAL REWARDS

The financial rewards of selling depend on the level of skill and sophistication needed to do the job. For example, salespeople who sell to businesses typically are paid more than are retail salespeople, because the buying process in businesses is more complex and difficult to manage. Exhibit 1.6 shows average 1992 salaries, including base salary, commissions, and bonuses, for salespeople at different levels.

Such salary averages can be very misleading. People in sales often make over $100,000 a year; some make over $1 million. Occasionally, the top salespeople in a firm will make more than the chief executive officer (CEO) of the firm.

However, many salespeople find selling to be personally as well as financially rewarding. The Profile at the beginning of this chapter describes the rewards that a teacher realized when she began selling Apple computers.

MANAGEMENT OPPORTUNITIES

Selling jobs provide a firm base for launching a business career. A study of senior managers reported that 28 percent of the presidents of the 1,000 largest US companies had marketing experience.[15] Corporate executives clearly recognize the importance of selling experience. Frank Cary, former chairman of the board of IBM, advised those who aspire to top jobs at IBM: "It's hard to find a better start than sales because you get thrown in contact with a great variety of situations and problems to solve. So I would recommend the sales track to anybody."[17]

Although selling can launch corporate careers, many entrepreneurs also work in sales before starting their own companies. For example, after a divorce left her on her own, Mary Kay Ash supported herself and her three small children by selling cleaning supplies at in-home demonstrations. She went on to start Mary Kay Cosmetics, now an international cosmetics firm with annual sales over $5 billion dollars. Ross Perot began his career selling computers for IBM. He started his own computer system management firm, EDS, which he eventually sold to General Motors, and, during his 1992 campaign for the U.S. presidency, received the most votes of any third-party candidate in history.

Even though selling offers opportunities for advancement, many salespeople promoted to management positions later return to selling. Ed Nunn sold for Enerpac Group, a Wisconsin tool manufacturer, for six years, and was offered the position of national sales manager—at a $10,000 pay cut. Everyone told him, "Oh, Ed, you gotta take it; it's good for your career." At first he liked training salespeople and working in the field with them. But as time passed, the administrative work, the meetings, and being tied to a schedule made him long to return to selling. One morning he realized the managerial life was not for him: "I was standing in an office getting chewed out because I came in at 8:20 instead of 8:00. I looked at my boss and said, 'What difference does it make? Sometimes I'm here till seven or eight at night.' And he said, 'But Ed, no one sees you then.' . . . I've never been big on details or hanging around the factory [office] for show. I want to be out doing something." So Nunn quit and went to work for another company as a salesperson.[18]

SUMMARY

In summary, you should study personal selling because we all use selling techniques. If you want to work in business, you need to know about selling because salespeople play a vital role in business activities. Finally, you might be interested in taking a job in selling. Selling jobs are inherently interesting because of the variety of people encountered and activities undertaken. In addition, selling offers opportunities for financial rewards and promotions.

This chapter considers the nature of personal selling, its role in the operations of a company, the roles and characteristics of successful salespeople, and the opportunities and rewards of a selling career.

As businesses move from the production era to the partnering era, the role of the salesperson in the organization changes. In the production era, salespeople were order takers. Then their role shifted to persuading customers to buy products in the sales era. Salespeople became more customer oriented with the advent of the marketing era and the adoption of the marketing concept as a business philosophy.

Now, salespeople are becoming relationship managers as businesses move into the partnering era.

Salespeople engage in a wide range of activities, including providing information on products and services to customers and employees within their firm. Most of us are not aware of many of these activities because the salespeople they meet most frequently work in retail stores. However, the most exciting and challenging sales positions are in business-to-business selling.

The specific duties and responsibilities of salespeople depend on the type of selling position; however, most salespeople engage in other tasks in addition to influencing customers. These tasks include managing customer relations, working with other people in their firms, reporting on activities in their territory, and traveling.

Sales jobs can be classified by the roles played by salespeople and their firms in the channel of distribution. The nature of the selling job is affected by whom salespeople work for and whether they sell to manufacturers, distributors, or retailers. Other factors affecting the nature of selling jobs are the customer's relationship to the salesperson's firm, the salesperson's duties, the importance of the buying decision to the customer, the place where the selling occurs, the tangibility of the benefits considered by the customer, and the degree to which the salesperson seeks a commitment from customers.

Research on the characteristics of effective salespeople indicates that many different personality types can be successful in sales. However, successful salespeople do share some common characteristics: They are highly motivated, dependable, ethical, knowledgeable, good communicators, and flexible.

KEY TERMS

distribution channel   *16*

field salespeople   *19*

inside salespeople   *19*

manufacturers' agents   *18*

marketing concept   *11*

marketing era   *12*

marketing mix   *7*

missionary salesperson   *18*

partnering era   *13*

personal selling   *6*

production era   *11*

retail salesperson   *16*

sales era   *11*

trade salesperson   *16*

QUESTIONS AND PROBLEMS

1. Linda Sanchez worked her way through college by selling in a local department store. She has done well on the job and is one of the top salespeople in the jewelry department. Last week, Linda was offered a job with Procter & Gamble (P&G) in trade selling. After training, she will be responsible for selling P&G products to small, owner-operated grocery stores. Tell her what the differences are between selling in a department store and her P&G sales job.

2. What are similarities and differences between teaching and selling?

3. How do you think the training programs for a sales position differ in a stock brokerage and a capital equipment manufacturer (e.g., General Electric robotics division)? Consider the programs in terms of length and content.

4. Would society benefit if large insurance companies decided to eliminate all of their salespeople and sell insurance through the mail, at a lower price to the customer?

5. Discuss the following myths about selling:
   a. Salespeople do not serve a useful role in society.
   b. Salespeople are born, not made.
   c. Selling is just a bag of tricks.
   d. A salesperson should never take no for an answer.
   e. A good salesperson can sell anything to anybody.

6. Many people have a negative impression of salespeople and careers in selling. Why do you think this negative opinion exists?

7. What rewards does a selling career offer?

8. Assume you are a sales manager and you need to recruit someone for the sales positions listed below. For each position, list the qualities you would want in the recruit.
   a. New-car salesperson.
   b. College textbook salesperson.
   c. Used-car salesperson.
   d. Salesperson selling laundry detergent to supermarkets.

9. Some outstanding salespeople are poor sales managers. Why? Compare and contrast the skills needed in sales with those needed in sales management.

10. Do you think that going to college helps a person become a more effective salesperson? Why or why not?

CASE PROBLEMS

CASE 1 • 1
CAL HERNANDEZ
CONTEMPLATES A SALES
CAREER

Cal Hernandez is a sophomore at Piedmont Junior College. He is talking with a group of friends about his selling course.

JOAN KELLY   Why are you taking that selling course?

CAL   Well, I've been thinking about what I would like to do when I graduate. I thought I'd like to go into sales. So I took the course to see what it was all about. Frankly, I am really excited about the course.

SALLY KEMP   But you've spent two years in college. Some of my friends went to work as salespeople in our local department store after graduation. You don't need a college education to be a salesperson.

CAL   I think there are a lot of sales jobs that do require a college degree. Maybe some of the jobs are different than selling in a department store.

SALLY KEMP   Selling is a real dog-eat-dog business. I don't think I'm aggressive enough to hack it in sales.

JOAN   But you sure wouldn't get bored. You meet new people all the time. Each sales call is different. I can see why Cal is excited about the course.

CAL   But I can't keep a poker face. And I blush whenever I try to hide the truth. How can I succeed in sales if I'm so transparent?

JOAN   I don't know. I think you could learn to control your feelings more with experience.

SALLY   How about the workload? You'd be on the road all the time, with no time for family life.

JOAN   At least you'd have an exciting job. Who wants a nine-to-five job sitting behind a desk? And think of all those weekday afternoons that you can take off and go sailing!

CAL   My parents are really against my going into sales. They say that people don't respect salespeople.

QUESTIONS

1. How would you reply to each statement made by Cal and his friends?
2. What could you tell Cal Hernandez to help him understand his friends' and parents' views on selling?

CASE 1 • 2
SONIA BRADLEY APPLIES
FOR A SALES JOB

Sonia Bradley is a senior at the University of Florida, majoring in marketing. Sonia has always been very interested in helping less fortunate people. Before enrolling at the university, she did volunteer work at a local hospital in Tampa. While attending the university, she has continued to do volunteer work in a homeless shelter.

Last summer she had an internship with Eckerd, a large retail drug store chain. She worked for a buyer who placed orders with pharmaceutical companies for prescription and nonprescription pharmaceuticals. Occasionally, the buyer would let her sit in on the meetings with salespeople from the pharmaceutical companies, but most of the time she did work analyzing sales patterns in the various stores.

Based on her internship experience, Sonia did some research about selling jobs with pharmaceutical companies. She read articles about the various companies and reviewed information in the Career Resource Center. She learned that the salespeople in large metropolitan areas, like Tampa, do very little overnight traveling. Each day they call on physicians in their territory, and also work on teams calling on the large hospitals in the district. The companies provide a car and pay for all travel expenses. The starting salaries are about $25,000 a year, with the potential for earning a bonus based on performance.

She interviewed with three pharmaceutical companies on campus, and Smithkline Beckman invited her for a second interview in Philadelphia. During the on-campus interview, Sonia found out that most of Smithkline's sales representatives had pharmacy degrees. Even though she does not have a pharmacy degree, Sonia feels she has the skills Smithkline is looking for. She has good grades, has been an officer in her sorority, and is active in the American Marketing Association student chapter on campus. Because she passed the initial interview, she feels that the pharmacy degree must not be necessary to get the job.

Sonia is preparing for her trip to Philadelphia and wants to make the most out of this opportunity.

QUESTIONS

1. What should Sonia do to prepare for her upcoming interview?
2. What kind of questions will the interviewers probably ask her? How should she answer these questions?
3. What should she do if someone emphasizes that a pharmacy degree is really necessary for this job?

ADDITIONAL REFERENCES

Blustain, Harvey. "From Hot Boxes to Open Systems: The Changing World of Computer Salespeople." *Journal of Personal Selling and Sales Management,* Spring 1922, pp. 67–73.

Ingram, Thomas; Charles Schwepker; and Don Hutson. "Why Salespeople Fail." *Industrial Marketing Management* 21 (August 1992), pp. 225–30.

Keenan, William, Jr.; and Martin Everett. "Put the Salesperson in Control." *Sales & Marketing Management,* May 1992, pp. 48–53.

Kelley, Bill. "Selling in a Man's World." *Sales & Marketing Management,* January 1991, pp. 28–35.

————. "Bucking the Snake Oil Syndrome." *Sales & Marketing Management,* October 1991, pp. 87–92.

Moncrief, William; Shannon Shipp; Charles Lamb; and David Cravens. "Examining the Roles of Telemarketing in Selling Strategy." *Journal of Personal Selling and Sales Management,* Summer 1989, pp. 1–12.

Powers, Thomas; William Koehler; and Warren Martin. "Selling from 1900 to 1949: A Historical Perspective." *Journal of Personal Selling and Sales Management,* November 1988, pp. 11–21.

Powers, Thomas; Warren Martin; H Rushing; and S Daniels. "Selling before 1900: A Historical Perspective." *Journal of Personal Selling and Sales Management,* Fall 1987, pp. 1–7.

Schul, Patrick; and Brent Wren. "The Emerging Role of Women in Industrial Selling: A Decade of Change." *Journal of Marketing* 56 (July 1992), pp. 38–54.

Sellers, Patricia. "How to Remake Your Sales Force." *Fortune,* May 4, 1992, pp. 98–103.

Swenson, Michael; William Swinyard; Fredrick Langrehr; and Scott Smith. "The Appeal of Personal Selling as a Career: A Decade Later." *Journal of Personal Selling and Sales Management,* Winter 1993, pp. 51–64.

Visanathan, Madhubalan; and Eric Olson. "The Implementation of Business Strategy: Implications for the Sales Function." *Journal of Personal Selling and Sales Management,* Winter 1993, pp. 34–50.

Wedell, Al; and Dave Hempeck. "Sales Force Automation: Here and Now." *Journal of Personal Selling and Sales Management,* August 1987, pp. 11–16.

Weilbaker, Dan; and Nancy Merritt. "Attracting Graduates to Sales Positions: The Role of Recruiter Knowledge." *Journal of Personal Selling and Sales Management,* Fall 1992, pp. 50–58.

Younger, Sandra Millers. "Savvy Selling in the Nineties." *Training & Development,* December 1992, pp. 13–17.

Building Partnering Relationships

P aul Baron, vice president of sales and marketing for Quaker Oats, emphasizes the changing nature of the selling environment. "The complexity of the sale has intensified tremendously in the last five or ten years. There's no longer a homogeneous sale. Every single sales event is an event itself. It's no longer just a product and a program. Now it's starting to be a product, the financial package around it, and how you can deliver."[1]

To cope with this complex and dynamic environment, buyers are demanding higher levels of service and product quality from fewer suppliers. Companies are looking for partners to help them gain an advantage over their competitors.[2] For example, IBM entered into a partnership with Microsoft to develop the DOS operating system used in its first generation personal computers.

In the first chapter we briefly discussed how the role of salespeople is changing as firms enter the partnering era. In this chapter we will explore in more depth the nature of relationship building in the partnering era. We begin by examining the different types of exchange relationships that salespeople are involved in. Then we review the characteristics of successful buyer-seller relationships. The chapter concludes with a review of how relationships develop over time and the activities of salespeople in relationship development. The specific activities salespeople engage in to develop and maintain good relationships with customers are discussed in more detail in Chapter 13.

Some questions answered in this chapter are:

What are the different types of relationships buyers and sellers have?
What are the characteristics of successful partnerships?
What are the benefits and risks in partnering relationships?
How do relationships develop over time?
What are the new responsibilities of salespeople in the partnering era?

"It's been my experience that many times a company buys from the *person* and not necessarily the company she represents," says Nancy Henderson. She feels that this is the result of her personal integrity in building relationships and has followed this philosophy in her 13-year career in professional sales. At ADP, she sells services and software to banks, who in turn sell her products to the bank's corporate customers as part of a total package for managing the corporation's cash and related assets. "My focus is always to deliver a reliable service and a total package. I work with the banks to customize our product so that it best fits their needs."

NANCY HENDERSON

ADP Financial Services

Henderson views her relationships in the industry as never short-term or one-time-only. "I always treat people as if our relationship is going to be long-term. This means being honest right from the start and never overselling my product. Customers respect me for this and trust me." Because she has worked for more than one company in the industry, she has found that the value of these relationships has remained even after she switched jobs.

Because Henderson sells a product that banks resell to their customers, she has to work very closely with her clients so they don't end up disappointing their customers. "In essence, my reputation becomes the bank's reputation. If I make a promise to them, they rely on it. They make commitments to their customers based on what I say. If it doesn't work, the bank associates are the ones in trouble. This demonstrates how essential it is for us to work closely at every step. It's imperative that there is open communication and mutual trust." In fact, she has such a good relationship with one of her banking customers that they asked if they could give her business cards with her name and the bank's name imprinted on them!

Another example of the trust she has established with her customers is the story she tells about one of her recent sales. "I worked for several months with a customer to sell a particular service. In the end they selected my service not only because of the benefits and flexibility it offered but also because they trusted me to provide continuous after-sale service. They weren't sure that the other vendors would stick with them after the sale was made. But the most amazing example of how strong our relationship was when, at the end of the entire selling process, the customer remarked that he had never seen a demonstration of the product. He had relied upon me to be the expert. And he had trusted me completely when it came to the product's capabilities."

To build that trust with her clients, Henderson is very careful to make only commitments that she can fulfill. Often this means developing an implementation plan with the customer. The plan not only ensures that customers know what their responsibilities are, but also makes commitments on behalf of ADP for when the product will be ready. "I've learned that you have to be honest and detailed and to clearly represent the amount of work that needs to be done by both parties. A relationship can be ruined if halfway through the project it's discovered that there is more work than anyone expected."

Henderson finds these partnerships a very satisfying aspect of her selling career. "The aspect of building relationships as part of the sales effort is important to me because I like to see other people succeed."

Types of Relationships

Each time a transaction occurs between a buyer and a seller, the buyer and the seller have a relationship. Some relationships may involve many transactions and last for years; others may only exist for the few minutes during which the exchange of goods for money is made.

In this section, we will describe four basic relationship types and their distinguishing characteristics. These relationships include one-time market transactions, and three types of long-term relationships: functional relationships, relational partnerships, and strategic partnerships.[3] The last two types of long-term relationships are called **partnerships** because in these types of relationships the buyer and seller have an ongoing, mutually beneficial relationship, with each party having concern for the other party's well-being. The characteristics of these relationship types are summarized in Exhibit 2.1.

One-Time Market Transactions

A one-time **market exchange** is a short-term transaction between a buyer and a seller who do not expect to be involved in future transactions with each other. For example, suppose you are driving on a highway to Florida for a spring vacation. The generator light in your car comes on. You stop at the next gas station and the service attendant says that you need a new generator for your car. The generator will cost $250, including installation. At this point, you might pay the quoted price, bargain with the service attendant for a lower price, or drive to another service station a block away and get a second opinion. After you select a service station, agree on a price, have the generator replaced, and pay for the service, you have completed a one-time market transaction. Neither you nor the service station expect to engage in future transactions.

This service attendant engages in a market transaction with a customer traveling on a highway. The customer and attendant do not anticipate interacting in the future, so they pursue their own short-term, self-interests during the interaction.

Courtesy Amoco Corporation.

E X H I B I T   2 . 1   TYPES OF RELATIONSHIPS BETWEEN BUYERS AND SELLERS

	Type of Relationship			
Factors Involved in the Relationship	**One-Time Market Transaction**	**Functional Relationship**	**Relational Partnership**	**Strategic Partnership**
Time horizon	Short term	Long term	Long term	Long term
Concern for other party	Low	Low	Medium	High
Trust	Low	Low	High	High
Investments in the relationship	Low	Low	Low	High
Nature of the relationship	Conflict, bargaining	Cooperation	Accommodation	Coordination

Price is the critical issue in market transactions. It serves as a rapid means of communicating the bases for the exchange. Because the parties in the transaction do not intend to do business together again, both the buyer and the seller in a market exchange pursue their own self-interests. In the example above, you try to pay the lowest price for the generator and the service station tries to charge the highest price for it. The service station is not concerned about your welfare, just as you are not concerned about the service station's welfare.

Market exchanges typically occur when buyers feel that the products offered by sellers are basically the same. The exchange involves a commodity product, and thus price is the critical decision factor.

Market transactions offer buyers and sellers a lot of flexibility. Buyers and sellers are not locked into a continuing relationship, and thus buyers can switch from one supplier to another to make the best possible deal. However, these minimal relationships do not work well when buyers want to exchange information and develop products that are tailored to their needs. This more complex transaction can not be conducted solely on the basis of price. Partnerships are needed to manage these types of transactions.

LONG-TERM RELATIONSHIPS

One-time market transactions represent a small portion of the relationships between buyers and sellers. Most transactions between buyers and sellers involve long-term relationships. The three types of long-term relationships shown in Exhibit 2.1 differ with respect to purpose, scope of activities, and level of investments made into the relationship.

Functional Relationships

Functional relationships are a series of one-time market exchanges linked together over time. They differ from market exchanges in that buyers find it easier to buy repeatedly from the same supplier rather than search for a new supplier every time an item is needed. However, the buyers and sellers in market exchanges and functional partnerships have the same orientation.[4]

Both parties are interested exclusively in their own profits and are unconcerned about the welfare of the other party. Basically, the buyer and the salesperson are always negotiating on how to "split up the pie"—who is going to make more in the transaction. Thus, a functional relationship is a **win-lose relationship,** because when one party gets a larger portion of the pie, the other party gets a smaller portion.

Neither the buyers nor the sellers in a functional relationship have any commitment to the relationship over the long term. Essentially, the buyer and seller work together to make sure that the exchange goes smoothly—the price is quoted, the order is received, products are delivered on time, and the payment for the products is made promptly—so that the relationship will be maintained.

Functional partnerships are very common in business. For example, a NYNEX buyer purchases office supplies—paper, file folders, pens, and pencils—for the company. However, the buyer and the office supply distributor have little interest in working closely together. The relationship between the buyer and distributor's salesperson is not critical to NYNEX's survival as a corporation. The purchase and sale of office supplies is a routine process. The buyer has the flexibility to buy from another distributor. However, the buyer probably won't go to another supplier unless some problems arise. Thus, the salesperson's job in a functional relationship is to make sure that these problems do not arise.

Functional relationships are common when the products bought are well defined and do not have a major impact on the company's performance. These type of transactions can be made without a lot of interpersonal interaction. Frequently, telephone salespeople are used to solicit orders in these types of relationships. When buyers require special services or information, personal relationships with salespeople become more important and the need for partnerships grows.

Relational Partnerships

Relational partnerships are long-term business relationships in which the buyer and salesperson have a close, trusting interpersonal relationship. As the founder of the country's largest department store chain, James Cash Penney once said, "All great businesses are built on friendship."

The buyers and salespeople in relational partnerships have higher levels of trust and longer time-span orientations than do people involved in functional relationships. They are concerned about each other's welfare, and want to work to develop programs that will be mutually beneficial.

Relational partnerships are essentially "good business" relationships. In market exchanges and functional relationships, the theme is bargaining to make the most money one can. People involved in relational partnerships believe that caring about the person, your partner, makes good economic sense.

The benefits of a relational partnership go beyond simple monetary rewards. Although both partners are striving to make money in the relationship, they are also trying to build a working relationship that will last for a long time.

This feed salesperson has developed a functional relationship with the farmer. The farmer trusts the salesperson to recommend the appropriate feed for his pigs. He knows that the salesperson is concerned about his farm when he makes his recommendations.

Courtesy Merck & Co.

For example, Bill Stack, manager of the Eastern Communication Region for General Electric's Information Services in Louisville, Kentucky, reports:

We had a client who was a vice president when his company became involved in a leveraged buyout. He was forced out of his job. Our sales rep actually carried the guy's resume around for months trying to help him connect with another job. Eventually, our client wound up with a small pharmaceutical company that was about to place an order with another vendor. He flew to the home office in London, stopped the order, and gave it to our sales rep strictly on the basis of their relationship and our past performance. That sale wound up being worth close to half a million dollars.[5]

Strong personal relationships are important in functional partnerships. These personal relationships lead to a cooperative climate between a salesperson and the customer. When both partners feel safe and stable in the relationship, open and honest communication can take place. The salesperson and buyer are interested in working together to solve problems. They are not concerned about little details because they trust each enough to know that these will be worked out.

Firms that want to build functional partnerships with their customers are very concerned about their reputation. They want to generate sales over the long term. Thus, they emphasize the reliability and quality of their products and salespeople. They are willing to be flexible when dealing with their customers.

In this chapter, we have been talking about business relationships, but these concepts also apply to personal relationships. A functional relationship is like an acquaintance whom you run into frequently, and a relational partnership is like a close friendship.

In a close friendship, you don't sit down every day to figure out whether you got your fair share from the relationship; you have confidence that over the long run the favors and support provided by the relationship will even out. You trust your friend to care about you, and trust you in return. You are not very concerned with how the "pie is split up" each day, because you are confident that, over the long run, each of you will get a fair share.

Lee has a strategic partnership with Hoechst Celanese, its fiber supplier. Hoechst Celanese invested in R&D to develop a fiber that enables Lee to make better-fitting jeans. Lee sells more jeans and Hoechst Celanese sells more fibers.

Courtesy Hoechst Celanese Corporation.

The relational partnerships, like close personal relationships, can be very rewarding. However, there are some costs and risks in these relationships. The partners have to make short-term sacrifices. For example, a buyer might be willing to wait longer for the delivery of some components because the buyer recognizes that the partner (the supplier) is having trouble with some new equipment. The buyer accepts the late delivery, trusting that the supplier will return the favor. For example, next year there might be a shortage of the components. The supplier will help its partner (the buyer) out and make sure that the buyer gets all of the components needed.

The development of mutual trust in a relational partnership provides a stepping stone to strategic partnership—the highest level of long-term relationships.

Strategic Partnerships

highest level

Strategic partnerships are the long-term business relationships in which the partners make significant investments to improve the profitability of both parties in the relationship. In these relationships, the partners have gone beyond trusting each other to putting their money where their mouths are. They have taken risks to expand the pie—to give the partnership a strategic advantage over other companies.

Thus, a strategic partnership is a **win-win relationship.** Both parties benefit, because the size of the pie has increased. Selling Scenario 2.1 describes

S E L L I N G   S C E N A R I O

2.1

Building a Partnership with Whirlpool

Robert Hall, corporate vice-president for purchasing, talks about what it takes to sell to Whirlpool: "If we go with a supplier, we want to form a strategic partnership. It's a mutual dependency relationship and we put a lot of trust in them, so we count on them not to disclose any information we have disclosed to them."

For 15 years, Wollin, a small plastics manufacturer near Whirlpool's corporate headquarters, called on its neighbor but never got an order. Finally, they broke through and got an order—for $400 worth of small parts. It took Wollin another two years of small trial orders to convince Whirlpool that it had the technical and production capabilities and the right people to supply parts for Whirlpool's washing machines.

When Whirlpool's washing machine moved its assembly operation to Ohio, Wollin built a plant a mile away. "I wrote them a letter notifying them," says Ewald Lehmann, CEO of Wollin. "We asked for no guarantees."

But Wollin got all of Whirlpool's business because of their partnering relationship. Even though Wollin is a much smaller company, Whirlpool relied on Wollin for specially designed plastic parts that were essential to the performance of Whirlpool's washing machines.

Source: Barry Rehfeld, "How Large Companies Buy," Personal Selling Power, September 1993, pp. 31–32. Copyright September 1993. Reprinted by permission.

the investments and risks taken by a small company to build a strategic partnership with Whirlpool.

Strategic partnerships are created explicitly for the purpose of uncovering and exploiting joint opportunities.[6] Members in strategic partnerships have a high level of dependence on and trust in each other, share goals and agree on how to accomplish those goals, and show a willingness to take risks, share confidential information, and make significant investments for the sake of the relationship.

For example, in the situation described in Selling Scenario 2.1, Whirlpool shared confidential information with Wollin about its design plans for a new, energy-efficient washing machine. With this information, Wollin used its expertise to develop some plastic parts tailored to the design plans. These unique parts were superior to the standard parts that could be purchased from several suppliers.

Whirlpool took a risk in sharing the information about its new product and eventually buying parts that were available from only one supplier. Wollin took a risk in designing parts without a firm order and producing parts that could be sold to only one customer. However, by taking these risks, the performance and eventual sales of the new washing machine were enhanced and both parties benefited.

Wal-Mart has made great strides in developing strategic partnering relationships with its vendors. Wal-Mart and many of their suppliers have created cross-functional teams composed of individuals from various areas of the firm such as marketing, finance, operations, distribution, and management information systems. Wal-Mart's teams work closely with similar

A strategic partnership is like a marriage. Both Penney and Levi Dockers are committed to their strategic relationship in good and not so good times.

Courtesy J.C. Penney Company.

teams from Procter & Gamble, Kraft General Foods, James River, Black & Decker, and many others. These teams work together to develop unique information systems and promotional programs tailored to markets served by Wal-Mart and its vendors.[7]

Similarly, Levi Strauss teams worked with JCPenney to create a specially designed area in the stores to display Docker merchandise. Then the teams developed sophisticated inventory control systems to make sure the stores were always stocked with the styles and sizes that were selling well. The result was that JCPenney is now Levi's largest customer worldwide. JCPenney also increased it profits, because it was able to offer a unique display and in-stock merchandise to its customers that were not available from competitive department stores.[8]

Moving from a relational to a strategic partnership is like moving from steady dating to marriage. When businesses enter into strategic partnerships, they are wedded to their partner for better or worse. For example, if the Levi's Docker merchandise had not sold well, JCPenney and Levi Strauss would have lost money. Strategic partnerships are risky, and they reduce flexibility. Once JCPenney formed a true strategic partnership with Levi Strauss, it could not "date around" with Levi Strauss's competitors.

In cultures outside the US, relationships are very important. In Japan, for example, several organizations may join together to form a **keiretsu,** or family of companies. These families of companies may include a bank, a transportation company, a manufacturing company, and distribution companies who share risks and rewards and jointly develop plans to exploit market opportunities. Keiretsus are strategic partnerships between several companies, rather than only two.

In the next section, we talk about the characteristics of successful relationships—relationships that have the potential for developing into strategic partnerships.

CHARACTERISTICS OF SUCCESSFUL RELATIONSHIPS

A good long-term relationship, or partnership, is one that accomplishes the goals of both parties. Some companies use the term *partnering* but do not really understand what it means. For example, Allan Weydahl, a regional sales director for Nalco, likes to work with

> a customer that says, 'Please quit talking about money, that's not the issue we're talking about. We're talking about product and how you're going to get it here and how we're going to use it.' That kind of partner is a joy to do business with. On the other hand, you get a company that calls us in and says 'We want a partnership,' and what they really want is to use their purchasing power to get the lowest possible price.[9]

Successful relationships involve growing the *mutual* benefits, as the partners learn to trust and depend on each other more and more. Additionally, the buyer and salesperson are able to resolve conflicts as they arise, settle differences, and compromise when necessary. At the foundations of successful, long-term relationships are (1) mutual trust, (2) open communication, (3) common goals, (4) a commitment to mutual gain, and (5) organizational support (see Exhibit 2.2).

▮ MUTUAL TRUST

The key to the development of successful, long-term customer relationships is trust. Lou Pritchett, former senior vice president of sales for Procter & Gamble, once said, "Cost reduction throughout the total system can be accomplished when trust replaces skepticism. Trusting suppliers, customers, and employees is one of the most effective, yet most underutilized, techniques available to management."[10]

Definition

Trust is a belief by one party that the other party will fulfill its obligations in a relationship.[11] Three aspects of trust are perceived dependability, capability or expertise, and concern for the other party.

Buyers trust salespeople when they are confident that the salespeople will follow through on promises and commitments made. To develop this confidence, the buyers must feel that the salespeople and their company

EXHIBIT 2.2

FOUNDATIONS OF
SUCCESSFUL RELATIONSHIPS

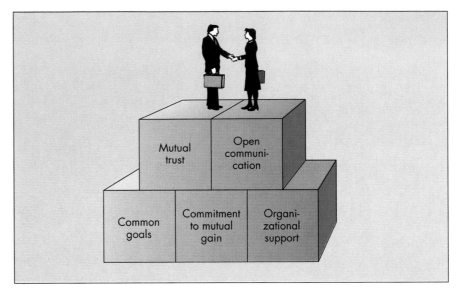

have the capability to meet their commitments. Finally, the buyers need to believe that the salespeople are concerned about the buyers' interests. Thus, if special circumstances arise and the initial promises need to be changed, the salespeople will consider the buyers' interest under the new circumstances.

When salespeople and buyers trust each other, they are more willing to share relevant ideas, clarify goals and problems, and communicate more efficiently. Information shared between the parties becomes increasingly comprehensive, accurate, and timely. There is less need for the salesperson and buyer to constantly monitor and check up on each other's actions, because they both believe that the other would not take advantage of them if given the opportunity.[12]

Without trust, the salesperson and buyer are unlikely to work closely together to achieve mutually beneficial outcomes, such as reduced distribution costs and improved product development. This is because these types of joint activities are typically risky. Sometimes the buyer and salesperson can't determine the precise outcome or payoff in advance, and success is not always guaranteed.

For example, an apparel manufacturer might want to be able to deliver new styles to its customers faster. To achieve this goal, it must get cooperation from its suppliers. The manufacturer has a better chance of realizing its goal by approaching a supplier who can visualize the benefits of working together with the manufacturer and is willing to take the risks associated with altering its normal routines. If the manufacturer and supplier trust each other, they will be more willing to try new and different ways of doing business, because they both know that their partner is similarly committed to the relationship. Further, they believe that any gains and losses resulting from their partnership will even out over the long run, so they are not afraid to sustain a short-term loss for the sake of gaining a greater long-term advantage.

Developing Trust

Buyers develop trust in salespeople when the salespeople consistently take the buyers' needs and interests into account. For example, salespeople who have a track record of consistent deliveries and reliable performance, and who cultivate a positive, interpersonal relationship with their customers, earn valuable trust.

Today's customers are especially sensitive to signs of unreliable performance. Unreliable performance, lack of smooth coordination, or an inability to communicate in a timely and accurate manner are signals that a long-term relationship may be difficult to successfully implement and manage over time.

Salespeople develop trust by going beyond the buyer's expectations. For example, John Dowling, a commercial real estate agent, negotiated a generous electricity allowance for one of his clients. The credit was to be applied to overtime air-conditioning charges, but when the bill came in, the credit Dowling had expected wasn't there—the electricity usage was much higher than he expected. In order to find out why, Dowling flew to New Orleans to check the client's meters. He took a hotel room across from the client's building and observed the building. He found five full floors of lights kept on at night. So the client began turning the lights off in the evenings, but the results still didn't satisfy Dowling. He sent in a team to investigate, and ultimately wound up installing motion detectors to help control the utility usage. Dowling's efforts to go the extra mile on a customer's behalf enabled him to create an incredible level of trust with his customers.[13]

▌COMMUNICATION

Open and honest communication is key to developing successful relationships. Buyers and salespeople in a relationship need to understand what is driving each other's business, their roles in the relationship, each firm's strategies, and any problems that arise over the course of the relationship.

Customer knowledge facilitates communications and builds trust. Ellen Manzo is an award-winning area manager with At&T Computer Systems in Parsippany, New Jersey. "It's critical to do a lot of account research," she explains, "especially if you're servicing a small number of accounts. I go to the library, I go through Dun & Bradstreet and news clipping services, and I get the last 18 months of articles on the company. I buy a share of stock in the company so that I receive all the proxy statements and quarterly information. I try to get on the customer's mailing list." Manzo also requires all her new salespeople to go through an extensive research exercise before they ever call on a customer, and she develops strategies for visits with her reps on major accounts.[14] (Chapter 5 focuses on approaches for improving communications.)

Cultural differences in communication style can be easily misunderstood and thus hinder open and honest communications. For example, all cultures have ways to avoid saying no, when they really mean no. In Japan, maintaining long-lasting stable relationships is very important. To avoid damaging a relationship, customers rarely say no directly. Some phrases used in Japan to say no indirectly are, "It's very difficult." "We'll think about it." "I'm not sure." Or leaving the room with an apology. In general, when Japanese customers do not say yes or no directly, it means that they want to say no.[15]

SHARED GOALS

Salespeople and customers must have common goals for a successful relationship to develop. Shared goals give both members of the relationship a strong incentive to pool their strengths and abilities, and exploit potential opportunities. There is also greater assurance that the other partner will not do anything to hinder goal achievement within the relationship.

For example, if Johnson & Johnson (J&J) and Kmart commit to reducing out-of-stock occurrences at the store level, then they both must work toward this goal. J&J can not fall behind on their shipments, and Kmart can not be lackadaisical about getting the product on the shelf in a timely manner. With a common goal, both firms have an incentive to cooperate, because they know that by doing so they will both be able to achieve a higher level of sales than before.

Shared goals also help to sustain the partnership when the expected benefit flows are not realized. If one J&J shipment fails to reach a Kmart store on time due to an uncontrollable event, like misrouting by a trucking firm, Kmart will not suddenly call off the whole arrangement. Instead, Kmart is likely to view the incident as a simple mistake and will remain in the relationship. This is because Kmart knows that J&J is committed to the same goal in the long run.

Clearly defined, measurable goals are also very important. Kmart and J&J might monitor the number of stockouts, late deliveries, order processing time, and sales every week or month to assess how well they are meeting their goals. Without this information, there is a significant risk that the partners may not agree that anything was actually done.

Effective measuring of performance is particularly critical in the early stages of the partnership. The achievement of explicitly stated goals lays the groundwork for a history of shared success, which serves as a powerful motivation for continuing the relationship and working closely together into the future.

COMMITMENT TO MUTUAL GAIN

Members in successful partnerships must actively work to create win-win relationships by looking for overlapping areas of opportunity in which both can prosper. For example, Clark Equipment Company manufactures forklift trucks, pallet trucks, and other mobile material-handling equipment. They recently began to integrate their partnering suppliers into their design process by sharing detailed information on costs, cost targets, profitability targets, and business strategies. By working closely with their suppliers, Clark improved their product quality and sales, which increased their orders for the vendors' products, outcomes that were mutually satisfying to both parties.[16]

The most successful relationships involve mutual dependency. One party is not more powerful than the other party. Mutual dependency creates a cooperative spirit. Both parties search for ways to expand the pie and minimize time spent on resolving conflicts of how to split the pie.

Credible Commitments

As a successful relationship develops, both parties make credible commitments to the relationship. **Credible commitments** are tangible investments in the relationship. They go beyond just making the hollow statement, "I want to be a partner"; credible commitments involve spending money to improve the products and services sold to the other party.[17]

For example, a firm may hire or train employees, invest in equipment, and develop computer and communication systems to meet the needs of a specific customer. These investments signal a partner's commitment to the relationship in the long run.

ORGANIZATIONAL SUPPORT

For relationships to succeed and grow, each firm in the relationship must provide their boundary-spanning employees—the purchasing agents and salespeople—with the necessary support.

Structure and Culture

Buy in @ all levels.

The organizational structure and management must support the salespeople or buyers in a partnering relationship. All employees in the firm need to "buy in" or, in other words, accept the salesperson and buyer's role in developing the partnership. Partnerships created at headquarters should be recognized and treated as such by local offices, and vice versa. Without the support of the respective companies, the partnership is destined to fail.

It is critically important for both firms to cultivate a partnering culture throughout their organizations. This can be difficult. Joe Durrett, senior vice president of sales at Kraft General Foods, notes that "the biggest difficulty is changing attitudes. You must reengineer what you have because there are no experienced salespeople you can bring into the company who relate to this team approach."[18] Selling Scenario 2.2 describes the resources that Baxter Healthcare directs toward building relationships.

Training

Firms need to train their salespeople to sell effectively in a relationship-building environment. Salespeople need to be taught how to identify customer needs and work with the customer to achieve better performance. Kraft General Foods (KGF) uses a program, called Navigator, to train their salespeople in partnering.

In this program, salespeople pretend to work for a KGF clone, Pathfinder Foods. Pathfinder sells to three hypothetical customers: a traditional supermarket chain, a discounter, and a distributor to independent grocers.

S E L L I N G   *S C E N A R I O*

2.2

Baxter Healthcare: Teaming with Customer Counterparts

One example of how closer customer-supplier ties are changing the role of a company's sales force comes from hospital supply giant Baxter Healthcare Corp. At Baxter, the emphasis on partnering has paradoxically "enabled us to increase our sales force at the same time that we have decreased it," says Baxter's Senior Vice President of Quality Leadership David Auld.

Auld estimates that in the past several years, "We have taken about 40 percent out of our sales force staff. Instead of focusing on the use of sales reps, Baxter has formed a joint relationship at every significant level of the two organizations," says Mr. Auld. In essence, every employee has taken on a sales role.

"Our senior people meet with the customer's senior people so that we understand what their mission is, what their strategy is, and what is important to them. Then we can go back and mobilize our resources to address those specifically," Mr. Auld explains.

"At the other end of the spectrum, Baxter has its warehouse workers team up with those working in the warehouses at the hospitals that are Baxter customers, so that our warehouseman, our picker, now is a salesman," says Mr. Auld. "We now have designated pickers, people in our warehouses who are designated to serve specific hospitals as customers, and two or three times a month they will jump on the delivery truck and ride it to that customer." During those visits, the designated pickers study the customer warehouse operations to try to figure out how Baxter can pack its shipments to make it easier for the customers to unload, unpack, and distribute the Baxter deliveries.

Much of the initial motivation for these closer linkages was to improve the efficiency of the interaction, to provide better customer service, and to cut costs of operation. "Baxter has found that the close relationships that develop create a formidable competitive barrier," Mr. Auld explains. "They bind the customer to us and make it difficult for anyone who might try to take the business away. What we have found is that these nonsales relationships, which are focused on issues that are relevant to the customer, are among the strongest selling features that we have."

Source: B.G. Yovovich, "Partnering at Its Best," *Business Marketing,* March 1992, pp. 36–37. Copyright March 1992. Reprinted by permission.

Salespeople are asked early on, "Which retailer has a competitive advantage in today's market?" Inevitably, every employee falls into the trap of trying to guess. No one ever gets it right. The right answer is all of the customers have the opportunity to be successful. Every salesperson should develop a unique sales strategy that will help his or her customer outsell its competition.[19]

Training is critical in helping salespeople identify ways to make it easier for the customer to do business with them. At Alcoa Aluminum, sales representatives are trained to look at what their customers do to a product that Alcoa could do for them.

For example, one salesperson noticed that customers stack materials in skids in various-sized stacks, sometimes 10 feet tall. When an order is pulled from inventory, a forklift driver must go into the stacks and pull a particular skid. Sometimes, the skids are not stacked with a packing ticket on the outside, so the driver has a hard time identifying the right skid. Alcoa

To be effective in building partnerships, salespeople must know how their products can provide benefits to customers. General Motors builds strong relationships with its dealers by offering extensive training for dealer salespeople on special leasing, insurance, and financing programs.

Photo courtesy GMAC Financial Services.

began to put a package ticket on both ends of the skid so that the driver can always see the package number, no matter how it is stacked.

Rewards

Reward systems on both sides of the relationship should be coordinated to encourage supportive behaviors. In the past, buyers were rewarded for wringing out concessions from the salespeople, salespeople were rewarded on the basis of sales volume. In a partnering relationship, rewarding short-term behaviors can be detrimental. Thus, companies are beginning to reward salespeople and buyers on the quality of the relationships they develop.[20]

PHASES OF RELATIONSHIP DEVELOPMENT

The preceding section reviewed the characteristics of successful buyer-seller relationships. In this section, we describe the process by which relationships develop the mutual trust, open communication, shared goals, and commitment to mutual gain described above.

Buyer-supplier relationships typically evolve through five stages: (1) awareness, (2) exploration, (3) expansion, (4) commitment, and (5) dissolutionment. These stages are illustrated in Exhibit 2.3.

■ AWARENESS

No interaction occurs between salespeople and buyers in the awareness phase. During the **awareness phase,** salespeople locate and qualify prospects, while buyers consider various sources of supply. Reputations in the marketplace and market shares are very important during this phase. Buyers will typically screen out potential suppliers based on what they know of the suppliers' products and service.

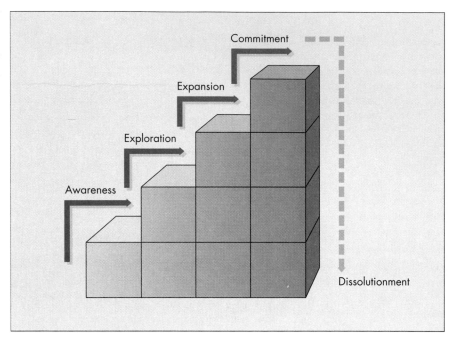

■ EXPLORATION

The **exploration phase** is a search and trial phase for the salespeople and buyers. Both parties will explore the potential benefits and costs involved in a relationship.[21]

Cheryl Ricketts-Basinger, a star account executive with Franklin International Institute in Pickerington, Ohio, describes a funnel-type approach that she commonly uses:

> I start with very broad questions and then go into the specifics. I usually start with an opening statement that begins something like this, "Franklin is really committed to making a positive difference in our client companies. In order for me to evaluate whether our program is a fit for your situation, I'd like to ask a few questions. Would you give me an overview of your company?"[22]

Her approach involves understanding the customer's philosophy, trends, mission statement, goals, industry trends, and so forth. She then narrows it to specific needs, problems, and challenges. Doing this allows her to determine how important the problems really are to the client. The final focus is on the potential payoff that will be achieved if the specific problems are solved.

In general, successful salespeople put greater emphasis on relationship development during the initial call than do less successful salespeople.[23] Higher-performing salespeople place more importance on determining a potential client's knowledge of the company and understanding a prospect's background, whereas lower-performing salespeople tend to be less sensitive to customer needs. Lower performers feel that it is more appropriate to explain each product benefit and make a complete presentation on the initial call than do higher-performing salespeople.

During the exploration phase, salespeople focus on understanding the customer's needs. This pharmaceutical salesperson is discussing the type of medical problems the physician encounters in her practice.

Courtesy PFIZER Inc.

Sometimes the salesperson and customer begin to negotiate possible terms of exchange in this phase. Buyers may place a trial order to assess product quality and the salesperson's management of the transaction.

The exploration phase may be very brief or extend over a long time period. Regardless of the length, it is important to remember that during this phase, the relationship is very fragile. The buyer and salesperson have made only minimal commitments and investments and, thus, the relationship can be terminated easily. The exploration phase is like starting to date someone.

▮ EXPANSION

When the salesperson and customer see potential in fostering the relationship, it moves into the expansion phase. The **expansion stage** involves significant efforts by both parties to investigate the potential benefits of a long-term relationship. The parties begin to share sensitive information, and customers place orders more frequently.

Salespeople work with customers to examine opportunities for expanding the relationship to other products and applications. They develop a better understanding of the customer's needs and help solve additional concerns. If the two are able to work well together over time, their trust and satisfaction with each other will grow, and they will be more willing to take risks together.

If a buyer develops trust in a salesperson, the buyer will be reluctant to switch to an untested supplier. Additionally, the customer is more likely to take risks, share confidential information that will help them both accomplish common goals, and work closely with the salesperson to achieve mutually beneficial outcomes. Basically, the expansion phase is like serious dating.

▎ COMMITMENT

In the **commitment phase,** the customer and salesperson have implicitly or explicitly pledged to continue the relationship for an extended period of time. Commitment represents the most advanced stage in a relationship. The customer and salesperson are so satisfied with the relationship that they become extremely loyal to each other. Both members are willing to make investments in the relationship.

In later chapters, we discuss "obtaining commitment" as a stage in the sales process. Commitment in the sales process means obtaining an order from the buyer in a specific transaction. The commitment stage in a relationship involves a promise by both parties to work together over many transactions. The benefits that each party receives from this stage are typically very difficult to achieve with alternative buyers and suppliers. At this point, the salesperson and customer have agreed-on roles, common goals, and plans for achieving these goals. They have worked with each other long enough and understand each other's cultures and needs to be able to predict with certainty how each would react or respond to various situations and possibilities. The high level of trust between them encourages them to freely discuss mutually beneficial opportunities and options.

THINKING IT THROUGH	Consider the steps that you went through in developing a close personal relationship. What were some of the events or activities that moved your relationship through the expansion stage to the commitment stage?

▎ DISSOLUTIONMENT

At every stage of the relationship development process, the relationship can move to a *dissolutionment phase* resulting in termination. Dissolution might occur because of a poor performance history, change in needs, better terms from an alternative partner, and so forth.

Dissolution is particularly important to understand when the members of a partnership have made large investments into the relationship and have developed a lot of strong attachments and interdependencies between the organizations. When such a relationship is terminated, its effects are felt throughout the entire organization and industry.

▎ SELLING IN THE PARTNERING ERA

In the partnering era, salespeople are relationship managers. They are responsible for making sure that their company develops the appropriate type of relationships with each of its customers. They are using increasingly sophisticated technologies to marshal their firm's resources toward solving customer problems, and moving the relationship through the phases described in the previous section. Although many American firms are just entering the partnering era, Selling Scenario 2.3 describes how the concept of relationship building is critical in Japanese selling.

Selling in Japan

Chuck Laughlin, the co-author of *Sumurai Selling: The Ancient Art of Service in Sales,* says that in Japan "a salesperson will spend a lot of time in the very early stages of developing a relationship and not even mention a company or product, [whereas] in the United States, the company and the product come out from the first call. We [in the United States] may be into the middle of the sales process within days [or] hours, where a Japanese selling person can spend a year building a relationship before beginning to introduce his product."

To make an initial contact with a customer, salespeople in Japan must have a formal introduction. For example, the president of the salesperson's company will make a formal request to the president of a potential customer firm to introduce his or her sales manager. After the sales manager makes the initial contact, he or she will introduce the salesperson.

To encourage salespeople to focus on the relationship and not just sales, Japanese companies pay their salespeople 100% salary with no incentive or commission based on the amount they sell. Salespeople are often referred to as "salarymen."

Source: Paula Champa, "How To Sell in Japan," *Selling,* December 1993, pp. 39–47.

Relationship Managers

As more companies evolve to the partnering era, the terms *personal selling* and *salesperson* no longer represent what people in this position do and are. These employees are becoming **relationship managers,** not simply salespeople. They are responsible for working with people in their company to develop problem solutions.

For example, until recently, Procter & Gamble did not have good relationships with major retailers. Retailers considered P&G salespeople to be very knowledgeable, but often felt they were arrogant, dictated what products to stock and how to display them, and had little regard for the customer's needs. Now, P&G salespeople manage employee teams that focus on developing good relationships with retailers. A team might include employees in finance, distribution, and manufacturing. When a major retailer complains about a late shipment, the P&G distribution team member talks to the retailer's transportation person to solve the problem.[24]

Using Technology to Increase Efficiency

Partnering relationships are built on effective communications. To improve communications with customers, salespeople are making greater use of computers, telecommunications, and videos.

Over 25 percent of the firms contacted in a recent survey used portable computers in their sales forces.[25] Computer use ranges from providing information during a sales call to analyzing a customer's problems. Ryder Truck developed a computer model that salespeople use to help customers compare the costs of leasing and purchasing trucks. The

Relationship building is a critical aspect of selling in Japan. The process of developing a relationship begins with a formal introduction of the salesperson and evolves over years.

Jose Pelaez/The Stock Market.

salesperson questions the customer about estimated mileage and the type of trucks needed, enters the answers into a laptop computer, hits a single key, and reviews the printout with the customer.

Companies are developing video presentations to demonstrate complex product benefits. According to Thomas Bird, president of Gould Inc.'s test and measurements division, "One of the problems in technical sales is that some salespeople do not exactly convey what the inventor or manufacturer had in mind when the product was designed." To overcome this problem, Gould spent $200,000 to produce videocassette presentations and $75,000 to equip salespeople with VCRs. The use of new technologies to improve selling effectiveness is discussed throughout the text.

Professionalism in Selling

As the rate of change in technology increases, as products become more complex, and as customers demand long-term relationships, salespeople need to develop a more professional approach to deal effectively with the business environment in the 1990s. A **professional** is someone who engages in an occupation requiring great skill or knowledge and whose capabilities are respected by co-workers. Most successful salespeople are professionals continually seeking to improve their skills.[26]

SUMMARY

As we discussed in Chapter 1, many businesses are moving from the marketing era into the partnering era. However, even in the partnering era, not all of transactions between buyers and sellers will be partnerships. Many exchanges will continue to be market transactions and functional relationships. In these types of relationships, the buyer and salesperson are interested only in the benefits they get from the transaction.

Relational and strategic partnership are characterized by a mutual concern of each party for the long-run welfare of the other party. Both of these type of partnerships are based on mutual trust. However, the strategic partnership involves the greatest commitment, because the parties are willing to make significant investments in the relationship.

Mutual trust, open communications, common goals, a commitment to mutual gains, and organizational support are key ingredients in successful relationships. These five factors form the foundation for win-win relationships between customers and salespeople.

Customers trust salespeople when they think the salesperson is dependable, capable, and concerned about their welfare. To build trust, salespeople need to be consistent in meeting the commitments they make to customers. They also need to demonstrate their concern for the well-being of the customer.

Relationships typically go through five phases: awareness, exploration, expansion, commitment, and dissolution. In each of these phases, salespeople play an important role.

In the partnering era, firms view salespeople as relationship managers. They provide the resources and incentive to motivate salespeople to seek partnering relationships with customers.

KEY TERMS

awareness phase *49*	partnership *36*
commitment phase *52*	professional *54*
credible commitments *47*	relational partnership *38*
dissolutionment phase *52*	relationship manager *53*
expansion phase *51*	strategic partnership *40*
exploration phase *50*	trust *43*
functional relationship *37*	win-lose relationship *38*
market exchange *36*	win-win relationship *41*

QUESTIONS AND PROBLEMS

1. Why do companies want to enter into partnering relationships?

2. What is the difference between a relational and a functional partnership?

3. Many companies seem to be calling salespeople by different titles, such as account executives, sales executives, or account managers. Why are companies using these different titles for employees that were formerly called salespeople?

4. What factors should a salesperson consider when deciding with which customers he or she wants to develop a close relationship?

5. When buyers and sellers negotiate over price, somebody wins and somebody loses. If the seller makes a price concession, the seller makes less money and the buyer makes more. How is it possible for a buyer and a seller to have a win–win relationship?

6. Are there situations in which a salesperson might not want to develop a partnering relationship with a customer? Why not?

7. Assume that you had a functional relationship with a buyer. The buyer no longer trusts you or your company because the last three orders came in late and there were defects in the product. The relationship is damaged and it can not be repaired. What would you be concerned about as this relationship dissolves? How would you manage the dissolution of this relationship to minimize the damage?

8. Do all relationships between buyers and sellers move from market transactions to strategic partnerships? What factors can stop the growth of relationships in this way?

CASE PROBLEMS

CASE 2 • 1
WHEN IT'S ONE CLIENT
OVER ANOTHER

Most days, Steve Kaplan wholeheartedly agrees with Mae West: "Too much of a good thing can be wonderful." For instance, Kaplan has always believed that he can never make too many sales. Then came the day he made one sale too many.

Kaplan is the owner and president of Sampling Corporation of America (SCA), a company that undertakes product sampling and promotional programs targeted toward children, teens, and teachers in elementary and secondary schools. Companies use these programs to get potential customers to try their products and to increase sales.

Most of the programs that SCA conducts are cooperative. Groups of products and coupons from different manufacturers are assembled and distributed to children in specific age groups. SCA offers an exclusive guarantee for each cooperative program. Once a firms has decided to participate in a program, competitive products will not be included in the package.

Kaplan's oldest and largest client, General Products (GP), was "challenged" in the shampoo category for a new promotion package directed toward the teenage female market. In other words, a competitor of GP's, Smith & Lynch (a firm larger than GP), wanted to take part in the program with its shampoo sample if GP decided not to participate.

After a week of deliberation, GP said it was not prepared to make a decision about participating in the teen promotion package. The client told Kaplan "to do what you have to do." And he did.

Kaplan told Smith & Lynch, a new client for SCA, that it had the shampoo slot in the promotion. And that was that . . . until GP phoned a week later, after the contract with Smith & Lynch was signed. GP changed its plans and wanted to be in the promotion package. Yes, it was late. Yes, there was one shampoo too many. Yes, it was Kaplan's largest client.

QUESTIONS

1. What should Kaplan do? He felt he had two options. First, he could ask Smith & Lynch to withdraw. After all, GP was Kaplan's largest and oldest client. Second, could tell GP the truth and honor the contract with Smith & Lynch. Kaplan had given GP the chance and he was now obligated to stand by his new client.

2. Can you think of any other options that are better?

CASE 2 • 2
TUPELO TABLE & CHAIR

Tupelo Table & Chair (TTC) manufactures and sells lower-priced dining room and dinette furniture to independent furniture stores across the South. Recently, Sears approached TTC about creating a special line of furniture to be sold only through Sears. The projected volume would be almost double TTC's current volume and would require TTC to build a new plant or drop all customers except their biggest account, a furniture retailer called Badcock's with 184 stores. Sears is willing to loan TTC half the money needed to build a new plant at prime rate (which is 3 percent lower than the bank's rate to TTC). The proposed agreement would last three years. During that time, Sears would provide TTC with market data to design products that would sell extremely well in exhange for sole rights to their choices of TTC's new products every year.

Nancy Troyer, TTC sales manager, and Roger Kennedy, TTC president, were discussing the pending offer. "Roger, I'm not sure this is the best thing for TTC. What kind of history does Sears have with vendors?" asked Nancy. "And what about Badcock's?" They're 28 percent of our business. Even building a new plant, we've got to cut 30 percent or more of our current clients. Do we cut Badcock's? They've been our best customer for near 30 years!"

Roger replied, "We've got no long-term agreement with them. And think of what Sears means for us in terms of profit. Our prices may be reduced by 10 percent but we don't have to pay the usual 15 percent commission on the sale! And we can take all that market data and do even better with our regular lines. In a few years, maybe build another plant and expand back into our old accounts."

"So who's going to take care of Sears?" she fumed. "Does this mean if we go with Sears, all of us in sales are out of jobs?"

QUESTIONS

1. What should TTC consider when evaluating a potential partnership with Sears? Should the relationship with Badcock's have any influence on their decision?

2. What does the brief dialog indicate about TTC's ability to partner? What, if anything, is TTC lacking to partner effectively, and how should they improve in those areas?

ADDITIONAL REFERENCES

Anderson, James, and James Narus. "Partnering as a Focussed Marketing Strategy." *California Management Review,* Spring 1991, pp. 24–34.

Berling, Robert. "The Emerging Approach to Business Strategy: Building a Relationship Advantage." *Business Horizons,* July–August 1993, pp. 16–27.

Dunn, Dan, and Claude Thomas. "Partnering with Customers." *Journal of Business and Industrial Marketing,* January 1994, pp. 13–24.

Farber, Barry, and Joyce Wycoff. "Relationship Building: Six Steps to Success." *Sales & Marketing Management,* April 1992, pp. 50–54.

Garry, Michael, and Glenn Synder. "Turning Partnerships into Reality." *Progressive Grocer,* September 1993, pp. 44–46.

Gassenheimer, Jule; Jay Sterling; and Robert Robicheaux. "Long-Term Channel Member Relationships." *International Journal of Physical Distribution and Material Management,* 12 (1989), pp. 15–28.

Hallen, Lars; Jan Johanson; and Nazeem Seyed-Mohamed. "Interfirm Adaptation in Business Relationships." *Journal of Marketing,* 55 (April 1991), pp. 29–37.

Hills, Cathy. "Making the Team." *Sales & Marketing Management,* February 1992, pp. 54–56.

Jackson, Barbara Bund. "Build Customer Relationships That Last." *Harvard Business Review,* November–December 1985, pp. 120–27.

Mohr, Jakki, and Robert Spekman. "Characteristics of Successful Partnerships: Attributes, Communication Behavior, and Conflict Resolution Techniques." *Strategic Management Journal,* February 1993, pp. 23–45.

Morgan, James, and Thomas Stundza. "Supply Strategy: Buyer-Supplier Alliances Just Don't Come Together." *Purchasing,* March 4, 1993, pp. 34B11–16.

Rosenbloom, Bert. "Motivating Your International Channel Partners." *Business Horizons,* 33 (March–April 1990), pp. 53–57.

Zemke, Ron. "Creating Customer Value." *Training,* September 1993, pp. 5–47.

Ethical and Legal Issues in Selling

Consider the following situation: You are a salesperson for a consumer electronics manufacturer and are negotiating a $100,000 sale with the buyer for a discount store chain. The buyer says, "I like your new large-screen TVs. I would really appreciate getting one as a gift." If you make the sale, you will get a commission of $7,000. It would cost you $2,000 to buy the TV and give it to the buyer. What would you do? Would it be illegal to give the gift to the buyer? Would it be unethical?

Everyone confronts situations that involve making ethical choices. However, ethics are particularly important in personal selling. Salespeople often have to balance their personal needs with the needs of their company and their customers. This chapter examines the salesperson's personal code of ethics and the laws that should govern the salesperson's behavior when these conflicts arise.

Some questions answered in this chapter are:

Why do salespeople need to develop their own code of ethics?
What ethical responsibilities do salespeople have toward themselves, their firm, and their customers?
Do ethics get in the way of being a successful salesperson?
What guidelines should salespeople consider when confronting situations involving an ethical issue?
What laws apply to personal selling?

While Rick Shih-Hsieh was getting his degree in computer sciences at Northwestern, he worked part time as a programmer for a computer retailer in Chicago. "I realized that programming is a real 'heads down' job. I like working with people. So after I graduated, I went to work for the retailer in sales, primarily to commercial accounts and educational institutions. Eventually I became the sales manager of two stores. But I missed spending time with customers. Also, as a manager, I had to depend on others to get the job done. In sales, my performance was due to my personal skills and effort. A couple of years ago I decided to go back into sales and took a job with IBM."

Shih-Hsieh is an IBM marketing specialist in Chicago. He is responsible for selling IBM's personal computers (PCs) and workstations to major accounts including Abbott Laboratories, United Airlines, and Baxter Healthcare.

"IBM has a strong ethical code of conduct for its employees and our customers know it. I don't run into obvious unethical situations like cheating on expense accounts or bribery. But I do see situations that are not black or white. There are a lot a subtleties in spur-of-the-moment communication, which is at the heart of personal selling. Having an overall sensitivity to ethical issues is important, but your most critical skill is an ability to recognize when an ethical issue is being raised and when your judgment is required. I always keep in the back of my mind that the next words out of my mouth could compromise my relationship with a customer.

"The most difficult situations are when you're under a great deal of pressure or the stakes are high. And sometimes people confuse being ethical with being timid. Then it's tempting to say and do things that bring in short-term results without considering the long-term implications. I've seen situations where competitors have shaded the truth and overpromised on the delivery and support they would offer to customers.

RICK SHIH-HSIEH

IBM

"For example, one of my biggest customers was going to place a half-million-dollar order for PCs, but he wanted delivery of 500 units in two months. I just couldn't commit to that tight of a delivery schedule. There was a shortage of a critical chip and we had already made commitments to customers for the chips we were going to receive over the next three months. I knew our competitors had the same problem we did, but one of them agreed to the delivery demands and got the order. I guess he decided to get the order and figure out how to dance around late deliveries later.

"I kept my manager and headquarters informed about the situation. One good thing about working for IBM is that management encourages dialogue; I had no qualms whatsoever about discussing this problem with them. They supported me all the way, even though we lost the order. But we weren't going to risk our long-term relationship with the customer over this. Of course, the other vendor couldn't deliver as promised. Now, the purchasing agent really respects me and this situation has strengthened our relationship. He knows that I'm going to be straight with him."

CONFLICTING NEEDS FACING SALESPEOPLE

We all have needs and values that guide our daily lives. But when you take a sales job with a firm, you now must consider the needs and values of the firm and your customers as well as your own personal needs.

Exhibit 3.1 displays the different objectives and needs of salespeople, their firms, and their customers. For example, both the company and its customers want to make profits. Should a salesperson tell a customer about problems his or her firm is having with a new product? Concealing this information might make it easier to make a sale, increase your company's profits, and enhance your success with the company, but it could decrease the customer's profits when the product does not perform adequately. In the situation described at the beginning of the chapter, the salesperson's moral values concerning bribes might be in conflict with his desire to be successful in his new job and the buyer's personal needs for a large-screen TV.

These conflicts often are not covered by company policies and procedures, and managers may not be available to provide advice. Thus, salespeople must make decisions on their own, relying on their ethical standards and understanding of the laws governing these situations.

As discussed in Chapter 2, most businesses try to develop long-term, mutually beneficial relationships with their customers. Salespeople are the official representatives of their companies. They are responsible for developing and maintaining customer loyalty. Loyalty is built on trust. Partnerships between buyers and sellers cannot develop when salespeople behave unethically or illegally.[1] Selling Scenario 3.1 illustrates that good ethics make for good business.

This chapter examines ethical and legal issues in personal selling. *Laws*, discussed in the second part of the chapter, dictate what salespeople should not do—what activities society has deemed clearly wrong. However, many situations are not covered by laws. Salespeople must then rely on their own code of ethics and/or their firm's and industry's code of ethics to determine the right thing to do. Ethical considerations are reviewed in the next section.

E X H I B I T   3 . 1

CONFLICTING OBJECTIVES

Company Objectives	Salesperson Objectives	Customer Objectives
Increase sales	Increase compensation	Reduce costs
Increase profits	Satisfy customers	Solve problems
Decrease sales costs	Receive recognition, promotion	Satisfy needs
	Maintain personal code of ethics	

S E L L I N G   S C E N A R I O

3.1

Maintaining Your Integrity

Alan Lesk's first call after his promotion to district manager was unforgettable. He met with the buyer of a major department store in Washington, D.C. The store was not doing much business with Maidenform, and the buyer was very uncooperative. On the way out of the store, Lesk met the buyer's boss and set up a meeting with some higher-level executives for later in the week.

When the day of the meeting arrived, Lesk was quite nervous making a presentation to nine department stores executives. In the middle of the presentation, the senior vice president stood up and asked Lesk point-blank how much rebate he was going to give, over and above the normal discounts, to do business with the store.

Lesk feared that the vice president might be asking for money under the table. Making a fast decision, he responded, "If this is what it takes to do business here, I don't want anything to do with it." As he started to walk out the door, the executives began laughing. They had been teasing him to see how far he would go to get more business.

This incident taught Lesk an important lesson: Never let people intimidate you into compromising your integrity. Also, don't lose your sense of humor. He made the sale, and the department store remains one of Maidenform's best customers.

Source: Adapted from "Strange Tales of Sales," *Sales & Marketing Management*, June 3, 1985, p. 46. Copyright June 1985. Reprinted by permission.

ETHICAL ISSUES

Ethics are the principles governing the behavior of an individual or group. These principles establish appropriate behavior. Defining the term is easy, but determining what those principles are is difficult. What one person thinks is right, another may consider wrong.

What is ethical can vary from country to country and from industry to industry. For example, offering bribes to overcome bureaucratic roadblocks is an accepted practice in Middle Eastern countries but is considered unethical, and even illegal, in the United States.

An ethical principle can change over time. For example, some years ago, doctors and lawyers who advertised their services were considered unethical. Today it is accepted as common practice.

Although there are no absolute rules for ethical behavior, each salesperson needs to develop a personal code of ethics. A code of ethics such as the following, helps salespeople in difficult situations:

- Should you tell customers about what one of their competitors is ordering from you?

- Is it all right to use a high-pressure sales approach when you know your product is the best for the customer's needs?

Ethical principles change over time. Twenty years ago it would have been considered unethical for this lawyer to have a display ad in the yellow pages.

AVAILABLE TO PRACTICE IN
➤ BANKRUPTCY   INJURIES ◄

BANKRUPTCY
• CHAPTER 7 DISCHARGE
• CHAPTER 13 PAYMENT PLAN
   WAGE DEDUCTION
STOP FORECLOSURES
   REPOSSESSIONS
   ANNOYING PHONE CALLS

INJURIES
• WORKERS COMPENSATION
• AUTOMOBILE COLLISIONS
• ACCIDENTS
• NO FEE UNLESS YOU COLLECT

Paul C. Sheils, J.D.
579-5871
110 W. Burlington   LAGRANGE

19 Years Serving Cook And DuPage
Free Consultation

Courtesy Paul C. Sheils, J.D.

- Should you sell a product to a customer if you know a better product exists for that application?
- Is it ethical to tell a customer about the poor performance features of a competing product?
- Should you put the cost of a hotel room on your expense account even though you stayed at a friend's house during the business trip?
- If your supervisor suggests that you pad your expense account to make extra money, should you do it?

THINKING IT THROUGH	*How* would you respond to each of these situations listed above? Why? Do you think others would respond the same way you would?

Some people hesitate to pursue a sales career, because they think selling will force them to compromise their principles. Students often think salespeople and sales managers are unethical. However, the results of a recent

EXHIBIT 3.2

ETHICAL STANDARDS OF
SALES MANAGERS AND
STUDENTS

Students and sales managers were asked to indicate their level of agreement with statements concerning ethics in sales. Their average responses on a 5-point scale, where 1 is strongly disagree and 5 is strongly agree, are shown below:

Statement	Level of Agreement	
	Managers	Students
Generally salespeople have high ethics.	3.61	3.11
I am unwilling to violate any company policies in order to make a sale.	3.43	2.98
I would always be ethical in sales.	4.23	3.63
Sales managers expect results even if a salesperson has to be a little unethical to get the sale.	1.97	3.16
I would never lie to a buyer.	3.95	4.17
If I had to, I would cheat just a little in order to make a sale.	2.36	2.01
It is more important to be unethical and make the sale than to be ethical and not make the sale.	1.68	2.19
Taking pens home from the office is unethical.	3.04	2.55
Dating one's boss is unethical.	2.95	2.65
Lying to one's boss is unethical.	4.65	3.96
If I knew for sure I couldn't get caught, I would be more willing to be unethical.	1.70	2.26

Source: J B DeConninck and D J Good, "Perceptual Differences of Sales Practitioners and Students Concerning Ethical Behavior," *Journal of Business Ethics,* Fall 1989, pp. 667–76. Copyright 1989. Reprinted by permission.

study (summarized in Exhibit 3.2) indicate that sales managers have a greater concern for ethical standards than college students do. Good ethics are good business! Sales managers and salespeople know that.[2]

Most companies want to develop long-term relationships with both their salespeople and their customers. To maintain good relationships, salespeople need to have a clear sense of right and wrong so their companies and customers can depend on them when questionable situations arise. Many companies have codes of ethics for their salespeople to guide them in making ethical decisions. An outline of Motorola's policy appears in Exhibit 3.3.

In the following sections, we discuss the ethical situations that salespeople may confront in their relationships with their customers, competitors, and colleagues (other salespeople).[3] (In Chapter 17, the company's ethical and legal obligations to its salespeople and society in general are reviewed.)

RELATIONSHIPS WITH CUSTOMERS

Areas of ethical concern involving customers include using deception; offering gifts, bribes, and entertainment; divulging confidential information; and back-door selling.

E X H I B I T 3 . 3	*Improper Use of Company Funds and Assets*
ETHICS POLICY FOR MOTOROLA SALESPEOPLE	The funds and assets of Motorola may not be used for influential gifts, illegal payments of any kind, or political contributions, whether legal or illegal.

Improper Use of Company Funds and Assets

The funds and assets of Motorola may not be used for influential gifts, illegal payments of any kind, or political contributions, whether legal or illegal.

The funds and assets of Motorola must be properly and accurately recorded on the books and records of Motorola.

Motorola shall not enter into, with dealers, distributors, agents, or consultants, any agreements that are not in compliance with U.S. laws and the laws of any other country that may be involved, or that provide for the payment of a commission or fee that is not commensurate with the services to be rendered.

Customer/Supplier/Government Relationships

Motorola will respect the confidence of its customers. Motorola will respect the laws, customs, and traditions of each country in which it operates but, in so doing, will not engage in any act or course of conduct that may violate U.S. laws or its business ethics. Employees of Motorola shall not accept payments, gifts, gratuities, or favors from customers or suppliers.

Conflict of Interest

A Motorola employee shall not be a supplier or a competitor of Motorola or be employed by a competitor, supplier, or customer of Motorola. A Motorola employee shall not engage in any activity where the skill and knowledge developed while in the employment of Motorola is transferred or applied to such activity in a way that results in a negative impact on the present or prospective business interest of Motorola.

A Motorola employee shall not have any relationship with any other business enterprise that might affect the employee's independence of judgment in transactions between Motorola and the other business enterprise.

A Motorola employee may not have any interest in any supplier or customer of Motorola that could compromise the employee's loyalty to Motorola.

Compliance with the Code of Conduct is a condition of employment. We urge you to read the complete code.

Should any questions remain, you are encouraged to consult your Motorola law department. In the world of business, your understanding and cooperation are essential. As in all things, Motorola cannot operate to the highest standards without you.

Source: Company document.

Deception

Deliberately presenting inaccurate information, or lying, to a customer is illegal. However, misleading customers by telling half-truths or withholding important information is a matter of ethics. Frequently, salespeople feel it is the customer's responsibility to uncover potential product problems. They answer questions but don't offer information that might make a sale more difficult. For example, a computer salesperson might tell a customer that the computer is IBM-compatible, but fail to inform the customer about some IBM software that will not operate on the computer.

Customers expect salespeople to be enthusiastic about their firm and its products. They recognize that this enthusiasm can result in a certain amount of exaggeration. Customers also expect salespeople to emphasize the positive aspects of their products and not spend much time talking about the negative aspects. But practicing **deception** by withholding information or telling "white lies" is clearly unethical. Such salespeople are taking

Most salespeople take customers to lunch occasionally. However, paying for a lavish meal can make a customer feel uncomfortable and is considered unethical.

Jose Pelaez/The Stock Market.

advantage of the trust customers place in them. When buyers uncover these deceptions, they will be reluctant to trust the salesperson in the future.

When salespeople fail to provide customers with all of the information about their products, they lose an opportunity to develop trust. By revealing both positive and negative information, salespeople can build up their credibility.

Bribes, Gifts, and Entertainment

Bribes and kickbacks may be illegal. **Bribes** are payments made to buyers to influence their purchase decisions, whereas **kickbacks** are payments made to buyers based on the amount of orders placed. A purchasing agent personally benefits from bribes, but bribes typically have negative consequences for the purchasing agent's firm, because the product's performance is not considered in buying decisions.

Determining what gifts and entertainment are acceptable and what are not brings up ethical issues.[4] To avoid these issues, more than half of the companies in a recent survey have set policies that forbid employees to accept gifts (more than pencils or coffee cups) or entertainment from suppliers.[5] These firms require that all gifts sent to the employee's home or office be returned. Wal-Mart (the largest retailer in the world) goes one step further, allowing contact between buyers and vendors only at business meetings at Wal-Mart's or the vendor's headquarters. On the other hand, many companies have no policy about receiving gifts or entertainment. Some unethical employees will accept and even solicit gifts although their company has a policy against such practices.

Taking customers to lunch is a commonly accepted business practice. Over 85 percent of surveyed salespeople indicated they take customers to lunch occasionally or frequently. However, less than half occasionally take

EXHIBIT 3.4

PURCHASING AGENTS'
ETHICAL JUDGMENTS OF
GIFT GIVING

Gift	Percentage of Purchasing Agents Considering Gifts to Be	
	Very Unethical	**Very Ethical**
Buying lunch	4%	56%
Providing entertainment such as a ticket to a sporting event	37%	17
Giving a customer a Christmas gift valued at:		
$10	30	20
$25	50	11
$50	71	6
Giving a prospect a Christmas gift valued at:		
$10	61	9
$25	78	5
$50	82	5

Source: I Fredrick Trawick and John Swan, "How Salespeople Err with Purchasers: Overstepping Ethical Bounds," *Journal of Business and Industrial Marketing* 3 (Summer 1988), pp. 5–11. Reprinted by permission.

customers to dinner or for a drink, and only 25 percent entertain customers with leisure activities such as golf or fishing.[6]

Exhibit 3.4 shows purchasing agents' general feelings about gifts. Typically they feel that accepting lunch is ethical but receiving gifts, even if they cost only $10, is unethical. Thus purchasing agents, in general, may not welcome gifts, and you should be careful about offering them.

If salespeople would like to give a gift out of friendship or invite a customer to lunch to develop a better business relationship, they should phrase the offer so that it can be easily refused by the customer. For example, the salesperson might say: "John, I know some buyers do not like to have business lunches with salespeople, although others feel differently. How do you feel about it?" *not* "John, would you like to have lunch with me today?" To develop a productive, long-term relationship, you need to avoid embarrassing customers by asking them to engage in activities they might see as unethical.

Even when customers encourage and accept gifts, lavish gifts and entertainment are both unethical and bad business. Treating a customer to a three-day fishing trip is no substitute for effective selling. Sales won this way are usually short-lived. Salespeople who offer expensive gifts to get orders may be blackmailed into continually providing these gifts to obtain orders in the future. Customers who can be bribed are likely to switch their business when presented with better offers.

Some guidelines for gift giving are:

- Check your motives for giving the gift. The gift should be given to foster a mutually beneficial long-term relationship, not to obligate or reward the customer for placing an order.

- Make sure the customer views the gift as a symbol of your appreciation and respect, with no strings attached.
- Make sure the gift does not violate the customer's or your firm's policies.
- Never give customers the impression that you are attempting to buy their business with a gift.

Special Treatment

Some customers try to take advantage of their status to get special treatment from salespeople. For example, a buyer might ask a salesperson to make a weekly check on the performance of equipment, even after the customer's employees have been thoroughly trained in the operation and maintenance of the equipment.

Providing this extra service may upset other customers, who do not get the special attention. In addition, the special service can reduce the salesperson's productivity. You should be diplomatic, but decline requests to provide unusual services.

Confidential Information

During sales calls, salespeople often encounter confidential company information such as new products under development, costs, and production schedules. Offering information about a customer's competitor in exchange for an order is unethical.

Long-term relationships can only develop when customers can trust salespeople to maintain confidentiality. By disclosing confidential information, salespeople will get a reputation for being untrustworthy. Even the customer who solicited the confidential information will not trust the salesperson, who will then be denied access to information needed to make an effective sales presentation.

Back-Door Selling

Sometimes purchasing agents require that all contacts with the prospect's employees be made through them. The purchasing agent insists that salespeople get their approval before meeting with other people involved in the purchase decision. This policy makes it difficult for a new supplier to get business from a customer using a competitor's products.

Salespeople engage in **back-door selling** when they ignore the purchasing agent's policy, go around his or her back, and contact other people involved in the purchasing decision directly. Back-door selling can be very risky and unethical. If the purchasing agent finds out, the salesperson might never be able to get an order. To avoid these potential problems, you need to convince the purchasing agent about the benefits to be gained by direct contact with other people in the customer's firm.

RELATIONSHIP WITH YOUR COMPANY

Because salespeople's activities in the field cannot be closely monitored, their employers trust them to act in the company's best interests. Professional salespeople do not abuse this trust. They put the interests of their company above self-interest. Taking this perspective may require them to make short-term sacrifices to achieve long-term benefits for their companies and themselves. Some problem areas in the salesperson-company relationship involve expense accounts, reporting work-time information and activities, and switching jobs.

Expense Accounts

Many companies provide their salespeople with cars and reimburse them for travel and entertainment expenses. Developing a reimbursement policy that prevents salespeople from cheating and still allows them the needed flexibility to cover their territory and entertain customers is almost impossible. And a lack of tight control can tempt salespeople to use their expense accounts to increase their income.

To do their job well, salespeople need to incur expenses. However, for them to use their expense accounts to overcome what they consider to be inadequate compensation is unethical. If you cannot live within the company compensation plan and expense policies, you have two ethical alternatives: (1) persuade the company to change its compensation plan or expense policy or (2) find another job.

In using the company's expense account, you should act as if you are spending your own money. Eat good food, but don't go to the most expensive restaurant in town. Stay in clean, comfortable, safe lodgings, but not in the best hotel or the best room in a hotel. When traveling, you should maintain the same standard of living and appearance that you do at home.

Reporting Work-Time Information and Activities

Employers expect their salespeople to work full time. Salespeople on salary are stealing from their employer when they waste time on coffee breaks, long lunches, or taking days off. Even salespeople paid by commission cheat their company if they don't work full time. Their income and company profits both decrease when they take time off.

To monitor work activities, many companies ask their salespeople to provide daily call reports. Most salespeople dislike this clerical task. Some provide false information, including calls they never made. Giving inaccurate information or bending the truth is clearly unethical. A failure to get an appointment with a customer is not a sales call. Providing a brief glimpse of a product is not a demonstration.

Switching Jobs

When salespeople decide to change jobs, they have an ethical responsibility to their employer. The company often makes a considerable investment in training salespeople and then provides them with confidential information about new products and programs. Over time, salespeople use this training and information to build strong relationships with their customers.

Salespeople may have good reasons to switch jobs. However, if you go to work for a competitor, you should not say negative things about your previous employer. Also, disclosing confidential information about your former employer's business is improper. The ethical approach to leaving a job includes:[7]

- Giving ample notice. If you leave a job during a busy time and with inadequate notice, your employer may suffer significant lost sales opportunities.

- Offering assistance during the transition phase. Help your replacement learn about your customers and territory.

- Don't burn your bridges. Don't say things in anger that may come back to haunt you. Remember that you may want to return to the company or ask the company for a reference in the future.

RELATIONSHIPS WITH COLLEAGUES

To be effective, salespeople need to work together with other salespeople. Unethical behavior by salespeople toward their co-workers, such as engaging in sexual harassment and taking advantage of colleagues, can weaken company morale and have a negative effect on the company's reputation.

Sexual Harassment

Sexual harassment is unwelcome sexual advances, requests for sexual favors, and other verbal (jokes and graffiti) and physical conduct. Harassment is not confined to requests for sexual favors in exchange for job considerations such as a raise or promotion; simply creating a hostile work environment can be considered sexual harassment.[8]

Unwelcome physical contact is sexual harassment. It is illegal and unethical.

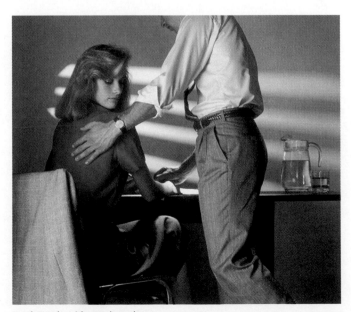

Frank Gardner/The Stock Market.

SELLING SCENARIO

3.2

Turning a Competitor's Negative Comments into a Sale

Steve Shilling is director of sales in New York City for Northern Telecom, a major international telecommunications firm. Using his knowledge of his own and competing products, he turned a competitor's attempt to discredit Northern Telecom products into an advantage.

When Shilling called on the communications manager of a large industrial company, he was surprised by the manager's skeptical, almost hostile attitude. He found out the reason for the chilly reception: A competitor had given the manager a long list of supposed drawbacks to Northern Telecom's products.

Instead of bad-mouthing the competitor, Shilling addressed each point on the list and demonstrated that many—although not all—were invalid. By calmly exposing the erroneous points and frankly admitting the valid ones, Shilling gained credibility and undermined the competitor. The customer became interested in talking with Shilling.

After discussing the customer's application, Shilling explained that his product could solve the problem but the competitor's could not, even though the latter's sales brochure indicated that it could. Shilling knew that this would provoke the purchasing agent, who favored the competitor, to prove him wrong. Shilling landed a $1 million contract when the purchasing agent found the competitor had made a false claim.

Source: Adapted from Edward Doherty, "How to Steal a Satisfied Customer," *Sales & Marketing Management*, March 1990, p. 42. Copyright 1990. Reprinted by permission.

Some actions that are considered sexual harassment are lewd sexual comments and gestures, sexual joking, showing obscene photographs, staring at a co-worker in a sexual manner, alleging that an employee got rewards by engaging in sexual acts, and commenting on an employee's moral reputation.[9]

THINKING IT THROUGH	*A*ssume you are a female who has recently graduated from college. You accept a sales trainee position and your sales manager is a middle-aged male. After several months on the job, he says to you, "I really think you're doing a good job. I like to develop a special relationship with the saleswomen who work for me. Let's have dinner tonight so we can get a start on that special relationship." What would you do?

Taking Advantage of Other Salespeople

Salespeople can behave unethically when they are too aggressive in achieving their own goals at the expense of their colleagues. For example, it is unethical to not relay a customer's phone message to another salesperson or make critical comments about a colleague to your boss. Colleagues usually discover such unethical behavior and return the lack of support.

RELATIONSHIPS WITH COMPETITORS

Clearly it is unethical and often illegal to make false claims about competitors' products or sabotage their efforts. For example, a salesperson who rearranges the display of a competitor's products to make it less appealing is being unethical. This type of behavior can backfire. When customers detect these practices, the reputation of the salespeople and their companies may be permanently damaged. Selling Scenario 3.2 recounts one such incident.

Another questionable tactic is criticizing a competitor's products or policies. Although you might be tempted to say negative things about a competitor, this approach usually does not work. Customers assume that you are biased toward your own company and its products and discount negative comments you make about the competition. Some customers may even be offended. If they have bought the competitor's products in the past, they may regard these comments as a criticism of their judgment.

A PERSONAL CODE OF ETHICS

Salespeople develop a sense of what is right and wrong—a standard of conduct—from family and friends long before they go to work. Although they should abide by their own code of ethics, they may be tempted to avoid difficult ethical choices by developing "logical" reasons for unethical conduct. For example, salespeople may use the following rationalizations:[10]

- All salespeople behave unethically in this situation.
- No one will be hurt by this behavior.
- This behavior is the lesser of two evils.
- This is the price one has to pay for being in business.

Salespeople use such reasoning to avoid feeling responsible for their behavior and being bound by ethical considerations.

Even though the pressure to make sales may tempt you to be unethical and act against your internal standards, maintaining an ethical self-image is important. Compromising ethical standards to achieve short-term gains can have adverse long-term effects. When you violate your own principles, you lose self-respect and confidence in your abilities. You may begin to think that the only way you can make sales is by being dishonest or unethical.

Short-term compromises also make long-term customer relationships more difficult to form. As discussed above, customers will be reluctant to deal with the salesperson again. Also, they may relate these experiences to business associates in other companies.

You can ask yourself some questions to determine whether a sales behavior or activity is unethical. These questions, listed in Exhibit 3.5, emphasize that ethical behavior is determined by widely accepted views of what is right and wrong. Thus, you should only engage in activities about which you would be proud to tell your family, friends, employer, and customers.

Your firm can strongly affect the ethical choices you will have to make. You should not take a job with a company whose products, policies, and conduct conflict with your standards. Self-respect suffers when you have to

EXHIBIT 3.5

CHECKLIST FOR MAKING
ETHICAL DECISIONS

1. Would I be embarrassed if a customer found out about this behavior?
2. Would my supervisor disapprove of this behavior?
3. Would most salespeople feel that this behavior is unusual?
4. Am I about to do this because I think I can get away with it?
5. Would I be upset if a salesperson did this to me?
6. Would my family or friends think less of me if I told them about engaging in this sales activity?
7. Am I concerned about the possible consequences of this behavior?
8. Would I be upset if this behavior or activity were publicized in a newspaper article?
9. Would society be worse off if everyone engaged in this behavior or activity?

If the answer to any of these questions is yes, then the behavior or activity is probably unethical and you should not do it.

compromise principles to please an employer. Before taking a sales job, investigate the company's procedures and selling approach to see if they conflict with your personal ethical standards.

LEGAL ISSUES

Laws codify, or classify, many ethical principles. Society has determined that some activities are clearly unethical, and has decided to use the legal system to prevent people from engaging in these activities. Salespeople who violate these laws can cause serious problems for themselves and their companies—problems more serious than just being considered unethical by a buyer. By engaging in illegal activities, you expose your firm to costly legal fees and hundreds of millions of dollars in fines.[11]

The activities of salespeople in the United States are affected by three forms of law: statutory, administrative, and common. **Statutory law** is based on legislation passed either by state legislatures or by Congress. The main statutory laws governing salespeople are the Uniform Commercial Code and antitrust laws. **Administrative laws** are established by local, state, or federal regulatory agencies. The Federal Trade Commission is the most active agency in developing administrative laws affecting salespeople. However, the Securities and Exchange Commission regulates stockbrokers, and the Food and Drug Administration regulates pharmaceutical salespeople. Finally, **common law** grows out of court decisions. Precedents set by these decisions fill in the gaps where no laws exist.

Current laws affecting salespeople are discussed here, but every year important new laws are developed and court decisions rendered. Thus, you should contact your firm for advice when a potential legal issue arises.[12]

UNIFORM COMMERCIAL CODE

The **Uniform Commercial Code (UCC)** is the legal guide to commercial practice in the United States. In its provisions, the code defines a number of terms related to salespeople.

Agency

A person who acts in place of his or her company is an **agent.** Authorized agents of a company have the authority to legally obligate their firm in a business transaction. This authorization to represent the company does not have to be in writing. Thus, as a salesperson, your statements and actions can legally bind your company and have significant financial impact.

Sale

The UCC defines a **sale** as "the transfer of title to goods by the seller to the buyer for a consideration known as price." A sale differs from a **contract to sell.** Any time a salesperson makes an offer and receives an unqualified acceptance, a contract exists. A sale is made when the contract is completed and title passes from the seller to the buyer.

The UCC also distinguishes between an offer and an invitation to negotiate. A sales presentation is usually considered to be an **invitation to negotiate.** An offer takes place when the salesperson quotes specific terms. The **offer** specifically states what the seller promises to deliver and what it expects from the buyer. If the buyer accepts these terms, the parties will have established a binding contract.

Salespeople are agents when they have the authority to make offers. However, most salespeople are not agents because they only have the power to solicit written offers from buyers. These written offers, called *orders,* become contracts when they are signed by an authorized representative in the salesperson's company. Sometimes these orders contain clauses stating that the firm is not obligated by its salesperson's statements. However, the buyer usually can have the contract nullified, and may even sue for damages, if salespeople make misleading statements, even though they are not official agents.

Title and Risk of Loss

If the terms of the contract specify **FOB (free on board) destination,** the seller has title until the goods are received at the destination. Any loss or damage during transportation is the responsibility of the seller. The buyer assumes this responsibility and risk if contract terms call for **FOB factory.** The UCC also defines when titles transfer for goods shipped COD (cash on delivery) and goods sold on consignment. Understanding the terms of the sale and who has title can be useful in resolving complaints about damaged merchandise.

Oral versus Written Agreements

In most cases, oral agreements between a salesperson and a customer are just as binding as written agreements. Normally, written agreements are required for sales over $500. Salespeople must be careful when signing written agreements, because they may be the legal representatives of their firm.

The Super Valu produce buyer on the right is inspecting a shipment of grapes from Chile. Since the produce was shipped FOB destination, he is not responsible for the merchandise until it arrives at the Super Valu warehouse.

Courtesy SUPERVALU INC.

Obligations and Performance

When the salesperson and customer agree on the terms of a contract, both firms must perform according to those terms. Performance must be in "good faith." Both parties must perform according to commonly accepted industry practices. Even if salespeople overstate the performance of their products, their firms have to provide the stated performance and meet the terms of the contract.

Warranties[13]

A **warranty** is an assurance by the seller that the products will perform as represented. Sometimes a warranty is called a *guarantee*.

The UCC distinguishes between two types of warranties, expressed and implied. An **expressed warranty** is an oral or written statement by the seller. An **implied warranty** is not actually stated but is still an obligation defined by law. For example, products sold using an oral or written description (the buyer never sees the products) carry an implied warranty that the products are of average quality. However, if the buyer inspects the product before placing an order, the implied warranty only applies to any performance aspects that would not have been found by the inspection. Typically, an implied warranty also guarantees that the product can be used in the manner stated by the seller.

Salespeople can create a warranty for their products through inadvertent comments and actions. For example, a chemical company was liable for a product that did not meet the performance standards promised by a

Factual statements made by this salesperson about a new analgesic are regarded as an expressed warranty. They legally obligate his company, particularly if the customer is unsophisticated.

Courtesy Merck & Co., Inc.

salesperson, even though the sales brochure contradicted the salesperson's claims for the product.

Salespeople can also offset the effects of warnings provided by a firm. For example, when securities salespeople indicated that legally required warnings in the documents describing the investment were unimportant and could be ignored, the company offering the securities was liable for millions of dollars when customers were disappointed with the financial returns from the securities.

Problems with warranties often arise when the sale is to a reseller (a distributor or retailer). The ultimate user—the reseller's customer—may complain about a product to the reseller. The reseller, in turn, tries to shift the responsibility to the manufacturer. Salespeople often have to investigate and resolve these issues.

MISREPRESENTATION OR SALES PUFFERY[14]

In their enthusiasm, salespeople may exaggerate the performance of products and even make false statements to get an order. Such misrepresentation can destroy a business relationship and may involve salespeople and their firms in lawsuits.

Over time, common and administrative laws have defined the difference between illegal misrepresentation and sales puffery. Not all statements made by salespeople have legal consequences.

Glowing descriptions, such as "Our service can't be beat," are considered to be opinions or sales puffery. Customers cannot reasonably rely on these statements. However, statements about the inherent capabilities of products or services, such as "Our system will reduce your inventory by

40 percent," may be treated as statements of fact and warranties. Here are examples of such statements found to be legally binding:

> This is a safe, dependable helicopter.
>
> Feel free to prescribe this drug to your patients, doctor. It's nonaddicting.
>
> This equipment will keep up with any other machine you are using and will work well with your other machines.

Factual statements become particularly strong indicators of an expressed warranty when salespeople sell complex products to unsophisticated buyers. In these situations, buyers rely on the technical expertise and integrity of the salespeople. However, when salespeople deal with knowledgeable buyers, the buyers are obligated to go beyond assertions made by salespeople and make their own investigation of the product's performance.[15]

US salespeople need to be aware of the both US laws and laws in the host country when they are selling internationally. All countries have laws regulating marketing and selling activities. In Canada, all claims and statements made in advertisements and sales presentations about comparisons with competitive products must pass the **credulous person standard.** This means the company and the salesperson have to pay damages if a reasonable person could misunderstand the statement. Thus, a statement like, "This is the strongest axle in Canada" might be considered puffery in the United States, but be viewed as misleading in Canada unless the firm had absolute evidence that the axle was stronger than any other axle sold in Canada.

To avoid legal and ethical problems with misrepresentation, you should try to educate customers thoroughly before concluding a sale. You should tell the customer as much about the specific performance of the product as possible. Unless your firm has test results concerning the product's performance, you should avoid offering an opinion about the product's specific benefits in the customer's application. If you don't have the answer to a customer's question, don't make a guess. Say that you don't know the answer and will get back to the customer with the information.

ILLEGAL BUSINESS PRACTICES

The Sherman Antitrust Act of 1890, the Clayton Act of 1914, the Federal Trade Commission Act of 1914, and the Robinson-Patman Act of 1934 prohibit unfair business practices that may lessen competition. These laws are used by the courts to create common law that defines the illegal business practices discussed here.

Business Defamation

Business defamation occurs when salespeople make unfair or untrue statements to customers about a competitor, its products, or its salespeople. These statements are illegal when they damage the competitor's reputation or the reputation of its salespeople. Some examples of false statements that have been found to be illegal are:

- Company X broke the law when it offered you a free case of toilet paper with every 12 cases you buy.
- Company X is going bankrupt.
- You shouldn't do business with Company X. Mr. Jones, the CEO, is really incompetent and dishonest.

You should avoid making negative comments about a competitor, its salespeople, or its products unless you have proof to support the statement.

Reciprocity

Reciprocity is a special relationship in which two companies agree to buy products from each other. For example, a manufacturer of computers agrees to use microprocessors from a component manufacturer if the component manufacturer agrees to buy its computers. Such interrelationships can lead to greater trust and cooperation between the firms. However, reciprocity agreements are illegal if one company forces another company to join in the agreement. Reciprocity is legal only when both parties consent to the agreement willingly.

not same as strat. allian.

Tying Agreements

In a **tying agreement,** a buyer is required to purchase one product in order to get another product. For example, a customer who wants to buy a copy machine is required to buy paper from the same company, or a distributor that wants to stock one product must stock the manufacturer's entire product line. Because they reduce competition, tying agreements typically are illegal. They are only legal when the seller can show that the products must be used together—that one product will not function properly unless the other product is used with it.

Tying agreements are also legal when a company's reputation depends on the proper functioning of equipment. Thus, a firm can be required to buy a service contract for equipment it purchases, but need not buy the contract from the manufacturer.

Conspiracy and Collusion

An agreement between competitors before customers are contacted is a **conspiracy,** whereas **collusion** refers to competitors working together while the customer is making a purchase decision. For example, competitors are conspiring when they get together and divide up a territory so that only one competitor will call on each prospect. Collusion occurs when competitors agree to charge the same price for equipment that a prospect is considering. These examples of collusion and conspiracy are illegal because they reduce competition.

Interference with Competitors

Salespeople may illegally interfere with competitors by:[16]

- Trying to get a customer to break a contract with a competitor.
- Tampering with a competitor's product.
- Confusing a competitor's market research by buying merchandise from stores.

Restrictions on Resellers

Numerous laws govern the relationship between manufacturers and resellers—wholesalers and retailers. [17] At one time, it was illegal for companies to establish a minimum price below which their distributors or retailers could not resell their products. Now this practice, **resale price maintenance,** is legal in some situations.

Manufacturers do not have to sell their products to any reseller that wants to buy them. Sellers can use their judgment to select resellers, as long as they announce, in advance, their selection criteria.

One sales practice considered unfair is providing special incentives to get a reseller's salespeople to push products. For example, salespeople for a cosmetics company may give a department store's cosmetics salespeople prizes based on the sales of their product. These special incentives, called **spiffs** (or **push money**), are legal only if the reseller knows and approves of the incentive and it is offered to all of the reseller's salespeople.

Price Discrimination

The Robinson-Patman Act became law because independent wholesalers and retailers wanted additional protection from the aggressive marketing tactics of large chain stores. Principally, the act forbids price discrimination in interstate commerce. While Robinson-Patman applies only to interstate commerce, most states have passed similar laws to govern sales transactions between buyers and sellers within the same state.

Court decisions related to the Robinson-Patman Act define **price discrimination** as a seller giving unjustified special prices, discounts, or services to some customers and not to others. To justify a special price or discount, the seller must prove that it results from (1) differences in the cost of manufacture, sale, or delivery; (2) differences in the quality or nature of the product delivered; or (3) an attempt to meet prices offered by competitors in a market. Thus, you must treat all customers equally. If you offer a price discount or special service to one customer, you must offer it to all customers.

Different prices can be charged, however, if the cost of doing business is different. For example, a customer who buys in large volume can be charged a lower price if the manufacturing and shipping charges for higher-volume orders are less.

Firms also may not offer special allowances to one reseller unless these allowances are made available to competing resellers. Because most resell-

The Robinson-Patman act requires salespeople to offer the same prices and services to the corner grocery store on the left and the supermarket on the right. Different prices can only be offered when the cost of doing business with these two customers differs.

Kent Knudson/Stock Imagery.

Courtesy SUPERVALU INC.; photo by James Schnepf.

ers compete in limited geographic areas, firms frequently offer allowances in specific regions of the country.

▌ GUIDELINES

To reduce the chances of violating laws governing sales practices, you should adopt the following guidelines:[18]

- Be sure that all specific statements about your product's performance, such as technical characteristics and useful life, are accurate.

- Be sure that all specific positive statements about performance can be supported by evidence. If you make strong positive statements that cannot be supported, use very general wording, such as "high quality" and "great value."

- If your customers do not pay attention to warnings and operating instructions, remind them to read this information. Never suggest that this information can be ignored.

- If customers contemplate using your product incorrectly or in an inappropriate application, caution them specifically about how the product should be used.

- Assess your customer's experience and knowledge. Your legal obligations are greater with unsophisticated customers.

- Don't make negative statements about a competitor's product, financial condition, or business practices. Never pass along rumors about competitors.

S E L L I N G   S C E N A R I O

3.3

Innocent Gift or Bribe?

Jerry Fadiman confronted an ethical problem in East Africa when a customer said, "Oh, and Bwana, I would like 1,000 shillings as *Zwandi,* my gift. And, as we are now friends, for *Chai,* bring an eight-band radio to my house when you visit." *Zwandi* and *Chai* can be interpreted as Swahili terms for "bribe." The request came at the conclusion of a negotiation. Fadiman had planned to follow American custom and buy the customer a drink to symbolically close the deal. But now he was faced with this request for money. Surprised by the request, he said, "I'm an American. I don't pay bribes," and walked away.

As Fadiman gained more knowledge of business practices in East Africa, he realized that he had made a mistake. Due to a limited command of English, the customer had framed his request as a command, but his statement was meant to be a request to participate in a local tradition. In East Africa, the traditional method for celebrating the beginning of a business relationship is to have a party and invite friends and business associates to meet the new business "partner." Both parties in the relationship pay for the party. The radio was intended to create a more festive atmosphere.

Source: Adapted from Jerry Fadiman, "A Traveler's Guide to Gifts and Bribes," *Harvard Business Review,* July–August 1986, pp. 122–36.

ETHICAL AND LEGAL ISSUES IN INTERNATIONAL SELLING

Ethical and legal issues are very complex when selling in international markets.[19] Value judgments and laws vary widely across cultures and countries. What is commonly accepted as right in one country can be completely unacceptable in another country. For example, a small payment to expedite the loading of a truck is considered a cost of doing business in some Middle Eastern countries, but may be viewed as a bribe in the United States. Selling Scenario 3.3 illustrates how differences in language can cause people to misinterpret gifts and bribes.

LUBRICATION AND SUBORDINATION

In many countries, there is a clear distinction between payments for lubrication and payments for subordination. **Lubrication** involves small sums of money or gifts, typically made to low-ranking managers or government officials, in countries where these payments are not illegal. The lubrication payments are to get the official or manager to do their job more rapidly—to process an order more quickly or to provide a copy of a request for a proposal. **Subordination** involves paying larger sums of money to higher-ranking officials to get them to do something that is illegal or to ignore an illegal act. Even in countries where bribery is common, subordination is considered to be unethical.[20]

Legal and ethical issues vary widely in different cultures. To sell effectively in Japan, this salesperson needs to have a good understanding about what behaviors are considered ethical and unethical in the customer's culture.

Neil Selkirk/TSW.

LEGAL ISSUES

US salespeople are subject to US laws, regardless of the country they are selling in. US laws prohibit participating in unauthorized boycotts, trading with enemies of the United States, or engaging in activities that adversely affect the US economy. Under the anti-boycott law, it is illegal for US firms and their salespeople to be involved in an unauthorized boycott of a foreign country. Any approach to cooperate in such a boycott must be reported. For example, a large hospital supply company was found guilty of violating this law when it closed its manufacturing plant in Israel to get its name off an Arab blacklist.

The **Foreign Corrupt Practices Act** makes it illegal for US companies to pay bribes to foreign officials. Violations of the law can result in sizable fines for company managers, employees, and agents that knowingly participate or authorize the payment of such bribes. However, an amendment to the act permits small lubrication payments when they are customary in a culture.

The US laws concerning bribery are much more restrictive than laws in other countries. For example, in Italy and Germany, bribes made outside the countries are clearly defined as legal and tax deductible.

SUMMARY

This chapter discusses the legal and ethical responsibilities of salespeople. These responsibilities are particularly important in personal selling, because salespeople may face conflicts between their personal standards and the standards of their firm and customers.

Salespeople's ethical standards determine how they will conduct relationships with their customers, employer, and competitors. Relations with customers involve the use of entertainment and gifts and the disclosure of confidential information.

Salespeople also need to have standards in dealing with their own company concerning expenses and job changes. Finally, salespeople must be careful in how they talk about competitors and treat competitive products.

Many companies have ethical standards that describe the behavior expected of their salespeople. In evaluating potential employers, salespeople should consider these standards.

Salespeople need to develop their own ethical standards of right and wrong. But they also need to develop their own standards, because salespeople encounter many situations not covered by company statements. Without personal standards, they will lose their self-respect and the respect of their company and customers. Good ethics are good business. Over the long run, salespeople with a good sense of ethics will be more successful than will salespeople who compromise their and society's ethics for short-term gain.

Statutory laws (such as the Uniform Commercial Code) and administrative law (such as Federal Trade Commission rulings) guide the activities of salespeople in the United States. Selling in international markets is quite complex, because salespeople need to be aware of differences in ethical judgements and laws, both those of the United States and those of the host country, related to sales activities.

KEY TERMS

administrative law   72
agent   73
back-door selling   67
bribes   65
business defamation   76
collusion   77
common law   72
conspiracy   77
contract to sell   73
credulous person standard   80
deception   64
ethics   60
expressed warranty   74
FOB destination   73
FOB factory   73
Foreign Corrupt Practices Act   81

implied warranty   74
invitation to negotiate   73
kickbacks   65
lubrication   80
offer   73
price discrimination   79
reciprocity   77
resale price maintenance   78
sale   73
sexual harassment   69
spiffs (push money)   78
statutory law   72
subordination   80
tying agreement   77
Uniform Commercial Code (UCC)   72
warranty   74

QUESTIONS AND PROBLEMS

 1. Consider each situation below and indicate whether the salesperson behaved illegally, unethically, or inappropriately, or if there was no problem with the behavior.

   a. The buyer's secretary asks you out as you are leaving the plant after making a sales call, and you accept.

   b. You have a customer that is about to place an order. You know that the product's price will be reduced in two weeks and you don't inform the buyer about the impending price reduction. If the buyer knew about the price reduction, she would wait two weeks to place the order.

   c. You accept an invitation from a buyer to take you out to dinner in appreciation for all of the support you have provided over the last three months.

   d. You ask a buyer about the experiences he has had with a competitor's products.

   e. You go directly to see the head of the engineering department because the buyer will not see you.

   f. You take the afternoon off after making a big sale.

2. For centuries, the guideline for business transactions was the Latin term *caveat emptor* (let the buyer beware). This principle suggests that the seller is not responsible for the buyer's welfare. Is this principle still appropriate in modern business transactions? Why or why not?

3. Why are salespeople more likely to confront ethical situations than are people in other occupations?

4. What should a salesperson do if he or she believes a competitor is making unethical statements about his or her product?

5. Is it ever appropriate to give gifts to customers? Why or why not?

6. If bribing buyers is common practice in an industry or country, what should a salesperson do?

7. Why are laws enacted to regulate the behavior of salespeople and firms?

8. Consider this statement: Sales managers, not salespeople, have to be concerned with the legal implications of selling activities. Do you agree with this statement? Why or why not?

9. Jim Hanson is a sales representative for a plastics manufacturer. His company has always had a policy of uniform pricing for all customers. One of his largest customers, Hoffman Container, always tries to bargain for special prices. The buyer is now threatening to use another supplier unless Jim agrees to a special price concession. Jim's sales manager has agreed to the concession. Jim has just gotten a similar-size order from one of Hoffman's competitors at a price 10 percent higher than Hoffman is demanding. What should Jim do? Does Jim have any responsibility to Hoffman's competitor?

10. In Selling Scenario 3.1, was Mr. Lesk's response to the vice president's question the best way to handle this situation? Can you think of a better response, one that would maintain integrity but not risk losing the business?

CASE PROBLEMS

CASE 3 • 1
CONFRONTING AN ETHICAL DILEMMA IN A NEW TERRITORY

Rich Romano received his BA in June 1994 and joined Toddlers, Inc., as a sales trainee. He expected to work for six to nine months as a trainee and then be assigned to a sales territory. Toddlers is a large manufacturer of children's wear, with annual sales in excess of $20 million. It employs 25 salespeople, who are paid a straight commission of 6 percent. They all report to the national sales manager, Susan Hoyt.

In November 1994, Ed Davis, the sales representative covering the Atlanta territory, died suddenly. Davis had been a longtime employee of Toddlers and was highly regarded for his selling abilities. When news of the sales rep's death reached headquarters, Hoyt asked Romano to take over the territory. She went on to explain that she was going on a four-week business trip to Europe and would be unable to introduce Romano to customers in the territory.

During his first two weeks in the territory, Romano visited most of its key customers. He made several sales and opened some new accounts. After this success, he felt confident enough to meet with the buyer for his largest account, Don Black of the Kiddie World chain. The previous year, Kiddie World had ordered $80,000 in merchandise. Romano, anxious to present the new spring line and to establish rapport with this key customer, arranged a dinner date with Black.

The dinner meeting went well. After some social conversation, Romano presented the new line and asked Black what he thought of it. Black said he was impressed but he was also considering two competitive lines. After Romano explained how Toddlers' line was superior, Black told Romano that Ed Davis had given him a $500 bonus before each season. Black said, "I hope we can work together the way Ed and I did. There are a lot of good lines and a lot of good salespeople, but Ed was something special."

QUESTION

1.   What would you do if you were in Rich Romano's position?

CASE 3 • 2
TO BRIBE OR NOT TO BRIBE

The Lodi Machine Tool Company has a one-person sales office in a large Latin American country. Frank Rothe has been in that country for 10 years and is retiring this year. His replacement is Bill Hunt, a top sales rep covering Texas and New Mexico.

Frank has been very successful in spite of his unique style and his refusal to conform with company policies. Some senior executives complained about Frank to the former CEO, who responded, "If he's making money—and he is—then leave the guy alone." However, the new CEO is reorganizing Lodi to be a global firm in which a loner like Frank would probably not fit in. In fact, the CEO specifically chose Bill to replace Frank because Bill is an organization person.

When Bill arrived at the Latin American Lodi office, Frank was on his way to inspect some Lodi machines. Some adjustments had to be made in the machines before they would be acceptable to the government agency buying them. After inspecting the machines, Bill and Frank had lunch.

FRANK   "Bill, did you see any problems with the S-27s we just looked at?"

BILL   "No, they looked fine to me."

FRANK   "I suspect this is one of the most sophisticated instances of bribe taking I've come across in my 10 years here. Most of the time they're more honest about their *mordidas* than this."

BILL   "What is *mordidas?*"

FRANK   "*Mordidas* is a little grease to expedite the action. It's a local word for a slight offering. You might call it a bribe."

BILL   "Do we pay bribes to get an order?"

FRANK   "Oh it depends on the situation, but it's something you have to deal with. Here's the story. When the S-27s arrived, we began uncrating them and right away the local engineer for the agency told me there is a vital defect with the machines. I agreed to have our staff engineer check all the machines and make the necessary adjustments, but he said there wasn't enough time for an engineer to come from the States. He said the machines could be adjusted locally. We could pay him and he would make the arrangements. What could I do? I paid him $1,200 for each machine."

BILL   "I don't like it. We've got good products and they are priced right. We give good service and keep plenty of spare parts in Latin America. Why should we have to pay bribes? In addition, paying bribes to a government official is illegal."

FRANK   "Look, you're not back in the States any longer. If you stop these payoffs your sales are going to go down, because our competitors from Germany, Italy, and Japan will pay them."

BILL   "I know. But wrong is wrong and we want to operate differently now. We want to expand our operation here and make a long-term commitment. One of the first thing we must avoid is unethical . . ."

FRANK   "But is it unethical? Everyone does it and the people here even pay *mordidas* to each other. Remember, 'When in Rome do as the Romans do.'"

BILL   "I can't buy that. We have to differentiate ourselves from the rest of our competition. Graft and unethical behavior have to be cut out to build lasting relationships. By taking the high road, we will strengthen our position."

FRANK   "I know it's hard to accept. Probably the most disturbing problem in these developing countries is graft. And frankly, we really don't know how to deal with it. It bothered me at first. But now I think it makes its own economic contribution because it's as much a part of the economic process as a payroll. Are we developers of wealth, helping to push the country to greater economic growth, or are we missionaries? Or should we be both?"

QUESTIONS

1. Is what Frank did ethical? Frank seems to imply that there is a difference between business activities in Latin America and those in the United States. Do you think there is a difference?

2. If Frank should not have paid the bribe, what should he have done, and what might have been the consequences?

3. What are Lodi's interests in this situation, and should they be considered?

CASE 3 • 3
EVALUATING ETHICAL
ASPECTS OF SELLING
BEHAVIORS

For each of the following situations, evaluate the salesperson's action and indicate what you think the appropriate action should be.

1. A salesperson picks up an order at a customer's plant but forgets to turn it in to the order processing department. After a few weeks, the customer calls to complain about the slow delivery. The salesperson realizes the order has not been turned in and immediately submits it. Then the salesperson tells the customer that the slow delivery is due to a mistake in the order processing department. The salesperson lays the blame on the order processing department because the truth might jeopardize future relations with the customer.

2. A customer gives a salesperson a suggestion. The salesperson does not turn in the idea to her company, even though the company's policy manual states that all customer ideas should be submitted with the monthly expense report. Instead, the salesperson quits her job and starts her own business, using the customer's suggestion.

3. A cosmetics manufacturer begins a program of providing extra incentives to retail clerks in cosmetics departments. The salespeople for the cosmetics company are instructed to contact retail clerks and offer them $1 for each item they sell from the manufacturer's product line. The company instructs the salespeople not to mention this program to the managements of the retail stores.

4. Mary Wilson, a retail salesclerk, uses a sales technique that enables her to increase her sales significantly. When customers are shopping for various items, Mary takes the item they seem to favor and immediately wraps it up. She then asks the shoppers if they need anything else. Mary has found that most shoppers will buy the item that has been wrapped.

5. A salesperson selling small business computers is asked by a customer if the computer has software for an inventory control system. The salesperson replies that an inventory control software package is available as part of the standard software system that comes with each unit. The salesperson has answered the question truthfully but has failed to mention that the inventory control software is only useful in a few special situations and probably will not meet the customer's needs.

6. A business major is being considered for a sales job. During the interview, the sales manager indicates that company officials want to meet the student's husband before offering her a job. Such a meeting is necessary, the company believes, because a salesperson's family can be helpful in influencing customers during social events.

7. The custom of the trade is that competitive firms submit bids based on specifications provided by the buyer; then the buyer places an order with the firm offering the lowest bid. After a salesperson submits a bid, the purchasing agent calls him and indicates that the bid is $100 too high. The buyer asks the salesperson to submit another bid at a price $100 lower.

8. A student interviews for a job. The job is attractive, but the salary is about $2,000 lower than those for other sales jobs. When the student tells the interviewer about the low salary, the interviewer says, "You can pick up about $50 a week by padding your expense account."

9. In some Latin American countries, a cash payoff to customers who do a favor for a salesperson is considered normal. A young, inexperienced salesperson is given the responsibility for sales in such a Latin American country. When a buyer confronts the salesperson with a demand for a cash payoff in return for a larger order, the salesperson complies.

ADDITIONAL REFERENCES

Bellizzi, Joseph, and Robert Hite. "Supervising Unethical Salesforce Behavior." *Journal of Marketing*, April 1989, pp. 36–47.

Boedecker, Karl; Fred Morgan; and Jeffery Stoltman. "Legal Dimensions of Salespersons' Statements: A Review and Managerial Suggestions." *Journal of Marketing,* January 1991, pp. 70–80.

"Businesses Are Signing Up for Ethics 101." *Business Week*, February 15, 1988, p. 57.

Dawson, Leslie. "Will Feminization Change the Ethics of the Sales Profession?" *Journal of Personal Selling and Sales Management* 11 (Winter 1992), pp. 21–32.

DeConinck, James B. "How Sales Managers Control Unethical Sales Force Behavior." *Journal of Business Ethics,* October 1992, pp. 789–98.

DeConinck, James B, and Paul Thistlethwaite. "Sales Managers' Perceptions of the Appropriate Response to Unethical Sales Force Behavior." *Journal of Applied Business Research* 8 (Winter 1991–1992), pp. 118–23.

Dubinsky, Alan, and Barbara Loken. "Analyzing Ethical Decision Making in Marketing." *Journal of Business Research,* Spring 1989, pp. 83–107.

Finn, William. "How to Make the Sale and Remain Ethical." *Sales & Marketing Management,* August 1988, p. 8.

Hunt, Shelby, and Scott Vitell. "A General Theory of Marketing Ethics." *Journal of Macromarketing,* Spring 1986, pp. 5–16.

Laczniak, Gene, and Patrick Murphy. *Marketing Ethics.* Lexington, Mass.: D.C. Heath, 1985.

Murphy, Patrick. "Implementing Business Ethics." *Journal of Business Ethics,* December 1988, pp. 910–21.

Trawick, I Fredrick; John Swan; and David Rink. "Industrial Buyer Evaluation of the Ethics of Salesperson Gift Giving: Value of the Gift and Customer versus Prospect Status." *Journal of Personal Selling and Sales Management,* Summer 1989, pp. 31–37.

Vaccaro, Joseph, and Derek Coward. "Managerial and Legal Implications of Price Haggling: A Sales Manager's Dilemma." *Journal of Personal Selling and Sales Management* 13 (Summer 1993), pp. 79–86.

Wotruba, Thomas. "A Comprehensive Framework for the Analysis of Ethical Behavior, with a Focus on Sales Organizations." *Journal of Personal Selling and Sales Management,* Spring 1990, pp. 29–42.

KNOWLEDGE AND SKILL REQUIREMENTS

The basis of effective personal selling is understanding the customer's needs and communicating how your product or service satisfies those needs. Part II provides information about the knowledge and skills needed to be an effective salesperson.

Chapter 4 focuses on customers—the process they go through in making purchase decisions and the factors they consider in evaluating alternatives. The chapter also outlines changes occurring in the way businesses buy products and services, and shows how these changes will affect what salespeople do.

Chapter 5 reviews communication principles. It explains how salespeople can collect information about their customers by listening, asking questions, and observing nonverbal behaviors. Methods for using verbal and nonverbal communication to influence customers are also discussed.

Effective selling requires salespeople to adapt both the style and content of their sales presentations to satisfy the needs of a customer. Chapter 6 discusses why flexibility is important and how salespeople can develop the knowledge to effectively practice adaptive selling.

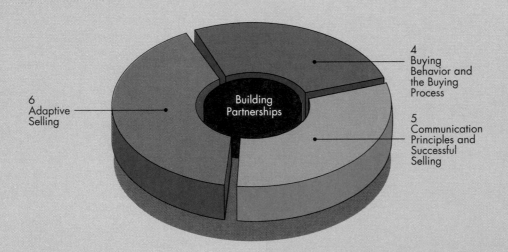

Buying Behavior and the Buying Process

S uperior customer knowledge enabled Bill Meyer, vice president of sales for Chemineer Corp., to snatch a million-dollar contract from a complacent competitor. Chemineer makes mixing equipment for chemical plants. When Meyer received an inquiry from a major chemical company, he assumed the inquiry was a mere formality because the chemical company bought all of its mixing equipment from a competitor. The key decision maker was very concerned about mechanical problems of mounting and supporting an unusually large mixing tank. Meyer found out who the other decision makers were and arranged for them to talk with customers using similar-sized tanks made by Chemineer.

Meanwhile, Chemineer's competitor was unaware of the customer's concerns. As the established supplier, they didn't keep on top of the customer's new needs. Chemineer won the contract, despite a slightly higher price, because Meyer knew more about the customer.[1]

To be effective, salespeople must know what their customers need, who will be involved in the purchase decision, and how the purchase decision will be made. The more salespeople know about their customers, the more effective they will be in satisfying those customers' needs.

Some questions answered in this chapter are:

What are the different types of customers?

How do organizations make purchase decisions?

What factors do organizations consider when evaluating products and services?

Who is involved in the buying decision?

What should salespeople do in the different types of buying situations?

What changes are occurring in organizational buying, and how will these changes affect salespeople?

Jim Groose is a regional manager for Sentry Equipment Corp. based in Oconomowoc, Wisconsin. Sentry manufactures systems for monitoring the performance of power plants that generate electricity. The outputs from its monitoring system are used to make adjustments in the operation of the power plant, which improves its efficiency.

"We really sell a wide range of products, from $500 components that customers reorder without much analysis to $5 million systems that might take four or five years to close a sale. To sell the systems, you have to get in on the ground floor—before the power plant is built. You need to work with the architects and project engineers that are designing the plant and make sure your system is in the design.

"It's really hard to sell a system into an existing plant. You have to convince the plant engineers, purchasing agent, and plant manager that a new system is going to provide a meaningful benefit. The key players are usually very risk averse. They take the position that 'if it isn't broke, don't fix it.' One approach that we take to reduce their risk is offering a 60-day demonstration of a piece of the system. We'll install a partial system, without charging them, and let the performance sell them."

As you can well imagine, when something costs millions of dollars, many people are involved in making the ultimate decision. Groose and his salespeople will deal with project and architect engineers, facility chemists, plant managers, secretaries, and purchasing agents before the job is finished. He finds that his degrees in chemistry and water resources management give him the ability to talk the same language as many of the technical people he'll deal with. "And sometimes they all have slightly different needs and problems that we're looking to solve. Sometimes it's difficult to walk a fine line among all the different motivations."

The decision process in industrial selling is distinct from most consumer products. "Most of our projects will take the form of a 'request for proposal or quote' from a prospective customer. Typically, in response, we'll provide a very detailed 50-page proposal to the customer. This will include drawings and spec sheets as well as the advantages and benefits of our system. Sometimes we'll also give a formal presentation to the buyer and project engineer. This gives us an opportunity to answer any questions and field any objections. Very often we can turn what the customer perceived as a negative into a positive.

"Usually there are at least two other bidders besides Sentry Equipment, so understanding the competition is also an issue for us. Of course, price and service are critical to customers, but we want to demonstrate that our system will do everything they're asking for and sometimes more."

JIM GROOSE

Sentry Equipment Corp.

TYPES OF CUSTOMERS

Salespeople interact with a wide of variety of customers, including business enterprises, government agencies, institutions, and consumers. Each of these customer types has different needs, and each requires unique selling approaches.

▌ BUSINESS ENTERPRISES

Business enterprises can be involved in three different types of buying situations: They make buying decisions as original equipment manufacturers (OEMs), end users, and resellers.

Original Equipment Manufacturers

When businesses purchase goods (components, subassemblies, raw and processed materials) to use them in products they produce, they are acting as **original equipment manufacturers (OEMs)**. For example, Intel produces microprocessors and sells them to OEM customers, such as IBM. The microprocessors directly affect the performance and cost of IBM's personal computers. Thus, quality and cost are important concerns for OEM purchases.[2]

Some components develop such a good reputation for quality that they help sell the OEM's products. For example, personal computer manufacturers advertise that Intel microprocessors are inside their computers. Thus, customers who believe Intel microprocessors offer superior performance will be more inclined to purchase a personal computer containing Intel microprocessors.

Salespeople working in the automobile industry can sell to companies that manufacture automobiles, dealers who resell automobiles, or consumers who use automobiles.

Courtesy Ford Motor Company.

Courtesy Ford Motor Company.

Most OEM products are standardized and purchased in large quantities on an annual contract. The purchasing department negotiates the contract with the supplier; however, engineering and production departments evaluate the products and can affect the choice of suppliers. When sellers custom design OEM products to buyers' specifications, the buyers' engineering and production areas have much more influence in the choice of vendor.

End Users

When businesses purchase goods and services to support their own production and operations, they are acting as **end users.** End-user buying situations include the purchase of capital equipment and maintenance, repair, and operating (MRO) supplies. **Capital equipment** items are major purchases, such as mainframe computers and machine tools, which are used by the business for a number of years. **MRO supplies** are minor purchases, such as paper towels and pencils, which have a short useful life.

Since capital equipment purchases typically require major financial commitments, many people, including high-level corporate executives, are involved in the purchase decision. Reliability, service, and support are often important considerations, because an equipment failure can shut down the customer's operation. Capital equipment customers often are more interested in operating cost than the initial purchase price, because the equipment will be used over a long period of time.

MRO supplies and services are not part of the finished product and do not support the production of the finished product. Thus, these purchases typically are less important to businesses. Purchasing agents usually oversee these buying decisions. Because they typically do not have time to evaluate all suppliers, they tend to purchase from vendors who have performed well in the past. Some professional services, such as accounting, advertising, and consulting, are more important to the company and may be treated as capital equipment purchases.[3]

Resellers

When products or services are bought with the intention of reselling them to businesses and consumers, the firms purchasing the products are acting as **resellers.** For example, an electronics distributor purchases large quantities of microprocessors from a semiconductor manufacturer and sells smaller quantities to a firm producing home security systems. Resellers come in many types, including retailers (restaurants, supermarkets, and department and discount stores) and distributors.

Because resellers do not use the products, they are primarily interested in the attractiveness of the products to their customers. For example, Du Pont promotes the benefits of Stainmaster© carpets to stimulate consumer demand and, thus, encourage carpet distributors and retailers to stock and sell it. Resellers are also interested in services provided by suppliers that make the resale of the product more profitable.[4] (The special needs of resellers and approaches for selling to them are discussed in Chapter 15.)

Note that the same customer can act as an OEM manufacturer, an end user, and a reseller. For example, Dell Computer makes OEM buying decisions when it purchases microprocessors for its computers; acts as an end

DuPont encourages retailers to buy its Stainmaster© carpet by advertising to the retailer's customers and stimulating demand.

Courtesy E.I. du Pont de Nemours and Company.

user when it buys a machine to bend sheet metal for the case in which the computer is housed; and functions as a reseller when it buys software to resell to its computer customers when they place an order.

GOVERNMENT

The largest customers for goods and services in the United States are federal, state, and local governments, which purchase over $1 trillion of goods and services annually. Selling to the government is highly specialized and often very frustrating. Government buyers typically develop detailed specifications for a product and then invite qualified suppliers to submit bids. A contract is awarded to the lowest bidder.[5] However, government agencies are beginning to purchase more commercial products with less red tape.[6]

Effective selling to government agencies requires a thorough knowledge of their unique procurement procedures and rules. Salespeople also need to know about projected needs so they can influence the development of the buying specifications. For example, Hershey sold a lot of specially designed

Desert Bars to the US Army during Operations Desert Shield and Desert Storm. These candy bars were designed to taste good and not melt in temperatures over 100° F.[7]

Many salespeople that sell in international arenas find themselves selling to government agencies, even though private companies may be their biggest customers in the US. For example, Northern Telecom, a Canadian company that manufactures and sells telephone equipment, would sell to a private company like IBM or GM in the US but to the Post, Telephone, and Telegraph (PTT) government agency in many countries in Europe, Asia, and Africa. While bid processes may be used, issues such as percentage of domestic product (countries may require a certain percentage of the product be manufactured or assembled locally) and exchange rates (the value of local currency in US dollars) are just as important as what the product actually does. In addition, different economic and political systems can make selling difficult. Add differences in culture and language, among others, and selling to foreign governments becomes a challenge.

INSTITUTIONS

similar to govt.

Another important customer group consists of public and private institutions, such as churches, hospitals, and colleges. Often these institutions have purchasing rules and procedures that are just as complex and rigid as those used by government agencies.

Packaged goods manufacturers, such as Heinz, sell to both resellers (supermarkets) and institutional customers (restaurants and hospitals). These customers have different needs and buying processes. Thus, Heinz has one sales force calling on supermarkets and another sales force selling different products to restaurants.

CONSUMERS

Consumers purchase products and services for use by themselves or by their families. A lot of salespeople sell insurance, automobiles, clothing, and real estate to consumers. However, most college graduates take sales jobs that involve selling to business enterprises, government agencies, or institutions. Thus, the examples in this text focus on these selling situations, and this chapter discusses organizational rather than consumer buying behavior.

ORGANIZATIONAL BUYING AND SELLING

The salespeople you encounter most frequently sell to consumers. They have a very different job than do the salespeople who call on organizations. Since the organizational buying process typically is more complex than the consumer buying process, selling to organizations often requires more skills and is more challenging.

COMPLEXITY OF THE BUYING PROCESS

The typical organizational purchase is much larger than the typical consumer purchase and can have an important effect on corporate performance. Organizations use highly trained, knowledgeable purchasing agents to make these decisions. Many other people in organizations get involved

S E L L I N G   S C E N A R I O

4.1

100 Sales Calls to Get a Big Order

GTE's traffic council spent three days hearing proposals from more than a dozen companies seeking the firm's freight forwarding business. Frank Perry (national account sales manager for Pilot Air Freight), John Edwards (Pilot's president), and Dick Morris (national sales manager) had to present their case quickly. Edwards said, "You get four minutes, so we could only show six slides. It was the shortest time I have ever talked in my life." After answering some questions and making minor changes in their proposal, the three headed home.

Frank Perry had first targeted GTE four years earlier, but the traffic people were not interested in talking with a new supplier. The company had just signed contracts with a number of other freight forwarders. Getting GTE interested in Pilot was difficult because decisions on buying freight forwarding service were made by a traffic council comprised of 25 decision makers from GTE installations across the country.

Pilot felt it had a shot at the business because its flexible service was well suited to GTE plants that work two and three shifts a day. Pilot promoted itself as the forwarder that would pick up and deliver 24 hours a day, but more than a year passed before anyone at GTE noticed.

Finally, two GTE plants agreed to give Pilot a tryout. Once Pilot established a reliable track record at these plants, other GTE plants began to use Pilot. While Perry made presentations to all the key buying influences at GTE, he counted on one or two of them to support him in the council meeting. "You need someone who will carry your cause in those meetings and be your spokesperson."

Pilot was awarded a three-year contract by this giant corporation. Over 100 sales calls to GTE plants across the country and three years of effort won the order, not that four-minute presentation.

Source: Adapted from Martin Everett, "This Is the Ultimate in Selling," *Sales & Marketing Management*, August 1989, pp. 28–29. Copyright August 1989. Reprinted by permission.

in purchase decisions, including engineers, production managers, business analysts, and senior executives.

Organizational buying decisions often involve extensive evaluations and negotiations over a period of time. The average time required to complete a purchase is five months, and during that time salespeople need to make many calls to gather and provide information. Selling Scenario 4.1 describes the time and effort required to make a major sale.

The complexity of organizational purchase decisions means that salespeople must be able to work effectively with a wide range of people. For example, when selling a new additive to a food processor such as Nabisco, an International Flavors and Fragrances salesperson might interact with advertising, product development, legal, production, quality control, and customer service people at Kraft/General Foods. The salesperson needs to know the technical and economic benefits to Nabisco and the benefits of the additive to consumers.

In addition, the salesperson must coordinate all areas of his or her own firm to assist in making the sale. The salesperson works with research and development to provide data on consumer taste tests, with production to meet the customer's delivery requirements, and with finance to set the purchasing terms. (Working effectively within your organization is discussed in more detail in Chapter 17.)

The complexity of organizational selling is increasing as more customers become global businesses. For example, Deere and Company has a special unit to coordinate worldwide purchases. The unit evaluates potential suppliers across the globe for each of its product lines and manufacturing facilities.[8] Thus, a salesperson selling fanbelts to Deere must work with the special corporate buying unit as well as the employees at each manufacturing location around the world.

DERIVED VERSUS DIRECT DEMAND

Organizational selling often requires salespeople to know about the customer's customers. Sales to OEMs and resellers are based on derived demand rather than direct demand. **Derived demand** means that purchases made by these customers ultimately depend on the demand for their products—either other organizations or consumers. For example, JR Simplot sells 1.5 billion pounds of potatoes to McDonald restaurants. Its sales depend on how many french fries McDonald's sells.[9] When demand is derived, salespeople must understand the needs of the ultimate user as well as those of the immediate customer.

Sometimes salespeople can stimulate the demand for their product by directing their efforts toward the ultimate customer. For example, Procter & Gamble salespeople set up in-store displays so consumers will buy more of their products. When the consumers do buy more, the supermarkets place more orders with Procter & Gamble.

ORGANIZATIONAL BUYING PROCESS

To effectively sell to organizations, salespeople need to understand how organizations make purchase decisions. This section discusses the steps in an organizational buying process, the different types of buying decisions, and the people involved in making the decisions.[10]

STEPS IN THE BUYING PROCESS

The eight steps in an organizational buying process are shown in Exhibit 4.1.

Recognizing a Need or Problem (Step 1)

The buying process starts when someone realizes that a problem exists. People in the customer's firm or outside salespeople can trigger this recognition. For example, the buying process described at the beginning of this chapter started when the chemical company's engineers recognized the need for a large mixing tank. Salespeople often trigger the buying process by demonstrating how their products can improve the efficiency of the customer's operation.

EXHIBIT 4.1

STEPS IN THE BUYING
PROCESS

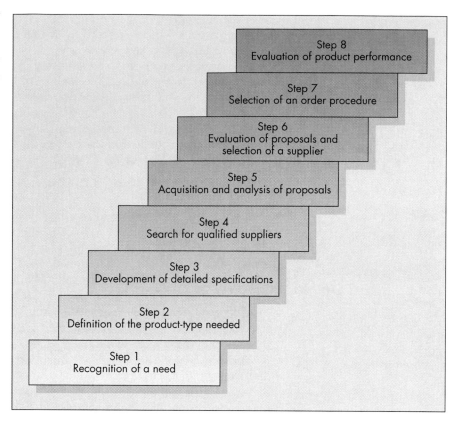

Defining the Type of Product Needed (Step 2)

After identifying a problem, organization members develop a general approach to solving it. For example, a production manager who concludes that the factory is not running efficiently recognizes a problem, but this may not lead to a purchase decision. The manager may think that the inefficiency is caused by poor supervision or unskilled workers.

However, a production equipment salesperson might work with the manager to analyze the situation and show how efficiency could be improved by purchasing some automated assembly equipment. When this occurs, the problem solution is defined in terms of purchasing a product or service—the automated assembly equipment needed—and the buying process moves to Step 3.

Development of Detailed Specification (Step 3)

In Step 3, the specifications for the product needed to solve the problem are written. Potential suppliers will use these specifications to develop proposals. The buyers will use them to objectively evaluate the proposals.

Steps 2 and 3 offer great opportunities for salespeople to influence the outcome of the buying process. Using their knowledge of their firm's products and the customer's needs, salespeople can help develop specifications that favor their particular product. For example, a Hyster forklift might have superior performance in terms of a small turning radius. Knowing this advantage and the customer's small, tightly packed warehouse, the Hyster salesperson might influence the customer to specify a very small turning radius for forklifts—a turning radius that can only be provided by Hyster forklifts. Competing salespeople, who first become aware of this procurement after the specifications are written, will be at a severe disadvantage.

Searching for Qualified Suppliers (Step 4)

After the specifications have been written, customers look for potential suppliers. The customers may simply contact previous suppliers or might go through an extensive search procedure, calling salespeople, asking for a list of customers, and checking with their customers on each supplier's financial stability and performance.

Acquiring and Analyzing Proposals (Step 5)

At Step 5, qualified suppliers are asked to submit proposals. Salespeople work with people in their company to develop their proposal.

Evaluation of Proposals and Selection of a Supplier (Step 6)

Next, the customer evaluates the proposals. (Some methods used to evaluate proposals are discussed later in this chapter.) After selecting a preferred supplier, further negotiations may take place concerning price, delivery, or specific performance features.

Placement of an Order and Receipt of Product (Step 7)

In Step 7, an order is placed with the selected supplier. The order goes to the supplier, who acknowledges receipt and commits to a delivery date. Eventually the product is shipped to the buying firm, which inspects the received goods and then pays the supplier for the product. During this step, salespeople need to make sure the paperwork is correct and their firm knows what has to be done to satisfy the customer's requirements.

Evaluation of Product Performance (Step 8)

In the final step of the purchasing process, the product's performance is evaluated. The evaluation may be a formal or informal assessment made by people involved in the buying process.[11]

Salespeople play an important role in this step. They need to work with the users to make sure the product performs well. In addition, salespeople need to work with purchasing agents to ensure that they are satisfied with the communications and delivery.

This after-sale support ensures that the salesperson's product will get a positive evaluation and he or she will be considered a qualified supplier in future procurement. This step is critical to establishing the successful long-term relationships discussed in Chapter 2. (Building relationships through after-sale support is discussed in more detail in Chapter 13.)

Creeping Commitment

Creeping commitment means that a customer becomes increasingly committed to a particular course of action as the customer goes through the steps in the buying process. As decisions are made at each step, the range of alternatives narrows; the customer becomes more and more committed to a specific course of action and even to a specific vendor. Thus, it is critical for salespeople to be very involved in the initial steps so they will have an opportunity to participate in the final steps.

For example, at the beginning of the chapter we discussed a capital equipment sale of mixing equipment. The salesperson was successful in this situation because he was involved in the initial stage of the buying process. He worked with the customer to identify the problem and specify the equipment needed to solve the problem. By the time the competitor realized that an opportunity existed, the customer was ready to buy mixing equipment provided by Chemineer.

THINKING IT THROUGH	*T*hink of a major decision you have made, such as buying a car or computer or finding an apartment and signing a lease. What steps did you go through in making this decision? Can you relate your decision-making process to the eight steps in the buying process? Did any decision you made early in the process affect any decision you made later in the process?

TYPES OF BUYING DECISIONS

Many purchase decisions are made without going through all of the eight steps described above. For example, a Frito-Lay salesperson may check the supply of his or her products in a supermarket, write out a purchase order to restock the shelves, and present it to the store manager. After recognizing the

A Frito-Lay salesperson takes inventory of snacks to prepare a refill order for the store manager to sign. In this situation, the manager will make a straight rebuy decision and not go through all eight steps in the buying process.

© Jay Brousseau.

problem of low stock, the manager simply signs the order (Step 6) without going through any of the other steps. However, if the Frito-Lay salesperson wanted the manager to devote more shelf space to Frito-Lay snacks, the manager might go through all eight steps in making and evaluating this decision.

Three types of buying decisions—new tasks, straight rebuys, and modified rebuys—are described in Exhibit 4.2, along with the strategies that salespeople need to use in each situation. In this exhibit, the "in" company is the seller that has provided the product or service to the company in the past, and the "out" company is the seller that is not or has not been a supplier to the customer.[12]

New Tasks

When a customer purchases a product or service for the first time, a **new task** situation occurs. Most purchase decisions involving capital equipment or the initial purchase of OEM products are new tasks.

Since the customer has not made the purchase decision in the past, the company's knowledge is limited and it goes through all eight steps of the buying process. In these situations, customers typically seek information from salespeople and welcome their knowledge.

From the salesperson's perspective, the initial buying process steps are critical in new-task situations. During these steps, the alert salesperson can help the customer define the characteristics of the needed product and develop the purchase specifications. By working with the customer in these initial steps, the salesperson can take advantage of creeping commitment and gain a significant advantage over the competition.

EXHIBIT 4.2   TYPES OF ORGANIZATIONAL BUYING DECISIONS

	New Task	Modified Rebuy	Straight Rebuy
Financial risks	High	Moderate	Low
Information search	Extensive	Limited	Minimal
Number of people involved in decision	Many	Few	One or two
Key steps in buying process	1, 2, 3, 8	3, 4, 5, 6, 8	5, 6, 7, 8
Key decision makers	Engineering	Production, purchasing	Purchasing
Selling strategies for in supplier	Monitor changes in company needs; provide information and technical advice	Act immediately to correct problems that arise; respond quickly to changes in customer needs	Reinforce relationships with customer; make sure the customer's needs are being satisfied
Selling strategies for out supplier	Suggest new approaches for reducing cost or increasing performance; provide information and technical advice	Respond to problems that customer has with existing supplier; encourage customer to consider alternative suppliers	Convince customer of potential benefits to be gained from reexamining requirements and suppliers; secure recognition as an alternative supplier

The final step, postpurchase evaluation, is also critical. Buyers making a new purchase decision are especially interested in evaluating results. They will use this information in making similar purchase decisions in the future.

Straight Rebuys

In **straight rebuy** situations, the customer buys the same product from the same source it used when the need arose previously. Since customers have purchased the product or service a number of times, they have considerable knowledge about their requirements and the potential vendors. MRO supplies and services and reorders of OEM components often are straight rebuy situations.

Typically, a straight rebuy is triggered by an internal event, such as a low inventory level. Since needs are easily recognized, specifications have been developed, and potential suppliers are identified, the latter steps of the buying process assume greater importance.

Some straight rebuys are computerized. For example, many hospitals use an automatic reorder system developed by Baxter, a manufacturer and distributor of medical supplies. When the inventory control system recognizes that levels of supplies such as tape, surgical sponges, or IV kits have dropped to a prespecified level, a purchase order is automatically generated and transmitted electronically to the nearest Baxter distribution center.

When price and delivery are acceptable, the company that provided the product in the past—the in company—will continue to get the orders. Salespeople for in companies want to maintain the status quo; they do not want the customer to consider new suppliers. Thus, they must make sure that orders are delivered on time and the products continue to get favorable evaluations.

Salespeople trying to break into a straight rebuy situation—those representing an out supplier—face a tough sales problem. Often they need to persuade a customer to change suppliers even though the present supplier is performing satisfactorily. In such situations, the salesperson hopes the present supplier will make a critical mistake, causing the customer to reevaluate suppliers. To break into a straight rebuy situation, salespeople need to provide very compelling information to motivate the customer to treat the purchase as a modified rebuy.

Modified Rebuys

In a **modified rebuy** situation, the customer has purchased the product or a similar product in the past but is interested in obtaining new information. This situation typically occurs when the in supplier performs unsatisfactorily, a new product becomes available, or the buying needs change. In such situations, sales representatives of the in suppliers need to convince customers to continue their present buying pattern. However, salespeople with out suppliers want customers to reevaluate the situation and actively consider switching vendors.

The successful sales rep will need to influence all the people taking part in the buying decision. The types of employees involved are discussed in the next section.

BUYING CENTER

A **buying center** is an informal, cross-department group of people involved in a purchase decision. People in the customer's organization become involved in a buying center because they have formal responsibilities for purchasing or they are important sources of information. In some cases, the buying center includes experts who are not full-time employees. For example, consultants usually specify the air conditioning equipment that will be used in a factory undergoing remodeling. Thus, the buying center defines the set of people who make or influence the purchase decision.[13]

Salespeople need to know the names and responsibilities of all people in the buying center for a purchase decision. The composition of the buying center may change for each purchase decision, particularly for new tasks, so salespeople frequently build detailed files for each customer, including organization charts and the responsibilities of each person. Even this information may need to be supplemented for specific buying situations.

The types of people typically involved in a buying center are discussed next.

The buying center for a cardiopulmonary system in a hospital may include the three types of people shown here—the operating room nurse (an end user), the surgeon operating on the patient (a gatekeeper), and the hospital administrator (a decider).

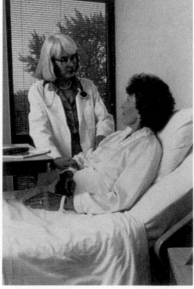

Charles Thatcher/TSW.

David Joel/TSW.

R. Rivera/Superstock.

▮ USERS

Users, such as the manufacturing-area personnel for OEM products and capital equipment, typically do not make the ultimate purchase decision. However, they often have considerable influence in the early and late steps of the buying process—need recognition, product definition, and postpurchase evaluation. Thus, users are particularly important in new tasks and modified rebuy situations. Salespeople often attempt to convert a straight rebuy to a modified rebuy by demonstrating superior product performance or a new benefit to users.

▮ INFLUENCERS

People inside or outside the organization who directly or indirectly influence the buying process are **influencers.** These members of the buying center may provide details on product specifications, criteria for evaluation proposals, or information about potential suppliers. For example, the marketing department can influence a purchase decision by indicating that the company's products would sell better if they included a particular supplier's components. Architects can play the critical role in the purchase of construction material by specifying suppliers, even though the ultimate purchase orders will be placed by the contractor responsible for constructing the building.

▮ GATEKEEPERS

Gatekeepers control the flow of information and may limit the alternatives considered. For example, the quality control and service departments may determine which potential suppliers are qualified sources.

Purchasing agents often play a gatekeeping role by determining which potential suppliers are to be notified about the purchase situation and are to have access to relevant information. In some companies, all contacts must be made through purchasing agents. They arrange meetings with other gatekeepers, influencers, and users; when dealing with such companies, salespeople are not allowed to contact these members of the buying center directly. When salespeople find purchasing agents restricting their access to important information, they are tempted to bypass the purchasing agents and make direct contact.[14] This backdoor approach can upset purchasing agents so much that they disqualify the salesperson's company from the purchase situation.

▮ E X H I B I T   4 . 3   IMPORTANCE OF BUYING CENTER MEMBERS IN BUYING PROCESS
FOR INTENSIVE MONITORING EQUIPMENT

Step in Buying Process	Physician	Nurses	Hospital Administrators	Engineers	Purchasing Agents
Need recognition	High	Low	Moderate	Low	Low
Specification development	High	High	Moderate	Moderate	Low
Analysis of proposal	High	High	Moderate	Moderate	Low
Selection of vendor	High	Low	High	Low	Moderate

Source: Adapted from Gene Laczniak, "An Empirical Study of Hospital Buying," *Industrial Marketing Management*, January 1979, p. 61.

S E L L I N G   *S C E N A R I O*

4.2

Keeping Track of the Buying Center

Gus Maikish heads a 21-person sales team responsible for IBM's business with a major New York City bank. The team includes two sales managers, four salespeople, two sales trainees, and 13 technical support people.

After two years in this position, Maikish is still meeting new buying influences in the bank. "There are many people involved in a major acquisition, and each one has a specific stake in the outcome. One will be concerned with reliability, another with processing speed, someone else with obsolescence."

To coordinate a major sale, Maikish uses a matrix. Each vertical column is labeled with the name of key influencers in a specific area of the bank, such as investment banking, securities trading, or data processing. Along the side of the matrix, he lists all of the factors that might be considered in evaluating the proposal (e.g., software availability, ease of user interface). Then, in the matrix squares, he checks off the factors important to each influencer.

Making the matrix sounds simple, but Maikish spends one to six months collecting this information. And because new influencers and needs emerge, the matrix is never finished: "The matrix may change by 75 percent during the course of selling the project, as the customer changes its mind and the decision criteria expand." Maikish is always jotting notes on file cards or scraps of paper as he and his sales team talk informally with people at the bank.

Source: Adapted from Martin Everett, "This Is the Ultimate in Selling," *Sales & Marketing Management,* August 1989, pp. 32–37. Copyright August 1989. Reprinted with permission.

▍DECIDERS

In any buying center, one or more members of the group—**deciders**—make the final choice. Determining who actually makes the purchase decision for an organization is often difficult. For straight rebuys, the purchasing agent usually selects the vendor and places the order. However, for new tasks, many people influence the decision, and several people must approve the decision and sign the purchase order.

In general, senior executives get more involved in important purchase decisions—those that have a greater effect on the performance of the organization. For example, the chief executive officer (CEO) and chief financial officer (CFO) would play an important role in purchasing a telephone system, because this network would have a significant impact on the day-to-day operations of the firm.

Effective selling hinges on knowledge of the people in the buying center and their involvement at different steps of the buying process. For example, a study of a hospital's purchase decision for expensive intensive-care monitoring equipment found that the buying center consisted of five types of people: physicians, nurses, hospital administrators, engineers, and purchasing agents. The importance of these buying center members in various stages of the process are shown in Exhibit 4.3.

Selling Scenario 4.2 describes the emphasis that Gus Maikish, an IBM account executive responsible for a major New York City bank, places on keeping track of this information.

In some countries, it is difficult to determine who are the members of the buying center. For example, in China, Craig McLaughlin from Texaco reports that salespeople frequently negotiate with representatives of the customer who do not have the authority to make a decision. In some cases, the delegation of authority is not clearly defined in the company. To identify the decision makers in the buying center, McLaughlin emphasizes that there is no point in discussing the situation unless they are willing to reveal their chain of command. "They may not necessarily give you a straight answer, and sometimes they may not even know themselves, but it's a step in the right direction."[15]

SUPPLIER EVALUATION AND CHOICE

At several steps in the buying process, members of the buying center evaluate alternative methods for solving a problem (Step 2), the qualifications of potential suppliers (Step 4), proposals submitted by potential suppliers (Step 5), and the performance of products purchased (Step 8). Based on these evaluations, they select potential suppliers and eventually choose a specific vendor.

The evaluation and selection of products and suppliers is affected by the needs of both the organization and the individuals making the decisions. In this section, we outline how the needs of the organization are considered in the decision-making process. The next section focuses on how the personal needs of buying center members affect the buying process.

MULTIATTRIBUTE MODEL OF ORGANIZATIONAL NEEDS

The evaluation method used by the buying center can be represented by a multiattribute model. We discuss this model in detail because firms actually use it in making purchase decisions.[16] Also, it provides a framework for developing sales strategies.

The **multiattribute model** is based on the idea that people view a product as a collection of characteristics, or attributes. They evaluate a product by considering how each characteristic satisfies the firm's needs

EXHIBIT 4.4

INFORMATION ABOUT LAPTOP COMPUTERS

Characteristic	Brand		
	Apex	Bell	Deltos
Reliability rating	Very good	Very good	Excellent
Weight (pounds)	2.0	4.5	7.5
Size (cubic inches)	168	305	551
Speed (clock rate in megahertz)	20	35	30
Internal memory (in megabytes)	80	100	120
Display visibility	Good	Very good	Excellent
Number of service centers in United States	700	300	100

and perhaps their individual needs. The following example examines a firm's decision to buy laptop computers for its sales force. The computers will be used by salespeople to keep track of information about customers and provide call reports to sales managers. At the end of each day, salespeople will call headquarters and transmit their call reports through a modem.

PERFORMANCE EVALUATION OF CHARACTERISTICS

Assume the company narrows its choice to three hypothetical brands: Apex, Bell, and Deltos. Exhibit 4.4 gives information the company collected about each of these brands. Note that the information goes beyond the physical characteristics of the product to include services provided by the potential suppliers.

Each buying center member, or the group as a whole in a meeting, might process this objective information and evaluate the laptop computers on each characteristic. These evaluations appear in Exhibit 4.5 as ratings on a 10-point scale, with 10 being the highest rating and 1 being the lowest.

How do members of the buying center use this set of evaluations to select a laptop computer? The final decision depends on the relationship between the performance evaluations and the company's needs. The buying center members need to consider the degree to which they are willing to sacrifice poor performance on one attribute for superior performance on another. The members of the buying center must make some trade-offs.

No one product will perform best on all characteristics. For example, Apex excels on size, weight, and availability of convenient service; Bell has superior speed; and Deltos provides better internal memory and display visibility.

IMPORTANCE WEIGHTS

In making an overall evaluation, the buying center member needs to consider the importance of each characteristic. These importance weights may differ from member to member. Consider two members of the buying center: the national sales manager and the director of management information systems (MIS). The national sales manager is particularly concerned

EXHIBIT 4.5

PERFORMANCE EVALUATION OF LAPTOP COMPUTERS

Characteristic	Brand Ratings		
	Apex	Bell	Deltos
Reliability	5	5	⑧
Weight	⑧	5	2
Size	⑧	6	4
Speed	3	⑧	6
Internal memory	3	5	⑧
Display visibility	2	4	6
Service availability	⑦	5	3

EXHIBIT 4.6   INFORMATION USED TO FORM AN OVERALL EVALUATION

Computer Characteristic	Importance Weights		Brand Performance Ratings		
	Sales Manager	**MIS Director**	**Apex**	**Bell**	**Deltos**
Reliability	4	4	5	5	8
Weight	6	2	8	5	2
Size	7	3	8	6	4
Speed	1	7	3	8	6
Internal memory	1	6	3	5	8
Display visibility	8	5	2	4	6
Service availability	3	3	7	5	3
Overall evaluation					
Sales manager's			167	152	143
MIS director's			130	169	177

about motivating his salespeople to use the laptop computers. He feels the laptops must be small and lightweight and have good screen visibility. On the other hand, the MIS director foresees using the laptop computers to transmit orders and customer inventory information to corporation headquarters. She feels expanded memory and processing speed will be critical for these future applications.

Exhibit 4.6 shows the importance these two buying center members place on each characteristic using a 10-point scale, with 10 representing very important and 1 representing very unimportant. In this illustration, the national sales manager and the MIS director differ in the importance they place on characteristics; however, both have the same evaluations of the brands' performance on the characteristics. In some cases, people may differ on both importance weights and performance ratings.

OVERALL EVALUATION

A person's overall evaluation of a product can be quantified by calculating the sum of the performance ratings multiplied by the importance weights. Thus, the sales manager's overall evaluation of Alpha would be:

$$
\begin{aligned}
4 \times 5 &= 20 \\
6 \times 8 &= 48 \\
7 \times 8 &= 56 \\
1 \times 3 &= 3 \\
1 \times 3 &= 3 \\
8 \times 2 &= 16 \\
3 \times 7 &= \underline{21} \\
&\ 167
\end{aligned}
$$

Using the national sales manager's and MIS director's importance weights, the overall evaluations, or scores, for the three laptop computer brands

This buyer needs a high-volume office copier. He places a lot of importance on the copier's speed and reliability. However, your instructor would probably place the highest importance on cost when buying a copier for a home office.

"It's my job to buy copiers. I have to make the right decision."

When buying high-volume copiers for your company, you have to make the right decision the first time.

That's why we're proud to offer The Corporate Line of highly productive high-volume copying systems—copiers uniquely created for the demands of companies like yours.

The Corporate Line, featuring the NP 6060, NP 9800 and the new NP 9850 copier-duplicator, offers a full range

of advanced high-volume copying systems designed to maximize productivity and uptime. The Corporate Line also features sophisticated document handling and finishing capabilities for complete stapled sets at the touch of a button.

The Corporate Line from Canon. For eleven years, America's #1 copier company. And now the new power in high-volume copying. To find out why we're the right decision for you, call 1-800-OK-CANON.

Official Copier of WorldCup '94 and U.S. National Team

Canon

Courtesy Canon U.S.A. Inc.

appear at the bottom of Exhibit 4.6. These scores indicate the level of benefits provided by the brands as seen by these two buying center members.

▮ VALUE OFFERED

The cost of the computers also needs to be considered in making the purchase decision. One approach for incorporating cost calculates the value—the benefits divided by the cost—for each laptop. The prices for the computers and their values are shown in Exhibit 4.7. The sales manager believes that Apex provides more value. He would probably buy this brand if he were the only person involved in the buying decision. On the other hand, the MIS director feels that Bell and Deltos offer the best value.

THINKING IT THROUGH	*If* you were selling the Bell computer to the national sales manager and MIS director depicted in the text and in Exhibits 4.6 and 4.7, how would you try to get them to believe that your computer provided more value than Apex or Deltos do? What numbers would you try to change?

EXHIBIT 4.7

VALUE OFFERED BY
EACH BRAND

Computer Brand	Overall Evaluation (Benefit Points)	÷	Cost of Computer	=	Assigned Value (Benefit Points per Dollar Spent)
Sales manager					
Apex	167		$1,050		0.16
Bell	152		1,100		0.14
Deltos	143		1,150		0.12
MIS manager					
Apex	130		$1,050		0.12
Bell	169		1,100		0.15
Deltos	177		1,150		0.15

SUPPLIER SELECTION

In this situation, the sales manager might be the key decision maker and the MIS director might be a gatekeeper. Rather than using the MIS director's overall evaluation, the buying center might simply ask her to serve as a gatekeeper and determine if these computers meet her minimum acceptable performance standards on speed and memory. Both laptops pass the minimum levels she established of a 20-megahertz clock rate and a 80-megabyte internal memory. Thus, the company would rely on the sales manager's evaluation and purchase Apex laptops for the sales force.

Many organizations use such a formal method to evaluate suppliers and proposals like the one demonstrated above. Each vendor is rated numerically on a number of characteristics. For example, National Can uses the following factors and weights to evaluate suppliers:

Factor	Weight
Competitive pricing	0.8
On-time delivery	0.9
Product quality	0.9
Emergency assistance	0.9
Communications	0.4
Technical service	0.4
Cost reduction suggestions	0.5
Inventory stocking program	0.3

New suppliers are rated on each factor from 0 (absolutely unacceptable) to 5 (excellent—top 10 percent of all suppliers). The ratings for each factor are multiplied by the factor weight, and a total score is calculated. Suppliers with scores higher than 18 are preferred suppliers; suppliers who score below 5 are unacceptable.

Even if a buying center or individual members do not go through the calculations described above, the multiattribute model is a good representation of their product evaluations, and can be used to predict product choices. Purchase decisions are made as if a formal multiattribute model were used.

IMPLICATIONS FOR SALESPEOPLE

How can salespeople use the multiattribute model to influence their customers' purchase decisions? First, the model indicates what information customers use in making their evaluations and purchase decisions. Thus, salespeople need to know the following information to develop a sales strategy:

competition 1. The suppliers or brands the customer is considering.

deter. attrib 2. The product characteristics being used in the evaluation.

perceived perf. of prod. on 3. The customer's rating of each product's performance on each dimension.

importance of ea. attrib. 4. The weights the customer attaches to each dimension.

With this knowledge, salespeople can use several strategies to influence purchase decisions. First, salespeople must be sure their product is among the brands being considered. Then they can try to change the customer's perception of their product's value. Some approaches for changing perceived value are:

Approach 1: Increase the performance rating for your product.

Approach 2: Decrease the rating for a competitive product.

Approach 3: Increase or decrease an importance weight.

Approach 4: Add a new dimension.

Approach 5: Decrease the price of your product.

Focus on ↑ value of determinant attrib. Assume you are selling the Bell computer and you want to influence the sales manager so that he believes your computer provides more value than does the Apex computer. Approach 1 involves altering the sales manager's belief about your product's performance. To raise his evaluation, you would try to have the sales manager perceive your computer as small and light. You might show him how easy it is to carry—how it better satisfies his need for portability. The objective of this demonstration would be to increase your rating on weight from 5 to 7 and your rating on size from 6 to 8.

You should focus on these two characteristics, because they are the most important to the sales manager. A small change in a performance evaluation on these characteristics will have a large impact on the overall evaluation. You would *not* want to spend much time influencing his performance evaluations on speed or internal memory, because these characteristics are not important to him. Of course, your objectives when selling to the MIS director would be different, because she places more importance on speed and internal memory.

This example illustrates a key principle in selling. In general, salespeople should focus primarily on product characteristics that are important to the customer—characteristics that satisfy the customer's needs. They should not focus on the areas of superior performance (such as speed in this example) that are not important to the customer.

Approach 2 involves decreasing the performance rating of Apex. This can be dangerous. Customers prefer dealing with salespeople who say good things about their products, not bad things about competitive products.

In Approach 3, you change the sales manager's importance weights. You want to increase the importance he places on a characteristic on which your product excels, such as speed, or decrease the importance of a characteristic on which your product performs poorly, such as display visibility. For example, you might try to convince the sales manager that a fast computer will decrease the time salespeople need to spend developing and transmitting reports.

Approach 4 encourages the sales manager to consider a new characteristic—one on which your product has superior performance. For example, suppose the sales manager and MIS director have not considered the availability of software. To add a new dimension, you might demonstrate a program specially developed for sales call reports and only usable with your computer.

Approach 5 is the simplest to implement: Simply drop your price. Typically, firms use this strategy as a last resort, because cutting prices decreases profits.

Each of these strategies illustrates the concept that salespeople need to adapt their selling approach to the needs of each customer. Using the multiattribute model, salespeople decide how to alter the content of their presentation—the benefits to be discussed—based on customer beliefs and needs. (Chapter 6 describes adaptive selling in more detail, and illustrates it in terms of the form of the presentation—the communication style the salesperson uses.)

INDIVIDUAL NEEDS OF BUYING CENTER MEMBERS

The multiattribute model illustrates how buying center members evaluate the degree to which alternative products satisfy organizational needs. However, buying center members are people. Their evaluations and choices are affected by their personal needs as well as the organization's needs.[17]

Types of Needs

Maslow developed a useful theory of needs, illustrated in Exhibit 4.8. He proposed that individuals have these five basic needs, and that higher-order needs become important to people only when their lower-order needs have been satisfied. For example, buying center members will only be interested in satisfying social needs when their physiological and safety needs have been satisfied.

Salespeople can influence members of the buying center by developing strategies to satisfy individual needs. For example, demonstrating how a new product will reduce costs and increase the purchasing agents' bonus would satisfy the purchasing agents' economic safety needs. Encouraging an engineer to recommend a product employing the latest technology might satisfy the engineer's need for self-esteem and recognition by his or her engineering peers.

EXHIBIT 4.8

MASLOW'S HIERARCHY OF
NEEDS

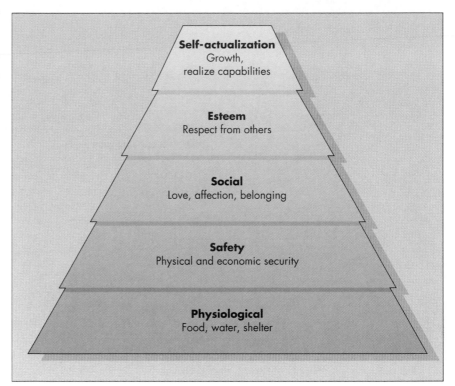

Risk Reduction

Members of the buying center tend to be more concerned about losing benefits they have now than about increasing their benefits. They place a lot of emphasis on avoiding taking risks that might result in poor decisions—decisions that can affect their personal reputations and rewards as well as their organization's performance. To reduce risk, buying center members may collect additional information, develop a loyalty to present suppliers, and/or spread the risk.[18]

methods

Exhibit 4.9 shows the sources of information used by buying center members. Customers, knowing that suppliers try to promote their own products, tend to question information received from vendors. Because noncommercial information comes from independent sources, customers usually view information from trade publications, colleagues, and outside consultants as more credible than information provided by salespeople and company advertising and sales literature.

Impersonal commercial information—advertising and sales literature—tends to be used more in the early steps of the buying process, but personal noncommercial sources are very important in the proposal evaluation and supplier selection steps. In addition, personal noncommercial sources assume even more importance for risky decisions—decisions that will have a significant impact on the organization and/or the buying center member.[19]

*Develop
vendor
loyalty*

Another way to reduce uncertainty and risk is to display **vendor loyalty** to suppliers—continue buying from suppliers that have proved satisfactory in the past. By converting buying decisions into straight rebuys, the

EXHIBIT 4.9

SOURCES OF INFORMATION

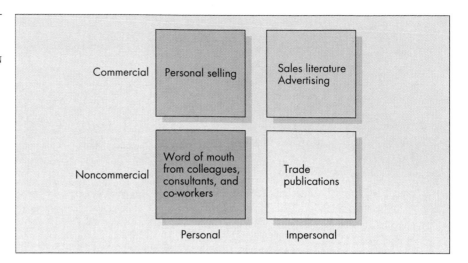

decisions become routine, minimizing the chances of a poor decision. Organizations tend to develop vendor loyalty in unimportant purchase decisions. In these situations, the potential benefits from new suppliers do not compensate for the costs of evaluating these suppliers.[20]

The consequences of choosing a poor supplier can be reduced by using more than one vendor. Rather than placing all orders for an OEM component with one supplier, a firm might elect to purchase 75 percent of their needs from one supplier and 25 percent from another. Thus, if a problem occurred with one supplier, another would be available to fill the firm's needs. If the product is proprietary—only available from one supplier—the buyer might insist that the supplier develop a second source for the component.

These risk reduction approaches present a major problem for salespeople working for out suppliers. To break this loyalty barrier, these salespeople need to develop trusting relationships with customers. They can build trust by offering performance guarantees or by consistently meeting personal commitments. Another approach would be to encourage buyers to place a small trial order so that the salesperson's company could demonstrate its capabilities. On the other hand, the salesperson for the in supplier wants to discourage buyers from considering new sources, even on a trial basis.

TRENDS IN ORGANIZATIONAL BUYING

The business environment is changing dramatically in the 1990s. Major changes include the increasing cost of raw materials, the development of new technologies, and increased competition from international firms and in deregulated industries. These changes put organizations under pressure to improve product quality, control the cost of purchased material, and minimize inventories. Some changes in organizational buying effected in response to these needs are discussed next.[21]

S E L L I N G   S C E N A R I O

4.3

The New Breed of Purchasing Managers

Al Mulvey, one of a new breed of purchasing managers, looks far beyond price in making his buying decisions. He is the vice president of purchasing and administration at J. I. Case (located in Racine, Wisconsin), a Tenneco subsidiary with annual sales of $2.5 billion. Mulvey has a degree in engineering and an MBA. He has taken courses in negotiating skills, international business, and value analysis.

Mulvey emphasizes that, in the past, purchasing agents and salespeople focused on "beating each other up over the amount of profit." Now he is more interested in discovering ways to reduce Case's manufacturing costs. "The ability to negotiate manufacturing costs requires an even stronger relationship with suppliers than it has in the past."

Mulvey wants salespeople to make a "technical infusion" into J. I. Case. A salesperson who spoke with him about Case's involvement in financial leases illustrates the concept. The salesperson had done his homework. He could talk knowledgeably about Case's customers and current suppliers, how prices were set, how leases were structured, and the tax advantages. The salesperson presented an opportunity for Case to carve a niche in the truck leasing business. According to Mulvey, "His work amounts to a technical infusion on the management side. His company is making a contribution to our business mission instead of coming to me and simply saying, 'Give me your business.' "

Source: Adapted from Edith Cohen, "A View from the Other Side," *Sales & Marketing Management,* June 1990, pp. 108–9. Copyright June 1990. Reprinted by permission.

INCREASING IMPORTANCE OF PURCHASING AGENTS

Most major firms have elevated their director of purchasing to the level of senior vice president to reflect the increasing importance of this function. Many have combined purchasing, transportation, inventory control, and warehouse activities in an all-encompassing materials management department.

To meet these new responsibilities, purchasing managers are upgrading their skills and placing more emphasis on the use of computer information and control systems. The National Association of Purchasing Management (NAPM) has a rigorous certification program requiring a minimum of three years of experience and formal coursework in quantitative techniques. To achieve certification, candidates must pass four examinations. Selling Scenario 4.3 illustrates the needs and sophistication of today's purchasing agents.

CENTRALIZED PURCHASING

Purchasing is becoming more centralized. Rather than having each manufacturing facility contract for supplies to meet its own production needs, more purchasing is done at a central location, such as corporate headquarters. Through centralization, purchasing agents can become specialists, concentrating on particular items and developing an extensive knowledge about the uses, specifications, and suppliers for those items.

For example, prior to 1984, each airline program at Boeing—737, 747, and 757—had its own purchasing department. To control costs, Boeing formed a Materials Division to coordinate Boeing's relationships with its vendors. The new division encourages standardization of parts across the existing and new airline designs. It promotes the development of long-term relationships with suppliers, involving them as early as possible in the design of new planes.[22]

To effectively sell to a centralized purchasing department, many firms use a national account management organization concept. In this type of sales organization, a *national account manager (NAM)* is given the responsibility for coordinating the firm's efforts to satisfy the needs of a major customer. The NAM will work directly with the centralized purchasing department and coordinate the activities of salespeople calling on decentralized locations.[23] In some cases, the customer actually determines who will call on their account. For example, Sherwin-Williams, the large paint supplier, lets Sears select the sales team that will service the Sears account.

Total Quality Management

Many firms have adopted a **total quality management** (**TQM**) approach to managing their business. TQM is a set of programs and policies designed to meet customer needs by delivering defect-free products when customers want them, 100 percent of the time. Management provides the resources and atmosphere to enable and encourage employees to meet the firm's quality goals. Each employee is given the appropriate tools and trained how to achieve total quality in his or her job.[24]

Firms that have adopted TQM programs expect their suppliers to provide support for their efforts to provide quality products. They often insist that suppliers also adopt TQM programs. Salespeople often need to describe how their firms will support the customer's TQM objectives.

Just in Time

The objective of a **just-in-time (JIT) inventory control** system is to minimize inventory by having frequent deliveries, sometimes daily, just in time for assembly into the final product.[25] In theory, each product delivered by a supplier must conform to the manufacturer's specifications every time. It must be delivered when needed, not earlier or later, and it must arrive in the exact quantity needed, not more or less. The ultimate goal is to eventually eliminate all inventory except products in production and transit.

To develop the close coordination needed for JIT systems, manufacturers tend to rely on one supplier. The selection criterion is not the lowest cost but rather the ability of the supplier to be flexible. In a JIT relationship, the salesperson becomes a facilitator, coordinator, and even marriage counselor in developing a selling team that works effectively with the customer's buying center.[26] (The manufacturer and supplier develop a strategic partnership, which was discussed in Chapter 2.)

Resellers are also interested in managing their inventories more efficiently. Retailers and distributors work closely with their suppliers to make sure that they minimize their inventory investment and are still able to satisfy the needs of their customers. These JIT inventory systems are referred to **quick response** or **efficient consumer response (ECR)** systems in a distribution channel context. (Partnering relationships involving these systems are discussed in more detail in Chapter 15.)

Material requirements planning (MRP) systems are an important element in JIT programs. These systems are used to forecast sales, develop a production schedule, and then order parts and raw materials with delivery dates that minimize the amount of inventory needed, thereby reducing costs.[27] Effective JIT requires that customers inform suppliers well in advance about their production schedules and needs.

Many firms use elaborate computer systems to keep track of inventories, orders, and deliveries. These systems help firms uncover and eliminate suppliers whose late deliveries and defective products cause scheduling

When selling to customers with a just-in-time production system, salespeople need to work closely with buyers to make sure that their parts are delivered at the right time, every time.

Courtesy Rockwell International.

problems. Some customers and suppliers link computer systems, sharing information about sales, production, and shipment and receipt of products.[28]

VALUE ANALYSIS

Obviously, customers want to satisfy their needs for quality products and on-time delivery at the lowest possible cost. **Value analysis** is one approach used to reduce costs and still provide the required level of performance.[29]

Members of the purchasing department and technical experts from engineering, production, or quality control usually form a team to undertake the analysis. The team begins by examining the product's function. Then members brainstorm to see if changes can be made in the design, materials, construction, or production process to reduce the product's costs but not its performance. Some questions addressed in this phase are:

Can the part be eliminated?

If the part is not standard, can a standard (and presumably less expensive) part be used?

Does the part have greater performance than needed in this application?

Are unnecessary machining or fine finishes specified?

Salespeople can use value analysis to get customers to consider a new product. This approach is particularly useful for the out supplier in a straight rebuy situation.[30]

Scott Paper Company's salespeople use value analysis to sell hand towels and toilet paper. Because Scott products are of high quality and sell at a premium price, Scott sales representatives have to prove that the products are worth the extra money. Using value analysis, they help purchasing agents determine how much it costs to use the product rather than how much the product costs. They focus on the price per use, such as the number of dries per case of paper towels, rather than the price per case. Scott even designed a paper towel dispenser to reduce the number of refills needed and, thus, reduce maintenance labor cost.

LIFE-CYCLE COSTING

Buyers are now taking a more sophisticated approach to evaluating the cost of equipment. Rather than simply focus on the purchased price, they consider installation costs, the cost of needed accessories, freight charges, estimated maintenance costs, and operating costs, including forecasts of energy costs.

Life-cycle costing is a method for determining the cost of equipment or supplies over their useful lives. Using this approach, salespeople can demonstrate that a product with a higher initial cost will have lower overall cost. An example of life-cycle costing appears in Exhibit 4.10. (Approaches that salespeople can use to demonstrate the value of their products to customers are discussed in more detail in Chapter 10.)

EXHIBIT 4.10

LIFE-CYCLE COSTING

	Product A	Product B
Initial cost	$ 35,000	$ 30,000
Life of machine	10 years	10 years
Power consumption per year	150 Mwh*	180 Mwh
Power cost at $30/Mwh	$ 45,000	$ 54,000
Estimated operating and maintenance cost over 10 years	$ 25,000	$ 30,000
Life-cycle cost	$105,000	$114,000

Note: A more thorough analysis would calculate the net present value of the cash flow associated with each product's purchase and use.

*Mwh = megawatt-hour.

GLOBAL SOURCING

Corporations no longer focus on buying from suppliers in their own country. Purchasing agents consider potential suppliers around the globe. For example, the $10,000 paid for General Motors' LeMans in 1991 consisted of:

- $3,000 for labor and assembly in South Korea.
- $1,850 for engines, transaxles, and electronics made in Japan.
- $700 for styling and design engineering in Germany.
- $400 for small components from Japan, Singapore, and Taiwan.
- $250 for advertising done in Britain.
- $50 for data processing in Barbados and Ireland.

These suppliers are not all independent companies. Some are General Motors subsidiaries and joint ventures. But the global sourcing for the LeMans illustrates the growing need for salespeople to recognize the global nature of competition and the importance of understanding the network of relationships that a customer has.[31]

LONG-TERM CUSTOMER–SUPPLIER RELATIONSHIPS

As we discussed in Chapters 1 and 2, organizational customers and suppliers are developing mutually dependent partnering relationships. The supplier needs the customer's orders to meet financial objectives; the customer needs the supplier and its salespeople to make sure that products are delivered when needed, that they perform to specifications and are reliable, and that spare parts and service are provided. This interdependency makes obtaining a specific purchase order only one point in a long-term relationship between the organizational buyer and seller.

To effectively manage these relationships, salespeople need to take a long-term perspective rather than focusing on getting a specific order. Each year, *Purchasing* magazine surveys its 100,000 readers to select the top 10 salespeople.[32] The characteristics of the 10 salespeople described in Exhibit

EXHIBIT 4.11 PURCHASING MAGAZINE'S TOP 10 SALESPEOPLE

Lisa Cortes, Avis Rent A Car,
Cincinnati, Ohio

She has helped in modifying our car rental reports to help us control costs . . . This translates into tens of thousands of dollars.

Steve, D'Ercole, Anixter,
Orlando, Florida

He talks with our work force and looks for and accepts ideas to improve his service while making suggestions of alternative materials to reduce cost . . . He has implemented a JIT program for wire, cable, lugs, and terminals . . . We figure he has saved us $100,000 to $150,000 in the past two years.

Warren Lundgren, Madison Kipp,
Madison, Wisconsin

A veritable fountain of information about value analysis . . . suggested the substitution of a bearing that achieved both weight reduction and a cost savings of $700,000 per year.

Mark Neill, Carpenter Technology,
Mansfield, Massachusetts

. . . has been instrumental in helping us achieve our continuous improvement goals.

Albert Osborn, Electrical Equipment,
Augusta, Georgia

Uncommon source of information and ideas. He keeps us copied and up to date on environmental issues, new efficiency products, and new technology.

Roger Setzke, PHH FleetAmerica,
Oakbrook, Illinois

He's proactive in providing valuable information without my asking . . . One of his recommendations has reduced our maintenance costs to 15 to 20 percent.

Kevin Thayer, Eaton Corp.,
Bloomington, Illinois

. . . a believer and practitioner of value analysis. He is always working to find a suitable substiutute to an obsolete pump or valve . . . He keeps us more competitive.

Michael Thomas, Hoeschst Celanese Corp.,
Brookfield, Wisconsin

In one case we called him in to recommend a plastic resin for a carburetor. He set up a team to meet our design needs, product testing, and delivery requirement. The team was able to meet and exceed specifications, improve product reliability, reduce warranty cost, and lower purchased cost.

Jack Townsend, Wheaton Tubing Products,
Des Plaines, Illinois

Played a vital role in protecting our company from the ravages of a serious world shortage of glass vials.

J R Wilcott, Doonan Truck & Equipment,
Wichita, Kansas

. . . acts quickly and solves all types of problems. He analyzed our route structure and determined we could downsize our fuel capacities on tractors. Based on the weight saving from the reduced fuel load we were able to eliminate the expense of aluminum wheels.

Source: "Are Your Suppliers' Reps Ready to Go to Bat for You," Reprinted from *Purchasing Magazine,* June 3, 1993, pp. 665–66. Copyright June 1993. Reprinted with permission.

4.11 emphasize the importance of developing partnerships with customers. Top salespeople share the following qualities: willingness to fight for the customer, thoroughness and follow through, preparation for sales calls, marketing knowledge, imagination, knowledge of buyers' needs, and knowledge of product line(s).

SUMMARY

Salespeople sell to many different types of customers, including consumers, business enterprises, government agencies, and institutions. This text focuses on selling to businesses rather than to consumers. Selling to organizations differs from selling to consumers because organizations are more concentrated, demand is derived, and the buying process is more complex.

The organization buying process can be divided into eight steps, beginning with the recognition of a need and ending with the evaluation of the product's performance. Each step involves a number of decisions. As organizations progress through these steps, decisions made at previous steps affect subsequent steps, leading to a creeping commitment. Thus, salespeople need to be involved as early as possible in the buying process.

The multiattribute model is a useful tool for understanding the factors considered by members of the buying center in making decisions. The model also indicates a number of strategies that salespeople can use to influence those decisions.

The length of the buying process and the role of different participants depend on the customer's past experiences. When customers have had considerable experience buying a product, the decision becomes routine—a straight rebuy. Few people are involved and the process is short. However, when customers have little experience buying a product—a new task—many people are involved and the process is quite lengthy.

The people involved in the buying process are referred to as the *buying center*. The buying center is composed of people who are users, influencers, gatekeepers, and deciders. Salespeople need to understand the roles played by buying center members to effectively influence their decisions.

Organizations in the 1990s are facing an increasingly dynamic and competitive environment. Organizational buying practices are changing to cope with the greater environmental uncertainties. Some of these changes are the increasing importance of purchasing agents, the longer-term orientation in evaluating costs and vendors, the use of computer systems for planning and inventory control, and the development of long-term relationships with selected vendors.

KEY TERMS

buying center 103
capital equipment 93
creeping commitment 100
deciders 105
derived demand 97
efficient consumer response
  (ECR) 117
end users 93
gatekeepers 104
influencers 104
just-in-time (JIT) inventory
  control 116
life-cycle costing 118
material requirements planning
  (MRP) 117

modified rebuy 102
MRO supplies 93
multiattribute model 106
new task 100
original equipment manufacturer
  (OEM) 92
quick response 117
resellers 93
straight rebuy 102
total quality management
  (TQM) 116
users 104
value analysis 118
vendor loyalty 113

QUESTIONS AND PROBLEMS

1. A manufacturing plant wants to buy a converter to reduce emissions and pollution. What differences in criteria for evaluating supplier proposals might be used by *(a)* the purchasing agent, *(b)* the engineering department, *(c)* the sales manager, and *(d)* the head of the legal department?

2. Assume that you are calling on a customer for the first time. You have just found out the customer needs a product such as the one you are selling. What questions would you ask in order to learn how to sell your product to the customer?

3. What are the implications of multiple buying influences for salespeople selling to organizations?

4. What factors determine the length of time and the number of people involved in a buying decision?

5. Stan Harris, a purchasing agent, views his decision to buy fluorescent lightbulbs for his factory as a routine purchase decision. Assume you are a salesperson working for a lighting distributor from which Stan does not order. How would you try to make a sale to Stan?

6. Buying centers are often made up of people from different areas in the organization (such as purchasing and engineering) who have different criteria for selecting products. How do these people with different needs ever reach a decision? What can a salesperson do to minimize the conflict between members of the buying center?

7. How does value analysis help the salesperson?

8. Purchasing agents may not have the same degree of technical knowledge that salespeople or users of a product possess. This difference in knowledge may cause tension between the salesperson and the agent. What can a salesperson do to reduce this tension?

9. Why might management place pressure on purchasing agents to buy from the lowest bidder? Why might a purchasing agent ignore this pressure and buy from a higher-priced bidder?

10. Under what conditions might loyalty to a supplier be economically efficient? When might it be inefficient or wasteful?

11. Assume that you work for a manufacturer selling office equipment to a dealer (reseller). In the opinion of your company, would you be more successful if you sold as much equipment to the dealer as possible or if you helped the dealer sell equipment to its customers? Would there be any difference between the long- and short-term effects of these two approaches? Why or why not? How could you, as a salesperson, help the dealer sell its inventory of your products?

CASE PROBLEMS

CASE 4 • 1
MEDICARE SUPPLIES

Ron Marks sells for Medicare Supplies, a pharmaceutical wholesaler. His customers include all the major hospitals in the Chicago area. One of them is Metropolitan Hospital, a public institution under pressure to cut costs.

Ron has experienced difficulties trying to convince Metropolitan's chief purchasing agent to buy HAB's travel-size toothbrushes in bulk. Ron wants this item included in the toiletries supply kit furnished to each patient. The kit already contains soap, hand lotion, a plastic pitcher, a tumbler, and a tabletop tub for sponge bathing.

The hospital purchasing agent has argued that the toothbrushes are not essential. Many patients bring their own, and those who don't can ask for a regular-size toothbrush from the hospital pharmacy. The purchasing agent claims that including even this small item would add too much to the patient's bill.

QUESTION

Using a multiattribute model, what strategies can Ron employ to convince the purchasing agent that this item should be added to the kit?

CASE 4 • 2
IMAGE SYSTEMS

On January 18, 1994, Ken Stillman, a sales engineer for Image Systems, learned that Shands University Hospital had placed an order with CT Technology for a magnetic resonance (MR) scanner. Stillman was very disappointed by the decision; he had been working on the sale for eight months. He reviewed his call reports to try to understand why Image Systems did not get the order.

BACKGROUND

The nuclear magnetic resonance scanner is relatively new in the field of diagnostic imaging. It combines a computer and a unique method for detecting the resonance of molecules in the body to provide patient images without using X-rays. With an MR scanner, radiologists can see sections of the body that cannot be seen with conventional X-ray equipment. The typical MR scanner costs from $500,000 to $1.5 million.

Image Systems sells conventional X-ray equipment in addition to computed tomography (CT) and (MR) scanners. The firm has an international reputation for advanced technology and excellent after-sales service. Image System's principal competitor is CT Technology.

MR SCANNER BUYERS

Most buyers of MR scanners are public or privately owned hospitals. Budgets for new equipment are set at the beginning of the year and must be spent by the end of the year. Hospitals tend to use formal procedures to make purchase decisions, including developing specifications and then requiring firms to provide bids based on these specs.

Typically, four groups of people take part in the buying decision: hospital radiologists, physicists, administrators, and people in supporting government agencies, which frequently provide funding. Radiologists are the doctors who actually use the equipment to make images and interpret them for physicians treating the patients. Physicists, the scientists in a university hospital, write technical specifications for the equipment. They have a good understanding of the state of the art in technology. Their principal concern is patient safety. Administrators, responsible for the financial well-being of the hospital, consider both potential revenues and the cost of the scanner. Administrators are typically wary about buying an expensive technological toy that may become obsolete in a few years. In some hospitals, administrators are the top decision makers; in others, they are simply buyers.

People in supporting agencies are usually not directly involved with the purchase decision, but they must approve the expenditure. They have the greatest influence over hospital administrators.

SHANDS UNIVERSITY HOSPITAL

Shands University Hospital is a large hospital associated with the University of Florida, servicing the Gainesville, Florida, community. The hospital, a leading teaching center, has an excellent radiology department. It has X-ray equipment from a number of companies, including CT Technology.

SALES CALLS ON SHANDS

June 5, 1993   Office received a call from Professor Stein, the head of the radiology department at Shands, regarding an MR scanner. I was assigned to make the call on the professor. Looked through the files to see if we had sold anything to the hospital before. We hadn't. Made an appointment to see Professor Stein on June 9.

June 9, 1993   Called on Professor Stein, who informed me of a recent decision by university directors to set aside funds next year for the purchase of the hospital's first MR scanner. The professor wanted to know what we had to offer. Told him the general features of our MR system. Gave him some brochures. He asked a few questions that led me to believe other companies had already come to see him. Told me to check with Dr. Chen, the hospital's physicist, regarding the specs. Made an appointment to see him again in 10 days. Called on Dr. Chen, who was not there. His secretary gave me a lengthy document, the scanner specs.

June 10, 1993   Read the specs last night. Looked like they had been copied straight from somebody's technical manual. Showed them to our product specialist, who confirmed my hunch that our system met and exceeded the specs. Made an appointment to see Dr. Chen next week.

June 15, 1993   Called on Dr. Chen. Told him about our system's features and the fact that we met all the specs set down on the document. He looked somewhat unimpressed. Left technical documents on our system with him.

June 19, 1993   Called on Professor Stein. He had read the material I had left with him. Looked sort of pleased with the features. Asked about our upgrading scheme. I told him we would upgrade the system as new features became available. Unlike other systems, ours can be made to accommodate the latest technology. There will be no risk of obsolescence for a long time. He was quite impressed. Also answered his questions regarding image manipulation, image processing speed, and our service capability. Just before I left, he inquired about our price. Told him I would have an informative quote for him at our next meeting. Made an appointment to see him on July 23, after he returned from his vacation. He told me to get in touch with Carl Hartmann, the hospital's top administrator, in the interim.

July 1, 1993   Called on Hartmann. It was difficult to get an appointment with him. Told him about our interest in supplying his hospital with our MR scanner, which met all the specs as defined by Dr. Chen. Also informed him of our excellent service capability. He wanted to know which other hospitals in the country had purchased our system. Told him I would drop him a list of buyers in a few days' time. He asked about the price. Gave him an informative quote of $1.1 million—a price my boss and I had arrived at since my visit to Professor Stein. He shook his head, saying, "Other scanners are cheaper by a wide margin." I explained that our price reflected the latest technology, which was incorporated into it. Also mentioned that the price differential was an investment that could pay for itself several times over through faster speed of operation. He was noncommittal. Before I left his office, he instructed me not to talk to anybody else about the price. Asked him if I could tell Dr. Stein. He said I should not. Left him with a lot of material on our system.

July 3, 1993 Took Hartmann a list of three other hospitals of a similar size that had installed our system. He was out. Left it with his secretary, who recognized me. Learned from her that at least two other firms, CT Technology and GE, were competing for the order. She also volunteered the information that "prices are so different, Mr. Hartmann is confused." She added that the final decision will be made by a committee made up of Hartmann, Professor Stein, and one other person whom she could not recall.

July 20, 1993 Called on Dr. Chen. Asked him if he had read the material on our system. He had, but did not have much to say. Repeated some of the key operational advantages our product enjoyed over those produced by others, including CT Technology and GE. Left him some more technical documents. On the way out, stopped by Hartmann's office. His secretary told me that we had received favorable comments from the hospitals using our system.

July 23, 1993 Professor Stein was flabbergasted to hear that I could not discuss our price with him. Told him of the hospital administrator's instructions to that effect. He was not convinced, especially when CT Technology had already revealed to him their quote of $900,000. When he had calmed down, he wanted to know if we were going to be at least competitive with the others. Told him our system was more advanced than CT Technology's. Promised him we would do our best to come up with an attractive offer. Then we talked about his vacation and sailing experience in the Florida Keys. He said he loved key lime pie.

August 15, 1993 Called to see if Hartmann had returned from his vacation. He had. While checking his calendar, his secretary told me that our system seemed to be the "radiologists' choice" but that Hartmann had not yet made up his mind.

August 30, 1993 Visited Hartmann, accompanied by the regional manager. Hartmann seemed bent on the price. He said, "All companies claim they have the latest technology." So he could not understand why our offer was "so much above the rest." He concluded that only a "very attractive price" could tip the balance in our favor. After repeating the operational advantages that our system enjoyed over others, including those produced by CT Technology and GE, my boss indicated that we were willing to lower our price to $1 million if the equipment was ordered before the end of the current year. Hartmann said he would consider the offer and seek "objective" expert opinion. He also said a decision would be made before Christmas.

September 15, 1993 Called on Professor Stein, who was too busy to see me for more than 10 minutes. He wanted to know if we had lowered our price since the last meeting with him. I said we had. He shook his head, saying laughingly, "Maybe that was not your best offer." He then wanted to know how fast we could make deliveries. Told him within six months. He did not respond.

October 2, 1993 Discussed with our regional manager the desirability of inviting one or more people from Shands to visit Image Systems' headquarters near Chicago. The three-day trip would have given the participants a chance to see the scope of the facilities and become better acquainted with MR scanner applications. The idea was finally rejected as inappropriate.

October 3, 1993 Dropped in to see Hartmann. He was busy, but had the time to ask for a formal "final offer" from us by November 1. On my way out, his secretary told me of "a lot of heated discussions" concerning which scanner seemed best suited for the hospital. She would not say more.

October 25, 1993 The question of price was raised in a meeting between the regional manager and the managing director. I had recommended a sizable cut in our price to win the order. The national sales manager seemed to agree with me. But the managing director was reluctant. His concern was that too much of a drop in price looked "unhealthy." He finally agreed to a final offer of $950,000. Made an appointment to see Hartmann later that week.

October 29, 1993   Took our offer of $950,000 in a sealed envelope to Hartmann. He did not open it but commented that he hoped the scanner question would be resolved soon to the "satisfaction of all concerned." Asked him how the decision was going to be made. He evaded the question but said he would notify us as soon as a decision was reached. Left his office feeling that our price had a good chance of being accepted.

November 20, 1993   Called on Professor Stein. He had nothing to tell me but that "the MR scanner is the last thing I like to talk about." Felt he was unhappy with the way things were going. Tried to make an appointment with Hartmann in November, but he was too busy.

December 5, 1993   Called on Hartmann, who told me that a decision would probably not be reached before January. He indicated that our price was "within the range" but that all the competing systems were being evaluated to see which seemed most appropriate for the hospital. He repeated that he would call us when a decision was reached.

January 18, 1994   Received a brief letter from Hartmann thanking Image Systems for participating in the bid for the MR scanner and informing it of the decision to place the order with CT Technology.

QUESTIONS

1. Who were the members of the buying center for the MR scanner? What important benefits were these buying center members seeking?

2. Why did Stillman lose the sale? What should he have done differently?

ADDITIONAL REFERENCES

Banting, Peter; Jozsef Beracs; and Andrew Gross. "The Industrial Buying Process in Capitalist and Socialist Countries." *Industrial Marketing Management*, May 1991, pp. 105–13.

Campenelli, Melissa. "The Secrets of America's Best Sales Forces. *Sales & Marketing Management*, January 1993, pp. 92–93.

Dawes, Philip; Grahame Dowling; and Paul Patterson. "Factors Affecting the Structure of Buying Centers for the Purchase of Professional Business Advisory Services." *International Journal of Research in Marketing*, August 1992, pp. 269–79.

Hahn, Chan; Charles Watts; and Kee Young Kim. "The Supplier Development Program: A Conceptual Model." *Journal of Purchasing and Materials Management*, Spring 1990, pp. 2–7.

Hayes, H. Michael, and Stephen Hartley. "How Industrial Buyers View Industrial Salespeople." *Industrial Marketing Management*, February 1989, pp. 73–80.

Hutt, Michael, and Thomas Speh. *Business Marketing Management*, 4th ed. Fort Worth, TX: Dryden Press, 1992.

Leendes, Michael. "Supplier Development." *Journal of Purchasing and Materials Management*, Spring 1989, pp. 10–15.

Reichard, Clifton. "Industrial Selling: Beyond Price and Persistence." *Harvard Business Review,* March–April 1985, pp. 127–33.

Samli, A. Coskun; Dhruv Grewal; and Sanjeev Mathur. "International Industrial Buyer Behavior: An Exploration and a Proposed Model." *Journal of the Academy of Marketing Sciences,* Summer 1988, pp. 19–29.

Scherring, Eberhard. *Purchasing Management*, Englewood Cliffs, NJ: Prentice Hall, 1989.

Sellers, Patricia. "How to Remake Your Sales Force." *Fortune,* May 1992, pp. 98–101.

Shipley, David; Conlin Egan; and Scott Edgett. "Meeting Source Selection Criteria: Direct versus Distributor Channels." *Industrial Marketing Management*, November 1991, pp. 297–304.

Communication Principles and Successful Selling

A stockbroker is telling a client about the benefits of buying stock in JCPenney. She says: "Penney is an excellent buy. Its price-earnings ratio is depressed because of uncertainties in GDP growth. But NAFTA offers great opportunities for expansion into Mexico." The stockbroker wants to communicate the benefits of buying stock in JCPenney, but the client may not interpret this message correctly because he is not familiar with the terms *NAFTA*, *GDP*, and *depressed price-earnings ratio*. The stockbroker might recognize the lack of understanding by observing the client's facial expression and then say, "Let me explain my reasoning in more detail." Or the client might try to understand the stockbroker's message by asking, "What does depressed price-earnings ratio mean?" But the client might be embarrassed by his lack of understanding and respond, "I don't think I am interested in buying stocks now."

Effective communication is a key element in building close personal and business relationships. To adapt your sales presentation to customers, you need to learn about their needs as well as communicate product benefits to them. The communication principles discussed in this chapter can help everyone, including salespeople, avoid misunderstandings and improve relationships.

Some questions answered in this chapter are:

What are the basic elements in the communication process?
Why are listening and questioning skills important?
How can salespeople develop listening skills to collect information about customers?
How do people communicate without using words?
What are the barriers to effective communication?

Christina Flores emphasizes that the key to her successful sales career is her ability to identify a customer's problem and propose a cost-effective solution. "But you really have to ask questions and listen to find out what the customer's *real* problem is.

"Just last week, I was talking with the data processing manager in a trucking firm. He told me about some problems he was having with a competitor's forms. He said that every once in a while they jam in the printer. Then I dug a little deeper and I discovered he really wasn't really concerned about the jamming. But he did think it was a waste of time to have to run the form through the printer twice. I analyzed the information he was printing on the form and proposed one of our forms that could do the job in one pass. If I had focused on the jamming problem, I probably would not have gotten a $10,000 order."

Flores is an account executive with the Business Forms Division of AT&T. She sells preprinted forms and labels used with business systems. AT&T's business strategy is selling specially designed, high-quality forms that improve the performance and lower the operating cost of the customer's system. "Some purchasing agents I work with don't see the big picture. They just want us to give them a lower price for the form they are already using. I don't want to get into a bidding war. I want to add value by providing a better solution."

To find a better solution, Flores spends a lot of time talking with the data processing (DP) people, who produce the reports, and the users of the information printed on the form. "Sometimes the users aren't aware of all the possibilities. I let them know how AT&T's forms can improve the accessibility or organization of their information. Of course, in order to do this I try to know as much as possible about their business. And I spend a lot of time just making sure everyone has all the information they need to make the best decision."

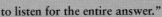
CHRISTINA FLORES
AT&T
Global Information Solutions

Because Flores has several customers in El Paso who have operations in Juarez, Mexico, she often makes calls across the border. "Fortunately for me , their English is better than my Spanish so most of the conversation will be in English. But it's easy for misunderstandings to occur; you have to listen much more carefully. You also speak slower, use more common terminology, and try to avoid jargon. There'll be lots of rephrasing and asking the same question in slightly different ways. I try not to interrupt and take time to listen for the entire answer."

Flores really enjoys meeting interesting people and learning about a wide variety of industries. She lives in Albuquerque, New Mexico, and covers a large territory in the Southwest including west Texas, New Mexico, and southern Colorado. That means a lot of traveling. Last year she put 20,000 miles on her car and about the same amount in the air. "But it's worth it. I enjoy my job and have a lot of independence."

THE COMMUNICATION PROCESS

Developing communication skills begins with understanding the communication process. The process has three basic elements: the sender, the message, and the receiver. How these elements relate is shown in Exhibit 5.1.

The process begins with the sender, the message source. In personal selling, this is a salesperson. However, in more general terms, the sender can be anyone who wishes to communicate an idea, such as a political candidate, a college professor, or a minister. The sender wants to communicate some thoughts and ideas to the receiver. Since the receiver cannot read the sender's mind, the sender must translate these ideas into words. The translation of thoughts into a message is **encoding.**

The sender's message is transmitted to the receiver by voice in a face-to-face interaction or over the telephone, or in a written form such as a letter or proposal. Then the receiver must decode the message and try to understand what the sender intended to communicate. **Decoding** involves interpreting the meaning of the received message.

COMMUNICATION ACCURACY

Communication is effective when the receiver accurately understands what the sender intended to transmit. When this does not happen, a communication breakdown occurs. Communication breakdowns can occur because (1) senders do not encode their ideas accurately, (2) receivers do not decode messages accurately, or (3) the message is distorted in the transmission process. The following sales interaction between a copier salesperson and a prospect illustrates the factors leading to communications breakdowns:

What the salesperson wants to say: "We have an entire line of copiers. But I think the Model 900 is ideally suited for your needs, because it provides the basic copying functions at a low price. It's our basic model."

What the salesperson says (encodes): "The Model 900 is our best-selling copier. It is designed to economically meet the copying needs of small businesses like yours."

What the customer hears: "The Model 900 is a low-price copier for small businesses."

What the customer thinks (decodes): "This company makes low-price copiers with limited features. They are designed for businesses that don't have much money to spend for a copier. We need a copier with more features. We should invest in a better copier that will meet our future needs."

What the customer says: "I don't think I'm interested in buying a copier now."

In this situation, the salesperson assumed that price was very important to the prospect, and the prospect misinterpreted the salesperson's message to indicate that the company only made low-price, low-performance copiers.

E X H I B I T   5 . 1   COMMUNICATION PROCESS

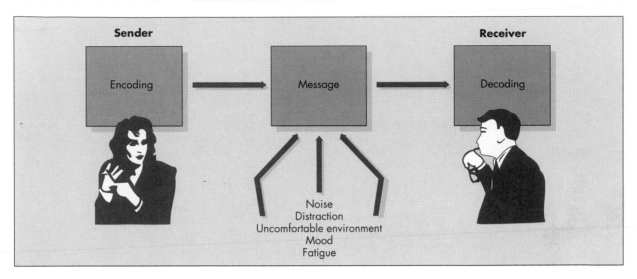

COMMUNICATION BARRIERS

Effective communication in selling involves more than telling prospects about the product; it involves an active, two-way exchange of ideas and thoughts. Some factors that can inhibit or distort communications are: (1) one-way flow of information, (2) noise, (3) uncomfortable environment, (4) bad mood, and (5) fatigue.

One-Way Flow of Information

Effective communication involves a two-way flow of information. As shown in Exhibit 5.2, the parties in **two-way communication** both send and receive information. Salespeople send messages to customers and receive feedback from them. Customers send messages (feedback) to salespeople and receive responses in turn.

Consider a salesperson who is demonstrating a complicated product to a customer. At some point in the presentation, a perplexed look comes across the customer's face. The salesperson receives this nonverbal message and then asks the customer what part of the presentation needs further explanation. The feedback provided by the customer's expression told the salesperson his message was not being received. The customer then sends verbal messages to the salesperson in the form of questions concerning the operation and benefits of the product.

Two-way communication is essential to the practice of adaptive selling. Without it, salespeople cannot determine the needs of the customer. In addition, feedback from customers enables the salesperson to make adjustments—to determine if messages about product benefits are being received accurately and to correct inaccuracies.

Two-way communication also provides the customer with greater satisfaction. People learn more when they participate. For example, when a professor lectures to you, you may lose interest. But you will pay much closer attention in class when the professor calls on you to be

EXHIBIT 5.2   TWO-WAY FLOW OF INFORMATION

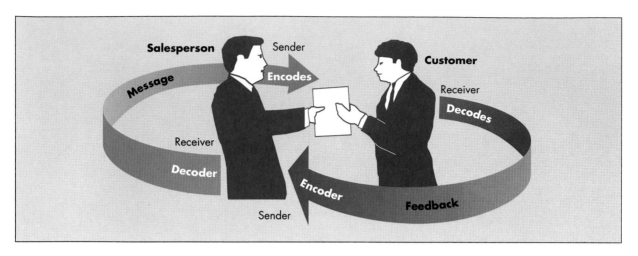

part of class discussion. Participation also leads to more enjoyment. People do not like being talked to without being able to ask questions or respond.

Noise

The exchange of information is inhibited when people are distracted by noise in the environment. **Noise** is sound unrelated to messages being exchanged by the salesperson and customer, such as ringing telephones or other conversations nearby. To improve communication, salespeople should attempt to minimize the amount of noise in the environment by closing a door to a room or suggesting that the meeting move to another, quieter place.

Uncomfortable Environment

People communicate most effectively when they are physically comfortable. If the room is too hot or cold, you should suggest changing the temperature, opening a window, or moving to another room. You and the prospect do not want to be thinking about the room temperature instead of listening to each other.

Mood

Occasionally, prospects may be in a bad mood. They might be angry or upset about something totally unrelated to the sales interaction and take out their frustration on you. If this situation arises, it is best to graciously end the conversation and come back another day when the customer is feeling better. You also need to recognize that when you are in a bad mood, you will not be an effective communicator.

Background noise on an air field can make effective communication difficult. This salesperson should attempt to move the meeting to a quieter location so the customer will not be distracted by the noise.

Walter Bibikow/The Image Bank.

Fatigue

Effective communications requires a lot of mental effort. When people are tired, they have difficulty listening and responding to customers. You need to schedule appointments with customers when both of you are prepared to work on the communication process.

THINKING IT THROUGH	*T*hink of a recent face-to-face interaction you had with another person when there was a communication breakdown. What caused the miscommunication? Was it two-way communication with feedback? Did noise affect the interaction?

MODES OF COMMUNICATION

Four modes for communicating with customers are shown in Exhibit 5.3. These modes are based on whether the salesperson is sending or receiving messages from the customer and what channel is being used to communicate—verbal or nonverbal. **Verbal communication** involves the transmission of words either in face-to-face communication, over a telephone, or through written messages. But messages are often communicated without words, through such nonverbal means as facial expressions and body movements. In the next sections, we discuss these four communication modes.

EXHIBIT 5.3

MODES OF
COMMUNICATIONS

Communication Channel	Sending Messages to Customer	Receiving Messages from Customer
Verbal	Asking questions Presenting information	Listening
Nonverbal	Using body language, voice characteristics, spacing, and appearance to send messages	Reading body language, voice characteristics

SENDING VERBAL MESSAGES TO CUSTOMERS

Messages communicated verbally are encoded into symbols called *words*. Words, however, are just symbols; they have different meanings to different people. Consider a presentation by a salesperson working for a fabric manufacturer. During the presentation, the salesperson indicates that the fabrics made by the company are of high quality, are durable, and their colors are *fast*. But will the prospect know what *fast* means? The dictionary lists over 30 definitions of *fast*. Some of them have to do with very different things, including eating habits, running, or behavior on a date. In this case, of course, the salesperson is pointing out that the colors will not fade despite frequent washing or dry cleaning.

EFFECTIVE USE OF WORDS

Each industry has its own trade jargon. A college textbook sales representative, for example, must know the meaning of such technical expressions as *test bank, transparency, quarters,* and *instructor's manual.* But salespeople cannot assume all of their customers will be familiar with this trade jargon. They need to check with their customers continually, to determine if their sales message is being interpreted properly.

Words have different meanings in different cultures and even in different regions of the United States. In England the hood of a car is called a *bonnet* and the trunk is called the *boot.* In Boston a *milkshake* is just syrup mixed with milk, while a *frappe* is ice cream, syrup, and milk mixed together. The words *ship* and *boat* have very different meaning to sailors.

Characteristics of Words

Words can be either abstract or concrete as well as emotional or neutral. Concrete, fact-oriented words and expressions usually convey more information and are less likely to be misinterpreted than are abstract conceptual words. The purity of water is communicated more effectively by saying, "The mineral content of this water is under one part per million," than by saying, "This water is pure."

Many words related to politics, gender, and race elicit strong emotional responses that inhibit effective communication. Politicians are particularly adept at using words that typically involve a positive emotional response.

Who could be against programs such as Truth in Lending, the Fair Deal, or the Right to Work?[1]

Using Effective Words

Words are tools. Word artists have the power to be soft and appealing or strong and powerful. They can use short words and phrases to demonstrate strength and force or to provide charm and grace (e.g. "clean, crisp copies"; "library quiet"). With practice, words may be used, like the notes of a musical scale, to create the proper mood.

In making sales presentations, you should choose words that have strength and descriptive quality. Avoid words such as *nice, pretty, good,* and *swell* and phrases that make you sound like an overeager salesperson such as "a great deal," "I guarantee you will . . . ," and "No problem!"

Every salesperson should be able to draw on a set of words to help present the features of a product or service. The words might form a simile, such as "This battery backup is like a spare tire"; a metaphor, such as "This machine is a real workhorse"; or a phrase drawing on a sensory appeal, such as "smooth as silk" and "strong as steel."

Painting Word Pictures

Salespeople can use word pictures to help customers understand the benefits of a product or a feature of the product. A **word picture** is a story designed to help the buyer visualize a point. For example, Exhibit 5.4 provides a word picture that a Jeep Cherokee salesperson might use when calling on a commercial real estate owner.

To use a word picture effectively, you need to paint as accurate and reliable a picture as possible. No attempt at puffery should be made. Word pictures should be honest attempts to help the buyer accurately visualize the situation.

Tailoring Words to the Customer

Effective communication happens only when salespeople use words familiar to the customer. Some salespeople think that using long words and technical jargon impresses customers. However, unfamiliar terms usually confuse customers and fail to communicate sales messages effectively. A good communication principle is to use short words and short sentences.[2] This principle particularly holds true when communicating with customers whose native language is not English.

Customers can have different styles of communicating. Some may be very visual; others may prefer an auditory communication mode; and some customers communicate in a feeling mode. Salespeople need to adapt their word choices to the customer's preferred communication style. Examples of effective words for the various styles are shown in Exhibit 5.5.

EXHIBIT 5.4

EXAMPLE OF A WORD
PICTURE

Situation

A Jeep Cherokee salesperson is calling on Jim, the owner of a commercial real estate firm. The goal of the word picture is to demonstrate the value of the four-wheel drive option.

Word Picture

Jim, picture for a moment the following situation. You've got this really hot prospect—let's call him Steve—for a remote resort development. You're in your current car, a Cadillac DeVille. You've been trying to get Steve up to the property for months, and this is his only free day for several weeks. The property, up in the northern Georgia mountains, is only accessible by an old logging road. The day is bright and sunny, and Steve is in a good mood.

When you reach the foot of the mountains, it turns cloudy and windy. As you wind up the old bumpy road, a light rain begins. You've just crossed a small bridge when a downpour starts; rain comes down like cats and dogs. You say, "Boy, it's getting a little messy, huh Steve?" And Steve looks a little worried.

Suddenly your car's tires start spinning. You're stuck in the mud. You realize it's at least four miles back to a phone, and you haven't even reached your destination. You mutter some apology and start to walk back to the last farmhouse you saw. Steve decides to join you but slips as he steps out of your car and falls flat on his face. You can't help laughing. It's either laugh or cry. Your day is shot, and so are your chances of a sale.

Now, let's replay the story, assuming you buy this Jeep Wagoneer we've been talking about. [Salesperson quickly repeats the first two paragraphs of this story, substituting Jeep Cherokee for Cadillac DeVille] Suddenly your car tires start spinning. You're stuck in the mud. Calmly you reach down and shift into four-wheel drive. The Jeep pulls out easily, and you reach the destination in about five minutes. Although it's raining, the prospect looks at the land and sees great potential. On the way back down the mountain, you discuss how Steve should go about making an offer on the property. Steve agrees to call you later in the day to discuss the details of his offer.

Jim, while I'm not the greatest at painting pictures, I hope I've made a point. Can you see why the four-wheel drive option is important for you, even though it does add to the base price of the car?

VOICE
CHARACTERISTICS

Your delivery of words affects how the customer will understand and evaluate your presentations. Good voice and speech habits are quite important for salespeople. The degree to which a customer receives a salesperson's message depends on the salesperson's **voice characteristics**: rate of speech, loudness, pitch, quality, and articulation.

Speech Rate

We normally speak at 120 to 160 words per minute. If you talk faster, you should consciously try to slow down when first meeting a customer and then gradually build up to your normal rate.

You also should vary your rate of speech, depending on the nature of the message and the environment in which the communication occurs. Simple messages can be delivered at faster rates, while more difficult concepts should be presented at slower rates. Speak more slowly in a noisy area. Conduct telephone calls at a lower speech rate, because the listener does not have visual information to help interpret the words. In general, vary the rate of speech to help maintain attention.

EXHIBIT 5.5

WORD CHOICES FOR
CUSTOMERS WITH
DIFFERENT ORIENTATIONS

Visual	Auditory	Feeling
analyze	announce	active
angle	articulate	affected
appear	audible	bearable
clarity	communicate	charge
cognizant	converse	concrete
conspicuous	discuss	emotional
demonstrate	dissonant	feel
dream	divulge	firm
examine	earshot	flow
focus	enunciate	foundation
foresee	gossip	grasp
glance	hear	grip
hindsight	hush	hanging
horizon	inquire	hassle
idea	interview	heated
illusion	listen	hold
image	mention	hustle
inspect	noise	intuition
look	oral	lukewarm
notice	proclaim	motion
obscure	pronounce	muddled
observe	remark	panicky
obvious	report	pressure
perception	roar	sensitive
perspective	rumor	set
picture	say	shallow
scene	shrill	softly
see	silence	solid
sight	squeal	structured
sketchy	state	support
survey	talk	tension
vague	tell	tied
view	tone	touch
vision	utter	unbearable
watch	vocal	unsettled
witness	voice	whipped

Source: Reprinted by permission of *Journal of Personal Selling and Sales Management* © 1983. William G. Nickels, Robert F. Everett, and Ronald Klein, "Rapport Building for Salespeople: A Neuro-Linguistic Approach," *Journal of Personal Selling and Sales Management,* November 1983, pp. 1–7.

Loudness

Loudness should be altered based on the nature of the communication situation, in a similar manner to speech rate. To avoid monotony, you should learn to vary the loudness of your speech. Loudness can also be varied to emphasize certain parts of the sales presentation, indicating to the customer that these parts are more important.

You should use customer reactions to determine the appropriate loudness. For example, if a customer backs away, you are talking too loud; if a customer leans closer, you are talking too softly.

Inflection

Inflection is the tone of speech. At the end of a sentence, the tone should decrease, indicating the completion of a thought. When the tone goes up at the end of a sentence, listeners often sense uncertainty in the speaker.

Articulation

Articulation refers to the production of recognizable sounds. Poor articulation has three common causes: (1) locked jaw, (2) lazy lips, and (3) lazy tongue. Articulation is best when the speaker opens his or her mouth properly; then the movements of the lips and tongue are unimpeded. When the lips are too close together, the enunciation of certain vowels and consonants suffers.

▍ ASKING QUESTIONS

Asking questioning is a critical element in effective verbal communications.[3] Questioning gets customers to participate in the sales interview. They have a chance to actively engage in conversation rather than just listen to a presentation. This holds the attention of the customer, who ends up learning and remembering more about the product. Questioning also shows the salesperson's interest in the customer and his or her problems. Finally, by asking questions, salespeople are able to collect information about customers and test their assumptions during all phases of the sales interaction, from prospecting to closing. A salesperson might have a lot of information about the customer before the sales call, but there is no guarantee that this precall information is accurate. Salespeople can use questions to either confirm or disprove the precall analysis. Some guidelines for asking good questions follow.

Encourage Longer Responses

Closed-ended questions can be answered by a word or short phrase. Such questions do not draw much information from the customer. **Open-ended questions,** questions for which there are no simple answers, encourage greater communication.

For example, the closed-ended question "Have you heard of our company?" will probably result in a simple yes or no answer. Then the salesperson will need to ask a follow-up, open-ended question, such as "Why haven't you heard of our company?" or "What have you heard about our company?" Some examples or closed- and open-ended questions are:

Closed-Ended Questions	Open-Ended Questions
Will Mr. Jones be back from vacation on Monday?	When will Mr. Jones be back from vacation?
Are you interested in buying laptop computers for your sales force?	Why haven't you bought laptop computers for your sales force?
Are you satisfied with your present supplier of aluminum cans?	What problems are you having with your present supplier of aluminum cans?

Space Out Questions

When salespeople ask several questions, one right after another, customers may feel threatened. They may think they are being interrogated rather than participating in a conversation. Some customers react by disclosing less, rather than more, information. For this reason, questions should be spaced out so the customer has time to answer each question in a relaxed atmosphere. One method for spacing out questions is encouraging prospects to elaborate on their responses. In this way, customers believe they are volunteering information rather than being forced to divulge it.

If you really need to ask a number of questions, you might ask a permission question first, such as:

SALESPERSON   "Do you mind if I ask you some questions about your operations so we can see if our products might be of use to you?"

Ask Short, Simple Questions

Questions that have two or more parts should be avoided. The customer may not know which part to answer, and the salesperson may not know which part has been answered. For example:

SALESPERSON   "How much time do you spend making your annual budget and your sales forecasts?"

CUSTOMER   "Oh, about three weeks."

Does this mean the customer spends three weeks on both tasks or only on one?

Long questions are hard to remember and to answer. For example:

SALESPERSON   "With so many complicated reports to prepare and review, is it difficult for you to determine your direct material and labor costs and determine how much shelf space to allocate to laundry detergent in the 20,000- and 40,000-square-foot stores?"

Long questions can lose the customer's attention. Some customers may be annoyed by questions that force them to ask the salesperson for clarification.

Avoid Leading Questions

Questions should not suggest an appropriate answer. Such questions may put words into the customer's mouth rather than drawing out what the customer actually thinks. For example:

SALESPERSON   "Why do you think this is a good product?"

CUSTOMER   "Well, you said it has a low price and is very reliable."

The salesperson's question encouraged a positive response and discouraged a negative one. Even though such questions may get the responses that you want to hear, they may mask the customer's true feelings.

Some questions that you can use to collect and maintain the flow of information from the customer are discussed below.

Questions to Collect Information

Questions used to collect information usually start with the word *who, what, where, how,* or *why.* Responses to these questions give you a better understanding of the prospect, the prospect's business, and the present competition. It is best to start by asking for publicly available information; such questions are the easiest to answer. Some examples of these questions are:

Where do you buy your components now?

Who uses the copier?

What is your policy concerning returns?

Why is the Edgewood plant relocating to Oregon?

How much are you paying for the resistors now?

The questions above are used to to uncover specific facts. Questions can also be used to understand the customer's feelings on a subject. Some examples of these questions are:

How do you feel about leasing versus buying trucks?

What's your reaction to the new government safety regulations?

How do you feel about increasing your component inventory?

At times, customers may be reluctant to express their feelings on a subject. In these situations, indirect questions can be used to get customer reactions. Such questions ask customers to respond to the known views of a third party:

Electronic News had a recent article on the increased use of microswitches. Do you find this to be the case?

The Apex air conditioner got a good rating in *Consumer Reports.* Do you think it will sell well to your customers?

Questions can also be used to get a customer to articulate a specific problem. For example, a salesperson selling a copier with an advantage in copy quality might use the following series of questions:

SALESPERSON   "The copier you're using to reproduce these proposals uses treated paper, doesn't it?"

CUSTOMER   "Yes, it does."

SALESPERSON   "Some of my other customers have told me that treated-paper copiers give a gray cast to their copies. Have you experienced that as well?"

CUSTOMER   "Well, yes. The paper this machine uses isn't the best. It's heavy and doesn't look very good."

Compare the previous conversation with one using a closed-ended question:

SALESPERSON   "The quality of the copies that you'll be making of these sales proposals will not be very good. Right?"

CUSTOMER   "It's OK."

When customers realize the disadvantage of their present product, you can illustrate the consequences of the disadvantage by asking additional questions:

SALESPERSON   "How does the high energy cost of running our equipment affect you?"

CUSTOMER   "Well, we don't like it."

SALESPERSON   "How does the faster speed of our equipment decrease your production costs?"

CUSTOMER   "The speed really helps us. That's why we bought your equipment."

SALESPERSON   "Does the speed justify the higher energy cost?"

CUSTOMER   "I think it does."

Questions to Maintain the Flow of Information

A good way to maintain the flow of information is to offer verbal and non-verbal encouragement, such as saying "Really?" "Uh-huh," "That's interesting," and "Is that so?" and nodding your head. Let's look at the effect of a sequence of these encouragement signals:

CUSTOMER   "Then this salesperson asked me if I was interested in getting lower costs than I was getting from Delta."

SALESPERSON   "That's interesting. Tell me more about that."

CUSTOMER   "Well, he said that at my current usage level he could save me about $25 a month."

SALESPERSON   "Do continue, please."

CUSTOMER   "Then came the kicker."

SALESPERSON   "Uh-huh?"

CUSTOMER   "When I asked about service, the whole picture changed."

SALESPERSON   "I see."

CUSTOMER   "In short, they were going to give me a lower cost, all right. But they weren't going to give me much in the way of service."

Another approach for maintaining the flow of information is to make positive requests for additional information, such as:

Can you give me an example of what you mean?

Please, tell me more about that.

The third type of approach for maintaining the flow of information is to make neutral statements that reaffirm or repeat a customer's comment or emotion. They allow you to dig deeper, and they stimulate customers to continue their thoughts in a logical manner. By reaffirming a customer's statement, you can respond to customers without agreeing or disagreeing with them. Some examples of these questions are:

You said you were dissatisfied with your present service?

So, you need the self-correcting feature?

Reaffirming a customer's statements is particularly effective with customers who are angry, upset, or in some other highly emotional state. Often, these emotions persist until the customer recognizes that the emotions are being acknowledged. For example:

CUSTOMER   "Look, I've just about had it with you, your company, and your pumps!"

SALESPERSON   "It's pretty obvious you're upset, Ms. Roberts."

CUSTOMER   "Of course I am. That's the third time this week the pump has gone on the fritz!"

By acknowledging customers' emotional states, salespeople let them know they're being heard, which usually reduces the level of negative feelings. This allows salespeople to focus on the problem causing the emotion.

LISTENING TO VERBAL COMMUNICATIONS FROM CUSTOMERS

Many people believe effective communication is achieved by talking a lot. Inexperienced salespeople often go into a selling situation thinking they have to outtalk the prospect. They are enthusiastic about their product and company, and they want to tell the prospect all they know. Salespeople who monopolize conversations cannot find out what customers need. Actually,

S E L L I N G   *S C E N A R I O*

5.1

Top Stockbroker at Merrill Lynch Sells by Listening

Richard Greene is the top producer at Merrill Lynch year after year. He and his three assistants manage 1,000 accounts from Merrill Lynch's Boston office. Each year he pays his assistants nearly $200,000 in bonuses from his own pocket.

Most of Greene's customers are executives in local firms. He establishes relationships with these clients by listening. "I don't go to a meeting with something to sell. I want information about the customer's risk profile so I can do the right job for him."

Greene understands that listening can win over clients:

If you talk, you'll like me. If I talk, I'll like you—but if I do the talking, my business will not be served. Now this fellow is the same as everyone else. His kids don't listen to him. His wife doesn't listen to him—and he doesn't listen to her . . . . Then all of a sudden he goes to breakfast with me. He starts to answer a question. And he doesn't get interrupted. Before his eggs cool, I have another client.

Source: Monci Jo Williams, "America's Best Salespeople," *Fortune*, October 26, 1987, pp. 128–29.

listening is probably the most critical aspect of effective communication. Selling Scenario 5.1 describes the success Merrill Lynch's top salesperson achieves by being a good listener.

People can speak at the rate of only 120 to 160 words per minute, but they can listen to over 800 words per minute. This difference is referred to as the **speaking-listening differential.** Because of this differential, people often become lazy listeners. They do not pay attention, and often remember only 50 percent of what is said immediately after they hear it.

Effective listening is not a passive activity. More than just hearing what the speaker is saying, good listeners project themselves into the mind of the speaker and attempt to feel the way the speaker feels. If a customer says she needs a small microphone, the salesperson needs to listen carefully to find out what the term *small* means to this particular customer, how small the microphone has to be, why a small microphone is needed, and what the customer will be willing to sacrifice to get a small microphone. Through effective listening, the salesperson can consider the customer's specific needs in recommending a type of microphone.

Effective listeners are actively thinking while they listen. They think about the conclusions toward which the speaker is building, evaluate the evidence being presented, and sort out important facts from irrelevant ones. **Active listening** also means that the listener attempts to draw out as much information as possible. Gestures can motivate a person to continue talking. Head nodding, eye contact, and an occasional "I see," "Tell me more," and "That's interesting" demonstrate an interest in and understanding of what is being said.

To be an effective listener, the salesperson on the left demonstrates an interest in what the customer is saying and actively thinks about questions for drawing out more information.

Photo courtesy GMAC Financial Services.

Suggestions for active listening include (1) repeating information, (2) restating or rephrasing information, (3) clarifying information, (4) summarizing the conversation, (5) tolerating silences, and (6) concentrating on the ideas being communicated.[4]

REPEATING INFORMATION

During a sales interaction, you should verify the information you are collecting from the customer. A useful way to verify information is to repeat, word for word, what has been said. This technique minimizes the chance of misunderstandings. For example:

CUSTOMER   "I'll take 15 cases of personal-size Ivory soap and 12 cases of family-size."

SALESPERSON   "Sure, Mr. Johnson. That will be 15 cases of personal-size and 12 cases of family-size."

CUSTOMER   "Wait a minute. I got that backward. I want 12 cases of personal-size and 15 cases of family-size."

SALESPERSON   "Fine. 12 personal and 15 family. Is that right?"

CUSTOMER   "Yes. That's what I want."

You need to be careful when using this technique—customers can get irritated with salespeople who echo everything they say.

RESTATING OR REPHRASING INFORMATION

To verify a customer's intent, you should restate the customer's comment in your own words. This ensures that you and the customer understand each other. For example:

CUSTOMER   "The service isn't quite what I had expected."

SALESPERSON   "I see, you're a little bit dissatisfied with the service we've been giving you."

CUSTOMER   "Oh no. As a matter of fact, I've been getting better service than I thought I would."

CLARIFYING INFORMATION

Another way to verify a customer's meaning is to ask questions designed to obtain additional information. These can give a more complete understanding of the customer's concerns. For example:

CUSTOMER   "Listen, I've tried everything. I just can't get this drill press to work properly."

SALESPERSON   "Just what is it that the drill press doesn't do?"

CUSTOMER   "Well, the rivets keep jamming inside the machine. Sometimes one rivet is inserted on top of the other."

SALESPERSON   "Would you describe for me the way you load the rivets onto the tray?"

CUSTOMER   "Well, first I push down the release lever and take the tray out. Then I push that little button and put the rivets in. Next I push the bottom again, put the tray in the machine, and push the lever."

SALESPERSON   "When you put the tray in, which side is up?"

CUSTOMER   "Does that make a difference?"

This exchange shows how a sequence of questions can give a clearer definition of the problem and help the salesperson determine its cause.

SUMMARIZING THE CONVERSATION

An important element of active listening is mentally summarizing points that have been made. At critical spots in the sales presentation, you should state your mentally prepared summary. Summarizing provides both salesperson and customer with a quick overview of what has taken place and lets them both focus on the issues that have been discussed. Summarizing also lets the salesperson change the direction of the conversation. For example:

CUSTOMER   ". . . So I told him I wasn't interested."

SALESPERSON   "Let me see if I have this straight. A salesperson called on you today and asked if you were interested in reducing your costs. He also said he could save you about $25 a month. But when you pursued the matter, you found out the dollar savings in costs were offset by reduced service."

CUSTOMER   "That's right."

SALESPERSON   "Well, I have your account records right here. Assuming you're interested in getting more for your dollar with regard to copy costs, I think there's a way we can help you—without having to worry about any decrease in the quality of service."

CUSTOMER   "Tell me more."

▌ TOLERATING SILENCES

This technique could more appropriately be titled, "Bite your tongue." At times during a sales presentation, a customer needs time to think. This can be triggered by a tough question or an issue that the customer might want to avoid.

While the customer is thinking, periods of silence occur. Salespeople may be uncomfortable during these silences and feel that they need to say something. However, the customer cannot think when the salesperson is talking. When you tolerate silences, you give customers a chance to sell themselves. The following conversation about setting an appointment demonstrates the benefits of tolerating silence:

SALESPERSON   "What day would you like me to call on you?"

CUSTOMER   "Just a minute. Let me think about that."

SALESPERSON   [silence]

CUSTOMER   "Okay, let's make it on Monday, the 22nd."

SALESPERSON   "Fine, Mrs. Quinn. What time would be most convenient?"

CUSTOMER   "Hmmm . . ."

SALESPERSON   [silence]

CUSTOMER   "Ten o'clock would be best for me."

▌ CONCENTRATING ON THE IDEAS BEING COMMUNICATED

Frequently, what customers say and how they say it can distract salespeople from the ideas the customers are actually trying to communicate. For example, you might react emotionally when customers use emotion-laden phrases such as "bad service" or "lousy product." Rather than getting angry, you should try to find out what upset the customer so. You should listen to the words from the customer's viewpoint instead of reacting from your own viewpoint.

▌ READING THE CUSTOMER'S NONVERBAL MESSAGES

When two people communicate with each other, spoken words play a surprisingly small part in the communication process. Words are responsible for only 40 percent of the information that people acquire in face-to-face communication. The voice characteristics account for 10 percent of the message received, and the remaining 50 percent comes from nonverbal

S E L L I N G   S C E N A R I O

5.2

Sherlock Holmes and Selling Skills

In an episode from *The Memoirs of Sherlock Holmes,* Holmes and Watson return to their Baker Street lodgings to learn from the pageboy that a man had called during their absence, waited impatiently for a while, then departed in a state of agitation, leaving his pipe behind on the table. Holmes picks the pipe up, examines it briefly, and makes the following observations to Watson:

Now it has, you see, been twice mended: once in the wooden stem and once in the amber. Each of those mends—done, as you observe, with silver bands—must have cost more than the pipe did originally. The man must value the pipe highly when he prefers to patch it up rather than buy a new one with the same money. . . . The owner is obviously a muscular man, left-handed, with an excellent set of teeth, careless in his habits, and with no need to practice economy.

So, what has this to do with selling? Surely the answer to that question is elementary. If Sherlock Holmes had not given up his paper route early in life to become a detective, he might well have gone on to become a superlative salesperson. His keen powers of observation would have provided him with so many clues about his prospects' needs, desires, attitudes, and emotions that he would have been able to make effective presentations.

It is no accident that the best salespeople are likely to be those who observe their prospects closely and listen attentively to what they have to say. At the beginning of the sales interview, the prospect is always a mystery: So much about him or her is unknown. Unfortunately, at the end of the interview, the prospect is still a mystery to many salespeople. The difference between the successful and unsuccessful salesperson is the ability to extract clues from the prospect.

Observing and listening are the two best ways to do this. Salespeople should emulate the keen eyes and ears and the analytical approach for which Sherlock Holmes was renowned.

Source: Craig Bridgman, "The Power of Observation," *Personal Selling Power,* October 1986, p. 10.

communications.[5] **Nonverbal communications** are forms of expression—body language, space, and appearance—that communicate thoughts and emotions without using words.

Nonverbal communications provide a lot of information to the receiver, because the sender has difficulty controlling it. Since senders have less control over nonverbal communications, receivers tend to trust these communications more than verbal statements. For example, a customer may claim to be happy about a salesperson's proposal and indicates her happiness by smiling. However, people can detect fake smiles very accurately. The salesperson who feels the smile is not genuine will discount the customer's words and think that the customer really is not pleased by the proposal.[6] Selling Scenario 5.2 comapres the observational powrs of Sherlock Holmes to those of successful salespeople.

Some nonverbal communications have more universal meaning than do verbal communications. The same facial muscles are used to communicate emotions such as happiness, anger, surprise, and fear in many different cultures. The cultural differences in nonverbal communications arise not from the meaning of the expressions, but from when to appropriately display the expression.[7]

Customers do communicate through body language. The opened, relaxed posture of the second customer from the left is a positive signal; however, the first customer on the left is displaying some underlying tension, and the third customer from the left is leaning away from the salesperson—a negative signal.

P. Rivera/Superstock.

▌ BODY LANGUAGE

Customers provide a lot of information through their body language. The elements of **body language** are body angle, facial expressions, arms, hands, and legs.[8] Each of these channels is important in face-to-face communication.

Body Angle

Back-and-forth motions indicate a positive outlook, while side-to-side movements suggest insecurity and doubt. Body movements directed toward a person indicate a positive regard, while leaning back or away suggests boredom, apprehension, or possible anger. Changes in position may indicate a customer wants to end the interview, strongly agrees or disagrees with what has been said, or wants to place an order.

Face

The face has many small muscles capable of communicating innumerable messages. Customers can use these muscles to indicate interest, expectation, concern, disapproval, or approval.

The eyes are the most important area of the face. The pupils of interested or excited people tend to enlarge. Thus, by looking at a customer's eyes, salespeople can often determine when their presentations have made an impression. For this reason, many Chinese jade buyers wear dark glasses so they can conceal their interest in specific items and bargain more effectively.

Eye position can indicate a customer's thought process.[9] Eyes focused straight ahead mean that a customer is passively receiving information but devoting little effort to analyzing the meaning and not really concentrating on the presentation. An intense eye contact for more than three seconds generally indicates customer displeasure. Staring indicates coldness, anger, or dislike.

Customers look away from the salesperson while they actively consider information in the sales presentation. When the customer's eyes are positioned to the left or right, the salesperson has succeeded in getting the customer involved in the presentation. A gaze to the right suggests customers are considering the logic and facts in the presentation, while gazing to the left suggests more intense concentration based on an emotional consideration. Eyes cast down offer the strongest signal of concentration. However, when customers cast their eyes down, they may be thinking, "How can I get my boss to buy this product?" or "How can I get out of this conversation?" When customers look away for an extended period, they want to end the meeting.

There are significant cultural differences concerning eye contact between individuals. In the United States, salespeople look some one directly in the eyes when speaking or listening to a customer. Direct eye contact is a sign of interest in what the customer is saying. However, in other cultures, looking someone in the eyes may be a sign of disrespect. For example:

- In Japan, looking subordinates directly in the eyes indicates that the subordinate has done something wrong. When a subordinate looks a supervisor directly in the eyes, the subordinate is displaying hostility.

- Arabs dislike eye contact, and Americans often feel that their eyes dart around. This, unfortunately, gives some Americans the impression that Arabs are shifty.

- Brazilians look at people directly even more than Americans do. Americans tend to find this direct eye contact over a long period of time to be disconcerting.[10]

Skin color and skin tautness are other facial cues. A customer whose face reddens is signaling that something is wrong. That blush can indicate either anger or embarrassment. Tension and anger show in a tightness around the cheeks, jawline, or neck.

Arms

A key factor in interpreting arm movements is intensity. Customers will use more arm movement when they are conveying an opinion. Broader and more vigorous movement indicates that the customer is more emphatic about the point being communicated verbally.

Hands

Hand gestures are very expressive. For example, open and relaxed hands are a positive signal, especially with palms facing up. Self-touching gestures typically indicate tension. Involuntary gestures, such as a tightening of a fist, are good indicators of true feelings.

The open hands on the left provide a positive buying signal to the salesperson. The intertwined hands in the middle indicate that the customer needs to express his power and authority. On the right, the customer is playing with his hands indicating underlying tension.

All photos Michael J. Hruby.

The meaning of hand gestures differs from one culture to another. For example, in the United States the thumbs-up expression means everything is all right, but in the Middle East is an obscene gesture. In Japan, the OK sign made by holding the thumb and forefinger in a circle symbolizes money but in France it indicates that something is worthless.[11]

Legs

When customers have uncrossed legs in an open position, they send a message of cooperation, confidence, and friendly interest. Legs crossed away from a salesperson suggest that the sales call is not going well.

Body Language Patterns

No single gesture or position defines a specific emotion or attitude. To interpret a customer's feelings, salespeople need to consider the pattern of the signals, via a number of channels. Exhibit 5.6 explains eight patterns of nonverbal expression.

| THINKING IT THROUGH | *T*urn on a television set but keep the sound off. Look at the actors. Can you determine their emotions by observing their body language? Look closely to see if you can detect the patterns of body language we have discussed. |

EXHIBIT 5.6   PATTERN OF NONVERBAL EXPRESSION

	Cues from the Five Channels				
Pattern	Body Angle	Face	Arms	Hands	Legs
Power dominance, superiority	Sitting astride chair. Exaggerated leaning over. Standing while others sit.	Piercing eye contact.	Hands on hips.	Hands behind neck. Hands behind back. Steepling (fingertips touching).	Leg over chair. Feet on desk.
Nervousness, submission, apprehension	Fidgeting. Shifting from side to side.	Head down. Minimum eye contact. Constant blinking.	Hands to face, hair. Rubbing back of neck.	Wringing hands. Fingers clasped.	
Disagreement, anger, skepticism	Turning body away.	Negative shake of head. Lips pursing. Eyes squinting. Chin thrusting out. Frown.	Arms crossed. Finger under collar.	Fist. Finger pointing. Hands gripping edge of desk.	Legs crossed.
Boredom, disinterest	Head in palm of hands.	Lack of eye contact. Looking at door, at watch, out window. Blank stare.		Playing with object on table. Shuffling papers. Drumming on table.	Tapping feet.
Suspicion, secretiveness, dishonesty	Moving body away. Sideways glance. Crossing arms or legs with body forward.	Avoiding eye contact. Squinting eyes. Smirking.	Touching nose while speaking. Pulling ear while speaking.	Fingers crossed.	Feet pointing toward exits.
Uncertainty, indecision	Pacing back and forth.	Head down or tilted. Biting lip. Shifting eyes left and right.	Pinching bridge of nose. Tugging at pants. Scratching head.	Pulling neck.	Look of concentration while tapping feet.
Evaluation	Head titled slightly. Ear turned toward speaker.	Slight blinking of eyes. Eye squinting. Eyebrows raised. Nodding.	Hand gripping chin. Putting glasses in mouth.	Putting index finger to lips.	Kicking foot slightly.
Cooperation, confidence, honesty	Learning forward in seat. Sitting far up in chair. Back and forth movement of body.	Good eye contact. Slight blinking. Smile.	Putting hands to chest. Free movement of arms and hands.	Open hands. Palms toward other person.	Legs uncrossed. Feet flat on floor.

Sending Messages to Customers Using Nonverbal Communications

The previous section discussed how salespeople can observe body language to develop a better understanding of their customers. Salespeople use body language, voice characteristics, spacing, and appearance to send messages to their customers. Selling Scenario 5.3 shows how Dan Rather altered his image by changing his nonverbal behavior.

Using Body Language

Body language can be used to communicate more effectively with customers. For example, salespeople should strive to use the cooperative cues shown in Exhibit 5.6. Cooperative cues indicate to customers that the salesperson sincerely wants to help them satisfy their needs. On the other hand, you should avoid using power cues. These cues will intimidate customers and make them uncomfortable.

Face

Nonverbal communications are very difficult to manage. Facial reactions are often involuntary, especially during stressful situations. Lips tense, foreheads wrinkle, and eyes glare without salespeople realizing they are disclosing their feelings to a customer. You will be able to control your facial reactions only with practice.

As with muscles anywhere else in the body, the coordination of facial muscles requires exercise. Actors realize this need and attend facial exercise classes to control their reactions. Salespeople, to some extent, are also performers and need to learn how to use their faces to communicate emotions.

Nothing creates rapport like a smile. The smile should appear natural and comfortable—not a smirk or the exaggerated grin of a clown. To achieve the right smile, stand before a mirror or a video camera, and place your lips in various smiling positions until you find a position that feels natural and comfortable. Then practice the smile until it becomes almost second nature.

Eye Contact

Appropriate eye contact varies from situation to situation. You should use direct eye contact when talking in front of a group to indicate sincerity, credibility, and trustworthiness. Glancing from face to face or staring at a wall has the opposite effect. However, staring can overpower customers and make them uncomfortable.

Hand Movements

Hand movements can have a dramatic impact. For example, when you expose the palm of the hand, you are indicating openness and receptivity. Slicing hand movements and pointing a finger are very strong signals and should be used to reinforce only the most important points. In most cases, pointing a finger should be avoided. It will remind customers of a parent scolding a child.

S E L L I N G *S C E N A R I O*

5.3

Changing Dan Rather from Public Defender to Public Servant

Before Dan Rather became anchor for the "CBS Evening News," he had won five Emmys and was considered to be the best White House correspondent in the history of broadcast journalism. With his extremely telegenic face, the network was confident that he would be able to replace Walter Cronkite, an institution in broadcast journalism. However, when Dan Rather became anchor, the rating for the CBS Evening News dropped dramatically.

Viewers were asked why they had this unexpected negative reaction to Rather. The research found that people used the following words to describe Rather and Cronkite:

Rather	Cronkite
Cold	Warm
Rigid	Flexible
Aggressive	Conciliatory
Self-oriented	Other-oriented
Seeks attention	Seeks privacy
Superior	Equal
Tense	Relaxed

The research indicated Dan Rather needed to adapt his body language from that of an aggressive reporter to his new role as a friendly and relaxed an-

chor. The following changes were made to successfully alter his image:

Body movements: Use more forward and backward motion to convey drive and energy. He abandoned his highly controlled posture that appears to be rigid and tense.

Facial expression: Display a broader range of emotions and increase frequency of smiling.

Eye movement: Avoid downward eye movements to read script. His eye movements made him appear to be cold, removed, and concerned only with facts—not with people. By using a TelePrompter to increase eye contact, he seemed more human.

Arm posture: Increase hand motion and arm movement to give a more relaxed appearance.

Unfortunately, these changes in body language were not enough to soften Rather's image with the public. Perhaps teaming him with Connie Chung will increase the connection between the "CBS Evening News" and its audience.

Source: Adapted from Gerhard Gschwandtner and Pat Garnett, *Non-Verbal Selling Power* (Englewood Cliffs, NJ: Prentice Hall, 1985), pp. 9–11.

Dan Rather

CBS Photography.

Walter Cronkite

CBS Photography.

When salespeople make presentations to a group, they often use too few hand gestures. Gestures should be used to drive home a point. But if you use too many gestures, acting like an orchestra conductor, people will begin to watch the hands and miss your words.

Posture and Body Movements

Shuffling one's feet and slumping both give an impression of a lack of self-confidence and self-discipline. On the other hand, an overly erect posture, such as that of a military cadet, suggests rigidity. You should let comfort be your guide when searching for the right posture.

To get an idea of what looks good and feels good, stand in front of a mirror and shift your weight until tension in your back and neck is at a minimum. Then gently pull your shoulders up and back, and elevate your head. Practice walking by taking a few steps. Keep the pace deliberate, not halting—deliberate movements indicate confidence and control.

Matching the Customer's Communication Style

Salespeople develop better rapport when they match the verbal and nonverbal behavior of their customers. For example, consider a salesperson from New York selling to a customer in Texas. Communication in this sales interaction will be effective only if the salesperson slows his or her rate of speech and avoids using expressions only another New Yorker would understand.

This matching process also extends to body language. Michael McCasky, writing in the *Harvard Business Review*, noted that "In moments of great rapport, a remarkable pattern of nonverbal communication can develop. Two people will mirror each other's movements—dropping a hand, shifting their body at exactly the same time."[12] The more customers and salespeople share language, speech patterns, and nonverbal behavior, the greater the sense of rapport and mutual understanding they will have.

SPACE AND PHYSICAL CONTACT

Distance during Interactions

The physical space between a customer and salesperson can affect the customer's reaction to a sales presentation. The four distance zones people use when interacting in business and social situations are shown in Exhibit 5.7. The intimate zone is primarily reserved for a person's most intimate relationships; the personal zone for close friends and those who share special interests; the social zone for business transactions and other impersonal relationships; and the public zone for speeches, teachers in classrooms, and passersby.[13] The exact sizes of the intimate and personal zones depend on age, gender, culture, and race.[14] For example, the social zone for Latin Americans is much closer than for North Americans. Latin Americans tend to conduct business transactions so close together that North Americans feel uncomfortable.

EXHIBIT 5.7   DISTANCE ZONE FOR INTERACTIONS

Customers may react negatively when salespeople invade their intimate or personal space. To show the negative reaction, they may assume a defensive posture by moving back or folding their arms. While approaching too close can generate a negative reaction, standing too far away can create an image of aloofness, conceit, or unsociability.

In general, salespeople should begin customer interactions at the far end of the social zone and not move closer until an initial rapport has been established. If the buyer indicates that a friendlier relationship has developed, the salesperson should move closer.

Touching

People fall into two touching groups: contact and noncontact. Contact people usually see noncontact people as cold and unfriendly. On the other hand, noncontact people view contact people as overly friendly and obtrusive.

While some customers may accept a hand on their back or their shoulder being touched, salespeople should limit touching to a handshake. Touching clearly enters a customer's intimate space and may be considered rude and threatening—an invasion.

▌APPEARANCE

Physical appearance, specifically dress style, is an aspect of nonverbal communication that affects the customer's evaluation of the salesperson. Salespeople need to dress in a manner that makes a good first impression on a customer, although they should not dress like fashion models. If salespeople overdress, their clothing might distract from their sales presentation. Proper attire and grooming, however, can give salespeople additional poise and confidence. Some suggestions for proper dress follow.[15]

Business clothes project an image of the salesperson, the salesperson's company, and the product. Salespeople will feel most comfortable using their own natural style plus some common sense. Standards of acceptable business dress vary in different areas of the country, so adapt your clothing style accordingly. Consider corporate culture, too. How do the executives of the company dress? What image do they project? Finally, remember the customer—the salesperson's business dress should make both of them comfortable.

Dress Like the Customer

The appropriate style of dress varies, depending on the person's occupation, social status, age, physical size, and geographic location. Salespeople can get some useful clues about appropriate styles by observing their customers. They should attempt to match the style of their customers and avoid dressing more stylishly or expensively. Dressing better than your customers may create an impression of greater authority, but also may make the customers feel uncomfortable and defensive.

Salespeople should wear classic dresses, suits, and accessories. High-fashion clothing should be avoided; it costs too much, goes out of style too soon, and may not look professional or businesslike unless the salesperson is working in the fashion industry.

Hints for Men

The suit is the focal garment in business dress, particularly when you are interacting with upper-middle-class decision makers. Choose color, material, fit, and accompanying garments and accessories carefully. In general, darker suits give a more authoritative image; lighter colors create a friendlier one. Pinstripes convey the most authority, followed in descending order by solids, chalk stripes, and plaids (which must be very subtle). Natural fibers such as wool (or wool-polyester blends that look and feel like wool) are preferable. They look better and wear better than most synthetics. Cottons and linens, while comfortable, wrinkle too easily.

The fit of the suit is also important. The pant waist should fit slightly above the navel and be horizontal to the ground. Plain-bottom cuffs should break in front and be longer in back than in front. Turned-up cuffs should be horizontal to the ground and the same length in both back and front. Jacket sleeves should come within 5 inches of the base of the thumb.

White-on-white patterns and solid white shirts are the most effective, adding credibility; blues and other pale pastels are also popular. Shirts, as a rule, should be lighter than the suit, and the tie darker than the shirt. Shirt stripes should always be close together, clearly defined, and of one coordinating color on a white background.

Ties are important indicators of the salesperson's status, credibility, and personality. A good rule is to wear suits and shirts in basic colors and let the tie provide the accent color. For example, the accent color for a navy

Salespeople should wear clothes similar to the clothes worn by their customers. This DowElanco agricultural chemical salesperson on the left dresses like the Mexican farmer on the right.

Courtesy Dow.

suit and white shirt can be provided by a striped red and navy tie. The tie tip should come just to the belt buckle, and its width should harmonize with the width of the suit lapels. The standard tie is 55 or 56 inches long; to make a good knot, it must have added material sewn into it. Bow ties give off negative signals, and tie pins and clasps are currently out of style. Silk is the best choice for tie material; it looks elegant and wears well. Polyester or a blend must look like silk to be effective. Wool or cotton is acceptable, too. Acetate and rayon tend to look cheap, however, and linen should be avoided because it wrinkles so easily. Solid ties with solid suits look good. Other acceptable tie patterns include polka dot, rep, club, Ivy League, repeating diamond, paisley, and basic plaid.

As for accessories, the less jewelry worn, the better. Stay away from bracelets and pins and wear simple, small cuff links. Shoes should be black, brown, or cordovan, in lace-up, wingtip, Gucci-type buckle, or all-leather slip-on styles. Never wear shoes with multiple colors, platforms, or high heels with business dress. Most belts are acceptable. Buckles should be small, clean, and traditional. Attaché cases are positive symbols of success.

Hints for Women

In 1977, when John Molloy wrote his *Dress for Success* book, businesswomen were advised to wear only very conservative navy or gray suits, tailored blouses, and string ties. They were entering professions dominated by men (such as selling), and they needed to give clear signals that they were serious about their jobs and were members of the company team. In those days, the more that women in these "uniforms" looked like men, the more easily they were accepted in the business world.

Today, thanks to those pioneers, women just beginning their careers have the luxury of dressing with more flair and style while still maintaining a dignified, professional look. Women in business can now signal that they are good at, and relaxed about, their jobs, and that they know the difference between business and private life.

Molloy's more recent research shows that a tailored suit is still the best choice for a woman bent on success. Today, a good business wardrobe still starts with navy, black, and gray suits worn with light-colored blouses. But you can also add suits in more cheerful shades, wool or silk dresses with jackets, and blazers with coordinated skirts. As with menswear, women's suits look and wear best in natural fibers or in blends that look and feel like natural fibers. Women should choose a suit whose jacket and skirt lengths complement their figure shape and height. It should be stylish without being so trendy so it will look dated in a short time.

Women's blouses have not much more variety than men's shirts in color, style, and fabric. Cotton and silk are the best fabric choices; they are much more professional looking than sheer polyester or slithery silk imitations. Keep blouses businesslike, feminine but tailored, soft but not see-through, plain or with small prints.

Choose shoes and hose to complement the costume. Black, brown, navy, or cordovan are always acceptable shoe colors. Tailored, classic pumps should have heels no higher than 1 or 1½ inches (especially if the job requires walking), and should be combined with neutral or color-coordinated hose to look both professional and feminine. Fishnet or patterned hose, ankle straps, chunky loafers, and trendy boots are best left for after-hours wear.

Accessories such as ties, scarves, simple pins, gold chains, and plain watches can make even a plain, dark suit look dressy and businesslike. Chunky jewelry and clanking bracelets are out. Silk scarves can add flair and a touch of color if tied or draped attractively. Scarves are becoming more popular and acceptable today than the so-called ties that were formerly a required part of the uniform.

The businesswoman's hairstyle should share many of the same characteristics as her clothes: subtle, formal, comfortable, and easy to care for. Hair length is not an issue, but it must be managed effectively.

ADJUSTING FOR CULTURAL DIFFERENCES

In international selling situations, salespeople need to recognize that business practices differ around the world.[16] For example, Americans tend to think that agreements require formal, written contracts. However, many other cultures have strong moral principles in which verbal agreements are just as binding as written agreements. People in these cultures may find an insistence on written contracts insulting, because they feel their honor is being questioned.

EXHIBIT 5·8

INTERACTING SUCCESSFULLY WITH JAPANESE CUSTOMERS

1. Present your overall objectives, indicating how each interrelates with the others. The Japanese do not like bits and pieces.
2. Never ask questions unless you are sure the customer can answer them. Give your questions to Japanese customers ahead of time, so they can prepare the answers and not lose face.
3. Be patient. The Japanese perceive impatience as a sign of weakness.
4. Don't fidget, jiggle your feet, or play with a pen. The Japanese view these nonverbal behaviors as showing a lack of sincere interest in the transaction.
5. Be aware of feelings and emotions and base your sales approach on them. The Japanese are not as much influenced by logical arguments as they are by feelings and emotions.
6. Don't complain. The Japanese identify complaining with whining.
7. Don't try to bargain. The Japanese prefer persuasion, not pressure. Bargaining makes them feel uncomfortable and insecure.
8. Be prepared for silence. The Japanese like to sit back and reflect. They do not feel that someone has to be talking all the time. The Japanese say, "Eloquence is silver. Silence is gold."
9. Remember that if you cannot understand the reactions or feelings of the Japanese, this does not mean that they are being deceptive.
10. Be thoroughly prepared with hard data, facts, and figures. Don't wing it. The Japanese often require more information than Americans normally do.

Source: "Selling to a Japanese," *Sales & Marketing Management*, July 1987, pp. 58–61.

Americans assume that all the terms in a contract, such as price and delivery, remain constant throughout the contract. However, Greek businesspeople view a contractual agreement as the initial step in the negotiation. After the agreement is signed, Greek customers will continue to negotiate, and they keep negotiating until the products or services are delivered. The common practice in Korea is to adjust the terms of a contract if changes occur in the economy or in the price of raw materials. Exhibit 5.8 provides some suggestions for selling effectively to Japanese customers.

USE OF LANGUAGE

Communication in international selling often takes place in English, because English is likely to be the only language that salespeople and customers have in common. To communicate effectively with customers whose native language is not English, salespeople need to be careful about the words and expressions they use. People who use English in international selling should:[17]

1. Use common English words that a customer would learn during the first two years of studying the language. For example, use *expense* rather than *expenditure,* or *stop* instead of *cease*.
2. Use words that do not have alternative meanings. For example, *right* has many alternative meanings, while *accurate* has fewer. When you use words that have several meanings, recognize that

Communication in international selling is often done in English. However, this American salesperson needs to use words and expressions that are understood unambiguously by his Japanese customers.

Loren Santow/TSW.

nonnative speakers will usually use the most common meaning to interpret what you are saying.

3. Avoid slang expressions particular to American culture, such as "slice of life," "struck out," "wade through the figures," and "run that by me again."

4. Use rules of grammar more strictly than you would in everyday speech. Make sure you express your thoughts in complete sentences, with a noun and a verb.

5. Use action-specific verbs, as in "*start* the motor," rather than action-general verbs, as in "*get* the motor going."

Even if you are careful about the words you use, misunderstandings can still arise because terms have different meanings, even among people from different English-speaking countries. For example, tabling a proposal in the United States means delaying a decision, while in England it means that immediate action is to be taken. In England, promising to do something by the end of day means doing it when they have finished what they are working on now, not within 24 hours. *Bombed* in England means the negotiations were successful, while is has the opposite meaning in the United States.

▌ TIME AND SCHEDULING

International salespeople need to understand the varying perceptions of time in general and the time it takes for business activities to occur in different countries. For example, in Latin American and Arab countries, people are not strict about keeping appointments at the designated time. If you show up for an appointment on time in these cultures, you might have to wait several hours for the meeting to start.

Lunch in Spain is at 3:00 PM; 12:00 noon in Germany; 1:00 PM in England; and 11:00 AM in Norway. In Greece, no one makes telephone calls between 2:00 PM and 5:00 PM. The British arrive at their desks at 9:30 AM, but like to do paperwork and have a cup of tea before getting any calls. The French, like the Germans, like to start early in the day, frequently having working breakfasts. Restaurants close at 9:00 PM in Norway, just when dinner is starting in Spain. The best time to reach high-level Western European executives is after 7:00 PM, when daily activities have slowed down and they are continuing to work for a few more hours. However, Germans start going home at 4:00 PM.[18]

SUMMARY

This chapter discusses the principles of communication and how they can be used to improve selling effectiveness and reduce misunderstandings. The communication process consists of a sender, who encodes information and transmits messages to a receiver, who decodes them. A communication breakdown can occur when the sender does a poor encoding job, when the receiver has difficulty decoding, and when noise interferes with the transmission of the message.

Effective communication requires a two-way flow of information. At different times in the interaction, both parties will act as sender and receiver. This two-way process enables salespeople to adapt their sales approach to the customer's needs and communication style.

Four communication modes discussed in this chapter are interpreting verbal and nonverbal communications from customers and sending verbal and nonverbal communications to customers. Listening is a valuable communication skill that enables salespeople to adapt effectively. To listen effectively, salespeople need to be actively thinking about what the customer is saying and how to draw out more information. Some suggestions for actively collecting more information from customers are: repeat, restate, clarify, summarize the customer's comments, and demonstrate an interest in what the customer is saying.

More than 50 percent of communication is nonverbal. Nonverbal messages sent by customers are conveyed by body language. The five channels of body-language communication are body angle, face, arms, hands, and legs. No single channel can be used to determine the feelings or attitudes of customers. Salespeople need to analyze the body-language pattern comprised of all five channels to determine when a customer is nervous, bored, or suspicious.

When communicating verbally with customers, salespeople must be careful to use words and expressions their customers will understand. Effective communication is facilitated through the use of concrete, neutral words rather than abstract, emotional words.

Asking questions gets the customer involved in the interaction and provides additional information that can be used to develop and adapt the sales presentation. Open-ended questions encourage longer responses. In addition, questions should be spaced out, short and simple, and not suggest an appropriate answer.

Salespeople can use nonverbal communication to convey information to customers. In addition to using the five channels of body language, salespeople need to know the appropriate distances between themselves and their customers for different types of communications and relationships.

Salespeople also communicate to their customers through their appearance. Physical appearance and dress can be used to create a favorable impression. In general, salespeople should try to dress like the customers they are calling on.

Finally, two-way communication increases when salespeople adjust their communication styles to the styles of their customers. In making such adjustments, salespeople need to be sensitive to cultural differences when selling internationally.

KEY TERMS

active listening   *143*
articulation   *138*
body language   *148*
closed-ended questions   *138*
decoding   *130*
encoding   *130*
inflection   *138*
noise   *132*

nonverbal communication   *147*
open-ended questions   *138*
speaking-listening differential   *143*
two-way communication   *131*
verbal communications   *133*
voice characteristics   *136*
word picture   *135*

QUESTIONS AND PROBLEMS

1. Understanding nonverbal communication is more important to salespeople than understanding verbal communication." Do you agree? Why or why not?

2. Identify what the following body language cues indicate:
   a. Tapping a finger or pencil on a desk.
   b. Stroking the chin and leaning forward.
   c. Leaning back in a chair, with arms folded across the chest.
   d. Sitting in the middle of a bench or sofa.
   e. Assuming the same posture as the person with whom you are communicating.

3. Why is two-way communication preferable to one-way communication?

4. Assume you are selling cosmetics to a family-owned drugstore. Make up three questions that are designed to initiate two-way communication with the prospect.

5. Define *communication*. Can listening habits be a barrier to communication? If so, how?

6. Which form of communication—verbal or nonverbal—is more believable? Why?

7. Many people do not like to hear the words *sell* or *sold*. Why would you be unlikely to say the following to a friend: "Look at the new personal computer I was sold yesterday."

8. Give two examples each of open-ended and closed-ended questions. Why do open-ended questions generally improve communications?

9. It is often said that a common outcome of communication is misunderstanding. Do you agree?

10. Ross Thomas is a 25-year-old computer salesperson who calls on insurance companies, banks, and department stores. He views himself as a "free thinker" and wears the latest apparel and hair styles. At the present time his

hair is quite long, giving him an "in" look. He buys casual clothing because it can be worn at work and for leisure activities. What advice would you give Ross about his appearance? Why? Should he dress differently when calling on banks and department stores?

11. Pay close attention to your professor's next lecture. How does he or she use body language and voice characteristics to emphasize important points?

CASE PROBLEMS

CASE 5 • 1
GENERAL FOODS
INTERNATIONAL COFFEE
FLAVORS

June Daniels, a sales representative for the Maxwell House Division of General Foods, calls on Jim Goodwin, the beverage buyer for Super Foods, a chain of 12 supermarkets headquartered in Denver, Colorado. Ms. Daniels is trying to persuade Mr. Goodwin to carry a new line of decaffeinated, flavored instant coffees.

DANIELS "How's business?"

GOODWIN "Well, now that you ask, sales have slowed down. I was just looking over our sales analysis and . . ."

DANIELS "Jim, maybe our new line of decaffeinated international flavors will add some excitement to the beverage section. They are really attracting a lot of attention. Did you see our ad in *Progressive Grocer?*"

GOODWIN "I saw the ad last week. I don't see how I can . . ."

DANIELS "Good! Then you know all about the test market results for the six new decaffeinated flavors. Our research shows that a lot of elderly consumers like having flavored coffee after dinner but are afraid that the caffeine will keep them up. The new line has done particularly well with the elderly segment."

GOODWIN "Well, I can understand the concern about caffeine, but . . ."

DANIELS "Everyone is more health conscious now. Customers really want more health foods—low fat, low cholesterol, no additives. We really think these decaffeinated coffees fit right into this trend. We have developed an exciting marketing program to get you to carry the new line. If you agree to stock four out of the six decaffeinated flavors and feature the line in your weekly ad, we'll give you a 20 percent discount on your first order and pay for the space in your weekly ad."

GOODWIN "I have to stock four flavors?"

DANIELS "I knew you'd be excited. We also can set a special in-store tasting for your customers."

GOODWIN "That sounds interesting. You know our target market is younger blue-collar workers. Do you have any data on which flavor sells best to that segment?"

DANIELS "They like all the flavors. Pick the ones you like and I'm sure they will sell well. The Suisse Mocha and Vienna Expresso are excellent. Can I take your order?"

GOODWIN   "I've got an appointment coming in soon. Could you leave some material that I can look through? I'll get back to you."

DANIELS   "Sure. I've got some brochures in my briefcase. Can we set up an appointment?"

GOODWIN   "Well, business has been really hectic. Let me give you a call. Thanks for stopping by."

QUESTIONS

1. Is Ms. Daniels a good listener?
2. What indicates that Daniels has something to learn about communications skills?
3. Rewrite this dialogue to show how Daniels should have handled this sales call.

CASE 5 • 2
GAINESVILLE OFFICE SUPPLY

Carlos Hernandez is a sales representative for Gainesville Office Supply Company. He has just walked into the office of Jim Jackson, the office manager for Bear Archery. Hernandez is 25 years old and has been working for Gainesville Office Supply for six months. He is dressed in a blue pinstripe suit. Jackson is a large man, about 50 years old, and is wearing a plaid flannel shirt and slacks. He is sitting behind his desk, leaning back in his chair with his arms crossed.

HERNANDEZ   (walking around the desk to shake hands with Jackson) "Good morning Mr. Jackson. It's a pleasure to meet you. How are you today?"

JACKSON   "I'm fine. I was expecting you 15 minutes ago. I have an appointment soon, so I don't have much time."

HERNANDEZ   "I'm only five minutes late. I got held up in the traffic around the mall."

JACKSON   (moving around in his chair and crossing his arms again) "Okay. Maybe it wasn't 15 minutes. What can I do for you?"

HERNANDEZ   "I would like to talk to you about our new program for providing office supplies more economically to our partners. The program . . ."

JACKSON   "Before you waste a lot of time, we just placed a large office supply order with Chestnut's. We really don't need supplies at this point."

HERNANDEZ   (crossing his arms, speech rate increases): "That's too bad. Our program could have reduced your office supply costs by 30 percent."

JACKSON   (uncrossing arms, leaning forward) "Really?"

HERNANDEZ   (starting to rise and putting on his coat) "Well, I guess I'm too late."

QUESTIONS

1. How could Hernandez have communicated better with Jackson using nonverbal methods?

2. How did Hernandez make a mistake in reading the nonverbal messages sent by Jackson?

ADDITIONAL REFERENCES

Bishop, Kathleen. "The Silent Language." *Training and Development Journal,* June 1985, pp. 36–37.

Brown, Steven. "The Use of Closed Influence Tactics by Salespeople: Incidence and Buyer Attributions." *Journal of Personal Selling and Sales Management,* 10 (Fall 1990), pp. 17–29.

Castelberry, Stephen, and C David Sheppard. "Effective Listening and Personal Selling." *Journal of Personal Selling and Sales Management,* 13 (Winter 1993), pp. 35–49.

Dawson, Lyndon; Barlow Soper; and Charles Pettijohn. "The Effects of Empathy on Salesperson Effectiveness." *Psychology & Marketing,* 9 (July/August 1992), pp. 297–310.

Dion, Paul, and Elaine Notarantonio. "Salesperson Communication Style: The Neglected Dimension in Sales Performance." *Journal of Business Communication,* 29 (Winter 1992), pp. 63–77.

Evans, Elaine. "Turn the Power of Linguistics into Sales Magic." *Personal Selling Power,* October 1990, pp. 38–40.

Gschwandtner, Laura B. "John Cleese Brings His Unique Body Language Savvy to the Sales World." *Personal Selling Power,* November–December 1989, pp. 8–11.

Gschwandtner, Laura B, and Gerhard Gschwandtner. "America's Best Known Salesman . . . Ed McMahon." *Personal Selling Power,* May–June 1989, pp. 8–11.

King, R H, and M B Booze. "Sales Training and Impression Management." *Journal of Personal Selling and Sales Management,* August 1986, pp. 51–60.

Molloy, John. *New Dress for Success.* New York: Warner, 1988.

Nerenberg, Gerald, and Juliet Nerenberg. "Reading Silent Signals." *Business Marketing,* July 1989, p. 20.

Rosenthal, Alan. "How to Improve Presentations." *Business Marketing,* June 1992, pp. 40–41.

Sharma, Arun. "The Persuasive Effects of Salesperson Credibility: Conceptual and Empirical Examination," *Journal of Personal Selling and Sales Management,* 10 (Fall 1990), pp. 71–80.

Adaptive Selling

*P*ersonal selling is the most effective marketing communication media because
salespeople can tailor their presentation to each customer. They
can ask questions to determine the customer's needs and make a
presentation to show how their product will satisfy those specific needs.
By listening and observing nonverbal behaviors, they can tell when the
presentation is not working and change their approach on the spot.

By comparison, advertising managers are restricted to delivering the same
advertising campaign to all customers. The message in the campaign may
work for the typical customer, but there will be a lot of customers with
different needs who will not be influenced by the message. It may take
months for an advertising manager to realize and change a campaign
that is not effective.

Effective salespeople take advantage of this unique opportunity. They
use their knowledge of the customer's buying process (Chapter 4) and
communication skills (Chapter 5) to learn about their customers and
select effective sales strategies. They adapt their selling strategy and
approach to the selling situation. This chapter examines how salespeople
can communicate effectively with their customers by practicing adaptive
selling.

Some questions answered in this chapter are:

What is adaptive selling?
Why is it important for salespeople to practice adaptive selling?
What kind of knowledge do salespeople need to practice
  adaptive selling?
How can salespeople acquire this knowledge?
What different approaches can salespeople use to adapt their
  sales strategy, presentation, and social style?

Peter Baidoo is an Executive Professional Representative, the highest-level sales position in the Merck Human Health Division. Baidoo's outstanding performance representing Merck in Stockton, California, earned him the prestigious Vice President's Award.

Pharmaceutical representatives are often thought of as partners with physicians in the health care delivery system. Merck wants its representatives to deliver information in the language and terminology of the health care professional. Their sales reps need to be knowledgeable about scientific product information, the needs of the medical practitioners in their territory, and market conditions.

"A new challenge we are facing is selling to health maintenance organizations (HMOs). HMOs have committees that make decisions as to what drugs can be prescribed by physicians in their organization. These committees can include physicians, nurses, pharmacy directors, purchasing agents, and business managers. They'll all have slightly different perspectives and be interested in a wide range of information, from the efficacy (effectiveness) and side effects of the drug to its dosage, convenience, cost, and generic availability. You really need to target your presentation to the varying needs and interests of the committee members.

"To be an effective representative, I also have to understand the needs of the doctors I call on—what types of patients they treat and what's important to them when they decide to prescribe a drug. I also need to be adaptive, attuned to the sales situation and the personality of the person I'm calling on.

PETER BAIDOO

Merck

"One thing that always changes is the amount of time a doctor will have for me. Usually you can tell just by how they welcome you into their offices. If the doctor is relaxed, sitting back in his or her chair, smiling and very friendly, I know I'll have lots of time. In this case I'll make a full presentation, giving all the details of the features, benefits, and limitations of several products.

"On the other hand, I can call on this same doctor the next month and find him or her very busy. Then I take a different approach. Standing in the outer office I'll have about 30 seconds to remind him or her of one of my products. I'll choose just one aspect to present, such as the effectiveness or convenience of the drug. In either case I'll always leave product literature for the doctor to review and starter samples.

"Of course, I always have a purpose in mind for every sales call, and adapting to the personality of the physician is also key to being successful. With an extrovert I'll get lots of interaction and questions. Sometimes it's easy to get off track, so I'll reiterate the features and benefits of my product and try to get a commitment before I leave.

"With an introvert it's just the opposite situation. There's usually very little spontaneous discussion; the doctor may just sit there and nod without taking a position on my presentation. Then I'll ask open-ended questions such as, 'Based on the information I've given you, how comfortable do you feel in prescribing this drug?' This kind of questioning will generate a response and help me to know what the doctor is thinking."

TYPES OF SALES PRESENTATIONS

Three types of presentations used by salespeople are: (1) the standard memorized presentation, (2) the outlined presentation, and (3) the customized presentation. These presentations illustrate the differences between adaptive and nonadaptive selling.[1]

STANDARD MEMORIZED PRESENTATION

The **standard memorized presentation,** also called a *canned presentation,* is a completely memorized sales presentation. The salesperson presents the same selling points in the same order to all customers. Typically, the presentation is developed by analyzing the presentations used by the company's most effective salespeople. The best features from these presentations are incorporated into a standard sales story. Some companies insist that their salespeople memorize the entire presentation and deliver it word for word. Others feel that salespeople should be free to make some adjustments to suit their own personalities.

The standard memorized presentation ensures that the salesperson will provide complete and accurate information about the firm's products and policies. Because it includes the best techniques and methods, the standard memorized presentation brings new salespeople up to speed quickly and gives them confidence. Repetition is reduced, saving time for both the buyer and the salesperson. This type of presentation is very effective in telemarketing and direct selling, because the salesperson contacts the customer once and must gain the customer's attention and commitment on that call in a short time period.

However, the standard memorized presentation is inflexible. It offers no opportunity for the salesperson to adapt the presentation. The standardized presentation encourages salespeople to talk too much about the product without paying attention to the needs of the buyer. The customer is discouraged from participating in the sales presentation and, thus, the salesperson does not have an opportunity to discover the customer's actual needs.

OUTLINED PRESENTATION

The **outlined presentation** is a pre-arranged presentation that outlines the most important sales points to be discussed when calling on a customer. Salespeople using an outlined presentation often have a standard introduction, standard answers to common objections raised by customers, and a standard method for getting the customer to place an order. An example of a outlined presentation appears in Exhibit 6.1.

Some companies provide their sales representatives with suggested outlines for selling each product. For example, a large pharmaceutical company instructs its salespeople to adhere to an outlined presentation. Upon entering the doctor's office, the salesperson is instructed to make an opening comment, offer a one-line promotional message, ask a question about needs, describe how the product meets that need, ask if the doctor understands, and then ask the doctor to consider prescribing the pharmaceutical.

Scenario: A Procter & Gamble Salesperson Calling on a Grocery Store Manager

Step Sales Point	Say Something Like This:
1. Introduction and reinforcement of past success.	"Good morning, Mr. Babcock. I was talking with one of your stockers, and he said our Crest end-of-aisle display was very popular with customers last weekend. He said he had to restock it about three times. Looks like you made a wise decision to go with that program."
2. Reiterate customer's needs.	"I know that profits and fast turns are what you are always looking for."
3. Introduce new Sure anti-perspirant campaign.	"We have a new campaign coming up for our Sure line."
4. Explain ad campaign and coupon drops.	"We will be running a new set of commercials on all three network news programs . . . also, we'll be adding an insert in the Sunday coupon section with a 35-cents-off coupon."
5. Explain case allowances.	"We are going to give you a $1.20 case allowance for every case of Sure you buy today."
6. Ask for end-of-aisle display and order of cases.	"I would propose that you erect an end-of-aisle display on Aisle 7 . . . and that you order 20 cases."
7. Thank manager for the order.	"Thank you, and I know the results will be just as good as they were for our Crest promotion."

An outlined presentation can be very effective because it is well organized. Two senior sales executives emphasize that salespeople should "Prepare an outline of points in the order in which you want to cover them and stick to it at all costs."[2] This type of sales presentation is more informal and natural than is the standard memorized presentation, and it provides more opportunity for the customer to participate in the sales interaction.

However, the increased flexibility has some drawbacks. The salesperson must be able to speak extemporaneously. There is also a greater chance that the salesperson will be sidetracked and not present all of the product's benefits. But the greatest limitation of the outlined presentation is its lack of flexibility. When delivering this presentation, the salesperson is encouraged to present a specific message, even though the customer may wish to discuss other issues that are not part of the outline. Some adaptability is permitted, but not as much as when the customized presentation is used.

CUSTOMIZED PRESENTATION

The **customized presentation** is a written and/or oral presentation based on a detailed analysis of the customer's needs. To develop the presentation, the sales representative gets the customer to agree to a needs analysis. The salesperson may bring in specialists, such as engineers or systems designers, to conduct the study. Then this information is analyzed and used to make the presentation.

This type of presentation offers an opportunity to use the communication principles discussed in the last chapter to discover the customer's needs and problems and propose the most effective solution for satisfying those needs. The customized presentation builds the customer's respect for the salesperson and his or her company. The customer recognizes the sales representative as a professional who is helping to solve problems, not just sell products. This view is an important step in developing a partnering relationship.

On the other hand, the customized presentation is time consuming and costly for the salespeople and their companies. The company specialists will spend valuable resources investigating the customer's needs with no guarantee that a sale will be made.

Each of the presentation types discussed above involves a different level of flexibility. Salespeople have the greatest opportunity to adapt their presentation to customer needs when using the customized presentation, and the least opportunity when using the standard memorized presentation. The importance of this opportunity to adapt sales presentations is discussed in the next section.

ADAPTIVE SELLING AND SALES SUCCESS

Salespeople practice **adaptive selling** when they use different sales presentations for different customers, and alter their sales presentation during a sales call based on the nature of the sales situation.[3] An extreme example of nonadaptive selling is using the standard memorized presentation (discussed above) since the same presentation is used for all customers. The customized presentation illustrates adaptive selling since the presentation is tailored to the specific needs of the customer.

To be effective, salespeople need to adapt their presentations to the sales situation. This seed salesperson is using a different approach selling to these small farmers than he would use selling to large corporate farmers.

Steve Leonard/TSW.

S E L L I N G   S C E N A R I O
6.1

Selling Corporate Jets

Michael Moore is the vice president of sales for Learjet Corporation's western region. He is one of Learjet's 10 salespeople who sell planes costing between $3.5 and $6.0 million. "It's a very complex sale," says Moore. "Over the course of a sale, you may speak to the chairman, attorneys, accountants, tax planners, and, if they have planes already, the pilot and maintenance people."

Moore breaks down his prospects into three categories: large corporations that already have planes, smaller companies whose owners are thinking of buying planes, and wealthy individuals. When selling to large corporations, the decision making is "almost totally rational. You don't have to convince them about the benefits of owning a jet. You take the engineering approach. It's a much more technical approach."

Moore calls the second group "concept buyers." These are often entrepreneurs who want a jet for business and are looking for a way to justify it. "Someone or something has put the idea in their head that they should own a jet. Maybe they are tired of missing meetings because of commercial travel . . . For them, it's more of an emotional decision."

Source: Adapted from Bill Kelley, "Ideal Selling Jobs," *Sales & Marketing Management*, December 1988, p. 20. Copyright 1988. Reprinted by permission.

Adaptive selling is featured in this textbook because it forces the salesperson to practice the marketing concept. It emphasizes the importance of satisfying customer needs and building long-term partnerships. Selling Scenario 6.1 illustrates how a Learjet sales executive adjusts his presentation for different customer types.

The communication principles described in Chapter 5 are required to practice adaptive selling successfully. For example, a Briggs & Stratton sales representative may believe a customer is interested in buying an economical, low-horsepower motor. While presenting the benefits of a low-cost motor, the sales rep discovers, by observing nonverbal behaviors, the customer is not interested in the discussion of overall operating costs. At this point, the rep asks some questions to find out if the customer would pay a higher price for a more efficient motor with lower operating costs. Based on the customer's response, the rep may adopt a new sales strategy, presenting a more efficient motor and demonstrating its low operating costs.

Selecting the appropriate sales strategy for a sales situation and making adjustments during the interaction are crucial to successful selling. Successful salespeople, when questioned about the best advice on selling they had ever received, emphasized the importance of being flexible and adaptive. For example, Don Perreault, vice president of sales and marketing for Transistor Electronics, remembers this advice:

Be a chameleon. Change colors to fit the terrain. As salespeople, we must be able to change our characters to satisfy the present needs of selling—in other words, you have to be able to wear many hats."[4]

Thomas Glickman, director of sales and marketing for Diamedix, emphasizes that adaptive selling requires creativity:

You have to be creative when you're looking for your customer's hot button, because each customer is different. Then you have to activate the hot button by being innovative in your sales approach."[5]

Practicing adaptive selling does not mean you should be dishonest with customers about your products or your personal feelings, or be someone you are not. Adaptive selling means that you should alter the content and form of your sales presentation so that customers will be able to absorb the information easily and find it relevant to their situation.

THINKING IT THROUGH	*D*o you act differently when you are living on campus compared to when you are living at home? How do you change your behavior when you go home over the school breaks? How (and why) do you behave when you go to a restaurant with a date? With some friends? With your parents?

The advantages and disadvantages of the three types of sale presentations illustrate the benefits and drawbacks of adaptive selling. Adaptive selling gives salespeople the opportunity to use the most effective sales presentation for each customer. However, uncovering needs, designing and delivering different presentations, and making adjustments requires a high level of skills. The objective of this textbook is to develop the skills required to practice adaptive selling and knowledge.

KNOWLEDGE AND ADAPTIVE SELLING

A key ingredient for effective selling is knowledge. Salespeople need to know about the products they are selling, the company they work for, and the customers they will be selling to.

Knowledge enables the salesperson to build self-confidence, gain the buyer's trust, satisfy customer needs, and practice adaptive selling. Customers today demand information about the products they buy. They seek the advice of salespeople. When salespeople have a thorough knowledge about their products and customers, they know they can provide a service to their customers. By becoming a reliable source of information, you will win the buyers' respect and trust.

PRODUCT AND COMPANY KNOWLEDGE

Salespeople need to have a lot of information about their company and its products. For example, a buyer might say, "I'm satisfied with our present supplier. I see no reason to change." The informed salesperson might respond, "Company X is a fine company. But last year our firm sold three times as many units. IBM, Xerox, and Apple gave us an outstanding

This Parker salesperson is discussing how the O-rings he sells will benefit the manufacturer of commercial motors in England. He emphasizes how the easy installation will reduce the manufacturing costs.

Courtesy Parker Hannifin Corporation.

vendor award. A *Purchasing* magazine survey of buyers reported that we were number one in on-time deliveries. Let me explain what this can mean for you."

Purchasing agents rate product knowledge as one of the most important attributes of good salespeople. Effective salespeople need to know how products are made, what services are provided with the products, how the products relate to other products, and how the products can satisfy customers' needs. For example, a buyer for men's suits might want specific information to judge the quality of the suit. You might need to tell the buyer about the fabric used in making the suit and the method used to sew the garment to support your claims about the quality of the suit.

In many situations, the service provided is more important than the performance of the product. Efficient servicing of capital equipment ensures the manufacturer that costly shutdowns will be minimized. Delays in providing service when equipment fails can result in substantial financial losses.

Customers often want salespeople to explain how their products will work with other products. For example, a salesperson selling a laser printer needs to know with which computers it can interface. The Kodak salesperson introducing a new film should know with which Kodak and Canon cameras it can and cannot be used.

But the most important knowledge is how the product will satisfy the customer's needs, not the technical details about the product. Customers are not interested in just the facts about a product; they are interested in what the product will do for them. The salesperson's job is to provide information about the features of a product and tell the customer how these features translate into benefits. For example, a wider hitting area (feature) in a golf club results in straighter and longer shots even when the ball is not hit perfectly (benefit).

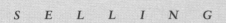

S E L L I N G   *S C E N A R I O*
6.2

Do Your Homework

Interviews with purchasing agents reveal the importance they place on a salesperson's knowledge.

> "Do your homework. Am I the one you want to see? I buy axles for our trucks. Don't call on me with your line of office supplies."

> "Read our annual report. Read anything you can about us. Follow the trades. Know ahead of time what we're up against in the market, what we're trying to do. If I offer to show you around, jump at the chance. Or better yet, ask me yourself."

> "Know your product inside and out. Or at least know how and where to get the answer for me—fast. Be ready to set up a meeting between your engineering people and ours."

> "With our new computer, it takes no time for me to pull up the facts on our relationship and the current market conditions. Use this to help us improve our relationship and solve our problems."

Source: Edith Cohen, "A View from the Other Side," *Sales & Marketing Management,* June 1990, p. 112. Copyright 1990. Reprinted by permission.

Salespeople also need to know about their competitors' products as well as their own, since they are frequently asked to compare their products to competitors'. A buyer for a meat packing plant might say, "The Model 41Z made by Company X is one of the most energy efficient refrigeration units in its size class," to which the salesperson might respond, "The Model 41Z certainly was a leader in energy efficiency when it was introduced in 1991. But our 800 series was designed using a new heat transfer technique that was not available in 1991. Tests show that our units have 10 to 15 percent greater energy efficiency than units using the older technology." Selling Scenario 6.2 illustrates the importance that purchasing agents place on the salesperson's knowledge.

Finally, international salespeople must recognize that customers in different cultures can seek different benefits for the same product. For example, Levi jeans are sold in over 70 countries. However, unique advertising themes are developed to appeal to customer needs in each country. Consumers in Brazil are strongly influenced by fashion trends in Europe, and thus advertisements shown in Brazil are filmed in Paris. In the United Kingdom, the advertising emphasizes that Levis are an American brand worn by cowboys in the Wild West. Australian ads focus strictly on the product benefits—the tight fit and durability.[6]

ORGANIZING KNOWLEDGE OF SALES SITUATIONS AND CUSTOMERS INTO CATEGORIES

Even more important than product and company knowledge, salespeople need detailed information about the different types of sales situations and customers they may encounter and what sales presentation works best in each situation. Theoretically, salespeople can treat each sales situation differently. In practice, however, they typically do not have time to develop unique strategies for each sales situation. Hence, effective sales people tend to categorize sales situations. Each category contains a

Outstanding performers in sales and sports organize their knowledge into categories. Troy Aikman's success is due to his ability to recognize different defenses and develop a strategy for responding to each of them. In a similar manner, successful salespeople are able to recognize different types of sales situations and use an appropriate sales strategy for the situation.

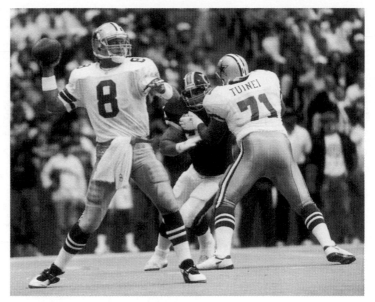

Wide World Photos/photo by Pat Sullivan.

description of the customer and the most effective presentation for that customer type.

By developing categories, salespeople reduce the complexity of selling and free up mental capacity to think more creatively; they also use knowledge gained through past experiences. When they encounter a customer with different needs than those they have dealt with previously—a customer who does not fit into an existing category—they add a new category to their repertoire. Salespeople with more categories, or customer types, have more selling approaches to use and, thus, have a greater opportunity to practice adaptive selling—to adjust their sales presentation to specific customer needs.[7]

The ability to organize knowledge into categories leads to better performance in many areas, not just personal selling. For example, sports stars such as Troy Aikman and Shaquille O'Neil organize their extensive knowledge into categories and have more categories than less skilled players. These categories describe types of defenses rather than types of sales situations. Aikman and O'Neil use cues, such as the positioning of the strong safety or the center, to recognize these defensive categories. For each pattern, they have a strategy, such as passing to the receiver with single coverage or posting up on the left side of the lane.[8]

The categories used by salespeople can focus on the benefits sought by the customer, the person's role in the buying center, the stage in the buying process, or the type of buying situation. In Chapter 4, for example, the multiattribute model illustrated how the importance customers place on benefits can be used to categorize customers and develop sales strategies. In that illustration, the national sales manager and MIS director differed in the importance they placed on laptop computer characteristics. This difference indicated the specific benefits a salesperson should focus on when making a presentation to each buying center member.[9]

Categories can help salespeople organize knowledge, but international salespeople need to avoid stereotyping buyers on the basis of their national origin. For example, Americans are often viewed as cold and unfriendly by people from other countries. Yet some Americans are amiables, some are drivers, some are expressives, and some are analyticals. The same holds true for buyers from other countries; when we see them as all the same, we lose precious information that enables us to adapt. Categories are useful when organizing knowledge but not when the categories become stereotypes.

APPROACHES FOR DEVELOPING KNOWLEDGE

Most knowledge about company products and policies, customer needs, and selling situations is acquired by salespeople through company training programs, analysis of company reports and trade publications, discussions with supervisors and other salespeople, and learning on the job.[10]

Tap the Knowledge from Sales Experts

Companies frequently tap the knowledge of their best salespeople and use this knowledge to train new salespeople. For example, a telecommunication company conducted in-depth interviews with its top performers. Through these interviews, they learned about the types of situations these salespeople encountered and what strategies they used in each situation. Exhibit 6.2 describes how the best salespeople categorized the sales situations they encountered.

The company developed role plays for each sales situation and used them when training new salespeople. Such role playing enabled their new salespeople to experience the variety of situations they would actually encounter on the job. The strategies recommended by the top salespeople served as a starting point for the trainees to develop their sales methods for handling these situations.

If your company does not tap the knowledge of sales experts, you can do it. When you meet senior salespeople at a meeting, you should ask them how they handle difficult situations you have encountered. For example, have they had any success selling Product X? What types of customers are they selling it to? What do they emphasize in their presentations?

Reading Manuals and Trade Publications

Information about your company, its products, and its competitors is available from many sources, including company sales manuals and newsletters, sales meetings, plant visits, and business and trade publications. In many large corporations, information is provided to salespeople during periodic training classes and sales meetings. But salespeople cannot rely on these formal programs as their only source of information; learning new information is a process that never ends.

Knowledgeable salespeople read sales bulletins and announcements from their company and articles in the trade publications about their customers and their industry. They ask company employees questions about new programs and products. They collect information about competitors from customers and by looking in on customer displays in trade shows.

EXHIBIT 6.2

SELLING SITUATIONS FOR TELECOMMUNICATION SERVICES

Sales Situation 1

The customer's telecommunication controls manager (TCM) is the major influence for purchases of telecommunication services. The following circumstance arises:
1. The TCM refuses to talk with the salesperson but the salesperson has support from other people in the buying center.
2. The TCM has done things that are illegal, dishonest, or not in customer firm's best interest.
3. All other alternative sales strategies for dealing with the TCM's refusal to interact with the salesperson have been tried.

Recommended Strategy: Confrontation—The salesperson should work with other members of the buying center and make the conflict between the TCM and the other members apparent to senior executives in the company.

Sales Situation 2

The TCM is committed to a supplier and refuses to permit the salesperson to contact other people in the organization who use telecommunication services.

Recommended Strategy: Competition—The salesperson should acknowledge differences of opinion with the TCM and establish an atmosphere of respect. Then the salesperson should develop relationships with users and provide a higher level of service to those groups than does the TCM.

Sales Situation 3

Disagreements arise on a specific issue. For example, the TCM insists on one method of solving problems that arise, and that method inhibits the selling team's activities.

Recommended Strategy: Compromise—The salesperson should offer an additional service to get the TCM to compromise on the area of disagreement.

Sales Situation 4

Differences in objectives arise between the salesperson and the TCM. For example, the TCM is interested primarily in new equipment, whereas the salesperson wants to promote new telecommunication applications.

Recommended Strategy: Nonaligned collaboration—The salesperson should reach an agreement that he or she will support the TCM's objectives but will be able to pursue his or her own objectives with users.

Sales Situation 5

Mutual agreement of roles, functions, goals, and methods exists between the TCM and the salesperson.

Recommended Strategy: Alliance—The salesperson serves as a consultant to the TCM's firm.

Sales Situation 6

The TCM has high respect and regard for the salesperson, although he or she lacks financial analysis skills or expertise in telecommunications.

Recommended Strategy: Supervisory—The salesperson directs the actions of the TCM but makes sure that his or her role is not recognized by other units in firm.

Source: Adapted from Harish Sujan, Barton Weitz, and Mita Sujan, "Increasing Sales Productivity by Getting Salespeople to Work Smarter," *Journal of Personal Selling and Sales Management,* August 1988, p. 15. Copyright 1988. Reprinted by permission.

Ask for Feedback on What You Are Doing

Frequently, the feedback you get from your supervisor focuses on your performance. For example, did you achieve your performance goals? However, diagnostic feedback is much more useful than is performance feedback for improving performance over the long run. **Diagnostic feedback** provides information about what you are doing right and what you are doing wrong. The difference between performance and diagnostic feedback is illustrated below:

> SALES MANAGER   "You didn't do a good job of selling that customer. You will need to improve if you want to sell him in the future."
>
> SALESPERSON   "Why do you think I didn't make the sale?"
>
> SALES MANAGER   "You stressed the low maintenance cost, but he wasn't interested in maintenance cost. Did you see how he kept looking around while you were talking about how cheap it is to maintain the product?"
>
> SALESPERSON   "What do you think I should do next time?"
>
> SALES MANAGER   "You might try spending more time finding his hot button. Maintenance cost isn't it."

The sales manager initially provided performance feedback, but the salesperson asked for diagnostic feedback. It provides reasons for sales successes and failures. With this information, you can build your knowledge of sales situations and improve your performance. You should ask your supervisors to analyze your performance, not simply evaluate it.

Analyze Successes and Failures

Salespeople encounter many different types of selling situations; thus, they have an opportunity to use different sales presentations. Sometimes they will use the wrong presentation and lose an order. Effective salespeople learn from their mistakes, using them to build a greater knowledge base. If salespeople disregard failures or blame the failures on someone else, they lose a valuable opportunity for learning. Salespeople should also try to learn from their successes. After making a sale, they should analyze what they did to achieve the outcome. Chapter 18 provides more information on how salespeople improve their skills throughout their careers.

When analyzing your performance, you need to assign the right reasons for the outcomes. There is a natural tendency for salespeople to take personal credit for successes and blame their company or competitors for failures. They might say, "I made that sale because I am great, a super salesperson," or "I lost that sale because my company's delivery was poor." Such reasoning does not help salespeople learn. It doesn't show them what to do in the future to make sales or avoid failures. Your performance analysis should focus on the sales strategies used, identifying the specific strategies causing the performance and determining if and how they should be changed in the future.

The key question when analyzing a sales situation is "Why?" If you first offer some reason over which you have no control, such as the competition was too tough or your products don't work well, think deeper and come up with reasons to which you can respond. Formulate strategies you can use to overcome competition or limitations in product performance.

Develop an Intrinsic Orientation to Your Work

People can have two types of orientation to their job—intrinsic and extrinsic. People with an **intrinsic orientation** get rewards from doing the job itself. They enjoy their work; they find it challenging and fun. People with an **extrinsic orientation** view their job as something that has to be done, either to get extrinsic rewards (e.g., more pay) or to avoid punishments (e.g., getting fired). For these people, their job provides extrinsic rewards, but doing the job itself is not rewarding. Most people get both types of rewards from their jobs, but they tend to emphasize one type over the other.

Selling frequently emphasizes extrinsic rewards. If you do well, you will make more money, get promoted, or win awards. This emphasis encourages you to work hard, but it can distract you from learning how to do your job better. You might begin to think you are just working for the money, and your job is not fun.

When salespeople find their job challenging and fun, they want to learn how to do it better. They view their job as a challenge—like a video game. They want to try new sales methods and learn from their successes and failures, so they can improve their score. Effective salespeople enjoy the challenge of selling. They like to try new selling methods, find new customers, sell new products, and figure out how to make a tough sale. If you find that you do not enjoy your selling job, you probably will not learn from your experiences and improve your performance.

SOCIAL STYLE MATRIX—A SALES TRAINING PROGRAM FOR BUILDING ADAPTIVE SELLING SKILLS

To be effective, salespeople need to use their knowledge about products and customers to adapt both the content of their sales presentations—the benefits they emphasize to customers and the needs they attempt to satisfy—and the style they use to communicate with their customers. The social style matrix is a popular training program that companies use to assist salespeople in adapting their communication style.

David Merrill and Roger Reid discovered patterns of communication behaviors, or social styles, that people use when interacting with each other.[11] They found that people who recognize and adjust to these behavior patterns have better relationships with other people. A sales training

EXHIBIT 6.3

INDICATORS OF
ASSERTIVENESS

Less Assertive	More Assertive
"Ask" oriented	"Tell" oriented
Go-along attitude	Take-charge attitude
Cooperative	Competitive
Supportive	Directive
Risk avoider	Risk taker
Makes decisions slowly	Makes decisions quickly
Lets others take initiative	Takes initiative
Leans backward	Leans forward
Indirect eye contact	Direct eye contact
Speaks slowly, softly	Speaks quickly, intensely
Moves deliberately	Moves rapidly
Makes few statements	Makes many statements
Expresses moderate opinions	Expresses strong opinions

program based on this research begins by helping trainees understand their own social style and identify their customers' styles. Then the trainees learn how to make appropriate adjustments in their sales behaviors to become more effective.

DIMENSIONS OF SOCIAL STYLES

In this training program, two critical dimensions used to understand social behavior are assertiveness and responsiveness.

Assertiveness

The degree to which people have opinions about issues and make their position clear to others publicly is called **assertiveness.** Having strong convictions does not make a person assertive; assertive people express their convictions publicly and attempt to influence others to accept their beliefs.

Assertive people speak out, make strong statements, and have a take-charge attitude. When under tension, they tend to confront the situation. Unassertive people rarely dominate a social situation, and they often keep their opinions to themselves. Some verbal and nonverbal behavioral indicators of assertiveness are shown in Exhibit 6.3.

Responsiveness

The second dimension, **responsiveness,** is based on how emotional people tend to get in social situations. Responsive people are those who readily express joy, anger, and sorrow. They appear more concerned with others and are informal and casual in social situations. Less responsive people devote more effort toward controlling their emotions. They are described as cautious, intellectual, serious, formal, and businesslike. Exhibit 6.4 lists some indicators of responsiveness.

EXHIBIT 6.4

INDICATORS OF
RESPONSIVENESS

Less Responsive	More Responsive
Controls emotions	Shows emotions
Cool, aloof	Warm, approachable
Task oriented	People oriented
Uses facts	Uses opinions
Serious	Playful
Impersonal, businesslike	Personable, friendly
Moves stiffly	Moves freely
Seldom gestures	Gestures frequently
Formal dress	Informal dress
Disciplined about time	Undisciplined about time
Controlled facial expressions	Animated facial expressions
Monotone voice	Many vocal inflections

CATEGORIES OF SOCIAL STYLES

The two dimensions of social style, assertiveness and responsiveness, form the **social style matrix** shown in Exhibit 6.5. Each quadrant of the matrix defines a social style type. Drivers are high in assertiveness and low in responsiveness. Expressives are high in assertiveness and high in responsiveness. Amiables are high in responsiveness and low in assertiveness. Finally, analyticals are low in both assertiveness and responsiveness.

Some well-known people illustrate these social styles. Former presidents Jimmy Carter and George Bush, TV commentator Ted Koppel, Mr. Spock in "Star Trek," and Data in "Star Trek: The Next Generation" are in full control of their emotions and are very thoughtful. They are examples of analyticals. By way of contrast, Lyndon Johnson, Muhammad Ali, Liza Minelli, Steve Martin, and Jesse Jackson are expressives. While more publicly emotional than Carter and Bush, they also appear to have more of a take-charge attitude.

Former president Ronald Reagen and media mogul Ted Turner illustrate the difference between amiables and drivers. Reagan's warm personality and unassuming manner demonstrate an amiable social style. In contrast, Turner's nonresponsive, high-control approach, coupled with an aggressive posture, is consistent with a driver social style. Other examples of drivers are Lucy in the "Peanuts" comic strip, Roseanne Arnold, Bart Simpson, and Dan Rather, whereas Jay Leno, Jerry Seinfeld, and Christine in "Coach" are famous amiables.

THINKING IT THROUGH

What do you think is your social style? Why do you think so? Can you think of times when you have been very assertive, very unassertive, very responsive, and very unresponsive?

EXHIBIT 6.5   SOCIAL STYLE MATRIX

All photos from Bettmann.

Drivers

Drivers are high on assertiveness and low on responsiveness. The slogan of drivers, who are task-oriented people, might be, "Let's get it done now, and get it done my way." Drivers have learned to work with others only because they must do so to get the job done, not because they enjoy people. They have a great desire to get ahead in their company and career.

Drivers are swift, efficient decision makers. They focus on the present and appear to have little concern with the past or future. They generally base their decisions on facts, take risks, and want to look at several alternatives before making a decision. Analyticals also like facts and data, but drivers want know how the facts affect results—the bottom line. They are not interested simply in technical information.

To influence a driver, salespeople need to use a direct, businesslike, organized presentation with quick action and follow-up. The effects of a purchase decision on profits should be emphasized in proposals.

Expressives

Expressives are high on assertiveness and high on responsiveness. Warm, approachable, intuitive, and competitive, expressives view power and poli

The body language of the buyer on the left suggests that he is a driver. He is engaging in direct eye contact with the salesperson and stating his view forcefully.

Courtesy Ceridian Corporation.

tics as important factors in their quest for personal rewards and recognition. While expressives are interested in personal relationships, their relationships are primarily with supporters and followers recruited to assist them in achieving their personal goals.

People with an expressive style focus on the future, directing their time and effort toward achieving their vision. They have little concern for practical details in present situations. Expressives base their decisions on their personal opinions and the opinions of others. They act quickly, take risks, but tend to be impatient and change their minds easily.

When selling to expressives, salespeople need to demonstrate how their products will help the customer achieve personal status and recognition. Expressives prefer sales presentations with product demonstrations and creative graphics rather than factual statements and technical detail. Also, testimonials from well-known firms and people appeal to expressives' need for status and recognition. Expressives respond to sales presentations that put them in the role of innovator, the first person to use a new product.

Amiables

Amiables are low on assertiveness and high on responsiveness. Close relationships and cooperation are important to amiables. They achieve their objectives by working with people, developing an atmosphere of mutual respect rather than using power and authority. Amiables tend to make decisions slowly, building a consensus among people involved in the decision. They avoid risks and change their opinions reluctantly.

Salespeople may have difficulty detecting an amiable's true feelings. Because amiables avoid conflict, they often say things to please others even though their personal thoughts differ. Therefore, salespeople need to build personal relationships with amiables. Amiables are particularly interested

The Wal-Mart buyer on the left is an analytical. If she develops a loyalty to this supplier, it will be because she feels that her well-reasoned decision does not need to be reexamined.

Courtesy Wal-Mart Stores, Inc.

in receiving guarantees about a product's performance. They do not like salespeople who agree to undertake activities and then do not follow through on commitments. Salespeople selling to amiables should stress the product's benefits in terms of its effects on the satisfaction of employees.

Analyticals

Analyticals are low on assertiveness and low on responsiveness. They like facts, principles, and logic. Suspicious of power and personal relationships, they strive to find a way to carry out a task without resorting to these influence methods.

Because they are strongly motivated to make the right decision, analyticals make decisions slowly, in a deliberate and disciplined manner. They systematically analyze the facts, using the past as an indication of future events.

Salespeople need to use solid, tangible evidence when making presentations to analyticals. Analyticals are also influenced by sales presentations that recognize their technical expertise and emphasize long-term benefits. They tend to disregard personal opinions. Both analyticals and amiables tend to develop loyalty toward suppliers. For amiables, the loyalty is based on personal relationships; analyticals' loyalty is based on their feeling that well-reasoned decisions do not need to be reexamined.

THINKING IT THROUGH	*I*f you were hiring salespeople, what social style would you look for? What are the strengths and weaknesses of the four social styles in terms of personal selling?

EXHIBIT 6.6

CUES FOR RECOGNIZING
SOCIAL STYLES

Social Style	Cues
Analytical	Technical background Achievement awards on wall Office is work oriented, showing much activity Conservative dress Likes solitary activities (e.g., reading, individual sports)
Driver	Technical background Achievement awards on wall No posters or slogans on office walls Calendar prominently displayed Furniture placed so contact with people is across desk Conservative dress Likes group activities (e.g., politics, team sports)
Amiable	Liberal arts background Office has friendly, open atmosphere Pictures of family displayed Personal mementos on wall Desk placed for open contact with people Casual or flamboyant dress Likes solitary activities (e.g., reading, individual sports)
Expressive	Liberal arts background Motivational slogan on wall Office has friendly, open atmosphere Cluttered, unorganized desk Desk placed for open contact with people Casual or flamboyant dress Likes group activities (e.g., politics, team sports)

IDENTIFYING CUSTOMERS' SOCIAL STYLES

Exhibit 6.6 lists some cues for identifying the social styles of customers or prospects. Salespeople can use their communication skills to observe the customer's behavior, listen to the customer, and ask questions to classify the customer.

Merrill and Reid caution that identifying style is difficult and requires close and careful observation. Salespeople should not jump to quick conclusions based on limited information. Some suggestions for making more accurate assessments are:

- Concentrate on the customer's behavior and disregard how you feel about the behavior. Don't let your judgment be clouded by your feelings about the customer or by thoughts about the customer's motives.

- Avoid assuming that specific jobs or functions are associated with a social style, such as "He must be an analytical because he is an engineer."

- Attempt to get customers to reveal their style rather than react to your style. Ask questions rather than making statements. For example, you might say, "I understand you are involved with setting industry standards for new plastic connectors. Can you tell me something about it?"

This salesperson is making a presentation to an analytical customer. He is emphasizing how the computer system works, rather than how it will increase company profits.

Courtesy Merck & Co., Inc.

- Test your assessments. Look for clues and information that may suggest you have made an incorrect assessment of a customer's social style. If you only look for confirming cues, you will be filtering out a lot of important information.

SOCIAL STYLES AND SELLING PRESENTATIONS

In addition to teaching trainees in the above-mentioned program how to assess social style, the trainees' social styles are assessed. Each is asked to have a group of his or her customers complete a questionnaire and mail it to the director of the training program. These responses are used to determine the trainee's style. Trainees frequently are surprised by the difference between their self-perceptions and the perceptions of their customers.

Interpreting self-ratings requires great caution. Self-assessments can be very misleading because we usually do not see ourselves the same way that others see us. When you rate yourself you know your own feelings, but others can only observe your behaviors. They don't know your thoughts or your intentions. We also vary our behavior from situation to situation. The indicators listed in Exhibits 6.3 and 6.4 merely show a tendency to be assertive or responsive.

Is there one best social style for a salesperson? No. None is "best" for all situations; each style has its strong points and weak points. Driver salespeople are efficient, determined, and decisive, but customers may also find them pushy and dominating. Expressives have enthusiasm, dramatic flair, and creativity but can also seem opinionated, undisciplined, and unstable. Analyticals are orderly, serious, and thorough, but customers may view them as cold, calculating, and stuffy. Finally, amiables are dependable, supportive, and personable but can also be undisciplined and inflexible.

EXHIBIT 6.7   CUSTOMER EXPECTATIONS BASED ON SOCIAL STYLE

| Area of Expectation | Customer's Social Style | | | |
	Driver	Expressive	Amiable	Analytical
Atmosphere in sales interview	Businesslike	Open, friendly	Open, honest	Businesslike
Salesperson's use of time	Effective, efficient	Leisurely, to develop relationship	Leisurely, to develop relationship	Thorough, accurate
Pace of interview	Quick	Quick	Deliberate	Deliberate
Information provided by salesperson	Salesperson's qualifications; value of products	What salesperson thinks; whom he/she knows	Evidence that salesperson is trustworthy, friendly	Evidence of salesperson's expertise in solving problem
Salesperson's actions to win customer acceptance	Documented evidence, stress results	Recognition and approval	Personal attention and interest	Evidence that salesperson has analyzed the situation
Presentation of benefits	*What* product can do	*Who* has used the product	*Why* product is best to solve problem	*How* product can solve the problem
Assistance to aid decision making	Explanation of options and probabilities	Testimonials	Guarantees and assurances	Evidence and offers of service

The sales training program based on the social style matrix emphasizes that effective selling involves more than communicating a product's benefits. Salespeople must also recognize the customer's needs and expectations. In the sales interaction, they should conduct themselves in a manner consistent with customer expectations. Exhibit 6.7 indicates the expectations of customers with different social styles.

Although each customer type requires a different sales presentation, the salesperson's personal social style tends to determine the sales technique he or she typical uses. For example, drivers tend to use a driver technique with all customer types. When interacting with an amiable customer, they will be efficient and businesslike even though the amiable customer would prefer to deal with a more relationship-oriented and friendly salesperson.

This sales training program emphasizes that to be effective with a variety of customer types, *salespeople must adapt their selling presentation to the customer's social style.* Versatility is the key to effective adaptive selling.

VERSATILITY

The effort that people make to increase the productivity of a relationship by adjusting to the needs of the other party is known as **versatility.** Versatile salespeople—those able to adapt their social style—are much more effective than are salespeople who do not adjust their sales presentation. Exhibit 6.8 compares behaviors of more versatile and less versatile people.

EXHIBIT 6·8

INDICATORS OF VERSATILITY

Less Versatile	More Versatile
Limited adaptability to others' needs	Able to adapt to others' needs
Specialist	Generalist
Well-defined interests	Broad interests
Firm on principles	Negotiates issues
Predictable	Unpredictable
Single-minded	Looks at many sides of an issue

EXHIBIT 6·9   ADJUSTING SOCIAL STYLES

	Adjustment	
Dimension	**Reduce**	**Increase**
Assertiveness	Ask for customer's opinion	Get to the point
	Acknowledge merits of customer's viewpoint	Don't be vague or ambiguous
		Volunteer information
	Listen without interruption	Be willing to disagree
	Be more deliberate; don't rush	Take a stand
	Let customer direct flow of conversation	Initiate conversation
Responsiveness	Become businesslike	Verbalize feelings
	Talk less	Express enthusiasm
	Restrain enthusiasm	Pay personal compliments
	Make decision based on facts	Spend time on relationships rather than business
	Stop and think	Socialize; engage in small talk
		Use nonverbal communication

As stated above, sales training programs based on the social style matrix suggest that effective salespeople adjust their social style to match their customer's style. For example, salespeople with a driver orientation need to become more emotional and less aggressive when selling to amiable customers. Analytical salespeople must increase their assertiveness and responsiveness when selling to expressive customers. Exhibit 6.9 shows some techniques for adjusting sales behaviors in terms of assertiveness and responsiveness.

THE ROLE OF KNOWLEDGE

The social style matrix illustrates the importance of knowledge, organized into categories, in determining selling effectiveness through adaptive selling. Sales training based on the social style matrix teaches salespeople the four customer categories, or types (driver, expressive, amiable, and analytical). Salespeople learn the cues for identifying them. Salespeople also learn what adjustments they need to make in their communication style to be effective with each customer type.

ALTERNATIVE TRAINING SYSTEMS FOR DEVELOPING ADAPTIVE SELLING SKILLS

The social style matrix developed by Merrill and Reid is one of several sales training methods based on customer classification schemes. Rather than using assertiveness and responsiveness, Buzzotta and Lefton use the dimensions of warm-hostile and dominant-submissive,[12] and Gerald Manning and Barry Reece use dominance and sociability dimensions to classify customers.[13] The Chailly Group classifies buyers into four categories—experts or gate swingers (nonusers), new users, experienced users, and routine users—based on their role in the purchase decision and the type of purchase decision.[14] Selling Scenario 6.3 describes a scheme for categorizing retail customers that a student developed during her summer internship, selling in a retail store.

EXPERT SYSTEMS

Expert systems have been developed to assist salespeople in understanding their customers and developing effective sales strategies.[15] A computer program that mimics a human expert is called an **expert system.** The program contains the knowledge, rules, and decision processes employed by experts and then uses these elements to solve problems, suggest strategies, and provide advice similar to that of an expert.

Some of these expert selling systems, such as the Sales Edge©, incorporate a model similar to the social style matrix described above. The Sales Edge expert system first asks salespeople to respond to a set of agree-disagree statements to assess their own personalities. Some of these statements are:

I like to take charge of situations.

I want social recognition at work.

I take more risks than most salespeople.

I desire feedback on my performance.

Then the computer program asks salespeople to describe a specific customer in terms of a set of adjectives, such as talkative, apprehensive, achieving, social, and independent. Using the self-assessment and the customer assessment, the computer program produces a sales strategy report containing six sections:

What to Expect from Your Customer

How to Succeed with Your Customer

Customer-Specific Preparation Strategy

Customer-Specific Opening Strategy

Customer-Specific Presentation Strategy

Customer-Specific Closing Strategy

S E L L I N G   S C E N A R I O

6.3

Customers Come in 31 Flavors

Cynthia Carter, a University of Florida undergraduate, spent 12 weeks as a paid summer intern in a JCPenney store. Working part of that time as a sales associate, she developed insights into how to effectively sell to different customer types. "Experienced sales associates recognize that customers come in all shapes, sizes, and flavors. Some are more pleasant to deal with, but the true skill of the successful sales associate lies in the ability to assist every type of customer, all 31 flavors." Carter described some of the "customer flavors" that she encountered during her internship:

The *vanilla customer* answers, "I'm just looking," to every question you ask or suggestion you offer. They're rather faceless and uninteresting, but they often actually need your assistance. It's most important that you don't threaten them by being overbearing, but simply let them know you are available when they realize they need your assistance.

The *I'll take four cones—chocolate, strawberry, bubble gum, and peanut butter and jelly— customer* has three screaming children with her, terrorizing the racks and dressing rooms. She doesn't have much time to shop. Ask her what she needs and she responds, "Anything that doesn't need ironing." She really needs your help. Give a "hanger gun" to her kids, sit her in a dressing room, find out her size, and bring her clothes to try on. She'll be very grateful for your help and will be back to spend money dressing her children.

The *"Why don't you have banana marshmallow swirl?" customer* gets very upset when she can't find what she wants. She freely criticizes the store for not having merchandise that *everyone* has. This customer needs to be handled with kid gloves. The key is to be *very* humble, *very* helpful, and *very* ready to point out similar items that the customer may find appealing. Use the JCPenney catalog as a backup, since items in the catalog can be delivered in two days. Remember, never lose your cool and never tell the customer she is wrong.

The *rum raisin customer* wants high quality and will pay high prices. Avoid the polyester/cotton blends and focus on the silks, suedes, and linens. Give a lot of personal attention and fashion-conscious advice. Stress add-on sales. If you can win her fashion trust, you can make a big sale.

The *tofu, granola sorbet customer* needs sturdy fabrics with lots of big pockets for rock collecting in Montana. Durability and practicality are much more important than fashion. Forget the 24-inch, triple-strand pearls and go for the Durango khaki outfit. She'll pay the price for the right clothes.

The *birthday cake customer* is a frantic husband, boyfriend, or father who realized over lunch that today is the big day and he forgot. He usually doesn't know her size or even her weight and height. You can try to guess, but the best bet is suggesting a nonform-fitting sweater or coordinating earrings and necklace. You need to take control of the occasion and offer concrete advice—and tell him that returns are handled most smoothly if he saves the receipt.

Source: Adapted from Michael Levy and Barton Weitz, *Retailing Management*, 2nd ed. (Burr Ridge, IL: Irwin, 1995).

Portions of a sales strategy report provided by the Sales Edge expert system appear in Exhibit 6.10.

The Sales Edge, like most expert systems, stores the information salespeople provide about their customers. As salespeople collect more information, assessments can be modified and updated, and revised sales strategy recommendations can be generated.

EXHIBIT 6.10   EXCERPTS FROM THE SALES EDGE© SALES STRATEGY REPORT

What to Expect

In dealing with Mr. J. B., you may feel he comes on heavy-handed, cocky, and with too much energy. Rather than feeling overwhelmed or stressed by him, you can turn his attributes to your advantage by letting him take the lead. This will give him the power he wants and allow you to collect information that you need . . .

How to Succeed

You Both Like to Work Quickly   Both you and Mr. J. B. are spontaneous and act with abruptness. Further, neither of you is particularly interested in all the details involved in the sale. Mr. J. B. is the type of buyer who will purchase based on a general, superficial product description. If possible, take some time to determine the fit of your product to Mr. J. B.'s needs and expectations. Remember that although Mr. J. B. may purchase impulsively, he may be dissatisfied later if the product does not perform to his satisfaction . . .

Mr. J. B. Will Want to Dominate . . .
Focus on Business . . .
Find Out What His Business Needs Are . . .
Plan to Answer Objections in an Expert Manner . . .
Expect Mr. J. B. to Take Risks . . .
Expect Mr. J. B. to Bargain Hard . . .
Business Facts Are What Counts . . .
Success and Achievement Are the Keys . . .
Apply Your Powers of Persuasion . . .

Customer-Specific Opening Strategies

1. *Establish a Balance of Social and Business Interests*   Since Mr. J. B. finds business exciting and is attracted to innovations and creative ideas, emphasize new and exciting ideas in your opening. Mr. J. B. is very social and will feel most comfortable if you are friendlier than you would normally be. Make an effort to be extra pleasant. Take an active interest in Mr. J. B. Show genuine, sincere interest in him and his business. Use compliments when you can.

2. *Needs Analysis: Mr. J. B. Knows What He Wants . . .*

Customer-Specific Presentation Strategies

1. *Innovations, Major Benefits, and Excitement*   It is essential for you to present your product to fulfill Mr. J. B.'s stated needs and to enhance his views and positions. Highlight areas of innovation; make your presentation exciting. Do not give extra details. Stick to the major features. Be persuasive. Do not hesitate to try to sell your product to Mr. J. B.; make him think he sold it himself. Move your presentation along at a quick pace.

2. *Deal with Stated Objections . . .*

Source: Robert Collins, "Artificial Intelligence in Personal Selling," *Journal of Personal Selling and Sales Management*, May 1984, pp. 58–66.

LIMITATIONS IN TRAINING METHODS

The training methods like the Social Style Matrix and the Sales Edge described in the previous sections are simply a first step in developing knowledge for practicing adaptive selling. They emphasize the need to practice adaptive selling—to use different presentations with different customers—and stimulate salespeople to base their sales presentations on an analysis of the customer. But these methods are limited; they present only a few types of customers, and classification is based on the form of communication (the social style), not on the content on the communication (the specific features and benefits stressed in the presentation).

S E L L I N G   S C E N A R I O
6.4

Preparing for Selling in the United States

NEC, the large Japanese computer manufacturer, has an extensive training program to prepare its employees to sell in the United States. The objective of the program is to make a graduate "smell like soy sauce when he talks to Japanese customers and smell like butter when he talks with foreigners." This statement refers to the traditional belief in Japan that Westerners give off a faint smell of butter.

The training lessons include table manners, cocktail party chit-chat, and English language jokes. They learn American clichés used in selling, such as "shooting from the hip," "going in cold," and "beating around the bush."

Sources: Bernard Wysocki, "Japanese Executives Going Overseas Take Anti-Shock Courses," *The Wall Street Journal,* January 12, 1987, p. 1; "High Technology Lip Service," *U.S. News and World Report,* December 26, 1988, pp. 112–14.

In addition, accurately fitting customers into the suggested categories is often very difficult. Customers act differently and have different needs in different sales encounters: A buyer might be very amiable when engaging in a new-task buying situation and be analytical when dealing with an "out" salesperson in a straight rebuy. Amiable buyers in a bad mood might act like drivers. By rigidly applying the classification rules, salespeople might actually limit their flexibility, reducing the adaptive selling behavior that these training methods emphasize.

Finally, the knowledge provided in these training programs is very general. It is not related to the specific types of customers to whom you will be selling or the specific products you will be selling. To be an effective salesperson, you need to develop knowledge about the specific sales situations you will encounter. Selling Scenario 6.4 describes how Japanese salespeople are trained to sell in the United States.

SUMMARY

By practicing adaptive selling, salespeople exploit the unique properties of personal selling as a marketing communication tool—the ability to tailor messages to individual customers and make on-the-spot adjustments. Extensive knowledge of customer and sales situation types is a key ingredient to effective adaptive selling.

To be effective, salespeople need to have considerable knowledge about the products they sell, the company for which they work, and the customer to whom they sell. In addition to knowing the facts, they need to understand how these facts relate to benefits that their customers are seeking.

Experienced salespeople organize customer knowledge into categories. Each category has cues for classifying customers or sales situations, and an effective sales presentation for customers in the category.

To develop more extensive knowledge of customers, salespeople need to use information from their firm's market research studies, ask for feedback, analyze their successes and failures, and develop an intrinsic orientation to their work.

The social style matrix, developed by Merrill and Reid, illustrates the concept of developing a categorical knowledge to facilitate adaptive selling. The matrix defines four customer categories based on a customer's responsiveness and assertiveness in sales interactions. To effectively interact with a customer, a salesperson needs to identify the customer's social style and adapt his or her style to match the customer's. The sales training program based on the social style matrix provides cues for identifying social style and presentations that salespeople can use to make adjustments.

The social styles matrix is one example of a categorical scheme that salespeople can use to improve their knowledge and adaptability. However, other schemes are used, and some have been incorporated into expert system computer programs.

KEY TERMS

adaptive selling *170*	expressives *182*
amiables *183*	extrinsic orientation *179*
analyticals *184*	intrinsic orientation *179*
assertiveness *180*	outlined presentation *168*
customized presentation *169*	responsiveness *180*
diagnostic feedback *178*	standard memorized presentation *168*
drivers *182*	social style matrix *181*
expert systems *189*	versatility *187*

QUESTIONS AND PROBLEMS

1. "A good salesperson can sell any customer." Do you agree? Why or why not?

2. Some people will say that salespeople should know everything about the products they sell and the company for which they work. Is it possible to have too much product knowledge? Why or why not?

3. Why do salespeople need to tell customers about the features or facts and the benefits of products in a sales presentation?

4. What do you think about the following statement? "Good salespeople need to be aggressive. They need to have powerful voices and a winning smile."

5. What social styles would you assign to the following people:
   a. Zonker in "Doonesbury."
   b. Clint Eastwood.
   c. Mike Wallace on "60 Minutes."
   d. Jessica Fletcher (Angela Lansbury) in "Murder, She Wrote."
   e. Roseanne.
   f. Seinfeld.

6. If you were an expressive, what adjustments would you make in selling to an amiable?

7. A salesperson who is a driver is preparing to deliver a presentation. What suggestions can you make to improve the salesperson's performance?

8. Henry Downs sells footballs, basketballs, volleyballs, and other rubber sporting goods products to sporting goods retailers. What facts about his company would a sporting goods retailer be interested in? Why would the retailer be interested in knowing these facts?

9. Assume that, during a sales call, a customer says, "Your computer software could never do everything you say it will." How would you respond to an analytical customer? An amiable customer?

10. The market research undertaken by a hospital supply company identified three types of hospitals. Traditional hospitals feel that patient satisfaction is based on the quality of medical staff, and that hospital supplies are unimportant. Private hospitals feel that supplies are important because they affect the staff's efficiency. Finally, marketing-oriented hospitals view supplies as an important element in creating a comfortable, customer service-oriented image. What type of sales presentation would you use if you were selling bedsheets and pillowcases to each of these hospital types? What products and benefits would you emphasize in each case?

CASE PROBLEMS

**CASE 6 • 1
RADIO PEEK**

Bob Stewart works for Radio PEEK in a city with a population of 80,000. PEEK competes against two other local radio stations. However, the local residents can receive the signals from seven radio stations in the large city located 45 miles away.

Advertising over a radio station is a relatively new experience for the owner of local retail stores. Bob knows he will need to sell them on the benefits of advertising on radio, and also sell them on advertising on PEEK. However, the local stations have found it difficult to sell time. None of the local stations have collected data to prove to prospects that advertising over local radio builds sales and profits.

QUESTIONS

1. What facts about PEEK, its competitors, and its potential customers could be useful to Bob in making sales presentations?

2. What benefits might the local retailers be seeking that could be satisfied by advertising on PEEK? Would these benefits sought be the same for all local retailers? How might they be different?

**CASE 6 • 2
USING THE SOCIAL STYLE
MATRIX TO DEVELOP SALES
PRESENTATIONS**

DICK SALMON

His office is pleasant and really looks "worked in." You notice a couple of file folders on the floor behind the desk. Two attractive nonbusiness posters (not framed) hang on the walls, along with four small, framed group photos. You notice a number of souvenirs on the desk. Chairs are comfortable and casually arranged. An assortment of snapshots is tucked in the frame of a family portrait on the desk.

Tom Johnson

Lots of things cover his walls: framed, autographed photos of sports notables; a Chamber of Commerce citizenship citation; children's colorful crayon drawings; and a large newspaper ad with a clever headline. Propped against a cabinet full of trophies stands a tennis bag with a racquet. You count at least eight stacks of papers and magazines. The visitors' chairs are pulled close to the desk.

Betsy Walker

Her office walls contain one oil painting and some nicely framed prints. A large stack of business periodicals rests on the credenza behind the desk. The pen and pencil set on the desk has an achievement plaque with Betsy's name on it. Although current work clutters the desk, the rest of the office is well organized. You notice a to-do list with today's date on it next to the telephone. The desk divides the room in two and separates you from the occupant.

Ivan Gorman

His office is relatively neat. Some nicely framed diplomas and achievement certificates decorate the walls. Two reference posters with helpful business data are pinned to the wall nearest the desk. The desk holds several in–out baskets, all well labeled. Two chairs are set up so that Ivan faces visitors directly across the desk.

Questions

1. Identify each customer's social style.
2. Outline the technique you would employ to sell to each customer.

CASE 6 • 3
CABLECAST

Gloria Sanchez is a salesperson for Cablecast, the company with the cable TV rights for the city of Cleveland and its surrounding suburbs. After Sanchez graduated from Cleveland State University with a BA in history, she went to work for the city in the community services department. When the economy slowed down, she was laid off and went to work for Cablecast, where she has been working in sales for two years. Sanchez is married, has two children, and is an active volunteer in programs for the homeless.

Sanchez is making her first call on Steve Watkins, the new director of advertising for the Cleveland National Bank. As Sanchez enters Watkins's office, she notices several graphs on the wall indicating the number of new accounts opened, total deposits, and market share over time. A plaque signifying Watkins's selection as Midwest Advertising Executive of the Year is prominently displayed.

SANCHEZ   (before taking a seat, Sanchez extends her hand warmly) "Good Morning, Mr. Watkins. This is really a beautiful day. How are you?"

WATKINS   (hesitating at first and then extending his hand) "I have just a few minutes to talk with you. My schedule is really tight today. Now tell me what you have to offer." (sits down without demonstrating an emotional response)

SANCHEZ   "Let me take a second to tell you why I made an appointment to see you. I was talking with Joan Waters at Fidelity Mutual Life Insurance. She said she met you at a recent Midwest Advertising Executives luncheon. She has been using Cablecast in her media plan and mentioned you might be interested in advertising on cable TV."

WATKINS   "I really can't remember Ms. Waters. You meet so many people at these luncheons."

SANCHEZ   "She really is an interesting woman. We worked together as volunteers in the Homeless in America program last fall. Are you involved in many community activities?"

WATKINS   "Not really." (looking at his watch)

SANCHEZ   "Well, Ms. Waters told me you were developing a new advertising campaign for the bank. I hear the campaign will stress customer service. I really think that is a great idea. Banks should be more concerned about providing good service."

WATKINS   "We did a lot of market research to develop this new campaign. Our research shows that customer service is particularly important to people in the eastern suburbs. We hope to increase our share of new deposits by 3 percent over the new six months. Tell me something about what you can do for us."

SANCHEZ   "I think we are the ideal media for your new campaign. Fidelity Mutual has been very pleased with the response to their commercials for homeowner insurance policies."

WATKINS   "That's interesting. What is its target market?"

SANCHEZ   "They have been targeting their campaign toward lower-income families in the western suburbs. Their homeowner policy sales doubled six months after they placed the first ads on cable TV."

WATKINS   "Doubled?"

SANCHEZ   "At least doubled, I think."

WATKINS   "Could you be more specific about your reach in the eastern suburbs? How many families subscribe to your cable TV service? How often do they watch the cable channels?"

SANCHEZ   "I don't have the specific information with me, but I know that our coverage is very good. More and more people are watching cable channels. You know . . ."

WATKINS   "Excuse me, but I have to go to another meeting. When you get some more specific information, why don't you leave it with my assistant."

QUESTIONS

1. What are Sanchez's and Watkins's communication styles? What do you base your assessments on?
2. How effective do you think Sanchez was on this sales call?
3. What adjustments should Sanchez have made in her sales presentation to increase her effectiveness?

ADDITIONAL REFERENCES

Bowers, Michael, and D. Layne Rich. "The Effect of Product and Market Factors on the Communication Styles of Salespeople." In Robert King (ed.), *Developments in Marketing Science*, vol. 14. Richmond, VA: Academy of Marketing Science, 1993, pp. 232–327.

Brown, Gene; Unal Boya; Neil Humphreys; and Robert Wilding. "Attributes and Behaviors of Salespeople Preferred by Buyers: High Socializing vs. Low Socializing Industrial Buyers." *Journal of Personal Selling and Sales Management*, Winter 1993, pp. 26–31.

Hwan, Dong Lee, and Richard Olshavsky. "Adapting to What? A Contingency Approach to Sales Interactions Based on a Comprehensive Model of Consumer Choice." In Chris Allen et al. (eds.), *Marketing Theory and Applications*. Chicago, IL; American Marketing Association, 1992, p. 224.

Kiechell, Walter. "How to Manage Salespeople." *Fortune*, March 14, 1988, p. 179.

Lambert, Douglas; Howard Marmorstein; and Arun Sharma. "The Accuracy of Salespersons' Perceptions of Their Customers: Conceptual Examination and an Empirical Study." *Journal of Personal Selling and Sales Management*, February 1990, pp. 1–9.

Miles, Morgan; Danny Arnold; and Henry Nash. "Adaptive Communication: The Adaptation of the Seller's Interpersonal Style to the Stage of the Dyad's Relationship and the Buyer's Communication Styles." *Journal of Personal Selling and Sales Management*, February 1990, pp. 21–29.

Vink, Jaap, and Wilem Verbeke. "Adaptive Selling and Organizational Characteristics: Suggestions for Future Research." *Journal of Personal Selling and Sales Management*, Winter 1993, pp. 16–23.

III

THE PARTNERSHIP PROCESS

P art I of this book provided a general introduction to the nature of selling jobs. In Part II we reviewed concepts of buyer behavior, communication principles, and the adaptive selling framework. In Part III we explore the activities required to build long-term relationships and partnerships. As the circular figure illustrates, these activities do not necessarily follow a step-by-step sequence; instead they occur throughout the partnership-building process.

Chapter 7 covers material on identifying prospects. Chapter 8 outlines how to gain precall information, plan each call, and make appointments effectively.

In Chapter 9 you will learn how to make a good impression. You will also discover techniques to effectively uncover the prospects' needs and then relate your solution to those needs.

The use of communication tools such as visual aids, samples, and demonstrations is covered in Chapter 10. Chapter 11 will help you learn how to respond helpfully to concerns raised by the buyer, while Chapter 12 will provide guidance in obtaining commitment. Finally, Chapter 13 summarizes methods and activities used to develop and enrich meaningful partnerships.

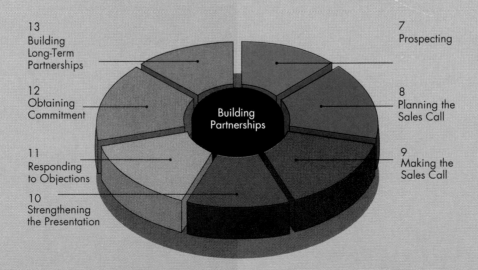

13
Building
Long-Term
Partnerships

12
Obtaining
Commitment

11
Responding
to Objections

10
Strengthening
the Presentation

7
Prospecting

8
Planning the
Sales Call

9
Making the
Sales Call

Building
Partnerships

Prospecting

One of the most important activities for most salespeople is locating qualified prospects. In fact, the selling process generally begins with prospecting. You can be the best salesperson in the world in terms of listening, asking questions, discovering needs, giving presentations, helpfully responding to objections, and obtaining commitment, but if you are calling on the wrong person or organization, it does you no good! This chapter provides resources to help you prospect effectively and efficiently.

Some questions answered in this chapter are:

Why is prospecting important for effective selling?

Are all sales leads good prospects? What are the characteristics of a qualified prospect?

How can prospects be identified?

How can the organization's promotional program be used in prospecting?

What elements are found in an effective prospecting plan, and how should it be developed?

How can a salesperson overcome a reluctance to prospect?

After graduating from the University of Georgia in 1987 with a BBA degree in marketing, Jerry Robison went to work for Merrell Dow Pharmaceuticals. In 1990 they merged with Marion Labs and are now known as Marion Merrell Dow Pharmaceuticals. Robison has really enjoyed his job as a pharmaceutical representative.

Robison began as a field representative, calling on doctors in a geographical area, and worked the area for four years. In 1991 he was promoted to an Institutional Representative, which is his present position. Basically, his job entails calling on doctors, administrators, and other health care professionals at several big teaching hospitals.

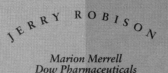

JERRY ROBISON

Marion Merrell
Dow Pharmaceuticals

Over the years Robison has won several awards, including Sales Representative of the Year for the Southeast Region in 1990 and Team Player Award in 1992. Robison said of his success, "I have reached or exceeded my performance goals each year with the company.

"I discuss our products with people with all levels of medical knowledge. Even the doctors I deal with range from medical students to attending staff doctors that write books on medical subjects. Dealing with such diverse groups is very challenging and can be very rewarding. To be successful, a representative must be able to talk on all knowledge levels and tailor the talk to the needs of the person he or she is dealing with.

"Basically my job is like any other sales job in that I am trying to find out what the doctor looks for in a product and who my competition is. I then show how my product can satisfy the doctor's needs better than the competition.

"Changing doctor prescribing habits is a long-term process where discussions build upon themselves. I must take good notes after my discussions so that when I see the doctor again, sometimes six weeks later, I can build upon our last discussion. It is a long-term process—in Atlanta it took four years for a doctor who was not prescribing Seldane at all to move to where he prescribed it for most of his patients. He started slow, prescribing it first only for very specific patients (e.g., elderly men). My notes over those four years were invaluable in helping the doctor move to prescribing the drug more.

"As in most fields, product knowledge is very important. I spend at least two hours each week (at night) reading medical journals so I can stay updated on the most current literature. The main journals I read include the *American Journal of Cardiology*, the *New England Journal of Medicine*, and the *Journal of the American Medical Association*, although I read others as appropriate for my drugs. We also have frequent meetings with other Marion Merrell Dow associates where we discuss the current literature. Having strong technical knowledge is a *requirement* if one wants to be successful.

"In my institutions there are thousands of people that I could call on if I had the time. Because I cannot be everywhere, I have to set priorities on who to see to make the most impact. This requires a lot of analyzing the business and determining tactics that will allow me to reach my goals. Tactics might include seeing the person more often, setting up a speaker program that meets their specific needs, and offering value-added services (like offering the Head of Residency a book for their library or setting up a journal club). It is very easy to get sidetracked in my job so I have to concentrate on the things that make the biggest difference.

"A career in sales can be very exciting and rewarding. Good luck in the future and may you be as happy in your career as I have been in mine."

IMPORTANCE OF PROSPECTING

The process of locating potential customers for a product or service is called **prospecting.** Having a list of prospects is critical to the success of both experienced and new salespeople. In fact, many experts note that prospecting is the *most* important activity a salesperson can do.

Today, extensive changes are taking place in population movements, in creation of new businesses and products, in shifting of businesses to new lines and expansion of old-line companies, and in methods of distribution. These changes are resulting in an estimated 15 to 20 percent annual turnover of customers. In addition, salespeople must find new customers to replace those that switch to competitors, go bankrupt, move out of the territory, merge with a noncustomer, or decide to do without the product or service. A salesperson may need to prospect even in existing accounts, due to mergers, downsizing by firms, and job changes or retirements of buyers. Thus, salespeople need to develop effective prospecting skills.

Prospecting is more important in some selling fields than in others. For example, the stockbroker or real estate sales representative with no effective prospecting plan usually doesn't last long in the business. In these sales positions, as a general rule, it takes 100 contacts to get 10 prospects who will listen to presentations, out of which 1 will buy. Each sale, then, represents a great deal of prospecting. It is also important in these fields to prospect continually. Some sales trainers relate this to your car's gas tank—you don't wait until you are on empty before you fill up!

Some sales positions, however, do not require as much emphasis on prospecting. For example, a Procter & Gamble sales representative in a certain geographic area would know all of the potential prospects for Crest toothpaste (all the grocery stores, drugstores, convenience stores, etc.) because they are easy to identify. For the same reason, a Pfizer Laboratories sales rep selling a cardiac medication can easily identify all of the cardiologists in a geographic territory. An IBM salesperson assigned only to one major account would not spend any time trying to locate new firms to call on. For these types of sales positions, prospecting as we normally think of it either does not occur or is a very simple task. This does *not* mean that we ignore these customers, however (as Chapter 13 will discuss).

CHARACTERISTICS OF A GOOD PROSPECT

Some salespeople make the mistake of considering everyone a prospect without first finding out whether he or she really provides opportunity to make a sale. Prospecting really begins with leads. A **lead** is a potential prospect, a person or organization that might or might not have what it takes to be a true prospect. As the next step, the salesperson qualifies the lead. If a salesperson determines that the lead is a good candidate for making a sale (has a need, ability to pay, etc.), then that person or organization becomes a **prospect.** Many leads will not become prospects. The process of determining if a lead is in fact a prospect is called **qualifying a lead.**

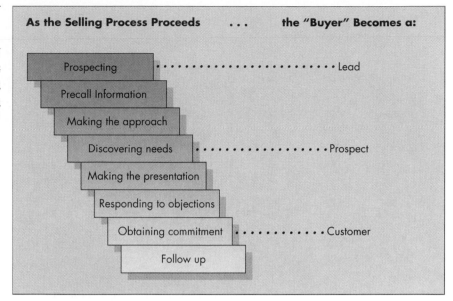

EXHIBIT 7.1

RELATIONSHIP BETWEEN
STEPS IN THE SELLING
PROCESS AND THE
DESIGNATION OF THE
"BUYER"

Exhibit 7.1 displays the relationship between the steps in the selling process and the terminology we use to refer to the "buyer."

Naturally, the amount of time spent trying to answer the question of who is a prospect varies for different types of selling. It depends on such factors as the type of product or service, the value of the salesperson's time, and the profit per sale. The following five questions will help qualify leads and pinpoint the good prospects:

1. Does the lead have a want or need that can be satisfied by the purchase of my products or services?
2. Does the lead have the ability to pay?
3. Does the lead have the authority to buy?
4. Can the lead be approached favorably?
5. Is the lead eligible to buy?

These questions can be asked about the person who is a lead, the lead's firm, or both. (Chapter 8 discusses how to begin gathering the information needed to answer these questions, and Chapter 9 provides further instruction on how to gather the remaining needed information during actual sales calls.) For now, let's look at each question a little closer.

DOES A WANT OR NEED EXIST?

Research has not supplied infallible answers to why customers buy, but it has found many reasons. As pointed out in Chapter 4, customers buy to satisfy practical needs as well as intangible needs, such as prestige or aesthetics.

Determining if leads need a salesperson's products or services is not always simple. Many firms use the telephone to assess needs. Sometimes an exploratory interview is conducted to determine whether a lead has needs

Progressive firms use telemarketers to qualify leads before sending a salesperson on a call.

Courtesy United Stationers.

that the seller's products can satisfy. And almost everyone has a need for some product lines; for example, practically every organization needs paper, desks, telephones, and fire insurance.

By using high-pressure tactics, sales may be made to those who do not need or really want a product. Such sales benefit no one. The buyer will resent making the purchase, and a potential long-term customer will be lost. The lead must want to solve his or her need to be considered a qualified prospect.

DOES THE LEAD HAVE THE ABILITY TO PAY?

The ability to pay for the products or services helps to separate leads from prospects. The commercial real estate agent usually checks the financial status of each client to determine the price range of office buildings to show. A client with annual profits of $100,000 and cash resources of $75,000 may be a genuine prospect for an office building selling in the $200,000 to $250,000 bracket. An agent would be wasting time, however, by showing this client an office building listed at $1 million. The client may have a real desire and need for the more expensive setting, but the client is still not a real prospect for the higher-priced office building if he or she doesn't have the resources to pay for it.

Ability to pay includes both cash and credit. Many companies subscribe to a rating service, such as Dun & Bradstreet or Moody's Industrial (see Exhibit 7.2). Salespeople can use this service to determine the financial status and credit rating of a lead. They can also qualify leads with information obtained from local credit agencies, consumer credit agencies like TRW, noncompetitive salespeople, and the Better Business Bureau.

Salespeople are sometimes surprised at credit ratings of their leads. Some big-name firms have poor ratings. Even the federal government does not always pay its bills on time. For example, in one study it was found that

EXHIBIT 7.2 MOODY'S: A SOURCE OF INFORMATION ABOUT COMPANIES

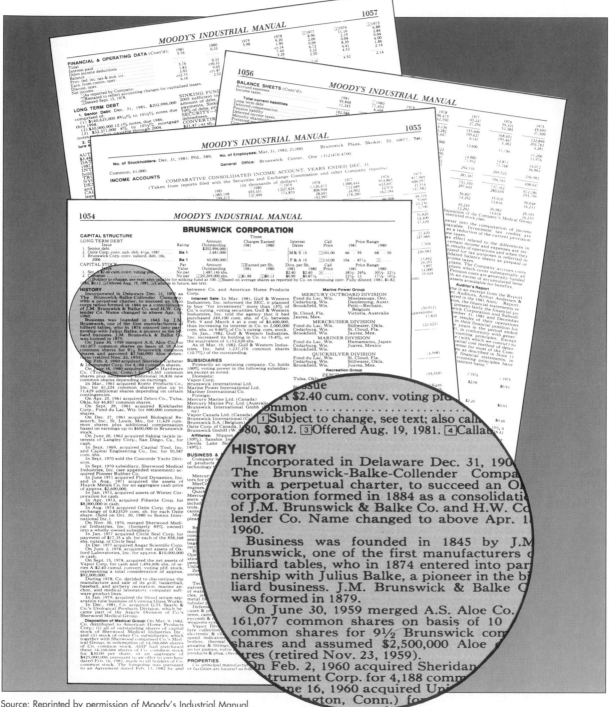

Source: Reprinted by permission of Moody's Industrial Manual.

the Justice Department makes over 16 percent of its payments late, while the State Department isn't far behind at 15 percent.[1]

DOES THE LEAD HAVE THE AUTHORITY TO BUY?

A lead may have a real need for a product and the ability to pay for it but lack the authority to make the purchase. Knowing who has this authority saves the salesperson time and effort and results in a higher percentage of closed sales. Dalcon Tool and Die, a machine tool company, planned its sales efforts assuming that its machines were being purchased by production managers. Careful analysis, however, showed that only 10 percent of the sales came from production executives. The rest came from engineers (44 percent), purchasing agents (29 percent), and others (17 percent), because they had the authority to make the purchase decision. Based on this survey, the company redirected its sales efforts toward engineers and purchasing agents, and profits increased by 22 percent over the next two-year period.

More and more firms are delegating their purchasing tasks to outside vendors.[2] These vendors, often called **systems integrators,** have the authority to buy products and services from others. Systems integrators usually assume complete responsibility for a project, from its beginning to follow-up servicing. An example would be Andersen Consulting, a division of Arthur Andersen & Co., acting as a systems integrator for the complete robotics system of a new Chrysler plant. In that scenario, every potential vendor would actually be selling to Andersen Consulting, not to Chrysler. When systems integrators are involved, salespeople need to delineate clearly who has the authority to purchase. Sometimes the overall buyer (Chrysler in our example) will retain veto power over potential vendors.

CAN THE LEAD BE APPROACHED FAVORABLY?

Some people may have a need, the ability to pay, and the authority to buy but still not qualify as prospects, because they are not accessible to the salesperson. For example, the president of a large bank, a major executive of a large manufacturing company, or the senior partner in a well-established law firm normally would not be accessible to a young college graduate starting out as a sales representative for an investment trust organization. Getting an interview with these people may be so difficult and the chances of making a sale so small that the sales representative eliminates them as possible prospects.

IS THE LEAD ELIGIBLE TO BUY?

Eligibility is an equally important factor in finding a genuine prospect. For example, a salesperson who works for a firm that requires a rather large minimum order should not call on leads that could never order in such volume. Likewise, if a representative sells exclusively to wholesalers, the salesperson should be certain the individuals he or she calls on are actually wholesalers, not retailers.

Another factor that may determine eligibility for a particular salesperson is the geographic location of the prospect. Most companies operate on the basis of exclusive sales territories. A salesperson working for such a company must consider whether the prospect is eligible, based on location, to buy from him or her.

Salespeople should also avoid targeting leads already covered by their corporate headquarters. Large customers or potential customers that are handled exclusively by company headquarters are often called **national accounts** or **house accounts.** For example, UNISYS considers the U.S. Air Force a national account; the local UNISYS salesperson located in Marietta, Georgia, should not try to solicit business from Dobbins Air Force Base in Marietta.

▌OTHER CRITERIA

Leads who meet the five criteria are generally considered excellent prospects. Some sellers, however, add additional criteria. For example, DEI Management Group instructs its salespeople to classify leads by their likelihood of buying. Salespeople may have a long list of people they feel need their product, can pay for it, have authority to buy it, and are approachable and eligible. If, however, these companies have absolutely no interest in buying, the salesperson should look elsewhere. Otherwise, the salesperson will just waste additional time on this lead and fail to prospect for better leads.

Other firms look at the timing of purchase to determine if a lead is really a good prospect. Some questions to consider include "How soon before the prospect's contract with our competitor expires?" and "Is a purchase decision really pending? How do we know?" Answers to these and other questions help a firm know if a prospect is worth pursuing at this time.

▌HOW AND WHERE TO OBTAIN LEADS

Prospecting sources and methods vary for different types of selling. A sales representative for commercial chemicals, for example, uses a different system than banking or office products salespeople would use. Exhibit 7.3 presents an overview of some of the most common lead-generating methods, which are described below.

▌SATISFIED CUSTOMERS

Both current and previously satisfied customers are the most effective sources for leads. Customers not only provide the potential for additional sales but also refer the seller to other prospects. Referrals of leads in the same industry are particularly useful, because the salesperson already has a better understanding of the unique needs of this type of organization (e.g., "If I have sold to a bank already, I have a better understanding of bank's needs").

As a result, developing a long-term trusting partnership with customers is critical. For example, Charlotte Jacobs, a Pitney Bowes representative in Cincinnati, stresses the importance of maintaining excellent rapport with current customers. Her territory consists solely of the national headquarters of 16 companies. Satisfied customers not only suggest opportunities elsewhere in their firms but also recommend Jacobs to other firms.[3]

EXHIBIT 7.3

OVERVIEW OF COMMON
SOURCES OF LEADS

Source	How Used
Satisfied customers	Current and previous customers are contacted for additional business and leads.
Endless chain	Salesperson attempts to secure at least one additional lead from each person he or she interviews.
Center of influence	Salesperson cultivates well-known, influential people in the territory who are willing to supply lead information.
Promotional activities	Salesperson ties into the company's direct mail, telemarketing, and shows to secure and qualify leads.
Lists and directories	Salesperson uses secondary data sources, which can be free or fee-based.
Canvassing	Salesperson tries to generate leads by calling on totally unfamiliar organizations.
Spotters	Salesperson pays someone for lead information.
Telemarketing	Salesperson uses phone and/or telemarketing staff to generate leads.
Sales letters	Salesperson writes personal letters to potential leads.
Other sources	Salesperson uses noncompeting salespeople, people in his or her own firm, social clubs, etc., to secure lead information.

(Chapter 13 provides more information about how to build relationships with your customers.)

ENDLESS-CHAIN METHOD

In the **endless-chain method,** sales representatives attempt to get at least one additional lead from each person they interview. This method works best when the source is a satisfied customer; however, it may also be used even when a prospect does not buy.

For example, at the conclusion of a meeting the following conversation might ensue:

SELLER   "Do you belong to any professional trade associations? Maybe you know of some other members who could use my services?"

BUYER   "Well, you know, maybe Harkins, and even Dudley, could use this service too."

SELLER   "You know a lot more about these people than I do. If you were me, who would you call first?"

BUYER   "Harkins, I would guess."

SELLER   "When I call Mr. Harkins, may I mention that we are doing some work with you?"

Some people object to having their names used as a means of opening the door to friends or business acquaintances. Others, particularly those who trust the salesperson and/or are enthusiastic over the products or services, will not hesitate to provide the names of additional prospects. They

EXHIBIT 7.4   EXAMPLE OF THE ENDLESS-CHAIN METHOD OF PROSPECTING

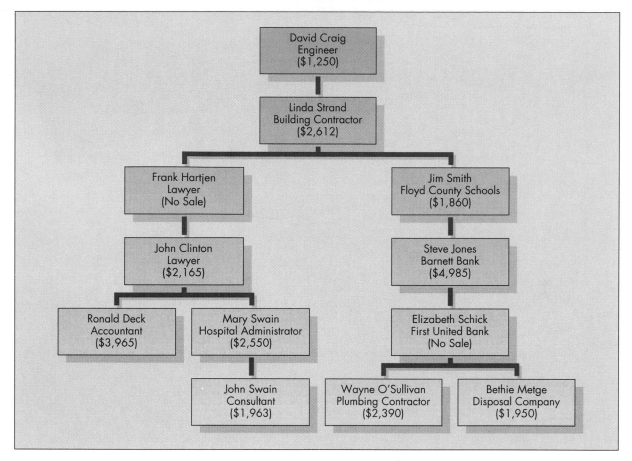

may even write a letter or card of introduction for the sales representative. The name of a lead provided by either a customer or a prospect, known as a **referred lead,** is generally considered to be the most successful type of lead. Exhibit 7.4 illustrates how a sales representative used the endless-chain method to produce $25,690 in business (selling fax machines) within a 30-day period. All the sales resulted directly or indirectly from the first referral from an engineer to whom the sales rep had sold a mere $1,250 of equipment.

CENTER-OF-INFLUENCE METHOD

In the **center-of-influence method,** the salesperson cultivates a relationship with well-known, influential people in the territory who are willing to supply lead information. Exhibit 7.5 illustrates the concept visually. Ross Perot understands the importance of centers of influence and prefers to call them "eagles." "You don't capture eagles by the flock," he says, "you catch them one at a time. When you catch one, you treasure it like a jewel."[4] A friend of one of the authors likes to call centers of influence "bell cows," because the rest of the "herd" follows their lead.

E X H I B I T 7 . 5

ILLUSTRATION OF THE
CENTER-OF-INFLUENCE
METHOD

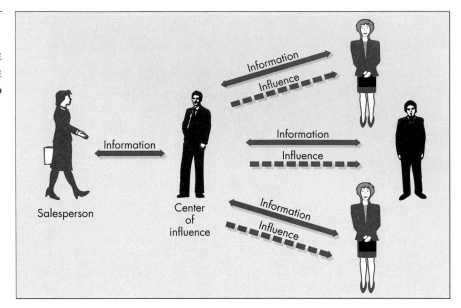

This method, as with the endless-chain method, works best if the center of influence is already a satisfied customer of the salesperson. Here is the way an industrial cleaning service salesperson used the center-of-influence method when meeting with a well-known and respected maintenance engineer:

> *"Now I've had the chance to explain my service, and you've had the opportunity to meet my cleaning crew. I wonder if you will do me a favor? You mentioned that it was probably the best-designed package you've ever seen. Can you think of any of your business associates who could benefit from such a plan? Does one come to your mind right away?"*

In industrial sales situations, the centers of influence are frequently people in important departments not directly involved in the purchase decision, such as quality control, equipment maintenance, and receiving. The salesperson keeps in close touch with these people over an extended period, solicits their help in a straightforward manner, and keeps them informed on sales that result from their aid.

One true story illustrates the method's use. A Xerox representative found that decision makers from several companies would get together and visit on occasion. These accounts formed a **buying community,** a small, informal group of people in similar positions who communicate regularly, both socially and professionally. The rep also found that one particular decision maker in that group, or community, would share the results of any sales call with the other members of the community. Thus, a call on that account had the power of seven calls. By working carefully with this center of influence, the rep closed nine orders among the seven accounts, with sales that totaled over $450,000!

Centers of influence may never buy. One church furnishings representative told of a pastor who suggested that the rep call on two other churches, both in the market for pews. The pastor who made the referral has not

EXHIBIT 7.6

DIRECT MAIL PIECE AND
REQUEST FOR ADDITIONAL
INFORMATION

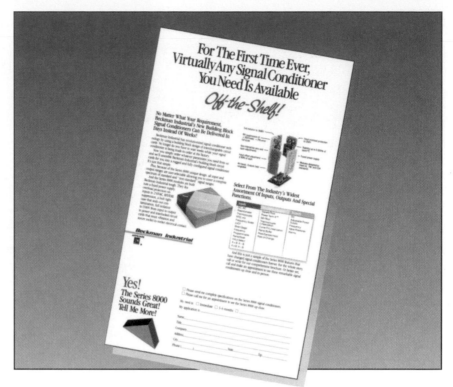

Source: Courtesy of Beckman Industrial. Used by permission.

purchased pews in over 10 years and probably won't for many more. But the rep continues to spend time with that pastor, who is an important center of influence in the pastoral community.

PROMOTIONAL
ACTIVITIES

generation techniques

Most companies elicit a steady supply of sales leads with advertising, catalogs, publicity, direct mail, trade shows, and seminars. Successful salespeople develop an effective system for utilizing and managing such leads.

Inquiries

Firms have developed sophisticated systems to generate inquiries from leads. For example, Beckman Industrial sends out direct mail to potential prospects for its signal conditioners (see Exhibit 7.6). The firm also places advertisements in trade publications, such as *Control Magazine*. A reader of the ad can request additional information by using the 800-number in the ad or by using the reader service card in the back of the magazine.

Beckman also participates in postcard packs. A **postcard pack** is a group of postcards (usually between 15 and 50 different cards) that provide information from a number of firms. Each firm has one card, usually describing one product or service. One side of Beckman's postcard contains

E X H I B I T   7 . 7   COVER LETTER, INFORMATION, AND BOUNCEBACK CARD FOR INQUIRIES

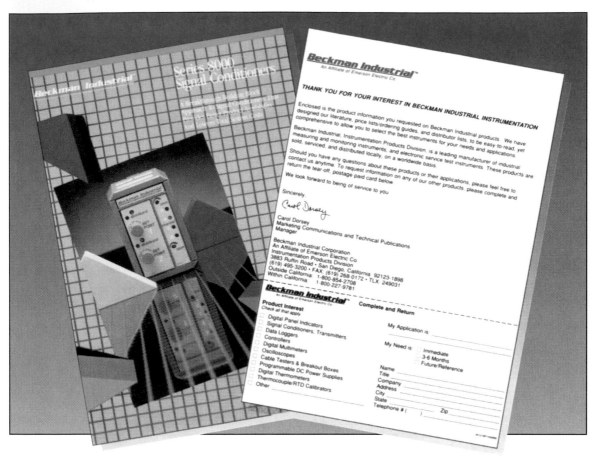

Source: Courtesy of Beckman Industrial. Used by permission.

information about a specific product or service (e.g., the Series 8000 signal conditioner). The other side, prestamped, carries Beckman's address. A company interested in learning more about Beckman's product simply fills in its name and address and drops the card in the mail.

Anyone who inquires about Beckman's products receives a cover letter, information about the advertised product, and a follow-up inquiry card (see Exhibit 7.7). A copy of the inquiry goes to the appropriate salesperson. Based on knowledge of the territory, the salesperson decides whether a personal follow-up is appropriate. If the inquirer returns the second inquiry card (frequently called a **bounceback card**), Beckman again notifies the salesperson. The salesperson then follows up on the lead with a visit or a phone call.

A growing trend is to tie the marketing promotion to an 800-number and the inquirer's fax machine. The prospect calls the 800-number, talks to a salesperson (or a voice-activated system, such as voice mail), and then is asked to supply his or her fax number. The requested information is sent within seconds, often while the salesperson is still on the phone with the prospect.[5]

Shows

Many companies display or demonstrate their products at trade shows, conventions, and fairs. They have sales representatives present to demonstrate their products to inquiring visitors, many of whom have not been called on by salespeople before.

Often, the primary function of salespeople at shows is to qualify leads for future follow-up. Typically, having only 5 to 10 minutes with a prospect, they need to get down to business and qualify the visitor quickly.[6] At other trade shows (e.g., furniture shows), salespeople actually sell and therefore generally spend more time with the buyer (as will be discussed in Chapter 15).

Seminars

Today, many firms use seminars to generate leads and provide information to prospective customers. For example, a local pharmaceutical representative for Pfizer Labs will set up a seminar for 8 to 10 cardiologists, inviting a nationally known research cardiologist to give a presentation to this group. The research specialist usually discusses some new technique or treatment being developed. During or after the presentation, the pharmaceutical representative for Pfizer Labs will describe how Pfizer's drug Procardia will help in the prevention of heart disease. Selling Scenario 7.1 explains how an industrial marketer successfully uses seminars to generate prospects.[7]

Trade shows and seminars are two effective activities that help salespeople discover and qualify leads.

Photo courtesy of Hewlett-Packard Company.

Richard Pasley/Stock Boston.

S E L L I N G   S C E N A R I O

7.1

Using Seminars as a Selling Tool

Andrew Corp., an Orland Park, Illinois, manufacturer of electronic communication equipment, may be one of the most savvy practitioners of business-to-business seminars, according to Allen J. Konopacki, a noted seminar consultant. Before it launched its first seminar series in early 1988, the company carefully orchestrated and pretested every facet of the program.

To target the right crowd, the company relied mainly on its own database, consisting largely of inquiries. Experts in the seminar field regard this core group as the most fruitful source of new business. For this year's series, Andrew Corp. also rented three trade magazine mailing lists and matched them with its own list to come up with a final registry of 43,000 names. The company likes to mix current customers with new prospects in a 1:2 ratio, figuring that satisfied clients not only may buy more but may also pass along word-of-mouth testimony about the company's products.

To reach its audience, the sales and marketing department prepared and sent out a four-page invitation to its free, daylong seminar. It detailed the topics to be covered, suggested who should attend, and asked for two names to be listed on a reply card or by way of an 800-number.

During the lunch break, sitting at each lunch table of 10 participants is a sales, marketing or telemarketing rep, who acts as a facilitator and sounding board. The reps' job, apart from presenting a company face to the group, is to gather reactions to the morning sessions, provide the names of contacts at Andrew Corp. (if asked), and request each attendee to fill out a one-page evaluation form.

The questionnaire, which takes about 10 minutes to complete, is the company's key vehicle for feedback. It asks such relevant questions as each person's reason for attending, his or her upcoming product requirements, and the status of any project—including installation date, value of total project, budgeting phase, and the name of the key decision maker. "We never try to close a sale at our seminars," says Hurt. "That comes later, after we evaluate the responses to the questionnaires."

A preliminary review starts right after lunch. The sales team separates the responses into three categories: (1) qualified leads—companies with projects and budgets approved and ready for implementation in less than one year; (2) companies with plans for a project and perhaps a tentative installation date; and (3) those with no set plans but who may be seeking information on the market and available products. The evaluations then travel to corporate headquarters, where the sales manager takes immediate action on those in the top-priority category.

Source: Adapted from Tom Murray, "Seminar Selling," *Sales & Marketing Management,* September 1990, pp. 54–58. Used by permission.

▮ LISTS AND DIRECTORIES

Individual sales representatives need to develop prospect lists of their own by referring to such sources as public records, telephone directories, Chamber of Commerce directories, newspapers, club memberships, and professional or trade membership lists. Secondary sources of information from public libraries can be useful. For example, industrial trade directories from most states are available. Exhibit 7.8 shows pages from the *New York State Industrial Directory.* Exhibit 7.9 lists some useful secondary sources.

Salespeople can purchase a number of prospecting directories and lead-generating publications. In fact, it has been estimated that "there are no fewer than *four* lists available of virtually every business phone number in

EXHIBIT 7.8

LEAD INFORMATION: PAGES
FROM THE *NEW YORK
STATE INDUSTRIAL
DIRECTORY*

Source: *MacRAE's New York State Industrial Directory.* Copyright © 1991 MacRAE's Blue Book, Inc., New York, NY. Reprinted by permission.

America."[8] For example, you can purchase, by geographical area, mailing lists for all gerontologists (specialists in geriatrics), Lions Clubs, T-shirt retailers, yacht owners, antique dealers, Catholic high schools, motel supply houses, nudists, multimillionaires, or pump wholesalers. Sources for these lists include *Alvin B. Zeller, Bresser's Directory Inc. Mailing Lists* (New York), *Lists of 14 Million Businesses* (American Business Lists, Omaha, Nebraska), and *Who's Wealthy in America* (Taft Group, Rockville, Maryland). Many of these directories now come on PC diskettes for easy access. Salespeople should keep in mind that purchased lists, regardless of the guarantee of accuracy, can have lots of errors.

Most lists are simply names and telephone numbers. However, prospecting systems can be much more elaborate. For example, construction firms in large cities can, for a fee, have access to computerized databases of planned construction projects that meet the user's criteria (e.g., type of work to be performed, amount budgeted for the project, method of payment,

■ E X H I B I T 7 . 9

PARTIAL LIST OF
SECONDARY SOURCES OF
LEAD INFORMATION

Middle Market Directory (Dun & Bradstreet). Lists 14,000 firms worth between $500,000 and $1 million.

Million Dollar Directory (Dun & Bradstreet). Lists names, addresses, and business lines of firms worth more than $1 million.

Thomas Register of American Manufacturers (Thomas). Annual that lists manufacturers by product classifications, company profits, and specific product information.

Encyclopedia of Associations (Gale). Lists 21,500 national associations, more than 4,000 international organizations, and more than 50,000 regional, state, and local organizations.

Standard & Poor's Register of Corporations, Directors, and Executives (Standard & Poor's). Annual publication listing names, titles, and addresses of over 50,000 firms.

Directory of Corporate Affiliations (Macmillan Directory Division). Lists 4,000 U.S. firms as well as their over-40,000 divisions, subsidiaries, and so on.

Moody's Industrial Directory (Moody's). Annual that lists names, type of business, and a brief financial statement for over 10,000 publicly held corporations.

U.S. Industrial Directory (Time). Annual that lists sales, employees, and financial statistics for the 500 largest industrial firms and 50 largest diversified service firms.

Trade Shows and Professional Exhibits Directory (Gale). Lists more than 3,200 trade shows, including location, timing, attendance expected, and so on.

World Scope: Industrial Company Profiles (Wright Investor's Service). Extensive coverage of 5,000 companies from 25 countries, within 27 major industry groupings.

National Trade and Professional Associations (Columbia Books). Lists over 6,200 trade and professional associations, along with pertinent information about each.

The International Corporate 1000 (Graham & Trotman). Profiles the 1,000 largest companies in the world—650 from Europe, South America, the Middle East, and the Pacific Basin and 350 from the United States and Canada.

etc.). Such lists obviously include much more than just names and phone numbers of leads.

In international selling situations, procuring lists can be much more difficult. One of the biggest problems in selling in Mexico under the NAFTA free trade agreement is that mailing lists and databases simply do not exist.[9] Nor is this phenomenon unique to Mexico—many firms dealing in international selling environments face similar problems.[10]

■ CANVASSING

Before learning about other prospecting methods, college students often assume salespeople spend most of their time making cold calls. Using the **cold canvass method,** or **cold calls,** a sales representative tries to generate leads for new business by calling on totally unfamiliar organizations. This method has been used extensively for a long time.

However, cold canvassing can waste a salesperson's time, as many companies have neither a need for the product nor the ability to pay for it. This stresses the importance of qualifying the lead quickly in a cold call so as not to waste time. Also, cold canvassing is seen as rude by many purchasing agents and other professionals.

In a survey, salespeople rated making cold calls as the part of the job they liked the least.[11] Thus, as mentioned earlier, most firms now encourage their salespeople to qualify leads instead of relying on the cold call.

Some companies use a selective type of cold canvass they refer to as a *blitz*. In a **blitz,** a large group of salespeople attempt to make calls on all of the prospective businesses in a given geographical territory on a specified day. For example, an office machine firm may target a specific four-block area in the city of Detroit, Michigan; bring in all of the salespeople from the surrounding areas; and then go out and in the period of one day call on every business located in that four-block area. The purpose is to generate leads for the local sales representative as well as to build camaraderie and a sense of unity among the salespeople.

THINKING IT THROUGH	*A*ssume your sales manager instructs you to make five cold canvass calls a day, although you simply do not have the time. Also, for the service you are selling, this method has proven to be a poor technique. When you question your manager, he says: "It worked for me. It'll work for you too!" What would you say in response? If he refuses to change his mind, what would you do?

SPOTTERS

Some salespeople use **spotters,** also called **bird dogs.** These individuals, for a fee, will provide leads for the salesperson. The sales rep sometimes pays the fee simply for the name of the lead but more often pays only if the lead ends up buying the product or service. Spotters are usually in a position to find out when someone is ready to make a purchase decision. For example, a PC Fix Inc. computer repairer working on a very old computer, for which parts are no longer available or are getting scarce, could turn the name over to a ComputerLand salesperson, who would then try to sell the lead a new computer system.[12]

A fairly recent development is the use of outside paid consultants to locate and qualify leads. This happens more often when small firms attempt to secure business with very large organizations. For example, Synesis Corp., a small firm specializing in computerized training, used the services of a consultant to identify and develop a lead; the result was a major contract with AT&T.[13]

TELEMARKETING

Increasingly, firms are relying on telemarketing to perform many functions that sales representatives used to perform. *Telemarketing* is the systematic and continuous program of communicating with customers and prospects via telephone and/or other person-to-person electronic media.[14] Telemarketing is not limited to consumer sales; as you will see, all of the examples used in this section involve real business-to-business companies. Telemarketing is now used to sell everything from 25-cent supplies to $10 million airplanes.

In **outbound telemarketing,** telephones are used to generate and then qualify leads. **Inbound telemarketing** involves a telephone number (usually an 800-number) that leads and/or customers can call for additional information. For example, Motorola Corporation's Communication Sector, which sells mobile communication systems to such diverse entities as contractors, hotels, and police stations, uses outbound telemarketing to generate and then qualify leads for its sales force. Qualified leads are turned over to field sales representatives if the order is large enough to warrant an outside sales rep. If the prospect needs a smaller system, a separate telemarketing salesperson will handle the account. Motorola also provides an 800-number for people who want more information about a product or service Motorola offers. Because of this excellent telemarketing organization, Motorola's field reps have more time to spend with qualified prospects and more time to develop long-term customer relations.

Active listening is just as important when conversing over the phone as when conversing in person. Take notes and restate the message or any action you have agreed to undertake. In addition, you will need to encourage two-way communication. If you have ever talked with two-year-olds over the phone, then you know that if you ask them a yes/no question, they tend to shake their heads "yes" or "no" rather than verbalize a response. Similarly, you cannot nod your head to encourage someone to continue talking on the phone. Instead, you must encourage conversations with verbal cues such as "Uh-huh," "I see," or "That's interesting." And, just as in active listening in a face-to-face conversation, you must be able to tolerate silences so that customers have an opportunity to ask questions, agree or disagree, or relate a point to their circumstances.

Limitations of Telephone Prospecting

While a wonderful tool that can enhance productivity for many salespeople, the telephone does have some limitations. First, customers may find telephone calls an annoying inconvenience. Unexpected calls may interrupt customers involved in meetings or concentrating on their work. When telephoning customers—in fact, at all times—salespeople need to respect the customer's privacy and not abuse the privilege.

Telephones limit communications to verbal messages. For this reason, the telephone may be a poor choice when salespeople need to show the product and its features and benefits. Nor can salespeople read customers' nonverbal cues in a telephone conversation. They may miss or misunderstand a customer's message.

Attracting and maintaining the customer's attention and interest is harder over the telephone. During face-to-face encounters, people are generally more polite and will concentrate on the person with whom they are talking. But customers talking on the telephone can engage in other activities; they may even continue to work or read a report or magazine.

Finally, saying no is much easier over the phone than in person. Because they cannot see the salesperson, customers may even be rude during telephone conversations. To end a phone conversation by hanging up is easy; to walk away from a face-to-face conversation with a salesperson is harder.

Salespeople need to be aware of these limitations. The telephone does present some advantages and can enhance productivity. But it does not replace face-to-face selling in all situations.

Tie-in with Other Tools

Firms are learning to use direct mail tied to inbound and outbound telemarketing to reach potential prospects effectively. For example, one firm offers a catalog to interested parties. After a request, the firm sends out a catalog and has a salesperson follow up with a phone call about a week after the catalog has been mailed. This phone call allows the salesperson to gauge the strength of the lead as a prospect.[15]

PROSPECTING VIA SALES LETTERS

Prospecting sales letters should be integrated into an overall prospecting plan. For example, Xerox salespeople who handle smaller businesses send prospecting sales letters every day. They follow up three days later with a telephone prospecting call and ask for an appointment for a personal visit. The telephone call begins with a question about the letter.

Like the telephone, sales letters have limitations. Once the message is sent, it cannot be modified to fit the prospect's style. The sender also has no chance to alter the message on the basis of feedback. Blanket mailings, then, can seem impersonal.

Because people in business receive so much mail, sales letters should be written with care. Think about the amount of junk mail that you receive and how much you throw away without a second glance. Sales letters must stand out to be successful.

One way to make sales letters stand out is to include a promotional item with the mailer. First National Bank of Shreveport, Louisiana, targeted certified public accountants for one mailer. The bank timed the mailers to arrive on April 16, the day after the federal income tax filing deadline. Included in each mailer was a small bottle of wine, a glass, and cheese and crackers—a party kit designed to celebrate the end of tax time. The bank followed up with telephone calls two days later, ultimately gaining 21 percent of the CPAs as new customers.

The salesperson must first consider the objective of the letter and the audience. What action does the salesperson desire from the reader? Why would the reader want to undertake that action? Why would the reader not want to undertake the action? These questions help guide the salesperson writing the letter.

Gain Attention

The opening paragraph must grab the reader's attention, just as a salesperson's approach must get a prospect's attention in a cold call. Two approaches that can work well in sales letters are the benefit approach and the curiosity approach. Exhibit 7.10 contains examples of both. They come from letters actually used to sell articles to magazines. Each opening gives

E X H I B I T 7 . 10

Sᴀʟᴇꜱ Lᴇᴛᴛᴇʀ Aᴘᴘʀᴏᴀᴄʜᴇꜱ

A. Curiosity Opener

August 29, 1994

Barbara Boeding, Editor
The American Salesman
424 N. Third St.
Burlington, IA 52601

Dear Ms. Boeding:

On the first day a new product was available for order taking, one sales rep had seven customers order for a total in sales of $450,000. Even more amazing, he only made one sales call on one prospect! How did he do it? By identifying and managing a "buying community."

B. Benefit Opener

September 29, 1994

Ms. Paulette S. Withers, Editor
Sales Manager's Bulletin
Bureau of Business Practice
24 Rope Ferry Rd.
Waterford, CT 06386

Dear Ms. Withers:

Field sales managers everywhere complain about a lack of support from their own organization. To get that support, though, they require better skills in working with other functional areas, such as manufacturing and administration. The proposed article, "Internal Marketing," will show your readers how to use their sales skills to develop stronger relationships with people in their own organization.

the readers a reason to continue reading, drawing them into the rest of the letter.

Present Benefits

The next paragraph or two, the body of the letter, will reflect the answers to the questions of why the reader would or would not want to take the desired action. Benefits of taking the action should be presented clearly, without jargon, and briefly. But the best-presented benefits are tailored to the specific individual, especially when the salesperson can refer to a recent conversation with the reader. Such a reference as the following example can truly personalize the letter:[16]

> As you said during my last visit, Ms. Powers, the most important factor is speed. The RX-4000 is the fastest lift available in its class, meaning that your dock personnel can handle the increases you are forecasting.

EXHIBIT 7.11

ACTION CLOSE (HOOK)

The action close in the letter must do four things:
1. Tell the reader what to do: **respond.** Avoid *if* ("If you'd like to try . . .") and *why not* ("Why not send in a check?"). They lack positive emphasis and encourage your reader to say *no.*
2. Make the action sound easy. Tell them to fill in the information on the reply card, sign the card (for credit sales), put the card and check (if payment is to accompany the order) in the envelope, and mail the envelope. If you provide an envelope and pay postage, stress those facts.
3. Offer a reason for acting promptly. Reasons for acting promptly are easy to identify when a product is seasonal or there is a genuine limit on the offer—time limit, scheduled price rise, limited supply, etc. Sometimes you may be able to offer a premium or a discount if the reader acts quickly. When these conditions do not exist, remind readers that the sooner they get the product, the sooner they can benefit from it; the sooner they contribute funds, the sooner their dollars can go to work to solve the problem.
4. End with a positive picture. Depict the reader enjoying the product (in a sales letter) or the reader's money working to solve the problem (in a fund-raising letter). The last sentence should never be a selfish request for money.

The action close can also remind readers of the central selling point, stress the guarantee, and mention when the customer will get the product.

Source: Kitty Locker, *Business and Administrative Communication* (Burr Ridge, IL: Irwin, 1989), p. 306.

If the salesperson and buyer do not know each other, part of the body of the letter should be used to increase credibility. References to satisfied customers, market research data, and other independent sources can be used to improve credibility. For example:

Inventory Management and Control magazine *rated the RX-4000 as not only the fastest but also the most trouble-free lift on the market.*

Seek Action

The final paragraph should seek commitment to the desired course of action. Whatever the action desired, the letter must specifically ask that it take place. Leave no doubt in the prospect's mind as to what he or she is supposed to do. Exhibit 7.11 details how the ending paragraph should tell the reader *what to do, make it sound easy, why it should be done now,* and *end with a positive picture.*

A postscript (PS) can also be effective. Postscripts stand out because of their location and should be used to make an important selling point. Alternatively, they can be used to emphasize the requested action, such as pointing out a deadline.

THINKING
IT
THROUGH

What do you hate most of all about junk mail? Can you see any patterns in the way junk mailings present their sales message? Could a field salesperson adapt some of their ideas to an industrial or trade selling situation?

■ E X H I B I T 7 . 1 2

PAGE FROM THE *SALES*
PROSPECTOR

APRIL 30, 1993

Sales Prospector.
A MACLEAN HUNTER ■ PUBLICATION

IOWA, MINNESOTA, NORTH DAKOTA, SOUTH DAKOTA, WISCONSIN

IOWA

BLOOMFIELD & OTTUMWA, IA -- <u>ResCare Inc.</u>, P.O. Box 932, Fairfield, IA 52556, contact John Kuster/Harvey Henley (515/472-1684), is planning a <u>$4 million expansion and renovation program</u>. Plans include a $1.2 million conversion of the Wapello County Care Facility in Ottumwa, IA 52501 into a mental health care facility. The facility will be able to accommodate 70 patients. Funding has also been allocated for a renovation of the Davis County Care Facility in Bloomfield, IA 52537. In addition, the company plans to build five fourplexes in Ottumwa and three fourplexes and a duplex in Bloomfield for independent living clients.

DES MOINES, IA -- The <u>Office of the U.S. Property & Fiscal Office for Iowa</u>, Camp Dodge, 7700 NW Beaver Dr., Johnston, IA 50131, contact 1LT. Esther L. Woods (515/252-4508), will issue solicitations May 18 and call general contract bids June 18 for a <u>$250,000 to $500,000 munitions maintenance facility</u> at the Iowa Air National Guard Base, Des Moines International Airport in Des Moines, IA. Plans for the project call for a stand-alone, 4,000 sq. ft. facility. Work on Sol. DAHA13-93-B-0006 includes site work, fencing, asphalt and PCC pavement, crushed rock, masonry walls, mechanical systems, electrical, water and other utilities and sewer lines.

LE MARS, IA -- UPDATE -- Ground was broken this month for a <u>$3.3 million expansion</u> planned by <u>Floyd Valley Hospital</u>, Hwy. 3E, Le Mars, IA 51031, contact Frank LaBonte, administrator (712/546-7871). As reported here November 18, 1992, the project involves construction of an addition to house outpatient services, a business office, physical therapy services and an emergency room. General contractor is <u>McHan Construction Inc.</u>, 1700 Riverside Blvd., Sioux City, IA 51109 (712/233-1471). <u>Proshaska & Associates</u>, 11317 Chicago Circle, Omaha, NE 68154 (402/334-0755), was architect.

SIOUX CITY, IA -- UPDATE -- The <u>City of Sioux City</u>, 6th and Douglas, Sioux City, IA, contact, Hank Sinda, city manager (712/279-6102), is evaluating plans for a new <u>city hall</u>. One proposal calls for maintaining the facility's clock tower and replacing the to-be-demolished city hall with a multimillion-dollar structure. The existing facility, which has had problems with cracking and uneven settling, is considered structurally deficient and possibly unsafe. This project was reported here July, 1991.

© 1993, Westgate Publishing Company, Inc.

The SALES PROSPECTOR® will increase your sales, boost your profits, and save you time and energy. Published twice monthly, it is a prospect research report for business people interested in industrial, commercial and institutional expansions and relocations in new or existing buildings. Reports are available for regional or national coverage. Subscription rates and coverage are shown on the last page, or call 1-800-752-4050.

Source: Used by permission of Westgate Publishing Company, Inc.

OTHER SOURCES OF LEADS

Many salespeople find leads through personal observation. For example, by reading trade journals carefully, salespeople can learn the names of the most important leaders (and, hence, decision makers) in the industry.[17] Sellers also read general business publications (such as *Business Week* and *The Wall Street Journal*) and the local newspapers and just keep their eyes open when they drive through their territory. Also, a number of fee-based publications provide the same current information. Exhibit 7.12 gives an example of the monthly *Sales Prospector* for the Iowa area. The information it provides allows the salesperson to spend more time actually selling.

Nonsales employees within your own firm can also provide leads. Some companies strongly encourage this. For example, Computer Specialists Inc., a computer service firm, pays its nonsales employees a bonus of up to $1,000 for any names of prospective customers they pass along. In one year, the program resulted in 75 leads and nine new accounts.[18]

Government agencies can supply lead information. For example, the Commerce Department has identified some of the hottest prospects in the new Economic Community to be searching for aircraft and aircraft parts, construction materials, computers and home electronics, and so forth.[19]

Other sources of leads include salespeople for noncompetitive but related products, and social and professional contacts from clubs and trade associations.

GETTING THE MOST OUT OF PROSPECTING

After salespeople separate leads from prospects, they carefully analyze the relative value of each prospect. This grading of prospects, or establishing a priority list, results in increased sales and the most efficient use of time and energy.

LEARN TO EFFECTIVELY QUALIFY AND EVALUATE PROSPECTS

Many companies conduct extensive research to determine what distinguishes a good prospect. For example, Metier Management Systems, a division of the Lockheed Corporation, identified 17 key criteria for assessing leads. Salespeople, in a monthly sales prospect review meeting (which often lasted four to six hours per salesperson), had to demonstrate that their leads were, in fact, actually qualified prospects.[20]

KEEP GOOD RECORDS

The information and the type of prospect file needed vary by type of business. Many industrial salespeople keep a file card for each customer and

Immediately after each sales call to a physician this salesperson from Merck Pharmaceuticals in Great Britain records the results of the visit and makes notes about future goals and activities.

Courtesy of Merck & Co., Inc.

E X H I B I T   7 . 1 3

PROSPECT CONTACT FORM
FOR AN ELECTRONIC
DISTRIBUTOR

ELECTRONIC COMPONENT INC.
Prospect Contact Form

Date _3/20/94_

Name of Contact _Jack Barry_ Telephone Number _(714) 833-1340_

Company _AIL Labs_   Type of Business _Instrument Mgr_

Address _2305 Campus Dr, Hinsdale, Chicago_

Position _Purchasing Agent_

Contact Needs _Interested in quick delivery needs source for metal L/on capacitors_

Present Suppliers _Wylie, Hamilton-Aunet_

Credit Rating _aa_   Annual Sales _$3M_

Annual Purchases of Components _$200K_

Types of Components Purchases

_____	Low-precision resistors	_____	RAMs
✓	Precision resistors	✓	Microprocessors
✓	Potentiometers	_____	LCDs
✓	Metal film caps	_____	LEDs
_____	MOS memory	_____	Bi-polar

Result of Visit _Still trying to get parts from Wylie_

Follow-Up _Call in two weeks_

each prospect. They complete a form after each contact. Exhibit 7.13 shows a form used by an electronic distributor.

Many salespeople now use PC laptop-based software packages to keep track of prospects. Salespeople for CONAM Inspection (a firm that sells lab services to industrial firms, water plants, and power plants) use the ACT package. A sample screen from the package appears in Exhibit 7.14. Notice that the salesperson can store and quickly retrieve all sorts of information, including important facts such as call objectives, notes about prior calls, "to-do" information, and reminders.

SET QUOTAS

Most effective prospecting plans include weekly and monthly quotas for obtaining new prospects. In the long run, prospecting goals are just as im-

EXHIBIT 7.14

SAMPLE SCREEN FROM THE
SOFTWARE PACKAGE ACT

```
File  Edit  Schedule  Clear  Write  Lookup  Phone  View  Report

    Name: Heldon Industries, Inc.        Addrs: 10321 Mockingbird Lane
 Contact: Samuels, Mr. Michael               : Suite 1230
   Phone: 214-491-2900  X: 279   CC:         :
   Title: Vice President of Sales       City: Dallas
     Sec: Donna                        State: TX
    Dear: Mr. Samuels                    ZIP: 75206

    Call:▼ 6/06/90    9:00 am   Re: Schedule meeting
 Meeting:  6/11/90    2:00 pm   Re: Product demonstration
   To-Do:▼ 6/05/90   10:00 am   Re: Prepare proposal

  Last Results: Very interested in new product line.
     Status/ID: Prospect                Referred by: Jack Winters

Next Objective: Close Sale             Probability: High
    Last Order $: 50,000                 Birthdate: 09/15/48
    YTD Revenue: 2,000,000             Wife's Name: Victoria

     Reminder: Had problems with previous company's customer support
       User 8:
       User 9:
 E:\ACT2\ACT                                   Name 494 of 934
 F1=Help  Tue 05-Jun-90  2:45 pm                  INS  SCROLL
```

Source: Used by permission of Conductor Software, Inc.

portant as are profit and sales goals, and quotas remind the salesperson to keep a constant lookout for new names to fill the prospect pipeline.

EVALUATE RESULTS

Salespeople need to evaluate the profitability of any sales resulting from various lead-generating activities instead of just counting the number of names that a particular method might yield. Study the methods used by the most successful salespeople in your firm, because salespeople differ greatly in their ability to judge the strength of leads.[21]

Analysis may show that the present system does not produce enough prospects or the right kind of prospects. Sales reps may, for example, depend entirely on referred names from company advertising or from the service department. If these two sources do not supply enough names to produce the sales volume desired, then other prospecting methods should be considered.

OVERCOME RELUCTANCE TO PROSPECTING

Many people stereotype salespeople as bold, adventurous, and somewhat abrasive. This view, that salespeople are fearless, is more fiction than fact. Salespeople often struggle with a reluctance to prospect that persists no matter how well they have been trained and how much they believe in the products they sell. Many people are uncomfortable when they initially contact other people, but for salespeople call reluctance can be a career-threatening condition.

Research shows a number of reasons for call reluctance.[22] Reasons include worrying about worst-case scenarios, spending too much time preparing, being overly concerned with looking successful, fear of making group presentations, guilt at having a career in selling, fear of appearing too pushy, feeling intimidated by persons of prestige or power, fear

S E L L I N G   *S C E N A R I O*

7.2

Prospect Even When Your Competitors Stop

John Paul Jones, senior territory manager for Monsanto, describes an unusual prospecting circumstance that led to a major sale.

"It was 1967 and I had been in sales for about three years. I was servicing western New York State. I was driving down the road in the middle of a terrible snowstorm on my way to a prospective client. I'm a native Floridian, so I was not prepared for that climate, and I was almost forced off the road. In desperation, I pulled into the parking lot of the Alliance Tool & Die Company to wait out the storm. While I was sitting there, I decided to go inside and see what local business conditions were like. I wasn't trying so much to make a sale as to maybe pick up a few leads.

"I went in and introduced myself to the manager and told him I'd been in Rochester six months and that the weather here stinks. I asked him if he needed a lot of plastic materials. He said no, but asked me what product I was pushing. I told him nylon and he told me that the chemical products division office of General Motors across the street was looking for nylon for about 18 different applications. He gave me the name of a person to speak to.

"To get there, I had to walk because of the weather. It was about 4 PM, and the person's receptionist told me he had a lot of appointments that day, but many of them canceled because of the snow, and he might see me. He did.

"Before I even took a seat, he asked me if we had the capacity to make 2 to 3 million pounds of nylon a year. Without blinking an eye, I said yes, even though I wasn't sure. He then told me that GM had to develop a special grade of the material and that we were just about six months behind our competitors. So I had to go back to our R&D people while our competitors were making inroads.

"Six months later, one of them pulled out of the competition because they didn't have the capability to take this on for the long term, and in the next 12 to 14 months another also dropped out.

"It took us a year to develop the product in the lab. But with two rivals dropping out, we eventually became the second source of supply for this material (DuPont became the first), which was used for the automobile emission control devices that were mandated by the Environmental Protection Agency.

"So a situation that I was forced into by a snowstorm turned out to be one of Monsanto's major products in the late 60s and early 70s."

Source: Reprinted from "Strange Tales of Sales," *Sales & Marketing Management*, June 3, 1985, p. 46. Used by permission.

of losing friends or family approval, fear of using the phone for prospecting, and having a compulsive need to argue, make excuses, or blame others.

Call reluctance can and must be overcome for successful selling. The following procedure is recommended for newly hired salespeople attempting to overcome call reluctance:

1. Listen to the excuses other salespeople give to justify their call-reluctance behavior.

2. Identify the excuses you use to avoid making calls.

3. Engage in role-playing exercises to experience how it feels to be free of call reluctance.

4. Have a supporting partner accompany you when contacting two or more strangers (prospects).

5. Make two more calls on strangers without the supporting partner.

6. Reenact the last two calls in front of a group.

7. Set specific goals for prospecting activity.

8. Recount your own successes, or those of others, that resulted from prospecting effectively. (Selling Scenario 7.2 tells how a prospecting situation turned out to be extremely profitable.)

SUMMARY

Locating prospective customers is the first step in the sales process. New prospects are needed to replace old customers lost for a variety of reasons and to replace lost contacts in existing customers (due to plant relocations, turnover, mergers, downsizing, etc.).

Not all sales leads qualify as good prospects. A qualified prospect has a need that can be satisfied by the salesperson's product, has the ability and authority to buy the product, can be approached by the salesperson, and is eligible to buy.

Many methods can be used for locating prospects. The best source is a satisfied customer. Salespeople sometimes obtain leads through their customers by using the endless-chain and center-of-influence methods. Companies provide leads to salespeople through promotional activities such as advertising, inquiries, telemarketing, trade shows, and seminars. Salespeople also can use lists and directories, cold canvassing (including blitzes), and spotters and other helpful contacts.

Effective prospecting requires development of a plan. The plan hinges on keeping good records, setting quotas, evaluating the results of the prospecting effort, experimenting with new methods, following through, and overcoming call reluctance.

KEY TERMS

bird dogs   217
blitz   217
bounceback card   212
buying community   210
center-of-influence method   209
cold calls   216
cold canvass method   216
endless-chain method   208
house accounts   207
inbound telemarketing   217

lead   202
national accounts   207
outbound telemarketing   217
postcard pack   211
prospect   202
prospecting   202
qualifying a lead   202
referred lead   209
spotters   217
systems integrators   206

QUESTIONS AND PROBLEMS

1. If you were a salesperson for the following companies, how would you develop a prospect list?
   a. A manufacturer of light airplanes for private buyers.
   b. A travel agency specializing in group tours.
   c. A manufacturer of heavy equipment for road construction.

2. How would you develop a prospect list under the following situations?
   a. You belong to a social organization on campus that needs to recruit new members.
   b. You are a marketing student about to graduate from college, and you want to find a full-time sales position.
   c. You, a veteran salesperson for Xerox copiers, are being transferred to Xerox's new office in Canton, China.

3. What information do you need to qualify the leads generated in each part of question 2?

4. What information should a salesperson collect to qualify leads for:
   a. A uniformed guard service?
   b. Sponsorship of a Little League baseball team?
   c. Paper for computer output?

5. "Salespeople should forget prospects who do not qualify." Comment on this statement.

6. Assume that you are starting a career as a stockbroker. Develop a system for rating prospects. The system should contain several important factors for qualifying prospects, and scales with which to rate the prospects on these factors. Use the system to rate five of your friends.

7. In industrial sales situations, several people influence the purchase decision. Suppose you have just completed an interview with an industrial prospect and believe you should contact other people in the company. How will you raise the subject with the prospect?

8. Salespeople are often reluctant to prospect for new customers. What advice would you give to a new salesperson to help him or her overcome reluctance to prospecting?

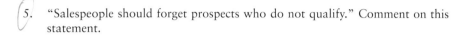

CASE PROBLEMS

CASE 7 • 1
FISHY BUSINESS

Jeff Berthiaume has been interested in tropical fish since he was a little boy. At age 6, he received his first fish; he has spent almost every waking moment since then thinking about fish. At age 16, he began work at a pet shop and read every book he could get his hands on that had *fish* in its title.

Jeff has set up a small fish collection and distribution operation—Fishy Business—in Long Beach, California. First he obtained financing for a 1,000-gallon tank in which to store the tropical fish before shipping them. Now he has outlined a system of distribution to retail pet stores, which consists of air shipping all fish in protected packages. Because of this system, he feels confident that he can service any customers located west of the Rocky Mountains.

Jeff has hired one part-time clerk to help with the books. Currently he does all of the diving needed to collect the fish; he loves that part of the operation.

Because his costs are so low, Jeff will be able to sell his tropical fish for about 10 percent less than his major competitor, Welsh Brothers, Inc. Welsh has been in business over 10 years and serves the entire US market. It is well known and respected due to its quality assurance program and excellent delivery record. Fishy Business will be able to offer the same level of service and guarantees.

Jeff is convinced that a good market exists for his product and service. The sale of tropical fish has grown by 10 percent per year over the last five years, and the trend is expected to continue for at least the next five years. One of his first problems is to obtain a list of prospects.

QUESTIONS
1. What prospecting methods should Jeff use?
2. How can Jeff qualify the leads he receives? What qualifying factors will be most important?
3. How can Jeff organize his prospecting activities? Who should be involved, and how will records be kept?

CASE 7 • 2
IDENTIFYING SHOWS TO USE IN OBTAINING LEADS

Many companies display or demonstrate their products or services at trade association shows, exhibitions, business machine shows, state fairs, and so forth. Sales reps usually obtain valuable leads at such shows. But where are these shows? When are they held? Whom do you contact if you want to participate? This exercise is designed to help improve your skill at answering these types of questions.

Consider the following products or services:

• Laptop personal computers.
• Complete janitorial service for large industrial plants.
• Large earth-moving equipment for road construction.
• Advertising and graphic design services.

For each product or service just listed, identify two shows that a salesperson could use for prospecting purposes, and answer the following questions. (Hint: See Exhibit 7–9 for some sources.)

QUESTIONS
1. What is the name and date of each show?
2. Who are the expected attendees of each show?
3. Who can you call or write for more information about each show?
4. What other information can you discover about each show (e.g., cost of booth space, expected number of attendees, number of vendors present, etc.)?

ADDITIONAL REFERENCES

Blue, Karen. "Closing the Loop: Hewlett-Packard's New Lead Management System." *Business Marketing,* October 1987, pp. 74–78.

Brady, Donald L. "Determining the Value of an Industrial Prospect: A Prospect Preference Index Model." *Journal of Personal Selling and Sales Management,* August 1987, pp. 27–32.

Brock, Richard T. "How to Get Quality Sales from Qualified Leads." *Sales & Marketing Management,* August 1990, pp. 94–95.

Collins, Robert H. "Microcomputer Systems to Handle Sales Leads: A Key to Increased Salesforce Productivity." *Journal of Personal Selling and Sales Management,* May 1985, pp. 78–83.

Dubin, Burt. "Referral Magic!" *Managers Magazine*, April 1990, pp. 8–15.

Emerick, Tracy. "The Trouble with Leads." *Sales & Marketing Management*, December 1992, pp. 57–79.

Falvey, Jack. "How to Get a Big Bang from Special Events." *Sales & Marketing Management*, October 1989, pp. 100–101.

Farber, Barry J, and Joyce Wycoff. "Relationships: Six Steps to Success," *Sales & Marketing Management*, April 1992, pp. 50–58.

Fishman, Steve. "The Art of Networking." *Success!* July–August 1985, pp. 36–43.

Good, Bill. *Prospecting Your Way to Sales Success.* New York: Scribner's, 1986.

Jolson, Marvin A. "Qualifying Sales Leads: The Tight and Loose Approaches." *Industrial Marketing Management*, August 1988, pp. 189–96.

————, and Thomas R Wotruba. "Prospecting: A New Look at This Old Challenge." *Journal of Personal Selling and Sales Management*, Fall 1992, pp. 59–66.

Messer, Carla, and James Alexander. "Classifying Your Customers." *Sales & Marketing Management*, July 1993, pp. 42–43.

Murray, Tom. "Seminar Selling." *Sales & Marketing Management*, September 1990, pp. 54–58ff.

"Prospecting Is Where the Gold Is." *Institutional Distribution*, May 15, 1990, pp. 70ff.

Rutherford, RD. "Make Your Sales Force Credit Smart." *Sales & Marketing Management*, November 1989, pp. 50–56.

Szymanski, David M, and Gilbert A Churchill, Jr. "Client Evaluation Cues: A Comparison of Successful and Unsuccessful Salespeople." *Journal of Marketing Research*, May 1990, pp. 163–74.

Tanner, John F. "Tapping into Your Buyer's Community." *American Salesman*, April 1990, pp. 3–6.

Van Doren, Doris C, and Thomas A Stickney. "How to Develop a Database for Sales Leads." *Industrial Marketing Management*, August 1990, pp. 201–8.

Planning the Sales Call

S alespeople are vulnerable to the great temptation to call on a prospect or customer without planning what to say and how to say it. Depending on spur-of-the-moment thinking is easy. However, all salespeople benefit from planning their calls in advance. This chapter discusses the kind of precall information you will need to gather and suggests where you can gather it, how to plan the sales call, and how to make appointments.

Some questions answered in this chapter are:

Why should salespeople plan their sales calls?

What precall information is needed about the individual prospect and the prospect's organization? How can this information be obtained?

What is involved in setting call objectives?

Should more than one objective be set for each call?

How can appointments be made effectively and efficiently?

After graduating with a BBA degree in 1992, Tracey Brill started selling for one of the largest firms in the grocery products industry. She felt lucky to get an offer from this firm because it seemed that everyone wanted to work for them. After a few months she found it wasn't the right job for her.

After a great deal of soul searching Tracey decided to accept a position with one of the leading pharmaceutical firms in the world—Bristol-Myers Squibb/Mead Johnson Laboratories Division, and she couldn't be happier. The firm provides excellent training, great incentives, and many other options for advancement. Everyone in her firm has been encouraging and motivational, which makes for an environment she loves to work in.

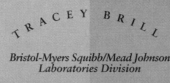

TRACEY BRILL

Bristol-Myers Squibb/Mead Johnson Laboratories Division

"Basically I call on OB/GYNs and family practitioners to 'detail' the benefits of our five different medications. Doctors will not always see pharmaceutical reps because there are too many of us and the doctors are too busy, so I really have to do my homework. Part of this involves determining who my best prospects are and then collecting precall information.

"First, I determine the doctor's specialty (OB/GYN, internal medicine, urology, neurology, etc.). You'd be surprised how many different kinds of doctors there are. Then I determine which, if any, of my products he or she might have a need for. Next, I try to determine the size of the doctor's practice. This will help me determine the number of samples to allocate and how frequently they would need me to call on them.

"To determine the size I simply become very observant by looking at the number of patients waiting, checking how many nurses the doctor has, counting the number of examining rooms, and listening how long it takes for a phone call to be picked up. These cues may be misleading because they are just a few pieces to a big puzzle.

"Precall planning is so important because the time I have to get my message across to the doctor is so limited. Before I enter any office I know what my objectives are for that call. I even set call objectives for the doctors that I know will not see me. It has happened that the doctors who 'don't see reps' will decide to give me a minute. If I blow this opportunity I may never have another chance to talk about my medications. Also, if I am well prepared this doctor may give me more than one minute.

"It is very important to get the doctor's attention. An effective method I have used on new calls is to bring in a tape recorder. I play a short recording of a telephone ringing and say 'That call could be one of your patients calling to complain about their estrogen replacement therapy, but not if they are on Estrace (my drug).' This gets his or her attention because doctors dislike phone calls from patients complaining about medication. I then make a statement (e.g., A study of 319 patients concluded that...) and then ask an opening probe.

"Most importantly my product knowledge is key. I spend my evenings reading several monthly medical journals and magazines so I know what 'new' information is published that relates to either my medications or my competitors. I read and reread all our studies and reference our training manuals so I will always be ready for any question. By continuously reading all this information I have strong technical knowledge that allows me to build and maintain credibility with physicians.

"Selling is fun. It is also a lot of hard work. I hope you find a selling job that you enjoy as much as I enjoy mine. Study hard in your selling class. It really pays off in the real world!"

WHY PLAN THE SALES CALL

Successful salespeople see advance planning of the sales interview as essential to achieving success in selling. The salesperson should remember that the buyer's time is valuable. Without planning the sales call, a salesperson quite easily may cover material in which the buyer has no interest, try to obtain an order even though that is an unrealistic expectation for this sales call, or strike off into areas that veer from what the buyer actually needs to hear. The result is wasted time and an annoyed prospect. However, with a clear plan for the call, the salesperson more likely will not only obtain commitment but also win the buyer's respect and confidence.

Salespeople should also remember the value of their own time. Proper planning helps them meet their call objectives efficiently as well as effectively. They then have more time to make additional calls, conduct research on this or other firms, fill out company reports, and complete other necessary tasks.

OBTAINING PRECALL INFORMATION

Often the difference between making and not making a sale depends on the amount of homework done by the salesperson before making the call. The more information the salesperson has about the prospect, the higher the probability of meeting the prospect's needs and making a sale.

However, the salesperson must be aware of the costs involved in collecting information. At some point, the time and effort put into collecting information become greater than the benefits obtained.

The following dialogue shows what can happen in a sales call made with inadequate precall information.

SALESPERSON   "Good morning, Mr. White. I'm Bob Thompson, the new sales rep for McNeil Clothing."

CUSTOMER   "My name is Wasits, not White."

SALESPERSON   "Oh! I'm sorry. I should have asked your secretary to spell your name when I called to make an appointment. I want to show you our new fall line. It is ideally suited for the growing teenage market."

CUSTOMER   "Most of our customers are middle-aged. I don't want to attract teenagers to my store. They make a lot of noise, and they bother the older customers."

SALESPERSON   "Well, we also have a line for the middle-aged market. Here's some photographs of the items in the line. *[Reaches into his pocket for a package of cigarettes.]* Would you like a cigarette? This has really been a tough day."

CUSTOMER   "I don't smoke, and smoking really bothers me. The smell gets into the clothing in our store. Please don't smoke."

Gathering information from individuals in the prospect's firm before making the call on the prospect is often a wise investment of time.

Courtesy ARA Services Inc.

By not obtaining precall information, this salesperson immediately encountered several embarrassing situations. With such a poor start, the salesperson is unlikely to obtain his call objective.

Clearly, a salesperson who has been calling regularly on a prospect or customer usually has no need to collect a lot of additional information; records and notes from prior calls will be adequate to prepare for the sales call. The same holds true for a new salesperson if the previous one kept good records. But before you make an initial call on a prospect, you will often expend considerable effort on collecting precall information about both the individual prospect and the prospect's company.

Don't expect this information gathering to be quick, easy, or cheap. For example, Tom Carnes, owner of a printing firm in Las Vegas, wanted to increase his sales in the legal market. He learned that paralegals usually control the flow of paper in law offices and that a professional association of paralegals existed. He decided to meet with the leader of that organization for two hours twice a month for two or three months to learn about the legal market, paying her $500 for each meeting. The efforts at gaining precall information paid off with sales of $600,000 in the first year alone.[1]

THE INDIVIDUAL PROSPECT

To obtain useful information about a prospect, salespeople should attempt to find answers to the following questions:

- What is the prospect's name? How does he or she pronounce it?
- What is the prospect's attitude toward salespeople in general, toward the salesperson's company, and toward products offered by the salesperson's company and its competitors?

- What are the prospect's job aspirations, attitudes toward risk, and level of self-confidence in decision making?
- What are the prospect's reference groups (clubs, professional organizations, family, etc.), and what are the norms of each group?
- What are the prospect's interests (hobbies, sports, reading, etc.), and what does the prospect not enjoy?
- What are some aspects of the prospect's background (education, family status, successes, failures)?
- What is the prospect's personality style (driver, amiable, analytical, expressive—see Chapter 6)?
- To whom does the prospect report? Does the prospect need to justify the purchase decision to this person?

If this list seems long, consider the fact that Harvey Mackay, one of the leading business writers of our century, actually lists 66 questions (the "Mackay 66") that a seller should know about a customer.[2] Most firms have developed their own unique list of questions that salespeople need to consider in order to call on a prospect successfully. Selling Scenario 8.1 powerfully illustrates the importance of gaining precall information about the prospect.

THE PROSPECT'S ORGANIZATION

Information about the prospect's company obviously helps the salesperson to better understand the environment in which he or she will be working. It allows the salesperson to more quickly identify problem areas and respond accordingly. Using up the prospect's time, which is always very valuable, is minimized. Answers to the following questions provide useful information about the prospect's organization:

- Is this a manufacturing, wholesaling, or retailing organization? How large is it? What products or services does it provide?
- What types of customers does the organization sell to? What benefits does the organization's target market seek?
- Who are the organization's primary competitors? How do the competitors differ in their business approach?
- How much does the organization purchase in the product category? Does the organization buy from several suppliers or only one? Why?
- Why does the organization buy from its present suppliers? Is it satisfied with them? Why or why not?
- Who are the other potential competitors? What are their strengths and weaknesses?
- Who are the people involved in the purchase decision for the product category? How do they fit into the formal organizational structure? Into the informal organizational

Precall Planning Pays Off!

Lynn Mapes, vice president and associate publisher of *Reader's Digest*, describes a memorable sales presentation.

One day about five years ago, a friend of mine at an advertising agency called to tell me there were some big changes under way at a company we had both worked with for years.

"They're putting carpeting in the halls," he said.

You see, the headquarters of this company had always looked more like a grade school than a corporate front office, complete with linoleum floors and walls adorned with pictures of their numerous plants—in other words, pretty dull. So the fact that they were putting down carpeting was something on the order of radical change.

"What are they putting on the walls?" I asked.

"Pictures that don't look like factories," he said.

This was obviously something serious. I soon discovered that a new president had been named, and among his first official acts was the face-lift at company headquarters. Perfect. This was the kind of innovator I thought would go for a big idea. But before we went in to make our pitch, we did a little research.

I got hold of every story that had ever been written on this guy—from *Ad Age, The Wall Street Journal*, even from their own annual report. I also called his secretary to get a copy of every speech he ever made. From this, we put together a presentation that was basically a distillation of all of the concepts and ideas he had put forth in his articles and speeches. I used this as my opening and quickly worked my way toward the big idea. From the research, it developed that what he wanted was a magazine of his own where he could say just what he wanted to say in his own way. I told him we would do the whole package—writing, designing, setting the type, and even distribution. Because we'd bind it into the *Reader's Digest*, his "magazine" would instantly have a circulation equivalent to the biggest magazine in the world.

After we had finished our presentation, he leaned back in his chair. "You know," he said, "you seem to know more about what we're trying to achieve than anybody I've talked to." Which just goes to show you that if you come at people with ideas *they* formulated, they tend to think you're smart.

Source: Reprinted from "Strange Tales of Sales," *Sales & Marketing Management*, June 3, 1985, p. 45. Used by permission.

---

structure? Who is most influential? Which of them carry great influence but are opposed to us (often called **influential adversaries**)?

- What current problems does the organization face?
- What policies does the organization have regarding salespeople, sales visits, purchasing, and pricing?
- What is the organization's financial position and its future?
- In what stage in the buying cycle is the organization?
- What other firms might the organization be considering (i.e., who are the seller's potential competitors)?

It's your first day on the job as a new salesperson. You were handed a stack of blank prospecting forms and told to fill them out completely for each new prospect. Most of the information you are requested to secure seems to make a lot of sense. However, you notice that you are asked to find out each prospect's attitude about military service and the names of each prospect's children. You don't feel comfortable asking for this kind of very personal information. What are you going to do?

SOURCES OF INFORMATION

To gather all of the information listed above for every prospect and organization is initially impossible. The goal is to gather what is both possible and profitable. Remember, the salesperson's time is also valuable!

Much information will be in the lists and directories from which the prospect's name came. It is possible that some information was gleaned at a trade show the prospect attended. Libraries also provide a wealth of information about publicly traded firms. Databases (e.g., NEXIS[3]) to which the salesperson can subscribe are available and can provide a wealth of knowledge.

Secretaries and receptionists of the prospect's firm usually are a source of the richest information. Use caution, however, because these important people are accustomed to having salespeople pry for all sorts of free information. Prioritize your questions and provide justification for asking them. Above all, treat secretaries and receptionists with genuine respect.

Also talk to noncompeting salespeople. In fact, one of the best sources of information is the prospect's own salespeople. Sales trainer Lee Boyan notes that "They are easy to reach because they return phone calls, they understand your situation, and are usually empathetic."[4]

Many other sources can provide information. Check your company's files to see if the prospect has ever done business with you before. Review any direct inquiries made by the prospect (from direct mail inquiries, through the telemarketing division of your firm, etc.). A center of influence will often be able to provide some information. Occasionally, a prospect will be important enough to warrant hiring an outside consultant to gather some of this information.

Don't expect companies to sit down and give you all of this information. According to Phil Farris, president of a leading training organization, gone are the days when salespeople would familiarize themselves with a company by dropping by the office and interviewing some managers. "Now because of time demands, customers no longer have time to educate salespeople. They say, 'If you don't know this stuff, I don't want to deal with you.'"[5]

To demonstrate the creativity possible in gathering information, Harvey Mackay relates how his first boss taught him to learn about competitive activity. Harvey and his boss

> *drove to our arch competitor's plant. We parked about 50 yards away from the shipping department and waited until the trucks began to exit to make the day's deliveries. The rest of the day, we followed those trucks. By the end of the day, we had a good idea of our competition's local customer base, obtained in record time and at no cost.*[6]

SETTING CALL OBJECTIVES

The most important step in planning is to set objectives for the call. Merely stating the objective of making a sale will not suffice. The customer's decision-making process involves many steps, and salespeople need to undertake many activities as they guide customers through the process.

Yet, as Neil Rackham, an internationally respected sales researcher, notes, "It's astonishing how rarely salespeople set themselves call objectives of any kind—let alone effective ones. Although most books on selling emphasize the importance of clear call objectives, it's rare to see these exhortations turned into practice."[7] Why is this true? Probably because many salespeople want to start *doing something,* instead of "wasting time" *planning.* But without a plan, you actually increase your chances of wasting time.

As a first step in setting objectives, the salesperson should review what has been learned from precall information gathering. Any call objectives should be based on the results of this review.

CRITERIA FOR EFFECTIVE OBJECTIVES

All objectives should be specific, realistic, and measurable. A call objective that meets only one or two of these criteria will be an ineffective guide for the salesperson. We will now examine each criterion in more detail.

An objective must be specific to be effective. It should state exactly what the salesperson hopes to accomplish, whom the objective targets are, and any other details (suggested order quantity, suggested dates for future meetings, length of time needed for a follow-up survey, etc.). Specific objectives also help the salesperson avoid "shooting from the hip" during the presentation and perhaps moving the prospect along too rapidly or too slowly.

Objectives must also be realistic. Often inexperienced salespeople have unrealistic expectations about the prospect's or customer's response in the sales call. For example, if Ford Motor Co. is currently using Firestone tires on all their models, a B.F. Goodrich salesperson who expects Ford to change over to B.F. Goodrich tires in the first few sales calls would be unrealistic. For objectives to be realistic, the salesperson needs to consider cultural factors. For example, some firms have a corporate culture of being extremely conservative. Creating change in such a culture is very time consuming and often frustrating for the seller. The national culture also becomes very important in selling to international prospects. When selling to Arab or Japanese businesses, you should plan to spend at least several meetings getting to know the other party. Selling in Russia is often still slowed down due to bureaucracy and incredible amounts of red tape. As these examples illustrate, culture is an important consideration in attempts to set realistic call objectives.

Finally, call objectives must be measurable so that salespeople can evaluate each sales call at its conclusion and determine if the objectives were met. For example, if a salesperson's stated objective was to "get acquainted with the prospect" or "establish rapport," how would the salesperson assess whether this goal was achieved? How can someone measure "getting acquainted?" To what extent would the salesperson have to be acquainted with the prospect in order to know that he or she achieved the sales call

To have the prospect sign an order for 100 pair of Levi's jeans.

To have the prospect agree to come to the Atlanta branch office sometime during the next two weeks for a hands-on demonstration of the copier.

To set up another appointment for one week from now, at which time the buyer will allow me to do a complete survey of her printing needs.

To learn the names of all other key players in this decision that the prospect can identify.

To inform the doctor of the revolutionary anticlogging mechanism that has been incorporated into our new drug and have her agree to read the pamphlet I will leave.

To have the buyer agree to pass my information along to the buying committee with his endorsement of my proposal.

To have the prospect agree to call several references that I will provide in order to develop further confidence and trust in my office cleaning business.

To schedule a co-op newspaper advertising program to be implemented in the next month.

To have the prospect agree to use our brand of computer paper for a trial period of one month.

To have the prospect agree on the first point (of our four-point program) and schedule another meeting in two days with an agenda of discussing the second point.

To have the retailer agree to allow us space for an end-of-aisle display for the summer promotion of Raid insect repellent.

To have the prospect initiate the necessary paperwork to allow us to be considered as a future vendor.

To have me fully understand and appreciate the principal risks that adopting my product would pose to the buyer.

objective? A more measurable sales call objective (which is also more specific and realistic) would be something like the following: "To get acquainted with the prospect by learning what clubs or organizations he belongs to, what sports he follows, what his professional background is, and how long he has held the current position." With this revised call objective, a salesperson could very simply determine if the objective was reached.

An easy way to help ensure that objectives are measurable is to set objectives that require a buyer's response. For example, achieving the objective of "make a follow-up appointment with the buyer" is easy to measure.

Successful salespeople in almost every industry have learned the importance of setting proper call objectives. For example, Dr Pepper's salespeople are required to set objectives for each call that are specific, measurable, and achievable, as well as compatible with the company's objectives (e.g., to have the grocer set up an end-of-aisle display that holds 50 cases of Dr Pepper during the next week's promotional campaign).[8] Pharmaceutical salespeople for CIBA-Geigy also set very clear objectives for each sales call they make on a physician. Then they lay out a series of objectives for subsequent calls so that they know exactly what they hope to accomplish over the next several visits. Some experts recommend that salespeople write down their call objectives on a piece of paper and keep them in view while

EXHIBIT 8.2 MULTIPLE-CALL OBJECTIVES OF A PANASONIC SALESPERSON SELLING TO JOHNSON ELECTRONICS

Overall Plan Developed on Oct. 1		Actual Call Results	
Expected Date of the Call	**Call Objective**	**Date of Call**	**Call Results**
Oct. 10	Secure normal repeat orders on K33 and K555 tape decks. Increase normal repeat order of K431 CD player from three to five units. Provide product information for new videodisk product V500.	Oct. 10	Obtained normal order of K33. Steve decided to drop K555 (refused to give a good reason). Only purchased four K431 players. Seemed responsive to V500 but needs a point-of-purchase (POP) display.
Oct. 17	Erect a front-counter POP display for V500 and secure a trial order of two units.	Oct. 18	Steve was out. His assistant didn't like the POP (thought it was too large!). Refused to use POP. Did order one V500. Told me about several complaints with K431.
Nov. 10	Secure normal repeat orders for K33, K555, and K431. Schedule one co-op newspaper ad for the next 30 days featuring V500. Secure an order for 10 V500s.	Nov. 8	Obtained normal orders. Steve agreed to co-op ad but only bought 5 V500s. Thinks the margins are too low.
Nov. 17	Secure normal repeat orders on K33, K555, and K431. Secure an order for 20 V500s.	Nov. 18	Obtained normal order on K33, but Steve refused to reorder K431. Claimed the competitor product (Sony) is selling much better. Obtained an order of 15 units of V500.

they are on the sales call. Having the objectives in sight helps the salesperson focus on the true goals of the sales call.[9] All of these examples have a common theme: The salesperson realizes the importance of setting specific, realistic, measurable call objectives. Exhibit 8.1 lists examples of call objectives that meet the above criteria.

SETTING OBJECTIVES FOR SEVERAL CALLS

By developing a series of very specific objectives for future calls, the salesperson can develop a comprehensive strategy for the prospect or customer. Exhibit 8.2 gives a set of call objectives for several visits over a period of time. The left side of the exhibit contains the long-term plan and each call objective that the Panasonic salesperson developed for Johnson Electronics. Note the logical strategy for introducing the new product, V500. On the right side of Exhibit 8.2 appear the actual call results.

The salesperson was not always 100 percent successful in achieving the call objectives; several subsequent ones needed to be modified. For example, because the meeting on October 10 resulted in the buyer dropping K555 tape decks, the call objectives on November 10 and November 17 needed to reflect that K555 was no longer a product carried by Johnson Electronics. The seller may also want to add a call objective for October 17, to

Even if the salesperson fails to achieve his primary call objective, he will be encouraged if he at least achieves his minimum call objective.

Courtesy Colgate-Palmolive Company.

discuss more about the situation with K555 (because of the outcome of the October 10 meeting) and perhaps try to reintroduce it. This example illustrates the importance of keeping good records, making any necessary adjustments in the long-term call objectives, and then preparing for the next sales call.

John Kirwan, a consultant specializing in major account selling, recommends that a salesperson include the following considerations when developing multicall objectives and strategies:[10]

- Have you made contact with all the key players? (If not, what will you say and how will you say it?)
- Do you understand all the business, technical, political, and personal issues involved? (If not, how can you discover them?)
- Do you know what your competitor's strengths, weaknesses, and strategies are? (If not, how will you learn?)

The key is to include consideration of these and related informational issues when setting multicall objectives.

Jim Hersma, sales vice president for a large sales force, has some specific advice about setting objectives:

The key objective of the first session is to have another chance to visit. What this allows you to do is have your standards relatively low because you are trying to build a long-term relationship. You should be very sensitive to an opportunity to establish a second visit. What you want to do is identify aspects of the business conversation that require follow up and make note of them . . . The key is not the first visit . . . it is the second, the third, the twenty-second visit.[11]

SETTING MORE THAN ONE CALL OBJECTIVE

Some salespeople have learned the importance of setting multiple objectives for a sales call. For example, I. Martin Jacknis, the president of Results Marketing, Inc., not only sets a **primary call objective** (the actual goal he hopes to achieve) before each sales call, he also sets a **minimum call objective** (the minimum he hopes to achieve). He realizes that at times the call does not go exactly as planned because sometimes a prospect is called away, the salesperson does not have all the facts necessary, and so forth. Although rarely met, a **visionary call objective,** the most optimistic objective that could occur, is also set. For example, the primary call objective of a Nestlé Foods rep might be to secure an order from a grocer for 10 cases of Nestlé Morsels for an upcoming coupon promotion. A minimum call objective would be to sell at least 5 cases, whereas a visionary call objective would be to sell 20 cases, set up an end-of-aisle display, and secure a retail price of $2.19.

Jacknis notes several benefits of multiple call objectives. First, they help take away the salesperson's fear of failure; most salespeople can at least achieve their stated minimum objective. Second, multiple objectives tend to be self-correcting. Salespeople who always reach their visionary objective realize they are probably setting their sights too low. On the other hand, if they rarely meet even their minimum objective, they probably are setting their goals too high.[12]

MAKING AN APPOINTMENT

After collecting information about the prospect and the prospect's firm and setting objectives, the next step is generally to make an appointment. Many sales managers insist that their salespeople make appointments before calling on prospects or customers. They have found from experience that working by appointment saves valuable selling time. One large sales organization has estimated that advance appointments increase the effectiveness of their sales force by at least one-third.

Appointments dignify the salesperson. Appointments get the sales process off to a good start by putting the salesperson and the prospect on the same level—equal participants in a legitimate sales interview. Appointments also increase the chances of seeing the right person and having uninterrupted time with the prospect. This section will describe how to see the right person at the right time and the right place, how to work through barriers, and how to phone for an appointment.

HOW TO MAKE APPOINTMENTS

Experienced sales representatives use different contact methods for different customers. They have found through trial and error that a certain method of making an appointment works well with a regular customer but may be entirely ineffective with a new prospect. (Keep in mind that in multicall situations, an appointment for the next call is usually made at the conclusion of the visit.) They have also found that knowledge of many different methods and techniques of making appointments is extremely helpful in obtaining sales interviews. Some of the basic principles and techniques are discussed here.

It is usually best to make an appointment for the next visit at the end of a call.

Sharon Hoogstraten.

▍THE RIGHT PERSON

Some experts argue the importance of going right to the top. When *Sales and Marketing Management* asked its Executive Advisory Panel "Should salespeople go over the heads of purchasing agents?" the majority responded with a conditional "Yes."[13] Terry Booten, a seasoned salesperson and sales training consultant agrees: "After years of selling there's a rule I always stick to: When I'm making my initial sales call, I go right to the top executive."[14] Why this advice? Booten notes several reasons: The president is most likely the one signing or at least okaying the check, it's the president's job to grow the business, only the president knows what the president really wants, the president knows the company's buying and investment criteria, and the president is usually the nicest person.

After carefully studying over 35,000 sales calls, Neil Rackham offers a radically different view from those just mentioned.[15] His research suggests that a salesperson should initially try to call on the **focus of receptivity,** that person who will listen receptively and provide the seller with needed valuable information. Note that this person may not be the decision maker or the one who understands all of the problems of the firm. The focus of receptivity, according to the research, will then lead the salesperson to the **focus of dissatisfaction,** the person who is most likely to perceive problems and dissatisfactions. Finally, the focus of dissatisfaction leads to the **focus of power,** that person who can approve action, prevent action, and/or influence action. Getting to the focus of power too quickly can lead to disaster, because the seller has not built a relationship and really learned the buyer's needs. In summary, Rackham notes that "There's a superstition in selling that the sooner you can get to the decision maker the better. Effective selling, so it's said, is going straight to the focus of power. That's a questionable belief."[16]

Of course, nothing is more frustrating that thinking you are making a final presentation only to realize you are not talking to the decision maker. To illustrate, a Nekoosa paper salesperson for years called mainly on printers. After a careful analysis of sales records and the sales potential, the salesperson concluded that the territory was not producing maximum sales volume. Many sales were lost because the printers lacked the authority to specify the brand of paper used by their clients. The sales representative solved this problem by contacting the printers' sales reps and finding out from them which clients normally specified a certain brand of paper when placing printing orders. The paper sales rep then contacted those printers' clients directly and explained the merits of the company's products to them.

 Is it okay to bypass normal channels when making calls? In other words, do firms frown on salespeople who bypass the traditional routine? The answer depends on many factors. Cultural norms always play a part. When asked if it is generally okay to bypass hierarchial lines, 75 percent of the Italians said "No," whereas only 22 percent of the Swedes said "No" (in the United States, 32 percent said "No").[17]

Frequently in industrial selling situations, no one person has the sole authority to buy a product. The salesperson may first be required to obtain the approval of a line organization representative or of an operating committee. For example, a forklift sales representative for Clarke found that he had to see the safety engineer, the methods engineer, the materials-handling engineer, and the general superintendent before he could sell the product to a certain manufacturing company. In this case, the salesperson should try to arrange a meeting with the entire group as well as with each individual.

▌ THE RIGHT TIME

Much has been written about the best time of day for sales interviews. Certain salespeople claim the best time to see prospects is right after lunch, when they are likely to be in a pleasant mood. Others try to get as many appointments as they can during the early morning hours because they believe the prospects or customers will be in a better frame of mind then. There is little agreement on this subject, for obviously the most opportune time to call will vary by customer and type of selling. The salesperson who calls on wholesale grocers, for example, may find from experience that the best time to call is from 9 AM to 11 AM and from 1:30 PM to 3:30 PM. A hospital rep, on the other hand, may discover that the most productive calls on surgeons are made between the hours of 8:30 AM and 10 AM and after 4 PM.

For most types of selling, the best hours of the day are from approximately 9 AM to 11:30 AM and from 1:30 PM to 4 PM. This is particularly true for business executives, who like to have the first part of the day free to read their mail and answer correspondence and the latter part of the day free to read and sign their letters. (Chapter 16 will provide more information about the proper time to make calls.)

Although the above hours may be the most favorable, salespeople need not restrict appointments to these times. Each soon learns the most favorable hours and days for each customer.

S E L L I N G   S C E N A R I O

8.2

Is This a Good Place to Make a Presentation?

Lisa Cole, a hospital specialist for Abbott Laboratories, describes how some environments can be distracting for making a presentation.

"Selling to the hospital industry is not always different for a woman than for a man. The traditional stereotypes of male doctors and female nurses have been rapidly dispersed in the past decade, and it's very common in urban hospitals to have relatively equal distribution.

"On some occasions, however, I have found that being a woman called for a little reshuffling of plans. For example, a couple of months ago, a doctor expressed an interest in seeing a product I carry. I made arrangements through the proper channels, per hospital policies, to show the product in the unit doctors' lounge the following Monday.

"When I showed up with the product, the doctor was rather shocked to discover that I was a woman. I had scheduled the appointment at his request with his receptionist, and she must have referred to me as 'the Abbott rep.' He was genuinely embarrassed as he explained that the unit doctors' lounge was also the dressing room. I agreed that I knew the product backward and forward—but I had never presented it blindfolded on a Monday morning! After we all had a few laughs, we moved the display and presentation to the general doctors' lounge, and it worked out great."

Source: Adapted from Lisa M. Cole, "What Do You Say to a Naked Doctor?" *Sales & Marketing Management,* April 1, 1985, p. 40. Used by permission.

THE RIGHT PLACE

The sales call must take place in an environment conducive to doing business. Often the salesperson has no say in where the call will take place. When appropriate, however, the salesperson should choose a place free of distraction for all parties. Selling Scenario 8.2 illustrates what can happen if this aspect of the call is not planned properly.

CULTIVATING RELATIONSHIPS WITH SUBORDINATES

Busy executives usually have one or more subordinates who plan and schedule interviews for them. These **barriers,** or **screens** as salespeople sometimes call them, often make seeing the boss rather difficult. For example, a secretary, usually feeling responsible for conserving his or her superior's time, tries to discover the true purpose of each salesperson's visit before granting an interview with the boss.

Salespeople should go out of their way to treat all subordinates with respect and courtesy. Why? First, because it is the right thing to do. Second, because they can truly be the key to your success or failure at their organization. They may not be able to buy your product, but they can often kill your chances for a sale.

Sales strategies have identified three basic ways of interacting with the screen. The salesperson can go "over the screen" by dropping names of people higher up in the organization. This might result in the screen allowing the seller in to see the boss right away for fear of getting into trouble. Or the salesperson can go "under the screen" by trying to make contact

Salespeople should work toward achieving a friendly relationship with the prospect's subordinates.

Courtesy Citibank.

with the prospect before or after the screen gets to work (or while the screen is on break). Finally, the salesperson can work "through the screen" by simply involving the screen in the process.

THINKING IT THROUGH	*D*o you see problems in working "over the screen"? How about working "under the screen"? What might this do to long-term relationship development?

TELEPHONING FOR APPOINTMENTS

There are several ways of making an appointment: in person, by mail, or by phone. Making an initial appointment in person would be nice (i.e., you could gather more precall information) but is usually too time consuming for the salesperson. Using the mail requires a lot of lead time and may also result in getting your letter misplaced or unread in the "junk mail" clutter. Therefore, the phone is most often used to make the initial appointment. Salespeople can save many hours by phoning to make appointments. But they need to use that instrument correctly and effectively. All of us have used telephones since childhood; many of us have developed bad habits that reduce our effectiveness when talking over the phone. Exhibit 8.3 presents a scenario for using the phone to make an appointment.

A potential customer might have objections—reasons for not granting an interview. The goal of the telephone call, however, is to make an appointment, not to sell the product or service. Exhibit 8.4 shows appropriate responses to common objections Xerox copier salespeople encounter when making appointments.

EXHIBIT 8.3

USING THE TELEPHONE TO
GAIN AN APPOINTMENT

1. State customer's name.	"Hello, Mr. Walker?" *(pause)*
2. State your name.	"This is Glen Scott, with Gamma Industries."
3. Check time.	"Did I call at a convenient time, or should I call later?" *(pause)*
4. State purpose and make presentation.	"I'm calling to let you know about our new office copier. It has more features than the present copiers and could be a real money saver."
5. Close.	"Could you put me on your calendar for 30 minutes next Monday or Tuesday?"
6. Show appreciation, restate time, or keep door open.	"Thank you, Mr. Walker. I'll be at your office at 9 AM on Tuesday."
	[or]
	"I appreciate your frankness, Mr. Walker. I'd like to get back to you in a couple of months. Would that be all right?"

EXHIBIT 8.4

RESPONSES TO OBJECTIONS
CONCERNING
APPOINTMENTS

Objection from a Secretary	Response
"I'm sorry, but Mr. Wilkes is busy now."	"What I have to say will only take a few minutes. Should I call back in a half-hour, or would you suggest I set up an appointment?"
"We already have a copier."	"That's fine. I want to talk to Mr. Wilkes about our new paper-flow system design for companies like yours."
"I take care of all the copying."	"That's fine, but I'm here to present what Xerox has to offer for a complete paper-flow system that integrates data transmission, report generation, and copiers. I'd like to speak to Mr. Wilkes about this total service."

Objection from the Prospect	Response
"Can't you mail the information to me?"	"Yes, I could. But everyone's situation is different, Mr. Wilkes, and our systems are individually tailored to meet the needs of each customer. Now . . . *[benefit statement and repeat request for appointment].*"
"Well, what is it you want to talk about?"	"It's difficult to explain the system over the telephone. In 15 minutes, I can demonstrate the savings you get from the system."
"You'd just be wasting your time. I'm not interested."	The general objection is hiding a specific objection. The salesperson needs to probe for the specific objection: "Do you say that because you don't copy many documents?"
"We had a Xerox copier once and didn't like it."	Probe for the specific reason of dissatisfaction and have a reply, but don't go too far. The objective is to get an appointment, not sell a copier.

Source: Courtesy of Xerox Corporation. Used by permission.

When salespeople call for appointments, prospects frequently ask questions about the product or service. But the salesperson should not be drawn into giving a sales presentation over the telephone. Again, the purpose of the call is to obtain an appointment, not to make a sale. In fact, some firms use their telemarketing staff to set appointments for salespeople in order to avoid being drawn into a complete sales presentation.

Some salespeople have their secretaries make telephone appointments for them. This often gives them greater prestige in the mind of the prospect or customer. If the secretary cannot obtain an appointment, the salesperson may make a second call, using a different approach.

At times, salespeople may have to use determination, persistence, and ingenuity to obtain interviews, but they should never resort to deceitful or dishonest tactics. The use of subterfuge to obtain appointments has no place in modern selling. Salespeople who select prospects carefully in terms of product needs should not have to conceal the purpose of the visit.

SUMMARY

This chapter stresses the importance of planning the sales call. Developing a clear plan saves time for both salespeople and customers. In addition, it helps salespeople increase their confidence and reduce strain.

As part of the planning process, salespeople need to gather as much information about the prospect as possible before the first call. They need information both about the individual prospect and about the prospect's organization. Sources of this information include lists and directories, secretaries and receptionists, noncompeting salespeople, direct inquiries made by the prospect, and other sources.

An effective call objective should be specific, realistic, and measurable. In situations requiring several calls, the salesperson should develop a plan with call objectives for each future call. Also, many salespeople benefit from setting multiple levels of objectives—primary, minimum, and visionary—for each call.

As a general rule, salespeople should make appointments before calling on customers. In this way, the salespeople can be sure they will talk to the right person.

A number of methods can be used for making appointments. Perhaps the most effective is the straightforward telephone approach. This includes stating the salesperson's name, establishing a link with the prospect or customer, stating the purpose of the call, and asking for an appointment.

KEY TERMS

barriers 246
focus of dissatisfaction 244
focus of power 244
focus of receptivity 244
influential adversaries 237

minimum call objective 243
primary call objective 243
screens 246
visionary call objective 243

QUESTIONS AND PROBLEMS

1. Suppose you belong to an organization that plans to hold an event for charity. In order for the event to be a success, it will need a great deal of community support, especially from local business.
   a. What sources would you use to identify potential sponsors?
   b. What information do you need to qualify them properly?

2. Setting call objectives takes time and effort on the part of the salesperson. Are there any situations in which it would not make sense for a salesperson to set a call objective? If so, what are they?

3. "Setting call objectives reduces my ability to be adaptable during the call." Respond to this salesperson's statement.

4. Evaluate the following objectives for a sales call:
    a. Show and demonstrate the entire line of 15 grinding wheels.
    b. Find out more about competitors' services under consideration.
    c. Increase the buyer's trust in my company.
    d. Determine which service the prospect is currently using and how much it costs.
    e. Have the buyer agree to hold our next meeting at some third location (other than either party's office).
    f. Get an order for 20 KA30 water purifiers.
    g. Make the buyer more comfortable with the fact that our firm has only been in business for one year.

5. Think for a moment about trying to secure a job. Assume you are going to have your second job interview next week with IBM for a sales position. Most candidates go through a set of four interviews. List your primary objective, minimum objective, and visionary objective.

6. Why is making appointments before visiting a customer desirable? Under what circumstances might the salesperson not need to make appointments?

7. Assume you are trying to sell air compressors to a large construction contractor. Your boss listed three possible objectives for your next call: sell two air compressors, sell 10 air compressors, and have the prospect watch a demonstration. Which is probably the primary objective, the minimum objective, and the visionary objective?

8. Evaluate the following approach for getting an appointment: "Mr. White, I'm going to be working in this area next week. When can I come by to tell you about our new product?"

9. Much attention is given to the best time of day for sales interviews. List the best time of day to call on the following types of individuals:
    a. A college professor (to sell textbooks).
    b. A lawyer (to sell investigative services).
    c. A product manager (to sell magazine ad space).
    d. A janitor (to sell janitorial supplies).
    e. A senior buyer at a grocery store's corporate headquarters (to sell a new food product).
    f. A computer operations supervisor (to sell repair services).
    g. An accountant (to sell fax machines).

10. Review the list of prospects in question 9 and identify:
    a. The worst time of day to call on each type of individual.
    b. The worst time of year to call on each type of individual.

CASE PROBLEMS

CASE 8 • 1
DUPLEX BUSINESS FORMS

Duplex distributes business forms for almost every office and business need. The company's main office is in the Chicago area. It sells products through regional and district offices in the United States. Sales representatives are usually assigned to specific geographic areas. However, in some larger cities, they are assigned certain key customers.

Robin Berglund, who sells in the Minneapolis area, has been with the company for 30 years and is planning to retire in six months. In general, he has done a fairly good job in his territory. 3M, however, has never given any business to Duplex. Berglund has called on the purchasing agent regularly but has never been able to obtain an order for Duplex business forms. The purchasing agent has told Berglund on several occasions that it is impossible to give Duplex any business because 3M has entered into an exclusive agreement for all printing work with a local concern, Twin Cities Printing. Berglund has heard indirectly that the Twin Cities Printing sales representative is a close friend of the purchasing agent.

Tammy Baumann has been a sales representative for Duplex for eight years. She worked three years in the Chicago area and during the last five years has been in the San Francisco area. Baumann, an excellent sales rep, has a fine background in office systems and methods work. The eastern regional sales executive has told Baumann she will take over Berglund's territory in Minneapolis when Berglund retires. Plans call for Baumann to work with Berglund in the Minneapolis area during the last month of his service. Telling Baumann of her new assignment, the sales manager said she wanted Berglund to introduce Baumann to the regular customers in the new territory. In addition she said, "Tammy, I want you to concentrate on getting some business from 3M. There is no reason why we shouldn't be getting some of that business. I told Berglund that I wanted you to spend whatever time was necessary to break that account open for us."

QUESTIONS

1. Assume that you are Tammy Baumann. List your call objectives for your first call with 3M. Develop a three-call follow-up schedule and list the objectives for each call.

2. What kind of information would you like to know about 3M? How could you obtain that information?

3. Assume the purchasing agent suggests that you call directly on 3M's vice president of purchasing. Also assume the purchasing agent refuses to help set up this meeting. Describe in detail how you would go about making such an appointment.

CASE 8 • 2
JUSTIN FOOD PRODUCTS

While Dan Erickson attended college, he worked nights at a large wholesale grocery warehouse operation, loading tractor-trailer trucks. The growth of sales of prepared salads so impressed him that he decided to go to work for Justin Food Products after he graduated. Justin Food, with $200 million in annual sales, is one of the largest national manufacturers of fresh salad products (prepackaged and refrigerated coleslaw, potato salad, chip dip, etc.).

After successfully selling for Justin Food for three years, Dan was promoted to key account manager for the Chicago region. In that position, he is responsible for calling on the corporate headquarters of some of the largest chains in the area. One of his toughest assignments is to get the Justin Food line of products into the Jewel Food Stores chain, which operates approximately 200 supermarkets in his region. According to past records, he needs to see Sarah Beckel, senior grocery buyer for Jewel and the key to getting the Justin Food line into the stores. Brian Davis, the president of Justin Food, made several calls on Beckel a few years ago but was not successful in getting the line into the Jewel stores.

Dan has scheduled an appointment with Sarah Beckel for three weeks from today. Over the phone, she was very noncommittal and seemed only mildly interested. She did mention that Jewel currently carries the LaBrother (a small regional supplier) line of prepared salads but that sales have been weak. She hinted that she leans toward deleting the LaBrother line and not replacing it, because primary demand for this type of product seems so small. Dan knows, though, that other grocery stores in his area actually exhibit strong demand for his products.

QUESTIONS

1. What kind of information should Dan gather about Sarah Beckel before he meets with her?

2. What kind of information should Dan gather about Jewel Food Stores before his meeting with Sarah?

3. What sources can Dan use to gather the needed information?

ADDITIONAL REFERENCES

Dunn, Dan T, Jr., and Claude A Thomas. "Strategy for Systems Sellers: A Grid Approach." *Journal of Personal Selling and Sales Management*, August 1986, pp. 1–10.

Fahner, Hal. "Call Reports That Tell It All." *Sales & Marketing Management*, November 12, 1984, pp. 50–53.

Grewal, Dhruv, and Arun Sharma. "The Effect of Salesforce Behavior on Customer Satisfaction: An Interactive Framework." *Journal of Personal Selling and Sales Management*, Summer 1991, pp. 13–24.

Henry, Porter. *Secrets of the Master Sellers.* New York: AMACOM, 1987.

Hunt, James M and Michael F Smith. "The Persuasive Impact of Two-Sided Selling Appeals for an Unknown Brand Name." *Journal of the Academy of Marketing Science*, Spring 1987, pp. 11–18.

Ingram, Thomas N; Charles H Schwepker, Jr.; and Don Hutson. "Why Salespeople Fail." *Industrial Marketing Management*, 1992, pp. 225–30.

Johnson, Mark. "How Computerization Can Organize a Sales Force: A System That Makes Planning Easy." *Business Marketing*, December 1985, pp. 98–100.

King, Ronald H, and Martha B Booze. "Sales Training and Impression Management." *Journal of Personal Selling and Sales Management*, August 1986, pp. 51–60.

Mayo, Edward, and Lance P Jarvis. "The Power of Persuasion: Lessons in Personal Selling from the White House." *Journal of Personal Selling and Sales Management*, Fall 1992, pp. 1–8.

O'Hara, Bradley S; James S Boles; and Mark W Johnston. "The Influence of Personal Variables on Salesperson Selling Orientation." *Journal of Personal Selling and Sales Management*, Winter 1991, pp. 61–68.

Reilly, Kate, and Eric Baron. "Teaching Salespeople the Five 'W's and the 'H' of Sales Call Planning." *Business Marketing*, August 1987, pp. 62–70.

Senne, Jeffrey. "Say Goodbye to Willie Loman." *Bank Marketing*, December 1988, pp. 23–24.

Sonnenberg, Frank K. "Presentations That Persuade." *Journal of Business Strategy*, September–October 1988, pp. 55–58.

Wilson, Harrell. "Over There: On Being a Stranger in a Strange Land." *Success*, May 1993, p. 8.

Wotruba, Thomas R. "The Evolution of Personal Selling." *Journal of Personal Selling and Sales Management*, Summer 1991, pp. 1–12.

Wotruba, Thomas R, and Stephen B Castleberry. "Job Analysis and Hiring Practices for National Account Marketing Positions." *Journal of Personal Selling and Sales Management*, Summer 1993, pp. 49–65.

Making the Sales Call

*A*t this point in the sales process, we assume that an appointment has been made, sufficient information about the prospect and his or her organization has been gathered, and the salesperson has developed strong objectives for the call. In this chapter, we will discuss how to make the actual sales call. (Exhibit 9.1 provides an organizing framework for our discussion.)

We will consider how to make a good impression and begin developing a long-term relationship. Also included is an examination of the initial needs assessment phase of a relationship and how to relate solutions to those needs. Finally, this chapter discusses the salesperson's need to be adaptable in order to make the sales call effectively.

Some questions answered in this chapter are:

How should the initial approach be made in order to make a good impression and gain the prospect's attention?

How can salespeople develop rapport and increase source credibility?

Why is discovering the prospect's needs important, and how can a salesperson accomplish this?

How can the salesperson most effectively relate the product/service features to the prospect's needs?

Why is it important in the call for the salesperson to make adjustments? How does the seller recognize that adjustments are needed?

Ron Woodyard attended the University of Georgia and graduated with a BBA in marketing in 1985. At that time, marketing included personal selling and sales management classes, and he felt that he would have a head start on a quality sales position after graduation. The pharmaceutical industry appealed to him because it is an ever-evolving, highly technical field that is virtually recession-proof. That is, there will always be a strong demand for high-quality pharmaceutical products. After researching several companies, Ron chose Pfizer Laboratories. It is recognized industrywide as having the most efficient, well-trained sales force to sell market-leading products. Pfizer's compensation package is also at the top of the industry.

In his five years with Pfizer, Woodyard has won numerous awards at the district (eight), regional (two), and national (three) levels and has been named to the exclusive Pacesetter Club three times. In addition, he has won several convention trips in which he was able to take his wife to exotic resort areas. As a result of his outstanding performance, he was promoted to the position of District Sales Manager.

"One important axiom in selling is that it is more of a science than an art. Rewards usually correlate directly with the number of calls made, the amount of time generated with each call, and the salesperson's ability to uncover and satisfy the needs of the customer.

"My first step in selling is to develop a weekly call itinerary. I prospect and gain all of the precall information I can about physicians so I make sure that I am calling on the most important, high-prescribing physicians most often. I then use this information to plan my individual

RON WOODYARD

Pfizer Labs

calls and set call objectives. For example, if Dr. Jones is a high prescriber of arthritic medications and he generally uses a competitor's drug first and my drug second, my objective for the next call would be to convince him to use my drug first, by showing a 'net gain' with my product when compared to my competitor's product.

"When I am in the doctor's office, I coach myself to listen intently to uncover important needs and adapt my presentation to those needs. I also sell benefits, not features. A doctor uses a drug not because it is given once daily but because it improves patient compliance to the medication. I always use a visual aid and demonstrate how my products work, which provides much better retention of the material I am covering.

"Perhaps the most exciting part of the call is uncovering and successfully responding to product objections. I was taught that 'an objection is nothing more than an opportunity in disguise.' Objections help me uncover needs, satisfy those needs, and gain commitment to use my product.

"Obtaining commitment is the most important part of my sales call. The close is simply finding out what the doctor uses and asking him to do something different. The one thing that differentiates the top performer from the average performer is the ability to ask for the business.

"Finally, by effectively practicing the above-mentioned variables for selling, the physician perceives me as a useful tool for increasing his or her product knowledge rather than as an absolute waste of time. Hence solid, long-term relationships are established."

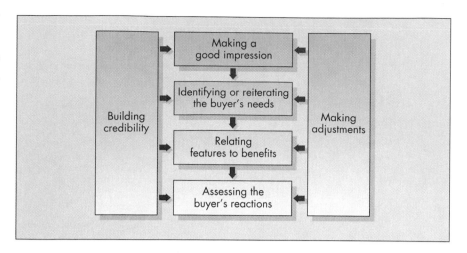

MAKING A GOOD IMPRESSION

Successful salespeople have learned the importance of making a good impression. When reps fail to arrive on time, make a poor entrance, fail to gain the buyer's interest, or lack rapport-building skill, it is difficult for them to secure commitment and build partnerships.[1] This section discusses how salespeople can manage the buyer's impression of them, often called **impression management.**

One of the most important ways of improving the buyer's impression is for the seller to be well prepared (as we discussed in Chapter 8). Some salespeople actually have a checklist of things to take to the presentation so they won't forget anything.

WAITING FOR THE PROSPECT

Being on time for your planned sales call is absolutely critical in order to avoid giving the buyer a negative impression. Because of this, salespeople often arrive a few minutes early and have to wait to see the prospect. Further, the prospect occasionally is running behind and lets the salesperson wait beyond the appointment time. Either or both scenarios can result in salespeople sitting and waiting, sometimes for long periods, for their prospects to see them.

Every salesperson must expect to spend a certain portion of each working day waiting for sales interviews. Successful salespeople make the best possible use of this time by working on reports, studying new-product information, planning and preparing for their next calls, and obtaining additional information about the prospect. (Chapter 16 covers time management more fully.)

Some sales managers instruct their sales representatives not to wait for any prospect, in normal circumstances, more than 15 minutes after the appointment time. Exceptions are necessary, of course, depending on the importance of the customer and the distance the salesperson has traveled. In all cases, salespeople should keep the sales call in perspective, realizing that their time is also valuable. (Chapter 16 discusses just how valuable that time really is!)

Sales calls can occur in practically every location.

Courtesy Kimberly-Clark Corporation.

Reproduced with permission of AT&T.

Courtesy 3M.

When the salesperson arrives, the receptionist may merely say, "I'll tell Mr. Jones that you are here." After the receptionist has spoken with Mr. Jones, the salesperson should ask approximately how long it will be. When the wait will be excessive and/or the salesperson has another appointment, it may be advisable to explain this tactfully and to ask for another appointment. Usually the secretary either will try to get the salesperson in to see the prospect more quickly or will make arrangements for a later appointment.

THE ENTRANCE

The first two minutes a salesperson spends with a prospect can be very important. Making a favorable first impression usually produces a prospect who is willing to listen. A negative first impression, on the other hand, sets up a barrier that may never be hurdled.

The entrance, like the presentation itself, can occur anywhere. For someone selling portable cellular telephones, for example, it can occur in a traditional office setting, with a farmer on his or her combine or tractor, or in the yard of a tow truck operator. The key is for the salesperson to be adaptable to the situation and to make an effective entrance for that particular scenario.

VERY FIRST IMPRESSIONS

Many salespeople make a poor impression without realizing it. They may know their customer's needs and their own product, but they overlook seemingly insignificant things that can create negative impressions. To avoid this, Ann Sabath suggests that salespeople use the business etiquette "Rules of Twelve":[2]

- The salesperson's 12 first words should include a form of "Thank you" (e.g., "Thank you for seeing me").
- The 12 inches from the shoulders up should suggest high-quality grooming (e.g., hair, collar, etc. are neat).
- The 12 first footsteps should reflect confidence by using erect posture, a lengthy stride, and a brisk pace.

And don't forget to smile! Watch what happens when you look at some-one and smile. In 99 out of 100 times, you will receive a smile in return.[3]

It is also important to remember prospects' names and how to pro-nounce them. There are many ways to try to remember names (e.g., you can associate their name with an animal that looks like they do). The key is to pronounce the prospect's name correctly.

THINKING IT THROUGH	*A*ssume you walk into a prospect's office very confidently, using erect posture and walking at a strong pace. When you offer your hand, you suddenly notice that the prospect is handicapped and has no right arm. What should you do and/or say?

▌ HANDSHAKING

Salespeople should not automatically extend their hand to a prospect, par-ticularly if the prospect is seated.[4] Shaking hands should be the prospect's choice. If the prospect offers a hand, the salesperson should respond with a firm but not overpowering handshake. We all remember the feeling of a limpid handshake—shaking a hand with little or no grip—or of a steel grip. Either impression is often lasting and negative. If you tend to have sweaty hands, carry a handkerchief.

Women should shake hands in the same manner as men. They should avoid offering their hand for a social handshake (palm facing down and level with the ground, with fingers drooping and pointing to the ground). Also, men should do nothing to force a social handshake from a woman in a business setting.

The salesperson selling in an international context needs to carefully consider cultural norms regarding the appropriateness of handshaking, bowing, and other forms of greeting. For example, the Chinese prefer no more than a slight bow in their greeting, while an Arab businessman may

---

Women should shake hands in the same manner as men.

Sharon Hoogstraten.

not only shake hands vigorously but also keep holding your hand for several seconds. A hug in Mexico communicates a trusting relationship, while for Germans such a gesture would be offensive because it suggests an inappropriate level of intimacy.

THE APPROPRIATE STANCE

When salespeople stand in front of their prospects, they must not appear to be either insecure or overly aggressive. A confident appearance can be achieved by:

Keeping feet about 12 inches apart to improve stability.

Standing at a 45- to 90-degree angle to the customer. Standing straight across from the customer can seem overly threatening.

Keeping the shoulders relaxed, and the arms off of the hips.

Standing 2 to 4 feet from the customer. Standing too close can be seen as threatening, while standing too far away gives an impersonal feeling.

As with handshaking, these guidelines need to be modified for regional and cultural differences. In some rural areas, hands on the hips indicate a relaxed posture and suggest a certain degree of informality and friendship. Arabs would probably see your hands on your hips as a threat or challenge. In Latin America, culture dictates that business conversations occur much closer than 2 to 4 feet.

SELECTING A SEAT

Many calls will not involve sitting down at all (e.g., talking to a store manager in a grocery store aisle, conversing with a foreman in a warehouse, asking questions of a surgeon in a post-op ward). When you will be seated for a call, the best arrangement is around a small table or at the side of the customer's desk. Salespeople need to be seated so they can observe all five channels of nonverbal communication—body angle, face, arms, hands, and legs (see Chapter 5)—and show brochures and other visual aids from a comfortable position.

When selecting a seat it is a good idea to look around and start to identify the prospect's social style and status (see Chapter 6), but be careful. For example, in the United States important decision makers usually have large, well-appointed private offices. In Kuwait, a high-ranking businessperson may have a small office and lots of interruptions. Don't take that to mean he or she is a low-ranking employee or is not interested.

Asking permission to sit down is usually unnecessary. The salesperson should read the prospect's nonverbal cues to determine the right time to be seated.

GETTING THE CUSTOMER'S ATTENTION

Getting the customer's attention is not a new concept. It is also the goal of many other activities you are familiar with (e.g., advertising, making new friends, writing an English composition, giving a speech).

Time is very valuable to prospects, and they concentrate their attention on the first few minutes with a salesperson to determine whether they will benefit from the interaction. The first few words the salesperson says often set the tone of the entire sales call. The **halo effect** (how and what you do in one thing changes a person's perceptions about other things you do) seems to operate in many sales calls. If you are perceived as effective at the beginning of the call, you will be perceived by the prospect as effective during the rest of the sales call (and vice versa).

Some experts argue that the customer's name should be used in the opening statement. Dale Carnegie, a master at developing relationships, said a person's name is "the sweetest and most important sound" to that person. Using a person's name indicates respect and a recognition of the unique qualities of the person. Others disagree with this logic. They claim that using the person's name, especially more than once in any length of time, sounds phony and insincere. Perhaps the best approach is to use the prospect's name in the opening, then use it sparingly during the rest of the call.

Some approaches to opening a sales call are described below. An **approach** is a method designed to get the prospect's attention and interest quickly and to make a smooth transition into the presentation topic. Because each prospect and sales situation differs, salespeople should be adaptable, able to use any of a variety of openings.

Introduction Approach

In the **introduction approach,** salespeople state their name and the name of their company, and they may hand the prospect their business card. Handing the prospect a business card helps the prospect remember the salesperson's name and firm. Prospects may not hear the name because they are busy sizing up the salesperson. Some salespeople think a business card can be distracting, and find that giving their card at the end of the interview is more effective.

The introduction approach is the simplest and perhaps least effective way of opening a sales call, because it is unlikely to generate much interest. It is used most often in conjunction with other methods. Here is a basic introduction approach:

"Mr. Fontaine, my name is John Locklear, and I'm with Best Foods."

Referral Approach

Using the name of a satisfied customer or a friend of the prospect can begin a sales call effectively. Salespeople frequently present letters of introduction or testimonials. The **referral approach** is often effective with amiables and expressives (see Chapter 6) because they like to focus on relationships.

Because prospects often will contact these references, salespeople should use only the names of individuals and companies to whom they would like the prospect to talk. Successful salespeople always gain permission from references prior to using them. Dropping names and stretching the truth concerning third parties will almost always backfire. Also, remember that "The right contact may get you in the door, but it's knowledge that gets and keeps the business."[5] Here are some examples of referral approaches:

"Ms. Lewis, I'm here at the suggestion of Mr. McQueen of Brock Control Systems, Inc. He thought you would be interested in our new marketing and sales productivity system."

"Mr. Braden, several of the other CPAs in town are now using our database management software package. Here are some letters they have written about what our service has meant to them."

Benefit Approach

Perhaps the most widely used sales call opening is the **benefit approach,** which focuses the prospect's attention on a product benefit. To be effective, the benefit must be of real interest to the prospect. Unless the salesperson knows the prospect's needs (either from good precall information gathering or from other visits), this approach cannot succeed. In addition, it should be specific—something the prospect can actually realize and something that can be substantiated during the presentation. The benefit approach, effective for drivers and analyticals (who like to get down to business rather quickly), gets right to the point. For example:

"Mr. Scofield, I would like to tell you about a copier that can reduce your copying costs by 15 percent."

"Your secretary can save one hour per day using the spelling checker and auto-merge features of this new version of WordPerfect's word-processing package."

"Ms. Twombly, AT&T can save your firm at least $100,000 by transmitting voice, data, and images all at the same time, over one line, using our new ISDN network."

Product Approach

The **product approach** involves actually demonstrating a product feature and benefit as soon as you walk up to the prospect. Its advantage is that it appeals to the prospect visually as well as verbally; handing the product to prospects for their examination adds even more involvement. This approach can be very effective for expressives. Here are several examples:

[Carrying a portable fax, 2½ × 6 × 12 inches, into an office] "Ms. Joyner, you spend a lot of time on the road as an investigative lawyer. Let me show you how this little fax machine can transform your car's cellular phone into an efficient, effective 'office.' "

[Handing the buyer a scarf made out of a new synthetic material] "Is it silk or something else?"

[Handing a photograph of a computer-controlled milling machine to a production manager] "How would you like to have this machine in your shop?"

Tracey Brill uses an interesting approach for her doctors that is sort of like a product approach for the service features of her product (a prescription drug): *[Playing a recording of a telephone ringing]* "That

The product approach can be an effective way to quickly grasp the customer's attention.

Courtesy of Merck & Co., Inc.

call could be one of your patients calling to complain about her estrogen replacement therapy, but not if she is on our drug."

Compliment Approach

Most people enjoy being praised or complimented, but such an approach poses a danger. Insincere flattery is often obvious and offensive to prospects. In using the **compliment approach,** the compliment must be both sincere and specific. Sincerity relates directly to specificity. For example, the compliment "Mr. Smith, congratulations on the cost savings you achieved through the recent reorganization" is far more effective than "Mr. Smith, you are really a good businessperson."

Also, complimenting the obvious will not be effective. Chances are that others have already complimented the prospect about obviously noteworthy things (e.g., a golf tournament trophy in the office, a much publicized and unusual fourth-quarter profit for the prospect's firm).

Be careful when using the compliment approach. One salesperson, when calling on a 55-year-old man, noticed a picture of a beautiful 25-year-old woman on the buyer's desk. The seller said, "You certainly have a beautiful daughter," to which the buyer replied, "That's my wife!" It's generally best to stick to neutral topics unless you are sure of your information.

The compliment approach can be effective for all personality types. Here are two examples:

> "I noticed as I walked in that you are carrying the new INX15 machines. They are going to set a new standard of excellence in your industry. You're the first dealer I've called on who is displaying them. It's perfect evidence of your innovativeness and quest for quality!"

"I was calling on one of your customers, Jackson Street Books, last week, and the owner just couldn't say enough good things about your service. It sure says a lot about your operation to have a customer just start praising you out of the blue."

Curiosity Approach

The **curiosity approach** arouses interest by making an unexpected comment that piques the prospect's curiosity. Use caution with this approach, however. It has been used by salespeople for hundreds of years, so the prospect may think of you as just a hard-selling, fast-talking salesperson instead of as a counselor with the prospect's needs uppermost in your mind. Be prepared to fully substantiate claims, such as the following, at some point during the presentation:

"Mr. Johnson, today is your luckiest day of the year."

"Ms. Ford, some of my customers have called me the hardest person in the world to reach."

"Ms. Rockdale, I would like to offer you the chance of getting all of your paper supplies free."

Question Approach

Beginning the conversation with a question or stating an interesting fact in the form of a question is the **question approach.** It gets the customer's attention, motivates a response, and initiates two-way communication. The following questions illustrate this approach:

"Ms. Garnett, what is your reaction to the brochure I sent you on our new telemarketing service?"

"Mr. Ledford, if I can show you a way to reduce your turnover, would you be interested?"

"Ms. Stiles, have you heard of the new free delivery service our firm is offering to doctor's offices such as yours?"

▌ DEVELOPING RAPPORT

Rapport in selling is a close, harmonious relationship founded on mutual trust. Ultimately, the goal of every salesperson should be to establish rapport with each customer. Often they can accomplish this with some friendly conversation early in the call. Part of this process involves identifying the prospect's social style and making necessary adjustments (see Chapter 6).

The talk about current news, hobbies, and the like that usually breaks the ice for the actual presentation is often referred to as **small talk.** Examples include:

"I understand you went to OSU? I graduated from there too, with a BBA degree in 1990!"

"Did you happen to see the Cowboys game on TV last night?"

"I was just talking to Jane Wester, the controller, downstairs. She and I are on the same softball team and wow, can she ever pitch a fast ball!"

Customers are more receptive to salespeople with whom they can identify—with whom they have something in common. Thus, salespeople will be more effective with customers with whom they establish such links as mutual friends, common hobbies, or attendance at the same schools. Successful salespeople engage in small talk more effectively by first performing **office scanning,** which is looking around at the prospect's environment for relevant topics to talk about.

Of course, salespeople should consider cultural and personality differences and adapt the extent of their nonbusiness conversation accordingly. For example, an AT&T rep would probably spend considerably less time in friendly conversation with a New York City office manager than with, say, a manager in a rural Texas town. Businesspeople in Africa place such value on establishing friendships that the norm calls for a great deal of friendly conversation before getting down to business. Amiables and expressives tend to enjoy such conversations, while drivers and analyticals may be less receptive to spending much time in nonbusiness conversation.

It is important to maintain rapport with all contacts within the buyer's organization. Selling Scenario 9.1 describes what can happen when a salesperson forgets to do this.

WHEN THINGS GO WRONG

Making and maintaining a good impression is important. How nice it would be if the beginning of every call went as smoothly as we have described here. Actually, things do go wrong sometimes. (Question 3 in Questions and Problems at the end of this chapter allows you to think about what you would do in some rather awkward situations. You should read them even if your professor doesn't assign them!)

The best line of defense when something goes wrong is to maintain the proper perspective and a sense of humor. It's probably not the first thing you've done wrong and probably won't be your last. A good example of a call going downhill fast is the following experience, related by a salesperson:

I pulled my right hand out of the pocket and stuck it forward enthusiastically to shake. Unfortunately, a ball of lint, about the size of a pea, had stuck to the tip of my fingers and was now drifting slowly down onto the document he had been reading. We both watched it descend, as compelling as the ball on New Year's Eve. We shook hands, anyway. I said, "Excuse me," and bent forward to blow the ball of lint off the document. As I did so, I put a dent in the front edge of his desk with my briefcase.[6]

The worst response by this salesperson would be to faint, scream, or totally lose control. Instead, a better response would include a sincere apology for the dent and an offer to pay for any repairs. Further, proper planning might have prevented this situation in the first place. If the salesperson had walked into the room with his hands out of his pockets, he would not have picked up the lint.

S E L L I N G   S C E N A R I O

9.1

Don't Forget Anyone

Don't ever underestimate or downplay anyone in the prospect's or client's organization. One salesperson in our company had done an excellent job of selling to a major account, her largest. In meetings, the vice president of marketing was her main contact and there were numerous other people in attendance, at most meetings. One of the circulation directors, who appeared to be fairly new, was also in most meetings, but the salesperson, who had a great relationship with the vice president of marketing, paid little attention to this circulation director. She essentially ignored the relationship with this lower-level manager.

Sure enough, when the vice president of marketing got promoted, and the circulation director became the new vice president of marketing, there was a problem. In spite of the great relationship the salesperson had with the previous vice president of marketing, and despite the fact that the salesperson had otherwise been doing a good job, the new vice president of marketing asked for a new salesperson.

Although this type of situation rarely happens (in fact, it has only happened twice in our company's history), the price paid by the salesperson can be enormous. It's the stuff of which ruined careers are made. The strategy is to treat *all* contacts at a prospect or client organization exactly as if they were your *main* contact.

Source: George J. Kiebala, Account Executive, Direct Marketing Technology, Inc., personal correspondence, May 5, 1993, used by permission.

Also, keep in mind that you are dealing with a prospect with a unique personality and an outlook that may not always be consistent with yours. Some can even be downright nasty! Zemke and Anderson[7] have identified five basic profiles of difficult customers and have provided appropriate labels:

- Egocentric Edgar (vain, self-centered).
- Bad-mouth Betty (cusses like a drunken sailor).
- Hysterical Harold (loves to scream and throw a tantrum when he doesn't get his way).
- Freeloading Freda (demands to get her dollar's worth, and everyone else's too).
- Dictatorial Dick (tells everyone what to do, but blames the salesperson if anything goes wrong).

The authors have several suggestions for dealing with people like these. Appeal to Egocentric Edgar's ego and don't let his ego destroy yours. Either ignore Bad-mouth Betty's language or force the issue head on (e.g., "I don't have to listen to that language" and hang up). Let Hysterical Harold vent his anger and then offer to take responsibility for solving his problem. For Freeloading Freda, give her what she wants—you won't have many like these and it doesn't pay to have a loud, unhappy customer. Fulfill Dictatorial Dick's request right away and stick to your game plan.

IDENTIFYING THE PROSPECT'S NEEDS

When sales representatives make a presentation, they can easily make the mistake of starting with product information rather than with a discussion of the prospect's needs. The experienced salesperson, however, attempts to find out the prospect's needs and problems at the start of the relationship. In fact, the salesperson is actually still qualifying the prospect while attempting to discover needs. Attention then turns to the specific features and benefits that will satisfy those needs.

Research continually demonstrates the importance of needs discovery. One analysis, by Huthwaite, Inc., of more than 35,000 sales calls in 23 countries over a 12-year period, revealed that what distinguished successful salespeople was their ability to discover the prospect's needs.[8] Discovering needs was more important than opening the call strategically, handling objections, or using closing techniques effectively.

Given the importance of needs discovery, it is not surprising that most sales training programs now teach salespeople how to discover the prospect's needs. How successful are these programs? According to a recent study, 87 percent of 432 buyers at firms of all sizes said that salespeople do not know how to ask the right questions about their company's needs.[9] Almost half said that the biggest problem with salespeople is that they talk too much. This information reinforces the importance of learning how to discover needs and letting the prospect talk.

As you discover needs, keep in mind that this process can be very uncomfortable for the prospect. The prospect might resent your suggesting that there could be a problem or a better way to do things. When faced with direct evidence that things could be better, the prospect might express fear (fear of losing his or her job if things are not corrected, or of things changing and the situation getting worse than it is now). Also, remember that there are tremendous differences in the amount of time/effort needed to discuss needs depending on the type of industry, the nature of the product, the length of the relationship with the buyer, and so forth. We will come back to this issue after examining methods of identifying needs.

REMEMBER TO COMMUNICATE EFFECTIVELY

Chapter 5 covered most of the important communication principles needed to effectively ask questions and be a better listener. In fact, it wouldn't be a bad idea to review that material now. Remember to speak naturally while asking these questions. You don't want to sound like you are a computer asking a set of boring questions, nor do you want to appear to be following a strict word-for-word outline that you learned in your sales training classes.[10]

Before beginning to ask questions, it is often a good idea to gain permission. For example, the seller can say something like, "Do you mind if I ask you a few questions so I can learn more about ways to serve your needs?" We will now briefly describe two of the most widely used systems of needs identification taught to salespeople today.

ASKING OPEN AND CLOSED QUESTIONS

In the first method of needs discovery, salespeople are taught to distinguish between open and closed questions and then encouraged to utilize more open questions. **Open questions** require the prospect to go beyond a simple yes/no response—they encourage the prospect to open up and share a great deal of useful information. For example:

> "What kinds of problems have the new federal guidelines caused for your division?"
>
> "What do you know about our firm?"
>
> "When you think of a quality sound system, what comes to mind?"

Closed questions require the prospect to simply answer yes or no or to offer a short, fill-in-the-blank type of response. Examples include:

> "Have you ever experienced computer downtime as a result of an electrical storm?"
>
> "Is fast delivery important for your firm?"
>
> "Customers have expressed a desire to have many features, including four channels, AC/DC power, a four-year warranty, and easily upgradable equipment. Which of these are important to you?"

In most cases, salespeople need to ask both open and closed questions. Open questions help paint the broad strokes of the situation, whereas closed questions help zero in on very specific problems and attitudes. Some trainers feel simple, closed questions are best at first. Prospects become accustomed to talking and start to open up. After a few closed questions, the salesperson moves to a series of open questions. At some point, he or she may revert back to closed questions again.

Also, some trainers suggest asking a **double-barreled question,** a question that asks more than one question at the same time (e.g., "Do you find your current machine to break down a lot, or do you follow the suggested maintenance schedule?"). The advantage of double-barreled questions is that if one part of the question is not applicable to this prospect, the other part might be. Of course, you never want to confuse the prospect, so these should be used carefully.

Exhibit 9.2 contains an illustrative dialogue of a bank selling a commercial checking account to a business. In this sales presentation, the salesperson's questions follow a logical flow. Note that follow-up probes are often necessary to clarify the prospect's responses. At the conclusion of asking open and closed questions, the salesperson should have a good feel for the needs and wants of the prospect. One final suggestion is to summarize the prospect's needs:

> "So, let me see if I have this right. You are looking for a checking account that pays interest on your unused balance and has a monthly statement . . . Is that correct?

This helps to solidify the needs in the prospect's mind and helps ensure that there are no other needs or wants that are hidden.

EXHIBIT 9.2

USING OPEN AND CLOSED
QUESTIONS TO DISCOVER
NEEDS

Salesperson's Probe	Prospect's Response
Have you ever done business with our bank before? [closed]	No, our firm has always used First of America Bank.
I assume, then, that your checking account is currently with First of America? [closed]	Yes.
If you could design an ideal checking account for your business, what would it look like? [open]	Well, it would pay interest on all idle money, have no service charges, and supply a good statement.
When you say "good statement," what exactly do you mean? [open]	It should come to us once a month, be easy to follow, and help us reconcile our books quickly.
Uh huh. Anything else in an ideal checking account? [open]	No, I guess that's about it.
What things, if any, about your checking account have dissatisfied you in the past? [open]	Having to pay so much for our checks! Also, sometimes when we have a question, the bank can't answer it quickly because the computers are down. That's frustrating!
Sure! Anything else dissatisfy you? [open]	Well, I really don't like the layout of the monthly statement we get now. It doesn't list checks in order; it has them listed by the date they cleared the bank.
Normally, what balance do you have on hand in your account? What minimum balance can you maintain? [closed]	About $8,500 now. We could keep a minimum of around $5,000, I guess.
Are you earning interest in your account now? [closed]	Yes, 3 percent of the average monthly balance if we maintain at least a $5,000 balance.
What kind of service charges are you paying now? [closed]	$25 per month, 25 cents per check, 10 cents per deposit.
[more questions]	
Is there anything else that I need to know before I begin telling you about our account? [open]	No, I think that just about covers it all.

SPIN TECHNIQUE

The SPIN method of discovering needs was developed by Huthwaite, Inc. after analyzing thousands of actual sales calls.[11] The results indicated that successful salespeople go through a logical needs identification sequence, which Huthwaite labeled **SPIN:** Situation questions, Problem questions, Implication questions, and Need payoff questions. SPIN works for those salespeople involved in a **major sale,** one that involves a long selling cycle, a large customer commitment, an ongoing relationship, and large risks for the prospect if a bad decision is made. Major sales can occur anywhere but often involve large, major, or national accounts. For example, both Johnson Wax and Firestone use SPIN for their major accounts but use other techniques for smaller accounts.

SPIN actually helps the prospect identify unrecognized problem areas. Often, when a salesperson simply asks an open question such as, "What problems are you having?" the prospect replies, "None!" The prospect isn't lying; he or she just may not realize that a problem exists. SPIN excels at helping prospects test their current opinions or perceptions of the situation.

Situation Questions

Early in the sales call, salespeople ask **situation questions,** general data-gathering questions about background and current facts. Because these are very broad in nature, successful salespeople learn to limit them; prospects quickly become bored or impatient if they hear too many of them. Inexperienced and unsuccessful reps tend to ask too many situation questions. In fact, many situation-type questions can be answered through precall information gathering and planning. If a salesperson asks too many situation questions, the prospect will think the salesperson is unprepared. Examples of situation questions include:

> "What's your position? How long have you been here?"
>
> "How many people do you employ? Is the number growing or shrinking?"
>
> "What kind of handling equipment are you using at present?"
>
> "How long have you had it? Did you buy or lease it?"

Problem Questions

When salespeople ask about specific difficulties, problems, or dissatisfactions the prospect has, they are asking **problem questions.** Experienced sales reps tend to ask many such questions. In smaller sales, the use of problem questions is strongly related to success. In major sales, however, the rep must ask additional kinds of questions in order to understand needs and obtain commitment. Here are several examples of problem questions:

> "Do you find your current machine difficult to repair?"
>
> "Have you experienced any problems with the overall quality of your forklifts?"
>
> "Do your operators ever complain that the noise level is too high?"

Implication Questions

Questions that logically follow one or more problem questions and are designed to help the prospect recognize the true ramifications of the problem are **implication questions.** Implication questions cannot be asked until some problem area has generally been identified (through problem questions). They attempt to motivate the prospect to search for a solution to the problem. Ultimately, implication questions set the stage so that the seriousness of the problem outweighs the cost of the solution (which the salesperson will offer later). Successful salespeople in major sales tend to ask lots of implication questions, such as:

> "What happens if you ship your customer a product that doesn't meet specs?"
>
> "Does paying overtime for your operators increase your costs?"
>
> "What does that do to your price, as compared to your competitors'?"
>
> "Does the slowness of your present system create any bottlenecks in other parts of the process?

Need Payoff Questions

When salespeople ask a question about the usefulness of solving a problem, they are asking a **need payoff question.** They want the prospect to focus attention on solving the problem rather than continually thinking about the problem itself. In contrast to implication questions, which are problem centered, need payoff questions are solution centered:

> "If I can show you a way to eliminate paying overtime for your operators and therefore reduce your cost, would you be interested?"
>
> "So, would you like to see a reduction in the number of products that don't meet quality specifications?"
>
> "Would an increase in the speed of your present system by 5 percent resolve the bottlenecks you currently experience?"

If the prospect responds negatively to a needs payoff question, then the salesperson has not identified a problem serious enough for the prospect to take action. The salesperson should probe further by asking additional problem questions, implication questions, and then a new need payoff question.

Conclusion

One critical advantage of SPIN is that the prospect defines the need. At no time during the questioning phase does the salesperson ever talk about his or her product. As a result, the prospect views the salesperson more as a consultant trying to help than as someone trying to push a product.

SPIN selling has been taught to thousands of salespeople in Fortune 500 firms. While many salespeople quickly learn to master the technique, others have more difficulty. The best advice is to practice each component and to plan implication and need payoff questions before each sales call. An abbreviated needs identification dialogue appears in Exhibit 9.3 to demonstrate all components of SPIN for someone who sells desktop publishing programs.

▌ REITERATING NEEDS

The extent to which one has to identify needs during any call depends on the extent and success of precall information gathering. The salesperson may fully identify the needs of the prospect before making the sales call. In that case, reiterating the needs early in the sales call is advisable, so both parties agree about what problem they are trying to solve. For example:

EXHIBIT 9.3

Using the SPIN
Technique to Sell
Desktop Publishing

Salesperson   "Do you ever send work out for typesetting?" [situation question]

Prospect   "Yes, about once a month we have to send work out because we are swamped."

Salesperson   "Is the cost of sending work out a burden?" [problem question]

Prospect   "Not really. It only costs about 5 percent more, and we just add that to the customer's bill."

Salesperson   "Do you get fast turnaround?" [problem question]

Prospect   "Well, now that you mention it, at times the turnaround is kind of slow. You see, we aren't given very high priority since we aren't big customers for the printer. We only use them when we have to, you know."

Salesperson   "What happens if you miss a deadline for your customer because the turnaround is slow?" [implication question]

Prospect   "That only happened once, but it was disastrous. John, the customer, really chewed me out, and we lost a lot of our credibility. Like I say, it only happened once, and I sure wouldn't like it to happen again to John—or any of our customers for that matter!"

Salesperson   "If I can show you a way to eliminate outside typesetting without having to increase your staff, would you be interested?" [need payoff question]

Prospect   "Sure, the more I think about it, the more I realize I have something of a time bomb here. Sooner or later, it's going to go off!"

"Mr. Jonesboro, based on our several phone conversations, it appears that you are looking for an advertising campaign that will position your product for the rapidly growing senior citizen market, at a cost under $100,000, using humor and a well-known older personality, and delivered in less than one month. Is that an accurate summary of your needs? Has anything changed since we talked last?"

Likewise, in multicall situations, going through a complete needs identification at every call is unnecessary. But it is still usually best to briefly reiterate the needs identified to that point:

"In my last call, we pretty much agreed that your number one concern is customer satisfaction with your inventory system. Is that correct? Has anything changed since we met last time, or is there anything else I need to know?"

Additional Considerations

How many questions can a salesperson ask to discover needs? It depends on the situation. Generally, as the risk of making the wrong decision goes up, so does the amount of time you can spend asking the prospect questions. For example, a Boeing salesperson could address an almost unlimited number of questions to United Air Lines, because the airline realizes the importance of having Boeing propose the right configuration of airplane. A salesperson for Johnson Wax calling on a local grocery store, on the other hand, has very little time to probe about needs before discussing an upcoming promotion and requesting an end-of-aisle display. Regardless of the situation, the salesperson should carefully prepare a set of questions to ask, in order to maximize the use of available time.

Occasionally the prospect will refuse to provide answers to important questions on the ground that the information is confidential or proprietary. The salesperson can do little except emphasize the reason for asking the questions. Ultimately, the prospect needs to trust the salesperson enough to divulge sensitive data. (Chapters 2 and 13 discuss trust-building strategies.)

At times, buyers do not answer questions because they honestly don't know the answer. The salesperson should then ask if the prospect could get the information in some way. If not, the salesperson often can ask the buyer's permission to probe further within the prospect's firm for the information.

On the other hand, some buyers will not only answer your question, they will appear to want to talk indefinitely. In general, the advice is to let them talk. This is particularly true for many cultures. For example, people in French-speaking countries love rhetoric (the act and art of speaking); attempts to cut them off will only frustrate and anger them.[12]

<table>
<tr>
<td>

T H I N K I N G
I T
T H R O U G H

</td>
<td>

When prospects reveal facts about their situations and needs, they often provide some very sensitive and confidential information. Assume that a prospect at Firm A reveals to you her firm's long-term strategy of securing business away from her competitor, Firm B. Also assume that you are close friends with the buyer of Firm B, which is one of your biggest customers. Further assume that Firm B is beginning to lose market share and you sense that this will result in your commissions falling off. You have at best a 50–50 chance of landing Firm A's business. Will you share the confidential information with Firm B's buyer? What are the long-term consequences of your proposed behavior?

</td>
</tr>
</table>

DEVELOPING A STRATEGY

Based on the needs identified, the salesperson should develop a strategy for how best to proceed to meet those needs. This includes sorting through the various options available to the seller to see what is best for this prospect. Decisions have to be made about the product or service to recommend, the optimum payment terms to present for consideration, service levels to suggest, and so forth. This part of the process is not always easy, and often requires the expertise of many people in the salesperson's firm.

RELATING FEATURES TO BENEFITS

As you move from learning about the prospect's needs into the presentation, you invariably begin to talk about your product. Knowledge of your product is not enough. To be an effective salesperson, you must relate your product to the prospect's unique situation. You do this by translating product features into benefits for solving the buyer's needs.

A **feature** is a quality or characteristic of the product or service. Every product has many features designed to help potential customers. A **benefit** is how a particular feature will help a particular buyer and is tied directly to the buying motives of the prospect. A benefit helps the prospect more

FEATURES AND BENEFITS OF
MARMOT SLEEPING BAGS

Features	Benefits
GORE-TEX outer shell	Keeps you warm and dry in adverse weather because GORE-TEX is waterproof, windproof, and breathable.
Contoured, sculpted hood with drawstring	Helps keep you warm and dry because your head is inside the bag and yet your breath vapor escapes outside the bag.
Machine washable and dryable	Since it can be cleaned inexpensively, it will save you money.
Silicone-dipped zipper	Prevents icing, which means you will be able to open it easily, even in the coldest conditions.
Filled with the finest goose down	You get excellent protection against cold weather since goose down is one of the best insulators available today.
Adjustable down	Since you can rearrange the down to suit the weather, you will be assured of comfort year-round.
Double down-filled draft tubes	Draft tubes keep the zipper area covered, which prevents cold drafts from coming in through the zippers. This will keep you warm and cozy.
Bag weighs 39 ounces	Easy for you to carry when backpacking into wilderness areas.
Lifetime warranty against defects in material or craftsmanship	You will never have to worry about hidden defects and can have complete confidence in the quality of the products.

fully answer the question, "What's in it for me?" (Exhibit 9.4 lists examples of features and sample benefits for an expensive sleeping bag.) The salesperson usually includes a word or phrase in order to make a smooth transition from features to benefits:

"This china is fired at 2,600° F, and what that means to you is that it will last longer. Since it is so sturdy, you will be able to hand it down to your children as an heirloom, which was one of your biggest concerns."

"This set of golf clubs has shallow-faced fairway woods, which means that you'll be able to get the ball into the air easier. That will certainly help give you the distance you said you were looking for."

"Our service hot line is open 24 hours a day, which means that even your third-shift operators can call if they have any questions. That should be a real help to you, since you said your third-shift supervisor was very inexperienced in dealing with problems."

Buyers are not interested in facts about the product or the company unless these facts help solve their wants or needs. The salesperson's job is to supply the facts and then point out what these features mean to the buyer in terms of benefits. In fact, given that the buyer helped by identifying his

Features	Benefits
Of Importance to the Final Consumer	
Trusted name brand	Since you trust the Jello brand name, you know that this is a high-quality product.
Only 60 calories per bar	You can enjoy a treat without worrying about its effect on your weight.
Real fruit in every bite	You are getting needed nutrition from a snack.
Only fruit and cream brand that comes in a variety pack	You will be able to meet the different flavor preferences of your family members.
Each pack has 12 bars	You get a better value by purchasing in this family-size pack. Also, you won't run out of snacks as quickly and have to make a trip back to the grocery store.
Of Importance to the Grocery Store	
Test marketed for 3 years	Because of this research, you are assured of a successful product and effective promotion; thus your risk is greatly reduced.
$10 million in consumer advertising will be spent in the next 18 months	Consumers will come to your store looking for the product.
40-cent coupon with front positioning in the national Sunday insert section	Consumers will want to take advantage of the coupon and will be looking in your freezer for the product.
At the suggested retail price of $3.39, your profit margin will be 20 percent	This has a 5 percent higher profit margin than other fruit and cream bars you sell, so you'll make more profit each time you sell a box.
All advertising will feature Bill Cosby	Both parents and children trust and enjoy Bill Cosby. This will increase their desire to purchase the product. As a result, they will come to the store looking for the product.
Trusted, name brand, 60 calories per bar, real fruit filling, comes in a variety pack, 12 bars in each pack (list of features important to final consumers)	Consumers will like the product and continue to purchase it. This will create fast turnover of the product and result in higher overall sales and profits.

or her needs, the salesperson's responsibility is then to prove how those needs can be satisfied. (Chapter 10 will more fully discuss how to offer proof of assertions.)

Buyers typically consider two or more competitive products when making a purchase decision. Thus, salespeople need to know more than just the benefits provided by their products. They need to know how the benefits of their products are superior or inferior to the benefits of competitive products.

Products have many, many features, and one product may possess a large number of features that are unique and exciting when compared to competitive offerings. Successful salespeople, rather than overload the customer with all of the great features, discuss only those that specifically address the needs of the prospect. For example, suppose a Panasonic salesperson calls on a prospect who is looking for a VCR to use only as a playback device for training tapes. In this situation, the Panasonic representative should not discuss or even mention that one feature of the VCR is that it is ready to hook up to cable systems, with no tuning needed. The buyer has absolutely no need for this feature. To talk about features of little interest to the customer is a waste of time.

Sometimes, when selling commodities it is important to sell the features/benefits of the seller's firm instead of the product. For example, Ray Hanson sells fasteners like bolts and nuts. He states, "In the fastener industry I have found that a generic product, such as a nut or bolt, doesn't have too many features and benefits. We talk to our potential customers about the features our company has, and how these could benefit them as our customers."[13]

When selling to resellers, salespeople have two sets of benefits to discuss with the prospect: what the features of the proposal will do for the reseller, and what the product features will do for the ultimate consumer of the product. Covering both sets of features and benefits is important. Exhibit 9.5 illustrates the two sets of features.

ASSESSING REACTIONS

While making a presentation, salespeople need to continually assess the reactions of their prospect.[14] It is important that the prospect agrees that the benefits described would actually help him or her. By listening to what buyers say and by observing their body language, salespeople can determine whether prospects are interested in the product. If buyers react favorably to the presentation and seem able to grasp the benefits of your solution, you will have less need to make alterations or adjustments. But if a prospect does not develop enthusiasm for the product, you will need to make some changes in the presentation.

USING NONVERBAL CUES

An important aspect of making adjustments is interpreting a prospect's reactions to the sales presentation. By observing the prospect's five channels of nonverbal communication, salespeople can determine how to proceed with their presentations. Exhibit 9.6 lists signals, or nonverbal cues, that salespeople who are sensitive to a prospect's body language can read. (Chapter 5 provides more detailed information about nonverbal cues.)

Positive nonverbal cues are encouraging for the salesperson, who should send the same cues to the prospect.[15] If the prospect gives mixed signals, the salesperson needs to ask open-ended questions to draw out the prospect's reasons for caution. Negative nonverbal signals indicate a serious problem, and the salesperson should refocus the discussion completely after probing for concerns. The best way to avoid negative signals is to deal effectively with mixed signals when they appear.

EXHIBIT 9.6   NONVERBAL CUES THAT SIGNAL PROSPECTS' REACTIONS

Channel	Positive	Mixed	Negative
Body angle	Upright, direct to salesperson	Leaning away from salesperson	Leaning far back or thrusting toward salesperson
Face	Friendly, smiling, enthusiastic	Tense, displeased, superior	Angry, determined, shaking head
Arms	Relaxed, open	Closed, tense	Tightly crossed or thrusting out
Hands	Relaxed, open	Clasped, fidgeting with objects	Fist, pointed finger
Legs	Uncrossed, crossed toward salesperson	Crossed away from salesperson	Tightly crossed away from salesperson

VERBAL PROBING

As salespeople proceed through a presentation, they must take the pulse of the situation. This is often called a **trial close.** For example, after discussing a particularly important feature that helps meet the prospect's needs, the salesperson should say something like:

> "How does that sound to you?"
>
> "Can you see how that feature helps solve the problem you have?"
>
> "Have I clearly explained this feature to you?"
>
> "You now know a little more about the service offering. Do you foresee any initial limitations to the service?"

The use of such probing questions helps achieve several things. First, it allows the salesperson to stop talking and encourages two-way conversations. Without such probing, a salesperson can turn into a rambling talker while the buyer becomes a passive listener. Second, probing lets the salesperson see if the buyer is listening and understanding what is being said. Third, the probe may show that the prospect is uninterested in what the salesperson is talking about. This allows the salesperson to redirect the conversation to areas of interest to the buyer. This kind of adjustment is necessary in almost every presentation and underscores the fact that the salesperson should not simply memorize a canned presentation that has to occur in a particular sequence.

You must listen. Often we hear what we want to hear (this is called **selective perception**). Everyone is guilty of this at times. For example, read the following sentence:[16]

> *Finished files are the result of years of scientific study combined with the experience of years.*

Now, quickly count the number of Fs in that sentence. Most non-native English speakers see all six Fs, while native English speakers see only three (they don't count the Fs in *of* because it is not considered an important word). The point is that once salespeople stop actively listening they miss many things the buyer is trying to communicate.

Nonverbal cues are important indicators to help salespeople know when to make adjustments. In this picture, even though all members of the buying team are looking at the salesperson they seem to be giving off different nonverbal cues. Can you interpret them?

Frank Herholdt/TSW.

MAKING ADJUSTMENTS

Salespeople can alter their presentations in many ways to obtain a favorable reaction. During the sales presentation, for example, salespeople can discover that the prospect simply does not believe they have the appropriate product knowledge. Rather than continue with the presentation, they should redirect their efforts toward establishing credibility in the eyes of the prospect.

Other adjustments might require collecting additional information about the prospect, developing a new sales strategy, or altering the style of presentation. For example, a salesperson may believe a prospect is interested in buying an economical, low-cost motor. While presenting the benefits of the lowest-cost motor, the salesperson discovers the prospect is interested in the motor's operating costs. At this point, the salesperson should ask some questions to find out if the prospect would be interested in paying a higher price for a more efficient motor with lower operating costs. On the basis of the prospect's response, the salesperson can adopt a new sales strategy, one that emphasizes operating efficiency rather than the motor's initial price. In this way, the sales presentation is shifted from features and benefits based on a low initial cost to features and benefits related to low operating costs.

BUILDING CREDIBILITY DURING THE CALL

To develop a close and harmonious relationship, the salesperson must be perceived as having **credibility:** He or she must be believable and reliable. A salesperson can take many actions during a sales call to develop such a perception.[17]

To establish credibility early in the sales call, clearly delineate the time you think the call will take and then stop when the time is up. How many times has a salesperson told you, "This will only take five minutes!" and 30 minutes later you still can't get rid of him or her? No doubt you would have perceived the salesperson as more credible if, after five minutes, he or she stated, "Well, I promised to take no more than five minutes, and I see our time is up. How would you like to proceed from here?" Jim Hersma, a sales vice president of a major firm, likes to ask for half an hour and only take 25 minutes.[18] Salespeople who learn how to accurately calculate the time needed for a call and who then stand by their promises will find much more success in establishing credibility.

Another way to establish credibility is to offer concrete evidence to back up verbal statements that you make. If you state, "It is estimated that over 40 percent of the households in America will own videocassette recorders by 1995," be prepared to offer proof of this assertion (e.g., hand the prospect a letter or article from a credible source). This topic will be discussed in greater detail in Chapter 10.

Many salespeople have found that the most effective way to establish credibility is to present a **balanced presentation** showing all sides of the situation—that is, to be totally honest. Thus, a salesperson might mention some things about the product that make it less than perfect or may speak positively about some exclusive feature of a competitor's product. Will this totally defeat the seller's chances of a sale? No. In fact, it increases the chances of building long-term commitment and rapport.[19]

For example, Gregg Hoffman, a realtor for Messina-Zunich Realty, exclusively uses a balanced presentation format. When showing a client a potential piece of property, Gregg identifies how the property will meet the prospect's needs and then goes on to point out any potential negative points as well (e.g., "You know, the traffic noise *will* be louder in the summer during the tourist season"). As a result of his honesty, Gregg is well respected, successful, and highly sought out as a realtor. Selling Scenario 9.2 provides another example of using a balanced presentation. Salespeople can keep customers happy and dedicated by helping them form correct, realistic expectations about the product or service.[20]

In selling complex products, sales representatives often must demonstrate product expertise at the beginning of the sales process. Salespeople can accomplish this by telling the customer, without bragging, about their special training or education. They can also strengthen credibility with excellent, insightful questions or comments. Salespeople who establish their expertise will have more credibility when they make their presentations. This is especially true for young-looking and inexperienced salespeople.

Tracey Brill, a salesperson for a large pharmecutical company, notes that a salesperson calling on doctors should never use a word if the seller doesn't know the exact definition. Some doctors may even test you on this. She relates an example of a call on one doctor:[21]

TRACEY   "Because 'Product X' acts as an agonist at the Kappa receptor, miosis will occur."

DOCTOR   "What does *miosis* mean?"

TRACEY   "It means the stage of disease during which intensity of signs and symptoms diminishes."

DOCTOR   "No! Miosis means contraction of the pupils."

S E L L I N G   S C E N A R I O   *S C E N A R I O*

9.2

Sell Yourself . . . the Orders Will Surely Follow

"You are always selling yourself. If you do that exceptionally well, the orders will surely follow. In today's highly competitive economy, where every product or service is viewed as a commodity, the relationship that you build with the customer is the most critical element in the selling process.

"I personally learned early in my sales career that a focus on the customer's needs was my most powerful sales tool. I learned this over 20 years ago, almost by accident, from an experience with a medical school professor. At that time I sold microscopes for the Instrument Division of the American Optical Company. The company was highly ethical and customer focused, so it always stressed that we must only sell what our customers really needed for their application. The goal of both the company and its salespeople was to always sell the best products that served our customers' needs and the medical community.

"I was making one of my twice-yearly trips to a large medical school in one of the Western states. I met a professor in the hall who asked me into his office to discuss a special application for a microscope. We had a long discussion in which he explained and then showed me in detail what he had to do in applying this new procedure. We had built a good relationship over several years. It was obvious that he wanted to buy now, and from me. That was great, except for one problem, my microscope might work but only with a great deal of difficulty, whereas our competitor, B&L, had a scope that seemed like it was specifically designed for his application.

"After a lot of soul searching, I did what I thought was right. I told him about the B&L scope and told him how to reach them to place an order. He was almost speechless and thanked me over and over again for my advice. As the days passed, I missed that order. I felt the empty spot in my wallet where that commission should have been.

"I visited the professor on my next trip and again he thanked me for my recommendation of the competitive microscope. He said it worked perfectly.

"Two years later I bumped into that same professor in a corridor and he asked me to stop by his office to discuss a specialized microscope. When I arrived, he told me the specifications of the scope he needed and it turned out that we had a perfect fit. What he needed was a very expensive industry standard microscope for his application. This was a type of microscope that could be supplied by all my competitors.

"When will you need the scope delivered?" It was a good thing I was sitting down when he replied, "I have the budget approved and we will need all of them when the remodeling of the classroom is completed." I don't remember exactly what I said, but I think I stuttered out something like, "Them?" "Yes," he replied, "We will need 25 scopes to equip the entire classroom." This was the largest order the company had ever received for this model. It was sold without a demonstration, or a sample, or a competitive bid. When I offered to send him a sample to look over, his reply made my day; no, no—it made my year: "I don't need to see it, I know you would only recommend what I really need, only the best."

"That experience taught me a lot, it gave me an understanding of the selling process that has served me well over many years, in many different industries, with all sorts of customers and products. What I am always selling is myself. What I mean is, I'm always selling my relationship with the customer, my credibility, my honesty, my expertise, my concern for my customer. Once I sell me . . . the rest is just a logical process of understanding my customers' needs, their goals, and what will create a true win–win relationship. If you can't create a win–win sale with your customer, never, never, accept anything else . . . since the ultimate loser will only be you."

Source: Bob Newzell is host and moderator of "Sales Talk," a one-hour talk/interview show on the Business Radio Network, which is heard on 85 stations around the United States. He is a speaker and sales trainer, and designs special sales training programs for companies across the country.

TRACEY   "I did look it up in the 1989 edition of *Taber's Encyclopedic Medical Dictionary*. I would be happy to bring it in next time I come in because I wouldn't want you to think I would use a phrase without knowing what it meant."

At this point the doctor walked out of the room and Tracey thought she had lost all credibility. Actually, he had just gone out and grabbed a dictionary. The first definition was the contraction of the pupils and the second was Tracey's definition. Tracey's definition, not the doctor's, fit the use of the term for this medication. The doctor then shook Tracey's hand and thanked her for teaching him a new word! The salesperson's credibility certainly increased.

SUMMARY

Salespeople need to make every effort possible to create a good impression during a sales call. The first few minutes with the prospect are important, and care should be taken to make an effective entrance by giving a good first impression, expressing confidence while standing and shaking hands, and selecting an appropriate seat.

The salesperson can use any of several methods to gain the prospect's attention. Salespeople should adopt the approach that is most effective for the prospect's personality style. Also of critical importance is the development of rapport with the prospect. This can often be enhanced by engaging in friendly conversation.

Before beginning any discussion of product information, the salesperson must first establish the prospect's needs. This can be accomplished by effective use of open and closed questions. The SPIN technique is very effective for discovering needs in the major sale. In subsequent calls, the salesperson should reiterate the prospect's needs.

Moving into a discussion of the proposed solution or alternatives, the salesperson translates features into benefits for the buyer. He or she also makes necessary adjustments in the presentation, based on feedback provided by nonverbal cues and verbal probing.

A close, harmonious relationship will enhance the whole selling process. The salesperson can build credibility by adhering to stated appointment lengths, backing up statements with proof, offering a balanced presentation, and establishing his or her credentials.

KEY TERMS

approach   *260*
balanced presentation   *278*
benefit   *272*
benefit approach   *261*
closed questions   *267*
compliment approach   *262*
credibility   *277*
curiosity approach   *263*
double-barreled question   *267*
feature   *272*
halo effect   *260*
implication questions   *269*
impression management   *256*
introduction approach   *260*

major sale   *268*
need payoff questions   *270*
office scanning   *264*
open questions   *267*
problem questions   *269*
product approach   *261*
question approach   *263*
rapport   *263*
referral approach   *260*
selective perception   *277*
situation questions   *269*
small talk   *263*
SPIN   *268*
trial close   *276*

Questions and Problems

1. Assume you are selling computer software packages to CPAs (certified public accountants). How long beyond the agreed-on appointment time would you be willing to wait in each of the following situations? Why?
   a. This is your first call on a very important CPA. She is the president of the local CPA organization. You have never met her, nor have you found out anything about her.
   b. This is your first call on one of the CPA partners of a two-partner firm. The other partner has already heard your presentation and was somewhat impressed.
   c. This is your first call on a small, sole-proprietorship CPA in a small town. You just started selling two weeks ago and have not closed any sales yet. The CPA is an expressive.
   d. You have achieved great success in your territory. This is your fifth call on one of the big CPAs in your city. You have a lot of software installation work to do this afternoon for other clients. This CPA is a driver, who rarely has more than 5 minutes of time to talk to you on a visit.

2. What approach method would you use for each prospect listed in question 1 in order to get his or her attention? Explain the reasons for your choices.

3. Occasionally things don't go the way you plan them to go. Describe what you would do in each of the following situations:
   a. You offer your hand for a handshake, and the prospect just looks at you.
   b. The seat your prospect offers you is uncomfortable, too low, or in direct sunlight.
   c. You use the referral approach, and the prospect says "I've never trusted that man anyway."
   d. You use the product approach, and the prospect just keeps playing with the product. You are afraid to move on into your presentation without her attention.
   e. You state, "This will only take 15 minutes"; then the prospect rambles and uses up most of your time in trivial chitchat. At the end of 15 minutes, you haven't accomplished your call objectives.
   f. In the middle of your presentation, the secretary rings in to inform your prospect that her next appointment has arrived at the front desk.
   g. Your hands start to tremble just before you go into the prospect's office.
   h. You are presenting your product. As you lean over to get something out of your briefcase, your pants or skirt splits open in the back, with an accompanying loud noise.
   i. You are at dinner with a prospect, and you accidently spill soup on your tie.

4. Think for a moment about trying to secure a sales job. Assume you are going to have an interview with a district manager of NCR next week for a sales position. What can you do to develop rapport and build credibility with her?

5. "I don't need to discover my prospect's needs. I sell toothpaste to grocery stores. I know what their needs are—a high profit margin and fast turnover of products!" Comment.

6. Assume you are selling automobile tires to a customer. Develop a series of open and closed questions to discover the prospect's needs.

7. Generate a list of SPIN questions, assuming that you represent your school's placement service. You are calling on a large business nearby that never hires college graduates from your school. Make any additional assumptions necessary.

8. Prepare a list of features and benefits that could be used in a presentation to other students at your college. The objective of the presentation is to encourage the students to enroll in your selling course.

9. In a selling situation between a salesperson and a prospect, much of what is said is really never heard, and part of what is heard is often misinterpreted by one or both of the parties. What techniques might a salesperson use to improve communication with a prospect?

10. "I always shake hands with anyone I call on. If I didn't shake hands, people would not trust me. Besides, it's common knowledge that you're supposed to shake hands in business settings. It makes you seem more friendly." Comment.

11. In what situations should a salesperson use the prospect's first name? When should a more formal salutation be used?

12. How long should a salesperson wait for the prospect? What factors influence your answer?

CASE PROBLEMS

CASE 9 • 1
BABY SOFT, INC.

Todd Bitner is a salesperson for Baby Soft Inc., a San Francisco firm that specializes in importing baby products for the U.S. market. Today he called on the corporate headquarters of Kmart in Troy, Michigan, to introduce a new line of diaper covers. Here is the dialogue that occurred between Todd and Ann Glavan, a senior buyer at Kmart:

TODD   *[walking up to Ann, handing her a diaper cover]* "Have you ever seen anything like that?"

ANN   *[quickly putting the cover on her desk and sitting down]* "I don't even know what it is! Weren't you going to tell me about a new baby swing?"

TODD   "No, I don't sell baby swings. You must have me mixed up with someone else. I'm Todd Bitner from Baby Soft, Inc."

ANN   "Oh. Well, what can I do for you?"

TODD   "I'm trying to sell you a new product that's hot on the market today. A washable, reusable poly/cotton diaper cover with velcro closures."

ANN   *[looking confused]* "What?"

TODD   "Let me ask you a few questions. What do you look for when trying to decide on a new product?"

ANN "I look for a product that has broad appeal to a wide range of customer types. Also, one that will supply Kmart with a good profit margin. Finally, the product should complement what we already sell and result in cross-selling opportunities."

TODD "What is your buying budget for diaper-related products this year?"

ANN "That's pretty confidential information. I'm not sure I want to reveal that to you."

TODD "That's okay. It won't make much difference in my presentation anyway. These diaper covers are so neat I know you'll want them regardless of how much you have budgeted to spend."

ANN "You sound awfully sure of yourself!"

TODD "I am sure of my product. These diaper covers are so hot today because they help the environment. With these convenient, easy-to-use covers, mothers can use cloth diapers and help save our over-burdened landfills. The covers have a pinless, wide-band velcro fastener; the outside is made of 65/35 percent knitted poly/cotton; the inside net next to baby's skin is 100 percent nylon; it has form-fitting elastic in the back; it has a 100 percent water-repellant vinyl cushioned elastic leg; . . ."

ANN *[interrupting]* "You're listing a lot of features! But how are these things selling?"

TODD "Great! Say, did I tell you that we have a money-back guarantee and that the covers are machine washable and dryable?"

ANN "I really don't know if you told me or not. What is our cost?"

TODD "$2.60 if you buy over 1,000 units, which shouldn't be too much to buy given the number of stores you have."

ANN "I wonder what our profit margin would be? What do you suggest for a retail price?"

TODD "That's up to you. These are a must buy this year, Ann. Can I sign you up for 1,000 units?"

ANN "I don't know. I don't know how they would fit in with our current products. I'm also worried about our profit margin."

TODD "If you buy today, we could have them delivered in four weeks. Okay?"

ANN "I need to think about it. Maybe you can come back in a few months if you're in the area."

TODD "Well, I think you should . . ."

ANN *[interrupting]* "I'm sorry, but I have a meeting upstairs in five minutes. Have a nice day."

QUESTIONS

1. Identify the attention-getting approach Todd used. Discuss its effectiveness and describe any ways in which it could be improved.

2. Did Todd develop rapport and build credibility? If so, how? If not, what could he have done in this area?

3. Evaluate Todd's attempt at discovering needs. Provide recommendations for improvement.

4. How well did Todd relate product features to Ann's needs? How could he have improved?

5. Was Todd sensitive enough to recognize when adjustments were necessary in his presentation? Suggest ways to improve.

CASE 9 • 2
DISCOVERING NEEDS:
A PREVIDEO EXERCISE

Lexington Medical Supply Company has been in the medical equipment and supplies industry for over 20 years. The staple of their business has been, until recently, laboratory chemicals and glassware.

Lexington has just introduced its first piece of automated equipment—a slide processor. The slide processor is a fully automated device that dramatically increases the speed at which slides for microscopic analysis can be prepared. As a result of carefully dispensing expensive processing chemicals, the unit can save laboratories considerable money on the use of these chemicals; the unit also saves on the labor overtime that is often incurred where a high volume of processing is required, or when laboratories are understaffed.

In the video segment you will watch Fred Hernandez, a rep of the Lexington Medical Supply Company, calling on Dr. Charlotte Walters, chief of pathology at Memorial Medical Center, the city's largest and most comprehensive healthcare facility. Fred has been speaking regularly with the laboratory supervisor, Curtis Mathews, and, with Curtis's support, they have arranged for Dr. Walters to see a demonstration of the slide processor.

Fred knows that both Curtis and Dr. Walters would like to modernize the operation of the laboratory, and Fred thinks that the purchase of the processor is a good place to start. Fred also knows that Dr. Walters will probably need the hospital administrator's approval for a purchase of this size.

The following are important features and benefits of the new slide processor:

Features	Benefits
1. Fully automated	Reduces need for human contact during processing procedures Frees technologists to do more challenging and interesting work, reducing boredom and turnover Ensures consistent and easily readable slides, which speeds slide analysis
2. High-speed operation	Completes an average day's workload in half the time it takes to process manually, thus reducing overtime expenses Eases processing backlogs
3. Precision chemical dispensing	Reduces significantly the use of expensive chemicals, thus cutting lab costs (savings on chemicals typically provide a payback on equipment in two years)

QUESTIONS

To help you think through how Fred *could* discover Dr. Walter's needs, answer the following questions:

1. Develop a set of open and closed questions to fully discover Dr. Walters's needs.

2. Next, develop a set of SPIN questions to discover Dr. Walters's needs.

3. Reread the material above and be prepared to watch the videotape in class. Watch how Fred *actually* discovered Dr. Walters's needs.

ADDITIONAL REFERENCES

Ailes, Roger. "The First Seven Seconds: Make First Impressions Work for You." *Success,* November 1988, p. 18.

Baum, Neil. "The Indispensable Salesperson: Ten Steps to Becoming the Salesperson They Can't Live Without." *Personal Selling Power,* March 1993, p. 54.

Beltramini, Richard F. "High Technology Salespeople's Information Acquisition Strategies." *Journal of Personal Selling and Sales Management,* May 1988, pp. 37–44.

Brown, Gene; Unal O Boya; Neil Humphreys; and Robert E Widing II. "Attributes and Behaviors of Salespeople Preferred by Buyers: High Socializing vs. Low Socializing Industrial Buyers." *Journal of Personal Selling and Sales Management,* Winter 1993, pp. 25–34.

Castleberry, Stephen B, and C David Shepherd. "Effective Interpersonal Listening and Personal Selling." *Journal of Personal Selling and Sales Management,* Winter 1993, pp. 35–50.

Clayton, Carl K. "Making Productive Interest Calls: Identifying and Meeting a Prospect's Needs Are the Major Goals." *Agri Marketing,* May 1990, pp. 99–101.

Conley, Claire. "Socratic Method of Selling: The Question Is the Answer." *American Salesman,* June 1990, pp. 3–7.

Gabriel, Gail. "Dialogue Selling." *Success,* May 1993, pp. 34–35.

George, William R; Patrick Kelly; and Claudia Marshall. "The Selling of Services: A Comprehensive Model." *Journal of Personal Selling and Sales Management,* August 1986, pp. 29–38.

Goolsby, Jerry R; Rosemary R Lagace; and Michael L. Boorom. "Psychological Adaptiveness and Sales Performance." *Journal of Personal Selling and Sales Management,* Spring 1992, pp. 51–66.

Gschwandtner, Gerhard, and Pat Garnett. *Non-Verbal Selling Power.* Englewood Cliffs, NJ: Prentice Hall, 1985.

Hanan, Mack. *Consultative Selling: The Hanan Formula for High-Margin Sales at High Levels.* New York: AMACOM, 1990.

Henthorne, Tony L; Michael S LaTour; and Alvin J Williams. "Initial Impressions in the Organizational Buyer-Seller Dyad: Sales Management Implications." *Journal of Personal Selling and Sales Management,* Summer 1992, pp. 57–66.

Mackintosh, Gerrard; Kenneth A Anglin; David M Szymanski; and James W Gentry. "Relationship Development in Selling: A Cognitive Analysis." *Journal of Personal Selling and Sales Management,* Fall 1992, pp. 23–34.

McElroy, James C; Paula C Morrow; and Sevo Eroglu. "The Atmospherics of Personal Selling." *Journal of Personal Selling and Sales Management,* Fall 1990, pp. 31–41.

Miller, Robert B, and Stephen E Heiman. *Strategic Selling: The Unique Sales System Proven Successful by America's Best Companies.* New York: Morrow, 1985.

Schlossberg, Howard. "Dawning of the Era of Emotion: Companies That Survive Will Go Beyond Satisfying Customers." *Marketing News,* February 15, 1993, p. 2ff.

Tsalikis, John; Oscar W DeShields, Jr.; and Michael S LaTour. "The Role of Accent on the Credibility and Effectiveness of the Salesperson." *Journal of Personal Selling and Sales Management*, Winter 1991, pp. 31–42.

Tullous, Raydel, and J Michael Munson. "Organizational Purchasing Analysis for Sales Management." *Journal of Personal Selling and Sales Management*, Spring 1992, pp. 15–26.

Zurier, Steve. "Consultative Selling Is Here! Distributors Emphasize Account Service over Order Taking." *Industrial Distribution*, July 1990, p. 49.

Strengthening the Presentation

W hile Chapter 9 outlined the mechanics of *what* to present (that is, features and benefits), Chapter 10 teaches *how* to present the material effectively. After studying this chapter, you should be able to bring your presentations "alive," keeping your prospects awake and interested as well as helping them remember what you said.

Some questions answered in this chapter are:

Why do salespeople need to strengthen their oral communication through the use of other tools, such as visual aids, samples, testimonials, and demonstrations?

What methods are available to strengthen the presentation?

How can salespeople most effectively utilize visual aids?

What are the secrets of a good demonstration?

How can a salesperson effectively sell to a group?

Having completed his BBA degree in marketing, Brian Vollmert began to start the job market search. He finally decided on an inside sales position with Sauber Manufacturing Company. Never heard of them? Neither had Vollmert until he started interviewing.

Sauber is one of the leading manufacturers of something that college students don't have much opportunity to buy—trailers and supplies for utilities. Have you ever seen your electric utility on the side of the road replacing wire or installing a new pole? If so, you probably also saw some of the equipment that he sells.

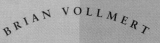

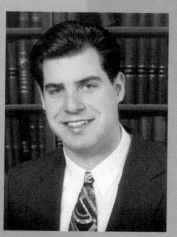

Sauber Manufacturing Co.

"Most of my selling occurs over the telephone (and we are talking about *large* ticket items; averages between $10,000 and $40,000 per unit). However, this can actually work in my favor. Although I'm young, compared to my buyers' age, they don't recognize this while on the phone and talk to me just as if I am 40.

"I've learned that it is important to learn exactly where they are coming from. I try to ask 'What do you view this type trailer you are considering buying as? Equipment? A tool? An investment?' In reality our products are all three, but by knowing their thoughts I can figure out which budget they plan to use for it and if they have any idea of the pricing.

"I always adapt to a particular customer. When bringing customers from the Chicago airport to our factory (in a rural setting) I have several different routes to choose from. If they love the country, I take the expressway for part, showing we're accessible, then I take back roads, passing cows, corn, and farms. If they would not appreciate this, then I take the expressway and stay on busy routes.

"It is always important to know where your competitors are located geographically. It's amazing how small the world really is. I once spent three weeks writing specs on

our tensioning equipment for a prospect only to find that this prospect gave my information directly to my competitor. Now, if I think that a local competitor could enter into the equation in the same way I ask the prospect tactfully and in a roundabout way 'why would you purchase our equipment with [this competitor] in your own backyard?' I would rather learn now than three weeks later!

"In sales you will probably learn to hate speaker phones. In one situation a customer, John, called about a problem that his mechanic, Al, and I were working on. John called me on his speaker phone and asked how my working relationship with Al was going. Al was in the room but kept quiet. I started speaking, then asked if Al happened to be nearby where he could add to the story. Al amazingly turned up and said 'Yes, I'm here.' Then I apologized and said, 'I'm sorry, I didn't mean to be rude, is there anyone else I should introduce myself to?' Fortunately, I had been honest in all I said before Al spoke up. Always tell the truth!

"In a manufacturing environment, include your shop people in as much as possible. They will be greater contributors and will help the customer and you. If the tables were turned, wouldn't you want it the same way? Neither one of us can exist without the other. There must be enormous respect between the office and plant or there will be trouble.

"Know when to send typed correspondence and when to include handwritten Post-Its. The Post-It portrays a personal relationship, more sincere and informal. In a time of mass-produced letters and signature stamps it is a nice thought knowing you were important enough to that person to spend time and effort. I use Post-Its a lot!"

EXHIBIT 10.1

BROCHURE WITH GREAT VISUAL APPEAL AS IT IS UNFOLDED

Courtesy National Cinema Network.

MODELS, SAMPLES, AND GIFTS

Visual selling aids such as models, samples, and gifts may be a good answer to the problem of getting and keeping buyer interest. Miniature models go to the interview as substitutes for products too large or bulky to transport easily. For example, Brink Locking Systems salespeople carry along a miniature working model of their electronic door locks when calling on prison security systems buyers. The model allows them to show how the various components work together to form a fail-safe security network.

Other salespeople use cross-section models to communicate more effectively with the buyer. For example, salespeople for Dixie Bearings use a cutaway model of a power transmission friction-reduction product. This helps the buyer, usually an industrial engineer, to clearly see how the product is constructed, resulting in greater confidence that the product will perform as described.

Some sales representatives even carry samples of large and bulky products. Fax machine salespeople for Ambassador Office Equipment have found it pays to bring along the types of machines they plan to sell. When the prospect wants a demonstration, the fax machine is available immediately. Experience has shown that anything can happen if the salesperson gets the interest of the prospect and then must return to the office to get a sample fax machine. Several more calls may be needed to secure an appointment for a demonstration.

Depending on the service or product, samples can make excellent sales aids. Food, office supplies, paper products, and long-distance services exemplify the many products or services that may be sold through the use of samples. Eli Lilly pharmaceutical salespeople almost always leave drug samples for doctors to distribute to their patients. If the drugs perform effectively, the doctor will begin prescribing the drug for other patients.

Getting samples into the buyer's hands is one of the best ways of helping the buyer evaluate a product.

Courtesy Ace Hardware Corporation.

Samples and gifts frequently help to maintain the prospect's interest after the call and serve as a reminder for prospects or customers who either buy or do not buy during the presentation. In a recent Johnson Wax sales campaign, salespeople called on buyers for major chains to describe the promotion. Salespeople walked into each buyer's office with a solid oak briefcase containing cans of aerosol Pledge, the product to be highlighted during the promotion. During the call, the sales representative demonstrated the Pledge furniture polish on the oak briefcase. At the conclusion of the visit, the rep gave the buyer not only the cans of Pledge but also the briefcase.

▌ TESTIMONIALS

Testimonials are statements, usually letters, written by satisfied users of a product or service. These letters commend the product or service and attest that the writer believes the product or service to be a good buy. For example, company representatives who sell air travel for major airlines have found case histories helpful in communicating sales points. American Airlines recounts actual experiences of business firms, showing the variety of problems that can be solved by air travel.

Progressive sales organizations use testimonials extensively. Relatively few products or services exist for which users cannot be found to testify. Testimonials are particularly useful when selling intangibles and relatively new and unusual products.

The effectiveness of a testimonial hinges on the skill with which it is used and a careful matching of satisfied user and prospect. In some situations, the testimony of a rival or a competitor of the prospective buyer would end all chance of closing the sale; in other cases, this type of testimony may be a strong factor in obtaining commitment. As much as possible, the person who writes the testimonial should be above reproach, well respected by his or her peers, and perhaps a center of influence. For example, when selling to certified public accountants (CPAs), a good source for a testimonial would be the president of the state's CPA association.

Before using a testimonial, you need to check with the person who wrote it and frequently reaffirm that he or she is still a happy, satisfied customer. One salesperson for UNISYS Computers routinely handed all prospects a testimonial from a satisfied customer of a new software package. But, unknown to the salesperson, the "satisfied customer" became an unsatisfied one and actually returned the software to UNISYS. (This happens to every vendor of software.) The salesperson kept handing out the letter until one of his prospects alerted him to the situation. He will never know how many other prospects lost interest after contacting that "satisfied customer."

Salespeople should not just hand out a testimonial to every prospect; such letters should be used only if they help to address the buyer's needs or concerns. For example, with a buyer concerned about service, the rep could use a testimonial that specifically mentions service. Also, prospects often discount testimonials, thinking: "I'll bet you used your only satisfied customer, probably a relative, to write this letter. Besides, it only talks about things in very general terms." This kind of thinking highlights the importance of using testimonials strategically rather than routinely.

▍ ELECTRONIC MEDIA

Slides, VCRs, computers, and projectors have become common equipment for the salesperson. Today's more sophisticated buyers are accustomed to watching cable TV and movies that include outstanding graphics, sound, and production. Effective salespeople respond to this trend by using electronic media.

Slides

Slides have been effective selling aids for many companies for years. For example, one structural timber firm used slides to convince buyers that laminated wood treated with waterproof glue was a good substitute for steel. Pictures of construction jobs in which laminated arches were actually being used were converted into a powerful slide show to communicate to architects and builders exactly how and where the company's product was used.

An advantage of slides has always been the relatively low cost of producing them. Also, salespeople can easily tailor the show to any buyer simply by removing and/or reordering the slides. The most effective slide shows utilize multiple projectors and multiple screens along with a stereo sound track. And thanks to new technology, slides can now be produced as easily as using a copying machine or computer.

COMPACT VCR/TV FOR
OFFICE PRESENTATIONS

SONY Corporation of America. Used by permission.

VCRs

Videocassette recorders (VCRs) are becoming a more important media tool for salespeople. VCRs improve on slides in that they portray action. Salespeople use VCRs to help the buyer see how quality is manufactured into the product (e.g., a tape showing the production process at the manufacturing plant), how others use the product or service (e.g., a tape showing a group of seniors enjoying the golf course at a retirement resort), promotional support offered with the product (e.g., a tape of the actual upcoming TV commercial for the product), and even testimonials from satisfied users. VCRs are not only used by salespeople in one-on-one and group presentations; they also see use at trade shows and for training the buyer's employees after the sale.

In the past, one of the greatest complaints against VCRs was that they were bulky and impossible to use in office settings. Technology, however, has alleviated these concerns, as Exhibit 10.2 illustrates.

Computers

More and more salespeople have adopted laptop computers for use in sales calls; the increase is dramatic. Not only do computers offer excellent visuals and graphics, they also allow the salesperson to perform what-if analyses much more easily and graphically. For example, a Procter & Gamble key account salesperson was using the computer to demonstrate how a new

EXHIBIT 10.3

COMPUTER IMAGES CAN BE
EASILY TRANSFERRED TO AN
OVERHEAD PROJECTOR

Courtesy of Kameny Spitzer Felix Advertising for Sharp Electronics Corporation, Professional Products Division.

P&G product would deliver more profit than would a competitor's product in the same shelf space. When the buyer asked what would happen if the P&G product sold for $1.69 instead of the $1.75 suggested price, the salesperson easily changed this one number in the spreadsheet program. Instantly all charts and graphs were corrected to illustrate the new pricing point, and comparisons were generated with the competitor's product.

Other salespeople use laptop computers to store large amounts of easily retrievable information. For example, Merck pharmaceutical salespeople carry laptops with a database of technical information, as well as complete copies of articles from medical journals. This allows them the flexibility to create completely unique presentations for each physician, based on the doctor's need for specific kinds of information.

Progressive firms are beginning to explore methods of utilizing high technology to its fullest. As Exhibit 10.3 shows, computers can be connected to overhead projectors for group presentations. IBM has developed a multimedia computer presentation that includes video, graphics, voice content, and an interactive touch screen.

M.D. Buyline, a firm that provides hospitals with information about negotiating for diagnostic medical equipment, equips each of its 20 field account executives with a laptop, a small 8-mm VCR, a speaker, a remote control unit and a projection panel.[3] During presentations, salespeople can switch from a 6-by-6 foot video presentation that includes video testimonials, to sales data. One advantage of this particular setup is that the prospect doesn't need to have a TV/VCR already in place.

Unfortunately, the high cost of technology prevents many from incorporating such tools in their presentations. Presentations with full-motion video can cost in the hundreds of thousands of dollars.[4] Also, high-tech

EXHIBIT 10.4   COLOR VIDEO PROJECTOR

Courtesy of Sharp Corporation. Used by permission.

equipment *can* be difficult to operate and prone to malfunction at the most embarrassing times (much like our Space Shuttle rockets).[5]

Projectors

Overhead projectors are another effective visual medium. The image projected on a wall can be up to 25 times larger than that on a written page, drawing more attention and creating greater impact. Such projectors are noiseless and simple to operate. Overhead transparencies can be made quickly and inexpensively on either a plain paper copier or an infrared transparency maker. New information, perhaps only available at the last minute, can be written on transparencies with a special marking pen. One model of projector weighs about 17 pounds, fits under an airplane seat, and looks like a briefcase. This medium can be used for presentations to individuals or to groups.

Other types of projectors are available, some capable of displaying action. For example, Exhibit 10.4 describes a color video projector used by salespeople and connectable to a VCR or computer.

PRODUCT DEMONSTRATIONS

One of the most effective methods of appealing to the buyer's senses is through product demonstration, or performance tests. Customers and prospects have a natural desire to prove the product's claims for themselves. Obviously the proof is much more satisfying and convincing to anyone who is a party to it. However, as Selling Scenario 10.1 discusses, the seller should be aware that some prospects will test your product for reasons other than

S E L L I N G · S C E N A R I O

10.1

Beware of Prospects That Are Too Interested

If a prospect is too focused on testing (your product or service) before giving you a try, or is putting an unusual amount of time and effort into the "mechanics" of a test, he or she may not be cognizant of the service aspect (i.e., the personal aspect of the buyer-seller relationship). Often a prospect such as this is, in fact, not interested in making a purchase decision, but rather wants to gather information for other reasons. These reasons might include providing competitive information to a friend or simply gathering information to present to management, or perhaps the prospect is looking to validate his or her current vendor's level of service—but with no intention of switching to a new vendor.

It's best to put selling efforts toward prospects who are committed to the idea of changing vendors and whose actions indicate a desire to learn more about the people, the product, the service, and the relationship that your company would provide. While this clearly does not hold true for all types of selling nor for all situations, when I look back and analyze what percentage of my business came from testing, almost none of our significant accounts tested us before deciding to move their business.

In two specific examples, our company, Direct Tech, expended a tremendous amount of effort, energy, and expense to compete against other "unknown" vendors for a large piece of business which, when the testing was done (and in both cases we had outperformed the other vendors), the decision was nonetheless to stay in-house.

Basically, forget testing, build a good solid relationship, use testimonials, use documentation and proof, then demonstrate superior follow-up and responsiveness—and the sale will be yours.

Source: George J. Kiebala, Account Executive, Direct Marketing Technology, Inc., personal correspondence, May 5, 1993, used by permission.

purchasing it. The following examples illustrate effective methods of demonstration for each specific situation encountered.

Paper sales representatives use demonstrations to sell quality. Having prospects hold two sheets of paper to the light, the reps point out that in a good grade of paper the fibers are evenly distributed, while in a poor grade of paper uneven distribution produces a mottled effect. To show opacity, they have the customer place a material with black lines on it under the sheet and check for show-through.

An enterprising NCR sales representative was having trouble convincing the buyer for a national retailer that NCR could provide service at all of the retailer's scattered outlets. On the next trip to the buyer, the sales representative brought along a bag of darts and a map marked with the chain's hundreds of stores and service locations. The buyer was invited to throw darts at the map, and then find the nearest stores. It was pointed out that the nearest NCR location for service was always within 50 miles. This helped win the company a multimillion-dollar order.

Farm equipment provides many opportunities for demonstrations. Power steering, quick connects and disconnects, and air-conditioning can be demonstrated effectively; buyers can see or feel such features to test

Getting the buyer actively involved is critical for effective product demonstrations.

Photo courtesy of Ted Kawalerski and Johnson & Johnson.

claims. Performance tests give buyers a chance to see the farm equipment perform over rough and smooth terrains as well as to try out the many features. Inviting the prospect to take the wheel and choose the route adds strength to the demonstration.

Some products can be sold best by getting prospects into the showroom for a hands-on product demonstration. Showrooms can be quite elaborate and effective. For example, Hewlett-Packard (HP) operates a medical marketing center in Germany. Prospects from across Europe can try all of HP's medical products. Patient responses are electronically simulated, which allows medical personnel to test the equipment in mock-emergency situations.

THINKING IT THROUGH

Many firms provide the salesperson with careful, detailed directions about how to conduct a sales demonstration successfully. One sales manager gave her salesperson these instructions:

"As you reach down to turn the machine on, try to distract the buyer's attention. While our literature claims the machine will start in 10 seconds, it is more like 45 seconds due to the microchips that we had to install under our cost-savings program. As you begin to print the daily activity log, have the buyer look at the log itself, not the screen. The screen will include an error message every time, and our engineers can't seem to find out how to correct it."

What is your reaction to these instructions? Assuming you are the salesperson, what would you say to your manager, and what would you do during the actual presentation?

The Hewlett-Packard demonstration center in Germany allows medical industry buyers to simulate actual emergencies and see how HP equipment can respond.

Photo courtesy of Hewlett-Packard Company.

A number of helpful hints for developing and engaging in effective demonstrations are:

1. Be prepared. Practice the demonstration until you become an expert. Plan for everything that could possibly go wrong.

2. Secure a proper place for the demonstration, one free of distractions for both you and the buyer. If the demonstration is at the buyer's office, make sure you have everything you need (e.g., power supply, lighting).

3. Check the equipment again to make sure it is in good working order prior to beginning the presentation. Have necessary backup parts and supplies (e.g., paper, bulbs).

4. Get the prospect involved in a meaningful way. If it is a group situation, plan which group members need to participate.

5. Always relate product features to the buyer's unique needs.

6. Make the demonstration an integral part of the overall presentation, not a separate, unrelated activity.

7. The demonstration should be simple, concise, and easily understood. Long, complicated demonstrations add to the possibility that the buyer may miss the point. Avoid any technical jargon, except with technically advanced buyers that you know will understand technical terms.

8. If your demonstration includes dead time—that is, time in which the machine is processing on its own—plan what you will do during this period of time. This is usually a great time to ask the buyer questions and have the buyer ask you questions.

9. Find out whether the prospect has already seen a competitor's prod-

S E L L I N G   S C E N A R I O

10.2

Demonstrations Can Backfire

Every salesperson has a favorite story to tell in answer to the question "Have you ever had anything go wrong during a demonstration?" Here are a few favorite stories.

Steve was demonstrating the ease of entering information into a computer program designed to generate monthly bills for electric utilities automatically. The buyer calmly sat there as Steve keyed in information for about 15 minutes. Then Steve said, "Now, all you have to do to generate those statements is to push this key, right here." The buyer, however, had his eye on a panel and a little switch near the back of the computer. "What's this red key for?" he said, as he opened the panel and pushed the switch. Unfortunately the little red key was a "kill button," which caused the computer to shut itself down, completely wiping out all of the data that Steve had put in. As the screen went blank, the buyer looked at Steve and said, "Oops!" To this day, Steve swears the buyer's act was premeditated.

Dave was demonstrating the ease of using a new copier. Suddenly, as often happens with copiers, the machine jammed. Dave calmly stated, "I'm really glad that happened. It gives me the chance to show you how easy it is to clear a jam in this machine." However, it wasn't that easy. As Dave opened the front panel to remove the offending piece of paper, a column of smoke rose from the machine. The paper was on fire! Dave not only got to show the prospect how to clear a jam, he also had to show the correct procedure for extinguishing fires. The buyer did not place an order for the copier but probably did buy a fire extinguisher for his office on the way back.

Demonstration failures aren't the exclusive territory of high-tech products. Sharon, as she demonstrated a plastic squeeze bottle to a group of potential buyers, asked, "Don't you just hate it when you shake and shake a bottle and the lotion just doesn't come out? Wouldn't it be nice if someone designed a bottle so the lotion would come out in nice, even increments?" At this, Sharon gave the bottle a rather substantial squeeze. Not only did the cap fly off, the lotion spewed all over the buyers at the front. Needless to say, Sharon took no orders that day.

Source: Personal information and Kathleen Hughes, "If You Show It Off and It Won't Work You Have a Problem," *The Wall Street Journal,* June 4, 1987, p. 1.

uct demonstration. If so, strategically include a demonstration of features the buyer liked about the competitor's product. Also plan to show how your product can meet the prospect's desires and do what the competitor's product won't do.

10. Find out if any buyers present at your demonstration have ever used your product before. Having them assist in the demonstration may be advantageous if they view your product favorably.

11. Probe during and after the demonstration. Make sure buyers understand the features and see how the product can help them. Also probe to see if buyers are interested in securing the product.

Remember Murphy's Law: What can go wrong will go wrong! And occasionally things do go wrong during a demonstration. Selling Scenario 10.2 provides several examples. If a demonstration "blows up" for whatever reason, your best strategy is usually to appeal to fate with a humorous tone of voice, like "Wow, have you ever seen anything get so messed up? I'll bet Congress couldn't have messed this up better than I have!" Don't let it embarrass or frustrate you. Life is not perfect, and sometimes things just don't work out the way you plan them. If it will help, just remember that prospects are also not perfect and sometimes they mess things up as well. Maintaining a cool and level head will probably impress the prospect with your ability to deal with a difficult situation. This may even increase your chances of a sale, since you are demonstrating your ability to handle stress (something that often occurs during the after-sale servicing of an account).

QUANTIFYING THE SOLUTION[6]

As mentioned in Chapter 2, one of the trends in buying is more sophisticated analyses by buyers. This section will explore methods available to help the buyer conduct these types of analyses.

Salespeople can strengthen the presentation by showing the prospect that the cost of the proposal is offset by added value; this is often called **quantifying the solution.** There are many methods of achieving this goal and we will examine some of the most common ones here (simple cost-benefit comparison, return on investment, net present value, payback period, and opportunity cost).

Quantifying the solution is more important in some situations than in others. Some products or services offer very little risk for the prospect (e.g., replacement parts or repairs). These products are so necessary for the continuation of the prospect's business that very little quantifying of the solution is usually needed. Other products offer moderate risk (e.g., expanding the production capacity of a plant for an existing successful product) or high risk (e.g., programs designed to reduce costs or increase sales—these offer higher risk because it is hard to calculate the exact magnitude of the potential savings or sales). For moderate- and high-risk situations, quantifying the solution becomes increasingly important. Finally, there are products that offer super-high risk (e.g., brand-new products or services—these are even riskier because *no* one can calculate costs or revenues with certainty). Attempts at quantifying the solution are imperative in super-high-risk situations. In summary, the higher the risk to the prospect, the more attention the salesperson should pay to quantifying the solution.

SIMPLE COST-BENEFIT ANALYSIS

Perhaps the simplest method of quantifying the solution is to list the costs to the buyer and the savings the buyer can expect from the investment, often called the **simple cost-benefit analysis.** Information needed to calculate savings must be supplied by the buyer in order to be realistic and meaningful. Exhibit 10.5 shows how one salesperson used a chart to compare the costs and benefits of purchasing a two-way radio system.

EXHIBIT 10.5

COST-BENEFIT ANALYSIS
FOR A MOBILE RADIO

Monthly Cost

Monthly equipment payment (five-year lease/purchase)*	$1,352.18
Monthly service agreement	295.00
Monthly broadcast fee	464.00
Total monthly cost for entire fleet	$2,111.18

Monthly Savings

Cost savings (per truck) by eliminating backtracking, unnecessary trips (based on $.21/mile × 20 miles × 22 days/month)	$ 92.40
Labor cost savings (per driver) by eliminating wasted time in backtracking, etc. ($6.50/hour × 25 minutes/day × 22 days/month)	59.58
Total cost savings per vehicle	151.98
Times number of vehicles	× 32
Total monthly cost savings for entire fleet	$4,863.36

	Years 1–5	Year 6+
Monthly savings	$ 4,863.36	$ 4,863.36
Less: Monthly cost	2,111.18	759.00*
Monthly benefit	2,752.18	4,104.36
Times months per year	× 12	× 12
Annual benefit	$33,026.16	$49,252.32

*Payment reflects ongoing cost of service agreement and broadcast fees.

COMPARATIVE
COST-BENEFIT
ANALYSIS

In many situations, the salesperson also provides a comparison of the present situation's costs with the value of the proposed solution. Or, the salesperson compares his or her product with a competitor's product. For example, a company with a premium-priced product may justify that higher price on the basis of offsetting costs in other areas. Or if productivity is enhanced, that increased productivity has economic value. In the example shown in Exhibit 10.6, the current washer must be changed three times as often as the new washer, while the new washer costs much more. If a prospect heard that you want $150 for a washer and he has been paying $25, he may say no immediately. Even if told it lasts longer, it appears that the new washer is twice as expensive ($15,000 per year versus $7,500).

But if you were able to identify other costs associated with changing the washer, such as overtime or lost production time, and you could quantify those costs (as Exhibit 10.6 shows) then you may be able to prove that the more expensive washer actually saves money. When quantifying costs, it is important to get the prospect to determine how much is lost dollar-

EXHIBIT 10.6   AN EXAMPLE OF A COMPARATIVE COST-BENEFIT ANALYSIS

	Your Current Washer			Our Proposal (The Maxi-Seal Washer)		
	Quantity	Cost	Total	Quantity	Cost	Total
Initial cost	300	$ 25	$ 7,500	100	$150	$15,000
Changing cost*	300	120	36,000	100	120	12,000
Total costs per year			$43,500			$27,000
Proposed savings				$16,500		

*Changing cost per unit = 8 hours × $15 labor = $120.

wise in production time or how much that overtime costs. Prospects will have greater faith in the numbers that they provide.

When we examine the proposal in Exhibit 10.6, we see that because the proposed washer is changed less often, the total costs per year are only $27,000, as compared to current costs of $43,500. This leads to a proposed savings of $16,500 per year!

RETURN ON INVESTMENT

The **return on investment** (ROI) is simply the net profits (or savings) expected from a given investment, expressed as a percentage of the investment:

$$\text{ROI} = \frac{\text{Net profits (or savings)}}{\text{Investment}}$$

Thus, if a new product costs $4,000 but saves the firm $5,000, the ROI is 25 percent ($5,000/$4,000 = 1.25). Many firms set a minimum ROI for any new products, services, or cost-saving programs. Salespeople need to discover the firm's minimum ROI or ROI expectations and then show that the proposal's ROI meets or exceeds those requirements. In the washer example, ROI would be calculated by taking the savings in labor hours ($36,000 − $12,000 = $24,000) and dividing by the investment. In this case, you would use the incremental cost of $7,500 and ROI equals 320 percent.

PAYBACK PERIOD

The **payback period** is the length of time it takes for the investment cash outflow to be returned in the form of cash inflows or savings. To calculate the payback period you simply add up estimated future cash inflows and divide into the investment cost. If expressed in years, the formula is:

$$\text{Payback period} = \frac{\text{Investment}}{\text{Savings (or profits) per year}}$$

Of course, the payback period could be expressed in days, weeks, months, or any other time period.

As an example, suppose a new machine costs $865,000, but will save the firm $120,000 per year in labor costs. The payback period is 7.2 years ($865,000/$120,000 per year = 7.2 years).

In the washer example, payback would be calculated by dividing $7,500 (incremental cost of the new washers per year) by $24,000 (savings in labor hours per year), which is .31 years. So in less than four months, the extra cost of the new washers is covered by the savings.

Thus, for the buyer the payback period indicates how quickly his or her investment money will come back to him or her. It can be a good measure of personal risk for a buyer. When a buyer makes a decision, his or her neck is "on the line," so to speak, until the investment money is at least recovered. Hence it's not surprising that buyers like to see small payback periods.

We have kept the discussion simple so you can understand the concept. In reality, the payback period would be calculated taking into account many other factors, such as investment tax credits and depreciation.

▍ NET PRESENT VALUE

As you may have learned in finance courses, money left idle loses value over time (i.e., a dollar today is worth more than a dollar next week) due to inflation and the firm's cost of capital. Thus, firms recalculate the value of future cash inflows into today's dollars (this is called *discounting the cash flows*). One tool to assess the validity of an opportunity is to calculate the **net present value** (NPV), which is simply the net value today of future cash inflows (i.e., discounted back to their present value today at the firm's cost of capital) minus the investment. The actual method of calculating NPV is beyond the scope of this book, but many computer programs and calculators can calculate NPV quite quickly and easily.

$$\text{Net present value} = \frac{\text{Future cash inflows discounted}}{\text{into today's dollars}} - \text{Investment}$$

As an example, let's assume that a $50 million investment will provide annual cash inflows over the next five years of $15 million per year. The cash inflows are discounted (at the firm's cost of capital) and the result is that they are actually worth $59 million in today's dollars. The NPV is thus $9 million ($59 million − $50 million).

Like ROI and payback period, many firms set a minimum NPV. In no case should the NPV be less than $0. Again, we have kept this discussion quite simple so you can understand the basic concept.

▍ OPPORTUNITY COST

The **opportunity cost** is the return a buyer would have earned from a different use of the same investment capital. Thus, a buyer could spend $100 million buying your new computer system, or buying a new $100 million production machine, or buying a $100 million controlling interest in another firm, and so forth.

Successful salespeople identify other realistic investment opportunities and then help the prospect compare the returns of the various options. These comparisons can be made using any of the techniques we have already discussed (simple cost-benefit analysis, ROI, payback period, NPV). For example, a salesperson might help the buyer determine the following information about the options identified:

	NPV	Payback Period
Buying a new telecommunications system	$1.6 million	3.6 years
Upgrading the current telecommun-ications system	$0.4 million	4.0 years

The key is that salespeople not forget that prospects have a multitude of ways to invest their money.

▍OTHER METHODS

There are many ways of quantifying the solution beyond our discussion here (e.g., turnover, contribution margin, accounting rate of return, after-tax cash flows). Salespeople should use those methods that are understandable to the prospect and that reflect the unique needs and concerns of the prospect.

When selling to resellers there are additional ways of quantifying the solution. (We will discuss these fully in Chapter 15.)

▍WRITTEN PROPOSALS

In some industries, written proposals are an important part of the selling process. As illustrated in the Dial Profit Story in Chapter 15, some proposals are simple adaptations of brochures developed by a corporate marketing department. But in industries that sell customized products, are involved in a large amount of needs-satisfaction selling, or require competitive bidding (such as many state and local governments require), a written proposal may be necessary for the buyer to organize and compare various offerings.

Proposals are also useful when the rep cannot see the decision maker. If, for example, the salesperson is calling on the Tempe, Arizona, office and the final decision will be made in the corporate office in Seattle, a proposal can be used to sell that home office decision maker.

▍RFP PROCESS

A document issued by a prospective buyer asking for a proposal may be called a **request for proposal (RFP)**, request for quote (RFQ), or request for bid (RFB). For brevity's sake, we will refer to all as RFPs.

The RFP should contain the customer's specifications for the desired product, including delivery schedules. RFPs are used when the customer has a firm idea of the product needed. From the salesperson's perspective, being a part of the specifying process makes sense. Using the needs identification process, the salesperson can assist the customer in identifying needs and specifying product characteristics. The result may be that the only product that can meet the specs is the one sold by that salesperson; when the resulting product truly meets the needs of the customer, that is only fair.

According to purchasers who issue RFPs, proposals that respond to an RFP should include:[7]

1. An executive summary containing pricing, time frames, and some product information.
2. Concise responses to questions, with direct references to the original RFP.

What buyers don't want are stacks of material that make them search for their answers; bids priced low in the expectation that the vendor can make it up later in add-ons, changes, and upgrades; and glossy marketing hype.

▮ WRITING PROPOSALS

Proposals do the selling job when the salesperson cannot be present. A key issue is keeping the customer's needs in mind. No matter what feature the salesperson likes best or how much information the salesperson's home office makes available, the only information the customer seeks is whether the product can satisfy the stated need at an affordable price.

Proposals, then, have three parts: (1) an executive summary, (2) a description of the current situation in relation to the proposed solution, and (3) a budget. When preparing proposals, salespeople can use the checklist that appears in Exhibit 10.7 to ensure that the proposal proves how the product will satisfy the buyer's needs.

Executive Summary

The **executive summary** provides, in one page or less, the total cost minus the total savings (including soft savings), a brief description of the problem to be solved, and a brief description of the proposed solution. It is designed to satisfy the concerns of an executive too busy or unwilling to read the entire proposal. The executive summary also serves to pique the interest of all readers by providing a quick glance at the benefits of the purchase.

Description/Proposed Solution

Many salespeople actually compare the current situation with the proposed solution on the same sheet. This is accomplished by listing problems with the current product or service in one column and describing how the proposed solution resolves those problems in a second column. The format resembles the Ben Franklin approach to gaining commitment, described in

A proposal must answer the following questions convincingly:

- *What Problem Are You Going to Solve?*

Show that you understand the problem and the organization's needs. Define the problem as the audience sees it, even if you believe that the presented problem is part of a larger problem that must first be solved.

- *How Are You Going to Solve It?*

Prove that your methods are feasible. Show that a solution can be found in the time available. Specify the topics you'll investigate. Explain how you'll gather data.

- *What Exactly Will You Provide for Us?*

Specify the tangible products you'll produce; explain how you'll evaluate them.

- *Can You Deliver on What You Promise?*

Show that you have the knowledge, the staff, and the facilities to do what you say you will. Describe your previous work in this area, your other qualifications, and the qualifications of any people who will be helping you.

- *What Benefits Can You Offer?*

In a sales proposal, several vendors may be able to supply the equipment needed. Show why the company should hire you. Discuss the benefits—direct and indirect—that your firm can provide.

- *When Will You Complete the Work?*

Provide a detailed schedule showing when each phase of the work will be completed.

- *How Much Will You Charge?*

Provide a detailed budget that includes costs for materials, salaries, and overhead costs.

Source: Kitty Locker, *Business and Administrative Communication* (Homewood, IL: Irwin, 1989), pp. 401–2.

Chapter 12. Such an approach has several advantages: It reminds the customer of the needs actually described in an earlier conversation or an RFP, and it can directly link the benefits of the proposed solution to satisfying those needs. Exhibit 10.8 provides a short example of such a format. If this proposal will be sent to the home office, the salesperson should make it clear that the present situation was identified by the customer's local personnel.

Some proposals are too complicated for such a simple approach. Discussion of the current situation and a description of the proposed solution may each require a separate chapter. Still, readers must be able to quickly relate characteristics of the proposed solution to the needs being met.

PRESENTING THE PROPOSAL

Prospects use proposals in many different ways. Proposals can be used to convince the home office that the local office needs your product, or proposals may be used to compare your product and terms of sale with those of your competitors. As we mentioned earlier, the intended use will influence the design of your proposal; it will also influence how you present the proposal.

Your Current Vendor (Quick Print)	Our Proposed Solution (Quickie Printers)
No delivery: You must bring it in, using 30 minutes per round trip	Free pickup and delivery: No time is lost driving to or from the copying store; receptionist can stay and do her job, with no more overtime.
Open 8 AM to 6 PM	Open 24 hours per day: overnight turnaround, which you need for most proposals and bids, now possible on all jobs at no extra cost; gives your marketing staff more time to prepare proposals and bids, resulting in more professional and profitable bids.
No special discounts	Preferred customer plan: Saves you 5 percent on every order, 10 percent on certain types of jobs; you get more productive workers, and copying for less!

Securing Local Support

When the proposal is going to be sent to the home office, it is wise to secure the support of the local decision maker. While that person is not the ultimate decision maker, the decision may rest on how much effort that person puts into getting the proposal accepted. Salespeople often use a "team effort" approach by asking the local recommending person how to assist in getting the proposal accepted. You may want to ask for permission to follow up with a phone call directly to the home office, offer to help write a recommendation letter, or ask for permission to have a national account rep or senior executive call on the prospect's home office.

Proposals and Buying Committees

Proposals are often used by buying centers to compare competitive offerings. The salesperson is asked to present the proposal to the buying committee. The challenge is that, as you learned in Chapter 4, buying center members play different roles and have different needs. Therefore, some parts of the presentation and the proposal will be of greater interest to each individual than others. Larry Boyd, sales representative for Quantum Medical, a manufacturer of sonogram equipment, solves this challenge by preparing a separate proposal for each member of the buying committee. Financial information, for example, is usually in the copy received by the hospital administrator.

Selling to Groups[8]

Selling to groups can be both rewarding and very frustrating. On the plus side, if you make an effective presentation every member of the prospect group becomes your ally. On the down side, groups behave like groups, with group standards and norms, and issues of status and group leadership.

When selling to groups, it is important for the salesperson to gather information about the needs and concerns of each individual who will attend: This should include a discovery *for each prospect group member*—his or her status within the group, authority, perceptions about the urgency of the problem, receptivity to ideas, major areas of interest and concern, key benefits for this person, likely resistance, and ways to handle this resistance.

It is important to develop not only objectives for the meeting, but also objectives for what the seller hopes to accomplish with each prospect present at the meeting. Planning may include the development of special visual aids for specific individuals present. The seller must expect many more objections and interruptions in a group setting as compared to selling to an individual.

During the presentation, it is usually best to create an informal atmosphere in which group members are encouraged to speak freely and the salesperson feels free to join the group's discussion. Thus, an informal location (e.g., a corner of a large room, as opposed to a formal conference room) is preferred. Avoid formal presentation methods like speeches that separate buyers and sellers into *them* vs. *us*. If the group members decide that the meeting is over, don't try to hold them.

Of course, most things you have learned about selling to individuals applies equally to groups. You should learn the names of group members and use them when appropriate. You should listen carefully and observe all nonverbal cues. When one member of the buying team is talking it is especially important to observe the cues being transmitted by the other members of the buying team who aren't currently talking to see if they are, in effect, agreeing or disagreeing with the speaker.

If the group meeting is actually a negotiation session, many more things must be considered. As a result, we have devoted an entire chapter (Chapter 14) to the topic of formal negotiations.

USING COMMUNICATION TOOLS EFFECTIVELY

Whatever methods are used to communicate with the buyer, they must be used effectively and efficiently. Several important hints for developing and using visual aids are:[9]

1. Don't place too much information on a visual; on a textual visual, don't use more than seven words per line nor more than seven lines per visual. Don't use complete sentences; the speaker should verbally provide the missing details.

2. Use bullets to emphasize key points.

3. When using tables and charts, don't overload the buyer with numbers. Use no more than five or six columns and drop all unnecessary zeros.

4. Clearly label each visual with a title. Label all columns and rows.

5. If possible, use graphics (e.g., diagrams, pie charts, bar charts) instead of tables. Tables are often needed if actual raw numbers are important; graphics are better at displaying trends and relationships.

EXHIBIT 10.9   VISUAL AIDS: A COMPARISON

Type of Visual	Relative Cost	Difficulty in Transporting	Complexity in Operating	Effective with Large Groups?
Portfolio	Low	No	Easy	No; unless you use an easel
Models/samples/gifts	Varies	No	Easy	Yes; if all have one
Testimonials	Low	No	Easy	Yes; if all have a copy
Slides	Medium	Little	Medium	Yes; with large screen
Regular TV/VCR	High	High	Medium	Yes
Compact TV/VCR	High	Little	Easy	No
Laptop computers	High	Medium	Hard	No; unless hooked up to projector
Overhead projectors	Medium	Medium	Easy	Yes
Color video projector	High	High	Medium	Yes
Product demonstrations	Varies	Varies	Varies	Maybe; need hands-on contact

6. Use consistent art styles, layouts, and scales for your collection of charts and figures. This will make it easier for the buyer to follow along.

7. Check your visuals closely for typographical errors, misspelled words, and other errors.

8. Make sure your buyer can see the visuals. For projected visuals, test to ensure that they can be easily seen from any seat in the room. When showing visuals in your portfolio, make sure the portfolio is turned so the buyer can see it easily.

9. Mark your visuals so you can find them easily. Arrange them in a logical order.

10. Don't let the visual interfere with your interaction. It should not be placed, like a wall, between you and the buyer. Also, look at the buyer, not at your visual; maintain eye contact with the buyer.

11. When using VCRs, make sure the video is fast-paced and relatively short. Don't show more than four minutes of a video at one time.

12. Maintain proper control of the visuals. Without control, buyers often thumb through catalogs or look ahead at visuals before the salesperson has adequately covered the current visual. Remove the visual after it has been used. This also cuts down on desk clutter and helps you be more organized. But be careful, you are there to meet the buyer's needs.

13. When discussing the visual, always relate features to benefits for the buyer.

14. Decide which visuals you can leave with the buyer, and have copies already made.

Although creating effective visuals is an art, the hints described here can help to maximize their usefulness. Exhibit 10.9 summarizes the strengths and weaknesses of a variety of visual aids.

SUMMARY

Strengthening communication with the buyer is important. It helps focus the buyer's attention, improves the buyer's understanding, helps the buyer remember what was said, and can create a sense of value.

Many methods of strengthening communication are available. Most salespeople have developed some sort of portfolio that includes charts, catalogs, brochures, pictures, and advertisements. Salespeople can also use models, samples, gifts, testimonials, and electronic media such as slides, VCRs, computers, and projectors.

A backbone of many sales presentations is the product demonstration. It allows the buyer to get hands-on experience with the product, something most other communication methods do not offer.

It is often important to quantify the solution so the buyer can evaluate the costs in relation to the benefits that he or she can derive from the proposal. Some of the more common methods of quantifying the solution include the simple cost-benefit analysis, return on investment, the payback period, net present value, and an understanding of opportunity cost.

All communication tools require skill and practice to be used effectively. Outstanding salespeople follow a number of guidelines to improve their use of visuals and to demonstrate their products more effectively.

KEY TERMS

executive summary   *309*
multiple-sense appeals   *290*
net present value   *307*
opportunity cost   *307*
payback period   *306*
portfolio   *292*

quantifying the solution   *304*
request for proposal (RFP)   *308*
return on investment   *306*
simple cost-benefit analysis   *304*
testimonials   *295*

QUESTIONS AND PROBLEMS

1. J.H. Patterson of National Cash Register fame trained sales representatives to "talk with their pencils." What advantages does the use of this type of sales aid offer?

2. A salesperson has planned a sales call to sell muffler components to an auto maker by developing a presentation around visual illustrations in an easel portfolio. She has placed the easel in front of her prospect, and she seats herself on the right side and begins her presentation. As she gets to the second page of the portfolio, the prospect picks it up and starts thumbing through it, looking at the pictures and illustrations. The prospect says, "Go ahead with your presentation. I can hear you while I glance through your portfolio."
   a. What should the salesperson do? Explain the reasons for the action you recommend.
   b. How can she effectively communicate product features of muffler components?

3. When it comes to making substantial outlays for farm machines, farmers understandably like to be shown the machines. Obviously, however, even the most enterprising sales representative cannot bring a complete selection of hay conditioners, harrows, or other machines to the farmer. The conventional sales rep relies on the power of words to convince farmers to visit the showroom. Can you think of a better way of making a presentation to the prospect in the home, or even in the field where the prospect may be working?

4. Assume you plan a flight demonstration to prove some of the claims you have made for a new-model Piper, Cessna, or Beechcraft airplane. Would the demonstration be the same for each of these three individuals: a nervous person, an economy-minded person, and a performance-minded person? Explain.

5. How could you demonstrate the following products?
   a. A stereo speaker in a showroom.
   b. A word processor in an office.
   c. Shatterproof plate glass in a factory.
   d. Air-conditioning in an industrial warehouse.
   e. A water purifier to a potential reseller.

6. What communication tools would you use to provide solid proof for the following concerns expressed by prospects?
   a. "No one has asked me to carry the product."
   b. "I think the costs are higher than my benefit from it."
   c. "I don't believe I could ever learn how to use that product feature."
   d. "I don't have time to go see your plant in New York. Further, I don't think your plant has the most modern equipment, which you'd need to order to produce a product of the quality we are looking for."
   e. "You look too young to service my account."
   f. "I'm not sure how your product compares to the competitor's product."

7. Visual aids have generally been described in this chapter as positive, useful tools for salespeople. When should they not be used? Are there any times when they could actually be detrimental to communication effectiveness?

8. Sometimes things don't go the way you plan them. What would you do in each of the following situations?
   a. The power goes off in the middle of a computer demonstration. As a result, you lose all of the data you have been inputting for the last eight minutes.
   b. The buyer says, "Look, I don't want to see a bunch of pictures and charts! Just tell me how you'll save me money."
   c. You involve the prospect by having her help you calculate the savings she will experience with your machine. While putting the last number in the calculator, she apparently hit the wrong key. As a result, she calculates the time needed to recoup her investment as 258 years instead of the actual 14 years.
   d. You hand the prospect a page from your price book. He takes it, looks at it, then opens his desk drawer and tosses it in. Because your industry has severe price competition, your company's policy forbids you to hand out your price sheet to anyone.
   e. You are showing your buyer some items in the portfolio, and you accidently knock it off the desk. The rings open up, and the pages scatter all over the floor.
   f. You offer the prospect a sample of your new food product. He tastes it, makes a face, and says, "That's really pretty awful tasting!"
   g. You are in the middle of using a computer to demonstrate return on investments at various pricing points. Suddenly you forget how to call up the next screen. No matter how hard you try, you just can't remember what to do next!
   h. You are in the middle of painting a word picture, and the buyer is interrupted by a phone call. The call lasts about five minutes. The buyer turns and says, "Now, where were we?"

9. What communication tools would you use to communicate the following facts?
   a. "We have been in business for over 100 years."
   b. "I am dependable."
   c. "Even though I've only been selling this product for two months, I do possess the necessary product knowledge."
   d. "I know our last product was a flop, but this product was developed with extensive test marketing."
   e. "Unlike our competitors, our company has never been sued by a customer."

10. Assume that you are selling a new sound system to a movie theater in your town. The system will cost $350,000. It is estimated that the new system will improve sound quality so much that more patrons will watch movies. You expect revenues to increase by $39,000 each year over the next 20 years. At the movie theater's cost of capital, the discounted cash inflows have a value today of $400,000. Based on this information:
    a. Calculate the return on investment.
    b. Calculate the payback period.
    c. Calculate the net present value.

CASE PROBLEMS

CASE 10 • 1
WDDO RADIO STATION

WDDO is a local radio station in Madison, Wisconsin, a city of 170,000 people. After the station was started 25 years ago, James Wensley, its owner and founder, emphasized public service programming rather than entertainment programming. The station was devoted exclusively to local and national news.

Last year Wensley sold the station to Tom Campbell. Campbell reviewed the station's ratings and advertising sales and decided to change its programming format. He also hired four advertising-time salespeople.

In designing the new format, Campbell used the following research data on the radio listening habits of Madison residents:

Women listen to the radio four hours a day, whereas men listen two hours a day.

Radio is preferred to television for coverage of fast-breaking news stories.

The WDDO all-news format captured an average of 20 percent of the radio audience.

The average age of radio purchasers is 26. Car radio owners listen to WDDO 40 percent of the time when they are driving.

Eighty percent of cars have radios.

The average car owner listens to the radio 30.2 minutes per day.

Radio listeners like to hear sincere, warm, friendly people.

WDDO is particularly popular during summer and winter vacations.

The new WDDO schedule has now been set, as shown in Case Exhibit 1.

QUESTIONS

Describe how you would use communication tools if you were attempting to sell WDDO advertising to the following leads. Fully prepare any visual aids you propose to use.

1. The promoter of a rock concert.

2. The largest car dealer in the city.

3. A small sporting goods store.

4. A large discount department store chain.

C A S E   E X H I B I T   1

Monday through Saturday

Morning*
12:00–4:00 Classical music
Host: John Michaels—music host and critic from Los Angeles

4:00–6:00 Call-in question-and-answer format
Host: Mike Lupin—recently on a national radio show

6:00–10:00 "Good Morning Show"—popular music plus news, weather, and interviews with personalities and local officials

Host: Jim Jackson—recently host of a similar program on most popular station in Minnesota

10:00–12:00 "Homemaker Show"—information on such subjects as cooking and child rearing

Host: Jennifer Fiddler—recently head of a consumer advocate group

Afternoon*
12:00–3:30 Popular music
Host: Debbie Rudder—host of local TV variety show

3:30–5:00 Rock music
Host: Mike Evans—recent college graduate

5:00–7:30 "News Roundup"—local and national news
Host: George Stein—longtime WDDO newscaster

7:30–10:00 Call-in comments on current events
Host: Ward Baxter—host for a similar TV program

10:00–12:00 Popular music
Host: Kamy Lutz—recently a disc jockey on a Chicago radio station

Sunday

Morning
12:00–6:00 Off the air

6:00–10:00 Religious services (noncommercial)

10:00–12:00 "Newsmakers"—interviews with local and national officials

Host: Jim Taylor—former University of Wisconsin political science professor

Afternoon
12:00–4:00 "Sport Event of the Week"—a major syndicated event

4:00–6:00 "News of the Week"
Host: Jim Taylor

6:00–8:00 Dance music
Host: Debbie Rudder

8:00–9:00 "Wall Street Summary"
Host: Jim Bettman—financial reporter for a local newspaper
9:00–12:00 Operatic music
Host: John Michaels

WDDO Rate Schedule

Class	Length of Spot	Number of Spots Purchased			
		1	10	50	100
AAA (Monday–Friday, 6:00–10:00 AM,	60 seconds	$200	$190	$175	$160
3:30–7:30 PM Saturday, 10:00–12:00 AM)	30	160	150	140	130
AA (Monday–Friday 10:00 AM–3:30 PM	10	100	90	80	75
7:30–10:00 PM Sunday, 9:00 AM–9:00 PM)	60	120	112	105	100
	30	100	90	85	80
A (all other times)	10	60	55	53	50
	60	85	80	75	65
	30	72	65	60	55
	100	45	40	38	35

*Every hour on the hour, five minutes are devoted to national and local headline news.

Consolidated Employee Benefits is a national provider of medical and hospital insurance programs to large- and medium-sized corporations. Consolidated sets the industry standard for progressive benefits administration. A sophisticated, computerized communications system links all 64 of its regional branch offices. Consolidated is proud of its record of offering its policyholders fast and accurate claims processing and customized benefits programs.

In the video segment you will watch, Dennis Savage, an account executive for Consolidated, is meeting with Tom Hong, vice president of personnel for Arrow Computers, and the benefits administrator, Pat Olsen. Dennis has had several meetings with Pat and has learned that Arrow intends to change its insurance carrier. He also knows that two other companies are vying for the account.

Dennis knows that the final decision on a new carrier will be made by Tom and the company treasurer, Jordon Gates. Dennis's objective is to get Tom to arrange for him to present a proposal to Gates.

The package that Dennis is selling has four main features:

Features	Benefits
Fully automated claims processing provides a standard turnaround of seven to ten days and, by special arrangement, a three- to five-day turnaround	Accelerates claims payments.
Highly trained claims administrators that review all claims rejected by system	Ensures reliable claims settlement.
	Reduces employee complaints about settlements.
Sixty-four regional claims offices located throughout the country	Meets growing company's need for conveniently located offices to ensure efficient service.
	Maintains local focus on available medical services.
	Provides quick, informed aid to employees from offices that are located nearby.
Computerized communications system linking all regional offices with computer terminals in client offices	Minimizes settlement problems by providing on-line reports.

QUESTIONS

To help you think how Dennis could strengthen the presentation to Tom and Pat, answer the following questions:

1. For each of the four features, list several ways in which Dennis can strengthen the presentation (e.g., charts, samples, letters, demonstrations, etc.). Make sure your suggestions will provide concrete proof of each asserted feature and benefit.

2. Describe any special tactics you would utilize with regard to strengthening the presentation under the following scenarios:
   a. Tom is a driver, Pat is analytical.
   b. Tom is an expressive, Pat is an expressive.

3. Reread the material above and be prepared to watch the videotape in class. Watch how Dennis actually strengthened the presentation. Make notes about what Dennis had to do before the meeting to prepare for using the tools he employed.

ADDITIONAL REFERENCES

"A Selection of Recent Presentation Products." *Business Marketing,* June 1992, p. 36+.

Andersen, Jeff. "Mastering Multimedia." *Sales and Marketing Management,* January 1993, pp. 55–58.

Boylan, Bob. "Overheads: Why They're Still No. 1." *Business Marketing,* January 1993, p. 57.

Brown, Priscilla C. "Color Helps the Sell." *Business Marketing,* January 1993, pp. 58–59.

"Demonstrating with Flair." *Institutional Distribution,* May 15, 1990, p. 106+.

Falvey, Jack. "Does Your Company Need First Aid for Its Visuals?" *Sales & Marketing Management,* July 1990, pp. 97–99.

Geco, Susan. "Making Company Tours Pay Off." *Inc.,* February 1993, p. 26.

"Giving Great Presentations." *Success,* May 1990, p. 30.

Kern, Richard. "Making Visual Aids Work for You." *Sales & Marketing Management,* February 1989, pp. 45–48.

Mayfield, Lee A. "Presentations: How to Do It Wrong," *Sales and Marketing Management,* July 1990, pp. 79–81.

Moine, Donald J. "Whatever You Sell, Sell It with a Story." *Personal Selling Power,* January–February 1989, pp. 28–30.

Mullich, Joe. "Polishing Your 'Image.' " *Business Marketing,* January 1993, p. 49+.

Phillips, Colman P. "The Not-so-Sweet Sound of Sales Talk." *Training,* September 1988, pp. 56–62.

Rehfeld, Barry. "How Large Companies Buy." *Personal Selling Power,* September 1993, pp. 26–33.

Rosenthal, Alan. "How to Improve Presentations: The Race Doesn't Always Go to the Slickest." *Business Marketing,* June 1992, pp. 40–41.

Sonnenberg, Frank K. "Presentations That Persuade." *Journal of Business Strategy,* September–October 1988, pp. 55–58.

Tartarella, Ron. "Picture This!" *Personal Selling Power,* September 1993, pp. 64–65.

Taylor, Thayer C. "Show and Tell That Sells." *Sales and Marketing Management,* April 1990, pp. 78–85.

"Wake Me When the Presentation Is Over," *Training,* January 1993, p. 65.

Walter, Joyce. "What Makes a Bad Presentation Bad?" *Folio,* September 1989, pp. 137–39.

Wisniewski, James Casimir. "How to Approach Doctors as Potential Customers." *Marketing News,* June 5, 1989, p. 7.

Responding to Objections

*A*ll salespeople encounter objections during the selling process. All buyers, at some time or other, voice an objection to something the salesperson says or does. In fact, some customers may raise irrational or irrelevant objections that have nothing to do with the product, the company, or the seller. Of course, buyers also raise valid concerns and questions.

Skill in responding to objections is just as necessary as skill in making appointments, conducting interviews, demonstrating, and obtaining commitment. When new salespeople realize buyers' objections are a normal and natural part of the sales process, they can treat such objections as sales opportunities.

Some questions answered in this chapter are:

When do buyers object?

What objections can be expected?

What preparation is necessary to respond to objections?

What methods and techniques are good to use when responding to objections?

Tia Kallas is an account executive for MetroVision Advertising in Chicago, Illinois. MetroVision sells advertising space on major cable networks such as ESPN, CNN, USA, Sportschannel, TNT, MTV, Nickelodeon, The Weather Channel, Discovery, and Headline News. Their target customers are local businesses, such as auto dealerships, restaurants, furniture stores, carpet and tile stores, and supermarkets. These businesses have the advantage of advertising on cable TV in their local area at a reasonable price.

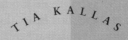

MetroVision Advertising

"MetroVision is a great company to work for. First of all, they are privately owned by Newhouse Publishing. Newhouse is a very strong firm (they own cable systems and newspapers and publish many magazines like *Vogue*, *Glamour*, and *Mademoiselle*). Second, MetroVision treats their employees very well. It is truly a family-oriented company. They always let you know you are appreciated. Finally, cable advertising is fun to sell!

"In the cable industry, one thing we have learned about getting our first appointment is to tell the prospect we would like 20 minutes of their time to get to know their business, not try and sell them something on the first call. And we do exactly what we say! Besides, it would be unfair for them if we tried to sell them without knowing how their business runs. Our approach works because it makes the prospect feel at ease on the first call.

"One objection I run into most often is 'cable television advertising is too expensive.' We feel this is not really an objection, just a misunderstanding. Once I present my rates they often say the prices are lower than they expected. It is amazing how people can get an idea in their head even though they have no basis for it.

"When it comes to giving quotes, there is one rule I have learned which is always give your best price first. If you find out you lost the sale to a competitor due to lower pricing, and you tell your client you can give them the same price or better, they say, 'why didn't you give me the best price first?' Of course, my firm would like to maximize its profits, but we feel this approach accomplishes this goal in the long run: We build trust, get the sale, and gain a business relationship.

"I've learned how important it is to build long-term relationships with your clients. When I sign a contract, the business doesn't stop there. I make sure I call them at least one a month and try to visit them once a month also. I have one client who likes to see me just to talk. If I get too busy and don't get a chance to see him one month, the next month I'm in he asks me where I've been. He has told me his rep from the other cable company signs a contract and he never sees her until it's renewal time."

EXHIBIT 11.2

FIVE MAJOR TYPES OF
OBJECTIONS

Need	*Source*
"I do not need the product or service."	"I don't like your company."
"I need more information."	"I don't like you."
"I've never done it that way before."	
"I'm just not interested."	*Price*
	"I have no money."
Product	"The value does not exceed the cost."
"I don't understand."	
"I don't like the product or service features."	*Time*
	"I need time to think about it."

require a collection service. Legitimate objections will arise when prospective buyers have not been qualified on all the essential characteristics of a prospect.

Salespeople may encounter objections such as "My business is different" or "I have no use for your service." These objections from an accurately qualified buyer show that the buyer is not convinced that a need exists. This could have been rectified with strong implication and need payoff questions (see Chapter 9).

If the salesperson cannot establish a need in the buyer's mind, that buyer can logically be expected to object. In **pioneer selling**—selling a new and different product, service, or idea—the salesperson has more difficulty establishing a need in the buyer's mind. For example, salespeople for Alpine Paper Company often hear "I don't think we need it" when the buyer is asked to carry a line of recycled paper products.

I NEED MORE INFORMATION

Some buyers offer objections in an attempt to get more information. They may have already decided they want the product or service but wish to fortify themselves with logical reasons they can use to justify the purchase to others. Also, the salesperson may not have provided enough proof about a particular benefit.

Conflict may also exist in the buyer's mind. One conflict could be a struggle taking place between the dictates of emotion and reason. The buyer may be trying to decide between two competitive products or between buying and not buying. Whatever the struggle, buyers who object to get more information are usually interested, and the possibility of commitment is good.

I'VE NEVER DONE IT THAT WAY BEFORE

Human beings are creatures of habit. Once they develop a routine or establish a custom, they tend to resist change. Fear or ignorance may be the basis for not wanting to try anything new or different. Businesspeople may resist anything new just because it is new or because they have no related experience to guide them in buying. The buyer's natural tendency to resist

Some buyers need more in-
formation before committing
themselves because they have
to justify their decision to
others.

Courtesy Caterpillar Inc.

buying a new product or changing from a satisfactory brand to a new one
can be found behind many objections.

It should be noted that some buyers have a habit of raising many
objections just to watch salespeople squirm and feel uncomfortable. (Fortunately there aren't many buyers like that!) For example, Peggy, a
manufacturer's salesperson for Walker Muffler, used to call on a large
auto parts store in an attempt to have the store carry her line of muf-
flers. Jackie, the store's buyer gave Peggy a tough time on her first two
calls. At the end of her second call, Peggy was so frustrated with the
manner in which she was being treated that she decided to never call
there again. However, as she was walking out of the store she ran into
a Goodyear rep who also called on Jackie, selling belts and hoses. Since
they were on somewhat friendly terms, Peggy admitted her frustrations to
the Goodyear rep. He replied "Oh, that's just the way Jackie operates. On
the third call he is always a nice guy. Just wait and see." Sure enough,
Peggy's next call on Jackie was not only pleasant, it was also productive!
Buyers like Jackie usually just want to see the sales rep work hard for the
order.

Habits and customs also help to somewhat insulate the prospect from
certain risks. For example, suppose you are selling a new line of office chairs
to Harry, a newly promoted assistant buyer. If Jane, the previous assistant
buyer and now the senior buyer, bought your competitor's product, Harry
would appear to take less risk by continuing to buy from your competitor.
If Harry buys from you, Jane may think, "I've been doing business with
the other firm for 15 years. Now, Harry, you come in and tell me I've been
doing it wrong all these years? I'm not sure you're going to be a good assistant buyer."

Sometimes buyers won't admit that they do not understand what the seller is talking about.

Martin Rogers/TSW.

I'M JUST NOT INTERESTED

Some prospects voice objections simply in an attempt to dismiss the salesperson. The prospect may not have enough time to devote to the interview, may not be interested in the product or service offered for sale, may not be in the mood to listen, or may have decided because of some unhappy experiences not to face further unpleasant interviews.

These objections occur when salespeople make a cold canvass or try to make an appointment. Particularly, overaggressive, rude, impolite, or pesky salespeople can expect prospects to use numerous excuses to keep them from making a presentation.

I DON'T UNDERSTAND

Sometimes objections arise because customers do not understand the salesperson's presentation. These objections may never be verbalized; meaning the seller must carefully observe the buyer's nonverbal cues. (See Chapter 5 for a discussion of nonverbals.) Misunderstandings frequently occur with customers unfamiliar with technical terms, unaware of the unique capabilities of a product, or uncertain about benefits arising from services provided with the product, such as warranties. Unfortunately, buyers often will not admit that they do not understand something.

For example, when desktop publishing programs were first made available for PC computers, a salesperson for an IBM distributor gave a presentation to a very busy plant manager of a consumer products firm. The new software would allow the manager to create and produce the plant's monthly newsletter to plant employees in-house, instead of sending the work out to be typeset and run. The manager, however, did not understand the new product's concept. He thought that the software would create the newsletter but that the firm would still have to send the work out to be typeset and run off. However, he did not want to appear stupid and simply told the salesperson that he was not interested. The rep never knew, until later when the manager bought a competitor's desktop publishing program, that the manager simply hadn't understood.

I Don't Like the Product or Service Features

Often the product or service has features that do not satisfy the buyer. At other times, the prospect will request features currently not available. Customers may say:

"I don't like the design."

"It doesn't taste good to me!"

"I wish you included free maintenance."

"We prefer printed circuits."

"I was looking for a lighter shade of red."

"I can't get my machines repaired quickly by your service technicians."

"It took a month for us to receive our last order."

I Don't Like Your Company

Most buyers, especially industrial buyers, are vitally interested in the sales representative's company because the buyer is put at risk if the seller's firm is not financially sound, can't continually produce the product, and so forth. They need to be satisfied with the company's financial standing, personnel, and business policies. Buyers may ask questions such as these:

"Isn't your company a new one in the field?"

"Is it true your company lost money last year?"

"How do I know you'll be in business next year?"

"Aren't you the firm that was indicted by a federal grand jury for price fixing?"

"Your company isn't very well known, is it?"

"Who does your designing?"

"Can your company give us the credit we have been receiving from other companies?"

"How do I know you can deliver on time?"

"Your company has a bad image in the industry."

Of course, buyers may not actually voice these concerns due to a desire to avoid appearing rude. But unvoiced questions about the sales rep's company may affect their decisions and the long-term relationships the sales rep is trying to establish.

I Don't Like You

Sometimes a salesperson's personality clashes with that of a prospect. Wise salespeople know they must do everything possible to adjust their manner to please the prospect. At times, however, doing business with some people appears impossible.

Prospects may object to a presentation or an appointment because they have taken a dislike to the salesperson or because they feel they can't trust the salesperson. Candid prospects may say:

"You seem too young to be selling these."

"You've never worked in my industry. How can you be trained to know what I need?"

"I don't like to do business with you."

"You're a pest! I don't have any time for you."

"You and I will never be able to do business."

More common, the prospect shields the real reason and says something like:

"We don't need any."

"Sorry, we're stocked up."

"I haven't any time today to discuss your proposition."

THINKING IT THROUGH	*A*ssume you have worked as a salesperson for an industrial chemical firm for six months. You attended a two-week "basic selling skill" course but have *not* yet attended any product knowledge training classes. You are making a call with your sales manager. The buyer says, "Gee, you look too young to be selling chemicals. Do you have a chemistry degree?" Before you get a chance to respond, your manager says, "Oh, he [meaning you] has already completed our one-month intensive product knowledge course. I guarantee he knows it all!" What would you say or do? What would you do if later the buyer asked you a technical question?

▌ I HAVE NO MONEY

Companies that have no money to buy the product may have been classified as prospects. As indicated in Chapter 7, the ability to pay is an important factor in lead qualification. An incomplete or poor job of qualifying may cause this objection to arise.

When leads say they can't afford a product, they may have a valid objection. If so, the salesperson should not waste time; new prospects should be contacted. Selling Scenario 11.1 describes how one seller responded to this objection.

▌ THE VALUE DOES NOT EXCEED THE COST

Most buyers must sacrifice something else in order to buy a product. The money spent for the product is not available for other things. When we buy as individuals, the choice may be between the down payment on a new car and a vacation trip; for businesses, it may be between expanding the plant and distributing a dividend.

S E L L I N G *S C E N A R I O*

11.1

How to Handle the "I Have No Money" Objection

With regards to the "I have no money" objection, one of the key responsibilities of a salesperson is to focus on the success of your product line. While calling on a Hallmark store last year, we noted that one of our key product lines, the Precious Moments figurines, occupied 20 feet of selling space. While attempting to place a reorder on this product line, the buyer suggested that they had no money or "open to buy" dollars.

From that point we calculated the square footage of our product line in relation to the entire store and then calculated the total dollars purchased and sold over the past 12 months. After our calculations, we determined that this particular Hallmark account was generating $260 per square foot of our product line, which is phenomenal for this industry.

After that calculation and explaining to the owner how we arrived at that amount, we then said, "Now, can you tell us that you don't have any money? What other product lines generate those type of dollars for you? May we possibly suggest you reduce your purchases in those other lines and transfer some of your dollars to this product category [Precious Moments figurines]?"

Needless to say, such an analysis of profits per square foot proved worthwhile and not only generated increased sales but also gave the store owner more confidence in the sales representative.

Source: Terry Michaels, personal correspondence, used with permission.

Usually, buyers object until they are sure the sacrifice is more than offset by the value of the product or services being acquired. Exhibit 11.3 shows this graphically. The question of value received often underlies customers' objections.

Whatever the price of a product, somebody will object that it is too high or out of line with the competition. Other common price objections are:

"I can't afford it."

"I can't afford to spend that much right now."

"I never accept the first price quoted by a salesperson."

"I was looking for a cheaper model."

"I don't care to invest that much—I'll use it only a short while."

"I can beat your price on these items."

"We can't make a reasonable profit if we have to pay that much for the merchandise."

"We always get a special discount."

"I'm going to wait for prices to come down."

Although objections about price occur more often than any other kind, they may just be masks to hide the real reason for the buyer's reluctance. (A more complete discussion of dealing with price objections appears in

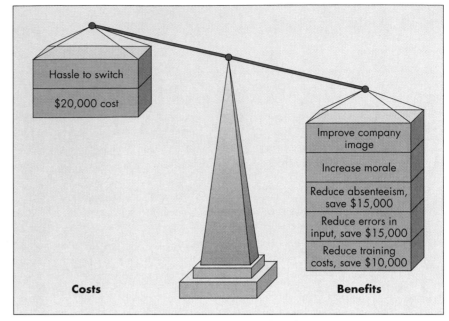

Note: If costs overweigh benefits, the decision will be not to buy. If benefits outweigh costs, the decision will be to buy.

the last section of this chapter.) Implicit in many price objections is the notion of product or service quality. Thus, the buyer stating that "your price is too high" might actually be thinking, "The quality is too low for such a high price."

I NEED TIME TO THINK ABOUT IT

Buyers often object to making a decision "now." Many, in fact, believe that postponing an action is an effective way to say no.

Salespeople can expect to hear objections such as the following, especially from analyticals and amiables (see Chapter 6):

"I haven't made up my mind."

"I want to think it over."

"I'd like to talk it over with my partner."

"See me on your next trip."

"I'm not ready to buy."

"I don't want to commit myself."

"I think I'll wait a while."

"I want to look around."

"I'm waiting until my inventory goes down."

"I want to turn in the old unit at the end of the season."

"Just leave me your literature. I'll study it and then let you know what we decide."

This buyer is providing non-verbal cues that say "I need more time to think about it."-

Paul Barton/The Stock Market.

OTHER OBJECTIONS SALESPEOPLE HEAR

Listing every possible objection that could ever occur under any situation would be impossible. However, the following are a number of additional examples of objections that salespeople often hear:

"I'm not interested."

"I'm satisfied with the company we use now."

"We have a reciprocity agreement with your competitor."

"We are all stocked up."

"We have no room for your line."

"There is no demand for your product."

"You'll have to see Mr. X."

"My brother-in-law is in the business."

"Your competitor just came out with a brand-new product that seems superior to yours."

"I've heard complaints from my friends who use your product."

"Sure, we can do business. But I need a little kickback to make it worth my time and trouble."

"I believe we might be able to do business if you are willing to start seeing me socially." (Selling Scenario 11.2 delves into this issue more fully.)

"It's a lot of hassle in paperwork and time to switch suppliers."

SELLING SCENARIO
11.2

Sexual Harassment on the Job

Probably the most frustrating situation is when the buyer sexually harasses the salesperson or requests some form of sexual favor before the "deal can be closed." Consider the following true situations and ask yourself what you would do in each case.

Susan Jayne sells oil products to industrial firms in the Midwest. Once, during the middle of the day, she parked her car in a multilevel car park. As she approached the elevator, one of her customers, Mark, a businessman from a major firm walked up. Riding up in the otherwise empty elevator with her, he suddenly grabbed Jayne and kissed her.

Paul Jarman works for a mortgage banker in the Southeast as a salesperson. He regularly calls on real estate agents and attempts to develop partnerships between his bank and the agencies. Recently he was faced with this dilemma. Three young, attractive female agents agreed to use Paul's bank exclusively—but only if he would agree to become each agent's sexual partner. Since the agents are very successful, if Paul agreed to their demands he would have earned an estimated $30,000 in commissions each year! Paul was convinced, however, that his wife would not be pleased with the arrangement.

Jeannette Holcomb is a drug retailer for Marion/Merrell-Dow Pharmaceuticals. She has regularly called on Dr. Howard Beane, a very respected and successful cardiologist, for the past three years. Today, as she was describing a new study that was just published, Dr. Beane placed his hand on her leg and said, "Jeannette, why haven't we ever gotten together?" Jeannette was shocked, especially since Dr. Bean's wife was one of his nurses and the office door was wide open!

Sexual harassment occurs in almost every industry. It has been a problem for females for years and now is a growing problem for males. Salespeople need to be prepared. How should you react? It depends on the situation. Linda Lynton offers several suggested responses: directly say "No," use humor, or walk away from the business.*

What did our real-world salespeople do in each situation? Susan looked Mark directly in the eye and said, "Mark don't you ever do that again!" He never did.

Paul decided to walk away from the business. He never explained to the agents his reason for not calling on them again.

Jeannette, in a somewhat disappointed tone of voice, softly told Dr. Beane: "We've done business for over three years. Let's not spoil it now." Dr. Beane never mentioned the topic again and continued to prescribe Jeannette's drug.

The situations are true. All names were changed to protect the victims.

*Linda Lynton, "The Dilemma of Sexual Harassment," *Sales & Marketing Management*, October 1989, pp. 67–71.

PREPARING TO RESPOND

DEVELOP A POSITIVE ATTITUDE

It takes careful thought and preparation to truly respond to objections in a helpful manner. Exhibit 11.4 overviews the activities of successful salespeople in this regard. To respond to objections effectively, nothing can substitute for having a positive attitude. It is important for sales reps not only to know how to successfully respond to objections but "also how to recognize problems for what they are—a logical extension of the selling

- They develop and maintain a positive attitude about objections.
- They relax and listen, never interrupting the buyer.
- They anticipate objections and prepare helpful responses.
- They forestall known concerns before they arise.
- They make sure the objection is not just an excuse.
- They are sincerely empathetic to the buyer's objections.

process rather than a personal affront to their own abilities."[1] Proper attitude is shown by answering sincerely, refraining from arguing or contradicting, and welcoming—even inviting—objections.

Just pretending to be empathetic is useless; buyers can see through it easily. And once the buyer gets the idea that the salesperson is talking for effect, regaining that buyer's confidence and respect will be almost impossible. Empathy shows as much in the tone of voice and facial expressions as in the actual words spoken.

The greatest evidence of sincerity, however, comes from the salesperson's actions. One successful advertising agency owner states: "I have always tried to sit on the same side of the table as my clients, to see problems through their eyes." Buyers want valid objections to be treated seriously; they want their ideas respected, not belittled. They look for empathetic understanding of their problems. Real objections are logical to the prospect, regardless of how irrational they may appear to the salesperson. Salespeople must have the attitude of and act as a helper, a counselor, and an adviser. To do this, they must treat the prospect as a friend, not a foe.

The temptation to prove the prospect wrong, to say "I told you so" or "I'm right and you're wrong," is always strong. This kind of attitude invites debate—encouraging, perhaps even forcing, the prospect to defend a position regardless of its merits. Egos get involved when prospects find their positions bluntly challenged. Most will try to defend their own opinions in these circumstances because they don't want to lose face. The sales presentation may then degenerate into a personal duel that the salesperson cannot possibly win. Arguing with, contradicting, and showing belligerence toward a prospect are negative, unwise actions.

The reality is that "a typical seller runs into more rejection in the course of a day than most of us have to absorb in weeks, if not months. From an emotional perspective, selling is a rough way to make a living. Your self-respect is on the line every time you walk through a customer's door."[2]

However, salespeople must remember that objections present sales opportunities.[3] People who object have at least some level of interest in what you are saying. Further, objections provide feedback as to what is really on the prospect's mind. To capitalize on these opportunities, salespeople must show they welcome any and all objections. They have to make the prospect believe they are sincerely glad the objection has been raised. This attitude shows in remarks such as:

"I can see just what you mean. I'd probably feel the same way."

"I'm glad you mentioned that, Mr. Atkinson."

"That certainly is a wise comment, Ms. Smith, and I can see your problem."

"If I were purchasing this product, I'd want an answer to that same question."

"Tell me about it."

In dealing with prospects and customers, truthfulness is an absolute necessity for dignity, confidence, and continued relations. Maintaining a positive attitude about objections will go a long way toward building goodwill.

ANTICIPATE OBJECTIONS

Salespeople must know that, at some time, objections will be made to almost everything concerning their product, their company, or themselves. Common sense requires that they prepare answers to objections certain to be raised (probably 80 percent or more can be anticipated), because few salespeople can answer objections effectively on the spur of the moment.

Many companies draw up lists of common objections and provide effective answers; the salesperson is encouraged to be familiar with these lists. Firms also help by videotaping practice role plays so the salesperson can become more proficient in anticipating objections and responding effectively in each situation.

Successful sales representatives may keep a notebook and record new objections they encounter, along with any new ideas for responses; they also pick up helpful suggestions at sales meetings. Successful reps, recognizing that different personality types may require different types of responses or proof, plan accordingly.

When salespeople know an objection will be raised, they should have good answers ready. This helps build confidence. Unanticipated or unanswerable objections can easily cause embarrassment and lost sales.

RELAX AND LISTEN—DO NOT INTERRUPT

When responding to an objection, listen first—then answer the objection. Allow the prospect to state a position completely. Do not interrupt with an answer, even though the objection to be stated is already apparent to you. Listen as though you've never heard that objection before. Ray Schmitz, a salesperson for Data Comm Networking, summarizes the view of many successful salespeople: "When speaking with a customer I have found silence to be as effective as anything."[4]

Too many salespeople conduct conversations somewhat like the following:

SALESPERSON   "Mr. Clark, from a survey of your operations, I'm convinced you're now spending more money repairing your own motors than you would by having us do the job for you—and really do it right!"

CUSTOMER   "I wonder if we are not doing it right ourselves. Your repair service may be good. But after all, you don't have to be exactly an electrical genius in order to be able to . . ."

SALESPERSON   "Just a minute now! Pardon me for interrupting, but there's a point I'd like to make right there! It isn't a matter of anyone being a genius. It's a matter of having a heavy investment of special motor repair equipment and supplies like vacuum impregnating tanks and lathes for banding armatures, boring bearings, and turning new shafts."

CUSTOMER   "Yeah, but you don't understand my point. What I'm driving at . . ."

SALESPERSON   "I know what you're driving at. And I assure you you're wrong! You forget that even if your own workers are smart cookies, they just can't do high-quality work without a lot of special equipment."

CUSTOMER   "But you still don't get my point! The idea I'm trying to get off my chest—if I can make myself clear on this third attempt—is this. The maintenance workers that we now have doing motor repair work . . ."

SALESPERSON   "Could more profitably spend their time on plant trouble-shooting! Right?"

CUSTOMER   "That isn't what I was going to say! I was trying to say that between their trouble jobs, instead of just sitting around and shooting the bull . . ."

SALESPERSON   "Now wait a minute, Mr. Clark. Wait jus-s-t a minute! Let me get a word in here! If you've got any notion that a good motor rewinding job can be done with somebody's left hand on an odd-moment basis, you got another think coming. And my survey here will prove it! Listen!"[5]

This type of attitude and interruptions will likely bring a quick end to the interview.

FORESTALL KNOWN CONCERNS

Good salespeople, after a period of experience and training, know that certain features of their products or services are vulnerable, are likely to be misunderstood, or are materially different from competitors' products. The salesperson may have products with limited features, may have to quote a price that seems high, may not be able to offer cash discounts, may have no service representatives in the immediate area, or may represent a new company in the field.

In these situations, salespeople often forestall the objection. To **forestall** is to prevent by doing something ahead of time. In selling, this means salespeople raise objections before the buyers have a chance to raise them. For example, one salesperson forestalled a concern about the different "feel" of an electronic typewriter this way:

I know you'll find the touch of the keyboard different, lighter than what you're used to on your electric typewriter. You're going to like that, though, because your hands won't get as tired. In almost every electronic I've sold, typists have taken only one day to get accustomed to the new feel, and then they swear that they would never go back to their electric again!

A salesperson might approach a price problem by saying, "You know, other buyers have been concerned that this product is expensive. Well, let me show you how little it will really cost you to get the best."

Some salespeople do such a good job of forestalling that buyers change their minds without ever going on record as objecting to the feature and then having to reverse themselves. Buyers are more willing to change their thinking when they do not feel constrained to defend a position they have already stated.

While not all objections can be preempted, the major ones can be spotted and forestalled during the presentation. Buyers have no need to raise an objection already stated—and answered—by the salesperson.

Forestalling can be even more important in written proposals, since immediate feedback between buyer and seller is not possible. These forestalled objections can be addressed throughout the proposal. For example, on the page describing delivery terms, the seller could insert a paragraph that begins: "You may be wondering how we can promise an eight-day delivery even though we have such a small production capacity. Actually, we are able to . . . because . . ."

Another option in forestalling objections in written proposals is to have a separate page or section entitled something like "Concerns You May Have with This Proposal." The section could then list the potential concerns and provide responses to them.

▮ EVALUATE OBJECTIONS

Objections may be classified as unsatisfied needs (i.e., real objections) or excuses. **Excuses** are concerns expressed by the buyer that mask the buyer's true objections. Thus, the comment "I can't afford it now" would simply be an excuse if the buyer honestly could afford it now but doesn't want to buy for some other reason.

An objection to buying is seldom stated as "I don't have any reason. I just don't want to buy." More common, the buyer or prospect gives a reason that appears at first to be a real objection: "I don't have the money" may be an excuse; "I can't use your product" may be an excuse. The tone of voice or the nature of the reason may provide evidence that the prospect is not offering a sincere objection.

Salespeople need to develop skill in evaluating objections. No exact formula has been devised to separate excuses from real objections. The circumstances will usually be a clue to the answer. In a cold canvass, when the prospect says, "I'm sorry, I don't have any money," the salesperson may conclude that the prospect doesn't want to hear the presentation. However, the same reason offered after a complete presentation has been made and data on the prospect have been gathered through observation and questioning may be valid. Salespeople must rely on observation, questioning (see the probing method described in Chapter 12), knowledge of why people buy, and experience to determine the validity of the reason offered for the objection.

In some situations, the buyer may honestly have difficulty in dealing with a particular salesperson. If the concern is real (i.e., not just an excuse), the seller's firm sometimes institutes a **turn over** (or TO), which simply means the account is given to a different salesperson. Unfortunately, this occasionally occurs because the buyer is sexist, racist, or otherwise prejudiced, or because the salesperson is not practicing adaptive selling behaviors.

EFFECTIVE RESPONSE METHODS

Any discussion of specific methods and techniques for responding to objections needs to emphasize that no one perfect method or technique exists for answering all objections completely. Some prospects, no matter what you do, will never feel that their objections have been adequately addressed.

In some instances, spending a lot of time trying to convince the prospect may not be wise. For example, when an industrial recycling salesperson contacts a prospect who says "I don't believe in recycling," the salesperson may better spend available time calling on some of the vast number of people who do.

Salespeople should develop a procedure for responding to objections. The following steps can be applied and adapted to most selling situations:

1. Listen carefully—don't interrupt. Let the prospect talk.
2. Repeat the prospect's objection. Make sure you understand the objection. Ask questions to permit the prospect to clarify objections. Acknowledge the apparent soundness of the prospect's opinion. In other words, agree as far as possible with the prospect's thinking before providing an answer.
3. Evaluate the objection. Determine whether the stated objection is real or just an excuse.
4. Decide on the method(s) to use in answering the objection. Some factors to be considered: the phase of the sales process in which the prospect raises the objection; the mood, or frame of mind, evidenced by the prospect; the reason for the objection; the personality type of the buyer; and the number of times the reason is advanced. Flexibility is critical.
5. Get a commitment from prospects. The answer to any objection must satisfy them if a sale is to result. Get them to agree that their objection has been answered.

This section will describe seven common methods for responding to objections.[6] As Exhibit 11.5 indicates, the first two, direct denial and indirect denial, are used only when the prospect makes an untrue statement. The next five methods—compensation, feel-felt-found, boomerang, pass-up, and postpone—are useful when the buyer raises a valid point or offers an opinion.

Before using any of the methods described in this section, salespeople almost always first need to probe to help the prospect clarify the concerns and to make sure they understand the objection.[7] If the prospect says, "Your service is not too good," the salesperson can probe by asking a question:

"Not too good?"

"What do you mean by not too good? Exactly what service are you referring to?"

"Is service very important to you?"

E X H I B I T   11 . 5

COMMON METHODS FOR
RESPONDING TO
OBJECTIONS

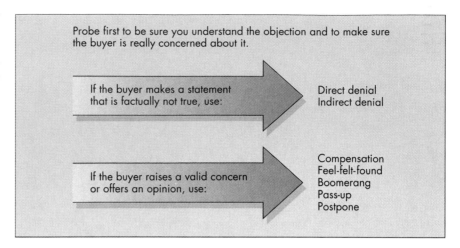

Probe first to be sure you understand the objection and to make sure the buyer is really concerned about it.

If the buyer makes a statement that is factually not true, use:

Direct denial
Indirect denial

If the buyer raises a valid concern or offers an opinion, use:

Compensation
Feel-felt-found
Boomerang
Pass-up
Postpone

"Can you explain what you mean?"

"I'm not sure I understand."

Many serious blunders have occurred because the salesperson did not understand the question, answered the wrong question, or failed to answer the objection fully.

For example, a sales training manager was listening to a sales training consultant talk about the services she could offer. At one point in the conversation the manager asked, "Has anyone in our industry, the electrical products industry specifically, ever used this training package before?" The rep for the consulting firm answered, "Sure, we have sold this package to several consumer products firms. Why just last week I received a nice letter from Gillette that had nothing but good things to say . . ." The manager did not buy the training package; he figured that if the rep for the consulting firm did not even know how to listen, then the sales training package she was selling couldn't be very good either. (Chapter 5 provided many helpful suggestions regarding the art of questioning and probing.)

DIRECT DENIAL

At times salespeople face objections based on incomplete or inaccurate information. They should respond by providing information or correcting facts. When using **direct denial,** the salesperson makes a relatively strong statement indicating the error the prospect has made. For example:

BUYER   "I am not interested in hearing about your guidance systems. Your firm was one of the companies recently indicted for fraud, conspiracy, and price fixing by a federal grand jury. I don't want to do business with such a firm."

SALESPERSON   "I'm not sure where you heard that, but it simply is not true. Our firm has never been involved in such activity, and our record is clean. If you would care to tell me the source of your information, I'm sure we can clear this up. Maybe you're confusing us with another firm."

No one likes to be told that he or she is wrong, so the direct denial must be used with caution. It is only appropriate when the objection is blatantly inaccurate and potentially devastating to the presentation. Salespeople must also possess facts to back up such a denial.

The direct denial should never be used if the prospect is merely stating an opinion or if the objection is true. For example, the direct denial would be inappropriate if the buyer stated the objection that "I don't like the feel of simulated leather products." Direct denial should be avoided even for a false statement if the objection is of trivial importance to the buyer. An indirect denial or pass-up method would be more appropriate in that case.

▌ INDIRECT DENIAL

In the **indirect denial** method, the salesperson denies the objection but attempts to soften the response. The salesperson takes the edge off the response by agreeing with the prospect that the objection is an important one. Prospects expect salespeople to disagree; instead, salespeople who recognize the sincerity of the objection will carefully respect the prospect's view. This avoids a direct contradiction and confrontation. To begin an answer, a salesperson would do well to agree with the prospect, but only to the extent that the agreement does not weaken the validity of the salesperson's later denial. For example:

> **BUYER**   "Your machines break down more often than most of your major competitors'."

> **SALESPERSON**   "I can see why you would feel that way. Just 10 years ago, that statement would have been right on target. However, things have changed with our new quality assurance program. In fact, just last year, Syncos Ratings, a well-respected independent rater of quality in our industry, rated us as number one in the industry for fewest breakdowns."

The important features of indirect denial are that salespeople recognize the position of the customer who makes the objection and then continue by introducing substantial evidence. The beginning statement should always be true and help the prospect know that the question was a good one. Examples of opening statements are:

"There is some truth to what you are saying."

"With the market the way it is today, I can certainly see why you're concerned about that."

"I'll bet 90 percent of the people I call on voice the same concern."

"That's really an excellent question, and it allows me the chance to clear up a misconception that perhaps I've given you."

Indirect denial should never be used if the prospect has raised a valid point or is merely expressing an opinion. It can be used for all personality types and would be especially effective for amiables and analyticals, because they like less assertive salespeople.

COMPENSATION METHOD

Every product has some advantages and some disadvantages, compared with competing products. Also, an absolutely perfect product or service has never been developed; the firm always has to make cost-benefit decisions about what features to include.

Buyers note these trade-offs and often object because the salesperson's product is less than perfect. The wise salesperson will admit that such objections are valid and then proceed to show any compensating advantages. This is called the **compensation method** of responding to objections. An example is:

> PROSPECT   "This machine only has four filling nozzles. Your competitor's has six nozzles."
>
> SALESPERSON   "You're absolutely right. It only has four nozzles, but it costs $4,000 less than the competitor's models and you said you needed a model that is priced in the lower range. Also, our nozzles are designed for easy maintenance. You only have to remove four screws to get to the filter screens. Most other models have at least 10 screws. That means downtime will be reduced considerably, which is something else you said you were very concerned about."

The compensation method is an explicit use of the multiattribute model discussed in Chapter 4. A low score on one attribute can be compensated for by a high score on another attribute. The method can be very effective for many objections and concerns. It seems most appropriate for analyticals, who are accustomed to conducting trade-off analyses. However, it is useful for all other personality types as well.

Of course, the buyer may not value the compensating advantages or may really need the features at issue (e.g., the prospect *must* have six nozzles in order to work with another piece of equipment already owned). In such cases, salespeople can recommend a different product (from their own line, if available, or from a competitor) or search for other prospects.

FEEL-FELT-FOUND METHOD

When buyers' objections reflect their own attitudes or opinions, the salesperson can show how others held similar views before trying the product or service. In this method, called the **feel-felt-found method,** the salesperson goes on to relate that others actually found their initial opinions to be unfounded after they tried the product:

> PROSPECT   "I don't think my customers will want to buy a CD player with all of these fancy features."
>
> SALESPERSON   "I can certainly see how you feel. Bob Scott, down the road in Houston, felt the same way when I first proposed that he sell these. However, he found that after he agreed to display them next to his current CD line, customers were very interested. In fact, he called me up four days later to order more."

The sequence of the feel-felt-found method is important, as is the person or persons identified in each stage. It should be "*I* can see how you feel . . . *others* felt the same way . . . yet *they* found." Inexperienced

An older buyer may question the credibility and knowledge of a much younger salesperson. In this situation the salesperson can use the feel-felt-found method to help resolve those concerns.

Time Systems, Inc.; photo by Al Payne.

salespeople often mix up the order or the parties identified (e.g., "yet you will find").

While the feel-felt-found technique is sound in principle, it should probably be used sparingly. Anyone with knowledge about selling (i.e., buyers) can easily spot this method and it may appear to be phony or canned.

Proof of the salesperson's assertion, in the form of a testimonial letter, strengthens the method. If a letter is not available, the salesperson might be able to supply the name and phone number of the third party. Always secure the third party's permission first, though. (See Chapter 10 for suggestions for references.)

Although the feel-felt-found method can be used for all personality types, it seems most appropriate for expressives and amiables. Both types tend to care more about what other people think and what other people are doing.

▮ BOOMERANG METHOD

By using the **boomerang method** of responding to objections, the salesperson turns the objection into a reason for acting now. It can be used in many situations (e.g., when making an appointment, during the presentation, when attempting to secure commitment, and in postsale situations):

PROSPECT   "I'm too busy to see you right now."

SALESPERSON   "I know you are busy, and that's the reason I would like to take 30 minutes of your time. I operate a service designed to save busy executives like yourself up to two hours out of every day."

The boomerang method requires care. It can appear very pushy and salesy. It sounds like a high-pressure sales tactic you would have heard from someone selling patent medicine in the 1800s (e.g., "You can't afford not to buy this amazing little bottle of Dr. Bob's Elixir!").

It does have useful applications, however. Often, the product or service is actually designed to save the buyer substantial amounts of time or money. If the buyer objects to spending either the time to listen or the money, the boomerang method may be a powerful tool to help the buyer see the benefit of investing these resources.

This method works with most personality types. Drivers may require the boomerang technique more often, since they tend to erect time constraints and other barriers and are less willing to listen to just any salesperson's presentation.

▌ Pass-Up Method

At times the buyer voices opinions or concerns more to vent frustration than anything else. When this occurs, your best strategy is often the **pass-up method:** simply let the buyer talk, acknowledge that you heard the concern, pause, and then move on to another topic.

BUYER "Hey, you use Madonna in your commercials, don't you? Sure you do. Now, I want to tell you that I don't like her style or what she stands for! Kids today need a role model they can look up to. What happened to the kind of role models we used to have? It just frustrates me the way rock stars get such a strong following these days!"

SALESPERSON "I certainly understand your concern. I remember my dad talking about some of his role models and the respect he had for them. *[Pause]* What were we talking about? Oh yes. I was telling you about the coupon drop we are planning."

In this example, the salesperson used the pass-up method because the buyer apparently was just blowing off steam. If the buyer really wanted some response from the salesperson, this would have become evident during the salesperson's pause; the buyer would have asked a direct question (e.g., "Can't you change your commercials?") or made a statement (e.g., "I refuse to do business with companies that use rock stars in their commercials!").

In reality, a salesperson can often do very little about some of a prospect's opinions. What are the chances that this salesperson's firm will pull a $5 million ad campaign just because one buyer objects? It's very doubtful that a firm would ever take such action (unless the buyer has tremendous power in the relationship).

Sometimes the salesperson can use the pass-up method by simply agreeing with the prospect and then moving on, which suggests to the buyer that the concern really shouldn't be much of an issue. For example:

BUYER "You want $25 for this little plastic bottle?!"

SELLER "Uh huh. Now, do you see this switch on this side? It's used if you ever need to . . ."

The pass-up method should not be used if the objection raised is factually false. Also, it should not be used if the salesperson, through probing, could help clarify the buyer's thinking on the topic. Experience is the key to making such a determination. The pass-up method, due to its very nature, should be used very sparingly.

T H I N K I N G **I T** **T H R O U G H**	*H*ow would you feel if someone used the pass-up method on you? Are there times it wouldn't bother you? Are there times it would really bother you?

▌ POSTPONE METHOD

In the early part of a sales interview, the prospect may raise objections that the salesperson would prefer to answer later in the presentation, after an opportunity has been given to discover the prospect's needs. Using the **postpone method,** the salesperson would ask permission to answer the question at a later time:

> **BUYER** *[very early in the call]* "How much does the air compressor cost?"
>
> **SALESPERSON** "If you don't mind, I would prefer to answer that question in a few minutes. I really can't tell you how much it will cost until I learn more about your air compressor needs and know what kind of features you are looking for."

The prospect will seldom refuse the request if the sales representative appears to be acting in good faith. The sales representative would then proceed with the presentation until the point at which the objection can best be answered.

Some objections are best answered when they occur; others can be responded to best by delaying the answer. Experience guides the sales representative. Take care not to treat an objection lightly or let it appear that you don't want to answer the question. Another danger in postponing is that the buyer will not be able to focus on what you are saying until his or her concern is addressed. (On the other hand, you are responsible for helping the buyer critically evaluate the solution offered; and often the buyer can process information effectively only after learning preliminary facts.)

Salespeople make the most use of the postponement technique when a price objection occurs early in the presentation. However, it can be utilized for almost any type of objection or question. For example, postponing discussions about guarantees, delivery schedules, implementation time frames, and certain unique product features until later in the presentation is often preferable.

What if the buyer is convinced that he or she deserves the answer right now? Then answer the objection now. You usually have more to lose by demanding that the buyer wait for information than by

E X H I B I T 11 . 6

RESPONDING TO
OBJECTIONS: USING
EACH METHOD

Objection: Your product's quality is too low.

Responses*

Direct denial: That simply is not true. Our product has been rated as the highest in the industry for the last three years.

Indirect denial: I can certainly see why you would be concerned about quality. Actually, though, our product has been rated as the highest in the industry for the last three years.

Compensation method: I agree that our quality is not as high as some of our competitors'. However, it was designed that way for consumers who are looking for a lower-priced alternative, perhaps just to use in a weekend cottage. So you see, our somewhat lower quality is actually offset by our much lower price.

Feel-felt-found: I can certainly understand how you feel. Mortimer Jiggs felt the same way before he bought the product. But after using it, he found that the quality was actually equal to that of other products.

Boomerang: The fact that the quality is lower than in other products is probably the very reason you should buy it. You said that some of your customers are looking for a low-priced product to buy for their grandchildren. This product fills that need.

Pass-up: I understand your concern. You know one of the things I always look for is how a product's quality stacks up against its cost. *[Pause]* Now, we were talking about . . .

Postpone That's an interesting point. Before discussing it fully, I would like to cover just two things that I think will help you better understand the product from a different perspective. Okay?

*These are not necessarily good answers to the stated objection. Also, the choice of method would depend on whether the objection is factual or not. Thus, the replies given in this table are just designed to differentiate the various methods.

simply providing the answer when the buyer strongly requests it. For example:

PROSPECT   "What are the delivery schedules of this new product?"

SALESPERSON   "I would really prefer to discuss that after we talk about our unique production process and extensive quality control measures."

PROSPECT   "No, I want to know now!"

SALESPERSON   "Well, keep in mind that my later discussion about the production process will shed new light on the topic. We anticipate a four- to five-month delivery time after the contract reaches our corporate headquarters."

USING THE METHODS

The seven methods just discussed appear in sales training courses across all industries and geographic boundaries. To help you more easily distinguish the differences among the various techniques, Exhibit 11.6 provides an example of the use of each method for the objection "Your product's quality is too low."

Salespeople often combine methods when answering an objection. For example, a price objection may initially be postponed, then later be discussed using the compensation method. At other times, several methods can be used in one answer:

BUYER   "I don't think this product will last as long as some of the other, more expensive competitive products."

SALESPERSON   "That's probably the very reason you should buy it. *[boomerang method]* It may not last quite as long, but it is less than half the cost of competitive products. *[compensation method]* I can certainly understand your concern, though. You know, Mark Hancock felt the way you do. He was concerned about the product's life. But after he used our product for one year, he found that its life expectancy didn't create any problems for his production staff. *[feel-felt-found method]*"

Before moving on with the presentation, the salesperson needs to make sure the buyer agrees that all objections have been completely answered. Without this commitment, the salesperson does not know that the buyer has understood the answer or that the buyer's concerns have been fully addressed. To achieve this commitment, the salesperson can use one or more of the following types of phrases:

"Did I answer your question?"

"Does that make sense?"

"Do you see why that is not as important as you originally thought?"

"I hope I haven't confused you."

"Do you have any more questions?"

THE PRICE OBJECTION

Sales managers continually hear from salespeople that price is the most frequently mentioned obstacle to obtaining commitment. In fact, about 20 percent of buyers are thought to buy purely on price (which means that a full 80 percent buy for reasons other than just price). As a result, all salespeople need to prepare for price objections.

Price is still an issue even between partnering firms. In fact, it appears that price haggling is on the increase.[8] As one observer noted, "Industry pundits have noted a trend within distribution toward partnerships in which price plays a limited role. But a simultaneous reality is that many customers continue to buy on price."[9]

The product's value must be established before time is spent discussing price. The value expected determines the price a prospect is willing to pay. The salesperson should build value to a point at which it is greater than the price asked, or there will be no sale. This cannot, as a rule, be accomplished during the early stages of the presentation.

EXHIBIT 11.7

LOOK BEFORE YOU CUT
PRICES! YOU MUST SELL
MORE TO BREAK EVEN

There is a business truism that says you can cut, cut, cut until you cut yourself out of business. This can certainly apply to cutting prices in an effort to increase profits. The two don't necessarily go together. For example: Select the gross profit presently being earned from those presented at the top of the chart. Follow the left column down until you line up with the proposed price cut. The intersected figure represents the percentage of increase in unit sales required in order to earn the same gross profit realized before the price cut. Obviously it helps to know this figure so you don't end up with a lot of work for nothing.

See for yourself: Assume your present gross margin is 25 percent, and you cut your selling price 10 percent. Locate the 25 percent column under Present Gross Profit. Now follow the column down until you line up with the 10 percent cut in selling price in the left-hand column. You will find you will need to sell 66.7 percent *more* units to earn the same margin dollars as at the previous price.

Present Gross Profit

Cut Price	5.0%	10.0%	15.0%	20.0%	25.0%	30.0%
1%	25.0	11.1	7.1	5.3	4.2	3.4
2	66.6	25.0	15.4	11.1	8.7	7.1
3	150.0	42.8	25.0	17.6	13.6	11.1
4	400.0	66.6	36.4	25.0	19.0	15.4
5	—	100.0	50.0	33.3	25.0	20.0
6	—	150.0	66.7	42.9	31.6	25.0
7	—	233.3	87.5	53.8	38.9	30.4
8	—	400.0	114.3	66.7	47.1	36.4
9	—	1000.0	150.0	81.8	56.3	42.9
10	—	—	200.0	100.0	**66.7**	50.0
11	—	—	275.0	122.2	78.6	57.9
12	—	—	400.0	150.0	92.3	66.7
13	—	—	650.0	185.7	108.3	76.5
14	—	—	1400.0	233.3	127.3	87.5
15	—	—	—	300.0	150.0	100.0
16	—	—	—	400.0	177.8	114.3
17	—	—	—	566.7	212.5	130.8
18	—	—	—	900.0	257.1	150.0
19	—	—	—	1900.0	316.7	172.7
20	—	—	—	—	400.0	200.0
21	—	—	—	—	525.0	233.3
22	—	—	—	—	733.3	275.0
23	—	—	—	—	1115.0	328.6
24	—	—	—	—	2400.0	400.0
25	—	—	—	—	—	500.0

Source: Vince Nall, President, Ideal Industries. Used by permission.

Price objections are best handled with a two-step approach. First, the salesperson should try to look at the objection from the customer's viewpoint, asking questions that can be used to better understand the customer's perspective:

"Too high in what respect, Mr. Jones?"

"Would you mind telling me why you think my price is too high?"

"Could you tell me how much we are out of line?"

"We are usually quite competitive on this model, so I am surprised you find our price high. Are the quotes you have for the same size engine?"

"What do you feel would be a fair price for this service?"

After you know more about the customer's perspective, your next step is to sell value and quality rather than price.[10] All customers would prefer to buy less-expensive products if they believe they will receive the same benefits. However, many customers will pay more for higher quality when the quality benefits and features are pointed out to them. Many high-quality products appear similar to lower-quality products; thus, salespeople need to emphasize the features that justify a price difference.

For example, a Premier Industrial salesperson, who sells industrial fasteners and supplies, may hear the objection "That bolt costs $750! I could buy it elsewhere for $75.00." The salesperson would reply, "Yes, but that bolt is inside the inner workings of your most important piece of production equipment. Let's say you buy that $75 bolt. How much employee time and production downtime would it take to disassemble the machine again and replace that one bolt?"

The salesperson would then engage in a complete cost-benefit analysis to further solidify his or her point.

One pharmaceutical salesperson often hears that her company's drug for migraines is too expensive. Her response is to paint a word picture:[11]

DOCTOR   "How much does this product cost?"

SALESPERSON   "It costs about $45. . . There are 15 doses per bottle, so it ends up about $3 per dose."

DOCTOR   "That's too much money!'

SALESPERSON   "Consider your patients who have to lie in the dark because their heads hurt so badly, they can't see straight, can't think straight, and are nauseous from this migraine pain. A price of $3 is really inexpensive to relieve these patients' pain, wouldn't you agree?"

Just telling customers about quality and value is not enough; they must be shown. Top salespeople use the communication tools discussed in Chapter 10 to describe more clearly the quality and value of the products. This includes such activities as demonstrating the product, showing test results and quality control procedures, using case histories, and offering testimonials.

Intangible features can also provide value that offsets price. Some of these features are:

1. Services. Good service in the form of faster deliveries, technical advice, and field assistance is but one of the intangibles that can spell value, savings, and profits to a customer.

2. Company reputation. For a customer tempted to buy on price alone, salespeople can emphasize the importance of having a thoroughly reliable source of supply: the salesperson's company. It has been demonstrated time and again that quality is measured by the reputation of the company behind it.

3. The salesperson. Customers value sales representatives who go out of their way to help with problems and promotions—salespeople who keep their word and follow through when they start something. These services are very valuable to customers.

Unfortunately, the first response of many salespeople to a price objection is to lower the price. Inexperienced salespeople, desiring to gain business, often quote the lowest possible price as quickly as possible. They forget that for a mutually beneficial long-term relationship to exist, their firm must make a fair profit. Also, by cutting prices, you have to sell more to maintain profit margins, as Exhibit 11.7 on page 346 clearly illustrates.

Keep in mind that buyers will respond to a seller in different ways, depending on their culture. For example, Germans are known as being thorough, systematic, and well prepared; but they are also rather dogmatic and thus lack flexibility and the desire to compromise.[12] As a result, it could be difficult to deal with a German who raises a price objection.

SUMMARY

Responding to objections is a vital part of a salesperson's responsibility. Objections may be offered at any time during the relationship between the buyer and salesperson. They are to be expected, even welcomed; and they must be handled with skill and empathy.

Buyers object for many reasons. They may have no money or they may not need the product. They may need more information or misunderstand some information already offered. They may be accustomed to another product, may not feel the value exceeds the cost, or may not like the product's features. They may want to get rid of the salesperson or may not trust the salesperson or his or her company. They may want time to think or may object for many other reasons.

Successful salespeople carefully prepare effective responses to buyers' concerns. They need to develop a positive attitude, not interrupt, anticipate known objections and forestall many of them, and learn how to evaluate objections.

Effective methods of responding to objections are available, and their success has been proven. Methods exist both for concerns that are not true and for objections that either are true or are just the buyer's opinion. Sensitivity in choosing the right method is vital. Nothing will substitute for developing skill at using them.

KEY TERMS

boomerang method *341*
compensation method *340*
direct denial *338*
excuses *336*
feel-felt-found method *340*
forestall *335*

indirect denial *339*
objection *322*
pass-up method *342*
pioneer selling *324*
postpone method *343*
turn over *336*

QUESTIONS AND
PROBLEMS

1. When making cold canvass calls, sales representatives often need to get through a "screen," such as a receptionist, secretary, or assistant, to reach the decision maker. How would you answer the following objections from a screen?
   a. "I'm sorry, but Mr. Harris is too busy right now."
   b. "We're cutting back on expenditures."
   c. "Could you just leave some literature?"
   d. "A representative of your company was here recently."
   e. "I really don't think we can afford your equipment."

2. Categorize each of the following into the five basic types of objections, and then illustrate one way to handle each:
   a. During a demonstration, the customer says, "You know, I really like your competitor's model."
   b. After a sales presentation, the doctor says, "You have a good drug there. Thanks for your time, and if I decide to prescribe it, I'm sure you'll find out."
   c. After the salesperson answers an objection, the prospect remarks, "I guess your product is all right, but—well, I don't think I need one just now. Thanks a lot."
   d. After a thorough presentation, the prospect answers, "No, I'm sorry, we just can't afford it."
   e. After the customer says, "Oh, no! That's really too much money. I've been looking at the same product in an industrial catalog, and I can buy the exact same product at a much lower price."

3. Mary Betando spent considerable time working with a prospective buyer. She thought a good order would be forthcoming on her next call. A portion of her conversation with the buyer went as follows:

   BUYER   "You know, I like your terms and the styling of your product. But how can I be sure the small parts will hold up and be available?"

   MARY   "We've never had any complaints on the parts, and I'm sure they will be easily available."

   BUYER   "You are sure of that?"

   MARY   "Well, I've never heard of any problems."

   BUYER   [appearing unconvinced and looking at some papers on his desk without glancing up] "I'll let you know later what I plan to do. Thanks for dropping by."

   Can you improve on Mary's answer? Suggest a more appropriate reply.

4. Discuss the differences between postponing an objection and forestalling an objection.

5. Occasionally, a buyer will offer several objections at one time. How would you respond if a buyer made the following comments without pausing? "Say, does this machine use 110 or 220 volts? What kind of service will you provide monthly? What is the estimated life of this equipment, and have you sold it to anyone else in the area?"

6. Indicate the appropriate action for the sales representative who encounters the following customer attitudes:
   a. "I like the things this copier can do—if it really does them. It's kind of hard to believe it'll give me reliable service, though, with all these features that could go wrong."
   b. "Let me be plain. Your company's reputation precedes you in this office. I've had more trouble with your company than you would care to hear."
   c. "That sounds fine. But there's really no reason to get rid of the copier I've got. It works well enough for anything I use it for."
   d. "I see what you're saying. This machine you're talking about could end up saving us some time and money."

7. You are planning on making calls to local high school students with your college admissions staff. Your objective is to help the students see the benefits of attending your college and then have them apply.
   a. Make a list of objections you may expect to encounter.
   b. What can you do to meet these objections effectively? List the answer you would propose and label the method used.

8. How would you attempt to answer the objection "Your new product will have more service problems than your competitor's product" in each of the following situations?
   a. You are calling on an amiable with whom you have been doing business for four years.
   b. You are calling on an expressive for the first time.
   c. You are calling on an analytical who bought one of your products three years ago but has bought nothing since.
   d. You are calling on a driver who currently uses your competitor's product.

9. To a secretary and her boss, you have been describing a new office chair that your firm just came out with. The chair is designed to relieve back strain while the sitter uses a personal computer. The secretary seems very interested and says, "I would really like that!" The boss says, "Well, if it's what you want, OK. How much does it cost?" At your reply, "This one is $498," the boss exclaims, "For that little thing?" What should you say or do?

10. Determining the real reason some customers or prospects habitually refuse to buy can be difficult. They may offer many excuses that disguise the true reason. Before a sale can be closed, the exact reason for not buying must be determined, and then the true objection must be answered to the prospect's satisfaction. Answering excuses satisfactorily does little good, because they are not the real hurdles to obtaining commitment. If a customer gives you several reasons for not buying your product, how can you determine whether the real reason has been stated? What technique would help uncover the real objection?

11. For each of the following objections, provide answers that clearly demonstrate the direct denial and indirect denial methods. Assume that each objection is not true.
   a. "Fishermen don't need a boat that goes this fast!"
   b. "The cost of replacing the air bag in the car will be too much."

  c. "I've heard that your firm is a pyramid organization. Products sold in
     that manner are usually a scam!"
  d. "Land is inexpensive in this rural area. It would be much easier and
     more cost effective to just develop a new landfill than to build this
     recycling operation you are discussing."
  e. "I heard your particle board is manufactured using resins that can
     cause cancer."
  f. "The scent of this L'Essence fragrance is not identical to the fragrance
     you say you are imitating."

12. For each of the following objections, provide answers that clearly
    demonstrate the compensation method, boomerang method, feel-felt-found
    method, postpone method, and pass-up method. Assume that all the
    objections are either true or are the prospect's opinion.
     a. "Midway Airlines does not fly to all the destinations to which our team
        needs to fly."
     b. "I don't think our customers will like the lighter tint of the lenses of
        your Revo sunglasses."
     c. "Your water purification units are not approved by the Environmental
        Protection Agency."
     d. "My customers have never asked for this new L'Oreal hair color product."
     e. "Your prices are the absolute highest in the plumbing tool industry."
     f. "I don't like the way you use female models in your Coors promotions
        at bars."

CASE PROBLEMS

CASE 11 • 1

DIAMOND BASEBALL
COMPANY

Jennifer Newman is a salesperson for Diamond Baseball Company, the world's largest producer of balls and bats. The company, founded in 1912, is one of the few
sporting good manufacturers that produce equipment approved by the major
leagues. At the factory in Tullahoma, Tennessee, 85 stitchers handsew the covers
on baseballs, turning out up to 5,000 balls per day.

The R-9, a reduced injury factor (RIF) baseball, was developed by Diamond in
order to reduce the number of injuries to children resulting from playing baseball.
A traditional baseball traveling at a speed of 60 miles per hour has a head injury
factor of 99 percent. The RIF ball has a risk factor of only 2 percent because the
solid core of the ball compresses over a larger area and for a longer period of time
upon impact, reducing the force of the impact. As a result, the probability of con-
cussion is decreased by 97 percent.

Although the R-9 uses different materials than do regular baseballs, no performance is lost. Tests conducted by Diamond show that RIF balls have essentially the
same bounce and rebound characteristics as does the traditional baseball. The RIF
ball is the same size and weight of the regular ball and the only "safe ball" that
meets standards set by the National Operating Committee on Standards for Athletic Equipment.

The ball has been approved by Little League and the American Amateur Baseball Congress; it is not approved for regular play at high school or professional
games. However, a recent ad for the R-9 included the endorsement of a well-known
and respected major league baseball player.

RIF balls have been on the market for six months. They are priced 15 percent
higher than traditional baseballs. Sales started off slowly but are building each day.
Jennifer has only sold the new balls in two of her 200 accounts.

Today, Jennifer is calling on Cheri Peters, the manager of Peters Sporting Goods, a small store that caters primarily to Little League teams and high school sports teams. Cheri runs a very profitable business because of her strong friendship with coaches in the area. Jennifer's objective is to secure an order of two cases of the RIF balls on this call.

Jennifer jotted down the following objections she thought she might encounter from Ms. Peters:

1. RIF baseballs are higher priced.
2. Won't there be a difference in performance?
3. I have experienced no problems with regular baseballs. We've had no concussions that I know about.
4. How do I know it will be widely accepted? I haven't had anyone ask for these RIF balls.
5. Won't a softer ball make kids feel wimpy?
6. I'm not sure the ball has proven itself. After all, sales have not been outstanding to this point!
7. Will the fact that young kids use a softer ball hinder their future performance?
8. I'm just old-fashioned. I like the use of the traditional ball.
9. Since I deal with the Little League a lot and I am pretty influential in this town, could you swing a deal my way? How about you and me splitting your commission on this first order?
10. The ballplayer you use in your advertising is not my favorite. I don't like his style or his team.

QUESTIONS

1. Provide a response to each objection listed. Include the name of the method you recommend.
2. What other objections might be raised?

CASE 11 • 2
RESPONDING TO
OBJECTIONS—A PREVIDEO
EXERCISE

Commercial Furniture Systems (CFS) is a manufacturer and importer of modular office furniture and accessories. CFS offers its clients traditional office furniture as well as its designer-influenced "Lugano Line." The Lugano Line was created specifically to meet the requirements of ultra-modern design applications and unusual office layout situations.

CFS has recently brought to market several new products, including "System-Tech" office workstations and a line of replaceable modular wall panels that are available in a number of different materials.

CFS is very proud of its newly developed computerized inventory and truck tracking system, an innovation that they feel will place them way ahead of their competition.

In the office furniture industry, it is not unusual for interior designers and furniture manufacturers (like CFS) to develop strong professional relationships. When these relationships occur, it is difficult for a competing manufacturer to gain recognition from a designer.

In this video segment, Catherine Craig, an account executive for CFS, is meeting with Joyce Lee, vice president of special projects for Clinton Associates, a large architectural design firm. Catherine was referred to Joyce by one of Clinton's clients. Catherine knows that Clinton has designed the interiors of several buildings for the Miller & Huntsman organization, and that in each case they have specified furniture from the Harrison Company. She also knows that Joyce is very happy with the Harrison Company.

Catherine's objective is to convince Joyce to review a proposal for the use of CFS products on a Miller & Huntsman project.

QUESTIONS

To help you think about the objections that Joyce Lee might raise in this meeting and how you think Catherine should respond, answer the following questions.

1. List objections you think might occur during this first meeting between Joyce and Catherine.

2. Describe how you would respond to each objection listed in question 1. Be sure to label the method you recommend.

3. Reread the material above and be prepared to watch the videotape in class. Watch for Joyce's *actual* objections and how Catherine responded. Evaluate Catherine's responses.

ADDITIONAL REFERENCES

Henry, Porter. *Secrets of the Master Sellers.* New York: AMACOM, 1987.

"How I Overcame Tough Objections." *Builder,* May 1991, p. 74.

Kern, Richard. "The Art of Overcoming Resistance." *Sales & Marketing Management,* March 1990, pp. 101–4.

Peterson, R T. "Sales Representatives' Utilization of Various Widely-Used Means of Answering Objections." *Proceedings of the American Marketing Association Educator's Conference,* 1987, pp. 119–24.

12

Obtaining Commitment

O btaining commitment does not stand apart and distinct from the total sales presentation. In fact, gaining commitment actually starts with the beginning of the sales process and succeeds only when the buyer becomes convinced that the decision to purchase is wise. If the sales representative fails to discover the prospect's needs or cannot meet those needs, then attempting to gain commitment is useless. If the prospect does buy under such circumstances, the end result will be negative, resulting in a poor relationship. Partnerships can only develop if the salesperson views obtaining commitment as a win-win objective. This chapter will teach you how to obtain commitment in an honest, straightforward way.

Some questions answered in this chapter are:

How much emphasis should be placed on closing the sale?

Why is obtaining commitment important?

What is the best time to obtain commitment?

What methods of securing commitment are available?

What should a salesperson do if the prospect says yes? What if the prospect says no?

What causes difficulties in obtaining commitment?

After graduating from Northern Illinois University in May 1992 with a degree in marketing (which included several courses in personal selling), Sheryl L. Koehler accepted a position with Wallace Computer Services. Since 1908, Wallace has provided organizations with innovative information-handling products and services with the broadest portfolio of products in the industry, including business forms, labels and labeling systems, office products, computer supplies, ribbons and rolls, direct response printing, and commercial printing.

SHERYL L. KOEHLER

Wallace Computer Services, Inc.

As a health care representative Sheryl calls on hospitals, HMOs, physician groups, software-related groups, blood banks, home health care organizations, and commercial laboratories to present these accounts with custom information-handling concepts. She chose Wallace due to their broad portfolio of products, their outstanding training program, and their recognized financial stability within the industry.

"During my first year with Wallace I was Sales Representative of the Month four times and I was also named Rookie of the Region out of 10 sales reps. I was also over my quota for the year, therefore a member of the 100% Club. I believe this is all due to working hard and working smart. Let me share a few stories from my first year.

"I was working on a large contract with a local hospital and my buyer continued to tell me that he needed more time to think about it. I asked how long and he said about four weeks. At that time I made an appointment with him for the same time, every week, for four weeks. I followed up each time with some samples of the paper (that our business forms utilize) and reminded him how much time he had before the decision was to be made. After four weeks I asked him for the order and he said yes! I found out that he was cautious about switching vendors because he did not know if I was reliable and if he could trust me to provide him with the service he desired. My constant contact with him before the sale helped alleviate his concerns.

"In another account, I learned that the purchasing department did not see any need to switch vendors. I met with various departments within the hospital and found that the largest department was not happy with the pricing or service offered by the current vendor. I built a strong relationship with the director of that department and the chief financial officer, who could override the director of purchasing's decisions. After months of hard work, presentations, and entertaining, I received an opportunity to work on the entire forms package in the hospital. I will be saving the hospital a substantial amount of money and providing a more efficient, automated network. An entire year of persistence really made the difference. However, it took me a year to make the customer realize that Wallace could offer the same products at a lower cost. (The current vendor has been in there for eight years.) Also, be aware that there are tremendous political obstacles to overcome in many selling situations.

"Not that I would want you to think that you always get the sale in the end. You don't. This is a very competitive industry and I have certainly heard my share of no's. Fortunately, Wallace is a strong company with excellent products and outstanding service, and that helps. Keep in mind that there will be peaks and valleys and maintain a positive attitude. Good luck to you!"

OBTAINING COMMITMENT TODAY

Asking for the buyer's business, often called **closing,** has always received a great deal of emphasis in sales training. Hundreds of books, audiocassettes, videocassettes, and seminar speakers have touted the importance of closing. By conventional wisdom, the key to success in any sale was to find a method or methods of closing that would make the decision maker say yes.

However, a more effective perspective on this topic has emerged. Tony Alessandra, a well-respected sales trainer, sums it up this way:

> Forget 150 ways to handle objections or 50 ways to close the sale. These are commando selling techniques or gimmicks that make up for not being good . . . The only way to develop a long-term relationship with a customer is to use a nonmanipulative, consultative selling technique. The key to nonmanipulative selling is trust. A good salesperson establishes trust by being candid, honest, forthright, and most of all a good listener.[1]

Another expert in sales management consulting and training states:

> Personally, I'm not a big fan of the "28-Ways-to-Close-a-Sale" books or systems. Putting cute names on closing techniques does little to build the skills necessary to close a sale. The famous minor-point close ("Do you want the blue one or the red one?") is an insult to the intelligence of both the sales professional and the buyer. It assumes gross indecisiveness on the part of the buyer and raises the possibility of losing a commitment altogether. Ploys of this sort are typical of manipulative or trick closes recommended in these systems. And while they may make good topic paragraphs in books or tapes and lend themselves to clever dramatizations in videos, they are, in reality, pure fiction. Being honest and straightforward about what you want is what works best in face-to-face situations with real customers. Closing is not trickery. It's an agreement to do business.[2]

Tim Conner, president of an international sales training organization, states:

> The emphasis in sales for decades has been on the "close" of the sale. I believe that this selling strategy is no longer appropriate given present consumers' attitudes, intelligence, and their need for practical solutions and increased information about products and services available to them today from a wide variety of organizations.[3]

Many writers have questioned heavy reliance on the close.[4] Senior managers of major firms are also beginning to question the usual emphasis placed on closing the sale. The vice president of training and development of a 900-member sales force told one of the authors:

> I have no desire to teach my reps how to close the sale. If they've done a good job of finding out the prospect's needs and demonstrated how they can meet those needs, then there is no use in relying on some fancy closing technique. Besides, prospects are sick of those methods anyway.

EXHIBIT 12.1

EXAMPLES OF
COMMITMENTS SALESPEOPLE
MAY ATTEMPT TO
OBTAIN*

To have the prospect *sign an order* for 100 pairs of Levi's jeans.

To have the prospect *agree to come* to the Atlanta branch office sometime during the next two weeks for a hands-on demonstration of the copier.

To *set up another appointment* for one week from now, at which time the buyer will allow a complete survey of her printing needs.

To *learn the names* of all other key players in this decision that the prospect can identify.

To *inform the doctor* of the revolutionary anticlogging mechanism that has been incorporated in our new drug and have her agree to read the pamphlet I will leave.

To have the buyer agree to *pass my information along* to the buying committee with his endorsement of my proposal.

To have the *prospect agree to call several references* that I will provide in order to develop further confidence and trust in my office cleaning business.

To *schedule a co-op newspaper advertising* program to be implemented in the next month.

To have the prospect agree to use our brand of computer paper for *a trial period* of one month.

To have the prospect *agree on the first point* (of our four-point program) and schedule another meeting in two days with an agenda of discussing the second point.

To have the retailer *agree to allow us space* for an end-of-aisle display for the summer promotion of Raid.

To have the *prospect initiate the paperwork* that would allow us to be considered as a future vendor.

To have me fully understand and *appreciate the principal risks* that adopting my product would pose to the buyer.

*Note the similarity between this table and Exhibit 8.1, which provides examples of call objectives. Actually a perfect positive relationship should exist between call objectives and closing attempts.

Finally, solid research has provided strong evidence with which to question heavy reliance on closing techniques. The research, based on more than 35,000 sales calls over 12 years, found that, in the major sale, reliance on closing techniques actually reduces the chances of making a sale.[5] Further, salespeople who were specifically trained in closing actually closed *fewer* sales. For very low-priced products (as in door-to-door magazine sales), however, closing techniques may increase the chances of a sale. As mentioned in Chapter 9, this research indicates that the most important activity of the salesperson is to discover the needs of the prospect.

So, why even cover closing at all? Because obtaining commitment is *critical* for the success of salespeople and the firms they work for. Unlike many other books, however, this chapter will cover the topic of obtaining commitment in a manner that is consistent with the theme of the book: developing and building long-term partnerships.

The process of obtaining commitment occurs throughout the natural, logical progression of any sales call. The general atmosphere and attitude of the sales call should continue as commitment is sought. Commitment, of course, is more than just securing an order, as Exhibit 12.1 illustrates, salespeople will attempt to obtain a commitment consistent with the objectives of that particular sales call.

IMPORTANCE OF SECURING FAVORABLE ACTION

Salespeople need to become proficient in obtaining commitment for at least three good reasons. First, if you truly discover unmet needs of your prospects, the sooner they can realize the benefits of your product or service the better. Second, your company's future success depends on goodwill and earning a profit. Finally, not only does securing commitment result in financial rewards for the salesperson, meeting needs is also intrinsically rewarding for the seller.

WHEN TO ATTEMPT TO OBTAIN COMMITMENT

Beginning salespeople frequently ask themselves these questions: Is there a right time to obtain commitment? How will customers let me know they are ready to buy? Should I make more than one attempt? What should I do if my first attempt fails?

The "right" time to attempt to gain commitment is when the buyer appears ready. Some salespeople say that one psychological moment in each sales presentation affords the best opportunity for this and, if this opportunity is bypassed, securing commitment will be difficult or impossible. This is not true. Seldom does one psychological moment govern the success or failure of a sales presentation.

Most buyers will commit themselves only when they clearly understand the benefits and costs of such a decision. At times this point occurs early in the call. A commitment to purchase a large system, however, will not usually occur until a complete presentation and several calls have been made and all questions have been answered.

To determine the appropriate time to request commitment, the salesperson should evaluate the situation. This includes listening to the buyer's comments, reading nonverbal cues, and gauging the buyer's response to probing.

BUYERS' COMMENTS

Customer's comments often indicate best that they are considering commitment. A prospect will seldom say, "All right, I'm ready to endorse this product to our buying committee." Customers may indicate, however, that they are about to make a decision (or that they have already made a decision) by saying one of the following:

> "I guess it would be better to get a new roof on this building before it rains."

> "How would we operate while the changeover of equipment is being made?"

> "If I come to your office to see a demonstration, could I bring my assistant along?"

> "If I do agree to go with this cooperative advertising program, do you have any ads already developed that I could use?"

The two buyers (on the left side of the photo) are providing nonverbal cues which can be interpreted as, "We're not yet convinced."

Courtesy of Kimberly-Clark Corporation.

"Do you have any facilities for training our employees in the use of the product?"

"How soon would you be able to deliver the equipment?"

"When would I be able to get this delivered?"

NONVERBAL CUES

As in every phase of the presentation, nonverbal cues serve as important indicators of the customer's state of mind. While attempting to gain commitment, the salesperson should use buyers' nonverbal signals to better identify their areas of concern and see if they are ready to commit. These nonverbals are commonly called **buying signals** or **closing cues.** Facial expressions most often indicate how ready the buyer is to make a commitment. Positive signals include eyes that are open and relaxed, face and mouth not covered with hands, a natural smile, and a relaxed forehead. The reverse of these indicate that the buyer is not yet ready to commit to your proposal.

Customers' actions also often indicate readiness to buy or make a commitment. For example, the prospective buyer of a fax machine may get a document and operate the machine or may place the machine on the table where it will be used. The industrial buyer may refer to a catalog to compare specifications with competing products. A doctor, told of a new drug, may pick up the pamphlet and begin to carefully read the indications and contraindications. A retailer considering whether to allow an end-of-aisle display may move to the end of an aisle and scan the layout. Any such actions may be signals for obtaining commitment; they should be viewed in the context of all available verbal and nonverbal cues.

BUYERS' RESPONSES TO PROBING

Obtaining commitment becomes much easier if the salesperson has continually taken the pulse of the situation with trial closes. Throughout the presentation, the salesperson should be asking questions such as:

"How does this sound to you so far?"

"Is there anything else you would like to know at this point?"

"Where would you like to go from here?"

"What do you think of what you've seen?"

"How does this compare with what you have seen of competing products?"

Buyers' responses to such questions provide good guidance regarding when the salesperson should attempt to obtain commitment. The response also helps the salesperson ensure that the buyer agrees that the benefits will accrue and are important.

HOW TO SUCCESSFULLY OBTAIN COMMITMENT

To achieve success in obtaining commitment, salespeople need to follow several principles: Maintain a positive attitude, let the customer set the pace, be assertive instead of aggressive, and sell the right product in the right amounts.

MAINTAIN A POSITIVE ATTITUDE

Confidence is contagious. Customers like to deal with salespeople who have confidence in themselves, their product, and their company. Any indication that salespeople think their presentation will receive an unfavorable reaction or that they have little chance of obtaining commitment is likely to be picked up by the customer.

Any skill is performed best with a positive attitude. The typist who fears errors will make many; the student who fears essay exams usually does poorly; ballplayers who know they cannot hit a certain pitch will probably get few hits; golfers who believe they will miss short putts usually do. So it is with salespeople. If they fear the customer will not accept their proposal, the chances are good they'll be right.

One manager related the example of a salesperson selling laundry detergent who unsuccessfully tried to convince a large discount chain to adopt a new liquid version of the product. When the rep's sales manager stopped by the account later in the week to follow up on a recent stockout problem, the buyer related his reasons for refusing the liquid Tide: "Listen, I know you guys are sharp. You probably wouldn't come out with a new product unless you had tons of data to back up your decision. But, honestly, the sales rep who calls on me is always so uptight and apprehensive that I was afraid to adopt the new product! Don't you guys teach them about having confidence?"

LET THE CUSTOMER SET THE PACE

Attempts to gain commitment must be geared to fit the varying reactions, needs, and personalities of each buyer. Thus, the sales representative needs to practice adaptive selling. (See Chapter 6 for a complete discussion of adaptive selling.)

Some buyers who react very slowly may need plenty of time to assimilate the material presented. They may ask the same question several times or show they do not understand the importance of certain product features. In these circumstances, the salesperson must deliver the presentation more slowly, and may have to repeat certain parts. Trying to rush buyers is unwise when they show they are not yet ready to commit.

As we discussed earlier in the book, buyers' decision-making styles vary greatly. Japanese and Chinese buyers tend to move more slowly and cautiously when evaluating a proposition. In contrast, buyers working for Fortune 500 firms located in the largest U.S. cities often tend to move much more quickly. The successful salesperson recognizes such potential differences and acts accordingly.

All prospects expect enough information from the salesperson to enable them to evaluate the product or service properly. The kinds of information and the speed with which it can be absorbed vary with different prospects. If salespeople know their prospects and customers well, they can judge the most effective pace to use.

THINKING IT THROUGH	*M*any sales trainers emphasize the importance of the seller maintaining complete control, including the pace of the interview. Do you agree? How could that help you gain commitment more easily? How could it hinder your attempts?

BE ASSERTIVE NOT AGGRESSIVE

Marvin Jolson identifies three types of salespeople: aggressive, submissive, and assertive.[6] **Aggressive** salespeople control the sales interaction but often do not gain commitment because they prejudge the customer's needs and fail to probe for information. Too busy talking to do much listening, they tend to push the buyer too soon, too often, and too vigorously. They

No one likes a pushy, aggressive salesperson.

David Lissy/Stock Imagery.

E X H I B I T 12 . 2 ASSERTIVE, AGGRESSIVE, AND SUBMISSIVE SALESPEOPLE'S HANDLING OF SALES ACTIVITIES

	Selling Style		
Selling Activity	**Aggressive**	**Submissive**	**Assertive**
Defining customer needs	Believe they are the best judge of customer's needs.	Accept customer's definition of needs.	Probe for need-related information that customer may not have volunteered.
Controlling the presentation	Minimize participation by customer	Permit customer to control presentation.	Encourage two-way communication and customer participation.
Closing the sale	Overwhelm customer; respond to objections without understanding	Assume customers will buy when ready.	Respond to objections, leading to somewhat automatic close.

might say, "I can't understand why you are hesitant," but they do not probe for reasons for the hesitancy.

Submissive salespeople often excel as socializers. With customers, they spend a lot of time talking about families, restaurants, and movies. They establish rapport quite effectively. They accept the customers' statements of needs and problems but do not probe to uncover any latent needs or opportunities. Submissive salespeople rarely try to obtain commitment.

Assertive salespeople are self-confident and positive. They maintain the proper perspective by being responsive to customer needs. Rather than aggressively creating new needs in customers through persuasion, they prospect for customers that truly need their products. To determine customer needs, they encourage customers through questioning to provide information. Their presentations emphasize an exchange of information rather than a one-way presentation. Exhibit 12.2 summarizes the differences between assertive, aggressive, and submissive salespeople's handling of the sales interview.

SELL THE RIGHT ITEM IN THE RIGHT AMOUNTS

The chance of obtaining commitment improves when the right product is sold in the right amount. Although this sounds obvious, it often is not followed.

For example, before selling two copiers, the office equipment sales representative must be sure that these two copiers, instead of only one copier or perhaps three, best fit the needs of the buyer's office. The chemical company sales representative selling to an industrial firm must know that one tank car of a chemical is more likely to fit the firm's needs than 10 55-gallon drums. The Johnson Wax sales rep who utilizes their "Sell to Potential" program knows the importance of selling not too few units (or the store will run out of stock during the promotion) and not too many units (or the store will be stuck with excess inventory after the promotion). Customers have long memories; they will refuse to do business with someone who oversells, and they may also lack confidence in someone who undersells. The chances to obtain commitment diminish rapidly when the salesperson tries to sell too many or too few units or the wrong grade or style of product.

Also, do not rely on trial orders often. If you do, you are not helping the prospect achieve his or her maximum potential. This could also result in a poor shelf position and/or a lack of enthusiasm on the part of the buyer.

Salespeople are likely to sell the right product in the right amounts if they keep a service attitude. For example, a large manufacturer of welding machines looks out for its customers' interests by maintaining a production design staff. This staff analyzes the use that a customer plans to make of the company's products. Recommendations are then made as to the right number and kinds of machines needed. Sometimes the analysis shows a need for fewer machines than the customer thought. In one case, the company sold a $4,000 machine instead of fulfilling the customer's request for eight $2,000 machines to do the same job. That manufacturer rightly believes that, although the first sale may be smaller if the right product is sold in the right amounts, repeat sales and goodwill always more than make up the difference.

EFFECTIVE METHODS AND TECHNIQUES

All commitments require a sacrifice from buyers. They must sacrifice money for the advantages the product or service provides. Making the decision to spend money for any one product may mean giving up other products. The buyer's sacrifice must be more than offset by the advantages that accrue from purchasing that particular product or service.

Studying successful methods and techniques enables salespeople to help prospects buy a product or service they want or need. Buyers sometimes have a need or a want and still hesitate to buy the product that will satisfy this want or need. For example, an industrial buyer for a candy manufacturer refused to commit to a change in sweeteners even though she had a need for a better raw material. Why? Because the sweetener rep had met with her on four separate occasions, and the buyer had difficulty remembering all that was said and agreed on. Had the salesperson used the correct method (the benefit summary method, to be discussed later in this section), commitment might have been obtained. We will explore several of the most important methods in this section.

DIRECT REQUEST

Perhaps the most straightforward, effective method of obtaining commitment is simply to ask for it. However, salespeople need to be wary of appearing overly aggressive when using this **direct request method**. It works best with decisive customers, like drivers, who appreciate getting down to business and not wasting time. Examples include:

"Can I put you down for 100 pairs of Model 63?"

"Can we meet with your engineer next Thursday to further discuss this?"

"Will you come to the home office for a hands-on demonstration?"

"Can you call the meeting next week?"

"Is it a deal?"

▍BENEFIT SUMMARY

Early in the interview, salespeople discover or reiterate the needs and problems of the prospect. Then, throughout the presentation, they show how their product can meet those needs. They do this by turning product or service features into benefits specifically for that buyer. When using the **benefit summary method,** the salesperson simply reminds the prospect of the agreed-on benefits of the proposal. The points mentioned in the benefit summary must be salient to the buyer, and the seller should not list any features that the buyer considers trivial. Also imperative is the salesperson's verifying that each major point discussed is understood by the buyer and could help solve the buyer's problem. This nonmanipulative method simply helps the buyer synthesize points covered in the presentation, in order to make a wise decision. For example, the salesperson attempting to obtain the buyer's commitment to pass on information to a buying committee with an endorsement of the proposal may engage in a dialogue such as this:

SALESPERSON   "You stated early in my visit that you were looking for a product of the highest quality, a vendor that could provide quick delivery, and adequate engineering support. As I've mentioned, our fasteners have been rated by an independent laboratory as providing 20 percent higher

Advertising by the seller's firm can help the salesperson obtain commitment.

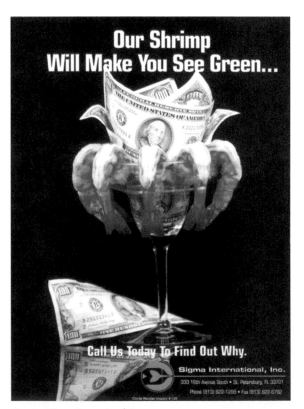

Courtesy Sigma International, Inc.

tensile strength than the closest competitor, resulting in a life expectancy of over four years. We also discussed the fact that our fasteners can be delivered to your location within 3 hours of your request, and that this holds true 24 hours a day. Finally, I discussed the fact that we have four engineers on staff whose sole responsibility is to work with existing customers in providing support and developing new specifications for new fasteners. Would you be willing to give this information to the buying committee along with your endorsement of the proposal?"

CUSTOMER   "Yes, I will present this at our next committee meeting, on Thursday. Would you be available to give a short presentation to the group at that time?"

One advantage of the benefit summary method over the direct request method is that the seller can help the buyer remember all the points discussed in the presentation. This becomes particularly important in long presentations and in selling situations involving several meetings prior to obtaining commitment. The salesperson cannot assume that the buyer will remember all the major points discussed in the presentation.

BALANCE SHEET METHOD

Sometimes referred to as the Ben Franklin method because he described using it to make decisions, the **balance sheet method** works with prospects who can't make a decision even though no reason for their behavior is apparent. Such a prospect may be asked to join the salesperson in listing the pros and cons of buying now or buying later, of buying the salesperson's product or that of a competitor, or of buying the product or not buying it at all.

The salesperson may start to obtain commitment with the following type of statement:

You know, Mr. Thacker, Ben Franklin was like you, always anxious to reach the right decisions and avoid the wrong ones. I suppose that's how you feel. Well, he suggested taking a piece of paper and writing all the reasons for deciding yes in one column and then listing the reasons for deciding no in a second column. He said that when you make this kind of graphic comparison, the correct decision becomes much more apparent.

As the salesperson relates this story, she gets things started by drawing a *T* on a plain piece of paper, placing captions on each side of the crossbar and leaving space below for the insertion of specific benefits or sales points. For example, assume the product is National Adhesives' hot-melt adhesive used to attach paper labels to plastic Classic Coke bottles. Coca-Cola is currently using a liquid adhesive made by Ajax Corporation. In this situation, the *T* might look like this:

Benefits of Adopting National Adhesive's Hot-Melt Method	Benefits of Staying with the Ajax Liquid Adhesives

Then the salesperson suggests, "Let's see how many reasons we can think of for your going with the National Adhesive system." The salesperson would write the benefits (not features) the customer has shown interest in on the left side of the *T*. Next, the salesperson would ask the customer to list reasons to stay with the Ajax company on the right side. Completed, the *T* lists should accurately reflect all the pros and cons of each possible decision. At that point the buyer is asked, "Which method do you think is the wisest?"

Done properly, the balance sheet method can be very effective. Especially appropriate for a buyer who is an analytical, it would make less sense for an expressive. However, the balance sheet approach takes time and may appear salesy. Also, the list of benefits of the product being sold won't always outnumber the list on the other side of the *T*.

▮ PROBING METHOD

In the **probing method,** sales representatives initially attempt to obtain commitment by simply asking for it (the direct request method). If unsuccessful, the rep uses a series of probing questions designed to discover the reason for the hesitation. Once the reason(s) becomes apparent, the salesperson asks a what-if question (e.g., "What if I could successfully resolve this concern? Would you be willing to commit?") An illustrative dialogue follows:

SALESPERSON   "Could we make an appointment for next week, at which time I would come in and do a complete survey of your needs? It shouldn't take more than three hours."

PROSPECT   "No, I don't think I am quite ready to take that step yet."

SALESPERSON   "There must be some reason why you are hesitating to go ahead now. Do you mind if I ask what it is?"

PROSPECT   "I'm just not convinced that your firm is large enough to handle a customer of our size."

SALESPERSON   "In addition to that, is there any other reason why you would not be willing to go ahead?"

PROSPECT   "No."

SALESPERSON   "If I can resolve the issue of our size, then you would allow me to conduct a survey?"

PROSPECT   "Well, I wouldn't exactly say that."

SALESPERSON   "Then there must be some other reason. May I ask what it is?"

PROSPECT   "Well, a friend of mine that uses your services told me that often your billing department sends him invoices for material he didn't want and didn't receive."

SALESPERSON   "In addition to that, is there any other reason for not going ahead now?"

PROSPECT   "No, those are my two concerns."

SALESPERSON   "If I could resolve those issues right now, would you be willing to set up an appointment for a survey?"

PROSPECT   "Sure."

This dialogue illustrates the importance of probing in obtaining commitment. The method attempts to bring to the table all issues of concern to the prospect. The salesperson does not claim to be able to resolve the issues but simply attempts to find out what the issues are. When probing has identified all of the issues, the salesperson should attempt to resolve them as soon as possible. After successfully dealing with the concerns of the buyer, the salesperson should then ask for a commitment.

Some sales trainers refer to the probing method just illustrated as the **magic eraser,** because it makes use of an imaginary temporary "eraser" (e.g., "*If* I can resolve your concern . . .") to set aside the buyer's concern for a moment. These trainers usually say that you shouldn't use the eraser phrase more than twice or it begins to sound canned.

There are many modifications of the probing method. One other way to achieve the same results is the following:

SALESPERSON   "Will you be willing to buy this product today?"

PROSPECT   "No, I don't think so."

SALESPERSON   "I really would like to get a better feel of where you are. On a scale of 1 to 10, with 1 being absolutely no purchase and 10 being purchase, where would you say you are?"

PROSPECT   "I would say I'm about a 6."

SALESPERSON   "If you don't mind me asking, what would it take to move you from a 6 to a 10?"

Also, it is important to always keep in mind cultural differences. For example, if a Japanese businesswoman wants to tell an American seller that she is not interested, she might state, "Your proposal would be very difficult" just to be polite. If the seller attempts to use the probing method the Japanese businesswoman might consider the seller to be pushy or a poor listener. In the same way, an Arab businessperson will never say no directly, a custom that helps either side avoid losing face.[7]

▮ OTHER METHODS

Literally hundreds of techniques and methods of obtaining commitment have been tried. Exhibit 12.3 lists a number of traditional methods. Most of these, however, tend to be ineffective with sophisticated customers. Neil Rackham provides an excellent illustration of this point in Selling Scenario 12.1.

EXHIBIT 12.3   Some Traditional Closing Methods

Method	How It Works	Remarks
Minor point close	The seller assumes that it is easier to get the prospect to decide on a very trivial point than on the whole proposition: "What color do you like, blue or red?" If the prospect makes the minor decision, the seller assumes the sale is made and begins writing up the order.	This can upset a prospect who feels he or she is being manipulated. No one wants to feel that he or she has been tricked into making a commitment. Even unsophisticated buyers easily spot this technique.
Continuous yes close	The seller, throughout the presentation, constantly asks questions for which the prospect most logically would answer yes. By the end of the discussion, the buyer is so accustomed to saying yes that when the order is requested, the natural response is yes.	This method is based on self-perception theory. As the presentation progresses, the buyer begins to perceive himself or herself as being "agreeable." At the close, the buyer wants to maintain this self-image and almost unthinkingly says yes. Use of this method can destroy long-term relationships if the buyer *later* feels manipulated.
Assumptive close	The seller, without asking for the order, simply begins to write it up. A variation is to fill out the order form as the prospect answers questions.	This does not even give the buyer the courtesy of agreeing. It can be perceived as being very pushy and manipulative.
Standing-room-only close	The seller attempts to obtain commitment by describing the negative consequences of waiting. For example, the seller may state, "If you can't decide now, I'll have to offer it to another customer."	This can be effective if the statement is true. However, if the prospect really does need to act quickly, this should probably be discussed earlier in the presentation. An earlier discussion would tend to reduce possible mistrust and feelings of being pushed without apparent necessity.
Benefit-in-reserve close	First the seller attempts to obtain commitment by another method. If unsuccessful, the seller says, "Oh, I forgot to tell you that if you order today I can offer you an additional 5 percent for your trade-in."	Although this method can be effective, it can also backfire easily. The buyer tends to think, "If I had agreed to your first attempt to obtain commitment, I would not have learned about this new enticement. What else do you have up your sleeves? If I wait longer, how much better will your offer be?" Use of this technique can also cause the buyer to seek additional concessions in every future sale attempt.
Emotional close	In this technique, the seller appeals to the buyer's emotions to close the sale. For example, the seller may say, "This really is a good deal. To be honest with you, I desperately need to secure an order today. As you know, I work on a straight commission basis. My wife is going to have surgery next week, and our insurance just won't cover . . ."	Many obvious problems arise with this method. It is an attempt to move away from focusing on the prospect's needs to focusing entirely on your own personal needs. It does not develop trust or respect.

SUMMARY

No method of obtaining commitment will work if the buyer does not trust the salesperson, the company, and the product. Gaining commitment should not require the use of tricky techniques or methods for forcing buyers to do something they don't want to do, nor should it involve making prospects buy something they don't need.

S E L L I N G   S C E N A R I O
12.1

Buyers Don't Like Tricky Closing Techniques

One of British Petroleum's senior buyers was particularly ill-disposed toward the use of closing techniques. "It's not closing itself that I object to," he told me, "it's the arrogant assumption that I'm stupid enough to be manipulated into buying through the use of tricks. Whenever a standard closing technique is used on me, it reduces the respect between us—it destroys the professional business relationship. But I've got my own way of dealing with it, as you'll see."

The following day I was watching an attempted sale and saw the buyer's method in action. The seller was in the vending machine business and supplied plastic cups. At one point in the call, he used an assumptive close, saying, "Mr. P., you've agreed that our cups are cheaper than your present supplier's, so

shall we make our first delivery of, say, 20,000 cups next month?" The buyer said nothing. He opened a drawer in his desk and slowly took out a box of 3 × 5 index cards. He shuffled through the box and selected one with Assumptive Close typed on it, placing it face upon his desk. "That's your first chance," he said. "I give people two. If you use just one more closing technique on me, then it's no sale. Just so you know what I'm watching for, look through these cards." And he handed the cards across his desk to the seller. On each card a well-known closing technique was typed. The seller went pale—but didn't try closing again.

Source: Neal Rackham, *Spin Selling* (New York: McGraw-Hill, 1988), pp. 34–35. Used by permission.

IF COMMITMENT IS OBTAINED

The salesperson's job is not over when commitment is obtained. In fact, in many ways the job is just beginning. This section will describe the salesperson's responsibilities that accrue after the buyer says yes.

CONFIRM THE CUSTOMER'S CHOICE

Customers like to believe they have chosen intelligently when they make a decision. After important decisions, they may feel a little insecure about whether the choice was a wise one. This is called **buyer's remorse** or **post-purchase dissonance.**

Successful salespeople reassure customers that their choice has been judicious. They may say:

"I know you will enjoy using your new office machines. You can plan on many months of trouble-free service. I'll call on you in about two weeks to make sure everything is operating smoothly. Be sure to call me if you need any help before then."

"Congratulations, Mr. Jacobs. You are going to be glad you decided to use our service. There is no finer service available. Now let's make certain you get off to the right start. Your first bulletin will arrive Tuesday, March 2."

One way to help customers feel good about their decision is to assure them they have made an intelligent choice. Remarks such as the following may also be appropriate:

"You've made an excellent choice. Other stores won't have a product like this for at least 30 days."

"This is an excellent model you've chosen. Did you see it advertised in last week's *Time?*"

"Your mechanics will thank you for ordering these tools. You will be able to get your work out much faster."

GET THE SIGNATURE

Many times, the buyer's signature formalizes a commitment. Signing the order is a natural part of a well-planned procedure. The order blank should be accessible, and the signing should appear to be a routine matter. Ordinarily the customer has decided to buy before being asked to sign the order. In other words, the signature on the order blank merely confirms that an agreement has already been reached. The decision to buy or not to buy should not focus on a signature.

The salesperson needs to remember several important points: Make the actual signing an easy, routine procedure; fill out the order blank accurately and promptly; and be careful not to exhibit any eagerness or excitement when the prospect is about to sign.

SHOW APPRECIATION

All buyers like to think their business is appreciated, even if they purchase only small quantities. Customers like to do business with salespeople who show that they want the business.

Salespeople may show appreciation by writing the purchaser a letter. This practice especially develops goodwill after large purchases and with new customers. Salespeople should always thank the purchaser personally; the thanks should be genuine, but not effusive.

CULTIVATE FOR FUTURE CALLS

In most fields of selling, obtaining commitment is not the end of a business transaction but rather only one part of a mutually profitable business relationship.[8] Obtaining commitment is only successful if it results in goodwill and future commitment. As Harvey Mackay stated:

My definition of a great salesperson is not someone who can get the order. Anyone can get the order if he or she is willing to make enough promises about price or delivery. A great salesperson is someone who can get the order—and the reorder—from a prospect who is already doing business with someone else.[9]

Customers like to do business with salespeople who do not lose interest immediately after securing commitment. What a salesperson does after commitment is achieved is called **follow up.**

To be welcomed on repeat calls, salespeople must be considerate of all of the parties involved in buying or using the product. Pronounce and spell all names correctly, explain and review the terms of the purchase so there

When commitment is not obtained it is important to make follow-up inquiries and learn the reason for the failure.

Courtesy Whirlpool Corporation.

can be no misunderstandings, and be sociable and cordial to subordinates as well as those in key positions. In addition, the buyer or user must get the service promised. The importance of this cannot be overemphasized. (Chapter 13 will provide detailed information about how to service the account and build a partnership.)

IF COMMITMENT IS NOT OBTAINED

Naturally, the salesperson does not always obtain the desired commitment. The salesperson should never take this personally (easier said than done). Doing everything right does not guarantee a sale. Some "prospects" really should not be considered prospects at all (because they have no real need, don't have the money, etc.), even though the salesperson has given one or more presentations.

THINKING IT THROUGH	*W*hat if the prospect *does* reject your proposal because he or she doesn't trust you (i.e., is rejecting you personally)? What would your reaction and response be?

In other cases, it might not even be in the best interests of the seller's firm for the buyer to say yes. For example, AT&T was invited to bid on a network system for a large regional bank. After studying the situation, AT&T decided to bail out of the running. Today the bank is involved in a major scandal and AT&T is glad it said no to the potential business.[10]

This section describes some of the common reasons for failing to obtain commitment and offers practical suggestions for salespeople who encounter rejection.

SOME REASONS FOR FAILURE

Wrong Attitudes

As discussed earlier in the chapter, salespeople need to have a positive attitude. A fear that obtaining commitment is going to be difficult may be impossible to hide. Inexperienced salespeople naturally will be concerned about their ability to obtain commitment; most of us have an innate fear of asking someone else to do anything. But all salespeople know that they need to focus on obtaining commitment in order to keep their jobs.

Some salespeople display unwarranted excitement when they see prospects are ready to commit. A salesperson who appears excited or overly eager may display nonverbal cues that suggest dishonesty or a lack of empathy. If this occurs, buyers may change their minds and refuse to commit.

One of the main reasons for salespeople's wrong attitudes toward obtaining commitment is the historical importance placed on closing the sale. It has often been viewed as a "win-lose" situation (i.e., "If I get the order, I win; if I don't get the order, they win"). Until salespeople see obtaining commitment as a positive occurrence for the buyer, these attitudes will persist.

Poor Presentation

Prospects or customers who do not understand the presentation or see the benefits of the purchase cannot be expected to buy. It is very important for the salesperson to use trial closes (see Chapter 9) and continually take the pulse of the interview.

A poor presentation can also be caused by haste. The salesperson who tries to deliver a 60-minute presentation in 20 minutes may neglect or omit important sales points. Foregoing the presentation may be better than delivering it hastily. Further, a sales presentation given at the wrong time or under unfavorable conditions is likely to be ineffective.

Poor Habits and Skills

Obtaining commitment requires proper habits and some measure of skill. The habit of talking too much rather than listening often causes otherwise good presentations to fail. Knowing when to quit talking is just as important as knowing what to say. Some salespeople become so fascinated by the sound of their own voices that they talk themselves out of sales that have already been made. A presentation that turns into a monologue is not likely to retain the buyer's interest.

DISCOVERING THE CAUSE

The real reasons for not obtaining commitment must be uncovered. Only then can salespeople proceed intelligently to eliminate the barriers. Some firms have developed sophisticated systems to follow up on lost sales. The BCI Consulting Group, acting as an independent third party, will perform this service for any sales force. Salespeople supply BCI with names and phone numbers of buyers who failed to buy. BCI then contacts these individuals to obtain objective feedback on both the client's company and its competitors. The consultant generates a report that identifies the reason(s) the buyer decided not to buy.[11]

SUGGESTIONS FOR DEALING WITH REJECTION

Maintain the Proper Perspective

The inexperienced salesperson's most important lesson probably is that when a buyer says no, the sales process has not necessarily ended. A no may mean "Not now" or "I need more information" or "Don't hurry me" or "I don't understand." A no answer should be a challenge to seek the reason behind the buyer's negative response.

In many fields of selling, the majority of prospects do not buy. The ratio of orders achieved to sales presentations may be $1:3$, $1:5$, $1:10$, or even $1:20$. Salespeople may tend to eliminate nonbuyers from the prospect list after one unsuccessful call. This may be sound practice in some cases; however, many sales happen on the second, third, fourth, or fifth call. When an earlier visit has not resulted in commitment, careful preparation for succeeding calls becomes more crucial.

The salesperson should have a clear objective for each sales call. When commitment cannot be obtained to meet that objective, the salesperson will often attempt to obtain commitment for a reduced request (a secondary or minimum objective). For example, the salesperson may attempt to gain a trial order instead of an actual order, or the sales representative may make a special offer (e.g., "I can give you an extra 50 cents a case on this order") or emphasize an impending event (e.g., "Due to deregulation I can't help but believe that our prices are going to start inching upward soon.").

Recommend Other Sources

The sales representative using the consultative selling philosophy (as described in Chapter 6) may recommend a competitor's product to solve the prospect's needs. When doing this, the sales rep should explain the reasons why his or her product does not meet the prospect's needs and then provide the name of the competitive product. One salesperson for a welding supply company keeps a current list of competitive products. When a customer requests an item that the salesperson can't supply, he volunteers the name of a competitor who can. No one need feel sorry for the salesperson, though; he is extremely successful. "I haven't been squeezed out by a competitor in more than three years," he reports.[12]

After recommending other sources, the sales rep should usually ask the prospect for names of people who might be able to buy the seller's product. Also, the salesperson should emphasize the desire to maintain contact with the prospect in the event that the seller's firm develops a competitive offering.

S E L L I N G   S C E N A R I O

12.2

Keep in Touch!

If there is one thing I have learned over the many years I have been selling, it is the importance of *persistence*. The computer systems we sell have extremely long sales cycles, sometimes approaching three years. We've even had prospects buy a competitor's system and use it for over a year before calling us back. Therefore, we have found it important to maintain contact with prospects, even if they give the order to another company. Our fragile egos often make this a difficult proposition.

The prospects must also be left with a way to "save face." We must not bludgeon them with "I told you so's." If they are having trouble with the competitor's system, they are now better prospects because they've learned that the least expensive solution may cost more in the long run. A lost sale simply means that the sales cycle has been extended. Besides, with computer technology becoming obsolete every three years, you will have another opportunity with each of them someday.

Source: Wayne B. Wilhelm, President, Computermax, personal correspondence, June 29, 1993, used with permission.

Good Manners Are Important

If obtaining commitment fails, no matter what the reason, the salesperson should react good-naturedly. Salespeople have to learn to accept no's if they expect to call on prospects again. Even if they don't obtain commitment, salespeople should thank prospects for their time. Arguing or showing disappointment gains nothing. The salesperson may plan to keep in contact with these prospects through an occasional phone call, a follow-up letter, or product literature mailings. One salesperson likes to make the following statement at the conclusion of any meeting in which commitment is not obtained: "I'll never annoy you, but if you don't mind, I'm going to keep in touch." Selling Scenario 12.2 describes how one salesperson finds that keeping in touch is important.

It is a good idea to leave something behind that will provide the prospect with a means of contacting you in the future. Vicki Whiteford, owner and salesperson for a courier service, leaves a Rolodex card with her name and number. "We figure even if everything else goes in the trash, they'll save the Rolodex card . . . . And if they get mad at their messenger [current courier service], they're likely to call us because our name is right in front of them."[13]

BRINGING THE INTERVIEW TO A CLOSE

Few buyers are interested in a prolonged visit after they commit. Obviously, the departure cannot be abrupt; the salesperson should complete the interview smoothly. Goodwill is never built by wasting the buyer's time after the business is concluded.

Remember that most sales take several calls to complete. If an order wasn't signed (and often this isn't even the objective of the call—see Chapter 8) and the prospect is interested in continuing to consider your proposal, you should leave with a clear action plan for all parties. An example of the kind of dialog that you might pursue is as follows:

SALESPERSON   "When will you have had a chance to look over this proposal?"

BUYER   "By the end of next week, probably."

SALESPERSON   "Great, I'll call on you in about 1½ weeks, okay?"

BUYER   "Sure, set up something with my secretary."

SALESPERSON   "Is there anything else I need to be doing for you before that next meeting?"

Always make sure the next step is clear for both parties.

SUMMARY

Commitment cannot be obtained by some magical or miraculous technique if the salesperson has failed to prepare the prospect throughout the presentation for making this decision. Salespeople should always attempt to gain commitment in a way that is consistent with the objectives of the meeting. Obtaining commitment begins with the salesperson's contact with the prospect. It can only succeed when all facets of the selling process fall into their proper place. All sellers need to keep in mind the old saying "People don't buy products or services—they buy solutions to their problems!"

The process of obtaining commitment is the logical progression of any sales call. Commitment is important for the customer, the seller's firm, and the seller as well. Commitments should result in a win–win situation for all parties concerned.

There is no one "right" time to obtain commitment. Salespeople should watch their prospects closely and recognize when to obtain commitment. Successful salespeople carefully monitor customers' comments, the buyer's nonverbal cues and actions, and the prospect's responses to probes.

To successfully obtain commitment, the salesperson needs to maintain a positive attitude, allow the customer to set the pace, be assertive rather than aggressive, and sell the right item in the right amounts. Engaging in these behaviors will result in a strong long-term relationship between buyer and seller.

No one method of obtaining commitment works best for each buyer. The direct request method is the simplest to use; however, the prospect often needs help in evaluating the proposal. In those instances, other methods may be more appropriate, such as the benefit summary, the balance sheet method, or the probing method. No method of obtaining commitment will work if a buyer does not trust the salesperson.

If commitment is obtained, sellers should immediately reassure customers that their choice has been judicious. The seller should show genuine appreciation as well as cultivate the relationship for future calls.

If commitment is not obtained, salespeople should analyze the reasons. Difficulties in obtaining commitment can be directly traced to wrong attitudes, a poor presentation, and/or poor habits and skills. Even if no commitment is obtained, the salesperson should thank the prospect for his or her time.

KEY TERMS

aggressive *361*
assertive *362*
balance sheet method *365*
benefit summary method *364*
buyer's remorse *369*
buying signals *359*
closing *356*

closing cues *359*
direct request method *363*
follow up *370*
magic eraser *367*
postpurchase dissonance *369*
probing method *366*
submissive *362*

QUESTIONS AND PROBLEMS

1. "The ABCs of closing are 'Always be closing.'" What is your reaction to this time-honored statement?

2. Obtaining commitment is just one skill needed by salespeople. Other skills include listening, discovering needs, helpfully responding to the concerns of prospects, managing your own nonverbal cues, and so on. How much time should be spent improving commitment-gaining skills as opposed to developing other skills?

3. You are selling copy machines for office use. After making a presentation that you think went rather well, you request the order and get this reply: "What you say sounds interesting, but I want some time to think it over. We'll probably go along with you, but I need some time to think about it." Your answer is "Well, OK. Would next Tuesday be a good day for me to come back?" Can you improve on the answer? How?

4. In 1919, a writer stated:

   There are a number of mechanical tricks which can be worked out as aids in closing and which frequently prove quite effective . . . One seller would stand at one of the old-style slanting desks, and after he had told his prospect where to sign, would toss his pencil carelessly upon the desk. Immediately it would begin to roll down to the floor, but he would not make the least effort to stop it. What more natural than the prospect himself should stop it? And lo! There he was with the pencil in his hand and ready to sign.[14]

   a. Would you label this seller as assertive or aggressive?
   b. Is this a trick or merely dramatization?
   c. Would a 1990s buyer respond positively to this behavior?

5. What if your boss tells you to consider your firm's welfare as more important than the buyer's welfare? What impact will that have on your attempts to obtain commitment?

6. "Selling doesn't begin until the prospect says no." Do you agree? If not, when does selling begin?

7. A sales manager once told his salesperson, "You know that when Mr. Jacobs told you no, he was saying no to your proposal—he was not rejecting you personally." Why is understanding that statement vital to all salespeople?

8. One successful salesperson assumes an attitude of indifference toward whether a commitment is obtained or not.
   a. Could this indifferent attitude help in obtaining commitment? If so, how?
   b. Are there any dangers inherent in giving this impression?

9. An old rule used by successful salespeople has been stated as: "First tell them what you're going to tell them; then tell them; and then tell them what you've told them."
   a. Do you believe this rule is sound? Why?
   b. Is this *all* that is necessary? When might the salesperson need to deviate from this rule?

10. One buyer stated: "All closing methods are devious and self-serving! How can a salesperson use a technique but still keep my needs totally in mind?" Comment.

11. Most of us have a natural fear of asking someone else to do something. What can you, as a student, do now to reduce such fear?

12. You are making a presentation to your closest friend, attempting to get him or her to agree to go on a long trip with you. Describe exactly what you would say to your friend, using each of the following methods (make any assumptions necessary):
    a. Direct request.
    b. Benefit summary.
    c. Balance sheet.
    d. Probing.

13. What laws govern this portion (obtaining commitment) of a sales presentation? (Refer back to Chapter 3, if needed.) How can a salesperson keep them in mind while attempting to gain commitment?

CASE PROBLEMS

CASE 12 • 1
SCHAEFFER'S FRAGRANCES, INC.

Schaeffer's Fragrances, Inc. makes and distributes fragrances for both men and women. The firm is known for recreating designer fragrances and selling them at wholesale prices. Schaeffer's Fragrances's motto is "Designer quality at a fraction of the price."

Lil Faugerstrom, a salesperson for Schaeffer's Fragrances, called on Adam Ratz, a buyer for Wal-Mart discount stores. The call objective was to have Adam agree to set up an appointment in the next several weeks with the full Wal-Mart buying committee and Lil. The latter portion of their conversation follows:

LIL "The fragrances are perfumes that are packaged conservatively in large, 3.3-ounce spray bottles. These perfumes are indistinguishable from the originals, except of course for the different packaging and labeling under the name Observe L'Essence."

ADAM "How can you be sure they are indistinguishable from the originals?"

LIL   "That's a good question. Schaeffer's Fragrances owns a $3 million piece of equipment that actually breaks down the original fragrances into their basic chemical elements."

ADAM   "But don't the original fragrances carry patent protection? Can't we get into trouble by selling these Schaeffer's Fragrances look-alikes?"

LIL   "It is perfectly legal to duplicate and sell a fragrance. Scents can't be patented. However, we cannot use the original product's name, bottle, or package. Have I answered your questions? Do you have any more concerns now?"

ADAM   "Yeah, I understand, and it all makes sense to me. No more questions right now."

LIL   "You are currently carrying several designer fragrances, including Giorgio, Poison, Drakkar Noir, and Polo. How are sales of those products?"

ADAM   "Very good. They are all heavily advertised, and people buy from us because we're cheaper than department stores."

LIL   "Great! According to our research, your sales of those products will not decline if you decide to include our products. Actually, our products appeal more to lower- and middle-income consumers who would like to realize the benefits of wearing a designer fragrance but are not able to afford it."

ADAM   *[leaning forward in his chair]* "That's interesting, but how do you *know* that they will sell in our stores? Wal-Mart is different from any other retailer in America, remember!"

LIL   "You're right. Wal-Mart is different. You try your best to offer high-quality name brands at affordable prices. You attempt to satisfy both men and women in all income brackets. Schaeffer's Fragrances can help you reach those goals. We have had successful introductions at other, smaller regional chain discount stores. In fact here's a letter from Mark Slonka at Big D Discount City in Athens, Ohio." *[hands Adam a letter and lets him read it in silence]*

ADAM   "Okay, okay. Well, what about advertising? How will customers know we are carrying the product?"

LIL   "We are currently running ads for Schaeffer's Fragrances in *Reader's Digest, Time,* and *Better Homes and Gardens.* Also, once your chain has purchased 1,000 bottles of our fragrances, our policy is to include your store's name in one of our magazine ads."

ADAM   "Pretty good. What happens if we overstock on some item? Can we send it back?"

LIL   "After a three-month trial period, we will buy back any bottles you would like to return at 90 percent of your cost. During the first three months, we hope to get a better handle on what brands Wal-Mart customers are looking for. Does that sound okay?"

ADAM   "Not bad."

LIL   "I would like to set up a meeting with the full buying committee of Wal-Mart in the next several weeks. Do you think that would be possible?"

ADAM   "Sure, we could probably do that next Friday."

LIL   "Will I have your endorsement at that meeting?"

ADAM   "We'll have to wait and see."

QUESTIONS

1.   Lil used the direct request method of obtaining commitment. Was that appropriate? Why or why not?

2.   Outline how you would attempt to obtain commitment, assuming that you use the following methods (add any assumptions necessary in order to develop the outline):
    a.   Benefit summary.
    b.   Balance sheet.
    c.   Probing.

3.   Although you have only been provided a portion of the conversation, evaluate Lil's performance in terms of:
    a.   Selling benefits, not just features.
    b.   Taking the buyer's pulse during the presentation.
    c.   Using communication aids to strengthen communication.
    d.   Responding to objections.
    e.   Attempting to obtain commitment at the proper time.

CASE 12 • 2
OBTAINING COMMITMENT:
A PREVIDEO EXERCISE

Brunswick Financial Services is an internationally recognized provider of diversified financial services. Founded over 50 years ago, Brunswick is now involved in stock brokerage, mutual fund portfolios, and corporate and individual retirement programs.

Brunswick offers 15 different investment portfolios ranging from low-risk and conservative to highly speculative. The more speculative the investment, the higher the risk and the greater the potential return on monies invested. Sales charges are based on a percentage of the amount of funds invested plus a fixed annual management fee.

Brunswick has built a reputation on the high quality of service that they provide for their clients and for their prompt payment of retirement benefits. Brunswick is particularly proud of a government-approved application form that it uses, which speeds the process of initiating a retirement program.

In this video segment, Ann Clark, an account representative for Brunswick, is calling on David Johnson, the founder and president of Johnson Foods, a manufacturer and distributor of gourmet food products. Prior to this meeting, Ann met with the company's comptroller, Joe Stone, about developing a proposal for a retirement program for Johnson's employees. Stone was very interested. He told her that it was an opportune time to start a pension plan for the tax benefits and the much-needed employee goodwill that the plan would generate. He also told her that Johnson would certainly have the last word and that Johnson was obstinate about even discussing the matter. Johnson is a very detail-oriented, somewhat distracted kind of person. Based on financial information received from Stone, Ann developed a written proposal that was reviewed by Stone. Johnson has repeatedly postponed meeting with Ann.

The following are the key features and benefits of Brunswick's proposal:

Features	Benefits
Fifteen investment funds with differing levels of investment security and potential return	Provides investors with the ability to choose a fund that meets their investment criteria. Helps ensure superior return on investments.
Simplified, government-approved application form	Keeps set-up time to a minimum; usually completed in less than two hours. Reduces government approval time.
Forty years of pension experience	Eases pensioners' transition into retirement. Provides information.
Investment advisors who discuss with the client company its investment goals and objectives	Increases confidence that money is invested in appropriate investment fund.
Flexicon (an adjustable contribution schedule that allows for contributions of up to 15 percent of annual earnings)	Prevents investors from being locked into a fixed contribution schedule.
Computerized benefits payment system	Ensures that retirees receive their checks in a timely manner.

QUESTIONS

To help you think about how Ann might attempt to obtain commitment from Johnson in this call (assume that the primary call objective is to have Johnson agree to set up a meeting for a formal presentation of Brunswick's offering), answer the following questions.

1. Outline how you would attempt to obtain commitment, assuming that you use the following methods (add any assumptions necessary in order to develop the outline):
   a. Direct request method.
   b. Benefit summary method.
   c. Balance sheet method.
   d. Probing method.

2. Based on the limited information you have, which method do you think would be most appropriate?

3. Reread the material above and be prepared to watch the videotape in class. Watch for Ann's *actual* method used to obtain commitment. Evaluate Ann's attempts at obtaining commitment.

ADDITIONAL REFERENCES

Badovick, Gordon J; Farrand J Hadaway; and Peter F Kaminski. "Attributions and Emotions: The Effects on Salesperson Motivation after Successful vs. Unsuccessful Quota Performance." *Journal of Personal Selling and Sales Management,* Summer 1992, pp. 1–12.

Conner, Tim. "The New Psychology of Closing Sales." *American Salesman,* September 1987, p. 25.

Falvey, Jack. "For the Best Close, Keep an Open Mind." *Sales & Marketing Management,* April 1990, pp. 10, 12.

Gibson, W David. "Holy Alliances!" *Sales and Marketing Management,* July 1993, pp. 85–87.

Gschwandtner, Gerhard. "Closing Signals via Body Signals." *Marketing Times,* September–October 1981, pp. 12–13.

Hanan, Mack. "When the Customer Buys, That's the Time to Start Selling." *Sales & Marketing Management,* March 15, 1982, pp. 96–98.

McCormack, Mark. "Customers Buy When They Want to." *Waco Tribune-Herald,* September 5, 1993, p. 1B+.

Strutton, David, and James R Lumpkin. "The Relationship between Optimism and Coping Styles of Salespeople." *Journal of Personal Selling and Sales Management,* Spring 1993, pp. 71–82.

Building Long-Term Partnerships

*T*he relationship between a salesperson and a customer seldom ends when a sale has been made. In fact, salespeople are finding the building of relationships and even partnerships with customers increasingly important. Such relationships help to ensure that customers will select the salespeople's products and services the next time they buy. This chapter provides insights into building a partnership with the buyer.

Future business can always be affected by elements beyond the control of the company or its sales representatives. However, one sure way to decrease future uncertainties lies in building solid, progressive business relationships with customers. These relationships, the topic of this chapter, may be developed through sound customer relations and proper servicing of accounts. The result of such relationships is additional selling opportunities.

Some questions answered in this chapter are:

How should salespeople stay in contact with customers?
What sales strategies exist to sell to current accounts?
What trends are influencing long-term buyer-seller relationships?
What techniques are important to use when handling complaints?

Pat Lynch Eaton is national account manager for The Freeman Companies, one of the largest service companies in the trade show industry. Her responsibility is to sell all of Freeman's services, including decorating convention halls for trade shows, building exhibits and trade show booths, and shipping and storing the booths between shows. Pat also assists in the installation of the booth at the show. "Working in the trade show industry is, to me, the ultimate challenge. I go to a city where I know no one and in three days produce a product." That product is a trade show exhibit.

PAT LYNCH EATON

The Freeman Companies

"For my customer, the exhibit is the culmination of a year's work. It is that exhibit manager's one chance to capture the attention of their customers, their management, and their board." In the trade show industry, an empty hall is converted to a cross between a glitzy shopping mall and the state fair. In only a few days, upwards of 30,000 potential buyers will walk in front of that booth. As Pat says, "We have one shot to get it right; we can't go back and make it all better if it doesn't work."

There are, according to Pat, several keys to relationships. First is understanding the customer's needs, "particularly their budget and their objective because it is my job to figure out how to achieve that objective within their budget." Another key factor is honesty, or trust. " I build both personal and professional lines of communication. I get to know my customers as people and it is my actions that show that I am honest; that I am worthy of their trust." These factors work together because, as Pat recognizes, without trust customers are reluctant to fully share their needs and their budget constraints.

Pat's personal philosophy is nothing new; it just works. "My dad always said, if you're going to do a job, do it right. If you empty the trash, make sure to get the last Kleenex. Buzzwords like TQM are simply new words for the basics." As Pat notes, she sells herself as well as her company. Therefore, "it is my personal reputation that is on the line so the job has to be done well."

Pat believes that leads to mutual admiration, for her customer and her company. "I have a personal concern for my customers' results, as well as respect for what they do. And they have the same for me and Freeman."

Sometimes this means doing things that other salespeople probably wouldn't consider. Like staying up until 2 AM, typing attendees' names and addresses into the computer because her customer's computer went down and all of the registration information was lost the day before a show opened.

Or like the time that the fire sprinkler system broke at the close of the first day of a music show. "The system dumped several hundred thousand gallons of water—on grand pianos, carpet, drapes—on everything." Pat got a work crew right in and they worked all night. When the show opened the next day, it appeared as though nothing had happened.

The downsizing during recent years has added new challenges to Pat's job. "I used to deal with someone who only did trade shows. Now the buyer I work with is personally responsible for trade shows, advertising, PR . . . everything." Because she took the time to get to know as many people as possible in her accounts, she has not had to build new partnerships with every personnel change. "Many salespeople work only with the main decision maker. But that person doesn't stay around as long anymore." Pat's customers, though, can count on her staying around to finish the job.

THE VALUE OF CUSTOMERS

To many students, the emphasis in selling may appear to be on getting that initial sale. But for most salespeople, sales increases from one year to the next are due to increasing the revenue from existing accounts. Even in industries where purchase decisions are made infrequently, salespeople gain a competitive advantage by maintaining partnering relationships with their customers, because when buying decisions need to be made those customers look to their partners first. For example, when Turner Broadcasting purchases satellite time for television broadcasting from Hughes Telecommunications, the contract is for the entire life of the satellite (which is 15 years or longer). Hughes may only launch a couple of satellites each year, but it is important for the Hughes salesperson to maintain a high-quality relationship with Turner, so that revenue is optimized through maximum customer satisfaction.

In this chapter, we will integrate the knowledge you have already gained in selling to new prospects with the material you covered in Chapter 2 on building partnerships, so that you can learn how to sell over the long term to the same accounts. We will also discuss how to handle those situations where customers are unhappy.

Customers are, of course, the primary revenue source for companies. But many businesspeople do not accurately understand the value of a customer. For example, if a company can retain only 2 to 5 percent more customers (instead of losing those customers to competition), the effect on the bottom line is the same as cutting costs by 10 percent.[1] Similarly, it takes an average of 7 sales calls to close a first sale, but only 3 to close a subsequent sale.[2] So it not only costs less, but it is also easier to sell to satisfied customers.

Customers are also worth more in terms of revenue than some salespeople recognize. For example, most car salespeople seem to think only of their immediate sale. But each customer is potentially worth hundreds of thousands of dollars in revenue over his or her lifetime. Exhibit 13.1 illustrates the value of a small attorney's office over a 20-year period for just a few salespeople. For example, if a copier salesperson were to sell all of the

EXHIBIT 13.1

SELECTED EXPENSES FOR A SMALL LAW FIRM

Item	Cost	Total
Copiers	5 @ $5,000	$25,000
Copying supplies	$50 per month	12,000
Fax machines	5 @ $2,000	10,000
Fax supplies	$20 per month	4,800
Telephone systems	3 @ $1,000	3,000
Other office supplies	$100 per month	24,000
Office furniture	$5,000	5,000
Total over 20 years		$83,800

copiers needed, total revenue would be at least $37,000. If that salesperson only thinks in terms of one sale, however, the customer is only worth about $5,000.

*H*ow much do you spend on gasoline each month? Now multiply that by 12. Assume you live in the same neighborhood during five years of school, so multiply that result by 5. That total is the amount of your gasoline purchases over your college career. Do you usually buy gasoline from one or two stations? If so, you are worth several thousand dollars as a customer to those stations! Is their service at a level equal to your value to the station?

THINKING IT THROUGH

Successfully retaining customers is important to all companies. One study showed, for example, that 65 percent of the average company's business comes from current, satisfied customers. Another study found the cost of acquiring a new customer to be five times the cost of properly servicing a current customer and retaining that customer's business! Some industries are only now beginning to recognize the value of retaining customers *because they lose customers as fast as they create new ones.* As you can see in Exhibit 13.2, it is like trying to fill up a pail with water when there is a hole in the bottom; the water leaks out as fast as you pour it in. The cellular phone industry, for example, is experiencing a disconnect rate of 30 to 45 percent per year. Those companies must replace a third to one-half of their customers each year, just to stay even![3]

Of course, we have already discussed the importance of good service in generating referrals and the importance of becoming a trusted member of the community in which your buyers operate so that more customers can be acquired. The value of satisfied customers is tremendous in so many ways that it makes good business sense to build the strongest possible relationships.

EXHIBIT 13.2

ACQUIRING AND LOSING CUSTOMERS
Some companies acquire new customers as fast as they lose old ones, like trying to fill a bucket with a hole in the bottom. Hence, there is no revenue growth.

BUILDING TRUST BUILDS PARTNERSHIPS

Trust is an important component of partnerships. As discussed in Chapter 2, there are several types of relationships between buyers and sellers. At one end of the spectrum are functional relationships, where each purchase is really thought of as a separate transaction by the buyer. Previous experience with the seller is considered, but future purchases are not based on any commitment to the seller.

But in partnerships, buyers do make commitments to purchase over time from sellers. They make these commitments because they feel that they can trust the seller. Trust is a combination of five factors: dependability, competence, customer orientation, honesty, and likability. In this section, we will discuss each of the five factors and how salespeople demonstrate their trustworthiness.

DEPENDABILITY

Dependability, or the buyer's perception that the salesperson (and the product and company represented) will live up to promises made, is not something that a salesperson can demonstrate immediately. Promises must be made and then kept. Early in the selling process, a salesperson can demonstrate dependability by calling at times agreed to, by showing up a few minutes early for appointments, and by providing information as promised.

Third-party references can be useful in proving dependability, especially if the salesperson has not yet had an opportunity to prove it personally. If the seller can point to a similar situation and illustrate, through the words of another customer, how the situation was resolved, dependability can be verified by the buyer. Some companies also prepare case studies of how they

Golf and other forms of entertaining are used less than most people realize, but can be an important way to show appreciation and build trusting, friendly relationships.

Lori Adamski Peek/TSW.

solved a particular customer's problem to aid salespeople in proving the company's dependability.

Product demonstrations, plant tours, and other special types of presentations can also illustrate dependability. A product demonstration can show how the product will work, even under difficult conditions. A buyer for component parts for appliances was concerned about one company's ability to produce the large volumes required. The salesperson offered a plant tour to prove that the company could live up to its promises for on-time delivery. When the buyer saw the size of the plant and watched the dedication of the employees to making quality products, she was convinced.

The salesperson's prior experience and training can also be used to prove dependability. For a company (and a salesperson) to remain in business, there must be some level of dependability. Length of experience, however, is a weak substitute for proving dependability with action.

As time goes on and the relationship grows, dependability is assumed by the buyer. For example, a buyer may say, "Well, let's call Sue at Mega. We know we can depend on her." At this point, the salesperson has developed a reputation within the account as dependable. But it doesn't stop there—reputations can spread beyond that account through the buyer's community. A reputation for dependability, however, can be quickly lost if the salesperson fails to continue to deliver as promised.

▌ COMPETENCE

Competence is the buyer's perception that the salesperson knows what he or she is talking about.[4] As you learned in earlier chapters, knowledge of the customer, the product, the industry, and the competition are all necessary to the success of the salesperson. It is through the use of this knowledge that a salesperson demonstrates competency. For example, when a pharmaceutical representative can discuss the treatment of a disease in medical terms, the physician is more likely to believe that the rep is medically competent.

Salespeople recognize the need to appear competent. Unfortunately, their recognition of the importance of competency may lead them to try to fake knowledge. Because buyers test the trustworthiness of a seller early in the relationship, they may ask questions just to see what the salesperson's response is.

Competency is demonstrated through the use of accurate information. Salespeople should never make up a response to a tough question; at the same time, salespeople should try to present information objectively. Buyers can tell when salespeople are exaggerating the performance of their product.

Kodak, which was named the top sales force in scientific/photographic equipment, creates competency through intensive training. Each salesperson undergoes 90 days of training before being sent into the field. Once in the field, salespeople are continually fed a stream of information that they can use to aid their customers. The result is a highly competent sales force that works in partnership with retailers, helping them run their business more successfully.[5]

CUSTOMER ORIENTATION

Customer orientation is the degree to which the salesperson puts the customer's needs first. Salespeople who think only of making sales are sales oriented rather than customer oriented. Buyers perceive salespeople as customer oriented when sellers stress benefits and solutions to problems over features. Buyers who perceive that the product is tailored to their unique requirements are likely to infer a customer orientation. Stating pros and cons can be perceived as being customer oriented, because understanding the cons also indicates that the salesperson understands the buyer's needs.

Emphasizing the salesperson's availability and desire to provide service also indicates a customer orientation. For example, "Call me anytime for anything that you need" is the type of statement that indicates availability. Offering the numbers for toll-free hotlines, voice mail, and similar concrete information indicates a desire to respond promptly to the buyer and can serve as proof of a customer orientation.

HONESTY

Honesty is both truthfulness and sincerity. While honesty is highly related to dependability ("We can count on you and your word because you are honest"), honesty is also related to how *candid* a salesperson is. For example, giving pros *and cons* can increase perceptions of honesty.

Honesty is also related to competency. As we said earlier, salespeople must be willing to admit that they do not know something, rather than trying to fake it. Otherwise, their honesty will be called into question.

A customer once asked, "Does your product SNA?" SNA was a new computer architecture that IBM had recently announced, but the salesperson represented a competing manufacturer. The salesperson replied, "No, not now and I don't know if we will, but I can find out." The customer's response was, "That's the first honest answer I've heard to that question." The salesperson eventually won a good portion of the customer's business, in part because she did not try to bluff her way through a tough question.

LIKEABILITY

Likeability, while a component of trust, may be the least important component, according to research.[6] **Likeability** refers to behaving in a friendly manner and finding a common ground between the buyer and seller. While not as important as other dimensions, salespeople should still attempt to find a common ground or interest with the buyer.

As you've probably noticed, the five dimensions of trust are highly interrelated. Honesty affects customer orientation, which also influences dependability, for example. Salespeople should recognize the interdependence of these factors, rather than simply focusing on one or two. For example, there once was a time when many salespeople emphasized only likeability. In today's market, professional salespeople must also be competent, dependable, honest, and customer oriented.

As we discussed in Chapter 2, relationships go through several stages, beginning with awareness and ending in dissolution. In this chapter, we are going to focus on the three stages in between awareness and dissolution: exploration, expansion, and commitment, as illustrated in Exhibit 13.3. As you read the rest of the chapter, you will see how trust is built and maintained throughout the life of the partnership.

EXHIBIT 13.3

THE THREE STAGES IN
BETWEEN AWARENESS AND
DISSOLUTION OF
PARTNERSHIP GROWTH

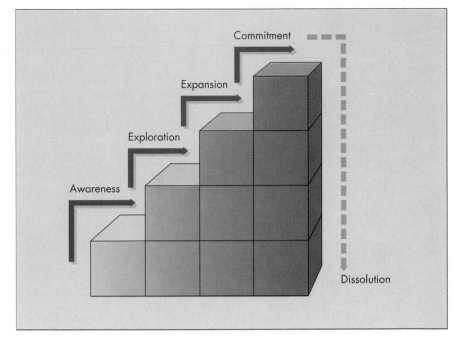

EXPLORATION

In the exploration stage, the relationship is defined through the development of expectations for each party. This means that each party explores what the other party offers. The buyer tests the seller's product, how the seller responds to requests, and other similar actions after the initial sale is made. At the same time, trust is developed, as are personal relationships.

Beginning the relationship properly is important if the relationship is going to last a long time. Keep in mind that the customer is excited about receiving the benefits of the product as promised by the salesperson. If the customer's initial experience with the product or with the company is bad, it may be extremely difficult to overcome. Beginning the relationship properly requires that the salesperson set the right expectations, monitor order processing, ensure proper use of the product, and assist in servicing the product.

SET THE RIGHT EXPECTATIONS

The best way to begin a relationship is for both parties to be aware of what the other expects. To a large degree, customers base their expectations on sales presentations.

Salespeople should make sure customers have reasonable expectations of product performance. If the salesperson exaggerates the capabilities of the product or the company, the customer will be disappointed. Admitting there has been a misunderstanding will not satisfy a customer who has registered a complaint. Avoiding complaints by setting proper expectations is best. Long-term relationships are begun by making an honest presentation of the product's capabilities and eliminating any misconceptions before the order is placed.

This United Stationers salesperson is working with the shipping department to make sure her customer's order is shipped promptly.

Courtesy United Stationers.

MONITOR ORDER PROCESSING

While many people may work on an order before it is shipped, the salesperson is ultimately responsible, at least in the eyes of the customer, for seeing that the product is shipped when promised. Salespeople should keep track of impending orders and inform buyers when the paperwork is delayed in the customer's plant. Orders placed directly with a salesperson should be transmitted to the factory immediately. Also, progress on orders in process should be closely monitored. If problems arise in filling the order, customers should be informed promptly; on the other hand, if the order can be filled sooner than promised, the customer should be notified so that the proper arrangements can be made. For example, a carpet company was able to install sooner than planned in a hotel that was being renovated. Unfortunately, because the carpet was installed early before some of the plumbing work was completed, the company had to remove a section that was ruined by the plumbers and replace it.

Shipping delays often occur when customers use outdated information in placing orders. Salespeople can prevent these delays and mistakes by making sure orders are accurate and complete. They should provide customers with the latest data sheets, product information, and descriptions of ordering procedures. Finally, they should review all orders for accuracy and completeness.

Fortunately, computers have made the sales representative's job easier. Salespeople can use hand-held terminals and laptop PCs to check on inventory and/or the status of an order. Progressive firms have introduced automated order systems. Computers are now available that allow the customer to sign a pad on the computer and the signature is sent electronically to the company, avoiding delays caused by mailing the contract.

Some firms, such as GE and Baxter Healthcare, facilitate the automatic placement of orders by having customers' terminals talk to their own computers. This boosts the productivity of both the salespeople and the purchasing managers they call on. As a result, salespeople spend less time writing orders and more time solving problems; buyers save on ordering and inventory costs. Computerized communication for order placement is particularly useful when managing a customer's needs worldwide. Elements such as time zones and language are minimized.

Monitoring order processing and other after-sale activities is critical to developing a partnership. Studies continually show buyers to be displeased with most salespeople in this respect. One study indicated that failure to follow through after the sale was the buyers' second biggest complaint against salespeople (talking too much was first).[7]

In two studies, buyers were asked to name the characteristics of excellent salespeople. The seller's ability to go to bat for the buyer within the seller's firm was the most important characteristic in one study and the second most important in the other.[8] Mike Rose, sales representative for Menasha Corp., sells packaging materials. He was named a top-ten sales representative by *Purchasing* magazine because of the way he represents his buyers to his company. For example, one customer had a problem with boxes popping open in shipment. Mike observed the problem and recognized that the dyes his company was using caused the adhesive to fail. He returned to his own company and persuaded them to invest in new dyes so that the adhesives would keep the boxes closed.[9]

ENSURE PROPER INITIAL USE OF THE PRODUCT OR SERVICE

+backup with post sale svc.

Customer dissatisfaction can occur just after delivery of a new product, especially if the product is technical or requires special installation. Customers unfamiliar with the product may have problems installing or using it. They may even damage the product through improper use. Many salespeople visit new customers right after initial deliveries so that they can ensure the correct use of the product. In this way, they can also help the customer realize the full potential benefits of the product.

Some buyers may be knowledgeable about how to use the basic features of a product or service, but if it is not operating at maximum efficiency, the wise salesperson will show the buyer how to get more profitable use out of it. Many firms have staffed a customer service department to aid salespeople in this task. It is still the salesperson's responsibility, however, to make sure that the customer service department takes proper care of each new customer.

One former product manager for a European Office equipment manufacturer reports that the company used to ship a typewriter to the US with a defective operator's manual. If the new owner followed the instructions exactly, there was no possible way to put in the ribbon. The manual was originally written in Italian, then poorly translated to English. To make matters worse, the product was re-designed, making the manual obsolete but they never changed it. In this situation, the salesperson had to ask the customer to call upon delivery of the product so that the rep could show how to install the ribbon. In international sales, companies often try to get by with manuals that emphasize diagrams rather than words in order to avoid translation problems. In these situations, salespeople should follow up with a personal visit to make sure that the customer gets off to a good start.

To be most effective, the salesperson should not wait until the user has trouble with the product and then point out remedies. The fewer difficulties allowed to occur, the greater will be the customer's confidence in the salesperson and the product.

In Biship's Stortford, England, a Thermofrost representative trains a TESCO store manager in proper maintenance of a Thermofrost display cooler. Getting customers off to the right start is important to building long and satisfying relationships.

Courtesy Parker Hannifin Corporation.

HANDLE CUSTOMER COMPLAINTS

Adjusting complaints receives special treatment here because of its importance in developing goodwill and maintaining partnerships. Complaints can occur at any time in the partnering process, not just during the exploration stage. Handling complaints properly is always important, but perhaps even more so in the early stages of a partnership. Attempts at establishing partnerships often collapse due to shortsightedness in handling customer complaints. Some firms spend thousands of dollars on advertising, but make the mistake of insulting customers who attempt to secure a satisfactory adjustment.

Complaints normally arise when the company and/or its products do not live up to the customer's expectations. Assuming the proper expectations were set, customers can be disappointed for any of the following reasons: (1) the product performs poorly, (2) it is being used improperly, or (3) the terms of a sales contract were not met. While salespeople cannot usually change the product or terms, they can affect these sources of complaints.

As we discussed earlier in this chapter, the cost of making the first sale is well known to be higher than the cost of repeat sales, so making every reasonable effort to keep customers in whom the company has invested time and money is good business. Also, many customers don't go to the trouble of complaining, so when a customer does attempt to secure satisfaction because of disappointment with a product or service, the producing company should view the complaint as an opportunity to prove that it is a reliable firm with which to do business.

One study showed that when a company fails in its dealings with a complainant, the latter will tell 10 people, on average, about the bad experience; those who are satisfied tell only 4 to 5 others. Also, estimates have been put forth that for every dissatisfied person who complains, 50 more just stop buying the product.[10]

Despite all the care manufacturers take to produce good products, unsatisfactory ones do find their way to the ultimate user or retailer. This inevitable situation, however, becomes alarming if the unsatisfactory products become too numerous.

Turning It Around

Sandy Garrett, manager of Personnel One Temporary and Permanent Placement in Tampa, Florida, held the phone away from her ear. The customer was shouting loud enough to be heard across the room.

"We deal with human beings; that's our product," notes Sandy. "And in this particular case, the people we sent to work for this account let us down. But as far as our client was concerned, it was Personnel One that let them down."

The client, a major insurance company headquartered in Tampa, had a data entry job that would take four temporary employees about three weeks to complete, including three days of training. Because of the training and the tight deadline, Sandy had asked for a three-week commitment from each person.

Unfortunately, one person's father died and she quit to be with her family. Another found a permanent job and quit, leaving two people to finish the job in less than two weeks. The customer wasn't interested, though, in why they left; the only thing the customer knew was that there was a deadline and it wasn't going to get met.

Sandy offered to come to their office and discuss alternatives, but the customer wanted none of that.

"The last thing I heard before he hung up on me was, 'Sandy, we can't depend on Personnel One. We're going to another agency.'" But whether he wanted to see her or not, Sandy developed two possible solutions and drove straight to her client's office.

"He still didn't want to see me when I arrived," she said. "But I had two options and asked him to just look at them." She presented two options because she wanted him to think of the decision as a choice between Personnel One and Personnel One, not Personnel One and a competitor.

"Each option would take care of his biggest concern, which was getting people trained and productive in order to meet the deadline. And in each option, we absorbed any additional cost." Sandy also reminded her client of everything that Personnel One had done right. But Sandy notes that, "The biggest factor, though, was that I personally and immediately went to see him. He knew then how much his business meant to me."

Sandy kept the client, and has since earned all of their temporary personnel business. "Turning around such a difficult client is a stressful challenge, but when you do it well, it is also intensely satisfying."

Most progressive companies have learned that an excellent way to handle customer complaints is through personal visits by sales representatives. This means the salesperson may have total responsibility for this portion of the company's public relations. Salespeople who carry this burden must be prepared to do an effective job. Selling Scenario 13.1 illustrates how one salesperson with the responsibility and authority for customer service was able to turn a customer's complaint around.

Complaints cannot be eliminated; they can only be reduced in frequency. The salesperson who knows complaints are inevitable can learn to handle them as a normal part of the job. The following discussion presents some techniques for responding to complaints; Exhibit 13.4 provides an overview.

EXHIBIT 13.4

- Encourage buyers to tell their story.
- Determine the facts.
- Offer a solution.
- Follow through with action.

Encourage Buyers to Tell Their Story

Some customers can become angry over real or imaginary grievances. They welcome the salesperson's visit as an opportunity to get complaints off their chests. Other buyers are less emotional in voicing complaints and give little evidence of irritation or anger, but the complaint is no less important.

In either case, customers need to tell their stories without interruption. Interruptions add to the fury and irritation of emotionally upset buyers. Reason seldom prevails when a grievance is discussed with an angry person. This makes it almost impossible to arrive at a settlement that is fair to all parties concerned until the customer has a chance to air the complaint and settle down.

The manner in which salespeople treat complaining customers determines the ease with which adjustments can be made. If salespeople get off to a poor start in the discussion, their chances of developing or maintaining a partnership diminish rapidly. Customers want a sympathetic reaction to their problems, whether real or imagined. They want their feelings to be acknowledged, their business to be recognized as important, and their grievances handled in a friendly manner. An antagonistic attitude, or an attitude that implies the customer is trying to cheat the company, seldom paves the way for a satisfactory adjustment. You can probably relate to this if you have ever had to return a defective product or get some kind of an adjustment made on a bill.

Good salespeople show that they are happy the grievance has been brought to their attention. After the customer describes the problem, the salesperson may express regret for any inconvenience. An attempt should then be made to talk about points of agreement. Agreeing with the customer as far as possible gets the process off to the right start.

Determine the Facts

It is easy to be influenced by a customer who is honestly and sincerely making a claim for an adjustment. An inexperienced salesperson might forget that many customers make their case for a claim as strong as possible. Emphasizing the points most likely to strengthen one's case is human nature. But the salesperson has a responsibility to the company, too. A satisfactory adjustment cannot be made until all the facts are known.

Whenever possible, the salesperson should examine, in the presence of the customer, the article or product claimed to be defective. Having the complaining customer tell and show the exact problem is a good idea. If the defect is evident, this may be unnecessary. In other instances, making certain the complaint is understood becomes necessary. The purpose of getting the facts is to determine the cause of the problem so that the proper solution can be provided.

Experienced salespeople soon learn that products may appear defective when actually nothing is wrong with them. For example, a buyer may complain that paint was applied exactly as directed but repainting became necessary in a short time, so the buyer concludes the paint was no good. However, the paint may have been spread too thin. Any good paint will cover just so much area. If the manufacturer recommends using a gallon of paint to cover 400 square feet with two coats, and the user covers 600 square feet with two coats, the unsatisfactory results are not the fault of the product. Or if an office equipment salesperson sells a fax machine that requires special paper, the machine is not at fault if the customer gets unsatisfactory results from a low-grade substitute paper.

On the other hand, salespeople should not assume that product or service failure is always the user's fault. They need an open mind to search for the facts in each case. Defective material may have found its way to the dealer's shelves, the wrong merchandise may have been shipped, the buyer may have been overcharged, or the buyer may have been billed for an invoice that was already paid. The facts may prove the company is at fault. Also, some companies have the policy that the customer is *always* right, in which case there is no need to establish *responsibility*. There is still a need, however, to determine what the cause was so the right solution can be offered.

Sometimes, investigation proves that neither the buyer nor the seller is at fault. For example, goods can be lost in transit or damaged because of improper handling by the transportation company. Or the salesperson may find that both buyer and seller have contributed to unsatisfactory results. Perhaps the buyer failed to follow printed instructions accurately, while the salesperson failed to instruct the buyer about precautions to take when using the product. Occasionally the reason for a failure cannot be determined at all. Obviously, this creates a problem in attempting to place responsibility.

In this phase of making an adjustment, salespeople must avoid giving the impression of stalling. The customer should know that the purpose of determining the facts is to permit a fair adjustment—that the inquiry is not being made in order to delay action or to avoid resolution.

Offer a Solution

After the customer tells his or her story and the facts are determined, the next step is to offer a solution. At this time, the company representative describes the process by which the company will resolve the complaint, and the rep should then gain agreement that the proposed solution is satisfactory.

Company policies vary, but many assign the responsibility for settling claims to the salesperson. Other companies require the salesperson to investigate claims and recommend a settlement to the home office. The proponents of both methods have good arguments to justify them. Some companies maintain that salespeople are in the best position to make adjustments fairly, promptly, and satisfactorily. This is especially true if the customer and salesperson are geographically distant from the home office.

Buyers appreciate salespeople who attempt to resolve complaints quickly. This salesperson is using the buyer's phone to track down a misplaced invoice.

Sharon Hoogstraten.

Others believe that permitting salespeople to only recommend a course of action ensures the customer of attention from a higher level of management. Therefore, the customer will be more likely to accept the action taken. Companies holding the latter view also claim that for many technical products the salesperson is not qualified to make a technical analysis of product difficulties.

Requiring salespeople to do the job when possible probably works best. Whatever the company policy, the customer desires quick action and fair treatment, and wants to know the reasons for the action. Nothing discourages a customer more than having action postponed indefinitely. While some decisions may take time, the salesperson should try to expedite action. The opportunity to develop a partnership may be lost if the time lapse is too great—even though action is taken in the customer's favor.

Decisions fair to the customer and to the company are a potent factor in building partnerships. Most customers are satisfied if they receive fair treatment. They must, however, be convinced of its fairness, and customers seldom are unless the reasoning behind the treatment is explained to them. The salesperson may need to review the guarantee provided with the product, or to explain the company's policy and why it is followed.

Some salespeople make disparaging remarks about their own company or managers. Blaming someone else in the company is a poor practice, because this can cause the customer to lose faith in both the salesperson and the company. Moreover, if the customer does not like the proposed solution, the salesperson trusted to make an adjustment or recommendation should shoulder the responsibility. Any disagreement on the action taken should be ironed out between the salesperson and the home office staff. The action, when reported to the customer, must be stated in a sound, convincing manner.

The action taken may vary with the circumstances. Some possible settlements when a product is unsatisfactory are:

1. Replace the product without cost to the customer.

2. Replace the product and charge the customer for labor or transportation costs only.

3. Replace the product and share all costs with the customer.

4. Replace the product but require the customer to pay part of the cost of the new product.

5. Instruct the customer on how to proceed with a claim against a third party.

6. Send the product to the factory for a decision.

Occasionally, customers make claims they know are unfair. Although they realize the company is not at fault, they still try to get a settlement. Fortunately, relatively few customers do this.

To assume that a customer is willfully trying to cheat the company would be unwise. He or she may honestly see a claim as legitimate even though the salesperson can clearly tell that the company is not at fault. The salesperson does well, then, to proceed cautiously and, if any doubt exists, to treat the claim as legitimate.

A salesperson convinced that a claim is dishonest has two ways to take action. First, he or she can give the buyer an opportunity to save face by suggesting that a third party may be to blame. For example, if a machine appears not to have been oiled for a long time, a salesperson may suggest, "Is it possible that your maintenance crew neglected to oil this machine?" Second, the salesperson can unmask the fraudulent claim and appeal to the customer's sense of fair play. This procedure may cause the loss of a customer. In some cases, however, the company may be better off without that customer.

Answers to the following questions often affect the action to be taken:

*   *What is the dollar value of the claim?* Many firms have established standard procedures for what they classify as small claims. For example, one moving and storage firm considers any claim under $200 to be too insignificant to investigate fully; thus, a refund check is issued automatically for a claim under this amount. Firms may also have a complete set of procedures and policies developed for every size of claim.

*   *How often has this customer made claims?* If the buyer has instituted many claims in the past, the company may need not only to resolve this specific complaint but also to conduct a more comprehensive investigation of all prior claims. Such a probe may reveal systematic flaws in the salesperson's company, product, or procedures. It may also spot similar deficiencies in the buyer's organization, or the salesperson may learn that the buyer is just hard to please and will complain regardless of the quality of the product or service.

*   *How will the action taken affect other customers?* The salesperson should assume that the action taken will be communicated to other prospects and customers. If the complaining customer is part of a buying community (Chapter 7 discussed these), chances are very

good that others will learn about the resolution of the claim. Thus, the salesperson must take actions necessary to maintain a positive presence in that community, possibly even providing a more generous solution than the merits of the case would dictate.

The solution that will be provided to the customer must be clearly communicated. The customer must perceive the settlement as being fair. When describing the settlement, the salesperson should carefully monitor all verbal and nonverbal cues to determine the customer's level of satisfaction. If the customer does not agree with the proposed course of action, the salesperson should seek ways to change the settlement or provide additional information as to why the settlement is fair to all parties.

Follow Through with Action

A fair settlement made in the customer's favor helps resell the company and its products or services. The salesperson has the chance to prove what the customer has been told for a long time—that the company will devote time and effort to keeping customers satisfied.

The salesperson who has authority only to recommend an adjustment must take care to report the facts of the case promptly and accurately to the home or branch office. The salesperson has the responsibility to act as a buffer between the customer and the company. After the claim is filed, contact must be maintained with the customer to see that the customer secures the promised settlement.

The salesperson also has a responsibility to educate the customer in order to forestall future claims. After a claim has been settled to the customer's satisfaction is a fine time to make some suggestions. For example, the industrial sales representative may provide a new set of directions on how to oil and clean a machine.

Many businesses have built great names by following the slogan "The customer is always right." This should be the attitude displayed by salespeople who plan to cultivate customers and to build goodwill for the company and themselves.

ACHIEVE CUSTOMER SATISFACTION

Although complaints always signal customer dissatisfaction, their absence doesn't necessarily mean that customers are happy. Customers probably voice only 1 in 20 of their concerns. They may speak out only when highly dissatisfied, or a big corporation's buyer may not be aware of problems until the product users blow their stacks. Lower levels of dissatisfaction still hurt sales. Salespeople should continuously monitor customers' levels of satisfaction and perceptions of product performance.

When the customer is satisfied, there is opportunity for further business. Complaints and dissatisfaction can occur at any time during the relationship, but during the exploration stage handling complaints well is one way to prove that you are committed to keeping that customer's business. When customers sense such commitment, whether through the handling of a complaint or through other forms of special attention, they may be ready to move to the expansion stage.

HFC's three regional customer service departments take care of many customer concerns daily. But as a salesperson, you may be the only customer service department your company has, and certainly the one on which your customers will want to depend.

Courtesy Household International, Inc.

EXPANSION

The next phase of the buyer-seller relationship is expansion. When a salesperson does a good job of identifying and satisfying needs and the beginnings of a partnership are in place, the opportunity is there for additional sales. Trust has developed, allowing the salesperson to focus on identifying additional needs and providing solutions. In this section, we are going to discuss how to increase sales from current customers to expand the relationship. Keep in mind, however, that the activities of the exploration stage (monitoring order processing, handling complaints, etc.) still apply.

There are several ways to maximize the selling opportunity each account represents. These include generating reorders, upgrading, full-line selling, and cross-selling.

GENERATING REPEAT ORDERS

In some situations, the most appropriate strategy is to generate repeat orders. For example, Cargill provides salt and other cooking ingredients to Kellog's. The best strategy for the Cargill salesperson may be to ensure that Kellog's continues to buy those ingredients from Cargill. Several methods can be used to improve the likelihood of reorders.

Be Present at Buying Time

One important method of ensuring reorders is to know how often and when the company makes decisions. For example, the salesperson who assisted your professor in choosing this textbook has already asked when book orders need to be in to the bookstore. The salesperson will then try to arrange a visit for just before that buying time.

Buyers don't always have regular buying cycles, which can make it difficult for salespeople to be present at buying time. In these situations, the seller still wants to be present in the buyer's mind. Two items that can help *reminders for buyers*

keep the seller present are catalogs and specialty advertising items. Catalogs are useful for buyers, who will usually refer to these when ready to buy. Specialty advertising items, like pens or desk calendars, also aid buyers in reordering, especially if the 800-number is easy to find. Florida Furniture Industries has used desk calendars for over 60 years as a reminder for furniture store buyers of whom to call when inventories are low.

Help in Servicing the Product

Most products need periodic maintenance and repair, and some mechanical and electronic products require routine adjustments. Such service requirements offer salespeople a chance to show buyers that their interest did not end with the delivery of the product. Salespeople should be able to make minor adjustments or take care of minor repairs. If they cannot put the product back into working order, they must notify the proper company representative. They should then check to see that the repairs have been completed in a timely manner and to the customer's complete satisfaction.

*Keep svc.
people up to date
(both customer &
own firm's)*

As we will discuss in Chapter 17, part of the salesperson's job is getting to know the company's maintenance and repair people. These repair people can act as the salesperson's eyes and ears when they make service calls. When a good relationship is established with service personnel, salespeople can learn of pending decisions or concerns and can take the necessary action.

Salespeople should monitor parts shipments just as they would any order; in addition, they should supply up-to-date service manuals and place buyers' names on the service mailing list. In this way, bulletins on maintenance and repair reach the proper people. If the customer's maintenance department in the plant is well informed about the product, user complaints fall off dramatically.

THINKING IT THROUGH	*S*ome customers take advantage of salespeople by trying to have them perform almost all of the routine maintenance on a product for free. What can you, as a salesperson, do to curb such requests? How do you know where to draw the line?

Provide Expert Guidance / *Assistance (total solutions)*

An industrial buyer or purchasing agent may need help in choosing a proper grade of oil or selecting a suitable floor cleaner. A buyer for a retail store may want help developing sales promotion ideas. Whether the buyer needs help in advertising, selling, or managing, good salespeople are prepared to offer worthwhile suggestions or services.

The salesperson usually prospers only if the buyer prospers. Obviously, unless buyers can use a product or service profitably or resell it at a profit, they have no need to continue buying from that product's seller.

Many firms have developed a team approach to providing guidance and suggestions. For example, General Telephone & Electronics Corporation (GTE) uses a systems approach to help develop and maintain the communication systems of its major accounts. The Major Account Service Team (MAST) is composed of marketing (as chairperson), engineering, service, supply, and traffic representatives. This interdepartmental approach brings together all skills required to provide expert guidance and suggestions to meet the expanding and sophisticated needs of large customers.

One salesperson was named a top-10 sales representative by *Purchasing* magazine because of his expert guidance. John Paduch, now vice president of sales for American Supply Co. of Gary, Indiana, saved one customer $1.4 million over five years through various ideas, such as showing how changing from stainless steel pipes and valves to cast iron saved $165,000 without any loss in quality. In addition, Paduch was able to assist the customer in reducing inventory by 47 percent. Such expert guidance led that customer to nominate John Paduch for *Purchasing's* top-10 sales rep award.[11]

UARCO's philosophy for success in the highly competitive field of selling business forms includes expert advice. Its forms management program makes it a business partner with, rather than merely a supplier to, its major accounts. Customers are shown how to control the costs of buying and using forms by such practices as redesigning existing forms, grouping forms for more economical ordering, keeping records of quantities on hand and on order, and keeping track of the dollar value of the inventory. UARCO's customers welcome such advice, leading to a high reorder rate.

Provide Special Assistance

Salespeople are in a unique position to offer many types of assistance to the buyer. This section will briefly mention a few of the types of assistance that salespeople can and do provide to their customers.

Salespeople engage in many activities. For example, a Nabisco salesperson serves as a bagger during the grand opening of a new grocery store. Procter & Gamble salespeople help in resetting (determining where products should go on) the shelves any time a grocery store decides to realign its shelf positions. Salespeople for Simmons help set up mattress displays in furniture stores. Makita power tool salespeople provide free demonstrations for customers of hardware stores. Most salespeople that sell to resellers will tidy up the shelves and physically restock them from the stockroom supplies. Salespeople also help train the reseller's employees in how to sell the products to the final consumers.

Gail Walker, of Marquis Communications (a trade show and special events service agency), worked in the booth at a trade show when one of her customer's salespeople got sick. She worked as if she were one of their employees. Providing such special assistance is one hallmark of excellence in selling. Good relationships are built faster and more soundly by the salesperson who does a little something extra for a customer—performing services over and above the salesperson's normal responsibilities.

▌ UPGRADING

Similar to generating reorders is the concept of upgrading. **Upgrading,** also called *upselling,* is convincing the customer to use a higher-quality product or a newer product. The salesperson seeks the upgrade because the new or better product serves the needs of the buyer more effectively than the old product did.

Upgrading is crucial to companies like Digital Equipment Corp. Digital recently launched the new Alpha AXP computer and industry experts agree that, for the new product to succeed, the company must secure upgrades from their old VAX products. Otherwise, as their customers find needs for newer equipment, they will turn to IBM or Hewlett-Packard, and Digital may lose their business forever.[12]

When upgrading, it is a good idea during the needs identification phase to emphasize that the initial decision was a good one. Now, however, needs or technology have changed and the newer product fits the customer's requirements better. Otherwise, what could occur is a perception by the buyer that the seller is trying to take advantage of the relationship to foist off a higher-priced product.

▌ FULL-LINE SELLING

Full-line selling is selling the entire line of associated products. For example, a Xerox copier salesperson may sell the copier but also wants to sell the dry ink and paper that the copier uses, and a service contract. Or a Campbell's Soup salesperson will ask a store to carry cream of potato soup as well as tomato soup.

When full-line selling, the emphasis is on helping the buyer realize the synergy of owning or carrying all of the products in that line. For example, the Xerox salesperson may emphasize the security in using Xerox supplies, whereas the Campbell's rep will point out that sales for all soups will increase if the assortment is broader.

In selling to retailers, a current trend in the area of full-line selling is category management (discussed in greater detail in Chapter 15). **Category management** is especially important in consumer packaged goods sales, such as processed foods sold to grocery stores. The salesperson from one supplier works closely with the retailer to create merchandising and marketing plans that boost sales for the entire product category, including competitive brands. Salespeople who develop category management partnerships recognize that when they improve their customer's sales, their own sales improve, too. For example, a Campbell's Soup rep would help Kroger develop marketing plans to sell soup, including Progresso and Kroger's Cost-Cutter brands. These plans would include promotion schedules, pricing plans, and display ideas. The challenge for the salesperson is growing category sales while growing profit for both Kroger and Campbells. It is a challenge that few suppliers have truly been able to meet.[13]

▌ CROSS-SELLING

Cross-selling is similar to full-line selling, except that the additional products sold are not directly associated with the initial products. For example, cross-selling occurs when the Xerox salesperson attempts to sell a fax machine to a copier customer, or when a Campbell's Soup Co. rep sells spaghetti sauce to a soup buyer. Cross-selling involves leveraging the

In Caracas, Venezuela, this Parker Hannifin salesperson is demonstrating fluid connectors to a customer who already purchases other Parker products. Cross-selling opportunities like this one involve leveraging existing relationships in order to identify needs for additional products.

Courtesy Parker Hannifin Corporation.

relationship with a buyer in order to identify needs for additional products. Again, trust in the selling organization and the salesperson already exist; therefore, the sale should not be as difficult as with a new customer, providing the needs exist.

Cross-selling is an important strategy in some industries, such as banking. MasterCard salespeople are training employees at several major banks in how to cross-sell MasterCard, following a test that improved branch sales by 20 percent. When someone opens a new checking account or seeks a loan, the employee also recommends a MasterCard. While aimed primarily at improving consumer credit card sales, the program will also help officers of the banks sell corporate cards to companies that are already clients of the banks.[14]

Some attempts at cross-selling, though, can resemble the initial sale, because the buying center may change. For example, the spaghetti sauce buyer may not be the same person who buys soups. If that is the case, the salesperson will have to begin a relationship with the new buyer, building trust and credibility.

TOTAL QUALITY MANAGEMENT AND ACCOUNT RELATIONSHIPS

Many companies are reviewing their purchasing habits because of the trend toward total quality management (TQM). TQM means many things, but one area with tremendous implications for salespeople is the area of buying. TQM originated in the US but was first fully implemented by the Japanese. Companies espousing a TQM philosophy are reducing the number of vendors with whom they do business in order to demand higher quality and other benefits from partnership-type relationships. The result is that some salespeople are finding receptive ears for full-line selling and cross-selling proposals, while others are losing business. For example, Xerox, including Fuji Xerox and Rank Xerox in Europe, reduced its number of vendors from 5,000 worldwide to 500 over a period of 10 years.[15] That means that 4,500 salespeople lost what was probably their biggest account, while

500 salespeople grew their sales tremendously through full-line selling and cross-selling. TQM and ISO 9000, a global quality standard, has increased global competition, making salespeople more important because of their role in satisfying customer needs. The trend to preferred supplier programs is strong. In only two years, the number of manufacturers with programs for developing preferred suppliers grew from approximately 67 percent to almost 80 percent.[16] In the next section, we will talk about how companies become preferred suppliers in the commitment phase of the relationship.

COMMITMENT

When the buyer–seller relationship has reached the commitment stage, there is a stated or implied pledge to continue the relationship, as was discussed in Chapter 2. Formally, this pledge may begin with the seller becoming a preferred supplier, which is a much greater level of commitment than those levels discussed in Chapter 12. While **preferred supplier** status may mean different things in different companies, in general it means that the supplier is assured a large percentage of the buyer's business and will get the first opportunity to earn new business.[17] For example, at Motorola, only preferred suppliers are eligible to bid on new-product programs.[18] Thus, *preferred supplier* is one term used for partnerships.

What does it take to become a preferred supplier? To become a preferred supplier for Bethlehem Steel, the supplier must pass several criteria (listed in Exhibit 13.5). In some cases, a Bethlehem preferred supplier is a distributor, not a manufacturer. In these cases, the supplier and Bethlehem Steel work in tandem to find the best manufacturers at the lowest prices, with the result being increases in sales volume and better volume discounts. Bethlehem Steel gets the lowest price possible at the required service level and the distributor makes more profit—a win-win opportunity.[19]

Note that upgrading, full-line selling, cross-selling, and handling complaints will continue to occur during the commitment stage. Because a commitment has been made by both parties to the partnership, however, expectations are greater. Handling complaints properly, appropriately upgrading or cross-selling, and fulfilling new needs are even more important because of the high level of commitment made to the partner.

Research finds that many buyers examine suppliers on criteria similar to that used by Bethlehem Steel.[20] While the salesperson may not have the ability to influence corporate culture, the salesperson does play an important role in managing the relationship and leading both sides into commitment.

SECURING COMMITMENT TO A PARTNERSHIP

When firms reach the commitment stage, elements in addition to trust become important. Along with the dimensions of trust such as competence and dependability (similar to Bethlehem's capability) and honesty (or ethics), there must be commitment to the partnership from the entire supplying organization, a culture that fits with the buyer's organizational culture, and channels of communication so open that it seems as though the seller and buyer are part of the same company.

EXHIBIT 13.5

PREFERRED SUPPLIER
CRITERIA FOR SUPPLIERS TO
BETHLEHEM STEEL

- Capability: The purchasing team examines manufacturing, shipping, and administrative capabilities. Because Bethlehem requires significant monitoring by suppliers, even paperwork is scrutinized.
- Organization: Are employees dedicated? Is the company flexible or bureaucratic? Can it change as we change?
- Financial health: Bethlehem reviews audited financial statements to determine if the supplier is managed well.
- Culture: Does the corporate culture fit with ours? Do we want the same things and do we work in similar ways? Can we get along?
- Willingness to commit: Suppliers must be willing to commit the resources necessary to serve the account. For many suppliers, this means a full-time representative on Bethlehem's site.
- Ethics: Is the supplier trustworthy?

Source: Adapted from Jean Graham, "A Simple Idea Saves $8 Million a Year," *Purchasing*, May 21, 1992, pp. 47–49.

Commitment Must Be Complete

Commitment to the relationship should permeate both organizations, from top management to the secretary who answers the phone. This means devoting the necessary resources to satisfy the customer's needs, even anticipating needs before the buyer does. It is often the responsibility of the salesperson to secure commitment from his or her own company. Senior management must be convinced of the benefits of partnering with a specific account and be willing to allow the salesperson to direct the resources necessary for the partnership. (We will discuss in Chapter 17 building the internal partnerships needed by the salesperson to coordinate those resources.)

Commitment also requires that all employees be empowered to handle the needs of the customer. For example, if the customer has a problem with a billing process, administration should be willing to work with the partner to develop a more satisfactory process. In a partnership, the customer should not have to rely on only the salesperson to satisfy its needs.

Communication

In the exploration stage, availability must be demonstrated, and we have already discussed the example of toll-free hotlines and voice mail so that the seller's organization can respond quickly to customer calls. But in the commitment phase of a partnership, the seller must take a proactive communication stance. This means actively seeking opportunities to communicate at times other than just when you have something to sell or a problem to resolve.

Salespeople should also encourage direct communication between similar functional areas. In previous stages, the two firms communicated through the buyer and the salesperson. If multi-level selling occurred, it occurred at even levels; that is, vice presidents talking to each other. But when two firms commit to a partnership, the boundaries between the two companies, at least in terms of communication, should blur, as illustrated in Exhibit 13.6.

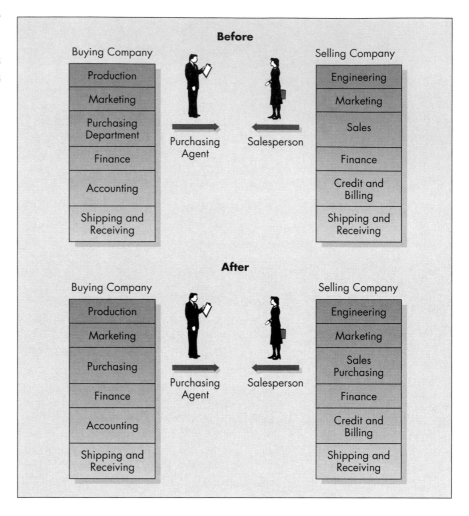

The buyer's production department, for example, should be able to communicate directly with the seller's engineering department if they need to work on a change in the product design, rather than going through the salesperson. While the salesperson would want to be aware of a product design change and ensure that engineering responded promptly to the customer's concern, direct communication means more accurate communication and a better understanding of the customer's needs. A better solution is more likely to result when there is direct communication.

Corporate Culture

Corporate culture is the values and beliefs held by senior management. A company's culture shapes the attitudes and actions of employees, and influences the development of policies and programs.[21] For example, consider the following scene. In a large room with concrete floors, there are a number of cubicles built out of plywood. In each cubicle is a card table, two folding chairs, and a poster that says "How low can you go?" Such is the scene in Bentonville, Arkansas, the corporate headquarters of Wal-Mart, where salespeople meet their buyers for Sam's Club and Wal-Mart. That room reflects Wal-Mart's culture of the lowest possible price.

A similar culture of constantly seeking ways to drive down costs is necessary for a seller to develop a partnership with Wal-Mart. A single salesperson is not going to change a company's corporate culture in order to secure a partnership with a buyer, but the salesperson must identify the type of culture held by both organizations and make an assessment of fit. Although a perfect match is not necessary, the salesperson must be ready to demonstrate that there is a fit. Offering lavish entertainment to a Wal-Mart buyer, for example, would not demonstrate a fit. Telling the buyer that you are staying at a Circle-6 Motel might.

Companies have often sought international partners as a way of entering foreign markets. Wal-Mart partnered with Cifra when Wal-Mart entered the Mexican market. Cifra provides distribution services and products to Wal-Mart for Sam's Club and Wal-Mart stores located in Mexico City, Monterrey, and Guadalajara. When partnering with companies from other countries, country culture differences as well as corporate culture differences can cause difficulties.

While the salesperson is not going to change a company's culture, the salesperson who seeks a partnering relationship is seeking change for both organizations. In the next section, we discuss what types of changes salespeople manage, and how.

SALESPERSON AS CHANGE AGENT

For revenue to grow over time in an account, it is important to recognize that the salesperson is **change agent,** or a cause of change in the organization. Each sale may involve some type of change; perhaps a change from a competitive product or simply a new version of the old one. Partnering, though, often requires that change is made in both the buying and selling organizations. For example, we discussed the case of John Paduch earlier, who saved his customer $1.4 million. To achieve those savings required that the buyer's company change the way they did business. As you can see in Selling Scenario 13.2, both ADS and Ciba-Geigy had to reorganize to partner.

Change is not easy, even when it is obviously beneficial. The objective is to manage change, such as changing from steel to iron pipe, in the buyer's organization while giving the appearance of stability. There are two critical elements to consider about change: the rate and the range of change. The **rate of change** refers to how fast the change is made, whereas the **range of change** refers to the degree to which the change affects the organization. Broad-range change affects many areas of the company, whereas narrow changes affect small areas. In general, the faster and broader the change, the more likely it will meet with resistance, as illustrated in Exhibit 13.7.[22]

To overcome resistance to change, the salesperson should consider several decisions. The first decision involves finding help in the buying organization for selling the proposal. Other important decisions are positioning the proposal, determining the necessary resources, and developing a time-based strategy.[23]

Creating a Partnership

How long does it take to create a partnership? In some ways, it takes years to create the trust needed to have a partnership. But once the decision is made, it can be only a matter of months before the elements of a solid partnership are in place. For Ciba-Geigy (a pharmaceutical manufacturer) and American Distribution Systems (ADS, a pharmaceutical distributor), it was six months from the initial meeting until the launch of the partnership program.

The process began with Ciba-Geigy identifying its needs as a buyer. Once those were identified, ADS and Ciba-Geigy began meeting to explore the possibility of a partnership. For several months, members of the two companies met and explored the possibilities of a partnership. During this period of discovery, the two organizations evaluated their compatibility and began to build the personal relationships necessary for a corporate partnership.

As Ciba-Geigy shared their vision for a joint effort, ADS recognized the need to create a cross-functional task force dedicated to making that vision a reality. This task force had the authority to make use of any of the company's resources and included personnel from information services, senior management, logistics planning, and operations. The task force became almost a company in a company. As

the task force worked with Ciba-Geigy personnel, they demonstrated their commitment to the relationship. Ciba-Geigy, too, displayed a collaborative culture by sharing information that would have previously been thought of as proprietary.

ADS submitted a proposal in October, but it took three more months of joint review and revision before the final Joint Operating Plan was completed. This complicated plan involved integrating systems of both companies.

But a plan alone is insufficient. For a partnership to become a reality, it must be implemented by many people who perceive an ownership, a personal commitment to the relationship. That feeling of ownership extends to continual examination of the process so that it can be improved. In fact, members of both companies scrutinize each other's processes and systems in order to create improvements.

To a large extent, the task force and other ADS employees who support Ciba-Geigy act as an extension of Ciba-Geigy, rather than a separate organization. They anticipate needs and create solutions in concert with Ciba-Geigy colleagues.

Source: Adapted from "Partnering for Performance," *NAMA Journal*, Fall 1992, pp. 6–9.

Champions

First, the choice of one or more champions must be made. **Champions**, also called *advocates* or *internal salespeople,* work for the buying firm in the areas most affected by the proposed change and work with the salesperson for the success of the proposal. These champions can build momentum for the proposal by selling in arenas or during times that are off limits to the salesperson. For example, a champion may be selling for the salesperson during a company picnic in a casual conversation with a co-worker.

Salespeople can help potential champions by providing them with all of the knowledge they will need. Knowledge builds confidence; champions will have the courage to speak up when they feel that they know what they are talking about. Salespeople can also motivate champions to participate fully

EXHIBIT 13.7

CHANGE AND RESISTANCE

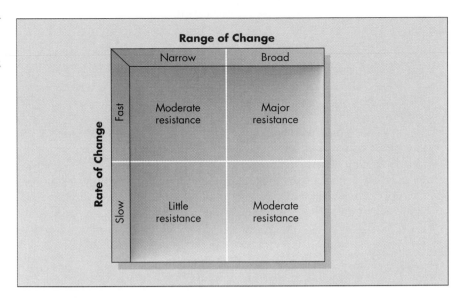

in the decision process by showing how the decision meets their needs as well as the overall needs of the company.

Positioning the Change

Positioning the change is similar to positioning a product in mass marketing, such as you may have learned in a principles of marketing course. In this case, however, the salesperson examines the specific needs and wants of the various constituencies in the account to position the change for the greatest likelihood of success. For example, Benson Bakery makes bread for restaurants. They were considering the purchase of equipment that would allow them to make bread and freeze it at the request of Steak and Ale, one of their major accounts. Hobart, which manufactures such equipment, could have positioned their equipment as delivering the best quality end-product (marketing's concern), or they could have positioned the equipment as the easiest to use and maintain (manufacturing's concern). Because manufacturing was not the key area in this decision, such a positioning may have been fatal.

Because salespeople are highly proactive in finding areas for improvement (or change) in their partners' organizations, positioning a change may determine who is involved in the decision. For example, suppose the IBM representative that calls on your school recognizes that the student computer labs are getting out of date. Is a proposal for new equipment primarily the domain of the computing support department, or is it the domain of faculty who teach computing classes? If the computer services department favors IBM but the users favor Apple, the IBM rep would be better served by positioning the change as the responsibility of the computer services department. Positioning the proposed change appropriately may spell success or failure for the proposal.

use
allies

EXHIBIT 13.8   TIME LINE FOR FRAM/CARQUEST STRATEGY

Month 1	Month 2	Month 3	Month 4	Month 5	Month 6
Visit director of marketing • **Primary objective:** Determine marketing needs • **Minimum objective:** Secure permission to see merchandising manager and advertising manager	Visit merchandising manager and advertising • **Primary objective:** Secure support in principle	Visit director of marketing • **Primary objective:** Specify objectives for new advertising plan and secure commitment in principle	Arrange tour of Fram facilities for VP of retail, marketing director, and advertising and merchandising managers	Submit plan to director of marketing for approval	Implement advertising program

Determining the Necessary Resources

in/outside both firms

The customer's needs may be beyond the salesperson's expertise. For example, Fram (a maker of auto parts) may be working with CarQuest (an auto parts retailer) to develop a major advertising program that will highlight their growing partnership. Such a change may require some selling to the advertising department at CarQuest. The Fram account representative will use the expert advice of Fram's own advertising department, their marketing research department, and probably marketing management as well. These experts may visit CarQuest with the account rep and aid in securing that change in CarQuest's advertising focus.

The salesperson must assess the situation and determine what resources are needed to secure the buyer's commitment. While the above example discusses allocation of personnel, salespeople have other resources, such as travel and entertainment budgets or sample supplies, that they manage. (We discuss how to build internal partnerships in order to effectively coordinate company resources in Chapter 17.)

Developing a Time-Based Strategy

The salesperson must determine a strategy for the proposed change and set that strategy against a timeline. This action accomplishes several objectives. First, the strategy is an outline of planned sales calls with primary and minimum call objectives determined for each call. Second, the timeline provides the salesperson with estimates of when each call should occur. Of course, objectives and planned times will change depending on the results of each call, but this type of planning is necessary to provide the salesperson with guidance for each call, to determine when resources are to be used, and to make sure that each call contributes to the visionary objective, as discussed in Chapter 8.

For example, the Fram salesperson may determine that calls need to be made on five individuals at CarQuest. A time-based strategy would indicate which person should be visited first and what should be accomplished during that visit, as well as the order of visits on the remaining four members of the buying center. The strategy would also alert the salesperson as to when the advertising personnel were needed; Exhibit 13.8 illustrates such a timeline.

COMMON PROBLEMS TO AVOID

There is a tendency to believe that once a customer has committed to a partnership less work is needed to maintain that relationship. That belief, however, is untrue. When salespeople subscribe to that belief, they fall victim to one or more of the common problems that can occur. As discussed in Chapter 2, the final stage for partnerships is dissolution, or breaking up. Several potential problems, including maintaining few personal relationships, failing to monitor competitive actions, and complacency, could lead to dissolution.

Limited Personal Relationships

Salespeople tend to call on buyers that they like; it is natural to want to spend time with friends. The result is that relationships are cultivated with only a few individuals in the account. Unfortunately for such salespeople, buyers may leave the organization, transfer to an unrelated area, or simply not participate in some decisions. Truly effective salespeople attempt to develop multiple relationships within an account.

One benefit of multiple relationships is that different champions can be selected for each proposal. Paul Kelly, a sales training consultant, suggests that after a proposal is decided on, review the process and identify the loudest opponent to the proposal in the buying organization. For the next proposal, solicit that person's support up front. The individual has already shown the courage and ability to fight for a position (even though it was against the salesperson's position), ideal qualities for a champion.[24]

Failing to Monitor Competitive Actions

No matter how strong the partnership is, competition will still want a piece of the business. And no matter how good the salesperson is, there will still be times when the account is vulnerable to competitive action. Accounts are most vulnerable when there is a personnel change (especially if the rep has developed relationships with a limited number of people in the account), when technology changes, or when major direction changes occur, such as a company starting a new division or entering a new market.

But the successful salesperson monitors competitive action even when the account seems invulnerable. For example, an insurance agency had all of the insurance business for over 10 years at a state university in Texas, but he failed to monitor competitive action at the state capitol and lost the account when another insurance agency found a sympathetic buyer in Austin. The loss of this one account cut his annual earnings by over 70 percent.

Monitoring competitive action can be as simple as checking the visitor's log at the front desk to see who has dropped by, or keeping up with competitive actions and asking buyers for their opinions. Frequently, developing relationships with the many potential influencers in an account will also keep you informed as to competitive actions. As each person is visited, questions and comments about competitors will arise, indicating the activity level of competition.

use inside contacts

Complacency

Perhaps the most common thief of good accounts is complacency. **Complacency** is, in sales terms, assuming that the business is yours and will always be yours. It is failing to continue to work as hard to keep the business as the salesperson did initially to earn the business. Complacency was the root cause of that insurance salesperson's failure to monitor the competition.

We opened this chapter discussing the value of customers. But just as a reminder, research indicates that customers are five times more likely to stop doing business with a company because of poor service.[25] While striving for excellence in relationships with customers is important, one millionaire salesperson says, "You beat 50 percent of the people in America just by working hard. You beat another 40 percent by being a person of honesty and integrity . . . The last 10 percent is a dogfight in the free-enterprise system."[26] His words are a strong reminder of the importance of avoiding complacency in customer relationships.

SUMMARY

Developing partnerships has become increasingly important for salespeople and their firms. Salespeople can develop partnerships and generate goodwill by servicing accounts properly and by strategically building relationships. Both salespeople and buyers benefit from partnering.

Many specific activities are necessary to ensure customer satisfaction and develop a partnering relationship. The salesperson must maintain the proper perspective, remember the customer between calls, build perceptions of trust, monitor order processing, ensure the proper initial use of the product or service, help in servicing the product, provide expert guidance and suggestions, and provide any necessary special assistance.

Probably few opportunities exist to develop goodwill comparable to those provided by the proper handling of customer complaints. Sales representatives ought to encourage and permit unhappy customers to tell their stories completely, fully, and without interruption. A sympathetic attitude to a real or an imaginary product or service failure cannot be overemphasized. After determining the facts, the salesperson should implement the solution promptly and monitor it to ensure that proper action is taken.

The appropriate solution will depend on many factors such as the seriousness of the problem, the dollar amount involved, and the value of the customer's account. A routine should be developed to make certain that every step is followed for handling complaints fairly and equitably.

KEY TERMS

category management *402*

champion *408*

change agent *407*

competence *387*

complacency *412*

corporate culture *406*

cross-selling *402*

customer orientation *388*

dependability *386*

full-line selling *402*

honesty *388*

likeability *388*

preferred supplier *404*

range of change *407*

rate of change *407*

upgrading *402*

QUESTIONS AND PROBLEMS

1. How can a salesperson lose by overselling a customer?

2. Explain how the art of listening can be applied to a situation in which a customer makes a complaint. What can applying this art accomplish?

3. If the company can't deliver an item on the date promised by the sales representative who sold it, what should the sales representative do? Would it matter which stage of the relationship the representative and customer were in?

4. Should a salesperson handle all complaints so that customers are completely satisfied? Explain why or why not. Would your answer change if you were in the exploration stage versus the commitment stage?

5. The soundest philosophy for building partnerships may be summed up in these words: "It's the little things that count." Identify six or eight "little things" a salesperson could do that will cost little or nothing but may be extremely valuable in building partnerships.

6. What is your reaction to the statement "The customer is always right"? Is it a sound basis for making adjustments and satisfying complaints? Can it be followed literally? Why or why not?

7. How would the actions of a salesperson vary over the course of a relationship? How would the actions of the buyer vary? If you believe the actions would not change greatly, why do you feel that way?

8. Would full-line selling, upgrading, or cross-selling change in the commitment stage? Why or why not?

9. What are the various ways that a salesperson can provide a potential champion with knowledge in order to build confidence? What types of knowledge will the champion need?

10. What are some factors that could lead to the dissolution of a partnership? What can the salesperson do to avoid these problems?

Case Problems

Case 13 • 1
Midwest Air Lines, Inc.

Midwest Air Lines, Inc., with headquarters in Detroit, Michigan, is one of the oldest regional passenger airlines in the United States. The corporation is proud of its reputation as a safe, efficient carrier.

A special analysis of plane reservations has revealed that some business executives with a long history of flying on Midwest Air Lines are no longer on its reservation lists. Midwest Air Lines knows these executives must be flying on a competitor or using other means of transportation.

In order to win back as many of them as possible, Midwest Air Lines management has instructed its sales representatives to call on all business executives who travel extensively and who no longer fly with Midwest Air Lines.

Jane Lacke, who has been with Midwest Air Lines for three years as a sales representative, selected the owner of a small chain of video rental stores, Dan Kemp, as her first contact. Lacke made an appointment with Kemp and the following interview took place:

LACKE   "Thought I'd stop around to see you Mr. Kemp. Haven't heard your name mentioned lately."

KEMP   "And you won't hear my name mentioned around your place again either. I'm through traveling with Midwest Air Lines. I'm sick and tired of being kicked around by your outfit. The last time I flew your line, I couldn't locate my baggage for over a week. And when you did return it, it was all bashed in."

LACKE   "How long ago did this happen?"

KEMP   "The last incident was seven months ago. Midwest seems to have a complex on baggage. You either lose 'em or crush 'em. I've read your ads about having the world's fastest and most modern airline. I've often thought that you probably have the world's most modern baggage smashers."

LACKE   "Oh, it can't be as bad as all that!"

KEMP   "You don't think so, eh? You ought to be on the receiving end of a damaged piece of luggage—corners bashed in, skin peeled off, handle ripped away. And you say, 'It can't be as bad as all that.'"

LACKE   "Well, of course, we are terribly sorry about it, and we are trying to cut down on that sort of thing."

KEMP   "I've heard that line before, but I haven't enough baggage to keep testing that statement. Moreover, you people just can't get a plane out of here on time. I have two buyers who travel by air at least once a month. I've told them to take your competitor."

LACKE   "Say, those new 767s of ours can beat anything they have to offer."

KEMP   "Says you, Ms. Lacke. My buyers take a 727 scheduled out of here one hour and a half after your great 767s—and as a rule they beat the 767s to their destination, usually because of your delayed departures. Hotels won't keep rooms, we miss connections—oh, it's just not worth it."

LACKE   "Well, Mr. Kemp, we are trying to cut down on delays. We are learning more about maintaining our newer equipment, and we feel that we are making headway."

KEMP   "I'm fed up with Midwest, and I'm not going to give you any more tries—not until you can really sell me that things are actually different. You haven't done a very good job so far."

Jane Lacke concluded the interview by saying she would certainly appreciate the opportunity to show that Midwest's service was all it was advertised to be.

Another Midwest sales representative, Tom Rogers, was the luncheon speaker for a local Rotary Club when the club celebrated Aviation Day. He talked about the operations of Midwest Air Lines in particular and about aviation problems in general. After the speech one of the Rotarians, Peggy Peifer, congratulated Rogers and said she enjoyed the talk. During the conversation, Rogers learned that Peifer was a former Midwest customer but had become disgruntled and was no longer flying with Midwest.

Rogers decided to call on Peifer. The following conversation took place about one week later:

ROGERS   "Ms. Peifer, it's kind of you to give me a hearing on your complaints about Midwest."

PEIFER   "Well, I felt I owed it to you after the way I criticized your company at our club the other day. You made a darn good speech, but when I thought about my experiences with Midwest, I got somewhat irritated."

ROGERS   "Tell me about the experience that is making you fly with our competitor."

PEIFER   "It wasn't one experience. It was a lot of the same old stuff over and over again. It was the repetition that got me down. I've used Midwest since the DC-3s, and I've always thought the world of your management—to such an extent that I'm a stockholder. And I don't invest my money without thoroughly investigating and knowing the company."

ROGERS   "I'm sorry that you feel the way you do about our company, Ms. Peifer. Specifically what did you experience?"

PEIFER   "Essentially I'm a short-haul commuter. The last time I flew Midwest, I had trouble getting a reservation. Although a round-trip reservation was finally confirmed, when I checked in at my destination, your agents said there was no record of it. I'll bet I spent 20 to 30 minutes at your ticket counter trying to get the reservation straightened out. They never did find any record of it and finally sold me space on a flight that left an hour later. But an hour with you people seems to be very unimportant. Also, your frequent flyer program is always changing. You are constantly increasing the mileage necessary to receive free trips.

"All of this reminds me about the time I was on a short flight of only 35 minutes, but we spent 45 minutes at the airport while your agents ran up and down the aisle counting heads and doing a lot of talking in the rear of the cabin. You waste more time in ticketing and boarding. You ought to be able to solve that kind of problem.

"And besides, there are those equipment delays. If you're going to be delayed several hours, tell us. You may lose my business that day, but I'll be back sooner than if you keep stalling me 15 minutes at a time. There's no point in my taking a plane for an hour's flight if I have to hang around an airport for an hour waiting for a delayed departure."

ROGERS   "You know, Ms. Peifer, if it weren't for the fact that we are getting those problems licked, I'd say you were justified in using other transportation."

PEIFER   "Getting them licked? How?"

ROGERS   "In the first place, we have recently installed a new reservations system geared to our current needs. Under this setup, we can usually confirm your going and return space immediately. You make only one call. One call does it all.

"In addition, we have installed a new loading procedure that has been extremely well received. And it's especially pertinent in your case as a commuter. If you have been ticketed before going to the airport and you have no luggage, you only need to wait for the loading announcement to enplane. That's a real time-saver and a convenience to the commuter passenger, isn't it, Ms. Peifer?"

PEIFER   "Yes, you're right. That boarding idea sounds great, and your 'one call' is an answer to a traveler's prayer, if it only works."

ROGERS   "It works, all right. How about giving us a chance to prove it?"

PEIFER   (laughing) "How about those delays? My sales representatives, unlike me, are long-haul passengers. They are using your competitors whenever possible, and your competitors are doing better by them, too."

ROGERS   "Well, I'm not going to deny we've had delays with our newer planes. Naturally it takes a while for our maintenance personnel to get the knowhow of new equipment. When we introduced our DC-7s and -8s, we had the same trouble, but we beat the problem. The same holds for our new 767s, but we are beating those, too. The record isn't perfect yet, but we are way ahead of where we were only three months ago. How about giving us another try?"

PEIFER   "And then have another piece of luggage crushed? All airlines are tough on baggage, but Midwest is near the top."

ROGERS   "I'll admit we haven't got an enviable record on that score. We have been putting on a campaign all over our system to eliminate damaged baggage. Management is trying its best to clean up that problem. If you will fly Midwest, I'm sure you will find an improvement on that point, too."

PEIFER   "Well, you seem confident things are better. I'll tell you. I'm planning a short trip in about 10 days. I was going to use your competition, but I might try Midwest again. I'll call you as soon as I determine the exact date. But let me warn you, this is only a trial. I'm not going to advise my sales representatives to travel with your company again until I see some real results. You've told me a good yarn—now we'll see."

ROGERS   "Thank you. That's a fair arrangement. I'll call you early next week to learn if you have set a definite date for your trip."

QUESTIONS

1. What do you believe to be the specific weaknesses and strengths of Lacke's interview?

2. What strengths and weaknesses did you observe in Rogers's interview?

3. Which of the two sales representatives, Lacke or Rogers, did the better job? Why?

CASE 13 • 2
TIMKEN ELECTRIC, INC.

Amy Cloud, account manager for Timken, was pondering her next move with Kidco, her largest account. Timken manufactures a line of pumps, electric motors, and controls that are sold to companies that use Timken's parts in manufacturing all kinds of equipment. Kidco, a maker of industrial heating and cooling units, had purchased Timken controls for the last five years, but also purchased controls from several small distributors for specific applications when Timken's products couldn't meet the specifications. Amy originally sold the controls by proving to the engineering department that Timken's quality could meet their specifications and by demonstrating the controls' accuracy and long life. Then she convinced the purchasing agent that the pricing would be more stable with one major vendor than with multiple distributors. Since then, Amy has heard no complaints about Timken's products. Kidco even allowed a trade magazine to write an article about Kidco's experience with Timken controls.

Early last year, Amy was able to persuade the purchasing agent for Kidco to switch to Timken electric motors for several applications. Although engineering was not involved in this decision, Amy had to prove to the purchasing agent that the products were as good as the ones they were currently purchasing. Amy estimated that Timken had about 30 percent of the Kidco motor business, 30 percent went to Visa SA from Mexico, and the remainder of the business belonged to Smart & Co., which actually distributed several lines of imported electric motors.

Last month, Amy received a call from the director of engineering asking for a meeting to discuss some issues with Timken motors. She was delighted, because one of the Timken engineers had suggested combining Timken motors and controls and shipping the units as one assembly. Amy felt that such a meeting would be a perfect opportunity to present the new idea. Amy created and presented a proposal to the engineering department that, if accepted, would mean doubling Timken's share of the electric motor business. The proposal would require some redesign by Kidco, but the savings over two years would be more than the redesign costs. After that, Kidco could increase profits by about 3 percent on those products. But several engineers pointed out that Timken was unwilling to manufacture controls for all of Kidco's needs and they were reluctant to make such a change with a company that was not willing to work closer with them. In addition, one engineer seemed very unhappy that the purchasing department had switched to Timken motors. She felt that the reject rate of 2 percent was too high; all of Kidco's other vendors were achieving lower than 1 percent rejects. At the conclusion of the meeting, the director of engineering said, "Amy, we've enjoyed a long and good relationship with Timken. And your idea is a good one. Right now, though, I don't think Timken is the company we should do that with. But we'll consider it and let you know."

QUESTIONS

1. In what stage of partnering is the relationship between Timken and Kidco?

2. Is there anything Amy could have done to set the stage for better acceptance of her proposal?

3. What should she do right now? If her visionary objective is to develop a strategic partnership with Kidco, is it still realistic? What should she do to achieve that visionary objective?

ADDITIONAL REFERENCES

Bryon, Dawn. "Beware the Purple Pigskin Clock!" *Sales & Marketing Management*, August 1990, pp. 74–80.

Donaton, Scott. "New Magazine Strategy: Marketing Partnerships with Advertisers Planned." *Advertising Age,* October 23, 1989, p. 1+.

Farber, Barry, and Joyce Wycoff. "Customer Service Evolution and Revolution." *Sales & Marketing Management*, May 1991, pp. 44–51.

————. "Relationships: Six Steps to Success." *Sales & Marketing Management*, April 1991, pp. 50–58.

Good, David. "Sales in the 1990s: A Decade of Development." *Review of Business,* Summer 1990, pp. 3–6.

Gronroos, Christian. "The Marketing Strategy Continuum: Towards a Marketing Concept for the 1990s." *Management Decision* 29, 1 (1991), pp. 7–13.

Hanan, Mack. *Consultative Selling.* New York: AMACOM, 1990.

Hayes, H. Michael, and Steven W. Hartley. "How Buyers View Industrial Salespeople." *Industrial Marketing Management,* May 1989, pp. 73–80.

Ingram, Thomas N. "Improving Sales Force Productivity: A Critical Examination of the Personal Selling Process." *Review of Business,* Summer 1990, pp. 7–12, 40.

Katz, Bernard. *How to Turn Customer Service into Customer Sales.* Lincolnwood, IL: NTC Business Books, 1988.

Lytle, John F. *What Do Your Customers Really Want?* Chicago: Probus Publishing Co., 1993.

Mackay, Harvey. *Beware the Naked Man Who Offers You His Shirt: Do What You Love, Love What You Do and Deliver More than You Promise.* New York: William Morrow, 1990.

Mercer, David. *High Level Selling.* Houston: Gulf Publishing, 1990.

"Partnering for Performance." *NAMA Journal,* Fall 1992, pp. 6–9.

Pollock, Ted. "Service—More Important Than Ever." *American Salesman,* September 1990, pp. 21–26.

Pritchett, Price. *Service Excellence.* Dallas: Pritchett and Associates, Inc., 1989.

Schenbelt, Derrick C. "Turning the Tables." *Sales & Marketing Management*, January 1993, pp. 22–23.

"Simple Idea Saves $8 Million A Year." *Purchasing,* May 21, 1992, pp. 47–49.

Szymanski, David M, and Gilbert A. Churchill, Jr. "Client Evaluation Cues: A Comparison of Successful and Unsuccessful Salespeople." *Journal of Marketing Research,* May 1990, pp. 163–74.

Teas, Kenneth. "Expectations, Performance Evaluation, and Consumers' Perceptions of Quality." *Journal of Marketing,* October 1993, pp. 18–34.

Willingham, Ron. *Hey, I'm the Customer.* Englewood Cliffs, NJ: Prentice Hall, 1992.

SPECIAL APPLICATIONS

*B*uilding on what you just learned in Part III about partnering, this section will cover several specific types of selling situations. In Chapter 14 you will learn about one form of selling that continues to grow in importance, formal negotiations. Topics include premeeting planning, opening the session, strategies and tactics, and how to effectively give and receive concessions.

Chapter 15 provides principles and guidance for the somewhat unique situation of selling to resellers. The chapter describes how salespeople aid resellers and discusses the role of supporting activities, for example, trade shows. Chapter 15 also contains information about national account managers and general terms and conditions of the sale.

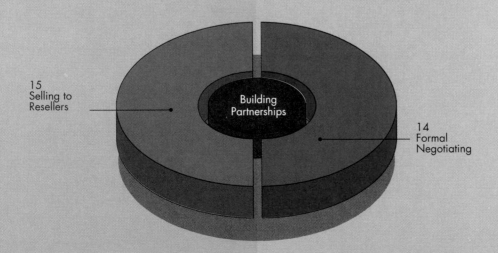

Formal Negotiating

We have all engaged in negotiations of some type. Most of these were informal (e.g., with your parents about attending a rock concert) and dealt with relatively minor issues—although they may have seemed deadly important to you at the time. This chapter discusses formal negotiations that occur between buyers and salespeople. The skills you will learn can also be used in your day-to-day negotiations with friends, parents, and people in authority positions.

Some questions answered in this chapter are:

What is negotiation selling? How does it differ from nonnegotiation selling?

In selling, what items can be negotiated?

What type of planning needs to occur prior to a negotiation meeting? How should a seller set objectives?

How can the negotiation session be effectively opened? What role does friendly conversation play?

What negotiation strategies and tactics do buyers use? How should negotiators respond?

What are the salesperson's guidelines for offering and requesting concessions?

Leon Montgomery, of Goodyear Tire & Rubber Company, has learned that paying attention and listening carefully are extremely important skills to cultivate, expecially for salespeople. He discusses his thoughts and experiences:

"During my 21 years in the sales and marketing business with the Goodyear Tire & Rubber Company (selling conveyer belting, industrial hose, and industrial V-belts), in both inside and outside sales capacities, I have come to appreciate the benefit and the value of paying attention. Although attention to details is vitally important in my routine sales activities I have to apply more exacting attention to details at engineering firms and other highly technical OEM-type customers. I call on engineering, design, and construction firms who build various kinds of power-generating facilities, the kind that utilize fossil fuel as the energy source. Engineers, by training and profession, are attentive to details—minute details—which for them can make the difference in their competitive edge and opportunity for being awarded construction contracts.

"With a degree in business administration, I had to learn how to work with engineers in the manner that they require, that is, close attention to details, in order to gain their confidence in my desire to be of support in their efforts. Much of the detail work with engineers is involved in studying and verifying the accuracy of drawings and blueprint-type specifications, as well as terms and conditions of sale as it relates to the value that my products are to add. In other words, detail work with engineers usually involves laborious paperwork.

"I have learned that attention to detail has as a prerequisite attention to listening. The importance of written and paperwork detail is often noted during verbal communication. That is, I have to employ the techniques of effective listening in order to get a clear understanding of what my customers expect from my product, my company, and from me. Attentive listening allows me to more effectively ask clarifying, fact finding-type questions that will confirm mutual understanding. I listen attentively by looking directly at them, blocking out distractions, making notations, and repeating key points and phrases.

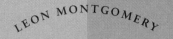

LEON MONTGOMERY

Goodyear Tire & Rubber Company

"That people do business with people is a well-known and obvious fact. Therefore, I always try to make an obvious point of paying attention to my customers as people. I have found that nearly all of my customers have something interesting about them when viewed as unique individuals. The vast array of experiences, hobbies, skills, and talents that I discover in my customers make it easy and fun to be attentive to them as people. I especially find it fun with the engineers when I am working with one of them and he shares, during a lunch or dinner, the details of his passion with a particular hobby, talent, or interest. One example is an engineer who is a 'Trekkie.' Therefore, whenever I come across something that I think is special and unique as an item of the Star Trek mania, I buy it and give it to him. The most rewarding relationships with my customers normally come as a result of knowing my customers as people first, and that makes them feel comfortable and confident in the work that I do with and for them.

"Paying attention to details, to listening, and to people does pay. Attention to details ensures accuracy and quality, while attention to listening and to people ensures understanding and instills confidence. My customers have confirmed the value of attentiveness as demonstrated in a steady annual increase in orders placed; and that gets my attention!"

THE NATURE OF NEGOTIATION

The decision-making process through which buyers and sellers resolve areas of conflict and/or arrive at agreements is called **negotiation.** Areas of conflict may include minor issues (e.g., who should attend future meetings) as well as major ones (e.g., cost per unit, exclusive purchase agreements). The ultimate goal of both parties should be to reduce or resolve the conflict.

Two basic philosophies guide negotiations. In **win-lose negotiating,** the negotiator attempts to win all the important concessions and thus triumph over the opponent. This resembles almost every competitive sport you've ever watched. In boxing, for example, one person is the winner and the other is, by definition, the loser.

In the second negotiating philosophy, **win-win negotiating,** the negotiator attempts to secure an agreement that satisfies both parties. You have probably experienced social situations similar to this. For example, if you want to attend a football game and your friend wants to attend a party, you may negotiate a mutual agreement that you both attend the first half of the game and still make it to most of the party. If this arrangement satisfies both you and your friend, you have engaged in win-win negotiating.

The discussion in this chapter assumes that your goal as the salesperson is to engage in win-win negotiating. In fact, this entire book has emphasized partnering, which is a win-win perspective. Partners attempt to find solutions that benefit both parties because they are concerned about the other party's welfare.

However, the buyer may be using a win-lose strategy, whereby the buyer hopes to win all major concessions and have the seller be the loser. To help you spot and prepare for such situations, we discuss many of these tactics as well.

NEGOTIATION VERSUS NONNEGOTIATION SELLING

How does negotiation differ from the sales presentations we've covered to this point in the book? In Chapters 8 through 12, we assumed that many factors are constants; they cannot be changed. For example, the price of an Allsteel Office chair model K316 has been set at $395. The Allsteel salesperson won't lower that price, unless, of course, the buyer agrees to purchase large quantities. Even then the buyer will just receive a standard quantity discount as outlined in the seller's price manual. In essence, the salesperson's price book and procedure manual form an inflexible set of rules. Period. If the buyer objects, an attempt to resolve the conflict will occur by using techniques discussed in Chapter 11 (e.g., compensation method, boomerang method).

In contrast, if the Allsteel seller enters formal negotiations with this same buyer, the price and delivery schedules will be subject to modification. The buyer neither expects nor wants the seller to come to the negotiation meeting with any standard price book. Instead, the buyer expects most policies, procedures, and prices to be truly negotiable.

Negotiations also differ from regular sales calls in that they generally involve more intensive planning and a larger number of people from the selling firm. Prenegotiation planning may go on for six months or more

Formal negotiations usually involve multiple buyers and multiple sellers.

Photo courtesy of GMAC Financial Services.

before the actual meeting takes place. Planning participants usually cover a wide spectrum of functional areas in the firm, such as production, marketing, sales, accounting, purchasing, and executive officers.

Finally, formal negotiations generally take place only for very large or important prospective buyers. For example, Quaker Oats might negotiate with some of the very large food chains like Jewel, Kroger, Safeway, and Cub Foods, but would not engage in a large, formal negotiation session with small local or "mom and pop" grocery stores. Negotiating is an expensive endeavor because it utilizes so much of so many important people's time. The firm only wants to invest the time and costs involved in negotiating if the long-term nature of the relationship and the importance of the customer justify the expense.

WHAT CAN BE NEGOTIATED?

If the customer is large or important enough, almost anything can be negotiated. Salespeople who have not been involved in negotiations before often find it hard to grasp the fact that so many areas are subject to discussion and change. The following areas are often negotiated between buyers and sellers:[1]

Inventory levels that the buyer must maintain.

Inventory levels that the seller must keep on hand to be able to restock the buyer quickly.

Details about the design of the product or service.

How the product will be manufactured.

Display allowances for resellers.

Advertising allowances and the amount of advertising done by the seller.

Sales promotion within the channel of distribution.

Delivery terms and conditions.

Retail and wholesale pricing points for resellers.

Prices and pricing allowances for volume purchases.

Amount and location of shelf positioning.

Special packaging and design features.

Service levels after the sale.

Disposing of unsold or obsolete merchandise.

Credit terms.

How complaints will be resolved.

Order entry and ease of monitoring orders.

Type and frequency of communication between the parties.

Performance guarantees and bonds.

In reality, no single negotiation session covers all of the areas listed. Each side comes to the bargaining table with a list of prioritized issues; only important points for which disagreement exists are discussed.

ARE YOU A GOOD NEGOTIATOR?

All of us are negotiators, some better than others. We have negotiated with parents, friends, professors, and, yes, sometimes even with enemies. Just because you may have engaged in many negotiations in your lifetime, however, does not mean that you are good at it.

The traits necessary to be successful at negotiating vary somewhat, depending on the situation and the parties involved. Some characteristics, however, are almost universal. For example, a good negotiator must have patience and endurance; after two hours of discussing the same issue, the negotiator needs the stamina and willingness to continue until an agreement is reached. Also, a willingness to take risks and the ability to tolerate ambiguity become especially critical in business negotiations because it is necessary to both accept and offer concessions during the meeting without complete information.

People with a fear of conflict usually make poor negotiators. In fact, some negotiating strategies are actually designed to increase the level of conflict in order to bring *all* of the issues to the table and reach an equitable settlement. Along the same lines, people who have a strong need to be liked by all people at all times tend to make very poor negotiators. Other undesirable traits include being closed-minded, unorganized, dishonest, and downright belligerent.

According to Laurel G. Bellows, past president of the Chicago Bar Association, women have special strengths and weaknesses as negotiators.[2] She claims that women are great at building relationships but are less adept at confrontational negotiation meetings. Her advice for women is to be thoroughly prepared, make use of men's stereotypes about women (let them treat you differently just because you are a woman), use silence as a tool instead of always responding, get help from a mentor, and be a chameleon (smile, complain, be tough, be aggressive, pour the coffee, etc.).

EXHIBIT 14.1   NEGOTIATION SKILLS SELF-INVENTORY

Place a check by each item that accurately reflects your personality and traits on an average, normal day.

_____ 1. Helpful	_____ 20. receptive
_____ 2. Risk taker	_____ 21. Easily influenced
_____ 3. Inconsistent	_____ 22. Enthusiastic
_____ 4. Persistent	_____ 23. Planner
_____ 5. Factual	_____ 24. Stingy
_____ 6. Use high pressure	_____ 25. Listener
_____ 7. Self-confident	_____ 26. Controlled
_____ 8. Practical	_____ 27. Thinks under pressure
_____ 9. Manipulative	_____ 28. Passive
_____ 10. Analytical	_____ 29. Economical
_____ 11. Arrogant	_____ 30. Gullible
_____ 12. Impatient	_____ 31. Afraid of conflict
_____ 13. Seek new approaches	_____ 32. Endurance
_____ 14. Tactful	_____ 33. Tolerate ambiguity
_____ 15. Perfectionist	_____ 34. Have strong need to be liked
_____ 16. Stubborn	_____ 35. Organized
_____ 17. Flexible	_____ 36. Honest
_____ 18. Competitive	_____ 37. Belligerent
_____ 19. Gambler	

How to score the checklist

All of the traits listed are positive except for the following negative traits: 3, 6, 9, 11, 12, 15, 16, 19, 21, 24, 28, 30, 31, 34, and 37. To arrive at a total score, give yourself one point for all positive traits and subtract one point for all negative traits. To interpret your total score: 19–22 excellent, 15–18 good, 11–14 fair.

Of course, cultural differences do exist.[3] For example, Brazilian managers believe competitiveness is more important in a negotiator than integrity. Chinese managers in Taiwan emphasize the negotiator's rational skills to a lesser extent than his or her interpersonal skills.

As the above indicates, being a truly excellent negotiator requires a very careful balance of traits and skills. Take a moment and complete the questionnaire in Exhibit 14.1 to rate your negotiating skills. Don't be discouraged by a low score—you can't easily change personality traits, but the rest of this chapter will offer suggestions for ways to improve your skills.

PLANNING FOR THE NEGOTIATION SESSION

"Preparation and planning are the most important parts of negotiation."[4] In Chapter 8, we discussed how to gather precall information and plan the sales call. All of that material is equally relevant when planning for an upcoming negotiation session—for example, learning everything possible about the buyer team and the buyer's organization.

The meetings the salesperson will have with the buyer prior to the actual negotiation session facilitate this. The buyer may also be, or have been, a customer of the salesperson, with the upcoming negotiation session designed to review contracts or specify a new working relationship. Even in such scenarios, negotiators will want to carefully review the players and learn as many facts about the situation as possible.

LOCATION

Plan to hold the negotiation at a location free from distraction for both teams. A neutral site, one owned by neither party, is usually best; it removes both teams from interruptions by business associates, and no one has a psychological (e.g., "home court") advantage. Experienced negotiators find the middle of the workweek best for negotiations and prefer morning to afternoon or evening (because people are more focused on their job and not on after-hours and weekend activities).

TIME ALLOTMENT

As you are probably aware, negotiations can take a tremendous amount of time. Some business negotiations take years to work out. But how much time should be set aside for one negotiation session? The answer depends on the negotiation objectives and the extent to which both sides will desire a win-win session. Studies have shown that high time pressure will produce nonagreements and poor outcomes when one or more sides takes a win lose perspective; but if both sides have a win-win perspective, high outcomes are achieved regardless of time pressure.[5]

NEGOTIATION OBJECTIVES

Power is a critical element when developing objectives.[6] The selling team must ask, "Do we need them more than they need us?" "What part of our service is most valuable to them?" "Can they get similar products elsewhere?" The best situation is when both parties share balanced power, although this is rare in practice.

In developing objectives for the session, keep in mind that the seller will almost certainly have to make concessions in the negotiation meeting. Thus, setting several objectives, or positions, is extremely important.

The **target position** is what your company hopes to achieve at the negotiation session. Your team should also establish a **minimum position,** the absolute minimum level you will accept. Finally, an **opening position**—the initial proposal—should be developed.

For example, for a Baxter salesperson negotiating the price for complete food service at a hospital, the target position could be $250,000, with a minimum position of $200,000 and an opening position of $300,000. In negotiations over service levels, the seller's opening position might be weekly delivery, the target position would be delivery twice a week, and the minimum position (the most the seller is willing to do) would be to deliver three times a week.

To allow for concessions, the opening position should reflect higher expectations than the target position. However, the buyer team may consider a very high target position unrealistic and may simply walk away. You have

Negotiations should occur in locations free of distractions. Because of frequent interruptions and the distraction of seeing other patrons, a restaurant is usually a poor place to conduct business.

R. Heinzer/SUPERSTOCK.

probably seen this happen in negotiations between countries that are at war. To avoid this, negotiators must be ready to support that opening position with solid information. Suppose the opening position for a Colgate-Palmolive negotiating team is to offer the grocer a display allowance of $1,000 (with a target position of offering $1,500). The team must be ready to prove that $1,000 is reasonable.

One team of experts recommends that negotiators plan for the upcoming meeting by employing the **mini-max strategy.**[7] This approach helps sellers understand and then prepare for the trade-offs that will undoubtedly occur in the negotiating session. The negotiator must answer four planning questions:

"What is the minimum that I can accept?"

"What is the maximum I can ask for without getting laughed out of the room?"

"What is the maximum I can give away?"

"What is the least I can offer without getting laughed out of the room?"

When developing objectives, negotiators need to sort out all issues that could arise in the meeting, prioritizing them by importance to the firm. They then develop a set of contingency plans to have a good idea, even before the meeting begins, of their reactions and responses to the buyer's suggestions. Talking this over beforehand helps the negotiation team avoid "giving away the store" during the heat of the negotiation session. It also allows the team to draw on the expertise of company experts who will not be present during the session.

EXHIBIT 14.2

COMPARING BUYER AND
SELLER PRICE POSITIONS

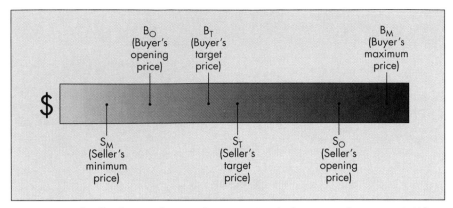

Note: See Howard Raiffa, *The Art and Science of Negotiation* (Cambridge, Mass.: Belknap Press, 1982) for a more complex discussion of mathematical formulations designed to predict negotiation outcomes under various states.

The buyer team also develops positions for the meeting. In Exhibit 14.2, we find a continuum that shows how the two sets of positions relate. With the positions illustrated, the parties can reach an agreement somewhere between the seller's minimum (S_M) and the buyer's maximum (B_M). However, if B_M fell to the left of S_M (had a lower maximum acceptable price), then no agreement could be reached; attempts at negotiation would be futile. For example, if the buyer is not willing to pay more than $200 ($B_M$) and the seller will not accept less than $250 ($S_M$), agreement is impossible. In general, the seller desires to move as far to the right of S_M (as high a price) as possible, and the buyer desires to move as far to the left of B_M (as low a price) as possible.

Negotiators need to try to anticipate these positions and evaluate them carefully. The more information collected about what the buyer hopes to accomplish, the better the negotiators will be able to manage the meeting and arrive at a win-win decision. Selling Scenario 14.1 discusses important aspects of anticipating these negotiating positions with an industry giant, IBM.

Negotiators create a plan to achieve their objectives. However, the chance of failure always exists. Thus, planners need to consider strategy revisions if the original plan should fail. The development of alternative paths to the same goal is known as **adaptive planning.**[8] For example, a firm may attempt to secure premium shelf position using any of the following strategies:

*   In return for a 5 percent price discount.
*   In return for credit terms of 3/10, net 30.
*   In return for a 50–50 co-op ad campaign.

The firm would attempt to secure the premium shelf position by using, for example, the first strategy. If that failed, they would move to the second strategy, and so forth.

Many firms will engage in a **brainstorming session** to try to develop strategies that will meet the firm's objectives. A brainstorming session is a meeting in which people are allowed to creatively explore different

Negotiating with IBM

Having International Business Machines Corp. (IBM) as a customer offers both enormous and obvious potential benefits. Purchase volumes can dwarf those of other major customers. For younger firms, an IBM contract often represents legitimacy—a springboard to recognition and respectability. And companies admitted to IBM's inner circle of favored suppliers may be rewarded with capital equipment, technical assistance, and even—on occasion—a role in IBM project planning.

But dealing with IBM also has a dark side. IBM has shrewdly structured its relationships with suppliers and potential suppliers to exploit fully its unique position as a high-volume, high-status purchaser. No other company demands as much. And no other company has so artfully refined the procedures for enforcing its demands.

Coming to Terms

Several suppliers make the point that IBM, particularly CCP (its component purchasing group in Poughkeepsie), is fair in negotiating prices. Former Intel manager Jeffrey Miller, for instance, says that CCP was generally willing to pay more for products that exceeded industry standards.

But suppliers also picture IBM as an extremely tough negotiator that routinely wins serious and unusual contract concessions. "Count your fingers before and after every meeting with IBM," counsels James Porter, publisher of the annual *Disk/Trend Report*. Says Finis Conner, former vice chairman of Seagate Technology's board of directors, "IBM is a very tough negotiator because of their volumes and the leverage they can exert."

Companies that want IBM's business at any price are doomed to pay it. Companies willing to challenge IBM on contract terms and insist on purchase orders can gain some measure of protection. Also, when IBM can turn to alternative sources of supply, the vendor is at an obvious disadvantage. But the supplier that has a unique product or technology or superior quality control must recognize and take advantage of its strengths. "It depends a lot on what the value of a product is to them. If you're the only guy that makes something they really need, you have a stronger position," says Jeffrey Miller of Adaptec.

Four times, according to Jim Watson, Quantum's vice president for marketing and sales, IBM and Quantum have sought to come to terms. Once, says Watson, Quantum was told that its disk drives were acceptable but too expensive—about $100 to $125 too high per unit. IBM also wanted Quantum to invest in new plant and production equipment that, according to Watson's calculations, would have cost the Milpitas, California firm $1.8 million. But IBM indicated that making such an investment still offered no guarantee of an IBM purchase order; the company would just have to take its chances. Then there was the matter of price reductions—which would be triggered not (as is generally the case) by the increasing volumes but simply by the passage of time. IBM also wanted Quantum to improve certain parameters in its standard products.

Quantum has declined to do business with IBM on IBM's terms. But Watson admits that he may wind up in business with IBM. The two companies continue to talk, and Watson reports that they are "coming closer and closer to amicable terms." If Quantum does eventually sign on with IBM, it will likely be under carefully negotiated terms that reflect the caution of the smaller company.

"It's always a high-risk thing to be selling to IBM, especially if you're thinking of a permanent marriage," concludes Porter. It would appear, though, that full and detailed awareness of the risks involved, a negotiating attitude every bit as tough and hardened as IBM's, and a willingness to walk away from the wrong deal probably constitute the most comprehensive available insurance.

Source: Adapted from Norm Alster, "Supplying to IBM: The Obligations of Victory," *Electronic Business*, October 15, 1985, pp. 40–47. Used by permission of Reed Publishing, U.S.A.

It is important for the salesperson's team to prepare for an upcoming negotiation session. Also, remember that the buyer's team is also planning!

Courtesy CSC Consulting.

methods of achieving goals. Firms also use computer software, like Negotiator Pro,[9] that is designed specifically to help salespeople prepare for negotiation sessions.

 Once again, cultural differences do exist. For example, Chinese and Russian businesspeople habitually use extreme initial offers, whereas Swedish businesspeople usually open with a price very close to their target position.[10]

TEAM SELECTION AND MANAGEMENT[11]

So far we have discussed negotiation as though it always involves a team of both buyers and sellers. Usually this is the case. However, negotiations do occur with only two people present: the buyer and the salesperson.

Teams offer both pros and cons. Because of team members' different backgrounds, the group as a whole tends to be more creative than one individual could be. Also, team members can help each other and reduce the chances of making a "stupid" mistake. However, the more participants, the more time generally required to reach agreement. Also, team members may voice differing opinions among themselves, or one member may address a topic outside his or her area of expertise. Such things can make the seller's team appear unprepared or divisive.

In general, the seller should have a team the size of the buyer's team. Otherwise the sellers may appear to be trying to exert more power or influence in the meeting. Whenever possible, strive for the fewest number. Unnecessarily large teams can get bogged down in details; also, the larger the team, generally the more difficult reaching a decision becomes.

Each team member should have a defined role in the session. For example, experts are often included to answer technical questions; executives are present as more authoritative speakers on behalf of the selling firm. Exhibit 14.3 lists the types of team members often chosen for negotiations. Many of these people take part in prenegotiation planning but do not actually attend the negotiation session.

Team members should possess the traits of good negotiators, although it often doesn't work out that way. For example, many technical experts have no tolerance for ambiguity and may fear conflict. As a result, the team

EXHIBIT 14.3

PEOPLE WHO SERVE ON THE
SELLING NEGOTIATION
TEAM

Title	Possible Role
Salesperson	Coordinates all functions.
Field sales manager (district manager, regional manager, etc.)	Provides additional local and regional information. Secures necessary local funding and support for planning and presentations. Offers information on competitors.
National sales manager/ vice president of sales	Serves as a liaison with corporate headquarters. Secures necessary corporate funding and staff support for planning and presentation. Offers competitive information.
National account salesperson/national accounts sales managers	Provides expertise and support in dealing with large customer issues. Offers information about competitors.
Marketing department senior executives, product managers, and staff	Provide suggestions for product/service applications. Supply market research information as well as information on packaging, new-product development, upcoming promotional campaigns, etc. Offer information about competitors.
Chief executive officer/ president	Serves as an authority figure. Facilitates quicker decisions regarding changes in current policy and procedures. As a peer, can relate well with buyer's senior officers.
Manufacturing executives and staff	Provide information on current scheduled production as well as the possibility/cost of any modifications in the schedule.
Purchasing executives and staff	Provide information about raw materials inflows. Offer suggestions about possible quantity discounts from suppliers.
Accounting and finance executives and staff	Source of cost accounting information. Supply corporate target returns on investment, cost estimates for any needed changes in the firm under various buying scenarios, and information on order entry, billing, and credit systems.
Data processing executives and staff	Provide information on current data processing systems and anticipated changes needed under various buying scenarios. Help ensure that needed periodic reports for the buyers can be generated in a timely fashion.
Training executives and staff	Provide training for negotiation effectiveness and conduct practice role plays. Also provide information and suggestions on anticipated buyer training necessary.
Outside consultants	Provide any kind of assistance necessary. Especially helpful if the firm has limited experience in negotiations or has not negotiated with this type of buyer before.

leader needs to help them see clearly what their role is, as well as what they should *not* get involved in, during the session.

The team leader will manage the actual negotiation session. With intimate knowledge of the buyers and their needs, salespeople often fill this post, rather than the executive on the team. When selecting a team leader, the seller's management needs to also consider the anticipated leader of the buyer team. It is unwise to choose a leader for the selling team who might be intimidated by the buyer's leader.

EXHIBIT 14.4

CONFLICT-HANDLING
BEHAVIOR MODES

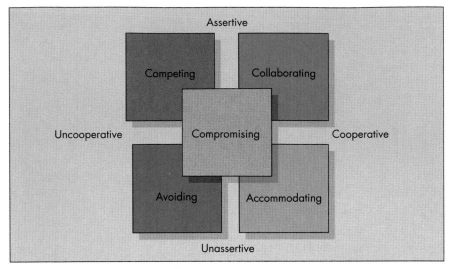

Source: Adapted from Kenneth Thomas, "Conflict and Conflict Management," in *The Handbook of Industrial and Organizational Psychology,* edited by Marvin Dunnette (Skokie, IL: Rand McNally, 1976).

The team usually develops rules about who will answer what kinds of questions, who should be the first to respond to a concession offered by the buyers, who will offer concessions from the seller's standpoint, and so on. A set of nonverbal and verbal signals is also developed so team members can communicate with each other. For example, they may agree that the salesperson taking out a breath mint signals all team members to stop talking and let the salesperson handle all issues; or when the executive places her red book inside her briefcase, the team should move toward its target position, and the salesperson should say, "OK, let's look at some alternatives."

To ensure that team members really understand their respective roles and that all rules and signals are clearly grasped, the team should practice. This usually involves a series of videotaped role-play situations. Many firms, like UARCO, involve their sales training department in this practice. Trainers, using detailed information supplied by the team, realistically play the roles of the buying team members.

INDIVIDUAL BEHAVIOR PATTERNS

The team leader needs to consider the personality style of each member of both teams in order to spot any problems and plan accordingly. Of course, one method would be to sort the members into analyticals, amiables, expressives, and drivers, based on the dimensions of assertiveness and responsiveness (see Chapter 6 for a full discussion). Others have developed personality profiles specifically for negotiations. One of the most widely used set of negotiation profiles will now be discussed.

A number of researchers, after studying actual conflict situations, arrived at a set of basic conflict-handling modes based on the dimensions of assertiveness and cooperativeness.[12] Exhibit 14.4 presents these five modes: competing, accommodating, avoiding, compromising, and collaborating. Note that these five styles are different than the social styles (drivers, amiables, expressives, and analyticals) we have been using in the rest of

People exhibit different conflict-handling modes. Can you spot someone in this photo in the competing mode? The avoiding mode? The collaborating mode?

Mug Shots/The Stock Market.

the book. Since all negotiations involve some degree of conflict, this typology is appropriate for use by salespeople preparing for a negotiation session.

People who resolve conflict in a **competing mode** are assertive and uncooperative. They tend to pursue their own goals and objectives, completely at the expense of the other party. Often power oriented, they usually surround themselves with subordinates (often called yes-men) who go along with their ideas. Team members who use the competing mode look for a win-lose agreement: they win, the other party loses.

Those in the **accommodating mode** are the exact opposite of competing people. Unassertive and highly cooperative, accommodators will neglect their own needs and desires in order to satisfy the concerns of the other party. In fact, they may seek a win-lose agreement, where *they* are the losers. Accommodators can be spotted by their excessive generosity; their constant, rapid yielding to another's point of view; and their obedience to someone else's order, even though it is obviously not something they desire to do.

Some people operate in the **avoiding mode,** an unassertive and uncooperative mode. These people don't attempt to resolve their own needs or the needs of others. In essence, they simply refuse to address the conflict at all. They don't strive for a win–win agreement; in fact, they don't strive for any agreement.

The **compromising mode** applies to people "in the middle" in terms of cooperativeness and assertiveness. A compromiser attempts to find a quick, mutually acceptable solution that partially satisfies both parties. A compromiser gives up more than a competing person but less than an accommodating person. In many ways, the compromiser does attempt to arrive at a win-win solution. However, the agreement reached does not usually maximize the satisfaction of the parties. For example, a compromising person might quickly suggest, "Let's just split the difference." Although this sounds great, a better solution may be reached—one that would please both parties more—with added discussion.

Finally, people in the **collaborating mode** are both assertive and cooperative. They seek to maximize the satisfaction of both parties and, hence, to reach a truly win-win solution. Collaborators have the motivation, skill, and determination to really dig into an issue or problem and explore all possible solutions. The best situation, from a negotiation standpoint, would be to have on both teams a number of people who generally use a collaborating mode.

As with the social style matrix described earlier, one person can exhibit different modes in different situations. For example, a buying negotiator who perceives that his or her position on an issue extremely vital to the long-term welfare of the company is correct may revert from a collaborating mode to a competing mode. Likewise, when potentially large damage could occur from confronting an issue, that same buyer might move to an avoiding mode.

INFORMATION CONTROL

What do buyers do while selling teams engage in preparation? They prepare, too! (Keep in mind that buyers have read more books and attended more seminars on negotiation than sellers have, because this training is one of their best negotitating tools.) They try to learn as much as they can about the seller's team and plans. This includes the seller's opening, target, and minimum positions. They also are interested in the seller's team membership and decision rules. As a result, the team leader needs to emphasize the need for security—don't give everyone access to all information. In fact, many team members (e.g., technical support) do not need to have complete and exhaustive knowledge of all of the facts surrounding the negotiation.

THE NEGOTIATION MEETING

At the negotiation meeting, the buyer team and seller team physically come together and deliberate about topics of importance to both parties, with the goal of arriving at decisions. As mentioned earlier, this meeting usually has been preceded by one or more smaller buyer–seller meetings designed to uncover needs and explore options. Informal phone conversations probably were used to set some aspect of the agenda, learn about team members who will be present, and so on. Also, the negotiation itself may require a series of sessions to resolve all issues.

PRELIMINARIES

Engaging in friendly conversation to break the ice before getting down to business is usually a good idea. Use this time to learn and use the names of all members on the buyer team. This is especially important in many international negotiation meetings. For example, the Japanese want to spend time developing a personal relationship before beginning negotiations. In fact, researchers have found that before negotiations begin, both sides must develop a working relationship that permits them to focus on the task.[13]

Every effort should also be made to ensure a comfortable environment for all parties. Arranging ahead of time for refreshments, proper climate control, appropriate size of room, adequate lighting, and layout of furniture will go far in establishing an environment conductive to negotiating.

Most negotiations occur at a rectangular table. Teams usually sit on opposite sides, with the leader of each team at the heads of the table. If possible, try to arrange for a round table or at least a seating arrangement that mixes members from each team together. This helps the parties feel like they are there to face a common task and fosters a win-win atmosphere.

If the buyer team has a win-lose philosophy, expect all kinds of ploys to be used. For example, the furniture may be too large or too small or may be uncomfortable to sit in. The buyers may sit in front of large windows to force you to stare directly into sunlight. You may discover that the sellers' seats are all placed beneath heat ducts and the heat is set too high. You should not continue with the meeting until all poor physical arrangements are resolved.

As much as possible, the selling team should establish a win-win environment. This environment can be facilitated by avoiding any verbal or nonverbal threatening gesture, remaining calm and courteous, and adopting an attitude of investigation and experimentation. The leader might even comment:

I can speak for my team that our goal is to reach agreements today that we can all be proud of. We come to this meeting with an open mind and look forward to exploring many avenues toward agreement. I am confident that we will both prosper and be more profitable as a result of this session.

THINKING IT THROUGH	**W**hat if you do everything in your power to establish a win-win attitude with the buyer team, but they insist on viewing the negotiation as a series of win-lose maneuvers? Since they won't play by win-win "rules," should you?

An **agenda,** a listing of what will and will not be discussed and in what sequence, is important for every negotiation session.[14] It helps set boundaries and keeps everyone on track. Exhibit 14.5 offers an example of a negotiation agenda. The selling team should come to the meeting with a preliminary typed agenda. Don't be surprised when the buyer team also comes with an agenda; if they do, the first thing to be negotiated is the agenda itself. In general, putting key issues as late in the agenda as possible is advantageous. This allows time for each party to learn the other's bargaining style and concession routines. Plus, agreement has already been reached on the minor issues, which, in a win–win situation, supports an atmosphere for reaching agreement on the major issues.

GENERAL GUIDELINES

To negotiate effectively, the seller team must put into practice the skills discussed throughout this book. For example, listening carefully is extremely important. This involves not only being silent when the buyer talks but also asking good probing questions to resolve confusion and misunderstanding.

The team leader must keep track of issues discussed or resolved. During complicated negotiations, many items may be discussed simultaneously. Also, some issues may be raised but not fully addressed before someone

Preliminary Agenda
Meeting between FiberCraft and Rome Industrial Inc.
Proposed New Spin Machine for 15 FiberCraft Plants
November 14, 1994

1. Introductions by participants.
2. Agree on the meeting agenda.
3. Issues:
   a. Who will design the new machine?
   b. Who will pay the costs of testing the machine?
   c. Who will have ownership rights on the new machine (if it is ever built for someone else)?
   d. Who will be responsible for maintaining and servicing the new machine during trial runs?
   e. Who will pay for any redesign work needed?
4. Coffee break.
5. Issues:
   a. How and when will the machines be set up in the 15 locations? Who will be responsible for installation?
   b. What percentage will be required for a down payment?
   c. What will the price be? Will there be any price escalation provisions? If not, how long is this price protected?
6. Summary of agreement.

raises a separate issue. The leader can provide great assistance by giving periodic status reports, including what has been resolved and the issues being discussed. More important, he or she can map out what still needs to be discussed. In essence, this mapping establishes a new agenda for the remainder of the negotiation session.

Once again, cultural differences are important in negotiations. For example, most Americans are uncomfortable with silence; most Japanese, on the other hand, are much more comfortable with extended periods of silence. Americans negotiating with Japanese businesspeople usually find this silence very stressful. Negotiators must prepare themselves for such probabilities and learn ways to reduce stress and cope in this situation.

Finally, keep in mind that people during negotiations need to save face. **Face** is defined as the person's desire for a positive identity or self-concept. Of course, people do not all strive for the same face (e.g., some want to appear "cool," some "macho," some "crass," etc.). Negotiators will at least try to maintain face and might even use the negotiation session to improve or strengthen this identity.[15]

DEALING WITH WIN-LOSE NEGOTIATORS

Many books have been written and many consultants have grown rich teaching both buyers and sellers strategies for effective negotiating. Unfortunately, many of these techniques are designed to achieve a win-lose situation. We will describe several to illustrate the types of tactics buyers might engage in during negotiations.[16] Knowledge will help the negotiating team defend its position under such attacks.

Both buyers and sellers occasionally engage in the win-lose strategies described here. However, because we are assuming that sellers will adopt a win-win perspective, this section will focus on how to handle buyers who engage in these techniques.

Good Guy–Bad Guy Routine

You've probably seen the **good guy–bad guy routine** if you watch many movies or police TV shows. A tough police detective interrogating the suspect gets a little rough. The detective uses bright lights and intimidation. After a few minutes, a second officer (who has been watching this) asks his or her companion to "go out and get some fresh air." While the tough detective (the bad guy) is outside, the other detective (the good guy) apologizes for his or her partner's actions. The good guy goes on to advise the crook to confess now and receive good treatment rather than wait and have the bad guy harass him or her some more.

Negotiators often try the same routine. One member of the buyer team (the bad guy) will make all sorts of outlandish statements and requests:

Look, we've got to buy these for no more than $15.00 each, and we must have credit terms of 2/10, net 60. After all the business we've given you in the past, I can't believe you won't agree to those terms!

Then another member of the buyer team (the good guy) will take over and appear to be offering a win-win solution by offering a lower demand:

Hang on, Jack. These are our friends. Sure we've given them a lot of business, but remember they've been good to us as well! I believe we should let them make a decent profit, so $15.50 would be more reasonable.

According to theory, the seller's negotiator is so relieved to find a friend that he or she jumps on the "good guy's" suggestion.

As an effective defense against such tactics, the selling team must know its position clearly and not let the buyer's strategy affect that. (Obviously, the selling team needs the ability to spot a good guy–bad guy tactic.) A good response might be:

We understand your concern. But based on all the facts of the situation, we still feel our proposal is a fair one for all parties involved.

Lowballing

You may also have experienced **lowballing;** it has been used for years by car dealers. The salesperson says, "This car sells for $9,965." After you agree to purchase it, what happens? "Oh, I forgot to tell you that we have to charge you for dealer prep and destination charges, as well as an undercoating already applied to the car. So let's see, the total comes to $11,450. Gee, I'm sorry I didn't mention those expenses before!" Most people go ahead and buy. Why? They have already verbally committed themselves and don't want to go against their agreement. Also, they don't want to start the search process over again.

The technique is also used in buyer-seller negotiations in industrial situations. For example, after the sellers have reached a final agreement with the buyer team, one of the buyer members says, "Oh, I forgot to mention that all of our new contracts must specify FOB destination and the seller must assume all shipping insurance expenses."

The best response to lowballing is to just say no. Remind the buyer team that the agreement has been finalized. The threat of lowballing underscores the importance of getting signatures on contracts and agreements as soon as possible. If the buyers insist on the new items, the selling team will simply be forced to reopen the negotiations. (Try this on car dealers too!)

A variation of lowballing, **nibbling,** is a small extra, or add-on, the buyer requests after the deal has been closed. Compared with lowballing, a nibble is a much smaller request. For example, one of the buyers may state, "Say, could you give us a one-time 5 percent discount on our first order? That would sure make our boss happy and make us look like we negotiated hard for her." Nibbling often works because the request is so small compared to the entire agreement.

The selling team's response to the nibble depends on the situation. It may be advantageous to go ahead and grant a truly small request that could be easily met. On the other hand, if the buyer team uses nibbling often, it may need to be restricted. Again, the best strategy is to agree on the seller's position before the meeting begins and set guidelines for potential nibbles. Often, the seller grants a nibble only if the buyer agrees to some small concession in return.

THINKING IT THROUGH	*S*uppose you are in a very important negotiation session and one of your teammates makes a statement that is not true. What will you do or say? What are the consequences of your action?

Emotional Outbursts

How do you react when a close friend suddenly starts crying, gets angry, or looks very sad? Most of us think, "What have *I* done to cause this?" We tend to feel guilty, become uneasy, and try to find a way to make the person stop crying. That's simply human nature.

Occasionally, buyer teams will appeal to your human nature by engaging in an **emotional outburst tactic.** For example, one of the buyers may look directly at you, shake his or her head sadly, slowly look down, and speak softly:

> *"I can't believe it's come to this. You know we can't afford that price. And we've been good partners all these years. I don't know what to say."*

This is followed by complete silence by the entire buyer team. They hope you will feel uncomfortable and give in to their demands. An extreme case would be where one or more buyers actually walk out of the room or begin to shout.

The selling team, once again, needs to recognize this behavior as the technique it is. Assuming no logical reason exists for the outburst, the negotiators should respond with a gentle but firm reminder of the merits of the offer and attempt to move the buyer group back into a win-win negotiating frame of mind.

Budget Limitation Tactic

In the **budget limitation tactic,** also called a **budget bogey,** the buyer team states something like the following:

> *The proposal looks great. We need every facet of the program you are proposing in order for it to work in our business. But our budget only allows us $250,000 total, including all costs. You'll have to come down from $300,000 to that number, or I'm afraid we can't afford it.*

This may be an absolutely true statement. If so, at least you know what you have to work with. Of course, claims of budget ceilings are sometimes just a ploy to try to get a lower price.

The best defense against budget limitations is to do your homework before going into the negotiation session. Learn as much as you can about budgets and maximums allowed. Have alternative programs or proposals ready that incorporate cost reduction measures. After being told of a budget limitation during the negotiation session, probe to make sure it is valid. Check the possibility of splitting the cost of the proposal over several fiscal years. Probe to find out if the buyer would be willing to accept more risk for a lower price or to have some of the installation work done by the buyer's staff. The salesperson can also help forestall this tactic by working closely with the buyer prior to the negotiation meeting, providing reasonable ballpark estimates of the cost of the proposal.

Browbeating

Sometimes buyers will attempt to alter your selling team's enthusiasm and self-respect by **browbeating** you. One buyer might make a comment like the following:

> *Say, I've been reading some pretty unflattering things about your company in* The Wall Street Journal *lately. Seems like you can't keep your unions happy or your nonunion employees from organizing. It must be tough to get out of bed and go to work every day, huh?*

If you feel less secure and slightly inferior after such a comment, then the tactic was successful.

You shouldn't let browbeating comments have an impact on you or your proposal. That's easier said than done, of course. Presumably, you were able to identify in prenegotiation meetings that this buyer had this type of personality. If so, you could prepare by simply telling yourself that browbeating is going to happen but that you won't let it affect your decisions. If you can make it through one such comment, buyers usually won't offer any more, because they can see that browbeating doesn't help achieve their goals.

The man to the left is engaging in browbeating (Your company has *never* been able to pull off a deal *this* big before!) in an attempt to make the selling team feel less secure and inferior.

SUPERSTOCK.

One response to such a statement would be to practice **negotiation jujitsu.**[17] In negotiation jujitsu, the salesperson steps away from the opponent's attack and then directs the opponent back to the issues being discussed. For example, the salesperson may say,

> *We are concerned about our employees and are working to resolve all problems as quickly as we can. If you have any ideas that would help us in this regard we would appreciate them. Now, we were discussing price . . .*

▮ MAKING CONCESSIONS

One of the most important activities in any negotiation is the granting and receiving of concessions from the other party. One party makes a **concession** when it agrees to change a position in some fashion. For example, if your opening price position was $500, you would be granting a concession if you agreed to lower the price to $450.

Based on many successful negotiations in a wide range of situations, a number of rules, or guidelines, have been formulated for making concessions effectively:[18]

1. Never make concessions until you have all of the buyer's demands and their opening position. Use probing to help reveal these.

2. Never make a concession unless you get one in return, and don't feel guilty about receiving a concession.

3. Concessions should gradually decrease in size. At first, you may be willing to offer "normal-size" concessions. As time goes on, however, you should make much smaller ones. This helps the prospect see that you are approaching your target position and are becoming much less willing to concede.

4. If a requested concession does not meet your objectives, don't be afraid simply to say, "No. I'm sorry, but I just can't do that."

5. All concessions you offer are tentative until the final agreement is reached and signed. Remember that you may have to take back one of your concessions if the situation changes.

6. Be confident and secure in your position and don't give concessions carelessly. If you don't follow this advice, your buyers may have less respect for your negotiating and business skills. Everyone wants to conduct business with someone who is sharp and who will still be in business in the future. Don't give the perception that you are not and will not.

7. Don't accept the buyer's first attempt at a concession. Chances are that the buyer has built in some leeway and is simply testing the water.

8. Help the buyer to see the value of any concessions you agree to. Don't assume that they will understand the total magnitude of your "generosity."

9. Start the negotiation without preconceived notions. Even though the prospects may have demanded certain concessions in the past, they may not do so in this negotiation meeting.

10. If, after making a concession, you realize you made some sort of mistake, tell the buyer and begin negotiating that issue again. For example, if you made a concession of delivery every two weeks instead of every four weeks but then realized that your fleet of trucks cannot make that route every two weeks, bring the issue back on the table for renegotiation.

11. Don't automatically agree to a "Let's just split the difference" offer by your buyers. Check out the offer to see how it compares to your target position.

12. Know when to stop. Don't keep trying to get and get and get even *if you are able.*

13. Use silence effectively. Studies have shown cultural differences in the negotiator's ability to use silence. For example, Brazilians make more initial concessions than Americans, who make more than the Japanese.[19]

The granting and receiving of concessions is often very complex and can result in the negotiations taking months or years to complete. For example, Selling Scenario 14.2 describes some of the unusual concessions resulting from 2½ year negotiations between PepsiCo and the Indian government.

OVERVIEW OF A SUCCESSFUL APPROACH

By setting the proper environment early in the meeting, you are well on your way to a successful negotiation. Remember to develop an agenda and be aware of win-lose strategies that can be used by buyers. Offer concessions strategically.

When the session is over, be sure to get any negotiated agreements in writing. If no formal contract is possible, at least summarize the agreements reached.

S E L L I N G   S C E N A R I O

14.2

Negotiations Can Take Years to Conclude

Ten years after Coca-Cola packed up and left India in a bitter row over the government's regulation of foreign businesses, its archrival PepsiCo won an equally bitter battle to return.

The government announced its approval for a $15.4 million joint venture linking PepsiCo with India's giant Tata Industries and Punjab Agro-Industries. The agreement brought the familiar taste of Pepsi to the 800 million–strong Indian market-place. The soft-drink component of the deal, only one part of the accord, was the element that spawned a 2½-year debate ultimately decided by a cabinet-level committee. The PepsiCo deal symbolized the bitter conflict between India's long-cherished ideals of self-reliance and Gandhi's goal of modernizing the nation's huge but antiquated industrial base in order to stimulate export earnings and economic growth.

The cabinet decision was part of a broad-based program to stimulate food processing with foreign input in a wide variety of products. A major component of the PepsiCo deal was the establishment, in troubled Punjab state, of a modern food-processing industry designed to process, package, and sell local fruit and vegetable produce.

The agreement gave PepsiCo slightly less than 40 percent of the new company, meeting Indian government limits on foreign ownership. The new venture guarantees the Indian government $5 in export earnings for every dollar it must spend on imports, answering yet another sensitive point on foreign operations in India.

PepsiCo spokesperson Rameah Vangal said, however, that his company is "fully committed" to living up to its part of the agreement. "This is perhaps the most scrutinized and controversial project in the country. It means a great deal to Pepsi," Vangal said.

Source: Adapted from Richard M. Weintraub, "After 2½-Year Fight, Pepsi Gains Approval to Enter Indian Market in Joint Venture," *Washington Post,* September 20, 1988, sec. E, p. 1d. Used by permission.

Studies have shown that more cooperation exists if both sides expect future interactions.[20] Keep in mind that your goal is to develop a long-term partnership with your buyer. This process can be aided by being level-headed, courteous, and, above all, honest. Also, don't try to get every concession possible out of your buyer. If you push too hard or too long, the buyer will get irritated and may even walk out. Never let this happen by being too greedy. Remember your goal: to reach a win-win settlement.

Summary

This chapter describes the way to engage in win-win negotiating. It also provides information about how buyers might engage in win-lose negotiating.

Almost anything can be negotiated. The areas of negotiation will depend on the needs of both parties and the extent of disagreement on major issues.

A successful salesperson is not necessarily a good negotiator. Important negotiator traits include patience and endurance, a willingness to take risks, a tolerance for ambiguity, the ability to deal with conflict, and the ability to engage in negotiation without worrying that every person present won't be your best friend.

As in regular sales calls, careful planning counts. This involves choosing the location, setting objectives, and developing and managing the negotiating team. The salesperson does not act alone in these tasks, but instead draws on the full resources of the firm.

Preliminaries are important in sales negotiation sessions. Friendly conversation and small talk can help reduce tensions and establish some degree of rapport. Agendas help set boundaries and keep the negotiation on track. Win-lose strategies that buyers use include a good guy–bad guy routine, lowballing, emotional outbursts, budget limitation, and browbeating. As much as possible, the salesperson should respond to any win-lose maneuvers calmly and with the intent of bringing the other side back to a win-win stance.

Concessions, by definition, will occur in every negotiation. Many guidelines have been established that can help negotiators avoid obvious problems. For example, no concession should be given unless the buyer gives a concession of equal value. Also, any concessions given are not formalized until the written agreement is signed; thus, all concessions are subject to removal, if appropriate.

KEY TERMS

accommodating mode *433*
adaptive planning *428*
agenda *435*
avoiding mode *433*
brainstorming session *428*
browbeating *439*
budget bogey *439*
budget limitation tactic *439*
collaborating mode *434*
competing mode *433*
compromising mode *433*
concession *440*
emotional outburst tactic *438*

face *436*
good guy–bad guy routine *437*
lowballing *437*
mini-max strategy *427*
minimum position *426*
negotiation *422*
negotiation jujitsu *440*
nibbling *438*
opening position *426*
target position *426*
win-lose negotiating *422*
win-win negotiating *422*

QUESTIONS AND PROBLEMS

1. What are the advantages of having a sales job that only involves selling by negotiation? What disadvantages could such a job have?

2. Think about recent encounters you either have had or have witnessed that involved negotiations. Did each party use a win-win perspective or a win-lose perspective? How do you know? (What clues did you use to make that determination?)

3. Salesperson Jim Lucas enjoys meeting people and helping them solve their problems. Although he is excited when he obtains commitment, he really went into selling because he has a strong need to make friends and develop relationships. He is very patient and not averse to take risks. Because his parents were in the military, he is accustomed to moving a lot and has developed quite a tolerance for ambiguity and new situations. Do you believe Jim will make a good negotiator? Why or why not?

4. "As a negotiator, solving your opponent's problem is your problem." Comment.

5. Assume that you are going to have your fourth and final job interview with Camadon, an office equipment firm, next Friday. Knowledgeable friends have told you that since you "passed" the first three interviews, you will be offered the job during the fourth interview. Also, you know that Camadon likes to negotiate with its new hires.
    a. Think about your own needs and desires for your first job (e.g., salary, expense reimbursement, benefits, geographic location, promotion cycle).
    b. For each need/desire listed, establish your target position, opening position, and minimum position.
    c. Camadon has probably also developed positions for each of your needs/desires. Describe how you might go about discovering these positions before next Friday's meeting.

6. Mary Joyner, a salesperson for Nabisco, is preparing for an important negotiation session with Kroger (a large national food chain) about an upcoming promotional campaign. Her boss has strongly suggested that he attend the meeting with her. The problem is that her boss is not a good negotiator; he tends to get angry, is unorganized, and tries to resolve conflict by talking nonstop and thus wearing the buyer team down with fatigue. Her boss definitely has a win-lose negotiating philosophy. What should Mary do?

7. "You are the worst possible person to have negotiate for yourself. You care too much about the outcome. Always let someone else negotiate for you." State your reaction to this statement. What implications does it have in industrial sales negotiations?

8. During the negotiation session, buyers make all kinds of statements. What would be your response to the following, assuming that each occurred early in the meeting?
    a. "We refuse to pay more than $3.20 each. That's our bottom line, take it or leave it!"
    b. "Come on, you've got to do better than that!"
    c. "You know, we're going to have to get anything we decide here today approved by our corporate management before we can sign any kind of a contract."
    d. "One of our buyers can't make it here for another hour. But let's go ahead and get started and see what progress we can make."
    e. "Tell you what, we need to see a detailed cost breakdown for each individual item in your proposal."

9. "Try to get a big concession from your opponent by giving away a small, insignificant concession yourself." Comment.

10. Negotiators have been known to lie during an important meeting. How can you tell whether buyers are lying or not? What should you do if you catch them telling a lie?

11. "If your opponent begins to use an unethical tactic, walk out of the room." Comment.

CASE PROBLEMS

CASE 14 • 1
YORK, INC.

Connie Johnson burst into her sales manager's office, smiling radiantly. "You won't believe it! I just convinced the buyer at Shoney's Restaurants to include York in his group of finalists for the new refrigeration contract. The meeting is in three weeks, and I'll need a lot of help from you in preparing for the negotiation session. They will negotiate with five potential vendors and then select the best one. The order could be worth over $2 million!"

Connie had worked for York for six months, and this was her first chance at a really big sale. York manufactures industrial refrigerators and freezers, air-conditioning systems, and refrigeration components for automobiles, homes, institutions, and so forth. Connie's division deals strictly with sales to large industrial users.

In the past, Shoney's has primarily used Westinghouse for its refrigeration needs. Just to be able to negotiate for the contract was truly an accomplishment on Connie's part.

Her sales manager, Manuel Rodriguez, was excited for her and immediately began to offer tips and suggestions. Part of the conversation that ensued follows:

MANUEL   "I couldn't be happier! I told you you could do it. Well, maybe you'll be able to join us in Hawaii for the Top Salesperson's Club after all."

CONNIE   "I sure hope so. I know, though, that the buyer at Shoney's is a tough cookie. He expects us to really come in with a terrific package."

MANUEL   "Sure, sure. But let's set some ground rules right now. You can't cut prices lower than 14 percent below your price book. Also, don't promise any better credit terms than 5/30, net 60 days. I want us to make a good profit and get paid quickly."

CONNIE   "Gee, that is a good discount, but I wonder if it will be enough. This has the potential of being one of our company's largest orders of the year. Don't you think we might be able to back off a little more?"

MANUEL   "I know you're hungry for this sale, but we can't give away the ship. Remember part of my bonus is based on net profit, not just sales volume. And don't ask my boss, Jim, or any of the higher-ranking sales managers for any better pricing. We need to be a team together—you and me."

CONNIE   "Any more tips?"

MANUEL   "I've got a drawer full of them. For example, any time you get a concession, give a very small one in return. But make a big deal out of it, like you're practically giving away the store! Okay? Remember, get big concessions, give insignificant, small ones."

CONNIE   "Won't they catch on to that? I mean, the buyer is no dope."

MANUEL   "Well, it's all in the execution, Connie. You not only need to *talk* about your concession, you also need to add a good mix of emotions in there. Look kind of teary; act kind of like you really need this sale. Heck, tell them your career depends on it. If you use your female charms well enough, they won't realize what a small concession you actually gave them."

CONNIE   "It sounds like I have a lot to learn. Can we start putting together a team soon to plan?"

MANUEL   "No need! You and I are the team! I've been in this business for 21 years and know all the ropes. No, we don't really need to get anyone else from York involved. Once we get the business, they'll know how great we are!"

CONNIE   "But if we got the national sales manager or divisional president involved, we might be able to get a better pricing package approved and *still* let you meet your profit quotas."

MANUEL   "Say, who's the expert here? Me or you? Trust me on this one. I won't let you down!"

QUESTIONS

1. Evaluate the dialogue. Identify potential problems that Connie may face in the upcoming planning and negotiation session.

2. Should Connie go over Manuel's head and try to get executives involved in this process? What would be the consequences of such an action?

3. Should Manuel attend the negotiation session? Why or why not?

4. If you could put together a selling team to help prepare and participate in the negotiations, what types of people would you choose?

5. Later in the conversation, Manuel indicated that lowballing often works when selling to large firms.
    a. Give an example of lowballing that Manuel might use with York.
    b. If you were Connie, what would be your reaction to Manuel's suggestions?

CASE 14 • 2
IDENTIFYING
CONFLICT-HANDLING
MODES

This chapter describes a number of basic conflict-handling modes that people use in negotiation. These include competing, collaborating, compromising, avoiding, and accommodating.

Carefully reread the section that describes these modes. Then identify someone you know that falls into *each* of the modes and answer the following questions for each of the five persons you have identified.

QUESTIONS

1. How do you know this person is "competing"? What specific behaviors of the person have you observed or heard about that support your assertion?

2. How do you (and/or others) interact with this person during a conflict situation? What do you do? How do you respond to this person's behavior? Is it effective?

3. Would you like to have this person on your team during an important negotiation session? Why or why not?

ADDITIONAL
REFERENCES

Cauthern, Cynthia R. "Moving Technical Support into the Sales Loop." *Sales & Marketing Management,* August 1990, pp. 58–61.

DeRose, Louis J. "Negotiating Value." *Sales & Marketing Management,* October 1990, pp. 108–9.

Falvey, Jack. "Team Selling: What It Is (and Isn't)." *Sales & Marketing Management,* June 1990, pp. 8–10.

Fisher, Roger, and William Ury. *Getting to Yes: Negotiating Agreement without Giving In,* 2nd ed. Boston: Houghton Mifflin, 1991.

Frank, Sergey. "Global Negotiating: Vivé Les Differences!" *Sales and Marketing Management,* May 1992, pp. 64–69.

Gschwandtner, Gerhard. "How to Sell in France." *Personal Selling Power,* July–August 1991, pp. 54–60.

Hall Lavinia (ed.). *Negotiation: Strategies for Mutual Gain.* Newbury Park, CA: Sage Publications, 1993.

Keiser, Thomas C. "Negotiating with a Customer You Can't Afford to Lose." *Harvard Business Review,* November–December 1988, pp. 30–33.

Keller, Robert E. *Sales Negotiation Handbook.* Englewood Cliffs, NJ: Prentice Hall, 1988.

Leritz, Len. *No-Fault Negotiating: A Practical Guide to the New Dealmaking Strategy That Lets Both Sides Win.* New York: Warner, 1987.

Morrison, William F. *The Prenegotiation Handbook.* New York: Wiley, 1985.

Perdue, Barbara C. "The Selling Firm's Negotiation Team in Rebuys of Component Parts." *Journal of Personal Selling and Sales Management,* November 1988, pp. 1–10.

Perdue, Barbara C.; Ralph L Day; and Ronald E Michaels. "Negotiation Styles of Industrial Buyers." *Industrial Marketing Management,* August 1986, pp. 171–76.

Richardson, Linda. *Winning Group Sales Presentations.* Homewood, IL: Dow Jones-Irwin, 1990.

Smith, Homer B. "How to Concede Strategically." *Sales & Marketing Management,* May 1988, pp. 79–80.

Selling to Resellers

S elling to resellers—the trade—differs somewhat from other forms of selling. In this chapter, we explore those differences. (The answers to the questions below will sometimes also apply to industrial or institutional sales, but in a different manner.) By examining the arena of trade selling, you will understand more fully the role of the salesperson in marketing a product, both from a strategic, or executive, viewpoint and from the perspective of the field sales representative. Also, you will more fully understand the different roles salespeople can play.

This chapter presents the world of trade selling. Trade selling, or selling to resellers, can seem different because many buyers and their organizations do not use the products they buy. While differences do exist, all of what you have learned to this point still applies. You will also find material in this chapter that applies to other arenas of selling as well.

Some questions answered in this chapter are:

What is a reseller?

How does buying for resale differ from other forms of buying?

What common terms and conditions apply to such sales, and how do they impact sales?

How does a salesperson aid resellers in merchandising the product?

What role do trade shows and markets play in the sale of goods to the trade?

How do national accounts managers interact with field salespeople?

What types of partnerships are formed with the trade?

Raja Farah has been out of college and working for Campbell's Soup Co. for two years, but has already enjoyed several promotions and earned her company's highest sales honor, the Merit Award. She received the award during and all-expense-paid trip to Hawaii. Awarded to only the top 100 of 1,400 salespeople, Raja is one of only a handful to ever win the award in less than five years.

What makes Raja so successful is the quality of relationships she has with her customers. "Often, I'll do something in a store and my manager will say, 'Raja, don't do that! We have to get permission first!' But then I'll ask my customer if it was okay, and they'll say, 'Oh, you know you didn't need to ask,' because they trust my judgment."

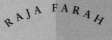

Campbell's Soup Co.

Raja has proven that her creative methods of merchandising Campbell's products and her scrupulous honesty make such trust worthwhile. "I earn a bonus for growing revenue in my territory. The only way I can do that is to grow profits for my customers. A customer will give you room to work when you have proven yourself worthy of their trust."

She notes that often competitors try to take away space that store managers have allotted to Campbell's. "One way that I prove myself trustworthy is that I never do that. And when it happens to me, I can use the store's planning diagram to prove that the space belonged to Campbell's." Sometimes she has to sell the manager back on that facing; that is, prove again that Campbell's deserves that space. Because she understands the needs of her accounts, she has never lost space.

Currently Raja handles 80 accounts, including two retail chains. In addition to soup, she sells Franco American pasta, V-8 juice, Swanson canned poultry, and other Campbell's products. With the chains, she designs a total marketing plan, including co-op advertising, in-store promotions, and other marketing strategies. "One chain likes to buy only things that are on special discounts. I managed to increase sales in the account the first year I had it, but not as much as I wanted to." Her strategy is to continue to build a relationship that will enable her to prove Campbell's profitability even without special discounts. "As I prove myself on each successive deal, they become more willing to work with me."

Raja recognizes that the grocery business is very competitive, but it is that competition that she finds so challenging. "I'm using everything I've learned in school and in the business to be successful. I have the opportunity to be creative in merchandising and marketing products through my customers. At the same time, I have a tremendous amount of responsibility to manage the profits for 80 stores and generate profitable revenue for Campbell's. Every day is different—and I love it that way!"

Many people can easily conjure up pictures of industrial salespeople selling the machinery that pounds away in a manufacturing plant or of a retail salesclerk assisting a shopper who is trying on a jacket. But selling to re-sellers, or the "trade," may be a little harder to picture.

WHAT IS THE TRADE?

The **trade** comprises all members of the channel of distribution that resell the product between the manufacturer and the user. Facilitators (e.g., banks, advertising agencies, transportation firms) would not be considered part of the trade, but wholesalers, retailers, and other distributors fall under its broad umbrella.

Many people think of the trade in terms of consumer package goods; that is, selling to the trade involves getting a product on the shelf of a grocer or a discounter such as Wal-Mart. But this is actually only a small part of trade selling.

Columbia 300, for example, is a major manufacturer of bowling balls. Its sales force is responsible for assisting bowling alleys, bowling pro shops, discount stores, and other retailers in merchandising and selling bowling balls. Columbia 300 sells to bowlers through retail outlets, as shown in Exhibit 15.1.

Broyhill, which manufactures furniture, provides another example. Their salespeople identify and sell Broyhill furniture to furniture retailers at annual furniture markets in High Point (North Carolina), Dallas, and Chicago. During the year, the reps assist their dealers in advertising, inventory management, and other merchandising tasks.

Not all trade selling involves selling consumer products through retailers; agricultural equipment is also sold through dealers. Brazos Farm and Equipment is a John Deere dealer. In Brazos's showroom, John Deere's salesperson sets up displays of John Deere toy tractors, lawn and garden equipment, and farm equipment parts and accessories. The sales represen-

Selling to the trade may involve helping grocery stores display consumer products or assisting individual distributors merchandise products such as pumps.

Courtesy Borden, Inc.; photo by Michael Hart.

Courtesy of WICOR Inc.

E X H I B I T   15 . 1

WHERE TRADE SALESPEOPLE
FIT IN CHANNELS OF
DISTRIBUTION

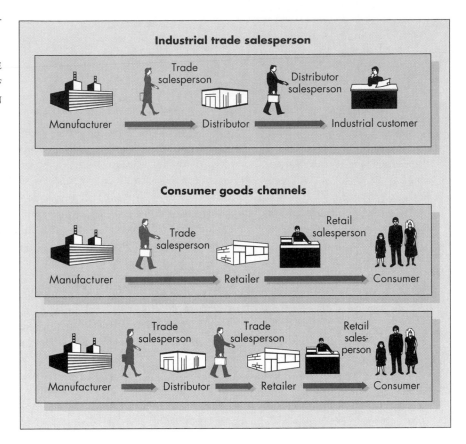

tative teaches Brazos salespeople how to sell John Deere tractors and farm implements. The rep also assists Brazos with the local advertising of Deere products. Keep in mind that dealers do not have to carry all of Deere's products or participate in all of Deere's marketing programs. Seeing that they do participate is the job of the Deere rep.

 Industrial products are also sold through resellers, or distributors, particularly when selling in other countries. Canon, for example, is a Japanese manufacturer of copiers, laser printers, faxes, and other office equipment. In the United States, they distribute these products through a network of dealers, although in Japan, they sell direct to users. In the United States, Canon reps call on dealers and train them in the selling and use of new products.

Trade goods can involve many types of products. Even when the final user is industrial or agricultural, trade salespeople are important to their buyers. As you can see in Selling Scenario 15.1, resellers want to build partnerships with their suppliers.

THE BATTLE FOR SHELF SPACE

When resellers are authorized dealers for one company's products and that company's products only, shelf space is not a concern. But in situations where resellers are authorized dealers for several products or for retailers such as department stores, grocery stores, and discount stores, salespeople wage a constant fight for shelf space.

S E L L I N G   S C E N A R I O

15.1

Salespeople Are Important Partners!

Caralee Bradbury, manager of George's Casual and Western Wear, recognizes the importance salespeople have in helping her and her store be successful. "We make better business decisions with the aid of knowledgeable salespeople," she declares.

"Knowing my customer is essential," says Caralee. She believes that the salesperson must study her final buyer in order to know what merchandise will sell best. Vendor salespeople have access to different customer information than she does. When a partnership is formed and partners each share the information they've collected, both parties profit.

Caralee notes that "Salespeople also bring imagination and fresh ideas." Salespeople visit many stores daily and gather creative ideas from each of the stores. The reseller, however, goes through the same routine each day. A salesperson is an outsider who can introduce new ways of producing business. "We trust our salespeople not to share our creative ideas with our direct competitors, but they call on many stores with whom we don't compete. So in those situations, the salesperson can be a creative asset."

Some of the creative ideas that Caralee has gotten from salespeople are anniversary sales, using joint promotions to create huge sales and customer giveaways, and other special events. "Salespeople also help us merchandise their products in our stores," she says. "When they understand our market, they can help us create the right in-store image that is supported by their marketing and really sells the product."

"We depend on our salespeople for more than just creative ideas, too." Caralee notes that sometimes a supplier does not want to accept returned defective merchandise. Then she depends on the salesperson to represent her case to the manufacturer. "The longer we work as a team, the more successful we both become because we understand each other. We're partners."

For example, Kraft, Liptons, and Rice-A-Roni all manufacture a noodles alfredo product. Each manufacturer's salesperson would like to have the best shelf space possible, but the best space can only go to one product. The other products have to make do with less space or poor quality position. The grocery store would like to assign shelf space in a way that maximizes total noodles alfredo sales, but the three salespeople are only interested in their brand's sales.

Sometimes the battle is not always ethical. One Noxell (Noxzema and Cover Girl cosmetics) rep described how she called on a pharmacy and discovered her products completely missing. A competitor had emptied the shelves of her products, moving them to the back room. The Noxell rep simply brought the lack of shelf space to the attention of the store manager, letting him draw his own conclusions. That unethical competitor was later asked to remove his products.

▎MIND SHARE

In selling to industrial distributors, manufacturers often talk of the battle for space as a battle for mind share. **Mind share** is the degree to which a manufacturer's product receives attention (occupies the mind) from the distributor. Industrial distributors may carry competing products that require some personal selling to the end user. In this case, the manufacturer wants his or her product recommended more often than the competitor's. When the products are sold at the user's site, the battle among manufacturers is for the distributor's mind share rather than shelf space.

For example, Panasonic manufactures electronic parts that other manufacturers use to make many types of products. They sell through distributors who also sell products produced by Panasonic's competitors. The distributors can recommend Panasonic or another product, and often there is no functional difference between the two. Panasonic would like to be the first brand recommended, or have the primary position in the mind of the distributor. As you will see in this chapter, Panasonic and other manufacturers seek to increase mind share through training and special promotions to the trade.

Trade Buyers

Like all salespeople, trade salespeople must convince customers that the products and services offered will satisfy their needs. But selling a product for resale differs in several ways from selling a product for personal or corporate use. The primary difference lies in the trade buyers' concern about their return on investment (ROI). All buyers focus somehow on their ROI. For example, when you buy a suit, you want to make sure that you will wear it enough (the return) to justify the price (the investment). But trade buyers approach ROI a little differently.

The primary reason that trade buyers approach ROI differently is that they deal with derived demand (discussed in Chapter 4). When trade buyers purchase a product for resale, they are concerned with whether their customers will also buy the product. Their ROI is not based on how well the product performs (such as how long the suit lasts), but how well the product sells.

To determine the projected ROI, resellers use a number of mathematical formulas. Trade buyers compare various profit projections by comparing their projected returns. One set of formulas that buyers use is the strategic profit model. We will focus on those elements of the strategic profit model influenced by the salesperson.

Strategic Profit Model

The **strategic profit model (SPM)** is a mathematical formula used to examine the impact of strategic decisions on profit. Retailers and other resellers often use the SPM to evaluate such actions as adding another product or engaging in a promotion.

The SPM uses several financial ratios in evaluating the performance of the overall store. Our interest here is in the evaluation of a product or marketing program that we may be selling to a retailer; the SPM also evaluates areas of performance that salespeople do not influence. Therefore, we are concerned with only gross margin ROI, or the portion of ROI related to the products that the trade salesperson sells to the reseller (see Exhibit 15.2). While we are discussing an evaluation of the future (i.e., what if they adopt this product or program), the same criteria can be used to assess a current product or prior program.

E X H I B I T   15 . 2   THE STRATEGIC PROFIT MODEL

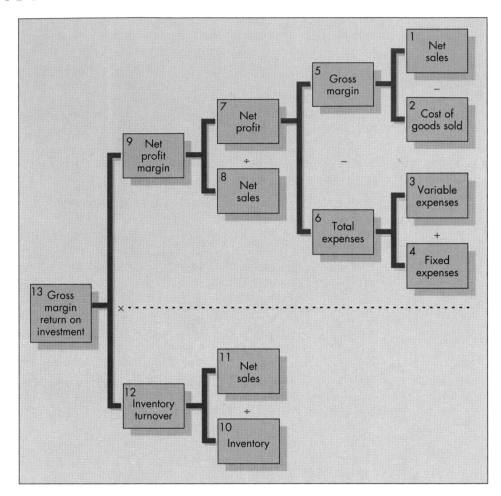

When evaluating a product or program, a trade buyer focuses on three things: how many will be sold, at what profit, and how fast the product will sell. The numerical answers to these questions are then converted into ratios that enable the buyer to compare the performance of various products or programs to objectives.

Net Sales

Of great interest to the trade buyer is how much sales revenue can be expected from a product or program. (When evaluating a product or program, trade buyers express sales in dollars rather than units, in order to evaluate the product or program's profitability.) But total sales does not accurately measure sales—people return products because of damage, improper fit, or for no apparent reason, and these returns must be subtracted in order to calculate net sales. **Net sales,** for our purposes, is total sales minus returns, in dollars, represented by Box 1 in Exhibit 15.2.

Another measure important to retailers is sales per square foot or sales per shelf foot. Of course, this measure won't be used by a John Deere dealer because space is not at such a premium, but the dealer will compare alternative uses of display space. In a grocery store or a department store, however, shelf and display space is a finite asset that has been filled to the maximum. Moreover, by the nature of retailing, only the fittest (most profitable) survive. Products are therefore evaluated by how well they use the space allocated to them.

The measure of how well products use space is the amount of sales dollars they generate. For example, if a retailer generates $50 per square foot in sales with Miami Fashion's products and only generates $45 with Sun-Coast, then Miami Fashion will get more space. SunCoast may be eliminated entirely.

Net Profit Margin

The profit on the product, expressed as a percentage of sales, is the **net profit margin** (or just *margin*). In mathematical terms,

$$\text{Net profit margin} = \frac{\text{Net profit}}{\text{Net sales}}$$

Net profit margin, or Box 9 in Exhibit 15.2, is influenced by the cost of goods sold (or the price charged to the reseller, Box 2 in the exhibit). Net profit margin is also influenced by the variable expenses (Box 3), which can be affected by costs associated with reselling the product. Salespeople, as we will see later in this chapter, can reduce those costs by reimbursing the store and through other means. Thus, salespeople can influence net profit (Box 7) in several ways, which can have a major impact on net profit margin.

Profit margin is an important factor when trade buyers consider a product or program. Many students confuse margin with markup, especially in practice role plays. Markup is the percentage of cost that the price for the product is increased. A trade buyer usually will be concerned with margin rather than markup when making the buying decision, but both margin and markup are important. The formula for markup is

$$\text{Markup} = \frac{(\text{Price} - \text{Cost})}{\text{Cost}}$$

The markdowns that retailers take off the selling price also affect margin. When they have a sale and say, "Everything is 15 percent off," they mean that everything is 15 percent off the regular retail price, not the cost to the store. Expenses are also calculated as a percentage of sales. Hence, to make it easier for buyers to calculate their profit margin, salespeople should quote profit margin in terms of suggested retail prices, not markup on the basis of retail cost.

For example, if Linz Jewelers buys a diamond ring for $1,000, they may sell it for $2,000. The markup is 100 percent when calculated as a percentage of cost: ($2,000 − $1,000)/$1,000. But profit margin is 50 percent: $1,000/$2,000 (multiply by 100 percent to convert to a percentage).

Turnover

There are several types of turnover that the trade can use to evaluate performance, but the type of turnover of interest to salespeople selling to the trade is inventory turnover. **Inventory turnover** measures how fast a product sells relative to how much inventory has to be carried. Inventory turnover (Box 12) measures how efficiently a reseller manages inventory. The reseller would like to have in the store only the amount needed for that day's sales, because inventory represents an expense until it has been sold, but obviously receiving daily delivery is impossible in most situations.

To fully understand the importance of inventory turnover, let's examine the impact that inventory has on the overall ROI. Inventory, Box 10, is often the largest current asset owned by a store. (Other current assets would include accounts receivable, or customer purchases made on credit.) Inventory makes up most of total current assets. The larger the inventory, the lower the inventory turnover (Box 12). The lower the inventory turnover, the lower the gross margin ROI (Box 13). If we were to examine overall ROI and include other current assets, the effects would be similar. A low inventory turnover would still lower overall ROI.

Calculated by dividing net sales (represented by Box 11 and is the same as Box 1) by inventory, the measure states the number of times that the firm sold an amount equal to the inventory it carried. In mathematical terms,

$$\text{Inventory turnover} = \frac{\text{Net sales}}{\text{Inventory}}$$

A reseller does not necessarily want to push turnover to the highest possible level—most easily accomplished by reducing inventory. Several negative consequences could result, including stockouts, increased ordering costs due to more frequent ordering, higher shipping costs, and loss of quantity discounts. Lowering prices can also increase turnover but may reduce profits because gross margin (Box 5) is lowered.

To improve inventory turnover, some resellers are working with manufacturers to develop efficient customer response systems. **Efficient customer response (ECR)** systems are distribution systems that drive inventory to the lowest possible levels, increase the frequency of shipping, and automate ordering and inventory control processes without the problems of stockouts and higher costs discussed earlier. Similar to just-in-time systems in manufacturing, these systems improve efficiency throughout the distribution channel. **Quick response** is a similar term, and refers to minimizing order quantities to the lowest level possible while increasing the speed of delivery in order to drive inventory turnover, accomplished by prepackaging certain combinations of products (*ECR* is primarily a grocery term, whereas *quick response* is used in other areas of retailing). One apparel manufacturer, Precision Fabric Group in North Carolina, even manufactures based on customer demand. If the retailer sells more of a certain color, they order more of that color, rather than a prepackaged combination. PFG can do this because they developed several weaving technologies that allow them to speed up the manufacturing process. Hence, they have a JIT manufacturing-through-retailing process.

Resellers use turnover to identify slow-selling merchandise, determine appropriate stock levels, and evaluate the buying process. Eliminating slow-moving goods, selling off excess inventory, and ordering at appropriate times can improve turnover. Turnover can also be improved by selecting reliable vendors. Less inventory is needed when the reseller doesn't have to carry extra stock just in case a shipment may be delayed. That is why ECR works best between partners; the partnership selection process (discussed in Chapters 2 and 13) would screen out vendors incapable of living up to the promises of ECR.

Turnover varies widely for different products. Jewelry, hardware, and furniture stores have lower turnover rates than do gas stations and grocery stores. As a result, the former need to make more profit from each sale and to maintain a wider assortment. Gas stations and grocery stores have lower margins but make up for that with higher unit sales volume.

Gross Margin ROI

When inventory turnover is multiplied by net profit margin, the buyer has determined the gross margin return on investment (Box 15). Keep in mind that this is a simplified version of ROI used to illustrate how a product is evaluated for purchase; overall ROI would include other assets and items not affected by a seller's program. If comparing two products, the buyer can insert the projected sales of each, the costs of each, the costs associated with reselling the products (less any support from the manufacturer), how much inventory must be kept on hand, and then calculate the return on investment. The choice would be made on the basis of which product had the best return on investment.

For example, Kmart was offered a large discount from a vendor if the vendor could begin shipping in bulk to Kmart's warehouses instead of directly to the stores. At first glance, the discount looked attractive because it lowered the cost of goods sold (Box 2), which should improve gross margin (Box 5), thus improving net profit (Box 7), net profit margin (Box 9) and ultimately ROI (Box 13).

But Kmart had other costs that would now be incurred, such as increased shipping from their warehouses to the stores, increased handling in order to break the vendor's large shipments down to the amount needed for each store, and increased inventory. The first two costs increased variable expenses (Box 3), while increased inventory (Box 10) hurt total current assets (Box 12), which hurt inventory turnover (Box 12). The overall result was lower ROI (Box 13). By forecasting these costs and applying the SPM, Kmart was able to avoid a costly decision.[1]

OTHER FACTORS TO CONSIDER

Unlike the hard financial aspects of reselling a product or evaluating the success of a marketing program, measuring the vendor's level of support is often not an objective process. Yet retailers and other resellers know that this, the "soft" side of supplier selection, is as important as the hard, financial side. In fact, the two are often highly related, as you can see in Selling Scenario 15.2.

S E L L I N G   S C E N A R I O

15.2

Partnering from the Retailers' Perspective

Based on a study conducted by the Meyers Research Center, retailers ask for only two things from manufacturers: equitable pricing programs and adequate brand support. In fact, when asked what goes into a partnership, retailers mentioned cost reduction programs, equitable deals from the manufacturer, and everyday low-price programs as often as they mentioned honesty and trust, sharing of cost and sales/market information, and customized programs.

It's no surprise, then, that retailers see the primary benefits as being lower costs and higher profits. Still, retailers feel that there are disadvantages to partnerships. Retailers are concerned about having enough in-house resources to deal with multiple partners, fear of becoming tied to one vendor, and are concerned that manufacturers are getting the better end of the deal. Half of the retailers participating in the study reported that they were currently involved in at least one partnership.

Even though retailers specify cost reduction and higher profits as major benefits and don't rank customized programs as a primary benefit, one difference does appear when asked who are the best partners and why. Among manufacturers, the best partners were Procter & Gamble, Coca-Cola, RJR/Nabisco, and Kraft/General Foods. When asked why these manufacturers made good partners, the most prominent answer was because they develop specific retail chain marketing programs. Manufacturers who provide retailers with special programs allow those retailers to offer their customers something special. And that is what retailers really want—something to compete with.

Source: Craig Miller, "What Do Retailers Really Want?" *Potentials in Marketing*, June 1993, p. 36.

Some of the dimensions on which vendors are evaluated include reliability, turnaround, facilitating functions, information, credit, and ethics. Other dimensions are risk and investment. Image represents the buyer's total perception of all of these.

Dimensions of Image

Image can mean many things, especially when one is selling to the trade. We will discuss the image that consumers hold of the selling firm as well as the image that buyers have of the salesperson. Both are important to the buyer in vendor selection.

IMAGE WITH CONSUMERS   The image that the consumer holds of a product is, the manufacturer hopes, the intended position. For example, Coca-Cola positioned Tab, a diet cola, as the diet cola for women because it contained calcium, something that Diet Coke does not have. As another example, Procter & Gamble has positioned Crest toothpaste as a cavity fighter, whereas Close-Up is positioned as a whitening toothpaste that improves sex appeal. Those manufacturers hope that consumers agree that

Tab is a diet cola for women, Crest is a cavity fighter, and Close-Up whitens teeth and improves sex appeal. A store might not carry both Crest and Close-Up if they had the same image.

What does this mean to a salesperson? That the product's and the company's image in the marketplace must be consistent with the image that the reseller wants to project. For example, a lawn and garden store that positioned itself as the lowest priced in town would not carry Snapper lawnmowers (premium priced, high-quality products), but rather would carry Murray mowers (affordable, with fewer features). If the same store positioned itself on the basis of top quality and service, it would want to carry Snapper, not Murray. Therefore, salespeople should consider the fit between their company's image and a retailer's image when prospecting for new distributors.

IMAGE IN THE TRADE   The vendor also has an image in the trade. This image, based on how the company treats its distributors, is separate from the position the company strives for in the marketplace. In the Coca-Cola example, Tab has its image in the marketplace. The Coca-Cola Company has an image among grocery stores separate from that for Tab. For example, Coca-Cola strives for an image of strong marketing support with its grocery store buyers.

Vendor image can be very important. For example, John Deere has a reputation among dealers of providing excellent support. This reputation made it easier for Deere to extend its product lines into lawn and garden equipment when times got tight in the agricultural market. New dealers for the new products were willing to invest with Deere because of that company's reputation for support.

When buyers evaluate a potential supplier's reputation, they consider such typical questions:

Is this company ethical? Does it fulfill its promises?

Will the supplier stand behind its offerings?

Is the supplier financially healthy? Will it be around to supply me over a period of time?

Is this supplier innovative or conservative?

Will I be treated fairly—given fair access to discounts, marketing support, delivery, and credit terms?

Salespeople play a big role in how their companies are viewed in the territory. Each salesperson has the opportunity to build a reputation or tear it down. Often the little things build a reputation, just as the little things build a relationship. As you review the above questions, you can see that being professional in the way you conduct yourself can have a very positive impact on the reputation of your company.

Doing business with a reputable company reduces risk for the buyer. Companies want partners they can trust. Confidence in the decision to select a partner is greater when the buyer recognizes that the supplying company is reputable.

SELLING TO RESELLERS

How do salespeople use this knowledge to be more effective in their jobs? As a first step, they understand that customers, the resellers, will be interested in their return on investment—a function of their total sales for the product, their profit margins, and how fast the product will sell. Professional salespeople also understand how their own performance will be evaluated by buyers, and how the buying process may work. Then salespeople must prepare to answer customers' questions and prove, using methods similar to the proof methods we discussed in Chapter 10, benefits for the buyer. Exhibit 15.3 relates how buyers buy to the proof processes that we now discuss.

▍USING THE SPM

Resellers evaluate many numbers and elements of marketing programs to make marketing and buying decisions. As you read earlier, however, these evaluations boil down to three questions, often asked in this order:

How much will sell (sales)?

At what profit (margin)?

How quickly and easily will it sell (turnover)?

The salesperson must show how the product will meet the reseller's needs on these three dimensions.

▍PROVING SALES

An important point to remember when selling to resellers is that they deal with derived demand, just as other organizational buyers do. Resellers are interested in whether their buyers will buy the product, not their own personal desire for the product. Students often forget this in practice presentations and spend too much time showing the buyer why the product

---

▍E X H I B I T   15 . 3

RELATIONSHIP OF HOW
BUYERS BUY TO PROOF
PROCESSES

What Trade Buyers Buy	How Salespeople Prove Benefits
Net sales	Selling history
	Market share
Net profit margin	Pricing terms
	Absorbing shipping costs
	Trade discounts
	Quantity discounts
	Promotional allowances
	Credit terms and financial discounts
	Marketing support
Inventory turnover	Selling history
	Market share
	Third-party proof
Image	Company history
	Turnaround

is so wonderful, forgetting to tie those features back to the buyer's need for strong sales. While the buyer for Foot Locker will want to know what is new and special about Nike's latest running shoe, the buyer is more interested in whether runners will find those features new and special and whether those runners will flock to Foot Locker stores to buy the shoe.

Using Selling History

Salespeople often use past sales experience to gain future sales. **Selling history** is defined as how well the vendor's product or line sold during the same season in the previous year. Selling history is the most important factor in vendor selection by department store buyers choosing clothing and accessories as well as housewares and appliances.[2] It is also important in other types of trade selling. For example, if you were selling a spring Raid (a leading bug killer) promotion to a grocer, you may want to remind that grocer that last spring's Raid promotion sold 50 cases in only one week. Because bugs come out in the spring and Raid's spring promotion this year is even better, surely that grocer will want to have at least 70 cases on hand to supply the coming demand! An example of how this might be presented is in Exhibit 15.4.

A sales representative trying to secure distribution through a new outlet has no selling history with that prospect to prove the selling power of the product or program, but success with similar dealers or retailers can be used. Be careful in such situations; you do not want to give away confidential information, such as how much your prospect's competitor is making. For example, you should not tell Macy's that Foley's sells 200 cases of your product per week. That would be unfair to Foley's, and unethical.

Using Market Share

One common method of proving that a product will sell is to show market share. **Market share** is the percentage of total market sales accounted for by one product. In mathematical terms,

$$\text{Market share} = \frac{\text{Brand sales}}{\text{Total product category sales}}$$

E X H I B I T   15 . 4

USING SELLING HISTORY TO
SELL MARGIN

Proposal for Budget Box Grocery Stores	
Last Spring's Off! Super Sale	**This Spring's Deep Woods Off! Sell-Out**
	New Off! product
50¢ coupon	50¢ coupon
$1 million national ad campaign	$1.3 million TV ad campaign
	$8 million print ad campaign
You sold **50 cases**	You sell **70 cases**
Profit **$736**	Profit **$1,176!**

A Dial representative will create an individual Profit Story for each customer, based on suggested order size, projected sales, and expected profits.

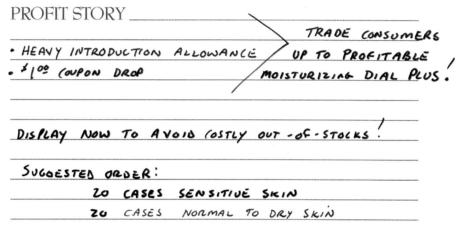

Courtesy of The Dial Corporation.

For example, to say that Dial has a 31 percent market share means that 31 percent of all deodorant soap sales are Dial products. Market share is most often used for consumer packaged goods, because markets are easily defined by product categories and data concerning sales of various products are readily available. But market share may not be as applicable in other industries, such as fashion goods and hardware, where markets may be ill-defined or data less readily available.

The way salespeople present market share information will vary depending on the type of buyer being dealt with. For example, an amiable can be told that "everyone loves this product—in fact, it is the leading product in the market," whereas an analytical will want to see the actual percentage. Such percentages are available from marketing research firms. In consumer package goods, commonly used measures of market share are provided by BehaviorScan and Nielsen's Retail Index. These services provide the percentage of products sold, by brand, in various categories. If you sell copiers to office suppliers, however, you would use data from

Salespeople use information from brochures like this to support their sales message. This brochure includes Nielsen and test market data for a new product to establish a selling history. Other brochures may include photos of coupon ads to show the company's advertising support and illustrations of the displays that are offered to retailers.

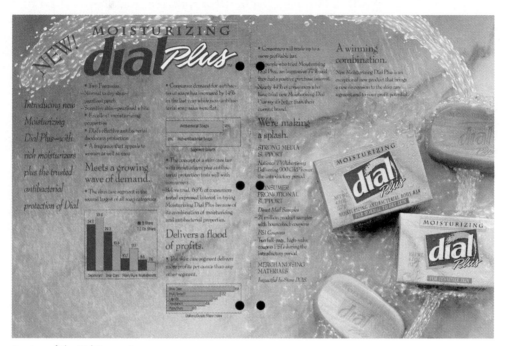

Courtesy of The Dial Corporation.

companies such as DataPro to support your claims for market share. Other market research companies provide similar market data for hardware, soft goods (linens, clothing, etc.), furniture, and other products—but, as previously noted, you may be less likely to use that data in those markets.

Other proof sources of market share include test market results, third-party sources such as articles in trade magazines, and company data that indicate sales growth, average volume per retailer, and other information. These sources can indicate increasing market share and that the product is selling, especially in the case of a new product. As you can see in the accompanying photo, Dial also included data to prove growing market demand for the new moisturizing Dial Plus product.

Selling Profit Margin

Net profit margin is the second most important factor considered by department store buyers. The importance of these two financial factors, selling history and margin, to department store buyers comes from the recognition that profits drive the store's activities. No matter how much a department store buyer likes a sweater, for example, if he or she doesn't think it will sell or can't be marked up enough to make a profit, then it won't be carried in the store.

How do resellers want to think about profit? In the largest amounts possible, just as they want to think about costs in the smallest amounts possible. For that reason, the salesperson should present profit totals. Consider the Raid example given earlier. Suppose that each case holds 24 cans of Raid and the wholesale price per can is $.69. Also suppose the rep suggests that the grocer sell the can for $1.39 (ignoring for the moment any coupons that might be used). The buyer is interested in total profit, or $1,176, rather than $.70 per can.

THINKING IT THROUGH	*S*hould a salesperson discuss costs only in terms of cost per can, and profits only in terms of total profit? If not, how could you achieve this emphasis ethically? Specifically, what would you say?

Terms and conditions of the sale also affect the seller's return. Knowledge of pricing, discounts, and credit policies is important because these policies affect the buyer's actual cost and ROI. In addition, if a salesperson misquotes a price, the selling company may be legally obligated to fill the order at that price, even if the rep and the company will lose money. But price is just one component of the terms and conditions of sale, which often become important determinants for the buyer because they affect profit.

Pricing Terms

Among the most common expressions used in quoting price are *list price, net price, guaranteed price, FOB price,* and *suggested retail price.* **List price** is the quoted or published price in a catalog or price list, from which buyers may receive discounts. **Net price** is the price buyers pay after all discounts and allowances have been subtracted. These would include quantity and other types of discounts that we will discuss shortly.

Suggested retail price is just that, the price at which the manufacturer suggests the store retail the product. The reseller, however, has no obligation to sell the product at that price. When presenting a product, the manufacturer's salesperson can suggest a retail price and base profit margin calculations on that price. However, to present margins and other sales-based information, the rep should also use any price the retailer has set. After all, that price is the one the retailer will use to make a decision.

Guaranteed prices are important during times of falling prices. For example, Apple may sell computers to retail stores at $500. If Apple decreases wholesale prices to $400 before a store can sell its inventory, the store has suffered an opportunity loss of $100 per computer. To encourage resellers to place larger orders, manufacturers may offer to protect the resellers' inventories with a guaranteed price. In our example, if Apple lowers its prices by $100, the retailer is refunded the $100 for each computer still in inventory. It would be the salesperson's job to verify the inventory and initiate the refund request.

Shipping Costs

The terms and conditions of sale include shipping costs. The seller who quotes an FOB (free on board) price agrees to load the goods on board a truck, freight car, or other means of transportation, but it may be up to the buyer to pay for transportation.

A great many variations exist in the use of **FOB,** but the term is used to specify the point at which the buyer assumes responsibility for both the goods and the costs of shipping them. Hence, FOB destination would mean that the buyer would take responsibility for the goods once they reach the buyer's location, and the seller would pay the freight.

Suppose Johnson Wax quotes an FOB origin. It will load the truck at its Racine, Wisconsin, plant, but the buyer bears the responsibility for paying for shipping. If Johnson Wax sold a truckload of Raid to Tom Thumb (a grocery chain headquartered in Dallas) under terms of FOB destination, then Johnson Wax would pay for shipping and would have the Raid delivered to Tom Thumb's Dallas warehouse, where the Tom Thumb warehouse personnel would unload the truck.

Trade Discounts

At times, the price a reseller will pay for a product is quoted in terms of a discount off of the list price, called a **trade discount.** For example, the manufacturer may offer the wholesaler a trade discount of 35 percent off.

Occasionally, the manufacturer may sell directly to a retailer. If so, the retailer may be quoted a smaller trade discount, for example, 20 percent of the list price. The wholesaler's discount would then be taken off the resulting retailer's cost. Hence, if the trade discounts are expressed as 20 and 35, the retailer pays 80 percent of suggested retail, and the wholesaler pays 35 percent less. Note that the wholesaler does not pay 45 percent of retail; the wholesaler's discount is taken from the retailer's cost. Exhibit 15.5 illustrates how the trade discount works. Trade discounts should provide a

EXHIBIT 15.5

TRADE DISCOUNT EXAMPLE

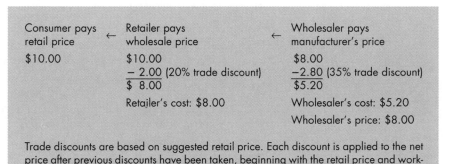

sufficient margin to cover the costs of the services rendered by the various middlemen and to give the middlemen a fair profit.

Most companies that use trade discounts classify their customers according to the trade discount allowed. However, when customers operate as both wholesalers and retailers, knowing which price to quote is difficult. Some manufacturers may then treat the trade discount as a quantity discount, offering the wholesale discount for larger orders and the retail discount for smaller quantities. Other manufacturers may only give the customer a retail discount, while still others may give the customer the wholesale discount, depending on the overall level of sales for the customer's retail and wholesale operations.

Quantity Discounts

Quantity discounts encourage large purchases by passing along savings resulting from reduced processing costs, and should not be confused with trade discounts (which are designed to provide the trade with profit). Quantity discounts are usually taken off the price after the trade discount is applied. Businesses offer two types of quantity discounts: (1) the single-order discount and (2) a cumulative discount. A typewriter company, for example, may offer a 10 percent discount on a single order for five or more typewriters—a single-order discount. That same company offering a cumulative discount might offer the 10 percent discount on all purchases over a one-year period, provided the customer purchases more than five. A **cumulative discount** is a quantity discount applied to purchases over a period of time, usually one year, rather than the quantity of a single order. The customer may sign an agreement at the beginning of the year promising to buy five or more, in which case the customer would be billed for each order at the discounted price (10 percent off). If the customer fails to purchase five typewriters, a single bill is sent at the end of the year for the amount of the discount (10 percent of the single-unit price times the number of typewriters actually purchased). Another method would be to bill the customer at the full price, then rebate the discount at the end of the year, depending on the actual number of typewriters purchased.

Promotional Allowance

Manufacturers often offer special allowances if resellers agree to promote their products. Clorox may offer a special discount to grocery stores if they agree to offer a special price for Clorox liquid bleach, advertise the special price in the local paper, and permit the Clorox rep to build an end-of-aisle display of Clorox products. This allowance, usually offered as a discount off the regular price, is separate from any cooperative advertising allowance (which would be based on the cost of advertising, not the amount of product purchased) or any other discount. The grocery trade refers to promotional allowances as a **deal,** the promotional discount offered to the retailer. The product is said to be "on deal." This promotional discount may be a quantity discount or may be in addition to regular quantity discounts.

Salespeople and their customers will use this advertising schedule to plan adequate inventories so that product will be available when consumers come in to buy.

	SEPT	OCT	NOV	DEC	JAN	FEB	MAR
ADVERTISING TELEVISION							
PRINT							
PROMOTION INTRODUCTORY ALLOWANCE							
ON-GOING ALLOWANCE							
PUMP							
REFILL							
COUPONING							
FSIs DIRECT MAIL							

THE DIAL CORPORATION

Courtesy of The Dial Corporation.

In the above example, Clorox may have their products on deal, with an extra quantity discount for the retailer.

Credit Terms and Financial Discounts

Most US sales are made on a credit basis, with certain discounts allowed for early payment. These cash discounts are the last discount taken, and like the others, are not added to other discount percentages. A common discount is 2/10, n/30, which means that the buyer can deduct 2 percent from the bill if it is paid within 10 days from the date of invoice. Otherwise, the full amount must be paid in 30 days. Another common discount is 2/10, EOM, which means that the 10-day period begins at the end of the month. A bill for $100 with terms of 2/10, EOM, and received January 10 could be paid with $98 by January 20, or with $100 by January 31, but on February 1 the payment would be late.

When selling to distributors in other countries, a company may ask customers to provide letters of credit. Letters of credit are like checks from your bank, except that the company cannot collect cash from a customer's letter of credit unless it is able to prove that the customer did not pay for the merchandise. Letters of credit are the most common method of international payment.

Buyers frequently request on their invoices **deferred datings,** which allows them to pay after the selling season, as an extra form of discount. In the golfing industry, for example, the big selling season is early spring. Golf pro shops ask to be billed at the end of the season, when they've sold enough products to be able to pay the bill.

▌ SELLING TURNOVER

When proving that the product will sell, the vendor does address turnover, or how quickly the product will sell. But in addition, the vendor provides marketing support so that the product will sell faster. Marketing support from the vendor improves the efficiency of the reseller. Vendor advertising, for example, should lead to greater product recognition by the consumer. The reseller has less selling to do, because the vendor's advertising has already presold the consumer, improving turnover. Note that Dial included its television advertising schedule on the brochure its salespeople used to introduce Liquid Dial, as seen in the photo on page 463. Buyers could rest assured that Dial would help them sell the product, which should positively influence turnover.

In summary, you now recognize the financial criteria on which product and marketing programs will be evaluated. The financial needs of the trade buyer have been quantified to some degree for you, and you have a better understanding of the ways to present a product's or program's financial capabilities.

Notice too, however, how support needs interact with financial needs. For example, turnover is determined in part by the level of inventory that must be carried. Inventory levels are affected by the level of service, specifically how promptly and reliably the company can deliver. How fast and how much a product sells will also be affected by the job the rep does in assisting that dealer or retailer in merchandising the product and by the effectiveness of the marketing program that the rep helps to create.

▌ SELLING IMAGE

How can a salesperson build the image of the company? Part of the proof will be in the pudding, or how well the salesperson serves prospects before they become customers. Returning phone calls, providing information or samples quickly, and delivering on promises will go a long way toward proving reliability.

If possible, salespeople should carry copies of business periodical or trade periodical articles about the company. Salespeople should also maintain a file of letters from satisfied customers. When a customer thanks you for service, ask for a letter. Not only can you document your level of service with other accounts, you can also prove your service skills to your management if the need arises.

Salespeople also sell image, and prove it with company history. For example, if a salesperson discovers that the buyer prefers carrying the products of innovative companies, the salesperson should remind the buyer of past innovations that the company developed. Then, when presented with the current innovation, the buyer sees this new product as part of an overall history of innovation.

A Goodyear salesperson can prove the company's record on quality by referring to Goodyear's many awards.

Courtesy The Goodyear Tire & Rubber Company.

One word of caution: Many sellers get too wrapped up in discussing how wonderful their company is; they don't make a connection to the buyer's needs, such as a concern about being treated fairly. Emphasizing your company's reputation is most effective when buyers can relate that reputation to their needs.

Turnaround

An important dimension of service, **turnaround** is how quickly you deliver a product or service after the customer orders it. The term is also used to describe how quickly you respond to a customer. Elsewhere in this book, you have read about the top salespeople as rated by their customers. Frequently, these customers considered turnaround under difficult situations as one important criterion for performance.

Turnaround is often a function of salespeople's ability to plan and their relationships with others in the company. As we will discuss in Chapter 17, salespeople need to develop strong relationships with colleagues in their company's order entry, billing, credit, and shipping departments in order to provide the desired level of service to customers.

At the same time, however, salespeople must plan their activities and sales calls to provide plenty of lead time. If normal delivery is two weeks, for example, salespeople would not want to wait to tell retailers about a promotion until two days before it starts. Retailers will want to know at least two weeks in advance so they can receive sufficient inventories of the promoted product, build their displays, and so forth.

We have discussed throughout this text how salespeople build long-term partnerships, and how important customer service and follow-up are in maintaining those partnerships. Turnaround can also relate to how fast

S E L L I N G   S C E N A R I O

15.3

Who Stole Bart's Butterfinger?

Nestlé acquired Butterfinger from RJR Nabisco in 1989, and has since increased sales by more than 70 percent. But not satisfied with those sales gains, Nestlé launched a major promotion involving Bart Simpson.

The company sought the aid of all Butterfinger consumers to find out who "Laid a Finger on Bart's Butterfinger." A push campaign involving advertising on Fox, NBC, several cable networks, radio advertising, and in-store displays was the largest ever for the brand. Special packaging also alerted consumers to the promotion.

When consumers purchased a Butterfinger, the label contained alibis for several of the characters from the hit TV show "The Simpsons." Customers used the wrappers to eliminate suspects, much as the game "Clue" is played. After all five alibis are collected, consumers sent their accusation to enter a $50,000 sweepstakes or to win one of 10,000 "Who Laid a Finger . . ." t-shirts.

Crucial to the success of the promotion was adequate supplies of the specially marked packages in retail outlets. Salespeople were responsible for clearing out old inventory and making sure that the trade had sufficient stock to deal with the increased demand.

Another important factor for success was selling the trade on the special display. This was no small task, because Halloween is a traditional high-volume candy sales period and every candy company wanted extra space. The sales force used sales aids describing the advertising and national sweepstakes to encourage chain store buyers to increase their inventories and allocate space for the special display. With the coordination and support of the sales force, Bart's loss was Nestlé's gain.

Source: Adapted from "Nestlé Casts a Major Caper," by Kerry J. Smith, *Promo: The International Magazine for Promotion Marketing,* September 1993, p. 9.

salespeople return phone calls and how quickly they handle credit requests and other problems. When customers know they can depend on the rep to turn their requests around on a timely basis, they will turn to that rep with more orders. As you can see in Selling Scenario 15.3, salespeople for Nestlé had to convince retailers of the expected success of the "Who Laid a Finger on Bart's Butterfinger" promotion so that the appropriate inventory could be ordered.

TRADE SHOWS, TRADE FAIRS, AND MERCHANDISE MARKETS

Another method of selling to the trade is to attend trade shows (see Chapter 6 for a discussion of using trade shows for prospecting), trade fairs, and merchandise markets. In some cases, a manufacturer lives or dies by how well it does in these special selling situations. Keith Clark, a company that manufactures office products such as calendars, depends heavily on the annual National Office Products Association show. Their salespeople report that selling year-round is easier due to the impression the company makes on prospects at the show.

Merchandise Markets

An important part of selling to resellers is **markets,** short-term sales (usually only a few days) held in large buildings that are like huge malls. The Dallas Market Center, for example, hosts separate markets for children's wear, western apparel, linens, and other soft goods. The sellers are the manufacturers or distributors, and they only sell to resellers, not to the public. Sellers may lease showroom space permanently or only during the market weeks. If they lease space permanently, they usually bring buyers in during off-market periods, or at times when there are no markets.

Buyers visit many vendors during markets, selecting the products they will carry for the next season. In some industries, almost all of the sales to resellers occur during markets. These industries include hardware, clothing, toys, and furniture. The major furniture markets are held in Dallas, Chicago, and High Point, North Carolina. Toys are marketed in an annual show in New York City and at other, minor shows. Major clothing markets are held for each season (such as fall and spring) in New York City, Paris, Dallas, and Los Angeles.

Trade Shows

Trade shows are short (usually less than a week) exhibitions of products by manufacturers and distributors. Trade shows, unlike markets, do not have permanent show space. Once the show is over, all vendors pack up and leave. The Specialty Advertising Association International (SAAI), for example, holds its annual trade show in Dallas each year. Vendors at this show are all manufacturers looking for dealers for their products; the end users of the products are not admitted. Dealers make an entire year's worth of purchases at the SAAI show, so the show is a make-or-break situation for many manufacturers.

Comdex, the largest computer trade show in the world, is usually held in Las Vegas. Comdex differs from SAAI's show in that it has a dual audience: Vendors exhibit to end users (industrial consumers) as well as to resellers. Another show with a dual audience is Networld, a show for computer networking products. A recent survey of Networld found that 40 percent of the vendors had promoting to dealers only as their primary objective, 40 percent were promoting to end users only, and 20 percent were looking for dealers and end users. Successful trade shows exist because they reach qualified buyers that might not otherwise be reached, as illustrated in Exhibit 15.6.

Even firms that do not use resellers may have salespeople involved in trade shows. Many trade shows have only customers as their audience. For example, the National Association of Legal Secretaries is a professional organization that promotes the welfare of legal secretaries. When they hold their annual convention, they also invite manufacturers of office equipment and other products to exhibit wares. The trade show is an adjunct of the convention, with the audience composed entirely of end users.

E X H I B I T   15.6   MORE BUYERS REPORT TRADE SHOWS AS EXTREMELY USEFUL
SOURCES OF INFORMATION.

Because so many buyers rely more on trade shows than ever before, selling
companies are increasing their use of trade shows.

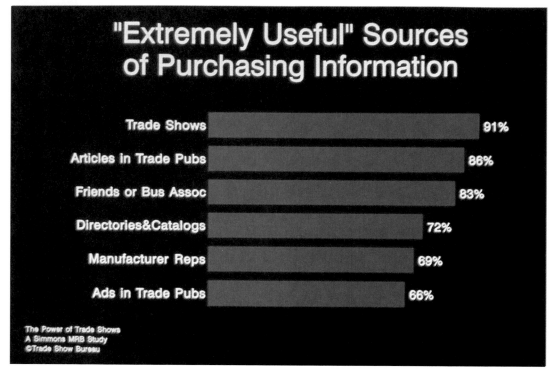

Courtesy of the Trade Show Bureau.

Trade Fairs

In Europe, trade shows are called **trade fairs.** In Hannover, Germany,
Europe's largest convention hall hosts many shows, including the Hannover
Fair, the European version of Comdex. This show attracts over half a million visitors from around the world and displays the products of 4,500
manufacturers from over 45 countries. Shows such as the Hannover Fair
can be extremely important for companies such as Microsoft and Novell
when looking for local dealers and distributors in other countries.

Trade shows and markets, then, are one activity that salespeople may
engage in, whether selling to resellers or consumers. These shows provide
excellent opportunities to locate prospects. Whereas the average number of
calls needed to close a sale is 4.6 without trade shows, the average number
of additional calls needed after exposure at a trade show is only .8. Thus,
closing a sale costs $1,158 without a trade show and only $334 with a
trade show, on average.[3] A company that employs a good system to track
those who visit the booth and uses that system to encourage a prompt
follow-up by salespeople can maximize the sales opportunities of trade
shows and markets.

Shows such as the FMI Food Expo and Comdex are important sources of leads, an opportunity to close sales, and a chance to strengthen ties to current customers.

Courtesy of the Trade Show Bureau.

Courtesy The Interface Group.

SELLING THROUGH THE TRADE

Manufacturers provide their salespeople with marketing programs that improve sales, margins, or turnover. These programs involve promotions to the trade, called *trade promotions*. **Trade promotions** are special offers made to resellers by the manufacturers, as opposed to promotions to consumers. Trade promotions, while influencing ROI, are best designed when they help the trade sell the product.

While most successful trade promotions involve supporting retailers' efforts to build traffic, one major area of conflict between manufacturers and retailers lies when the manufacturers' concern is exclusively with the sales of their products. Retailers' concern is not about the sales of a particular product but about the store's overall sales. Therefore, while manufacturers advertise and promote to sell their product, retailers advertise and promote to generate store traffic and sell anything.

Trade promotions work best when the manufacturer understands the retailers' advertising and promotion needs and works to satisfy those needs in a way that also meets the manufacturer's needs. For example, Kiwi (a manufacturer of footwear accessories such as shoe polish and athletic shoe cleaner) aids retailers in many ways, but the specific assistance for a given store depends on the store's needs. Merchandising materials that help display the product in the store are supported by ads in sport magazines, and if the retailer also needs local advertising help, Kiwi can provide that, too.[4]

OBJECTIVES OF TRADE PROMOTIONS

Trade promotions have one or more general objectives, including:

1. Gain retailer support for a manufacturer's promotion.
2. Launch a new product.
3. Widen distribution, including getting new distributors, more shelf space, or better shelf space.

These objectives illustrate the dilemma that trade promotions pose for most salespeople. Something is going to have to change in that store. Objective 1 means that attention and resources have to be diverted away from a current marketing program to the salesperson's program. Objectives 2 and 3 mean that another product will have to be taken off the shelf or given less room.

Keep in mind that a retailer's decisions often involve such trade-offs; being able to prove turnover and margins will help you if you are selling trade promotions to retailers.

TYPES OF TRADE PROMOTIONS

Manufacturers use two major types of promotion strategies, often in tandem. The **pull** strategy is designed to stimulate demand among consumers for the manufacturer's product. The **push** strategy is designed to stimulate sales efforts by the manufacturer's salespeople and/or the sales efforts by resellers.

Pull Strategies

Pull strategies are designed to pull consumers into the stores to buy the manufacturer's products. They include the use of national advertising campaigns, contests and sweepstakes for consumers, promotions such as the Pillsbury Bake-Off, and other means.

The importance of salespeople to a successful promotional campaign is illustrated by their actions when a manufacturer offers a coupon in a **freestanding insert (FSI)**. (When you shake your Sunday paper and all of those coupon ads fall out, you have shaken out the FSIs.) Creative salespeople will tell retailers that FSIs are coming up, to secure a special display and plan inventory. Then the retailer can maximize the sales of that product with the coupon without affecting the store's profit margin.

Manufacturers may have a co-op advertising program as part of their pull strategy. **Co-op advertising,** short for cooperative advertising, means that the manufacturer will pay some of the store's advertising costs. The manufacturer may provide the advertisement original, and the retailer will simply insert its name and address into the ad. Alternatively, the retailer may combine several co-op ads into one large ad. While the co-op ad does require marketing effort by the retailer, it is not considered a push strategy because the ad's purpose is to pull people into the store. The retailer may be reimbursed for a percentage of the advertising costs or may be offered a discount off the price of the product.

Manufacturers in many businesses offer co-op advertising, although the consumer package goods industry is the heaviest user. Other users include the fashion industry, some hardware manufacturers such as Stanley and Black & Decker, and home appliances manufacturers.

Manufacturers may also combine co-op advertising with a national promotional campaign. When you see a manufacturer's ad that says "at participating dealers," you are seeing a national promotional campaign that depends on the salespeople securing the participation of resellers. Those salespeople may also help the participating dealers properly display the promoted products and their in-store advertising to support the promotion.

Push Strategies

Salespeople and their companies often combine pull promotions with a program that encourages resellers to participate. Promotions that encourage reseller participation and support are push promotions. Push promotions include contests and extra incentives for the reseller's salespeople, special display incentives, and special pricing incentives.

FEATURES   Sometimes the manufacturer will offer additional discounts (called *deals,* as mentioned earlier) if the retailer will **feature** a product—that is, put the product on sale with a lower price, advertise it, and perhaps build a special display. When your grocery store advertises its weekly specials, those products are this week's features. For example, you may see an ad for Coke at $2.49 a 12-pack at your local grocery store. When you go into the store, you see a stack of Coca-Cola products at the end of the first aisle, with a special sign hanging from the ceiling announcing the special price. The store benefits because Coca-Cola may have paid for the special attention through co-op advertising allowances and special display incentives.

Salespeople play a major role in seeing that stores successfully feature their products. Neither the store nor the manufacturer wants to just sell at lower prices. Without the additional advertising and in-store promotion (either through an end-of-aisle display or some other special display), the sales volume will not increase enough to offset the lower price. The salesperson usually builds the display, sees that the retailer receives originals of any advertising, and ensures a proper inventory for the sale.

Deals can create problems. Sometimes retailers do not pass the savings on to their customers. Instead, because they can price the product for any amount, they keep the retail price at its regular level and pocket the extra earnings.

A similar problem is that the reseller may buy a larger than normal amount in order to take advantage of the lower price. At first glance, this seems okay. But some resellers may purchase an entire year's inventory at the low price, called **buying forward.** Such a large order is much greater than what the manufacturer anticipated for the special promotion period. Buying forward can cause the manufacturer's production plans to get out of whack in relation to real demand, because the manufacturer expects orders to return to normal levels after the promotion period. But the reseller who bought forward places no more orders that year. Buying forward can create serious problems for manufacturers.

CONTESTS   Some trade promotions are just like contests for the company's own salespeople. Top dealers may win trips to exotic places, or they may be able to pick out merchandise from a catalog, paying with "dollars" earned through top sales performance. Some trade promotions actually reward the top salespeople of the reseller directly, rather than the reseller. Robert Wagner, while a student at Baylor University, worked part time for a local Montgomery Ward selling computers and stereos. During the Christmas season, he sold enough IBM computers to place among IBM's top ten retailer salespeople, earning him an all-expense-paid trip to the Super Bowl. These types of trade promotions are used when a personal selling effort is required by the retailer.

PUSH MONEY   Similar to contests are spiffs, or push money. Like a commission, **spiffs** or **push money (PM)** are paid directly to the retailer's salespeople by the manufacturer for selling the manufacturer's product. But the reseller's salespeople can only earn PM for a short period of time and for a specific product, unlike a regular commission. Spiffs work well only when the promotion requires a personal selling effort by the retailer's salespeople.

THINKING IT THROUGH	*H*ow would you feel if you knew the stereo salesperson you were buying from could receive a spiff for selling you a particular product? Would you feel any different if you knew that the salesperson was paid straight commission, no matter which product was sold?

Some retailers discourage the use of PM, because they do not want products pushed on buyers and because the products may not be the best products for their customers. Other retailers frown on PM because they feel that it causes their sales staff to turn its attention to products that may be less profitable to the store than others. Salespeople, however, may appreciate the opportunity to earn extra money.

PARTNERING WITH THE TRADE

Throughout this book, the emphasis has been on developing strategic partnerships with buyers whenever possible. Just as in all other selling arenas, selling to resellers has been revolutionized by the concept of partnerships. And, as you have seen in this chapter, partnering is important to strategies such as efficient customer response and quick response systems. In this section, we'll take a closer look at two strategies related to partnering, training the trade and category management.

TRAINING THE TRADE

An important dimension of partnering with resellers is training their sales staff. While not a promotion strategy per se, training the trade may be necessary to enable a retailer's sales force to sell the product. The manufacturer's salespeople may be responsible for training the salespeople of the resellers in how a product operates and how it should be sold.

For example, we mentioned Kiwi earlier in this chapter, which has adopted a strategy of trade promotions involving advertising and merchandising. Their main competitor, SecondWind, uses an entirely different strategy based primarily on training the trade. Part of their training is delivered through two free videos, one that trains the retailer on how to merchandise SecondWind products and one that focuses entirely on selling SecondWind shoe accessories at the time of a shoe sale (this is like asking if you want fries with your Big Mac). They are planning another video, one that teaches retail salespeople how to sell any specific product in their line of shoe cleaners, deodorizers, laces, insoles, cleats, and replacement spikes.[5]

In some situations, the salesperson needs to teach general selling skills first (the purpose of SecondWind's first sales training video). Some companies have product specialists to assist salespeople with the training task, but the responsibility lies solely with the salesperson in many cases. Without such training, the reseller's salespeople will not have the knowledge or confidence to successfully sell the product, and the resellers do not have the expertise to conduct the training.

Training the trade is more important in situations requiring personal selling by the reseller. For example, office supply stores often sell office equipment and furniture. These products require active prospecting and selling skills that focus on needs satisfaction. The stores' salespeople need training so that they can sell the office equipment and furniture appropriate to the buyer's needs.

If customers require service, training may also be necessary. Salesclerks need to know the service procedures of the manufacturer so that the customer receives good service. Clerks may also be asked how something works or what is needed to solve a customer's problem (which is the purpose of the second sales training video from SecondWind). These situations may not require active selling, but a knowledgeable salesclerk can mean the difference between a satisfied customer and an irate ex-customer.

CATEGORY MANAGEMENT

Category management is a process by which retailers and manufacturers jointly plan and implement marketing programs to improve the performance of an entire product category (including competitive products) for mutual benefit.[6] Category management is a process of maximizing profits for the entire category (for the retailer) through efficiently using pricing, promotion, point-of-purchase merchandising, and other techniques. Perhaps the most important tool is information.[7] The supplier has information that was previously unavailable to the retailer through any other source. While the retailer knew everything that went on in that store and therefore knew the impact of displays and special prices, the retailer didn't know the segmentation structure of the category's market, consumption trends, new product trends, and key influences on the category by region, market, or other division. Such information can be crucial to the success of a promotion strategy.

Category management has opened the communication channels. By sharing such information in the form of fact-based presentations that educate buyers, salespeople and buyers create joint marketing and promotion programs. These joint programs are more effective than the old method of each independently creating a marketing program. But it isn't just marketing programs that are affected. Logistics, finance, and other phases of both companies' operations are affected by category management and partnership programs such as ECR.

One benefit of category management for the seller is that it can reduce forward buying for that salesperson's brand, but there is pressure to lower the usual price. With open communication, an average price can be agreed to that is more than a deal price but less than the regular price. The manufacturer will still save money because of more efficient manufacturing due to regular ordering, and can actually make more profit.

For example, a dried fruit company examined market data (from IRI, a marketing research company) for Dallas and realized that one chain of stores accounted for 8.3 percent of all edible food sales but only 6.3 percent for dried fruits.[8] Closer examination revealed that raisins, the major component of the dried fruit category, were selling at a rate half that of most other chains in the market. Further analysis indicated that raisin sales were actually decreasing at that chain, although increasing for the total market. What was that chain doing wrong?

By examining data from the retailer and comparing it to their own data, the company learned that 34.4 percent of all Dallas raisin sales are produced through promotions, but that amount fell to 15.3 percent at that particular chain. Incremental raisin sales due to promotions was 16.1 percent of all raisin sales, but only 5.4 percent for the store. Additional data showed that the chain promoted raisins fewer times and less heavily than did other stores in the market. A joint review between the company and the chain resulted in a promotion program to improve raisin sales. One event in the program was a baking promotion that did not involve a specific raisin company's brand, but was designed to simply increase raisin sales.

Category management began as a grocery store–consumer packaged goods strategy. But this particular form of partnering is spreading to other types of resellers such as Wal-Mart, sporting goods retailers, and others.

SUMMARY

Many students can easily picture how to sell a product to someone who will use it, but they have a little more difficulty understanding how to sell to resellers. Those who buy to resell, including wholesalers, distributors, and retailers, are called the *trade*. Trade buyers buy what sells, buy marketing support, and buy profits.

Industrial trade salespeople speak of their battle as one for mind share. Each salesperson wants his or her product, rather than a competitor's, to be recommended whenever possible by the distributor's sales staff. Because the distributor's sales staff is key to selling the product to the user, mind share, rather than shelf space, is more important.

To help in evaluating products and vendors, trade buyers use the strategic profit model (SPM). This model evaluates a product or store by examining net sales, net profit margin, and inventory turnover. When introducing a product or program, salespeople can use selling history, market share, and the others' results to prove how well a product can sell. Financial aspects such as the terms and conditions of the sale are also important.

Buyers also evaluate the product's image and the vendor's reputation. Reputation is often proven by taking care of the little things (as discussed in previous chapters).

Trade promotions are offered to the trade in an effort to stimulate sales. Pull strategies include advertising directly to the consumer, sponsoring contests, offering coupons, and the like. Push strategies include using push money, sponsoring contests for the retailer's salespeople, and building displays.

Merchandise markets, trade shows, and trade fairs can play a major role in a firm's sales efforts. In some industries, most of the sales are gained at a market. Trade shows and trade fairs are important when selling to certain types of industrial users, as well as to resellers and end-users.

Training the trade, an important dimension of service in many industries, may be needed to enable resellers' salespeople to sell the product well. The manufacturer's sales rep often performs this task.

Selling to resellers involves different benefits, but many of the same principles still apply. Many people find personal fulfillment in the challenges and rewards of selling to the trade.

KEY TERMS

buying forward 475
category management 477
co-op advertising 474
cumulative discount 466
deal 466
deferred dating 468
efficient customer response (ECR) 456
feature 475
FOB 465
freestanding insert (FSI) 474
guaranteed price 464
inventory turnover 456
list price 464
market share 461
markets 471
mind share 452
net price 464

net profit margin 455
net sales 454
pull 474
push 474
push money (PM) 476
quick response 456
selling history 461
spiffs 476
strategic profit model (SPM) 453
suggested retail price 464
trade 450
trade discount 465
trade fairs 472
trade promotions 473
trade shows 471
turnaround 469

QUESTIONS AND PROBLEMS

1. Some students fail to see how anyone could get excited selling household cleaning products to resellers. But some people enjoy this job a great deal. What differences do you think might be present in the attitudes of the two groups to account for their different perspectives?

2. Is encouraging buyers to order a large quantity so they can get a better quantity discount always a good idea? Why or why not?

3. The list price for a man's shirt is $20. Your company offers trade discounts of 20 percent and 30 percent to retailers and wholesalers, respectively. If shirts are ordered in quantities greater than 4 dozen, wholesalers receive an extra 5 percent discount. A wholesaler places an order for 12 dozen shirts. What does the wholesaler pay? If terms are 2/10, n30 and the wholesaler pays in five days, what price does the wholesaler pay?

4. Profit and turnover seem to be two natural enemies. Discuss how the manufacturer's salesperson can influence both in a positive way for the reseller.

5. What types of point-of-purchase displays would be effective for promoting desktop calculators? Personal computers? House paint?

6. Assume you sell cleaning supplies. How would your presentation differ when you sell to a store versus when you sell to a janitorial service company?

7. The most common complaint of resellers is a lack of support by vendors. Give your opinion as to why this is true.

8. What effect would an upcoming "Spring Cleaning" national ad campaign by Endust have on the activities of Endust salespeople?

9. One problem with promotional discounts is that some resellers do not pass them on to their customers but pocket the extra profit. Another problem with promotions in general occurs when some resellers do not participate. Why would resellers not participate fully in a manufacturer's promotional programs? What effect would this have on the manufacturer's image? The reseller's image?

10. What role do trade shows play in the overall marketing process? How does the role differ if one is selling through resellers versus selling directly to users?

11. Discuss store loyalty versus brand loyalty. How would each affect the sales efforts of a manufacturer's salesperson? Would these concepts have any effect on a category management program?

12. How is category management different from other forms of partnering? What impact do the *buyer's* customers have on any partnering relationship?

CASE PROBLEMS

CASE 15 • 1
CLEAN RITE COMPANY

Clean Rite offers several specialized cleaning cloths (such as simulated chamois cloths for washing cars, "Bag of Rags" for general cleaning, and "Shop Towels" for use in the garage), brushes, and brooms. The company, in business for over 20 years, has enjoyed a growth rate of over 15 percent per year. The company does no advertising, nor has it offered co-op advertising in the past. In grocery stores, the products are set up in a standard 4-foot display that uses pegboard to allow for the varying height of the brushes and brooms. In stores with an auto department, the company also displays the Shop Towels, chamois-like cloths, and other car-cleaning products.

Recently, the company introduced a fishnet "Bug Sponge." This sponge is covered with fishnet to provide extra scrubbing strength. Originally designed to clean bugs off cars, the sponges have a wide range of uses. They can be used for scouring in the kitchen or cleaning in the bathroom. Two sponges come in a small plastic bag with cardboard folded and stapled over the top; the unit can be hung on a peg on a pegboard.

As a sales representative for Clean Rite, you are planning tomorrow's activities. You want to call on the following stores:

- Budget-Box Grocery. This is a small, family-owned grocery store in a poorer part of town. It currently has only the 4-foot display, with no separate auto products area.

- Buy Lo Grocery. You will call on the nongrocery item buyer for Buy Lo, a four-store chain of midsize grocery stores. These stores have the pegboard display in the auto section.

- Florentine's. Florentine's, a regional discount chain, has 32 stores over a four-state area. Clean Rite is an approved vendor. You are calling on the only store in your territory that carries no Clean Rite products. The manager has told you that he doesn't want Clean Rite because he already carries S.A.M.S. (a competitor) and doesn't want the hassle of two vendors. You have collected data to show that Clean Rite outsells S.A.M.S. in the other stores by an average of 10 percent.

- Rhodes. Rhodes carries only S.A.M.S. in their 12 grocery stores. You called Rhodes headquarters by phone because it isn't in your territory, and found that all buying is done by local managers. They do not use an approved vendor list. When you visited this store last month, the manager did not have time to talk. She had never heard of Clean Rite, but did say you could come back when she had more time. You set up an appointment for tomorrow.

QUESTIONS

1. Keeping in mind why trade buyers buy, what strategies will you use to introduce the Bug Sponge (and/or Clean Rite) to these stores?

2. How will you maximize the number of facings for Bug Sponge in each store?

3. Assume that the Budget-Box buyer is an analytical, the Buy Lo buyer is an amiable, the Florentine's buyer is an expressive, and the Rhodes buyer is a driver. How would you prove/dramatize the benefits for each buyer?

4. In what category does Bug Sponge fit? What disadvantages would you face if you tried a category management program with each of these stores? How would you go about presenting a category management program?

CASE 15 • 2
B. A. JACKSON & CO.

B. A. Jackson & Co., a midwestern business started in 1912, has grown into one of the largest privately held consumer products companies in the United States. Their products range from dishwashing detergent to bathroom cleaners to air fresheners and other cleaning products. Recently, the company signed an agreement with Rabun, a European manufacturer of personal care products, including toothpaste, deodorant, and other similar products. Jackson will market Rabun products in the United States, and Rabun will market Jackson products in Europe.

Jack Starling, a Jackson sales representative, is visiting Bob Bauer, buyer for Bauer Brothers, an independent grocery chain of four stores in Central Florida. (Bob, a grandson of one of the founders, is 29 years old.) Jack has three objectives for this sales call:

1. Obtain an end-of-aisle display for a pallet display order for delivery in three weeks. This pallet pack would contain a mixture of Jackson cleaning products and would support a "Spring Cleaning" promotion that includes a freestanding insert in the local papers, with coupons for 25 cents off all Jackson products in the display.

2. Persuade Bauer to feature the products in a Wednesday newspaper ad.

3. Introduce Bauer to the Rabun products and obtain at least one facing per product on a trial basis.

During the sales call, the following conversation took place:

JACK   "Hi, Bob. How are you?"

BOB   "Doing well, Jack. Can always do better, of course."

JACK   "Of course, and that's why I'm here, Bob. Spring, as you know, is the time when many people do a lot of cleaning. And to help them do that and to make you money, Jackson has developed a "Spring Cleaning" promotion that will include an FSI and a special display for those stores that feature the products. Because of your success with last year's spring promo, I wanted to visit you first."

BOB   "Refresh my memory. I don't remember last spring as being all that good."

JACK   "As you recall, we set up an end-of-aisle display and gave you a promotional allowance that you passed on to your customers. Coupled with our national advertising, you were able to increase your margin on the products by 5 percent, sold out all of the 30 cases in the display during the first 10 days of the promotion in each store, and enjoyed revenue of over $700."

BOB   "Will there be coupons in this year's FSI?"

JACK   "Yes, Bob, a 25-cent coupon for each of Jackson's cleaning products."

BOB   "Jack, I really don't like coupons. They slow the checkers down and hold up the lines."

JACK   "I know you don't, Bob, but it turns out that coupon users spend an average of $32 more than those who don't use coupons. *[hands Bob a chart comparing average purchases with coupons versus those without]* If you'll feature the products in your ads, you'll bring in those high-volume shoppers, plus we'll take off another $1.50 per case. How does that sound?"

BOB   "That sounds OK, but what do I need to do?"

JACK   "Nothing except give us the OK. I'll have a display sent to each of your stores, and all your stocker will have to do is move it to the end of the aisle, take the shrinkwrap off, and put up the sign that will be with the product. Plus I have an ad slick here for you to put in your ad on the Wednesdays during the promotion."

BOB   "OK, Jack, I think I'll go with that. When is the promotion again?"

JACK   "It's in three weeks."

BOB   "Sounds good. *[writes out a note]* Well, thanks for coming by. Give this to my secretary, and you'll get a purchase order."

JACK   "Great! I'm glad that you will work with us on this promotion. But I wanted to also visit with you about a new line of products."

BOB   *[interrupts]* "All you guys have a new line. The stores are crammed with your stuff already!"

JACK   "Well, I sometimes wish that were true. Then it would be easier for me to have our promotions running all the time!" *[laughs]*

BOB   *[smiles]* "You know what I mean."

JACK   "Anyway, the new products are personal care products. We've launched these with a significant television campaign. The brand name is Rabun, and Rabun is the second-leading personal care brand in Europe. We're confident that with the support of leading grocers like Bauer Brothers, Rabun will perform well in this country, too."

BOB   "Jack, this isn't Europe. You're up against the big guns here. I don't see how you can expect me to give you any space."

JACK   "I understand how you feel, Bob. Phil and Missy Thompson of Thompson Family Grocery felt the same way, but they tried Rabun before we started the TV campaign and were quite pleased with the sales."

BOB   "Do you have any information on the products? I would need to know how many SKUs you want, how it will affect the other products, and so forth."

JACK   "I thought you might want that information, so I prepared this proposal. It shows the line of Rabun products, suggested retail, your cost, and your margin. If you'll authorize one facing per product, I believe you'll see a turnover rate of greater than two cases per month for each product."

BOB   "Sounds good, Jack, but I haven't seen the TV campaign. I think I'll wait a while on this one."

JACK   "I can appreciate your desire to consider this carefully. What would it take for you to carry Rabun?"

BOB   "I don't know, Jack. I can't see any reason why anyone would want to buy these products."

JACK   "Rabun is positioned as a family line of products, with different products for different members of the family. For example, children's toothpaste needs are different than an adult's. Rabun's toothpaste has a single adult pack, a single child pack, and a combo pack with a tube for Mom and Dad and a tube for the children in one box. That's just one example of the innovative packaging for Rabun."

BOB   "I still don't know, Jack. I think I'll pass until I see the TV campaign and hear some feedback from customers."

JACK   "While you think it over, Bob, I'd like you to try the Rabun line of products. Here's a sample pack for you and your family."

BOB   "Thanks, Jack. *[stands]* Thanks for coming by today."

JACK   *[also stands]* "Thank you for your time, Bob. I'm sure you will be very happy with the results of our Spring Cleaning promo. And next time I visit, I want to hear what you think of the Rabun products."

BOB   "Sure thing, Jack."

QUESTIONS

1. Identify how Jack proved sales for the Spring Cleaning promotion and evaluate his presentation.
2. Evaluate Jack's methods of handling objections and gaining commitment.
3. Why did Jack fail to obtain facings for the Rabun products? What should he have done differently?
4. What should Jack do now?

CASE 15 • 3
THE BIG PUSH

Bright and early on a Monday morning, Tim Wagner found himself in the upstairs room at Cupp's, a local breakfast establishment. Tim is a part-time campus rep for Stereo Town, selling stereos and other electronics to other students. Recently, he closed a big sale with the Sociology department with the help of Pam, his store manager. They sold over $100,000 of Panasonic video equipment to the school.

This morning, all of the Stereo Town salespeople were there, along with Pam and the rep from Sharp, for a rare Monday morning sales meeting. Breakfast was on Sharp, and Tim found himself enjoying the eggs and bacon that he never seemed to have time to make for himself.

Near the end of the meal, the Sharp rep stood up at the head of the table. "Thank you all for coming here so early in the morning," she began, and was interrupted by a chorus of thank yous for the breakfast from the salespeople. "Oh, you are all very welcome. The reason I asked Pam to bring you all together is because Stereo Town has long been a strong retailer for me and for Sharp products and I wanted to first offer this breakfast as a thank you for all of your hard work. Second, I wanted to tell you personally of an exciting sales incentive campaign that we have for the next month."

She walked over to an easel that had a large flipchart. As she pulled over the blank first page to reveal Sharp's slogan, "From Sharp minds come Sharp products," she said, "As you know, Sharp has kept new products coming that have really helped you make a lot of money." She flipped the page and pointed to several enlarged product photographs. "Here are several new products that will be arriving in your store around Thanksgiving, just in time for the Christmas season." She described each one, and each description was followed by applause.

"But as you know, we'll need room on the shelves for these products. That's why my company has authorized the first direct incentive program ever for you, the Stereo Town salespeople." She flipped the page to uncover a large dollar sign.

"For each of the products on the list that Pam is passing out that you sell, Sharp will pay you an extra $25 spiff." The salespeople broke out into wild clapping and a few cheers. "And, every rep who earns $100 in spiffs will also earn 100 points that can be used to purchase merchandise in the prize catalog that Pam is passing out." She was interrupted again by cheers.

Flipping the page to a picture of a sunny tropical beach, she continued, "The top rep in my district as of December 1 wins, are you ready for this? A trip to the Bahamas!" The reps went wild.

The rest of the meeting involved strategies to switch customers from other products to Sharp, how to present features and benefits of various Sharp products, and all of the details involving the contest.

Three days later, Tim was in the store demonstrating a couple of stereos, a Sharp and a Moyashita. Pam had priced the Sharp so that it was now only a few dollars more than the Moyashita, to help the salespeople move the Sharp.

"Gee, Tim, I really like the looks of the Moyashita," said the customer. The Moyashita did have a more futuristic look than the Sharp's more traditional lines.

"That's true, Bill, but looks aren't everything. If I were you, I'd have the Sharp for the sound it produces."

"I just don't hear the difference."

"Well, it is your decision, Bill. So you want to take the Moyashita?" Tim asked. Bill nodded yes. Even with the sale, Tim was slightly disappointed. He was having some difficulty pushing those Sharps compared to some of the other salespeople.

A couple of weeks later, the Panasonic rep called Tim at home. After some small talk and questions about the new video center in the Sociology department, he asked Tim why sales were down at Stereo Town.

"Have you talked to Pam about that?" Tim asked.

"Yes, but I don't get a straight answer. I get the feeling she's hiding something."

"Well, we're having a contest on some other products," admitted Tim.

"Hmm. I wonder what it would take to make Panasonic a player. Well, thanks Tim. And sell a few Panasonics, okay?"

"Sure thing," replied Tim. After he hung up, he thought about the contest. He got out the catalog and leafed through it, thinking about what he wanted to win.

QUESTIONS

1. Did Tim do anything unethical in the above scenario?

2. Strategically, why is Sharp using the promotion program? What other reasons would cause them to use a push program?

3. Why would Pam agree to it? How would it affect her relationships with other vendors?

4. Based on the success with the Sociology department, the Panasonic rep believed he was building a partnership with Pam and Stereo Town. Now, he's not so sure. What should he do?

ADDITIONAL REFERENCES	Berman, Barry, and Joel R Evans. *Retail Management: A Strategic Approach.* New York: Macmillan, 1989.

Candler, Julie. "How to Choose a Distributor." *Nation's Business,* August 1993, pp. 45–46.

"Donnelly Reports Account-Specific Increase in Promotion Spending." *Sales and Marketing Strategies & News,* July–August 1993, p. 35.

Hawes, John M; Kenneth E Mast; and John E Swan. "Trust Earning Perceptions of Sellers and Buyers." *Journal of Personal Selling and Sales Management,* Spring 1989, pp. 1–8.

Hoyt, Christopher W. "Co-Marketing Joins Marketing Lexicon." *PROMO: The International Magazine for Promotion Marketing,* March 1993, p. 90.

_____. "Co-Marketing Questions & Answers." *PROMO: The International Magazine for Promotion Marketing,* August 1993, p. 44.

Miller, Craig. "What Do Retailers Really Want?" *Potentials in Marketing,* June 1993, p. 36.

Schultz, Don E. *Strategic Advertising Campaigns.* Lincolnwood, Ill.: NTC Business Books, 1990.

Sharma, Arun. "The Persuasive Effect of Salesperson Credibility: Conceptual and Empirical Examination." *Journal of Personal Selling and Sales Management,* Fall 1990, pp. 71–80.

Smith, Kerry E. "Trade Promotion vs. Trade Spending, Part I." *PROMO: The International Magazine for Promotion Marketing.* February 1993, pp. 10–14, 32, 75.

_____. "Trade Promotion vs. Trade Spending, Part II." *PROMO: The International Magazine for Promotion Marketing,* March 1993, pp. 52–56.

Whittemore, Meg. "Trade Shows' Direct Appeal." *Nation's Business,* August 1993, pp. 48–50.

SALESPERSON AS MANAGER

*T*his section discusses a little-known but very important element of the profession of selling. Salespeople, by the very nature of their jobs, are managers, too. As you can see by the circle diagram, salespeople must manage their territory and their time, manage the resources within their company, and manage their careers. In Chapter 16 we discuss techniques that salespeople use to manage their time and other resources effectively. Chapter 17 presents many of the company resources that salespeople manage, and discusses methods of building internal partnerships to deliver superior customer satisfaction. In Chapter 18 you will learn valuable lessons for managing your career, beginning with how to get your career started. Even if you choose a career or initial job outside of sales, you will find the information in this section useful for improving your effectiveness.

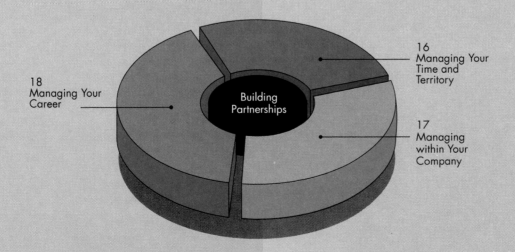

Managing Your Time and Territory

M any salespeople work in the field, their only contact with the office by telephone, computer, and fax. Because no one tells them when to start working or when to quit for the day, they must be self-sufficient. Their success or failure depends on their own efforts.

Salespeople have more individual freedom than almost any other type of employee. With that freedom comes the responsibility to manage themselves. Self-management involves using their scarcest resource, time, so that they get the most out of their other resources, their customers, and their skills.

Some questions answered in this chapter are:

How should territories be managed?

Why is time so valuable for salespeople?

What can you do to "create" more selling time?

What should you consider when devising a territory strategy?

How should you analyze your daily activities and your sales calls?

How do salespeople evaluate their own performance so that they can improve?

Time and account management really became important to Bill Arend, sales representative for SOS Technology, when he was working on the company's largest single sale. His company sells emergency response training and equipment to companies. While OSHA requires companies to have trained CPR and first-aid personnel on site, some managers don't recognize the need for full service, such as that provided by SOS. Such was the case with this account. The company had 59 locations around the country, and SOS had placed units in only 6. Bill walked in thinking he was going to easily add the other 53 when the customer said, "Bill, it appears from this Department of Labor memo that I don't have to have your equipment. In fact, it may be illegal. So I'd like to cancel all of our locations that have SOS."

Bill's first reaction was to sell. But when he saw that memo, he realized trying to persuade the buyer that the memo was wrong was not the best approach. "What I did was promise to find out more about it, because I had never seen the memo before." So, just as if he was working on a term paper, Bill went to the Houston Public Library. Then he was up until after 2 AM, working on a 30-page proposal documenting that the Department of Labor memo referred to a different product and illustrating the need for SOS products and service in all 59 locations. "I felt like I was back in school, and about to take the hardest final exam of my life."

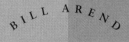

BILL AREND

SOS Technology

The bottom line was that the buyer believed in Bill's research. But then came the task of getting all 59 locations trained and the equipment installed as soon as possible. "The day after we trained the staff at one location, one of their customers had a heart attack. The staff was able to administer CPR and oxygen, saving his life," says Bill. "I hate to think what might have happened if I had put them off a day or two." Yet, that is the kind of total commitment that it takes to prioritize activities. "My customers know that when I promise to act, I will act. At the same time, I don't make promises for my time that I don't think I can keep," Bill states.

One of those promises is to himself and his wife. "Because your perfomance in sales is dependent on what you do, it is possible to allow yourself to be consumed by everything that could be done. So I have to constantly keep a balanced perspective by prioritizing activities with my wife and for myself."

This balanced approach must be working. Only 11 months after graduating from college, Bill was promoted to general sales manager, responsible for hiring, training, and managing some people twice his age. "It is a challenge, but a good one. Perhaps the toughest aspect, though, is simply finding enough time."

Many salespeople view their sales job as if they were running their own small business. Like independent business owners, they have the freedom to establish marketing programs, advertising, and sales strategies while ringing up sales. For example, Gary Wolfe sells chemicals. He has the responsibility for deciding how his company's products will be advertised and promoted in central Texas, his territory. He arranges seminars for his prospects and he is responsible for booking booth space at local business trade shows. Gary also decides which products to emphasize, the types of companies he will visit, and the strategies he will use to entice buyers to switch to his products. Just like the owner of a small business, Gary allocates marketing resources to generate the highest profit.

But just like a small business owner, Gary also has many demands on his time that can take away from selling activities. Filling out paperwork, learning new products, and performing similar duties can take up a great deal of time.

Managing time and territory is often a question of how to allocate resources. Allocating resources, like time, is a difficult management process that, when done well, often spells the difference between stellar and average performance. Many times, it is difficult to know what is really important and what only seems important. In this chapter, we will discuss how to manage your time. Building on what you have learned about the many activities of salespeople, we will also provide strategies for allocating resources among accounts, or managing your territory.

THE SELF-MANAGEMENT PROCESS

There are four stages to the self-management process in selling. The first stage is setting goals, or determining what is to be accomplished. The second stage is allocating resources and determining strategies so those goals can be met. In the third stage, the salesperson implements the time management strategy by making sales calls, sending direct mail pieces, or ex-

Sales managers often ask salespeople to publicly state their sales goals because these managers recognize the importance of setting personal sales objectives.

Photo courtesy GMAC Financial Services.

E X H I B I T   16.1

THE SELF-MANAGEMENT
PROCESS

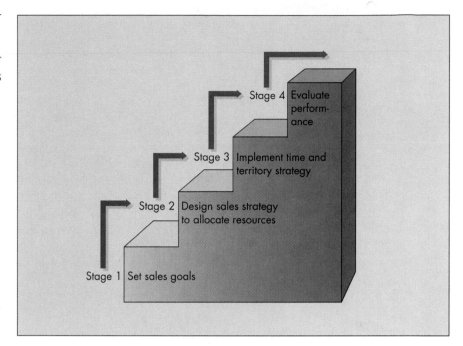

ecuting whatever action the strategy calls for. In the fourth and final stage, the salesperson evaluates performance to determine if the goals will be reached and the strategy was effective or if the goals cannot be reached and the strategy must change. This process is illustrated in Exhibit 16.1 and will serve as an outline for this chapter.

SETTING GOALS

NEED FOR GOALS

The first step in managing any worthwhile endeavor is to consider what makes it worthwhile and what you want to accomplish. Salespeople need to examine their careers in the same way. Career goals and objectives should reflect personal ambitions and desires, so that the individual can create the desired sort of lifestyle, as illustrated in Exhibit 16.2. When career goals reflect personal ambitions, the salesperson is more committed to achieving those goals.

To achieve career objectives, sales goals must be set. These sales goals provide some of the means by which personal objectives can be reached. Sales goals also guide the salesperson's decisions as to which activities to perform, when to perform those activities, whom to see, and how to sell.

The salesperson without goals will drift around the territory, wasting time and energy. Sales calls will not relate to any objectives and could be minimally productive or even harmful to the sales process. The result will be poor performance and, eventually, the need to find another job.

In Chapter 8, you learned that salespeople should set visionary, primary, and minimum call objectives so that the activities during the call would serve the purpose of bringing them closer to those objectives. The same can

E X H I B I T   16 . 2

THE RELATIONSHIP
OF GOALS
Career goals are devised from
lifestyle objectives. Sales goals
should reflect career goals.
While activities lead to sales,
performance goals are usually
set first. Then using
conversion goals, activity
goals are set.

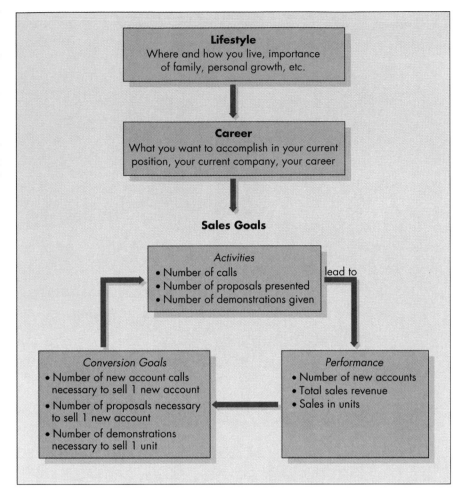

be said for setting sales goals. When sales goals are set properly and ad-
hered to, the salesperson has a guide to direct activities.

NATURE OF GOALS

As you read in Chapter 8, goals should be specific and measurable, reachable yet challenging, and time-based. Goals should be *specific and measurable* so that you know when they have been met. For example, setting a
goal of making better presentations is laudable, but how would the salesperson know if the presentations were better or worse? A more helpful goal
would be to increase the number of sales resulting from those presentations. The best goal would be a specific increase, such as 10 percent. Then
there would be no question in the salesperson's mind as to the achievement of the goal.

Goals should also be *reachable, yet challenging.* One purpose of setting
goals for yourself is to motivate yourself. If goals are reached too easily,
then little is accomplished. Challenging goals, then, are more motivating.
But if the goals are too challenging, or if they are unreachable, then the
salesperson may give up.

EXHIBIT 16.3

GOAL CALCULATIONS

Monthly earnings goal (performance goal):	$2,000
Commission per sale:	$ 250
$2,000 earnings ÷ $250 per sale = 8 sales	
Monthly sales goal (performance goal):	8
Closings goal (conversion goal):	10%
8 sales × 10 prospects per sale = 80 prospects	
Monthly prospect goal (performance goal):	80
Prospects per calls goal (conversion goal):	1 in 3
80 prospects × 3 calls per prospect = 240 calls	
Monthly sales calls goal (activity goal):	240
240 calls ÷ 20 working days per month = 12 calls	
Daily sales calls goal (activity goal):	12

Goals should also be *time-based*, that is, the goals should have deadlines. Putting a deadline on the goal provides more guidance to the salesperson and creates a sense of urgency that can be motivating. Without a deadline, the goal is not specific enough and the salesperson may be able to drag on forever, never reaching the goal but thinking that progress is being made. Imagine the motivational difference in setting a goal of a 10 percent increase in sales with no deadline versus a goal of a 10 percent increase for the next month. In the first instance there is no sense of urgency, of needing to work toward that goal *now*. Without a deadline, the goal has little motivational value.

THINKING IT THROUGH	**W**hat types of goals have you set for yourself in your college career? For specific classes? How would these goals meet the criteria of specific and measurable, reachable yet challenging, and time-based?

ESTABLISHING SALES GOALS

Salespeople need to set three types of sales goals: performance, activity, and conversions. While many salespeople focus only on how many sales they get, setting all three types of goals is necessary to achieve the highest possible success.

Performance Goals

Goals relating to outcomes are **performance goals.** In sales, outcomes such as the size of a commission or bonus check, the amount of sales revenue generated or number of sales generated, and the number of prospects identified are common performance goals. For example, the rep in Exhibit 16.3 set a performance goal of $2,000 in commissions and another performance goal of eight sales. Revenue quotas are an example of goals set by the company, but each salesperson should also consider setting personally relevant goals. For example, you may want to set higher goals so that you can achieve higher earnings. People are more committed to achieving goals they set themselves. That commitment makes achieving them more likely. Performance goals should be set first, because attaining certain performance levels is of primary importance to both the organization and the salesperson.

Performance goals can also be less quantifiable, such as setting a goal of improving your presentation skills. But even that type of goal should be measurable in terms of how many customers agreed to buy. Personal development goals, such as improving presentation skills, are important to long-term professional growth. Every person, whether in sales or other fields, should have some personal development goals. Not only will reaching these goals improve overall job performance, but personal satisfaction will also increase. But like all performance goals, these goals should meet the criteria of being specific, challenging, and time-based.

Activity Goals

Salespeople also set activity goals. **Activity goals** are behavioral objectives: the number of calls made in a day, the number of demonstrations performed, and so on. Activity goals reflect how hard the salesperson wishes to work. The company may set some activity goals for salespeople, such as a quota of sales calls to be made each week. In Exhibit 16.3, two activity goals are listed: 240 sales calls per month and 12 per day.

All activity goals are intermediate goals; that is, achieving them should ultimately translate into achievement of performance goals. As David Fields, vice president of sales for Zellerbach, a Mead company (a distributor of paper products), says, "You can't do sales. You do activities that generate sales." Activity goals help you know what activities you have to do in order to ultimately achieve your performance goals.

But activity goals and performance goals are not enough. For example, a salesperson may have goals of achieving 10 sales and making 160 calls in one month. The salesperson may get 10 sales but make 220 calls. That salesperson had to work much harder than someone who managed to get 10 sales in only 160 calls. That is why salespeople should also set conversion goals.

Conversion Goals

Conversion goals are measures of salesperson efficiency. Conversons reflect how efficiently the salesperson would like to work, or be working smarter. Unlike performance goals, conversion goals express *relative* accomplishments, such as the number of sales relative to the number of calls made, or the number of customers divided by the number of prospects. The higher the ratio, the more efficient the salesperson is. Exhibit 16.3 lists two conversion goals: closing 10 percent of all prospects and finding one prospect for every three calls. In our example above, a rep who made 10 sales while making 160 calls could sell 4 or 5 more if making 220 calls.

Conversion goals are important because they reflect how efficiently the salesperson uses resources, such as time, to accomplish performance goals. For example, Freeman Exhibit Company builds custom trade show exhibits. Customers often ask for booth designs (called *speculative designs*) before the purchase is made in order to evaluate the offerings of various competitors. Creating a custom booth design is a lot of work for a designer and the cost can be high. If a salesperson has a low conversion rate for speculative designs, then overall profits will be lowered because the cost for the unsold designs must still be covered. If the rep can increase the conversion rate, then the overall costs for unsold designs is lower, increasing profits.

As was mentioned earlier in the book, salespeople can choose to work smarter or harder (or both). Working smarter should be reflected in conversion goals. For example, a salesperson may be performing at a conversion rate of 10 percent. A **conversion rate** resembles a batting average; it is calculated by taking the number of sales and dividing by the number of calls. (Conversion rates can also be calculated for the number of cold calls necessary to identify a prospect, the number of demonstrations closed divided by the number of demonstrations given, etc.) Reaching a conversion goal of 12 percent (closing 1 out of 8 instead of 1 out of 10) would reflect some improvement in the way the salesperson operates—some method of working smarter. Working harder would involve the actual performing of activities (e.g., making more calls).

From a salesperson's personal perspective, it is important to remember that the salesperson has limited time to make sales calls. Using that time in the best manner can mean the difference between success and failure. Salespeople want to engage in the activities most likely to lead to success; measuring conversions tells them which activities those are. For example, a salesperson may have two sales strategies. If A generated 10 sales and B generated 8 sales, the salesperson may think A is the better strategy. But if A required 30 sales calls and B only 20, the salesperson would be better off using strategy B. Thirty sales calls would have generated 12 sales with strategy B.

Performance and conversion goals are the basis for activity goals. Suppose a sale is worth $250 in commission. If a rep wants to earn $2,000 per month (a performance goal), then eight sales are needed each month. If the salesperson sees closing 1 out of 10 prospects as a realistic conversion goal, then a second performance goal results: The rep must identify 80 prospects to yield 8 closings. If the rep can identify one prospect for every 3 sales calls (another conversion goal), 240 sales calls (an activity goal) must be made. Assuming 20 working days in a month, the rep must make 12 sales calls each day (another activity goal). Thus, activity goals need to be the last type of goals set, because activity goals will be determined by the desired level of performance at a certain rate of conversion.

Even though the conversion analysis results in a goal of 12 calls each day, that conversion rate is affected by the strategy employed by the salesperson. Sales calls take time, which is one of many important resources that must be allocated properly in order to achieve sales goals. We discuss how resources are allocated in the next section.

ALLOCATING RESOURCES

The second stage of the time and territory management process is to develop a strategy that allocates resources properly. These resources are allocated to different sales strategies used with different types of accounts with the purpose of achieving sales goals in the most effective and efficient manner possible. The process of allocating resources is very important for Van Martin, salesperson for a construction company, as you can see in Selling Scenario 16.1.

RESOURCES TO BE ALLOCATED

Salespeople manage many resources. Some of these are physical resources, like free samples, demonstration products, trial products, brochures, direct mail budgets, and other marketing resources. Each of these physical resources represents a cost to the company, but to the salesperson, these are investments. Salespeople consider physical resources as investments because resources must be managed wisely in order to generate the best possible return. Although financial investments may return dividends or price increases, the salesperson's investments should yield sales.

In addition, a key resource that salespeople manage is time. Time is limited and not all of a salesperson's work time can be spent making sales calls. Some time must be spent in meetings, learning new products, preparing reports for management, and other nonselling duties. So it is important to manage time wisely. As we will discuss in the next chapter, salespeople also coordinate many of the company's other departments in order to serve customers well. Salespeople must learn how to allocate these resources in ways that generate the greatest level of sales.

WHERE TO ALLOCATE RESOURCES

The allocation of resources for salespeople is often a question of finding the customers or companies that are most likely to buy, then allocating selling resources to maximize the opportunity they offer. Just as you may have learned in principles of marketing, some market segments are more profitable than others. And just as the company's marketing executive tries to determine which segments are more profitable so that marketing plans can be directed toward those segments, salespeople examine their markets in order to allocate their selling resources. Maximizing the opportunity means finding profitable ways to satisfy the greatest number of customers. In this section, we discuss how to analyze the market so that you can identify potential customers who are most likely to buy, so that resources will be allocated properly.

ACCOUNT CLASSIFICATION AND RESOURCE ALLOCATION

Not all customers have the same buying potential, just as we learned earlier that not all sales activities have the same results. The salesperson has to concentrate on the most profitable customers and minimize effort spent with customers that offer little opportunity for profitable sales. The proportion of unprofitable accounts is usually greater than one would think.

SELLING SCENARIO

16.1

Selling in Two (or 20) Places at Once

In tough economic times, companies often downsize their work forces. Yet those who are left are required to maintain the high quality of work and results that had been achieved with larger staffs. Such is the case of Van Martin, vice president of business development at a large general contracting firm. His position involves locating prospective construction projects, negotiating contracts, and getting a chance to respond to RFPs. Initially, he was one of five national vice presidents in the marketing department. Over a period of three years, this number was reduced to one.

How does one person do the job of five? "I became more selective of the companies I spent my time with. I try to concentrate on quality companies that have multiple high-profile projects. I began categorizing prospective companies as top priority, secondary, and low probability," Van explained.

Once they are categorized, Van spends a lot of time researching his top prospects in order to gain as much knowledge about the companies and their decision makers as possible. Although he does a lot of this himself, what he can he delegates to his assistants and others in the company in order to have more time to build partnerships with clients.

To find new prospects, Van has established a strong network. After a good working relationship has been created with a person at one of these priority companies, this person becomes a great source for other potential prospects. "I refer to these key contacts as *network coaches.* They can coach me through the structure of their own companies as well as provide insight on other prospective companies. This networking is invaluable."

Van is able to maximize his face-to-face time with customers by using the telephone and writing letters. His first contact with a potential lead furnished by a network coach is often by telephone. Once he has made this initial contact, he follows up with a letter and a brochure. These letters lay the groundwork that gives his company the opportunity to make a proposal on any given service. Van then follows up with another telephone call.

"If you don't have the basic fundamentals down—good telephone, written, and communication skills, you'll never get the opportunity for a face-to-face meeting." Also, by using letters and the telephone to find out ahead of time what will be expected, meetings can be more beneficial. It is important that Van do research on the client and company to find out their background and assess their needs and requirements. The all-important meeting with a prospective client is the start of building a partnership with him or her, and is more productive because of that research.

Van must then write a proposal for a project. That proposal describes the firm's "partnership attitude"—their belief that they operate as partners with the property owner, developer, financing companies, architects, and others involved in a project. His company wins bids not because they are the low bidder (they are not), but because this partnership attitude is real and reduces many risks for the property owner.

Says Van, "Thanks to the telephone, mail, and fax, I can make this strategy work." And worked it has. Van's company has continued to grow, even though Van is the only business development officer left.

As a rule, 80 percent of the sales in a territory come from only 20 percent of the customers. Therefore, salespeople should classify customers on the basis of their sales potential to avoid spending too much time and other resources with low-potential accounts, so that they can achieve their sales goals.

Computer software, such as ACT!, can be used to analyze an account's history (left) and plan future sales activities (right).

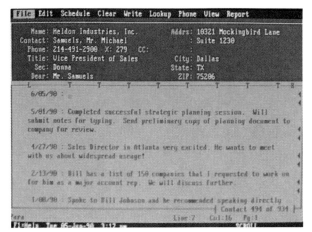

Courtesy of Symantec.

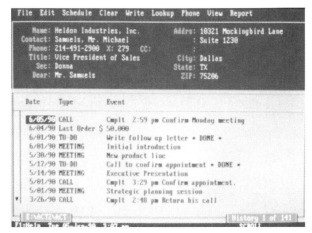

Courtesy of Symantec.

Customer management is not just a time management issue. Managing customers includes allocating all of the resources at the rep's disposal in the most productive manner. Of these resources, time may be the most important, but salespeople also manage sample and demonstration inventories, direct mail budgets, printed materials, and other resources.

ABC Analysis

The simplest classification scheme, called **ABC analysis,** ranks accounts by sales potential. The idea is that the accounts with the greatest sales potential deserve the most attention. Using the 80/20 rule, the salesperson identifies the 20 percent of accounts that (could) buy the most and calls those A accounts. The other 80 percent are B accounts, and noncustomers (or accounts with low potential for sales) are C accounts. This is how Marion/Merrell Dow classifies physicians, and how Johnson Wax classifies retail stores. Federal Express studied buying habits of their customers and realized that 1 percent of their accounts generated 50 percent of their revenue—they might call these A++ accounts! An example of an account analysis appears in Exhibit 16.4. As you can see, Sam Thompson has used estimated potential to classify accounts so that he can allocate sales calls to those accounts with the greatest potential.

Classification schemes can be used to generate call plans. Marion/Merrell Dow salespeople call on A physicians every two weeks, B physicians every six weeks, and on C physicians only when they have nothing else to do (which is rare). This way, they spend the most time with physicians who are heavy users of their products and account for the highest sales levels. ABC classification schemes only work well in industries that require regular contact with the same accounts, such as consumer package goods and pharmaceuticals. Some industries (e.g., plant equipment, medical equipment, and other capital products) may require numerous sales calls until

EXHIBIT 16.4   ACCOUNT CLASSIFICATION

Salesperson: Sam Thompson		A. Analysis of Call Pattern: 1994			
Customer Type	Number of Customers Contacted	Number of Calls	Average Calls per Customer	Sales Volume	Average Sales per Call
A	16	121	7.0	$212,516	$1,756
B	21	154	7.3	116,451	756
C	32	226	7.0	78,010	345
D	59	320	5.4	53,882	168
Total	128	821		$460,859	561

B. Annual Territory Sales Plan (dollars in thousands)

Account	Actual Sales			Estimated Potential	1995 Forecasted Sales	Number of Calls Allocated	Classification
	1992	1993	1994				
Allied Foods	$100	$110	$160	$250	$160	48	A
Pic N–Save	75	75	90	300	115	48	A
Wright Grocers	40	50	60	175	90	24	B
H.E.B.	20	30	30	150	30	24	B
Piggly Wiggly	10	10	25	100	55	18	C
Sal's Superstore	0	0	30	100	80	18	C
Buy-Rite	0	0	0	80	75	18	C
Tom Thumb	0	10	20	75	70	18	C
Apple Tree	0	5	12	60	60	12	D
Buy Lo	0	0	10	60	50	12	D
Whyte's Family Foods	10	8	9	50	40	12	D

the product is sold. After that sale, another sale may be unlikely for several years, and the number of sales calls may diminish. Then A, B, and C classification may not be very helpful.

Salespeople in some industries find grid and market analysis methods more useful than ABC analysis. They have learned that simply allocating sales activities on the basis of sales potential may lead to inefficiencies. For example, satisfied customers may need fewer calls to maximize great potential than accounts of equal potential that are loyal to a competitor.

Grid Analysis

The **sales call allocation grid** classifies accounts on the basis of the company's competitive position with an account along with the account's sales potential. Like ABC analysis, the purpose of classifying accounts using grid analysis is to determine which accounts are worth receiving more resources. Using this method, each account in a salesperson's territory falls

EXHIBIT 16.5

SALES CALL ALLOCATION GRID

		Strength of Position	
		Strong	**Weak**
Account Opportunity	**High**	**Segment 1** Attractiveness: Accounts are very attractive because they offer high opportunity, and the sales organization has a strong position. Sales call strategy: Accounts should receive a high level of sales calls because they are the sales organization's most attractive accounts.	**Segment 2** Attractiveness: Accounts are potentially attractive because they offer high opportunity, but the sales organization currently has a weak position with accounts. Sales call strategy: Accounts should receive a high level of sales calls to strengthen the sales organization's position.
	Low	**Segment 3** Attractiveness: Accounts are somewhat attractive because the sales organization has a strong position, but future opportunity is limited. Sales call strategy: Accounts should receive a moderate level of sales calls to maintain the current strength of the sales organization's position.	**Segment 4** Attractiveness: Accounts are very unattractive because they offer low opportunity, and the sales organization has a weak position. Sales call strategy: Accounts should receive minimal level of sales calls and efforts made to selectively eliminate or replace personal sales calls with telephone sales calls, direct mail, etc.

Source: Raymond W. LaForge, Clifford E. Young, and B. Curtis Hamm, "Increasing Sales Productivity through Improved Sales Call Allocation Strategies," *Journal of Personal Selling and Sales Management,* November 1983, pp. 53–59.

into one of the four segments shown in Exhibit 16.5. The classification is determined by the salesperson's evaluation of the account on the following two dimensions:

1. The **account opportunity** dimension indicates how much the customer needs the product and whether it is able to buy the product. Some factors the salesperson can consider when determining account opportunity are the account's potential, growth rate, and financial condition. This rating is similar to the ABC analysis and is a measure of total sales potential. Again, the idea is that accounts with the greatest potential deserve the greatest resources.

2. The **strength of position** dimension indicates how strong the salesperson and company are in selling the account. Some factors that determine strength of position are present share of account's purchases of the product, attitude of account toward the company and salesperson, and relationship between the salesperson and the key decision makers in the account. The strength of position helps the salesperson understand what level

of sales are *likely* in the account. The account opportunity may be tremendous, say $1 million. But if the account has always purchased another brand, your strength of position is weak and your real potential is something much less than $1 million.

The appropriate sales call strategy depends on the grid segment into which the account falls. Accounts with high potential and a strong position are very attractive, because the salesperson should be able to sell large amounts relatively easily. Thus, these attractive accounts should receive the highest level of sales calls. For example, if you have an account that likes your product, has established a budget for your product, and you know they need 300 units per year, then you may consider that a Segment 1 account (assuming that 300 units is a high number) and plan to allocate more calls to that account.

But if competition has a three-year contract with the account, the salesperson would be better off spending less time with that account. The account may buy 3,000 units per year, but you have little chance of getting any of that business. By classifying the account as a Segment 2, you would recognize that the most appropriate strategy is to strengthen your position in the account. The sales call allocation grid, then, aids salespeople in determining where, by account, to spend time in order to meet sales goals.

Market Analysis

Market analysis can be performed after the grid analysis. **Market analysis** is the evaluation of opportunity within segments in the overall territory (or market) in order to determine allocation of time and other resources. Market analysis is a process of looking for patterns in the types of accounts found in Segments 1 and 2 of the grid analysis, and can be helpful in determining prospecting and other selling efforts. For example, a Quickie's commercial print representative in Dallas found that training departments accounted for 25 percent of the Segment 1 accounts analyzed in the grid analysis, the most of any type of account. Training departments would then be a primary market for that rep, meaning that the rep should concentrate prospecting efforts on training departments.

The salesperson can then examine past experience with those Segment 1 accounts to plan for sales calls on similar accounts. Subsequent analysis of the Quickies rep's call reports pinpointed the primary decision maker and influencers in the typical training department, as well as reasons why they choose outside printing services. Resources such as time and direct mail dollars were then allocated to this market niche. The salesperson was able to create an effective sales presentation specifically for training departments and used it to capture over 60 percent of that market. Quickie's calls this approach *niche marketing* because the representative looks for **niches,** or small segments in the market with high potential and a strong position for Quickie's. For example, in Exhibit 16.6 the representative has listed the types of accounts in Segment 1. Two other niches seem to offer great opportunity for that rep, along with the training department niche. When used for niche analysis, the technique is especially helpful in determining where to prospect.

E X H I B I T   16 . 6

MARKET ANALYSIS EXAMPLE
Based on an assessment of
current accounts, this
salesperson has identified a
market niche—training
departments—with great
potential, and developed a
strategy to sell to training
departments in noncustomer
accounts.

Segment 1 Account Types (Number of Accounts)
Training departments (12)
Corporate attorneys/legal departments (8)
Marketing departments (7)
Miscellaneous (24)

Niche Analysis: Training Department Needs
1. Quality.
2. Binding.
3. Graphics and layout help.
4. Quick turnaround.
5. One to three major jobs per month.

Strategy
Use current corporate accounts and contacts to identify noncustomer training departments. Sell preferred copy account, use of graphics designer, and free binding.

Key Contact
Training director

INVESTING IN ACCOUNTS

Such planning as grid and market analysis should result in more effective use of the opportunity presented by accounts. This relates to the improved use of time, which is allocated to the appropriate accounts. But developing good strategies is more than developing good time-use plans; strategies require the use of other resources besides time.

Salespeople invest time, free samples or trials, customer training, displays, and other resources in their customers. For example, the Quickie's rep invested money in direct mail to training departments of certain corporations in her territory. Recall the free displays in the Dial brochure in Chapter 15, which were investments in launching new Moisturizing Dial. Pharmaceutical reps receive a limited number of free samples to distribute; account analysis enables them to use those samples where they should result in the largest sales. Market and grid analysis helps salespeople determine where to invest resources—samples, training aids, displays, and so forth. Sales costs, or costs associated with the use of such resources, are not always costs in the traditional sense but investments in an asset called customers. This asset generates nearly all of a corporation's revenue. Viewed from this perspective, formulating a strategy to allocate resources to maintaining or developing customers becomes much more important.

IMPLEMENTING THE TIME MANAGEMENT STRATEGY

Time is a limited resource. Once spent, it cannot be regained. How salespeople choose to use their time often means the difference between superstar success and average performance. In this section, we discuss the value of a salesperson's time and how to plan for its efficient use.

▍ VALUE OF TIME

The old axiom "Time is money" certainly applies to selling. If you work 8 hours a day for 240 days out of a year, you will work 1,920 hours that year. If you earn $30,000, each of those hours will be worth $15.63. An hour of time would be worth $20.84 if your earnings climbed to $40,000. Looking at your time another way, you would have to sell $208 worth of product per hour to earn $40,000 if you earned a 10 percent commission!

The typical salesperson spends only 920 hours in front of customers. The other 1,000 hours are spent waiting, traveling, doing paperwork, or in sales meetings. Thus, as a typical salesperson, you really have to be twice as good, selling $434 worth of products every hour in order to earn that $40,000 commission.

The lesson from this analysis is clear. Salespeople must make every hour count in order to be successful. Time is a resource that cannot be replaced if wasted. But salespeople can easily waste time; after all, no one really knows how they spend their time. They could be calling on customers or they might be playing tennis, taking extra coffee breaks, or engaging in social rather than business conversations with customers.

THINKING IT THROUGH	*H*ow do you plan your time now? How much of it do others schedule, and how much of it are you free to allocate? What do you do to make sure you spend your time wisely?

▍ DAILY ACTIVITY PLANNING

To be effective time planners, salespeople must have a good understanding of their own work habits. For example, some people tend to procrastinate in getting the day started, while others may want to knock off early. If you are a late riser, you may want to schedule early appointments to force yourself to get started. On the other hand, if your problem is heading for home too early, then schedule late appointments so that you work a full day. The salesperson in Exhibit 16.7 has scheduled an early appointment to get the day started.

Guidelines

Salespeople need to include time for prospecting and customer care in their daily activities. Some minimize the time for such activities because they think sales do not occur on such calls, but prospects and happy customers feed future sales. Columbia 300 (a leading manufacturer of bowling balls and related products) salespeople are required to handle customer care calls before 9 AM and after 4 PM, and to schedule prospecting activities between 10 AM and noon and between 2 PM and 3 PM. The remaining time is for scheduled appointments. The company bases these guidelines on its experience with buyers and when they are available.

Premier Industrial has a far different selling schedule. Its buyers are plant maintenance technicians who often arrive before the first shift, sometimes as early as 5:30 AM, to perform maintenance before the day's production

EXHIBIT 16.7   SAMPLE DAILY PLAN

Scheduling Worksheet

Day: __Wednesday__   Date: __June 2__   Location: __Cincinnati__

Hours	Appointments and Events	Type of Activity	Deadline	Estimated Time Involvement	Results Anticipated or Required
8:30	Jones Int'l	Sales call		60 min.	Make presentation to Dave Carey, VP eng. Demonstrate x35 tester.
10:00	D. Squares Systems	Service		20 min.	Drop off new catalog to Sue Jabbar in purchasing
10:45	Diamond Mfgr.	Sales call		15 min.	Deliver proposal to Jim O'hara in purchasing, Pick up order
11:15	Quad Distributor	Service		15 min.	Get OK to work with new sales people from Jill Conner
4:15	Write proposal for Wilkes Tool	Paperwork	Due 6/7	60 min.	Have manager review tomorrow morning.
5:15	Get sample for delivery tomorrow to Cube	Paperwork	.	5 min.	
5:20	Prepare schedule for tomorrow	Planning		30 min.	

begins. Premier expects its salespeople to begin prospecting at 5:30 AM, because buyers are available for cold calls at that hour.

Such planning guides are designed to maximize **prime selling time,** the time of day that a salesperson is most likely to see a buyer. That prime selling time will vary, depending on the industry of the buyer. For example, a good time to call on bankers is late afternoon, after the bank has closed to customers. But late afternoon is a bad time to call on physicians, who are then making rounds at the hospital or trying to catch up on a full day's schedule of patients. Prime selling time should be devoted to sales calls, with the rest of the day used for nonselling activities such as servicing accounts, doing paperwork, or getting information from the home office.

Prime selling time can also vary from country to country. In the US, prime selling time is usually 9 AM to 4 PM with the noon hour off for lunch. In Mexico, however, lunch starts later and ends much later, generally from 12:30 to 2:00 PM; offices may not close until 7 PM. In Great Britain, prime selling time starts later; a British Telecom rep may not begin making calls until 10 AM. Prime selling time depends on many factors, including the country you are in.

EXHIBIT 16.8

ACTIVITIES PLANNING
PROCESS

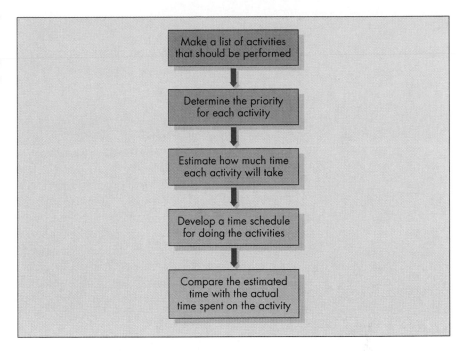

Planning Process

A process exists to help you plan your daily activities, with or without the aid of planning guides. This process can even help you now, as a student, take more control of your time and use it effectively.

As shown in Exhibit 16.8 you begin by making a to-do list. Then you determine the priority for each activity on your list. Many executives rank activities as A, B, or C, with A activities requiring immediate action, B activities being of secondary importance, and C activities being done only if time allows. You can correlate these A, B, and C activities to the A, B, and C accounts discussed earlier, as well as activities such as paperwork and training. Prioritizing activities helps you choose which activities to perform first.

Note, however, there is a difference between activities that seem urgent and activities that are important. For example, when the phone rings, most people stop whatever they are doing to answer it. The ringing phone seems urgent. Sometimes activities such as requests from managers or even customers may have that same sense of urgency—the desire to stop and drop everything to handle the request is called the "tyranny of the urgent." Yet, like most phone calls, those requests may not be as important as other tasks that must be done. Successful businesspeople learn to recognize what is truly urgent, and prioritize those activities first.

As the next step, estimate the time required for each activity. In a sales situation, as we mentioned earlier, time must be set aside for customer care and prospecting. The amount of time depends on the activity goals set earlier and how long each call should take. But salespeople often have unique activities such as special sales calls, demonstrations, customer training, and sales meetings to plan for as well. Time must also be set aside for planning and paperwork.

Your next step, developing an effective time schedule, requires estimating the amount of time such activities will require. Be sure, as a follow-up, to compare how long an activity actually took with how long you thought it would take. Such comparisons can help you plan more accurately in the future.

Need for Flexibility

Although working out a daily plan is important, times will arise when the plan should be laid aside. You cannot accurately judge the time needed for each sales call, and hastily concluding a sales presentation just to stick to a schedule would be foolish. If more time at one account will mean better sales results, then the schedule should be revised.

To plan for the unexpected, you should schedule a visit to the prime prospect first. In the terms discussed earlier, this would be an A account or activity. Then the next best potential customer should be visited (providing the travel time is reasonable), and so forth. If an emergency causes a change of plans, at least the calls most likely to result in sales have been made.

▌ MAKING MORE CALLS

Making daily plans and developing efficient routes are important steps toward better time use. But think if you could make just one more call per day. Using our analysis from the beginning of this chapter and Exhibit 16.3, this would mean 240 more calls per year, which is like adding one more month to the year!

Some salespeople develop an "out Tuesday, back Friday" complex. They can offer many reasons why they need to be back in the office or at home on Monday and Friday afternoons. Such a behavior pattern, however, means the salesperson makes 20 to 30 percent fewer calls than a salesperson who works a full week.

To get the most out of a territory, the sales representative must make full use of all available days. For example, the days before or after holidays are often seen as bad selling days. Hence, while your competition takes those extra days off, you can be working and making sales calls they would miss. The same reasoning applies to bad weather—bad weather reduces competition and makes things easier for the salesperson who doesn't find excuses to take it easy.

Salespeople can use certain techniques to increase the time they spend in front of customers selling instead of traveling. These are routing and zoning techniques.

Routing

Routing is a method of planning sales calls to minimize travel time. Two types of sales call patterns, routine and variable, can be more efficient with effective routing. Using **routine call patterns,** a salesperson sees the same customers regularly. For example, Marion/Merrell Dow pharmaceutical salespeople's call plans enable them to see all important doctors in their territory at least once each six weeks. Certain types of doctors (those that see large numbers of certain types of patients) may be in the plan to be visited every two weeks. The salesperson repeats the pattern every six weeks, ensuring the proper call level.

Variable call patterns occur when the salesperson must call on different accounts. Routing techniques are useful, but the salesperson may not repeat the call plan on a cyclical basis.

The four types of routing plans, **circular routing, leapfrog routing, straight-line routing,** and **cloverleaf routing,** are illustrated in Exhibit 16.9. If a Marion/Merrell Dow rep used the cloverleaf method (with six leaves

E X H I B I T   16 . 9   TYPES OF ROUTING PLANS

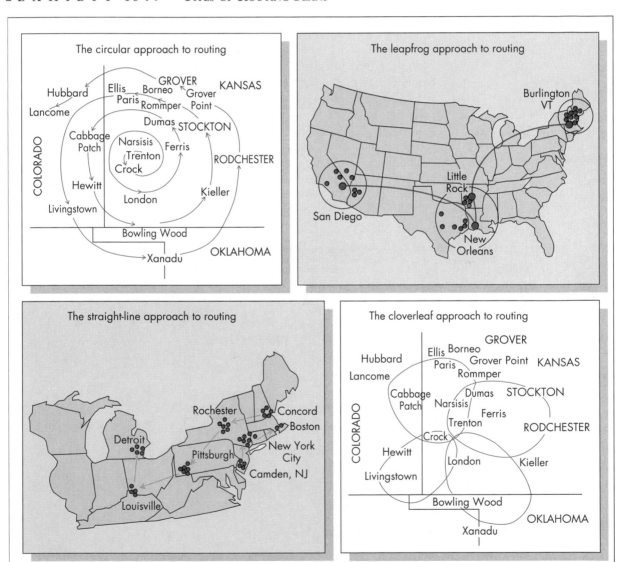

Source: Adapted from *Selling: The Personal Force in Marketing,* by W.J.E. Crissy, H. Cunningham, and Isabella Cunningham, Copyright 1977 by John Wiley & Sons, Inc. New York.

instead of four) for a routine call pattern, every sixth Tuesday would find that salesperson in the same spot. But a salesperson with variable call patterns could use the cloverleaf method to plan sales calls for an upcoming week, and then use straight-line the next week. The pattern would vary depending on the demands of the customers and the salesperson's ability to schedule calls at convenient times.

Zoning

Zoning is dividing the territory into zones based on ease of travel and concentration of customers, in order to minimize travel time. First, the salesperson locates concentrations of accounts on a map. For example, an office supply salesperson may find that many accounts are located downtown, with other concentrations around the airport, in an industrial park, and in a part of town where two highways cross near a rail line. Each of those areas would be the center of a zone. The salesperson then plans to spend a day, for example, in each zone. If your territory were zoned like the one in Exhibit 16.10, you might spend Monday in Zone 1, Tuesday in Zone 2, and so forth.

Zoning works best for compact territories or for situations where salespeople do not call regularly on the same accounts. (In a large territory, such as the entire Midwest, a salesperson is more likely to use leapfrog routes, but the principle is similar.) By calling on customers that are in a relatively small area, travel time between calls can be minimized.

EXHIBIT 16.10

Zoning a Sales Territory
A salesperson may work in Zone 1 on Monday, Zone 2 on Tuesday, and so forth.

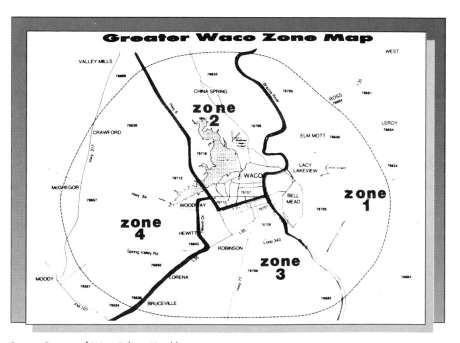

Source: Courtesy of *Waco Tribune-Herald*.

Salespeople can also combine zoning with routing, using a circular approach within a zone, for example. When zones are designed properly, travel time between accounts should be minimal.

Using Mail and Telephone

Customer contacts should not always be in-person sales calls. As many companies have learned, some sales objectives can be accomplished by the phone or through the mail. For example, some customer care calls can be handled by simply calling the customer and asking if everything is okay. The customer may appreciate the phone call more because it takes less time away from other pressing responsibilities. The salesperson may be able to make more customer care calls, increasing the number of contacts with customers. Keep in mind, though, that not all customer care should be handled by phone. As you recall from Chapter 13, there are many reasons, such as reorders and cross-selling, to continue to make sales calls in person to current customers.

Similarly, the telephone and direct mail can be used profitably when prospecting, as we discussed in Chapter 7. More calls, or customer contacts, can be made just as effectively with judicious use of the mail and telephone.

HANDLING PAPERWORK AND REPORTS

Every sales job requires preparing reports for management. All salespeople complain about such paperwork, but it is important. As we will discuss later, paperwork can provide information that helps a salesperson determine what should be improved. The information also helps management decide what types of marketing plans work and should be used again. Therefore, every salesperson should learn to handle paperwork efficiently.

Using waiting time to complete paperwork is efficient.

Kay Chernush/The Image Bank.

Paperwork time is less productive than time spent selling to customers, so getting it completed in the least possible time is important. Salespeople can do several things to minimize the impact of paperwork on their prime selling time.

First, salespeople should think positively about paperwork. Although less productive than selling, it can increase their productivity and the productivity of the company's marketing programs by facilitating a detailed review of selling activities and marketing programs.

Second, salespeople should not let paperwork accumulate. We once knew of a salesperson who never did expense reports. He finally offered a summer intern 10 percent if she would complete his expense reports for the previous 12 months. This deal cost him $600, plus he was essentially lending the company $500 per month, interest free.

Routine reports should be completed daily. Nonproductive time (e.g., time spent waiting for a customer) can be used for paperwork. Call reports and account records should be updated immediately after the call so that important points are remembered and any follow-up actions can be planned.

Finally, salespeople should set aside a block of nonselling time for paperwork. It can be done quicker if one concentrates on it and avoids interruptions. Setting aside a small amount of time at the beginning or end of each day for writing thank-you and follow-up notes and completing reports saves prime selling time for selling activities while ensuring that you keep up with your paperwork.

USING THE COMPUTER IN SALES

Account Analysis

The latest generation of sales automation software products are designed to let the salesperson know where each account stands in the selling cycle. In Chapter 7, we discussed how accounts move through several stages, from lead to prospect to customer. These software products aid salespeople in determining which accounts are leads, which are prospects, and which are customers. The software can even be used to identify needs and recommend solutions.

For example, Paine Webber uses a software package that analyzes a prospect's financial condition, then recommends the appropriate types and levels of insurance. In the commercial insurance field, the information may need to be gathered over several sales calls. The computer is used to record the lead's answers. When enough information is gathered and entered into the computer, the software generates a proposal. Based on decision rules concerning the level of commitment by the buyer and activity in the account (such as how many people have been interviewed), the software classifies the account as a lead or a prospect.

BellSouth uses the Strategic Account Manager (Blackstone and Cullen, Atlanta, Georgia). With the aid of the computer, they diagram the account's organization chart, which is useful in understanding decision processes. In addition, the software keeps track of what each account purchases, notes the salesperson makes after each call, and personnel movement in the account. This account history is very useful in designing sales strategies.

Sales Reps Are More Productive with Computers

The sales department can be the most critical area in which speed and efficiency can be increased with automation. RealWorld Corp., a 10-year-old company in Concord, New Hampshire, was using a manual system of tracking prospects, creating reports, writing orders, and evaluating performance. Developing its own software, which it calls Sales Management Solutions, the company integrated activity reports, proposal creation, and the ability to generate orders. The package also interfaces with the accounting system so that reps can have commissions and expenses generated. Calendar features, including a tickler system, were also built into the package.

Before implementing the software for all 35 salespeople, the company tested one salesperson using the software against two who continued with the manual system. Over several months, the first rep increased revenues 22 percent. The other two showed increases of only 2 to 7 percent.

The software was made available to all salespeople only after training. Then they used both systems together for one month. Side-by-side comparisons of the efficiency of the two systems convinced the salespeople that the computer system was the best way to go. The results, in terms of sales, have confirmed their feelings. Since the system was installed, sales have increased 10 to 20 percent across the entire sales force.

Source: Sam Licciardi, "Paper-Pushing Sales Reps Are Less Productive," *Marketing News*, November 12, 1990, p. 15.

Minolta Business Systems compiles some of the data from its account management software in order to profile the overall market. For example, if they want to know the organization size most likely to buy a certain product, they can extract that information from the database of account records that were entered in by salespeople. Minolta can then use that profile to create a mailing or telemarketing campaign to noncustomers, introducing them to that product. Those noncustomers that respond are profitable leads for the field salespeople.

Scheduling

Many of the same account management programs that salespeople use to identify and analyze accounts incorporate time planning elements. This software can generate to-do lists and calendars through a tickler file or by listing certain customer types. A **tickler file** is a file or calendar that salespeople use to remember when to call specific accounts. For example, if Customer A said to call back in 90 days, the computer would remind ("tickle") the salesperson in 90 days to call that customer. Or if the company just introduced a product that can knock out Competitor B, then the computer can generate a list of prospects with products from Competitor B; the salesperson then has a list of prospects for the new product. As you can see in Selling Scenario 16.2, RealWorld developed its own computer system to manage schedules.

Paperwork

Many companies, such as IBM, provide their salespeople with laptop computers. These computers can be hooked up to the company's mainframe to access customer information and process other paperwork automatically. Salespeople who travel can then complete their paperwork while in a hotel, airport waiting area, and other places. Salespeople calling on accounts overseas can also file reports or check the status of orders even though the home office may be closed due to time zone differences.

Computers can help international selling organizations operate smoothly by reducing communication barriers between the field and home office. For example, IBM has a division headquartered in Austin, Texas, but has salespeople scattered around the globe. Salespeople in London, for example, can fax or send requests via computer for pricing, product information, order status, and so forth. The Austin office may receive those requests during the night, local time, and then respond to the requests first thing in the morning. The London salespeople receive their information via fax or computer without having to wait for the Austin office to open. Computers and fax machines add flexibility, enabling communication in spite of large differences in time.

Some account management packages include territory management capabilities. These packages allow salespeople to track their performance by calculating conversion rates, commissions, expenses, and other important figures.

Such technology enables salespeople to file reports more quickly. The Minolta Business Systems salespeople file their sales call reports via electronic mail, which are then used to create the database mentioned earlier. **Electronic mail (E-mail)** enables users to send documents from one computer to another over telephone lines (or other communication lines). Other

---

Technology such as pagers and laptops help salespeople maximize the use of their time in the field.

© 1991 Alan MacWeeney.

Sharon Hoogstraten

companies use facsimile (also called **fax**) machines to transmit reports, contracts, disputed bills, and other paperwork. Faxes have the advantage over electronic mail of being able to send documents to anyone who has a fax machine, while electronic mail requires that the receiver be part of the same computer network. Fax machines can also scan and send written documents, including signatures, that electronic mail cannot send.

To manage your time wisely, you must exploit a scarce resource in the most effective manner possible. Your objective is to make as many quality calls as possible by reserving prime selling time for selling activities. Routing, zoning, goal setting, and other methods of planning and scheduling time will help you maximize your prime selling time.

SUMMARY

A sales territory can be viewed as a small business. Territory salespeople have the freedom to establish programs and strategies. They manage a number of resources, including physical resources such as sample inventory, displays, demonstration equipment, and perhaps a company vehicle. More important, they manage their time, their customers, and their skills.

Managing a territory involves setting performance, activity, and conversion goals. Salespeople use these goals to allocate time to various activities and to manage customers.

To manage customers well, the salesperson must analyze their potential. Accounts can be classified using the ABC method or the sales call allocation grid. These analyses tell how much effort should be put into each account. Market analyses then help in identifying patterns within a territory. Salespeople can use these patterns to develop account sales strategies.

More calls (working harder) can be accomplished by pushing nonselling activities, such as paperwork, to nonselling time. Also, selling time can be used more efficiently. For example, routing and zoning techniques enable the salesperson to spend more prime selling time in front of customers instead of behind the steering wheel of a car.

Effective planning of your day requires that you set aside time for important activities such as prospecting and still make the appropriate number of sales appointments. Using the full workweek and employing technology such as telephones, computers, and fax machines can help you stay ahead of competition.

Finally, salespeople must also manage their skills. Managing skills involves choosing how to make sales calls and improving the way you sell. Improvement requires that you first understand what you do well and what needs improvement. Evaluating your performance can provide you with that insight.

KEY TERMS

ABC analysis   *498*
account opportunity   *500*
activity goals   *494*
circular routing   *507*
cloverleaf routing   *507*
conversion goals   *494*
conversion rate   *495*
electronic mail (E-mail)   *512*
fax   *513*
leapfrog routing   *507*
market analysis   *501*

niches   *501*
performance goals   *493*
prime selling time   *504*
routine call patterns   *506*
routing   *506*
sales call allocation grid   *499*
straight-line routing   *507*
strength of position   *500*
tickler file   *511*
variable call patterns   *507*
zoning   *508*

QUESTIONS AND PROBLEMS

1. After reading the material in this chapter, a salesperson protests: "That's no fun. I like to play tennis every other afternoon. If I have to hustle every minute of every day, then forget it. I'll get another job!" What would you tell this salesperson?

2. Many companies call their salespeople *territory managers* or *account managers*. Is this an accurate designation of their job? Why or why not? If not, when would it be an appropriate job title?

3. Compare and contrast the special problems of self-management for a computer salesperson who works in a computer store with those of a computer salesperson who only calls on customers in their offices.

4. Shakespeare wrote, "To thine own self be true." How would you apply this statement to your planning and development activities?

5. What factors are important for classifying customers? Why? How would these factors change depending on the industry?

6. Distinguish between routing and scheduling, and between routing and zoning. Explain how routing and scheduling can interact to complicate the planning of an efficient day's work.

7. How might a life insurance salesperson increase the number of calls made per day? A manufacturing equipment salesperson? An office supplies representative? A furniture manufacturing representative who sells to furniture stores?

8. Sales managers know that making more sales calls results in more sales. Should sales managers encourage salespeople to continually increase the number of calls made each week? Explain your answer.

9. What sales reports would you want to use if you were a salesperson? How would you use them? How could a computer help you with those reports?

10. Do you ever find yourself "burning the midnight oil" to study or to finish an assignment? What self-management principles could you use to avoid "all-nighters"?

CASE PROBLEMS

CASE 16 • 1
SCHEDULING SALES CALLS

Your company, Sierra Office Furniture, distributes several lines of office furniture. Yesterday you worked with another salesperson, Bill Briggs, in the hopes that you would learn something. The following exchanges typify what you observed.

AT H.L. MENCKEN CO.

> **BILL** *[to the facilities director]* "Kerry, we've got a new promotion for desks and chairs that I want to tell you about."

KERRY   "That sounds great, Bill. What's up?"
[45 minutes later]

KERRY   "Well, thanks for the information, Bill. I'll let you know if we decide to do anything."
Afterward, Bill said, "They placed about a $10,000 order two years ago, but I haven't gotten them to do anything since."

AT HOLMES MANUFACTURING

BILL   *[to the office administrator]* "Hi, Betty. We thought we'd stop in and see if you had that purchase order ready for the new filing cabinets."

BETTY   "Gee, Bill, I'm really swamped today, trying to get ready for a board meeting. You'll have to come back next week."
Afterward, Bill said, "Man, I've never seen a board that meets that much. Must be at least once a week."
AT AUSTIN MIRROR CO.

BILL   *[to the receptionist]* "We'd like to see the person that handles office furniture."

RECEPTIONIST   "I'm sorry, but she only sees salespeople on Friday mornings after 9."

AT SPRING CREEK FOODS

BILL   *[to the vice president of operations]* "Jack, as you recall, we set up this appointment to review your furniture requirements for the new Loganville center."

JACK   "Listen, I know we had an appointment, but I can only spare you about 15 minutes. Mondays are just that way."
Afterward, Bill said, "I wish my routing plan could get me here on another day; Mondays are always bad for him."

QUESTIONS

1. What does Bill need to learn about territory management?
2. How can a salesperson determine whether the time of sales calls is significant?

CASE 16 • 2
NORTHERN FARM
EQUIPMENT: A DAY WITH
A FARM EQUIPMENT
SALESPERSON

"We sell a lot of farm equipment throughout this river bottom area," said Bob Hart, sales representative for Lang Implement Company, the Northern Farm Equipment Company dealer in Quincy, Illinois. Hart's territory lies on both sides of the Mississippi, in Illinois and Missouri. He covers it in a Northern pickup truck so he can go right out to his prospects when they are working in the field. Hart often meets his customers in an open-collar shirt, a leather jacket, and a felt hat that he rarely removes. In fact, Hart usually dresses more like one of his customers than like a sales representative. He knows the problems of his customers, and he talks their language. He is proud of his ability to "run a tractor around a barnyard and tell pretty well by the sound whether or not the rear end is OK."
Hart has spelled out some of his ideas on selling farm equipment:

The first thing I do is get around to enough doors and barn lots to find a person interested in buying something. During this time of year, there may be weeks when

I'm never in the office except in the morning before I start out on my calls. If you expect to sell farm equipment, you have to go out to the customer. And I usually have plenty of customers to call on. I do, however, want to spend some time in the store. A person who tends to business in the store can sell a lot of equipment and get a good many leads for future action.

When you go to some farmers, you can sit and talk all day if you want; and then they'll invite you in for dinner. It's a great temptation to waste time this way when you're out in the country. When I drive into a place, I always assume the customer is as busy as I am, so 30 minutes is about as long as I stay. I follow a plan of talking business while I'm there, and when I see it's time to leave, I leave. Often, I stop at one place and find that my customer is not going to buy anything. But sometimes the customer will say, "Hart, you ought to go down the road and see Albert Fowler. He's planning on buying a new tractor. Now don't you tell him I told you, but I heard that the John Deere people were out there the other day." When I get a lead like this, instead of going directly to Fowler's place, if he's a next-door neighbor, I go down the road, and then maybe the next morning I stop at the Fowler farm. If he doesn't say anything about the tractor deal, I pass the time of day with him for a while. Then our conversation naturally drifts into a discussion about his tractor.

If customers want to buy something that I don't think they should buy because it doesn't fit their needs, I always try to talk them out of it. I may lose an immediate sale by doing this, but in the long run, I have found that this procedure pays big dividends. The only time I mention anything about a competitive tractor is when the customer brings the subject up first. I prepare myself for such an occasion by studying up on the literature of all competitive machines.

Whenever you try to talk about everything on a tractor, you get your customer confused. I usually stress one or two major features, such as fuel efficiency or the 24-speed transmission. After I get the customer sold on that, then I mention the hydraulic system, which has special features on our tractors.

When I drive from one customer's place to the next, I usually listen to the car radio. This is very helpful, as I always pick up the community news and the market information everybody is talking about. A lot of people will tell you that the price of hogs or cattle dropped off yesterday and they don't know if they ought to buy anything from you. But if you catch that market news, maybe you can answer right back that they went up 50 cents today.

By putting such selling techniques as these into practice, Bob Hart has helped Lang Implement Company stay in the running with the best of its seven competitors in Quincy.

Bob Hart drove 60 miles on March 4, spending the morning in Missouri and the afternoon in Illinois. He made eight calls and talked to two customers at the store. His efforts bore some fruit, but the day also produced its share of blind alleys and frustrations. Arriving at one stop, he learned that the farmer had gone into Quincy to see him. Efforts to find another farmer at the grain elevator ended in failure. He found Harvey Ireland ringing pigs and had to talk business with him above the pigs' shrill, incessant squealing. Ireland finally decided not to deal.

Right after lunch, Hart drove up to see Glenn Mugdalen (who was in partnership with his brother, Orville) about the possibility of trading for a baler. Glenn's wife, Martha, came out to meet him when she heard the dog bark.

BOB   "What do you have Glenn doing today?"

MARTHA   "Well, he's sowing clover seed."

BOB   "What's he doing sowing clover seed—as muddy as it is?"

MARTHA   "Well, I tell you, he looked like a mud turtle. But he's sowing clover seed."

BOB   "What have Orville and Glenn decided on that baler?"

MARTHA   "You go over and see Orville. Have you been over there?"

BOB   "No, I haven't."

MARTHA   "He has all the statistics, and I think when you get over there, you'll get your answer."

BOB   "Thank you a lot, Martha. I'll go right over to see Orville to find out what was decided on that baler."

Hart found Orville preparing to go into the fields with fertilizer. They passed the time of day before Bob got down to business:

BOB   "I stopped over at Glenn's and talked with Martha. She said you had all the answers about the baler."

ORVILLE   "Yes, sir. Well, I wish I did know all the answers about the baler."

BOB   "If you go ahead and trade balers with us now, it'll help us to get rid of the used one."

ORVILLE   "After thinking it over, we just kind of thought we'd be better off by having this one fixed."

BOB   "You want us to pick it up then?"

ORVILLE   "I believe so."

BOB   "We can pick it up any time. That's all right with us if you want to fix it and don't want to trade. And while we've got it down there fixing it, you might take a notion to go ahead and trade."

ORVILLE   "That's right. I believe that's about as good a way as any to do it."

BOB   "Another thing. I want to see what we can do on that tractor deal . . ."

But 15 minutes of earnest talk in Orville's barnyard failed to bring the two men to terms on anything but repairing the baler (although a few days later, Orville did buy a new fast hitch for his tractor).

Bob Hart's hit rate was considerably less than eight for eight on March 4. But every minute he wasn't on the road, he was selling. Bob made two sales on March 4. Both were corn planters. One of the buyers came to him at the store after he made a pitch at the farm. He made the other sale because he went out after it.

Bill Adams owns 400 acres near LaGrange, Missouri, about 12 miles from Quincy. Hart had talked to him before about buying a new eight-row planter, using his old John Deere planter as a trade-in. Hart had also agreed to sell Adams's old crawler for him. On the morning of March 4, Hart crossed the river to LaGrange and found Adams at the wheel of his Case-IH tractor, hauling feed.

The following conversation ended in a sale:

BOB   "You know what I stopped for. We're going to trade that John Deere corn planter for that new Northern."

BILL   "Just as soon as you sell that crawler."

BOB   "They pick it up yet?"

BILL   "Nope."

BOB   "Well, they're going to pick it up. Now listen. On that cash part of it, you know we're not going to worry about that. But corn planting may be over before we get that crawler sold, and you know you want that new planter. What do you say we trade this morning?"

BILL   "I have to get some cash—that's all there is to it."

BOB   "I know you haven't bought anything yet for which you haven't paid cash. But here's our point on the planter. What we're in a hurry for is to get the used one sold because you can wait too long and then you'll have to carry it over another year. That's when you lose money. How long would I have to carry you?"

BILL   "You might have to carry me till harvest."

BOB   "Aw, I don't think so. You know you're going to buy that planter."

BILL   "Oh, I can get by."

BOB   "Doggone it, I'd sure like to trade with you. I want to look at that planter of yours again."

At this point, Hart went into a shed to check the trade-in planter. When he came out, Adams waited while Hart returned to his pickup to do some figuring. The conversation began again when Hart finished.

BOB   "Well, here's what I'll do. I'll bring that new planter over here for $9,300."

BILL   "$9,300. Hmm. Let's see how you figured, Bob."

BOB   "That's putting a lot of money in your planter."

BILL   "You're taking that forage harvester in on that, aren't you, Bob—for $1,200?"

BOB   "No. Doggone it, I can't."
[short pause]

BILL   "You're still asking a lot of money, Bob."

BOB   "But that's giving you an awfully good deal on the planter, too, you must remember. If you keep yours, you're going to have to put runners on it. Six of them—that's $270. With this new one, you'd be getting a high-speed planter that will plant accurately."

BILL   "Is that a good hill-drop planter?"

BOB   "It sure is. It'll hill drop 211 hills a minute. In other words, if you're spacing 40 inches apart, it'll hill drop at 6 miles an hour and put 95 percent of the grain in a hole the size of a silver dollar. Also think of the productivity gain in upgrading from your current six-row unit to this eight-row. You'll cover one-third more with each pass."
[long silence while Bill Adams thinks it over]

BILL   "That's a lot of money, Bob. It's a good trade, but . . ." *[another long pause]*

BOB   "You can see our point. Here it is the fourth of March, and people are buying this equipment now. We don't want to wait around too long."
[another pause]

BILL   "Aw, I don't know. You always make me a good deal, Bob."

BOB   "Sure I do. Why don't you let me write the order this morning? Let's see, that price is \$14,500. I'm giving you \$5,200 on your planter. That's \$9,300 difference."

BILL   "By the time this thaw is over, I'm liable to have to put all that money for a planter into gravel for these roads."

BOB   "Well, you don't have to pay for that planter today. Tell me when you would pay for it."

BILL   *[pausing]* "Reckon I can get the job done with that planter?"

BOB   "I know you can, because we'll come out and get it started for you."

BILL   "Are you going to get somebody over here to get the fuel injectors on this tractor straightened out?"

BOB   "Sure, I'll get it fixed for you—get somebody out here right away. Can you pay me by April 15th? That wouldn't crowd you any, would it?"

BILL   "Give me until the 15th of May. That'll give me a chance to sell some of the bred heifers."

BOB   "OK, let me write it up."
[At this point, Bob begins to write]

BILL   "Better give me \$5,500 for my planter, Bob."

BOB   "I'm giving you \$5,200."

BILL   "Well, I know, but it looks so much better."

BOB   "Well, OK. You just sign here. And thanks a lot to you, Bill. I'm sure you'll be happy about it."

"The greatest thing we've got to sell is goodwill," Bob Hart says. "If we keep the customer's goodwill, we'll keep our fair share of the business. Courtesy calls pay real dividends in this business. About 80 percent of Lang Implement's sales are repeat business. The first sale to a person is a hard one to make. The next one comes easier, and the one after that even easier. By this time, the customers come back because they like the way they've been treated."

QUESTIONS

1. How well do you think Bob Hart utilized his time on March 4? What, if any, suggestions would you make to Bob to improve his efforts?

2. If you were Bob Hart, what criteria would you use to evaluate the effectiveness of your sales efforts in that territory?

ADDITIONAL REFERENCES

Carl, Robert L. "How a Salesperson Can Make More Profit—Stop Procrastinating." *American Salesman,* July 1989, pp. 10–13.

Clayton, Carl K. "How to Manage Your Time and Territory for Better Sales Results." *Personal Selling Power,* January 1990, p. 46.

Klein, Matthew H. "Move Over, Indiana Jones!" *Sales & Marketing Management,* February 1990, pp. 88–89.

Messer, Carla; Michael Lyons; and James Alexander. "Classifying Your Customers." *Sales & Marketing Management,* July 1993, pp. 42–43.

Parasuraman, A. "An Approach for Allocating Sales Call Effort. *Industrial Marketing Management,* Winter 1987, pp. 75–79.

PSP Editors. "Seven Thieves of Time That Can Steal Your Sales Away." *Personal Selling Power,* January 1990, pp. 48–49.

Sauers, Daniel A; James B Hunt; and Ken Bass. "Behavioral Self-Management as a Supplement to External Sales Force Controls." *Journal of Personal Selling and Sales Management,* Summer 1990, pp. 17–28.

Schiffman, Stephan. "Prospect Management: Avoiding the Ups and Downs of Sales." *American Salesman,* September 1989, pp. 3–5.

Sujan, Harish; Barton A Weitz; and Mita Sujan. "Increasing Sales Productivity by Getting Salespeople to Work Smarter." *Journal of Personal Selling and Sales Management,* August 1988, pp. 9–20.

Taylor, Thayer C. "From Selling Aid to Taskmaster." *Sales & Marketing Management,* May 1991, pp. 69–73.

Weeks, William A, and Lynn R Kahle. "Salespeople's Time Use and Performance." *Journal of Personal Selling and Sales Management,* Winter 1990, pp. 29–38.

Managing within Your Company

S alespeople, who manage and coordinate many elements of the firm's marketing mix, are often called territory managers. And of course they work with and can become sales managers. In this chapter, we explore how salespeople manage their work within their company to achieve their sales goals and create customer satisfaction.

As you read in the previous chapter, to be a successful salesperson requires that you manage time and territory. But success also requires that salespeople manage their company's resources to satisfy customers by coordinating the company's manufacturing, shipping, customer service, even the sales manager, in order to fulfill a customer's needs.

Some questions answered in this chapter are:

What areas of the company work with salespeople to satisfy customer needs?

How do salespeople coordinate the efforts of various functional areas of the company?

How do salespeople work with sales managers? With sales executives?

How do company policies, such as compensation plans, influence salespeople?

How do salespeople work within the company to resolve ethical issues?

What is the organizational structure and how does that influence salesperson activities?

Ron Williams, director of national accounts for Champion Products (makers of sports apparel), is a salesperson. The only thing is, he sells for the customer. "I find myself selling the needs of the customer to senior management, manufacturing, customer service, or merchandising every day."

When you only have a few accounts, and they are all key accounts like Foot Locker or JCPenney, Ron notes that you don't have the luxury of saying you can't take care of their problems, as they will go find someone else who will. For Ron, there is no one else. "That's why I am constantly proving to our executives or our manufacturing people why it is essential for us to take care of a particular customer's needs.

"The challenge, the exciting thing about this position is that I help make the vision of my company come true every day, while at the same time helping my customers achieve the vision they have for their stores," says Ron. He finds that his internal customers (those people he serves in manufacturing, order entry, shipping, local sales, and upper management) are willing to make concessions when they see how their work accomplishes Champion's vision. "When I'm successful, my customer is happy, and my colleagues in the company feel more fulfilled because they know they've done something that moved the whole company along."

Champion uses independent sales agents to handle local stores, including the local stores of key accounts. These agents call on mom-and-pop sports stores as well as the Foot Locker in your mall. Champion's regional sales managers help the agents by providing training and support. Ron, whose specialty is sporting goods stores, and his counterpart, who handles department stores, work directly with accounts and with the regional managers and

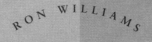

RON WILLIAMS

Champion Products

local agents. "My goal is to develop partnerships where we all win, whether it is just me and the buyer, or the agent, the manager, and a whole chain of buyers."

For example, one sporting goods chain had a shipment of shirts that it wanted to return. Champion, however, did not want to take the shirts back. "The shirts would sell," notes Ron, "they just weren't a good fit for that particular chain." Ron found himself selling the customer's position to his vice president of sales. "Fortunately, I won that one. Now the customer is happy and we're able to do a lot more business with them."

Ron also represents the customer when working with Champion's merchandising and advertising departments. Whether it is a gift with purchase, a cooperative advertising plan, or a concept shop (which is a Champion boutique inside a sporting goods or department store), Ron must create a plan for building the success of his retail partner while at the same time satisfying the needs of the various departments within Champion. "Many times, when I am working with my own merchandising or advertising people, I am the customer, I am Foot Locker or Merle Harmon's Fan Fair.

"What it all boils down to is making Champion work for the customer. If a customer needs a sweatshirt with the Champion logo on the left chest and we normally make it with a large logo across the front, I've got to get the order in on time so that manufacturing can schedule it without driving their costs way up and making them upset, I've got to get order entry to put the order into our billing system so that the invoice gets to the customer at the right time without messing up their budget, then get shipping to get the shirts to the customer in time for the advertising campaign that I need to design with our coop advertising department. That's an exciting challenge!"

BUILDING INTERNAL PARTNERSHIPS

To effectively coordinate the efforts of the many areas of a company, the salesperson must develop partnerships with the individuals in those areas. **Internal partnerships** are partnering relationships between a salesperson and another member of the same company. These partnerships should be dedicated to satisfying customer needs.

THE IMPORTANCE OF INTERNAL PARTNERSHIPS

By definition, a sales representative represents something. Students often think that the title means that the salesperson only represents a company or product, but at times the salesperson must represent the customer to the company. For example, the salesperson may have to convince the warehouse manager to ship a customer's product next in order to meet a special deadline. The salesperson does not have the authority to order the manager to ship the product, but must use persuasion. Or the rep may have to negotiate with production to get a product manufactured to a customer's specifications. Sometimes success in landing a sale may depend on the salesperson's ability to manage such company efforts.

This ability to work with groups inside the company can directly affect the rep's pocketbook. One of your authors, while selling for a major corporation, had an opportunity to earn a large bonus by making 30 sales. He had 31 orders, but a sale wasn't a sale until the product was delivered. Unfortunately, two orders were delivered after the deadline, and he did not get the bonus.

In tracking down the slow deliveries, the hapless salesperson learned that the order entry clerk had delayed processing the orders. A little probing uncovered the reason: She was upset with the way he prepared his paperwork! Her performance was evaluated on how quickly an order was delivered, but his sloppy paperwork always slowed her down and got her into trouble. Delaying work on his orders was her way of getting his attention.

It surely worked! For several months after that, he enlisted her help in filling out the paperwork properly before he turned it in. After that, she never had a problem with his orders. And when it was needed to meet a customer's requirements, she would prioritize his orders.

So salespeople not only sell a company, its products, and its services to customers, they also must sell their customers' needs to their company. Additionally, they must adapt to satisfy the needs and desires of those who influence their performance. Salespeople who develop successful partnerships are successful because they understand the needs of their partners. Dave Fields, in Selling Scenario 17-1 (see pp. 526–27), is one salesperson who has been successful with the help of internal partners.

SELLING INTERNALLY

To do a good job for customers, salespeople must often rely on personnel in other areas of the firm to do their respective jobs well. But how well those other employees assist salespeople may be a function of the relationship the salesperson has already established with them. That relationship should be a partnership, just like the one that you want to establish with

EXHIBIT 17.1

FIVE TIPS FOR SELLING
INTERNALLY

1. Understand that it's your problem. Accept responsibility for gaining the support of the internal staff.
2. Probe to find out and understand the personal and professional needs of the internal customer.
3. Use arguments for support that adequately address internal customers' needs as well as your own.
4. Do not spend time or energy resenting the internal customers' inability to understand or accept your sense of urgency. Rather, spend this time fruitfully by trying to figure out how you can better communicate your needs in a manner that will increase the internal customers' sense of urgency to the level you need.
5. Never personalize any issues.

Source: Roy Karr, "The Task of Selling Internally," *The Selling Advantage* (a twice-monthly publication in a fast-read format), 2(2) 715 Lancaster Ave., Bryn Mawr, PA 19010.

customers. To establish the appropriate partnership, invest time in understanding their needs and then work to satisfy those needs.

As summarized in Exhibit 17.1, the first step is to recognize that it is *the salesperson's responsibility* to develop relationships with other departments. Rarely is there any incentive for other departments to take the initiative. Salespeople who have the attitude "They should help me because it is their job to serve me," are frustrated by the lack of support they receive. The better perspective is "How can I serve them so we can serve the customer better?"

Use questioning skills such as SPIN to understand the personal and professional needs of the personnel in other departments. Salespeople have excellent communication skills but sometimes fail to use these skills when dealing with internal customers and support groups. SPIN and active listening are just as important to understanding the needs of colleagues as these skills are to satisfying customer needs. Keep in mind, too, that the salesperson cannot simply order a colleague to do what is wanted. But if a salesperson can show that doing what the salesperson wants will also meet the needs of the colleague, then the salesperson is more likely to receive the desired aid. Just as in selling the external customer, persuasion requires that the other person's needs be met as well as the salesperson's. *Show how their needs can be met* while meeting your needs and those of your customer.

People from other departments, except for billing and customer service, do not have direct contact with the customer. Therefore, they do not feel the same sense of urgency that is felt by the customer or the salesperson. Successful internal sellers can *communicate that sense of urgency* by relating to the needs of the internal customer. Just as with external customers, salespeople need to communicate the need to act now. Salespeople do this by securing commitment to the desired course of action. And just as with external customers, be sure to say "thank you" when someone agrees to provide you with the support you've requested.

Selling to internal customers also means to *keep issues professional*. Personal relationships can and should be developed. But when conflicts arise, focus on the issue, not the person. Personalizing conflict makes it seem bigger and harder to resolve. For example, rather than saying "Why won't

S E L L I N G   S C E N A R I O

17.1

Internal Partners

C. David Fields, vice president and general manager of Zellerbach Lexington, manages the sales and distribution of paper products in the central United States. His career has included stints as a salesperson for Xerox Corporation and in commercial real estate. In the following interview, Dave shares his experience in building internal partnerships.

Q. "What internal groups are critical to a sales rep's success?"

D. F. "There are three groups in any organization that are critical to a salesperson's success and these groups will vary depending on the type of business. But in general, these groups are (1) the receptionist/secretarial group, (2) the customer service group (order entry, credit, billing, and delivery scheduling), and (3) the technical or product service group (those who handle product complaints or technical service)."

Q. "Why do you list the receptionist/secretarial group?"

D. F. "These are the first people that customers see when they come to our office or the first they talk to on the phone. They can set the tone for anything that follows. How they react to you and your customers depends on how you treat them. If you have respect for them as professionals in their positions, they will treat you as a professional and, in turn, handle your phone calls and administrative needs accordingly."

Q. "How do you show respect for them?"

D. F. "When they ask you for information about something, it is because they have been asked by management to gather the information. If you show respect by responding in a timely and accurate manner, they will treat your requests in the same way. When I was a sales rep, I had a great working relationship with our

sales team secretary. When I turned in a proposal to be typed, mine always seemed to get done first."

Q. "What other ways can the secretarial group help you?"

D. F. "The handling of customers' phone calls is very important. The message taker can either simply record a message on a pink message pad or can ask a few extra questions, which can save you time or even handle the problem for you. The manner in which that customer's call is handled may be determined by your attitude and behavior toward the message taker. You reap what you sow."

Q. "Tell me about the customer service group . . . they only process paperwork. Why are they important?"

D. F. "You are right, they process paperwork, a lot of paperwork. They generally are buried in the office and never get to see a real customer. Their world is made better or worse by how well you (the salesperson) do your paperwork. If the order and the supporting documents are complete and accurate, then their job is easier and less stressful. They, in turn, can make your job less stressful."

Q. "How can you make their job less stressful?"

D. F. "Each company is different, but I have never seen a company that would not let an employee go see a customer. My first suggestion is that you include this group in your business. Take them to see a customer, especially one with whom they have had phone conversations. I had an experience with this last year that has made many commission dollars for one of my salespeople. He took our billing clerk, Cathy, to

continued

lunch with one of his customers. At lunch, Cathy learned that Janet, the customer's purchasing agent, was from the same small town. A great conversation followed (in which the rep had very little to say) and since then our business with that account has grown significantly. The rep would be the first to admit that Cathy has been a great help in this account."

Q. "What else can you do?"

D. F. "Do not make every situation an emergency. Good sales reps need every order now; that is the nature of the beast. However, like the little boy who cried "Wolf," the customer support group will not be able to recognize real emergencies from false ones. If you are accurate, complete, and on time with paperwork and let them process the regular orders in the proper time limits, they will move heaven and hell when you come to them in an emergency. Of course, if you set realistic expectations with your customers, you will have fewer emergencies."

Q. "Tell me about the product service group."

D. F. "This group usually sees a customer when that customer is mad. Very seldom do they get calls when things are running smoothly. When a rep has lunch or breakfast with this group regularly, the rep can share successes with them, especially when the customer's satisfaction with service helped make a sale. These service reps can also share with you problems and opportunities in accounts. If a customer has a training issue, solve it so that their employees operate equipment properly, which will save on service calls. If, during an installation, a part is missing, go get it so that the tech rep can stay on site and work. And when you get good feedback from a customer on the service rep, tell the service manager. By developing partnerships with your service reps, your business will grow and your customers will be better served."

Q. "Is there anything else you want to add?"

D. F. "Yes. Although good sales reps have independent natures and are self-motivated, the true professionals know and respect the team that supports them. The power of that team can be great."

you do this?" ask "If you can't do this, how can we resolve the customer's concern?" This type of statement focuses the other individual on resolving the real problem, rather than arguing about company policy or personal competence.

Salespeople must work with many elements of their organization. In fact, few jobs require the boundary spanning coordination and management skill that the sales job needs. In the next section, we will examine the many areas of the company with which the salesperson works, what their needs are, and how they partner with the salesperson to deliver customer satisfaction.

COMPANY AREAS IMPORTANT TO SALESPEOPLE

The sales force interacts with many areas of the firm. Salespeople work with manufacturing, sales administration, customer service, and personnel. In some industries requiring customization of products, engineering is a department important to salespeople. Finance can get into the picture as well when that department determines which customers receive credit and what

Salespeople who work closely with people in areas such as shipping and manufacturing can count on their internal partners' support when a customer needs it.

Courtesy Duplex Products, Inc.

Chuck Keeler/TSW.

price is charged. Additionally, salespeople work with members of their own department and the marketing department.

▌MANUFACTURING

Grafo Regia S.A. is a packaging and labeling firm in Monterrey, Mexico. Their clients include companies such as Kellogg, and they print labels and boxes that are used around the world. A key competitive advantage for Grafo Regia is their ability to deliver small or large orders faster than most of their competitors. Because the primary competitive advantage is based on manufacturing, the sales managers and salespeople spend a great deal of time in the factory, learning the manufacturing processes. More important, these salespeople have personal relationships established with workers at every level in the plant. Salespeople even play on manufacturing softball teams in a local corporate league, although they may have to fly home from Kellogg's headquarters in Battle Creek, Michigan, to make a game.

These personal relationships enable Grafo Regia to respond much quicker to customer needs. If Kellogg needs to change a Frosted Flakes package to include a promotion involving David Robinson (a basketball player for the San Antonio Spurs) just for the San Antonio market, Grafo Regia can do it faster than anyone else. One main reason is that manufacturing and sales are on the same team and are not viewed as separate entities.

In general, manufacturing is concerned with producing product at the lowest possible cost. In most cases, this means that they want long production runs, little customization, and low inventories. Customers, however, want their purchase shipped immediately and custom-made to their exact specifications. Salespeople may have to negotiate compromises between both manufacturing and the customer. Salespeople should also develop relationships with manufacturing so that accurate promises and guarantees can be made to customers.

▌ ADMINISTRATION

The functions of order entry, billing, credit, and employee compensation require that each company have an administrative department. This department processes orders and sees that the salesperson gets paid for them. Employees in this area (as we have discussed earlier) are often evaluated on how quickly they process orders and how quickly the company receives customer payment. Salespeople can greatly influence both processes, with substantial personal benefit to themselves.

Understanding the needs of the credit department, for example, and assisting it in collecting payments can better position the salesperson to help customers receive credit later. A credit representative who knows that you will help collect a payment when there is a problem is more likely to grant credit to one of your customers, and you have already read about the importance of working with order entry personnel.

▌ SHIPPING

The scheduling of product shipments may be part of sales administration or manufacturing, or it may stand alone. In any case, salespeople need the help of the shipping department. When salespeople make special promises to expedite a delivery, they actually must depend on shipping to carry out the promise. Shipping managers focus on costs, and they often keep their costs in control by planning efficient shipping routes and moving products quickly through warehouses. Expedited or special-handling deliveries can interfere with plans for efficient shipping. Salespeople who make promises that shipping cannot or will not fulfill are left with egg on their faces. John Munn, a Coca-Cola key accounts representative, will help load and drive a delivery truck when one of his accounts needs an expedited shipment so that his promise is fulfilled with minimal interruption in the warehouse.

▌ CUSTOMER SERVICE

Salespeople also need to interact with customer service. Perhaps this is obvious, but many salespeople arrogantly ignore the information obtained by customer service representatives. A technician who fixes the company's products often goes into more customers' offices or plants than the salesperson does. The technician has earlier warning concerning a customer's switch to a competitor, a change in customer needs, or failure of a product to satisfy. For example, if an IBM technician spies a new DEC computer in the customer's office, the technician can ask if the DEC unit is on trial. If a good working relationship exists between the technician and the salesperson, the technician will warn the salesperson that the account is considering a competitive product. Close relationships and support of customer or technical service representatives not only means better customer service, but faster and more direct information flow to the salesperson. This information will help you gain and keep customers.

Salespeople, in turn, can help customer service by setting proper expectations for product performance with customers, training customers in the proper use of the product, and handling complaints promptly. Technicians are evaluated on the number of service calls they make each day and how long the product works between service calls, among other things. Salespeople can reduce some service calls by setting the right expectations for product performance. Salespeople can also extend the amount of time between calls by training customers in the proper use of the product and in preventive maintenance. An important by-product of such actions should be higher customer satisfaction.

▮ MARKETING

Sales is part of marketing in some firms and separate from marketing in others. Marketing and sales should be highly coordinated because their functions are closely related. Both are concerned with providing the right product to the customer in the most efficient and effective manner. Sales acts as the eyes and ears of marketing, while marketing develops the promotions and products that salespeople sell. Salespeople act as eyes and ears by informing the marketing department of competitive actions, customer trends, and other important market information. Marketing serves salespeople by taking that information and using it to create promotional programs or to design new products. Marketing is also responsible for generating leads through trade show exhibiting, direct mail programs, advertising, and public relations.

▮ SALES

Within any sales force, there may be several types of salespeople. As you have learned from earlier chapters, there may be global account managers working with the largest accounts while other representatives handle the rest of the customers, and there are sales executives and sales managers with whom the salesperson must interact. How these people work together is the subject of the next section.

▮ PARTNERS IN THE SALES ORGANIZATION

The sales function may be organized in many different ways, but no matter how it is organized, it is rarely perfect. There is usually some customer overlap between salespeople, meaning that several salespeople may have to work together to serve the needs of one account. Customer needs may require direct customer contact with the sales executive as well as the salesperson. At the same time, the salesperson must operate in an environment that is influenced by the policies and procedures created by that same sales executive and executed by the salesperson's immediate manager. In this section, we will explore the sales organization, beginning at the top of the organization chart and working down.

▌ SALES EXECUTIVES

Sales executives play a vital role in determining the company's strategies with respect to new products, new markets, sales forecasts, prices, and competition. They determine the size and organization of the sales force, develop annual and long-range plans, and monitor and control sales efforts. Duties of the sales executive include forecasting overall sales, budgeting, setting sales quotas, and designing compensation programs.

Size and Organization of the Sales Force

The sales executive determines how many salespeople are needed to achieve the company's sales and customer satisfaction targets. In addition, the executive must determine what type of salespeople are needed. For example, it is the sales executive who determines if global account management is needed. There are many other alternative types of salespeople that can be selected, which we will discuss later in this chapter. For now, though, keep in mind that the sales executive determines the level of customer satisfaction necessary to achieve sales objectives, and then designs a sales force to achieve those goals. How that sales force is put together is important, because salespeople often have to work together to deliver appropriate customer service and to successfully accomplish sales goals. We will also discuss different organizing mechanisms when we discuss integrative selling.

Forecasting

Sales executives use a number of techniques to arrive at sales forecasts. One of the most widely used techniques is **bottoms-up forecasting,** or simply adding each salesperson's own forecast into a forecast for total company sales. At each level of management, the forecast would normally be adjusted, based on the manager's experience and broader perspective. This technique allows the information to come from the people closest to the market—the salespeople. Also, the forecast comes from the people with the responsibility for making those sales. But salespeople tend to be optimistic and may overestimate sales, or they may underestimate future sales if they know that their bonuses depend on exceeding forecasts or if they feel that their quotas will be raised.

Salespeople are especially important to the forecasting process when the executive is attempting to forecast international sales.[1] Statistics used in the United States to forecast sales are often not available in other countries. Government statistics in those countries may be unreliable if available. Therefore, the only reliable forecasting mechanism is the salesperson's own idea of what can be sold. For example, Harley-Davidson depends heavily on their salespeople in other countries for accurate forecasts of motorcycle sales. Harley-Davidson's international sales are more than 20 percent of total sales, making such forecasts important to Harley's planning. Salespeople are the most important source of market information in international markets.

Expense Budgets

Managers sometimes use expense budgets to control costs. An expense budget may be expressed in dollars (e.g., the salesperson is allowed to spend up to $500) or as a percentage of sales volume (e.g., expenses cannot go over 10 percent of sales). A regional manager or salesperson may be awarded a bonus for spending less than the budget allocates. However, such a bonus may encourage the salesperson to underspend, which could hurt sales performance. For example, if a salesperson refuses to give out samples, customers may not be able to visualize how the product will work, so some may not buy. The salesperson has reduced expenses but hurt sales.

While salespeople may have limited input into a budget, they do spend the money. Ultimately, it is the salesperson's responsibility to manage the territorial budget. Not only do you have control over how much is spent and whether your expenditures are over or under budget, but more important, you decide where resources are placed. As you recall from Chapter 16, these resources, such as samples and trial units or direct mailers, are investments in future sales. If you use these unwisely, you may still meet your expense budget but fail to meet your sales quota.

Control and Quota Setting

The sales executive faces the challenge of setting up a balanced control system that will encourage each sales manager and salesperson to maximize his or her individual results through effective self-control. As we have pointed out throughout this text, salespeople operate somewhat independently. However, the control system that management devises can help salespeople better manage themselves.

Quotas serve as a useful technique for controlling the sales force. **Quotas** represent a quantitative minimum level of acceptable performance for a specific time period. A **sales quota** is the minimum number of sales in units, while a **revenue quota** is the minimum amount of sales revenue necessary for acceptable performance. Often sales quotas are simple breakdowns of the company's total sales forecast. Thus, the total of all sales quotas equals the sales forecast. Other types of quotas can also be used. Understanding quotas is important to the salesperson because performance relative to quota is evaluated by management.

Profit quotas or **gross margin quotas** are minimum levels of acceptable profit or gross margin performance. These quotas motivate the sales force to sell more profitable products or to sell to more profitable customers. Some companies assign points to each product, based on the product's gross margin. More points are assigned to higher-margin products. The salesperson can then meet a point quota by selling either a lot of low-margin products or fewer high-margin products. For example, assume that an office equipment company sells fax machines and copiers. The profit margin (not including salesperson compensation) on copiers is 30 percent, but only 20 percent on fax machines. Copiers may be worth 3 points each, while faxes are worth 2. If the salesperson's quota is 12 points, the quota can be reached by selling 4 copiers or 6 faxes or some combination of both.

Activity quotas, similar to the activity goals we discussed in the last chapter, are minimal expectations of activities for each salesperson. These quotas are set by the company to control the activities of the sales force. This type of quota is more important in situations where the sales cycle is long and sales are few, because activities can be observed more frequently than sales. For example, for some medical equipment, the sales cycle is longer than one year and a salesperson may sell only one or two units each quarter. Having a monthly sales target in this case would be inappropriate, but requiring a certain minimum number of calls to be made is reasonable. The assumption made by management is that if the salesperson is doing the proper activities, then sales will follow. Activities for which quotas may be established include the number of demonstrations, total customer calls, number of calls on prospects, or number of displays set up.

THINKING IT THROUGH	*H*ow would you respond if you felt you were making as many calls as possible during the workweek, yet your manager demanded that you make more? The manager's reasoning is that if you make more, you will sell more. How would your response change if you were not meeting your sales quota? If you were selling twice your sales quota?

Compensation and Evaluation

An important task of the sales executive is to establish the company's basic compensation and evaluation system. The compensation system must satisfy the needs of both the salespeople and the company. You, as a salesperson, need an equitable, stable, understandable system that motivates you to meet your objectives. The company, however, needs a system that encourages you to sell products at a profitable price and in the right amounts.

Salespeople want a system that bases rewards on efforts and results. Compensation must also be uniform within the company and in line with that received by competitors' salespeople. If competitors' salespeople earn more, you would want to leave and work for that competitor. But your company expects the compensation system to attract and keep good salespeople and to encourage you to do specific things. The system should reward outstanding performance while achieving the proper balance between sales results and costs.

Compensation often relates to quotas. As with quotas, salespeople who perceive the system as unfair may give up or leave the firm. A stable compensation system ensures that salespeople can reap the benefits of their efforts, while a constantly changing system may find them dizzily changing their activities but never making any money. A system that is not understandable will be ignored.

Key account management requires planning and coordination, often among several salespeople. Sales executives must see that compensation plans recognize and reward each person's contribution appropriately.

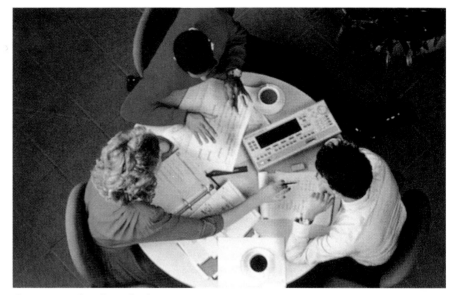

Photo courtesy of Hewlett-Packard Company.

TYPES OF COMPENSATION   The sales executive decides how much income will be based on salary or incentive pay. The salesperson may receive a **salary,** a regular payment regardless of performance, whereas **incentive pay** is tied to some level of performance. There are two types of incentives: commission and bonus. **Commission** is incentive pay paid for an individual sale, whereas **bonus** is incentive pay given for overall performance in one or more areas of performance. For example, a bonus may be paid for acquiring a certain number of new customers, for reaching a specified level of total sales in units, or for selling a certain amount of a new product.

TYPES OF COMPENSATION PLANS   Sales executives can choose to pay salespeople a straight salary, a straight commission, or some combination of salary, commission, and/or bonus. Most firms opt for some combination of salary and bonus or salary and commission. Fewer than 4 percent pay only commission, and slightly less than 5 percent pay only salary. Exhibit 17.2 illustrates how the types of compensation plans would work.

Under the **straight salary** method, a salesperson receives a fixed amount of money for work during a specified time. Salespeople are assured of a steady income and can develop a sense of loyalty to their customers. The company also has more control over the salesperson. Because your income does not depend directly on results, the company can ask you to do things in the best interest of the company, even though these activities may not lead to immediate sales. Straight salary, however, provides little financial incentive for salespeople to sell more. For example, in Exhibit 17.2, the salesperson receives $3,500 per month, no matter how much is sold.

EXHIBIT 17.2

How Different Types of
Compensation Plans Pay

| | | | **Amount Paid to Salesperson** | | |
Month	Sales Revenue	Straight Salary	Straight Commission*	Combination†	Point Plan
January	$50,000 6 copiers 10 faxes	$3,500	$5,000	$1,500 (salary) 3,000 (commission) 4,500 (total)	$3,800
February	$60,000 6 copiers 15 faxes	3,500	6,000	1,500 (salary) 3,600 (commission) 5,100 (total)	4,800
March	$20,000 2 copiers 5 faxes	3,500	2,000	1,500 (salary) 1,200 (commission) 2,700 (total)	1,600

*Commission plan pays 10% of sales revenue.

†Commission portion pays 6% of sales revenue.

Note: Copiers are worth 3 points, faxes worth 2, each point is worth $100 in commission. Also, the commission rates are used for example purposes only, to illustrate how compensation schemes work. Point plans, for example, do not necessarily always yield the lowest compensation.

Straight salary plans are used when sales require long periods of negotiation, when a team of salespeople is involved and individual results cannot be measured, or when other aspects of the marketing mix (e.g., advertising) are more important than the salesperson's efforts in generating sales (e.g., in trade selling of consumer products). Most sales trainees also receive a straight salary.

A **straight commission** plan pays a certain amount per sale, and the plan includes a base and a rate but does not include a salary. The **commission base,** the item from which commission is determined, will often be unit sales, dollar sales, or gross margin. The **commission rate,** which determines the amount paid, is expressed as a percentage of the base (e.g., 10 percent of sales or 8 percent of gross margin) or as a dollar amount (e.g., $100 per sale). Exhibit 17.2 illustrates two straight commission plans, one that pays 10 percent of sales revenue and a point plan that pays $100 per point (using the copier and fax example we discussed previously).

Commission plans often include a draw. A **draw** is money paid to the salesperson against future commissions, a loan that guarantees a stable cash flow. For example, a salesperson could receive a draw of $1,000 per month. If the salesperson earns less than $1,000 in commissions during one month, he or she would still receive $1,000. The difference between the earned commission and the draw would be paid back in months when the salesperson earned over $1,000. An example is presented in Exhibit 17.3.

Straight commission plans have the advantage of tying the salesperson's compensation directly to performance, providing more financial incentive. But salespeople on straight commission have little company loyalty and certainly are less willing to perform activities, such as paperwork, that do not directly lead to sales. Xerox experimented with such a plan but found that customer service suffered, as did company loyalty among salespeople.

EXHIBIT 17.3

AN EXAMPLE OF A DRAW
COMPENSATION PLAN

Month	Draw	Commission Earned	Payment to Salesperson	Balance Owed to Company
January	$1,000	$ 0	$1,000	$1,000
February	1,000	1,500	1,000	500
March	1,000	2,000	1,500	0

Companies that do not emphasize service to customers or do not antici-pate long-term customer relationships (e.g., a company selling kitchen appliances directly to consumers) typically use commission plans. Such plans are also used when the sales force includes many part-timers, because part-timers can earn more when their pay is tied to their performance. Also, part-timers may need the extra motivation that straight commission can provide.

Under bonus plans, salespeople receive a lump-sum payment for a cer-tain level of performance over a specified time. Bonuses resemble commis-sions, but the amount paid depends on total performance, not each indi-vidual sale. Bonuses, awarded monthly, quarterly, or annually, are always used in conjunction with salary and/or commissions in combination plans. For example, a bonus could be added to any of the compensation plans illustrated in Exhibit 17.2.

Sales executives frequently combine two or three of the basic methods to form the compensation plan. **Combination** plans, also called *salary-plus-commission,* provide salary and commission, and offer the greatest flexibil-ity for motivating and controlling the activities of salespeople. The plans can incorporate the advantages and avoid the disadvantages of using any of the basic plans alone. Note in Exhibit 17.2 that the straight salary plan pays a higher salary than the combination plan, but the difference can be offset by the incentive portion.

The main disadvantage of combination plans lies in their complexity. Salespeople confused by this complexity could unknowingly perform the wrong activities; sales managers affected by the complexity could uninten-tionally design a program that rewards the wrong activities. Using the of-fice equipment example above, if faxes and copiers were worth the same commission (for example, $100 per sale), the salesperson would sell what-ever was easiest to sell. If faxes were easier to sell than copiers, the firm may make less money, because salespeople would expend all of their effort selling a lower-profit product unless the volume sold made up for the lower margin. Even then, however, the firm may be stuck with a warehouse of unsold copiers.

Management uses salary-plus-commission plans to motivate salespeople (through commissions) to increase revenues while, at the same time, to con-tinue to perform nonselling activities (paid for with salary) such as customer service. When management wants to develop long-term customer relations, salary-plus-bonus plans are used so that less emphasis is placed on getting new (and commissionable) sales. Bonus plans are also used when the sales effort involves a team of people.

*A*s a buyer, which plan would you prefer your salesperson to work under? Which would you prefer if you were a salesperson? Can you anticipate conflicts that could occur between buyer and seller because of the type of compensation plan?

Ethics and the Sales Executive

Part of a sales executive's job is to determine corporate policy concerning what is considered ethical and what is not, and how unethical behavior will be investigated and punished. In addition, the sales executive must ensure that other policies, such as the performance measurement and compensation policies, also support the ethics of the organization. When performance measurement and compensation policies reward only outcomes, there may be a greater tendency on the part of salespeople to act unethically because of pressure to achieve and a culture supporting the credo "the end justifies the means." But when behavioral performance measurement systems are also in place, the compensation system can reward those who do things the right way.[2] While unethical behaviors may result in short-term gain (and therefore may accidentally be rewarded in an outcome-only compensation scheme), unethical behaviors can have serious long-term effects.

Sales executives must therefore develop a culture that creates behavioral norms of how things should be done and what behaviors will not be tolerated. Such a culture can be enhanced through the development of formal policy, training courses on ethics, ethics review boards, and an **open-door policy.** Open-door policies are general management techniques that allow subordinates to bypass immediate managers and take concerns straight to upper management when the subordinates feel a lack of support from the immediate manager. Open-door policies enhance an ethical culture, because salespeople can feel free to discuss troublesome issues that may involve their managers with someone in a position to respond. Ethics review boards may function in the same way, providing expert advice to salespeople who are unsure of the ethical consequences of an action. **Ethics review boards** may consist of experts inside and outside the company who are responsible for reviewing ethics policies, investigating allegations of unethical behavior, and acting as a sounding board for employees. Sales executives play an important role in determining how the corporate culture will support ethical activity by salespeople.

Salespeople also have the right to expect ethical treatment from their company. Fair treatment concerning compensation, promoting policies, territory allocation, and other actions should be delivered. Compensation is probably the area with the most common concerns, although problems do arise in all areas. Compensation problems can include slow payment, hidden caps, or compensation plan changes after the sale.

For example, one company paid their salespeople a straight commission of about 10 percent. When a salesperson sold one major account $11 million dollars worth of product, the company changed her commission plan to a salary plus commission in order to cut her payment. In another example, a company refused to pay a salesperson all of his commission because he earned more than the vice president of sales. The company claimed that there was a **cap**, or limit, on earnings. Caps are not unethical; what was unethical was that the salesperson was not made aware of the cap prior to selling. Although some problems do occur, most companies want to hire and keep good salespeople, and most businesspeople are ethical.

THINKING IT THROUGH	*S*hould schools have ethics review boards? What advantages would there be for the student? For the teacher? Would salespeople reap the same types of benefits if their companies had ethics review boards?

▌ FIELD SALES MANAGERS

Most salespeople report directly to a sales manager who reports, in turn, to the sales executive. This first level manager, or **field sales manager,** has a job that is similar to the sales executive. It involves the same management processes of planning, organizing, directing, coordinating, and controlling. However, the jobs differ in implementation of these processes because the field sales manager has responsibility for a smaller portion of the firm. Sales managers also have responsibility for recruiting (discussed in Chapter 18), training, and motivating salespeople and evaluating their performance.

Planning

As mentioned before, a company's sales planning often starts at the grass roots—in the field, where salesperson and customer meet face to face. The field sales manager is responsible for knowing what takes place in the territories of his or her salespeople. Field sales managers who have good communication with their salespeople can be the most effective conduits of market information for the company.

Some salespeople, because of their independence, do not welcome what they see as intrusions into their selling time or their business. As a result, they may be unwilling to provide management with the requested information, or they may respond slowly or with reports that are filled out inaccurately. But cooperating is usually to their advantage, because more accurate information should result in better marketing and sales plans and programs.

Organizing and Coordinating

Field sales managers are responsible for organizing and coordinating local sales efforts, because they have the local market knowledge necessary to develop such efforts. For example, a Goodyear truck tire sales manager in the Southeast would develop plans for selling to logging companies, whereas a similar manager in Texas would have salespeople calling on oil well service companies. In addition, it may be up to the local manager to

Central Transportation's Ad Hoc Organization Provides Whatever the Customer Needs

Central Transportation Systems is an agent for United Van Lines, representing the moving and storage company all across Texas. Central does not haul freight, but does act as an agent for United's freight services. Central also moves (or contracts for United to move) office furniture when companies relocate, household goods when companies relocate their personnel or when people move on their own, and trade show equipment for companies.

The many different services that Central can offer makes handling commercial accounts difficult. According to Dick Crovisier, sales manager for the company's Austin location, a company is likely to have a different decision maker for each service. "The person who handles trade shows is probably in the marketing department, while the human resources manager may work with us for employee residential moves, and yet another manager from another department may request our heavy machinery moving services," says Dick. "Although ordinarily one account rep might be responsible for all of the account's business, sometimes expertise of other

salespeople is required to handle the needs of each department."

Accounts are assigned to specific account managers, usually based on whoever sells the account first. But Dick expects account managers to bring in colleagues when their expertise is required. "Our account managers are professionals, so they have the authority to make their own decisions, but they also have the responsibility to bring in the business. Once we have a portion of an account's business, our salespeople want to leverage our performance in that area to gain the rest of the account's work. We might have as many as four salespeople working with the account, coordinated by the original account manager."

Dick believes that "Part of my job is to make sure that my salespeople are using their talents wisely. Each salesperson brings unique gifts, knowledge, and skills to the job. One of the aspects I like most about my job is helping each one achieve as much as he or she possibly can while also contributing the most to our team."

determine which salesperson is responsible for which account through the development of sales territories. Selling Scenario 17.2 illustrates how one local manager has organized his local sales force.

Some local sales managers are also given enough flexibility to determine the number and type of salespeople they will employ, but in larger companies that is the responsibility of the sales executive. We will discuss the different types of salespeople and how they work together later in this chapter.

Evaluating Performance

Field sales managers are responsible for evaluating the performance of their salespeople. The easiest method of evaluating performance is to simply add up the amount of sales that the salesperson makes. But sales managers must also rate their salespeople's customer service level, product knowledge, and other, less tangible aspects. Some companies, such as Federal Express, use customer satisfaction surveys to evaluate salespeople. In other companies,

EXHIBIT 17.4

BEHAVIORAL OBSERVATION SCALE (BOS)

	Almost Never						Almost Always
1. Checks deliveries to see if they have arrived on time.	1	2	3	4	5	6	7
2. Files sales reports on time.	1	2	3	4	5	6	7
3. Uses promotional brochures and correspondence with potential accounts.	1	2	3	4	5	6	7
4. Monitors competitive activities.	1	2	3	4	5	6	7
5. Brushes up on selling techniques.	1	2	3	4	5	6	7
6. Reads marketing research reports.	1	2	3	4	5	6	7
7. Prospects for new accounts.	1	2	3	4	5	6	7
8. Makes service calls.	1	2	3	4	5	6	7
9. Answers customer inquiries when they occur.	1	2	3	4	5	6	7

the manager rates each salesperson, using evaluation forms that list the desired aspects. (An example of an evaluation form appears in Exhibit 17.4.) Such evaluations help managers determine training needs, promotions, and pay raises.

The records and reports salespeople submit also play an important role in communicating their activities to the sales manager. The manager then uses these reports to evaluate performance in a manner similar to the way the salesperson would. But these written reports are not enough; sales managers should also make calls with salespeople in order to directly observe their performance. These observations can be the basis for recommendations for improving individual performance or for commending outstanding performance. Other information, such as customer response to a new strategy, can be gained by making calls. This information should be shared with upper management to improve strategies.

THINKING IT THROUGH

*D*o you ever feel a conflict between what you want to accomplish in a class and the activities that you have to perform in order to receive the grade you desire? The grade is a form of performance evaluation given by a teacher, instead of a manager. What factors would lead to such a conflict in a sales position?

Training

The sales manager trains new hires and provides refresher training for experienced salespeople. To determine what refresher training they need, managers often use information gathered while observing salespeople making sales calls. Content of training for new salespeople may be determined by a sales executive, but the field sales manager is often responsible for carrying out the training.

Professional salespeople constantly seek to upgrade their sales. This salesperson for Flair Personnel is receiving some pointers from his sales manager.

Courtesy MSI International, Atlanta, Georgia; photo by Ann States.

Most experienced salespeople welcome training when they see that it will improve their sales. Unfortunately, often training is viewed as an inconvenience, taking away from precious selling time. Additional sales training can be useful when the organization makes a real commitment to it. Follow-up in the field is often necessary to assist the experienced salesperson practice what was learned in the training session. If the commitment isn't there from the company, the experienced rep is liable to slip back into old habits. You should continue to welcome training, no matter how successful you are. There is always the opportunity to improve your performance, or at least achieve the same level with less effort.

Ethics and the Field Sales Manager

The field sales manager has a responsibility to communicate and support all company policies, including ethics policies. Salespeople often ask managers for direction on how to handle ethical problems, and it is usually the sales manager who is the first to investigate complaints of unethical behavior.

Salespeople, however, may find themselves faced with a sales manager who encourages them to engage in unethical behavior. When that situation occurs, a salesperson has several options to choose from in order to avoid engaging in such behavior.[3] Perhaps the most obvious is to find another job, but that is not always the best solution. If the organizational culture supports the unethical request, however, finding another job may be the only choice. Exhibit 17.5 lists choices available to the salesperson.

Another choice is to blow the whistle, or report the unethical request, if the salesperson has adequate evidence (if adequate evidence is not available, sometimes simply threatening to blow the whistle may work). If this choice of action is followed, the salesperson must be ready to accept such additional consequences as a perception of disloyalty, retaliation by the manager, or other consequences. However, if senior management is sincere in efforts to promote ethical behavior, steps should be taken to minimize

EXHIBIT 17.5

STRATEGIES FOR HANDLING
UNETHICAL REQUESTS FROM
A MANAGER

Leave the organization, or ask for a transfer.
Negotiate an alternative course of action.
Blow the whistle, internally or externally.
Threaten to blow the whistle.
Appeal to a higher authority.
Agree to the demand, but fail to carry it out.
Deny to comply with the request.
Ignore the request.

those negative outcomes. If an open-door policy or an ethics review board exists, the salesperson can take the concern to higher levels for review. For example, the salesperson could say, "I'm not sure that is appropriate. I'd like to get the opinion of the ethics review board." If the action is unethical, it is possible that the sales manager will back down at that point. It is also possible that the manager will try to coerce the salesperson into not applying to the ethics review board; if that is the case, another course of action may prove to be a better choice.

Another strategy is to negotiate an alternative. This response requires that the salesperson identify an alternative course of action with a high probability of success. For example, if a sales manager tells the salesperson to offer a prospect a bribe, the salesperson should be prepared to prove that a price reduction would be just as effective. Similar to negotiation is to simply ignore the request. The salesperson may say to the manager that the request was carried out, when in fact it was not; the potential problem with this is that the salesperson has admitted to carrying out an unethical act (even though it was not done), which can lead to future problems. Finally, another response is to simply deny the request. Denial can be a dangerous action in that it opens the salesperson to possible retaliation, particularly retaliation that is not obviously linked to the denial, such as denying access to training or reducing the size of the salesperson's territory.

The salesperson's choice of action will depend on how much proof is available, what alternative actions exist to the unethical action, and the type of relationship with the manager. Other factors to consider are the ethical climate of the organization, whether an open-door policy exists, and similar factors. The salesperson, however, is always in control of his or her behavior. Never should a salesperson rationalize away a behavior by placing responsibility on the sales manager.

SALESPEOPLE AS PARTNERS

There are many types of salespeople, including telemarketing representatives, field salespeople, product specialists, and account specialists. Often there is some overlap in responsibilities. As in the Shell example, two or more salespeople may have responsibilities to serve the same customers.

Geographic Salespeople

Most sales departments are organized geographically. A **geographic salesperson** is assigned a specific geographic territory in which to sell all of the company's products and services. Companies often combine geographic territories into larger branches, zones, or regions. For example, Eli Lilly has geographic regions that include 50 or more salespeople. Each Lilly salesperson has responsibility for a specific geographic area; for example, one rep may call on physicians in a portion of Dallas, using zip code boundaries to determine the territory. That rep may have all physicians in zip codes 75212, 75213, 75218, 75239, 75240, and 75252. Geographic salespeople also work with other types of salespeople, as will be discussed.

Account Salespeople

There are several ways that companies may organize salespeople by account. We have already discussed some of these types, such as NAMs. Another common form of specialization has some salespeople develop new accounts while others maintain existing accounts. Developing new accounts requires different skills than maintaining an already sold account. One RCA radio communications division uses field salespeople to develop new accounts and a telemarketing sales force to maintain the accounts. The field salespeople must identify prospects from noncustomers and sell the product. Once the RCA product has been installed, the account becomes the responsibility of the telemarketing sales force.

Similar customers often have similar needs, while different types of customers may have very different needs for the same product. In such cases, salespeople may specialize in calling on only one or a few customer types, although they sell the same products. NCR has different sales forces for calling on manufacturing companies and retail and financial companies. Andritz, an international heavy machinery company, has salespeople who sell only to paper producers and other salespeople who sell only to wastewater treatment plants, even though the same product is being sold. Some Procter & Gamble salespeople call on central buying offices for grocery store chains; others call on food wholesalers.

Companies also divide their customers on the basis of size. Large customers, sometimes called **key accounts,** may have a salesperson assigned only to that account; in some cases, a small sales force may be assigned to one large account. Amdahl, a computer and telecommunications company, has an account executive, a systems engineer, and a customer support representative assigned to each of certain large accounts.

In other firms, one company executive coordinates all of the salespeople who call on an account throughout the nation or the world. As mentioned in earlier chapters, these executives are called *national accounts managers (NAM)* or *global accounts managers (GAM)*. Moore Business Forms has been one of the leaders in using global accounts managers. Previously, the Paris rep would sell to American Express' European office, the Tokyo rep to American Express' Asian office, and so forth. Now, American Express has a centralized purchasing office but needs national or global implemen-

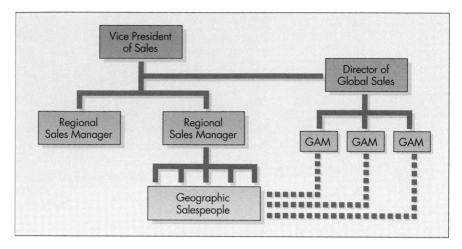

tation. The Moore GAM who serves American Express may call on their headquarters, but American Express still needs Moore's support in Europe and Asia. The GAM would coordinate sales support from the Paris and Tokyo sales representatives for delivery and postdelivery services.

The local geographic rep's responsibility may involve coordinating delivery with the local customer. This coordination may also require customer training on the product or working with a local store manager to set up displays, plan inventories, and so on. Local reps should also look for sales opportunities in the customer's location and provide this information to the GAM. They often become the eyes and ears of the GAM and provide early notice of opportunities or threats in the account, just a service rep can for the geographic rep. GAMs often report directly to the vice president of sales or to a director of global sales, as illustrated in Exhibit 17.6, but work with geographic reps.

Note, however, that **house accounts** differ from key accounts. A house account is handled by a sales or marketing executive in addition to that executive's regular duties, and no commission is paid on any sales from that account. House accounts are often key accounts, but not all key accounts are house accounts. The main point is that house accounts have no true salesperson. Wal-Mart has negotiated to be a house account with some suppliers on the basis that Wal-Mart will save money when the suppliers pass on the salesperson's commission or salary savings. General Dynamics attempted the same strategy when buying, but abandoned it when they realized that lower costs also meant reduced service.

Product Specialists

When companies have diverse products, their salespeople often specialize by types of products. Johnson & Johnson, which sells baby products, has two specialized sales forces: the disposable-products sales force and the toiletries products sales force. Hewlett-Packard has separate sales forces that specialize in selling computers, electronic test instruments, electronic components, medical test equipment, or analytical test equipment. Each sales force has its own regional, district, and area sales managers. Insuror's of

Texas has salespeople who specialize in auto insurance, others who specialize in homeowner's insurance, and still others who specialize in medical and disability insurance. But all Insuror's salespeople operate under the same sales management structure. Irrespective of the management structure, sometimes the technical knowledge requirements are so great that organizing territories by product makes sense.

In addition to management responsibilities similar to those for geographic reps, product salespeople must also coordinate their activities with those of salespeople from other divisions. Success can be greater for all involved when leads and customer information is shared. For example, a Hewlett-Packard test instrument salesperson may have a customer who is also a prospect for electronic components. Sharing that information with the electronic component rep can help build a relationship that can pay off with leads for test instruments.

Inside versus Outside

Our discussion to this point has focused on outside salespeople, called **field salespeople;** that is, salespeople who sell at the customer's location. **Inside salespeople** sell at their own company's location. Inside salespeople can be salespeople who handle walk-in customers or telemarketing salespeople, or they may handle both duties. For example, a plumbing supply distributor may sell entirely to plumbers, and employ inside salespeople who sell to those plumbers who come into the distributorship to buy products.

As we discussed in Chapter 7, some telemarketing salespeople are used to provide leads for field salespeople. But there are other types of telemarketing salespeople: account managers, field support reps, and customer service reps.[4] A telemarketer who is an account manager has the same responsibilities and duties as a field salesperson, except that all business is conducted over the phone.

Sales teams are one approach to integrating selling efforts by multiple salespeople who call on the same accounts. This sales team is planning a sales strategy for a key account.

Courtesy 3M.

A **field support rep** is a telemarketer that works with field salespeople, and does more than prospect for leads. The field support rep may also cross-sell, upgrade, or seek reorders. Together with field salespeople, field support reps develop account strategies, handle customer concerns, and perform similar duties. We will discuss these further when we discuss team selling strategies later in this chapter.

Customer service reps are in-bound salespeople that handle customer concerns. **In-bound** means that they respond to telephone calls placed by customers, rather than **out-bound,** which means that the telemarketer makes the phone call (prospectors, account managers, and field support telemarketers are out-bound reps). For example, there is an 800 telephone number on the back of a tube of Crest toothpaste. Call that number and you will be speaking with an in-bound customer service rep.

▌ SALES TEAMS

A recent innovation in integrated selling is the use of sales teams. Amdahl's team approach to some key accounts is an example of a sales team. This concept is being used by companies that recognize that they can best build partnerships by empowering one person—the account manager—to represent the organization. In **team selling,** a group of salespeople supports a single account. Each person on the team brings a different area of expertise or handles different responsibilities.

Before adopting team selling, companies might have had one salesperson for each product line. For example, Xerox once had separate copier salespeople, duplicator salespeople, supply salespeople, telecopier (fax) salespeople, printer salespeople, computer workstation salespeople, and communication network salespeople all calling on the same buyer. Custom-

▌ E X H I B I T   1 7 . 7

TEAM SELLING
ORGANIZATION
In team selling, product specialists work with account managers. Account managers have total account responsibility, but product specialists are responsible for sales and service of only a limited portion of the product line, and may work with several account managers.

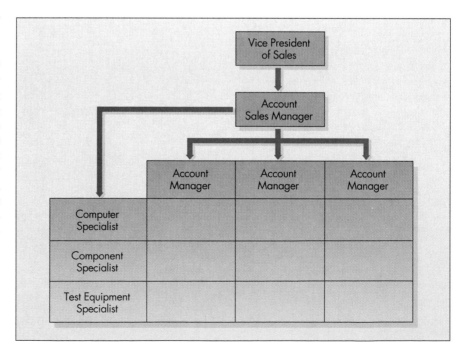

EXHIBIT 17.8

SALES TEAMS MAY BE
FORMED FOR MULTILEVEL
SELLING

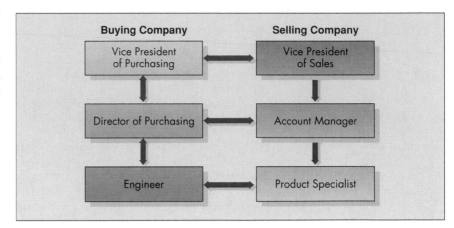

ers got tired of seeing as many as seven salespeople from Xerox. Now one account manager calls on the buyer, bringing in product specialists as needed. Exhibit 17.7 illustrates how a sales team might be organized.

In an extension of team selling, **multilevel selling,** members of the sales organization at various levels call on their counterparts in the buying organization. (As charted in Exhibit 17.8, the vice president of sales calls on a vice president of purchasing.) Multilevel selling can take place without a formal multilevel sales team if the account representative requests upper-level management's involvement in the sale. For example, you may ask your company's vice president of sales to call on the vice president of operations at a prospect's company to secure top-level support for your proposal.

Another type of sales team is made up of the field rep and the field support rep (see Exhibit 17.9). Some companies use one telemarketer for each field salesperson, whereas other companies may have several salespeople working with a telemarketer. The telemarketer performs as many selling tasks as possible over the telephone. But when a sales call is needed at the customer's location, the field support rep makes the appointment for the field rep. Good communication and joint planning is necessary to avoid overbooking the field rep, as well as to prevent duplication of effort.

EXHIBIT 17.9

INSIDE/OUTSIDE
SALES TEAM
Sometimes an inside rep or field support rep works with accounts over the phone while his or her partner, the field rep, makes calls at the customer's location.

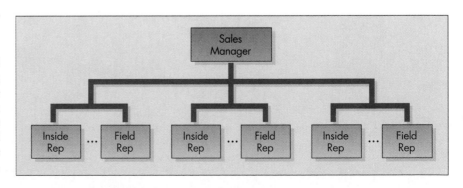

SUMMARY

As a salesperson, you begin to manage resources and build internal partners. To be successful, salespeople build partnerships with people in order entry, credit, billing, and shipping, as well as sales and marketing. These partnerships allow salespeople to keep the promises they make to customers when those promises must be carried out by someone else.

In the sales organization, salespeople work with, and for, a sales executive and a field sales manager. The sales executive determines policy and maintains financial control over the sales organization. Salespeople participate in the development of forecasts that the sales executive uses in the planning process.

Another policy decision involves the method of compensation for the sales force. The four basic methods are straight salary, straight commission, bonus, and a combination. Straight commission plans provide strong financial incentive for salespeople but leave the company with little control over their activities. Salary plans, on the other hand, give greater control to the company but offer less incentive for salespeople to work hard.

Sales executives are also responsible for creating a culture that supports ethical activities. Policies (e.g., as open-door policies) can encourage salespeople to act ethically. Ethical review boards are also useful in reviewing ethics policies, investigating potential ethics violations, and counseling salespeople who have concerns about the ethics of possible actions.

The main functions of the field sales manager are planning, organizing, directing, coordinating, motivating, evaluating, and training salespeople. Field sales managers are also responsible for implementing ethics policies. Sometimes, however, salespeople are faced with unethical requests from their managers. If that occurs, salespeople can choose from several courses of actions, such as blowing the whistle or appealing to an ethics review board.

Partnerships must be built within the sales force, too. Some examples include team selling with product specialists, inside/outside teams, or multilevel selling.

KEY TERMS

QUESTIONS AND PROBLEMS

1. You are one sale shy of achieving this month's quota, and today is the 29th. You finally close a deal but then the credit department tells you that the customer won't get credit (and they can't pay cash), shipping tells you they don't have the product in stock, and sales administration says unless the order is shipped tomorrow by 5:00 PM, it won't count toward this month's

quota. What will you do? What could you have done to prevent this from happening?

2. A company that rents office equipment to businesses pays its salespeople a commission equal to the first month's rent. However, if the customer cancels or fails to pay its bills, the commission is taken back. Is this fair? Why would the company have this plan?

3. What is the role of the geographic salesperson in a national or global account? Assume you were a NAM. What would you do to ensure the support of geographic reps?

4. How is team selling different from multilevel selling? How does the role of the account manager vary between the two? (Consider especially the account manager's role in coordinating internally.)

5. To what extent should salespeople be allowed to manage themselves? What risks do you take as a sales manager when you allow self-management? How can you minimize those risks?

6. Explain how compensation plans could affect cooperation between salespeople.

7. Assume your sales manager is working with you to evaluate your performance. As the sales call progresses, your manager begins to take over, ultimately dominating the call. How would you handle this? Why might this occur?

8. An experienced salesperson argues against salaries: "I don't like subsidizing poor performers. If you paid us straight commission, we'd know who could make it and who couldn't. Sure, it may take a while to get rid of the deadwood; but after that, sales would skyrocket!" Explain why you agree or disagree with this statement.

9. It took you four months to find a job and you were almost out of money when you finally landed the position. But today your boss asked you to do something unethical. You aren't sure what the corporate culture is yet because you are new at the company. How do you respond?

CASE PROBLEMS

CASE 17 • 1
STRUCTURAL STEEL
INDUSTRIES

It was nearly 5:00 on Friday afternoon when Charlie got the call from Westmont Construction. "Charlie, you gotta get someone out here now!" hollered Jack Westmont, owner of Westmont Construction. "You guys tried to slip some foreign steel into our job, and now we gotta rip it all out. But we aren't going to do it. You are, and it better be done by Monday!"

Charlie could tell that Jack was furious, and he had every right to be. Jack's company was building a major complex at the naval base in San Diego. Because it was a job for the federal government, the specs called for all U.S. steel. Somehow, steel from Structural Steel's Mexican supplier had been mixed with the domestic steel and sent to Westmont. If a navy inspector had seen it, Jack might even have had to forfeit a performance bond.

EXHIBIT 1   SSI ORGANIZATION CHART

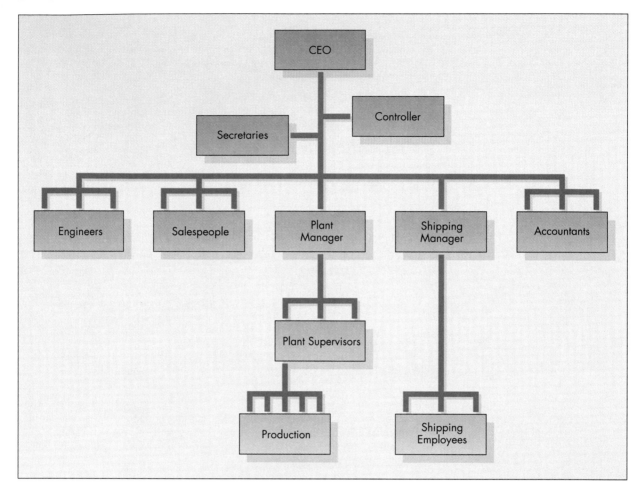

Structural Steel Industries (SSI) is a division of a larger steel fabricator. Steel fabricators take stock steel and make it into products. Miscellaneous steel fabricators, such as SSI, make custom steel components. SSI takes I-beams and other stock steel products and prepares them for assembly at a construction site. It cuts the steel to size, drills the holes for the rivets, and makes special beams and other steel products customized for specific buildings.

The company, a small division, employs 45 welders and production workers (including a plant manager and four supervisors), 10 employees in shipping (including the shipping manager), 2 engineers, 3 salespeople, 3 project managers who work with salespeople and engineers to prepare bids, a controller, 2 secretaries, and Charlie (the chief executive officer).

Everyone from the plant supervisors on up (see Exhibit 1) talks with customers directly. Because the jobs are custom, a lot of communication takes place between the contractor, the architect, and SSI to make sure that everything is done just right.

In addition to a high degree of customer contact, each job requires a great deal of communication within SSI. As the flowchart in Exhibit 2 shows, all areas of the organization must interact throughout the project to ensure that SSI meets customer specifications.

EXHIBIT 2

PROCESS FOR FILLING AN
ORDER

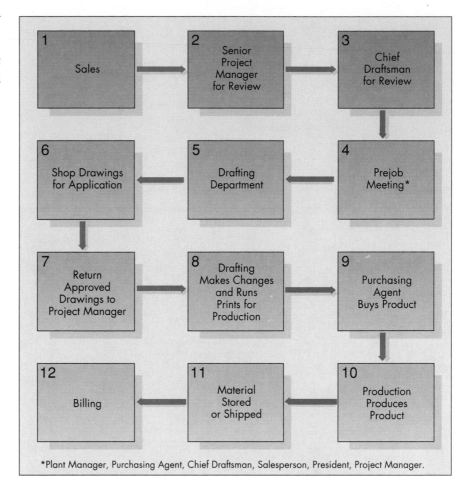

*Plant Manager, Purchasing Agent, Chief Draftsman, Salesperson, President, Project Manager.

After dealing with Jack, Charlie hung up the phone and buzzed Mary Longren, the project manager for Westmont's project. "Mary, who worked on the Westmont project?" Charlie queried.

"I did. Why?" she replied.

"I know you did. I meant who was the engineer and who inspected the goods before shipping. I just heard from Jack Westmont. Seems as though some of the steel was from a Mexican mill."

"Oh great, just what we need. When is he building the structure?" she asked.

"He's already started. He wanted us to go to San Diego and rip the material out ourselves, but I've got him calmed down somewhat," Charlie replied.

"Was it all Mexican steel?"

Charlie sighed. "No, only about 40 percent. The good news is that only about half of that was installed before they realized the problem. But they can't do anything until we ship the right steel."

Mary muttered something that Charlie didn't quite catch. Then she said, "OK, I'll go get Manuel and Mark and get manufacturing going." Mary hung up the phone and then slapped her desk in disgust. To her ceiling, she said, "Why can't we get this right? Is it that difficult?" She left her office to find Manuel, the production manager, and Mark, the shipping manager.

She quickly located the two among a crowd at the break lounge. She glanced at her watch; it was a few minutes after 5:00. Mark and several others were laughing loudly as Manuel described his weekend plans.

"You can forget those plans," interrupted Mary. "Westmont called. It seems that 40 percent of the steel we shipped was from a Mexican mill. That's a federal job, so it all has to be domestic steel."

"Well, we can get to it next week," Manuel replied, with his hands on his hips.

" 'Fraid not, Manuel. Charlie wants it out this weekend."

"No way, Mary! We can't get all of that done this weekend. That was a full-week job." Manuel was almost shouting.

"Then we'll just have to get out what we can," she stated, noticing that Mark was smirking. "You can forget your weekend plans too, pal. You've got to get us domestic steel and get this shipped to San Diego as soon as a truckload is ready."

"Well, we'll just see about that," said Mark, slamming a Coke can into a trash container. "C'mon Manuel, let's go see Charlie." The two walked off, talking animatedly to each other. A few production workers got up and started to walk out.

"Hey, you guys can just wait right there!" yelled Mary. "You are going to get plenty of overtime today. And if you don't want it, Charlie will help you find another place to work." One worker acted as if he didn't hear and kept right on going. Two turned around and returned to the break area.

On Monday, Angela Davis, the salesperson who handled the Westmont account, called Charlie. "I got your message, boss. What's up?" she asked.

"Westmont got Mexican steel. We've managed to ship a little more than half of the stuff he had already installed, but it will be Wednesday before the final shipment goes out."

"That's just terrific. What's the matter with those people in manufacturing? Can't they read specs?" Angela asked. Westmont wasn't her largest customer, but it was one of her biggest, a class-A account.

"Well, Angela," Charlie replied, pausing for effect, "it wasn't on the specs. Nothing manufacturing got said domestic only."

"But they should have known. It was a federal job!" she protested.

"Why should they have known? Anyway, you better call Jack Westmont and let him know what's happening. I'll let you talk to Mark next so you can get the full shipment schedule." Charlie transferred Angela to Mark. As Charlie hung up, he wondered where he was going to make up for the loss he was taking on the Westmont project.

Angela was in no mood for polite conversation when she finally reached Jack at the construction site. "Jack, this is Angela. Have you received the first emergency shipment yet?"

"No, we haven't. But it better get here soon. My guys are just sitting around." Jack sounded grim.

"You should get it any time now. I talked to Mark, and it went out about 5:00 this morning, so it should be there by 9:00."

"Look, sister. If it ain't here by 9:00, you might as well keep it. I can't afford to do business with you guys any longer." The line went dead as Jack hung up. Mary slumped against the wall of the pay phone booth, wondering what could go wrong next.

QUESTIONS

1. Who was primarily responsible for the Westmont project mistake? Who else was responsible? Why?

2. What can be done to prevent these problems in the future, and who should make those corrections?

3. Identify the managers that would be involved in a project and discuss what their priorities would be (e.g., the engineer would be most interested in the design itself).

CASE 17 • 2
WRT, INC. (A)*

Fred Johnson recently completed his MBA at the University of North Carolina—Chapel Hill with a concentration in marketing. After a series of interviews, he was hired by an electronic components division of WRT, Inc. as an industrial sales engineer. Johnson, who had served as an electronics officer in the United States Air Force, had no previous sales experience. During his MBA program at UNC—Chapel Hill, Johnson had taken numerous marketing courses. However, sales management and salesperson conduct were mentioned only briefly in these courses.

Johnson spent his first few weeks trying to get acclimated to the new job. Most of his time was spent familiarizing himself with a list of prospective clients and a series of product manuals. He was also encouraged to set up tours of the production facility and arrange meetings with product engineers. Toward the end of this initial orientation period, the human resources manager sent out a memo to all sales and customer service personnel announcing that a series of 30-minute sales-information videotapes would be shown on Monday mornings for those who were in the office. Anyone who was out of town during these presentations could check the appropriate tapes out overnight from the human resources department. When sales and customer service personnel attended the first meeting, they learned that the tape series focused exclusively on consumer sales. The human resources manager apologized for the consumer orientation, claimed that industrial videotapes were not available, and suggested that sales and customer service personnel should adapt the presented material to their own situations.

Two months after being hired, Johnson finally traveled to his sales territory in California and Arizona. Upon arriving in Los Angeles he was met by Jack Simpson, a former sales manager, who had previously been responsible for the area for over five years. The two of them then called on established accounts and, at first, Johnson watched Simpson handle himself with customers. Johnson, who wanted to appear enthusiastic, began asking questions and attempting to participate in the sales calls. After the trip, Johnson felt he was finally beginning to understand the WRT system and corporate philosophy.

Within a week of Johnson's return to the corporate offices, his boss requested a detailed five-year sales plan that was to include all territories, companies, and products. When Johnson explained he had been with the company for just over two months, he was told to do the best he could.

QUESTIONS

1. Why might Fred Johnson feel uncertain about how to proceed with a five-year plan?

2. What sales training areas should he have received that he did not? How could that training have enabled him to begin building internal partnerships with other areas of the company?

3. How could the training with Jack Simpson have been improved?

*This case was written by Earl Honeycutt and John Ford, Old Dominion University.

Case 17 • 3
WRT, Inc. (B)*

This case is to follow the WRT, Inc. (A) case, and it again involves Fred Johnson, a recent industrial sales recruit, who just completed a three-month period of orientation at the home office and in the field. Fred had been back for two weeks when the following letter arrived through distribution from the division manager:

> TO: *Fred Johnson, Sales Engineer*
> *Geoff LeBlanc, Sales Engineer*
> *J. C. Jones, Application Engineer*
> *Lynn Castleberry, Customer Service Manager*
> FROM: *Al Kraus, Division Manager*
> SUBJECT: *Training Program*
>
> *Over the past few months, we have hired a number of new personnel who have limited knowledge of our product line. In order to rectify this situation, I have asked each product engineer to meet with you and present the engineering aspects and technical specifications of their product line. Classes will be held in our conference room beginning Monday, March 15, from 9:00–12:00 noon, and will continue for the following six Mondays at the same time. Personnel who are on the road will be expected to make up missed material on their own time.*

At some point in the future, I will administer a test to each attendee. Those unwilling or unable to learn the presented material will be asked to find a position elsewhere. I know that I can count on each of you to devote the time and effort to master the information presented at these sessions.

Early the next morning, Fred Johnson's best friend at WRT, Inc., Geoff LeBlanc, stopped by for coffee. Geoff was quite concerned about the tone and nature of the division manager's letter. Geoff had previously worked for Westinghouse, Inc. and he was contemplating returning there. After talking with LeBlanc about the first three months at WRT, the lack of formal training, and the letter from the division manager, Johnson began to wonder if he too might have made a mistake by joining the company.

QUESTIONS

1. Do you see any problems with the training program announced in the letter? Has this manager built partnerships with his salespeople? Are partnerships possible? If so, how would, you as a salesperson, try to build a partnership? If not, describe the type of relationship you would strive for with this manager.

2. Is fear an appropriate motivator in this case? If not, how would you have written the letter?

EPILOGUE

Geoff LeBlanc did, in fact, leave WRT a month later and return to his previous job at Westinghouse. Fred Johnson also left WRT a year later due to job frustrations and his disenchantment with the overall methods employed by WRT upper management.

*This case was written by Earl Honeycutt and John Ford, Old Dominion University.

ADDITIONAL REFERENCES

Avila, Ramon A; Edward F Fern; and O Karl Mann. "Unraveling Criteria for Assessing the Performance of Salespeople: A Causal Analysis." *Journal of Personal Selling & Sales Management*, May 1988, pp. 45–54.

Boone, Louis E, and John C Milewicz. "Is Professional Selling the Route to the Top of the Corporate Hierarchy?" *Journal of Personal Selling & Sales Management,* Spring 1989, pp. 42–45.

Cardozo, Richard, and Shannon Shipp. "New Selling Methods Are Changing Industrial Sales Management." *Business Horizons,* September–October 1987, pp. 23–28.

Cauthern, Cynthia R. "Moving Technical Support into the Sales Loop." *Sales & Marketing Management,* August 1990, pp. 58–61.

Cespedes, Frank V; Stephen X Doyle; and Robert J Freedman. "Teamwork for Today's Selling." *Harvard Business Review,* March–April 1989, pp. 44–55.

Falvey, Jack. "Team Selling: What It Is (and Isn't)." *Sales & Marketing Management,* June 1990, pp. 8–10.

Lagace, Rosemary R. "Leader-Member Exchange: Antecedents and Consequences of the Cadre and Hired-Hand." *Journal of Personal Selling & Sales Management,* Winter 1990, pp. 11-20.

Morris, Michael H; Ramon Avila; and Eugene Teeple. "Sales Management as an Entrepreneurial Activity." *Journal of Personal Selling & Sales Management,* Spring 1990, pp. 1–15.

Rutherford, R D. "Make Your Sales Force Credit Smart." *Sales & Marketing Management,* November 1989, pp. 50–55.

St. John, Caron H, and Earnest H Hall, Jr. "The Interdependency between Marketing and Manufacturing." *Industrial Marketing Management,* Fall, 1991, pp. 223–229.

Strahle, William, and Rosann L Spiro. "Linking Marketing Share Strategies to Sales-Force Objectives, Activities, and Compensation Policies." *Journal of Personal Selling & Sales Management,* August 1986, pp. 11–18.

Tyagi, Pradeep, and Carl Block. "Monetary Incentives and Salesmen Performance." *Industrial Marketing Management,* Fall 1983, pp. 263–69.

CHAPTER

18

Managing Your Career

*I*n this chapter you will find the answers to many questions concerning how to start and develop a successful career in sales and marketing. Your first sale will involve selling yourself—to land that first position. But job searching is not always selling. As you will see, other activities are also necessary during the hiring process. That hiring process can be repeated each time you are considered for a promotion. Whether you decide to enter sales as a career or use it as a lauching pad for a career in marketing, or if you decide that you are better suited for another career, you will find this chapter helpful in getting your career started.

Some questions answered in this chapter are:

What entry-level jobs are available to new college graduates?

Where does one find these jobs?

How should I go about getting interviews and what should I do when I have an interview?

Besides interviews, what other selection procedures might I go through?

What career paths are available in sales?

How can I prepare myself for a promotion into management?

He had just swallowed the last of the barium sulfate the nurse told him to drink when he realized what he had always heard was true. Life is too short to work in a career you don't enjoy, regardless of how much you make. Now, with the beginnings of gastrointestinal problems, he was going to do something about it. After the x-rays were over he went back to his office and wrote his resignation letter. Finally he would do what he always wanted to do. Sell.

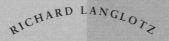

RICHARD LANGLOTZ

Minolta Business Systems

Eight plus years before that day Richard Langlotz, fresh out of the Air Force, went to work for the Southland Corporation as a store clerk at a 7-Eleven in Denton, Texas. His plan was to finish his marketing degree and go into sales. One year prior to completion of his degree, Southland offered him a job in their management team. After four years in the Air Force and three years working as a clerk, the money looked good. He was about to get married, so the opportunity to build on the three years he had at Southland looked like a great career move. Besides, he could always finish his degree at night and join the marketing department at Southland. He spent the next five years gaining the reputation as a top-notch field manager, but didn't go back to school.

Now, at the age of 34, with the beginnings of stomach problems, he was going to change careers. He finished his marketing degree at the University of North Texas and set out to find a good match for his talents and prospective employers. The first thing he found out was that several of the companies he had selected to interview with were not interested in a 34-year-old seeking an entry-level sales position. Only one company was willing to take the risk: Minolta Business Systems in Ft. Worth, Texas, selling copiers.

It didn't take long for Richard to verify what he knew all along. His experiences in management and in the Air Force were going to help. He had learned about people, the decision-making process, and what it took to make a good business decision. The first few months were typical for a new salesperson; sales were hard to come by. But Richard was still convinced that he had made the right move.

Beginning in the fourth month, Richard's sales skyrocketed. He ended his first year at Minolta with a 400 percent sales increase in his territory, was promoted through three sales positions, and made Minolta's President Club. After 15 months with Minolta, Richard was promoted to branch sales manager.

In looking back Richard said, "I was able to apply my experiences from the service and Southland to selling situations. Understanding business and people helped me understand the true needs of my customers and better help them with the decision-making process. It's hard to believe that I actually get paid to do this. To top it off, I haven't had a stomach problem since I came to Minolta."

Landing that first career position is an exciting moment that you may be looking forward to. But the job search is just the first task in managing your career. Like the chess player who is thinking two or three moves ahead, you must also think ahead about later opportunities. And also like the chess player, you must maintain some flexibility so that your career isn't checkmated if one strategy does not work.

Sales is a great place to begin a career. Salespeople gain first-hand customer knowledge that is necessary to be successful in later positions. Because salespeople must represent the entire company, they learn about many aspects of the business, as well as many of the people in various parts of the company. All of this knowledge can be put to use later as your career progresses.

OPPORTUNITIES IN SELLING

Selling offers many opportunities. About 4 million people are engaged in nonretail sales, with nearly a million new jobs expected in the next decade. Professional sales is second only to grade school teaching in new job growth. As you can see in Exhibit 18.1, there is strong growth in many sectors for new salespeople.

The number of sales positions is growing at a rate faster than for other types of positions. This fast-paced growth bodes well for marketing students, because most will begin their careers as salespeople. Corporate executives clearly recognize the importance of selling experience in any marketing career. You may recall the quote in an earlier chapter from Frank Cary, former chairman of the board of IBM, recommending selling as a great place to begin a career. Many people have also found career satisfaction by staying in sales throughout their working life.

Whether the career is sales or any other field, there are similar questions to consider when searching for a job. We will focus these questions, however, on the search for a sales position. We also explore how to land the first position. As part of that discussion, we examine how companies make hiring decisions. The chapter concludes with tips on how to build selling and management skills while managing a career.

E X H I B I T   1 8 . 1

NEW JOBS IN SALES

Source	Number of Jobs (in Thousands)
Sales, commodities	212
Sales, mining, manufacturing, and wholesale	209
Sales, retail durables and services	156
Insurance sales	31
Real estate sales	28

Source: U.S. Dept. of Labor, *Occupational Outlook Quarterly*, Spring 1993, pp. 13–23.

INTERNATIONAL OPPORTUNITIES

International opportunities are unlikely for most entry-level salespeople, but some entry-level marketing or sales positions can lead to international sales. Students who seek international opportunities may do well to begin with foreign companies doing business in the United States. International opportunities are also more likely with small companies already engaged in international business, especially for salespeople who have proved their abilities in a domestic sales position. Students who desire international sales should prepare themselves by learning the language of the people with whom they would like to do business and by participating in exchange or foreign study programs. There is no substitute for living in a culture in order to learn it.

MAKING A GOOD MATCH

The keys to being successful and happy lie in finding a good match between what you need and desire in a position and the positions that companies offer. The first step, then, is to understand yourself; what you need and what you have to offer. Then you must consider what each company needs and what each company has to offer. As illustrated in Exhibit 18.2, a good match means that your needs are satisfied by what the company offers and that what you offer satisfies the company's needs.

UNDERSTANDING YOURSELF

Shakespeare said, "To thine own self be true," but this presupposes that you know yourself. In order to be true to yourself, you must know who you are, what you need, and what you can offer others. To know these things about yourself require substantial self-examination. We will pose some questions that can help you know yourself.

EXHIBIT 18.2

A GOOD MATCH BETWEEN SALESPERSON AND COMPANY

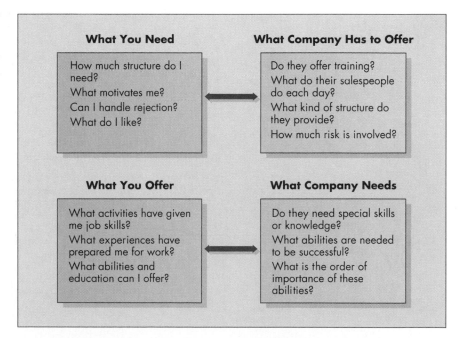

Many salespeople thrive in the recognition their superior results bring them, such as these four Mary Kay salespeople, just introduced to an audience of thousands of their peers as pink Cadillac winners.

Courtesy Mary Kay Cosmetics.

Understanding Your Needs

The first step to making a good match between what you have to offer and a company's position is to determine what it is you need. Important questions to consider include:

1. *Structure.* Can you work well when assignments are ambiguous or do you need a lot of instruction? Do you need deadlines that others set or do you set your own deadlines? If you are uncomfortable when left on your own, then you may need structure in your work life. Many sales positions, such as missionary and trade sales, are in a structured environment with well-defined procedures and routines. Other positions, however, require the salesperson to operate without much guidance or structure.

2. *Motivation.* Will it be financial incentives or personal recognition or simply job satisfaction that gets you going? Probably it will be some combination of the three, but try to determine the relative value of each to you. Then you can weigh compensation plans, recognition programs, and other factors when considering which sales position is right for you. You may want to review the section in Chapter 17 that discusses compensation plan types, to aid you in determining what plan would best suit your needs.

3. *Stress and rejection.* How much can you handle? Are you a risk-taker or do you prefer more secure activities? What do you do when faced with stress? With rejection? These are important questions in understanding what you need from a sales position. For example, capital equipment sales jobs can be high-stress positions, because sales are few and far between. Other jobs can

require you to wade through many rejections before finding a sale. If you thrive on that kind of challenge, then the rewards can be very gratifying.

4. *Interest*. What do you find interesting? Mechanical or technical topics? Merchandising? Art or fashion? You cannot sell something that bores you. You would just bore and annoy the customer.

Understanding What You Have to Offer

Other questions that help you understand the person you are may be available through your college's placement center. You must also take inventory of what you bring to the job:

1. *Skills.* What activities and experiences provided you with certain skills? What did you learn from those experiences and your education that you can apply to a career? Keep in mind that it is not the activities you participated in that matter to hiring companies; it is what you learned by participating that counts.

2. *Knowledge*. College has provided you with many areas of knowledge, but you have also probably learned much by participating in hobbies and other interests. For example, you may have special computer knowledge that would be useful in selling software, or you may have participated in a particular sport that makes you well-suited to sell equipment to sporting goods stores.

3. *Qualities and traits*. Every person is different, with his or her own personality. What part of your personality adds value for your potential employer? Are you detail oriented and systematic? Are you highly creative? In other words, what can you bring to the job that is uniquely you?

Your answers to these questions provide you with a list of what you have to offer to companies. Then, when you are in an interview, you can present these features that make you a desirable candidate.

When to Ask These Questions

Unfortunately, many students wait until just before graduation before seriously considering what type of career they desire. While it is not always realistic to expect every student to map out a life plan prior to the senior year, asking questions such as these as early as possible can guide a student to better course selection, better use of learning opportunities, and ultimately, a better career decision. Then the student can begin actively searching for the job at the beginning of the senior year so that graduation signals the beginning of a career, not a career search.

Understanding the Company

While developing a good feel for who you are and what you have to offer companies, you should also explore what is available and the companies that offer those positions. First we will discuss what sources of information are available to you, and then we address how to evaluate what you learn about the companies and their positions.

Sources of Job Information

There are numerous sources of written information about industries and jobs that will help you locate companies and information about them. As you may have discovered in other classes, such as marketing research, basic industry information is available in the *U.S. Industrial Outlook* published by the U.S. Department of Commerce. In addition to a general profile, the *Outlook* provides a five-year forecast for almost 350 industries. *Standard and Poor's Industry Surveys* can also provide you with industry information.

Magazines such as *Business Week, Money, Fortune,* and *Forbes* also contain helpful industry information. Once you locate an industry, you should also begin reading trade magazines for that industry. For example, *Communications News* is a trade publication for the telecommunications industry and is full of information on various telecommunications vendors. Magazines also exist for certain positions, such as *Sales & Marketing Management* for sales and marketing managers, or *Exhibitor Times* for people who manage trade show exhibits. Most magazines of this type publish annual salary surveys and job forecasts.

Your placement center may also contain recruiting brochures for various companies. While you may not be at the point of researching specific companies, you can use these as starting points to understand the needs of various industries.

The best sources of information are personal. Find people who currently hold the positions you are researching. You can find them by simply calling the local sales office for that company or by calling their customers (e.g., you can talk to physicians about pharmaceutical companies). You should be able to find salespeople and their customers willing to talk to you if you start your search early enough to give them time to visit when it is convenient for them. Other ways to meet salespeople and sales managers include visiting job fairs at your campus; visiting trade shows; and getting leads from friends, parents, community leaders (see Chapter 7 on prospecting), and your professors. In addition, whenever you prepare a term paper, you can include interviews with managers in the field. Term paper research can be a great opportunity to begin to know people who can help you later during a job search.

Most students won't make this effort. Yet remember that you may be competing with as many as 200 students at five or more colleges for that position you really want. One of our former students used these techniques to find a job in the steel industry. When he began to interview, he called company presidents, whom he had met at trade shows and steel industry association meetings. When he interviewed, he was knowledgeable about the industry because his term papers were often about that industry. And

Campus career service centers sponsor career fairs, an opportunity for you to meet and visit with employment representatives of many companies. Shown here is the Career Exchange Center at Triton College in Illinois.

Both photos courtesy Triton College.

when he got a job, he won the position over someone with several years of experience.

What the Company Has to Offer

When you meet a salesperson or sales manager, you should ask about compensation and recognition programs, training, career opportunities, and other information to determine if the company truly offers benefits to satisfy your needs. You should also explore daily activities of the salesperson, likes and dislikes about the job, and what that person thinks it takes to be successful. This information will help you determine if a match exists.

For example, if you need structure, you should look for a sales position in which your day is structured for you. Any industry that relies on repeated sales calls to the same accounts is more likely to be highly structured. Industries with a structured sales day include consumer packaged goods sales (Procter & Gamble, Quaker Oats, etc.) or pharmaceutical sales (Marion/ Merrell Dow, Eli Lilly Co., etc.). Even these sales positions, however, offer some flexibility and independence. Office and industrial equipment sales would provide much less structure when the emphasis is on getting new accounts.

Knowing your comfort level with risk and your need for incentives should assist you in picking a company with a compensation program that is right for you. If you need the security of a salary, look for companies in trade sales, some equipment sales, or missionary sales. But if you like the risk of straight commission, which can often be matched with greater financial rewards for success, then explore careers in such areas as convention sales, financial services, and other straight commission jobs.

Other factors to consider may include the size of the company and its promotion policies, particularly if the company is foreign. Many companies have a "promote from within" policy, which means that whenever possible they will fill positions with people who are already employees. Such policies are very attractive if you seek career growth into management. If the company is foreign-owned, however, there may be a level in the company where they want to staff positions with people from their own country.

Take advantage of interests you already have. If you are intrigued by medical science, then seek a medical sales position. If merchandising excites you, then a position selling to the trade would be appropriate. A bar of soap by itself is not exciting, but for some people helping customers find ways to market that bar of soap is.

An important trend to be aware of is the increasing use of on-the-job training, or at least delaying formal training. Many companies are providing little sales training at the start, emphasizing product and company knowledge in its place and reducing the initial training time to a few days or a week. Then, after six months or so in the field, the new rep is brought in for sales training. The thinking behind this strategy is that some aspects of sales training have little impact unless the trainee has a better understanding of what happens in the field. You may have noticed in this class that the instructor emphasizes topics that you may think are not that important, but your perception would be different if you have had some experience.

Another reason for the trend is the combination of high turnover and rising training costs for new hires. Xerox used to have to wait 18 months before covering the training costs of a new hire, yet the time with the greatest likelihood for losing a rep is within the first year. Now, some of those training costs are delayed so that if turnover occurs, less investment is lost. In addition, the new salesperson is in the field making some sales, which helps cover the cost. However, as a potential new hire, you need to be aware of the training offered by a company, and whether that training meets your needs.

What the Company Needs

At this point in your job search, you may have narrowed your selection to a group of industries or companies. At a minimum, you have a good picture of what a company should offer to land you as a salesperson. The next step is to find a company that needs you. Finding out what a company needs will require some research, but you will find it to be fun and rewarding.

Many Fortune 500 companies have changed their hiring policies for entry-level positions. In the past, they would recruit heavily at college campuses for beginning salespeople. Today, some of those companies, such as Xerox Corporation, hire only experienced salespeople. But many excellent opportunities exist in small companies. Richard Langlotz (featured at the beginning of this chapter) and Bill Arend (featured at the beginning of Chapter 16) both began selling with smaller companies and found the ex-

S E L L I N G   S C E N A R I O

18.1

Big or Small—A State of Mind?

Wade Hallisey works for a company that many people haven't heard of: Rollins Leasing. Even though they are traded on the New York Stock Exchange, employ 2,600 people, and generate $400 million in revenue a year, Rollins does not enjoy the name recognition among the general public that competitors such as Ryder Truck Leasing or Penske has. But according to Wade, Rollins does have the reputation where it counts: with its customers.

"Ask anyone in the business, and they'll tell you that Rollins is the most professional leasing company," says Wade. He attributes that reputation to small company flexibility and family pride. "The Rollins family still owns over 20 percent of the company, so they instill a personal pride in providing customer service. And we've always run lean [with few layers of management], which gives me greater flexibility in meeting my customers' needs."

Wade also likes the structured freedom at Rollins. "They provide me with goals, sales strategies, and excellent training, but they also give me the freedom to serve my market as I see fit. I think that is one benefit that a company of this size can provide."

But not all small companies are wonderful to work for. His first experience lasted only three months. "Training consisted of being introduced to everyone in the home office. I had no clear idea of how they wanted me to sell the product." Wade also reports that the company had no clear organization chart, with responsibilities and authority so ill-defined in the corporate office to the point that he was unsure who his boss was.

Quickly, he learned that the company also had different ethical standards than those he was willing to accept. Because of a conflict over the way a customer was treated, he left the company.

"After leaving them, I was more interested in a company with more square footage vertically than horizontally—in other words, I wanted to work on the 16th floor of a major corporation instead of on the shop floor of truck leasing company. But I've learned that it takes professional selling to sell a $20,000 leasing contract on the shop floor, and I've also realized that I get a great deal of satisfaction when I do close those big deals." As Wade says, "We may be small, but we're solid. And I'm building a solid sales career with Rollins."

perience to be very rewarding. Selling Scenario 18.1 discusses Wade Hallisey's experience in entry-level selling for two small businesses.

In general, companies look for three qualities in salespeople: good communication skills, self-motivation, and a positive and enthusiastic attitude.[1] Al Lynch, CEO of JCPenney International, adds quantitative skills, or an ability to ask the right questions, to this list.

Companies in certain industries may also desire related technical skills or knowledge, such as medical knowledge for the field of pharmaceutical sales, computer skills for computer sales, and so forth. If you desire to enter a field requiring specialized knowledge or skills, now is the time to begin learning that knowledge. Not only will you already have the knowledge when you begin to search for a position, but you will also have demonstrated self-motivation and the right kind of attitude by taking on the task of acquiring that knowledge and skill.

THE RECRUITING PROCESS

Early in this book, we discussed the buying process, so that we could understand the purchase decision that buyers make. Now we will take a look at the recruiting process, so that you can understand how companies will be viewing you as a candidate for a sales job or any other position.

SELECTING SALESPEOPLE

In recent years, companies have made considerable progress in screening and selecting salespeople. Most have discarded the myth that there is a "sales type" who will be successful selling anything to anybody. Instead, they seek people who match the requirements of a specific position. To do this, they use a number of methods to gain information and determine if a good match is made.

Applicant Information Sources

To determine if a match exists between the job requirements and the applicant's abilities, information about the applicant must be collected. Companies use five important sources of information: application forms, references, tests, personal interviews, and assessment centers. We will discuss each of these from the perspective of the company so that you can understand how these are used to make hiring decisions, but we will also discuss how you should use these sources of information so that you can present yourself accurately and positively.

The **application form** is a preprinted form that the candidate completes. You have probably already filled these out for part-time jobs you may have had. The form should include factual questions concerning the profile that the company established for the position. Responses on the form are also useful for structuring the personal interview. Resumes can act as application forms, but are often are too individualized and must be supplemented with an application form (we will discuss resumes in greater detail later in this chapter).

Contacting **references,** or people who know the applicant, is a good way to validate information on the application form. References can also supplement the information with personal observations. The most frequently contacted references are former employers. Other references are co-workers, leaders of social or religious organizations, and professors. You should also be aware that some organizations try to develop relationships with faculty so that they can receive leads on excellent candidates before visiting the placement office. Professors recommend students who have demonstrated in class the qualities desired by the recruiting companies.

Keep in mind when you select references that companies want references that can validate information about you. Choose references that provide different information, such as one character reference, one educational reference, and one work-related reference.

Experienced sales managers expect to hear favorable comments from an applicant's references. More useful information may be contained in unusual comments, gestures, faint praise, or hesitant responses that may indicate a problem. Before you offer someone's name as a reference, ask for permission. At this time, you should be able to tell if the person is willing to give you a good recommendation.

Intelligence, ability, personality, and interest **tests** provide information about a potential salesperson that cannot be obtained readily from other sources. Tests can also correct misjudgments made by sales managers who want to act on "gut feelings."

Several types of tests may be given. H.R. Challey Inc. designs tests to determine a person's psychological aptitude for different sales situations. IBM requires sales candidates to demonstrate technical aptitude through a test. Many companies require candidates to pass a math test, because of the importance of calculating price correctly. Tests are also given that indicate a candidate's ethical nature. Companies may require candidates to take tests in all of these categories before offering a position.

The important point to remember about tests is to remain relaxed. If the test is a valid selection tool, then you should be happy with the outcome no matter what that may be. If you feel that the test is not valid, that is it does not predict your ability to be successful for that job, you may want to present your feelings to the recruiter. Be prepared to back up your line of reasoning with facts and experiences that illustrate that you are a good candidate for the position.

Interviews are an important source of information for recruiters. Companies now give more attention to conducting multiple interviews in the selection process because sometimes candidates have only slight differences. Multiple interviews can improve a recruiter's chances of observing the differences and selecting the best candidate. We will discuss interviews in more detail later in the chapter.

Companies sometimes evaluate candidates at centrally located **assessment centers**. In addition to being used for testing and personal interviews, these locations may be used to simulate portions of the job. Simulating the job serves two purposes. First, the simulation provides managers with an opportunity to see candidates responding to a joblike situation. Second, candidates can experience the job and determine if the job fits them. For example, Merrill Lynch sometimes places broker-candidates in an office and simulates two hours of customer telephone calls. As many as half of the candidates may then decide that being a stockbroker is not right for them, and Merrill Lynch can also evaluate the candidates' abilities in a lifelike setting.

Companies will use many sources of information in making a hiring decision, perhaps even asking for a copy of a videotaped presentation you may make for this class. These sources are actually selling opportunities for you. You can present yourself and learn about the job at the same time, continuing your evaluation of the match.

| LANDING THE SALES POSITION | Companies take a number of steps to ensure that a good match will occur. But it is up to you, the candidate, to make the company aware of the desire and skills that you have. In this section, we will examine more closely how you can present your qualifications well and land that sales position.

▌ PREPARING THE RESUME

The resume is the brochure in your marketing plan. As such, it needs to tell the recruiter why you should be hired. Recruiters scan a resume for only 20 seconds before deciding whether to study it more carefully.[2] Whether you choose the conventional style or the functional style of resume, the purpose is to sell your skills and experience.

Conventional Resumes

Conventional resumes are a form of life history, organized by type of experience. The three categories of experience most often used are educational, work, and activities/hobbies (see the example in Exhibit 18.3). Although it is easier to create conventional resumes, it is also easier to fail to

▌ E X H I B I T   1 8 . 3

CONVENTIONAL RESUME
EXAMPLE

Cheryl McSwain

After June 1:
435 Wayward View, Apt. B
State College, PA 10303
203/555-1289

Present Address:
612 Homer
Aurora, CO 86475
804/555-9183

Career Objective: Sales in the telecommunications industry

Education:
Colorado University, Boulder, Colorado
Bachelor of Business Administration, June 1995
Major: Marketing
GPA: 3.25 on 4.0 scale

Major Subjects: Other Subjects:
Personal Selling   Microcomputing
Sales Management   Local Area Networks Management
Industrial Marketing   Telecommunications

Emphasized selling and sales management in computing and telecommunications. Learned SPIN, social styles, and other adaptive selling techniques. Studied LANWORKS and Novell network management.

Work Experience: Sales Representative, The Lariat (CU Campus Newspaper)
Practiced sales skills in making cold calls
and selling advertising
Fall 1993 to present

Camp Counselor, Camp Kanatcook
Learned customer service and leadership skills
Summers, 1992, 1993, 1994

Scholarships and Honors:
University Merit Scholar ($2,000/year, 2 years)
Top Sales Student, Spring 1994
Dean's List, 3 semesters

Activities:
Member, Alpha Delta Pi Sorority
Rush Chair, 1993
Motivated members to actively recruit; interviewed candidates for selection
Homecoming Float Chair, 1992
Managed float building; sorority awarded second in float competition
Women's Soccer Team, four years
Captain, 1994–95
Led team to conference championship, Fall 1994

emphasize important points. To avoid making this mistake, follow this simple procedure:

- List education, work experience, and activities.
- Write out what you gained in each experience that will help you prove that you have the desired qualities.
- Emphasize what you learned and that you have the desired qualities under each heading.

For example, the resume in Exhibit 18.3 is designed for a student interested in a sales career. Note how skills gained in this class are emphasized in addition to GPA and major. The candidate has also chosen to focus on customer service skills gained as a camp counselor, a job that would otherwise be overlooked by a recruiter. Rather than just listing herself as a member of the soccer team, she highlights the leadership skills she gained as captain.

Functional Resumes

Functional resumes reverse the content and titles of the conventional resume, organizing by what the candidate can do or has learned, rather than by types of experience. As you can see in Exhibit 18.4, an advantage to this type of resume is that it highlights more forcefully what the candidate can do.

When preparing this type of resume, you may want to begin by listing your qualities that you think will help you get the job. Narrow this list to three or four, then list activities and experiences that prove that you have those skills and abilities. The qualities are the headings for the resume, while the activities and experiences provide evidence that you really do have those qualities. One difficulty with this type of resume is that one past job, for example, may relate to several qualities. If that is the case, emphasize the activity within the job that provided you with the experience for each specific quality.

The Career Objective

As you've probably noticed, both sample resumes list a career objective. The career objective is important because it identifies immediately the desired position. One question that many students ask is what to do when interviewing for several types of positions; for example, interviewing for retail management with one company and sales with another. The solution is to create several resumes, each listing a different objective, then use whichever version is most appropriate for a particular company. The worst solution is to not use one; potential employers then have to guess what you want.

Cheryl McSwain

After June 1:
435 Wayward View, Apt. B
State College, PA 10303
203/555-1289

Present Address:
612 Homer
Aurora, CO 86475
804/555-9183

Career Objective: Sales in the telecommunications industry

Sales and Customer Service Experience:
Studied SPIN and adaptive selling techniques in Personal Selling.
Sold advertising in The Lariat, campus newspaper. Responsibilities included making cold calls, presenting advertising strategies, and closing sales.
Performed customer service tasks as Camp Counselor at Camp Kanatcook.
Served as the primary parent contact during drop-off and pick-up periods, answering parent queries, resolving parental concerns, and similar responsibilities.

Management and Leadership Experience:
Studied Situational Management in Sales Management.
Served as Rush Chair for sorority. Responsible for motivating members to recruit new members and developed and implemented a sales training seminar so members would present the sorority favorably within University guidelines.
Managed Homecoming float project. Sorority awarded second place in float competition.
Captained the Women's Varsity Soccer team to a conference championship.

Telecommunications Skills and Experience:
Studied LANWORKS and Novell network management in Telecommunications.
Designed, as a term project, a Novell-based LAN for a small manufacturing business.
Purchased and installed a 6-computer network in parents' wholesaling business.

Scholarships and Honors:
University Merit Scholar ($2,000/year, 2 years)
Top Sales Student, Spring 1994
Dean's List, 3 semesters

Students should begin examining different industries as early as possible, as we suggested earlier. As graduation looms closer and the time for serious job hunting arrives, your knowledge of the industries and companies that you would like to work for puts you a step ahead. You also understand the process that the company will go through in searching for a new salesperson.

Using Personal Contacts

More important, you have already begun to make personal contacts in those fields—contacts that you can now use to gain interviews. Those same salespeople and sales managers who gave you information before to help you with term projects will usually be happy to introduce you to the person in charge of recruiting. Contacts that you made at job fairs and trade shows can also be helpful.

THINKING IT THROUGH	*M*any students feel uncomfortable asking for favors from people they barely know. How can you overcome such feelings of discomfort? Why would someone want to help you find places to interview? What obligations do you have to people who provide you with the names of job contacts?

Using Employment Advertisements

Responding to newspaper advertisements can also lead to job interviews. You will want to carefully interpret employment advertisements, and then respond effectively to them.

INTERPRETING EMPLOYMENT ADVERTISEMENTS   All ads are designed to sell, and employment ads are no different. But what sounds great on paper may not be wonderful in reality. Here are some phrases that can often be found in such ads, and how you should interpret them:[3]

"Independent contractor": You will work on straight commission with no employee benefits. You will probably receive no training and little, if any, support.

"Earn up to $_____ " (another variation is "Our top rep made $100,000 last year"): You need to know what the average person makes, and what the average first-year earnings are, not what the top rep made or the upper limit. Another variation is "Unlimited income" (see "independent contractor"). The job could still be desirable, but you need to find out what reality is before accepting a position.

"Sales manager trainee": This is another title for sales representative. Don't be put off or overly encouraged by high-sounding titles.

"Bonuses paid weekly": Other versions include "Daily commissions" or "Weekly commissions." These are high-pressure jobs and probably involve high-pressure sales.

"Ten salespeople needed now!": That's because everyone quit. This company uses salespeople, then discards them.

In an ad, you should look for two things: what the company needs and what it has to offer. The company should provide concrete information concerning training, compensation plan (although not necessarily the amount), amount of travel to expect, and type of product or service you will sell. You should also expect to find the qualifications that the company desires, including experience and education. If you don't have the experience now, call and ask how to get the experience. Be specific: "What companies should I pursue that will give me the experience you are looking for?"

Want ads can be a good source of job leads; but care should be taken when interpreting claims made in some ads.

Michael J. Hruby.

RESPONDING TO ADVERTISEMENTS   Many ads will ask you to write and may have a blind box number. A blind box number is given when the company name is not included in the ad; the box number is usually at the address of the newspaper. For example, the ad may say to send a resume to Box 000, care of the *Dallas Morning News*. Don't be put off by the lack of company name; the ad may be placed by a company such as IBM that would otherwise receive a large number of unqualified applicants. Companies used blind box numbers for many legitimate reasons.

Writing the Cover Letter

When you write in response to an ad, you are writing a sales letter. As with any sales letter, it should be focused on what you can do for them, not what you expect from them. The letter should start with an attention-getter. One example might be:

> *In today's economy, you need someone who can become productive quickly as a territory representative. Based on your ad in the* Dallas Morning News, *I believe that I am that person.*

This attention-getter is direct, focused on a probable need, and includes a link to the ad. The probability of getting response to this attention-getter is far greater than if you simply said:

> *Please consider me for your territory representative position, advertised in the* Dallas Morning News.

because the attention-getter tells why you should be considered.

The body of the letter should center on two or three reasons why you should be hired. For example, if you have the qualities of self-motivation and leadership, spend two paragraphs relating each to the position. Use your resume as proof. For example:

> *A territory representative position often requires self-motivation. As you can see from the attached resume, I demonstrated self-motivation as a sales representative for the campus newspaper, as a volunteer for the local food bank, and as a member of the Dean's Honor Roll during two of the last four semesters.*

The letter should close with a request for action. Ask for an interview and suggest times that you are available. For example:

> *Please call me so that we can explore your exciting opportunity further. My schedule allows me to meet with you on Tuesday or Thursday afternoons.*

No response does not necessarily mean that you have been rejected; follow up with a phone call if you do not hear anything within a week. One student got a job because he called to verify that the sales manager had received his resume. She had never seen it but was impressed enough with the student's phone call to arrange an appointment. Sometimes letters are lost or delayed, and you would not want a company to miss out on the opportunity to hire you because of the mail!

▌ THE INTERVIEW ITSELF

Many students do not realize how much competition exists for the best entry-level sales positions, or perhaps they do not know what companies look for in new employees. Students often act as if they are shopping for a job. Job shoppers, however, are not seriously considered by recruiters, who are usually astute enough to quickly pick up on the students' lack of interest. If the job shopper does become interested, it is probably too late because the recruiter has already discounted this applicant. Like it or not, you are really competing for a job. As in any competition, success requires preparation and practice.

Preparing for the Interview

Students who know something about the company and its industry are leading the competition. You have already looked for company and industry information in the library, in business reference books, and in periodicals. You have also interviewed the company's customers, salespeople, and sales managers. You can use this knowledge to demonstrate your self-motivation and positive attitude, two of the top three characteristics that sales managers look for in sales candidates. The other top characteristic, communication skills, you will find easier to demonstrate with the confidence you gain from proper preparation.

In addition to building knowledge of the "customer," you must also plan your responses to the questions you will be asked. Exhibit 18.5 lists standard questions that you might hear.

EXHIBIT 18.5

FREQUENTLY ASKED
INTERVIEW QUESTIONS

1. What are your long-range and short-range goals and objectives? When and why did you establish these goals, and how are you preparing yourself to achieve them?

2. What do you consider to be your greatest strengths and weaknesses?

3. Why did you choose the career for which you are preparing?

4. How do you think a friend or professor who knows you well would describe you?

5. Why should I hire you?

6. In what ways do you think you can make a contribution to our company?

7. Do you think your grades are a good indication of your academic achievement?

8. What major problem have you encountered, and how did you deal with it?

9. What do you know about our company? Why are you seeking a position with us?

10. If you were hiring a graduate for this position, what qualities would you look for?

Source: Baylor University Career Services Center.

Scenario questions are very popular with recruiters. These questions ask what would the candidate do in a certain situation involving actions of competitors. For example, "What would you do if a customer told you something negative about your product that you knew to be untrue, and the customer's source of information was your competitor?" This scenario question tests ethics toward competitors and the ability to handle a delicate situation. Other such questions test the candidate's response to rejection, ability to plan, and other characteristics. You can best prepare for these types of questions with this class and by placing yourself in the situations described in the cases and exercises in this book. You may also want to review the questions at the ends of the chapters.

Sales has several unusual characteristics, such as travel, that influence the type of questions asked. For example, if significant travel is a part of the position, you may be asked something like: "Travel is an important part of this job, and you may be away from home about three nights per week. Would you be able and willing to travel as needed by the job?" However, questions such as "What is your marital status? Do you plan to have a family? Will that impact on your ability to travel?" are illegal and you do not have to answer them. Exhibit 18.6 lists questions that are inappropriate, as well as appropriate questions that you may have to answer.

At some point during the interview, the recruiter will ask if you have any questions. In addition to the standard questions concerning pay, training, and benefits, prepare questions unlikely to have been answered already. For example, suppose your research has uncovered the fact that the company was awarded the Malcolm Baldrige Award for Quality; you might plan to ask what the company did to win that award.

You may also want to plan questions about the interviewer's career, how it got started, and what positions he or she has held. These questions work best when you are truly interested in the response; otherwise, you could sound insincere. Answers to these questions can give you a personal insight into the company. Also, you may often find yourself working for the interviewer, so the answers to your questions may help you decide whether you like and can work with this person.

EXHIBIT 18.6

EXAMPLES OF LEGAL AND
ILLEGAL QUESTIONS

Subject	Legal Questions	Illegal Questions
Name	Have you ever used another name?	What is your maiden name?
Residence	Where do you live?	Do you own or rent your home?
Birthplace or national origin	Can you, after employment, verify your right to work in the United States?	Where were you born? Where were your parents born?
Marital or family status	Statement of company policy regarding assignment of work of employees who are related. Statement of company policy concerning travel and "Can you accept this policy?	With whom do you reside? Are you married? Do you plan a family?
Arrest or criminal record	Have you ever been convicted of a felony? (Such a question must be accompanied by a statement that a conviction will not necessarily disqualify the applicant.)	Have you ever been arrested?

Source: Baylor University Career Services Center.

Other important subjects to ask about are career advancement opportunities, typical first-year responsibilities, and corporate personality. You also need to know how financially stable the company is, but you can find this information for public firms in the library. If the firm is privately owned, ask about its financial stability.

Finally, it may seem trivial, but shine your shoes! You are interviewing for a professional position, so look professional. A student once showed up for an interview dressed in cut-off shorts and a T-shirt. The interviewer assumed the student didn't care enough to dress for the interview, and ended the interview before it began. If you don't look the part now, they won't see you in the part.

IN THE INTERVIEW

The job interview is much like any other sales call. It contains an approach, needs identification, presentation, and gaining commitment. There are, however, several important differences because both parties are identifying needs and making presentations.

The Approach

Social amenities will begin the interview. You will not need the same type of attention-getter that you would on a cold call. However, you may want to include an attention-getter in your greeting. For example, use a compliment approach, such as "It must be very exciting to work for a Malcolm Baldrige Award winner."

Interviews at a college place-ment center may be only the first in a series of interviews and evaluations for a candi-date.

Sharon Hoogstraten.

Needs Identification

One difference between sales calls and job interviews is that both par-ties have needs that have probably been defined before the meeting (in a sales call, SPIN helps you assist the buyer to define needs). Questions such as "Are you willing to relocate" not only identify your needs, but also assist the recruiter in determining if the company's needs are met as well.

Take notes during the interview, especially when asking about the com-pany, so that you can evaluate if your needs are met. Carry a portfolio with extra resumes and blank paper and pen for note taking. You may want to ask, "Do you mind if I take notes? This information is important to me, and I don't want to forget anything."

Try to determine early whether your interviewer is a sales manager or a personnel manager. Personnel managers may have a difficult time telling you about the job itself, its daily activities, and so forth; they may only be able to outline such things as training and employee benefits. Sales manag-ers, however, can tell you a lot about the job, perhaps to the point of de-scribing the actual territory you will occupy.

Personnel managers do not like being asked about salary; you'll find that many people will advise you not to ask about money on the first in-terview. On the other hand, you are making an important decision. Why waste your time or theirs if the salary is much lower than your other alter-natives? Sales managers are less likely to mind, but just in case, you may want to preface a question about earnings by saying, "Compensation is as important a consideration as training and other benefits for me when mak-ing a decision. Can you tell me the approximate earnings of a first-year salesperson?" You will probably get a range rather than a specific figure. You also could wait until a later meeting to ask about earnings.

People who prefer security desire compensation plans with an emphasis on salary. Other people like the potential rewards of straight commission. If either is important to you, do ask about the type of compensation plan in the first meeting. For example, you should ask, "What type of compensation plan do you offer: salary, straight commission, or a combination of salary plus commission or bonus?"

Presentation

Features alone are not persuasive in interviews, just as features alone do not persuade buyers to purchase products. The US Army Recruiting Command uses a technique to sell the Army that can be useful in interviewing. The technique is called **FEB,** which stands for feature, evidence, benefit. For example, Cheryl Swain (see Exhibit 18.3) might say: "I was a camp counselor for two summers at Camp Kanatcook (F), as you can see on my resume (E). This experience taught me customer service skills that you will appreciate when I sell for you. (B)"

Be able to back it up.

If asked to describe yourself, use features to prove benefits. Recruiters will appreciate specific evidence that can back up your claims. For example, if you say you like people and that is why you think you would be a good salesperson, be prepared to demonstrate how your love of people has translated into action.

THINKING IT THROUGH	*H*ow would you describe yourself in terms of *features?* How could you prove those features to a recruiter? What needs would be satisfied by those features so they could become benefits?

Keep in mind that the interviewer also will be taking notes. Writing answers down takes the interviewer longer than it takes for you to speak. Once the question is answered sufficiently, stop and allow the interviewer time to write. Many applicants feel that they should continue talking; the silence of waiting is too much to bear. Stay silent, however; otherwise, you may talk yourself out of a sale.

Gaining Commitment

If interviewing for a sales position, one that will probably require skill at gaining commitment, sales managers will want to see if the candidate has that skill. Be prepared to close the interview with some form of gaining commitment. For example, "I'm very excited about this opportunity. What is our next step?"

Be sure to learn when you can expect to hear from that company, confirm that deadline, and write it down. You may want to say: "So I'll receive a call or a letter within the next two weeks. Let's see, that would be the 21st, right?"

Asking for commitment and confirming the information signals your professionalism and your organizational and selling skills.

Special Types of Interviews

You can face many types of interviews: disguised interviews, stress interviews, and panel interviews, among others. **Disguised interviews,** or interviews where the candidate is unaware that the interviewer is evaluating the candidate, are common at college placement offices. In the lobby you may meet a **greeter,** probably a recent graduate of your college, who will try to help you relax before a scheduled interview and offer you an opportunity to ask questions about the job and the company. Although you can obtain a lot of good information from a greeter, you may want to save some for the real interview. You may also want to repeat some questions in the interview to check for consistency. Keep in mind that the greeter is also interviewing you, even though it seems like friendly conversation. Keep your enthusiasm high and your nerves low.

A **stress interview** is designed to place the candidate under severe stress in order to see how the candidate reacts. Stress interviews have been criticized as being unfair, because the type of stress that one feels on a job interview often differs from the type of stress that one would actually feel on the job. Using one stress interview tactic, the interviewer asks the applicant to reveal something personal, such as a time when the person felt hurt. Once the situation has been described, the interviewer may mock the applicant, saying that the situation wasn't that personal or that hurtful and surely the applicant can dig deeper. Another stress tactic is to ask the interviewee to sell something like a pencil or table.

You probably will not see stress interviews at a college placement office, but you could be faced with one at some point in the job process. You may find it helpful to deal with a stress interview by treating it as a game (e.g., say to yourself, "She's just trying to stress me out; I wonder how far she will go if I don't react"). Of course, you may simply refuse to play the game, either by terminating the interview or by changing the subject. If you terminate the interview, you will probably not get the job.

In **panel interviews,** you will encounter multiple interviewers. During a panel interview, try to make eye contact with each interviewer. Keep your eyes on each person for at least three seconds at a time; anything less than that and you are simply sweeping the room. When asked a question, begin your answer by directing it to the questioner, but then shift your attention to the group. By speaking to the group, you keep all interviewers involved and avoid a two-person conversation.

Group interviews are similar to panel interviews, but include several candidates as well as several interviewers. Group interviews may take place in a conference room or around a dinner table. If you find yourself in a group interview, avoid trying to top the stories of the other candidates. Treat social occasions during office or plant visits as interviews, and avoid alcohol or overeating. As with stress interviews, the key is to maintain your cool while being yourself. You can't do that if you overindulge.

Panel interviews require special tactics by the candidate to keep all interviewers involved.

Sharon Hoogstraten.

Follow-Up

Regardless of the type of interview, you should send a thank-you note shortly afterward. Send one to the greeter, if possible (so you will probably want to get this person's business card). If you had a panel interview, find out who the contact person is and write to that person. After thanking the person in the first paragraph, write a paragraph that summarizes the interview. Focus your summary on the reasons why you should be hired. In the final paragraph, reiterate your thanks and end with an assumptive statement, such as "I look forward to seeing you again."

If you do not hear by the target date, contact the person. Call if the interviewer was a sales manager; write if a personnel manager spoke with you. Sales managers will appreciate the saleslike perseverance; personnel managers may not. Within another week, call the personnel manager also. Simply ask for the status of your application rather than whether you got the job or not. The process of deciding may have taken longer than expected, or other delays may have arisen. You need to know where you stand, however, so that you can take advantage of alternatives, if possible.

INTERVIEWING NEVER ENDS

Even if you spend your entire career with one company, your job interviewing days are not over once you land that first job; you will interview for promotions as well. Some companies even interview candidates for admission to management development programs. The same techniques apply in all these cases. You will still need to prepare properly, conduct the interview professionally, close for some level of commitment, and follow up.

MANAGING YOUR CAREER GOALS

Mary Kay Cosmetics encourages its salespeople to plan family time first, religious time second, Mary Kay time third. This company recognizes the importance of sales employees leading a balanced life. As independent salespeople, they could easily allow their jobs to run their lives rather than maintaining control. But with the company's encouragement, they set time aside to keep their lives balanced.

An important aspect of career management is to set life-based objectives, then use those to determine your career objectives. A manager at MSI Steel keeps a photo of a ranch on his desk. It is not his ranch, but it resembles the one where he wants to raise his family. Keeping this life-based objective in front of him has helped him make career decisions. Career decisions must be compatible with family and personal objectives.

You may want to run the marketing operations of a company. Keeping that, or any, objective in mind, and remembering your reasons for setting that objective, will help you map out a career with which you can be happy.

MAKING THE TRANSITION FROM COLLEGE TO CAREER

That first year after college is unique and important in anyone's life. How this transition is handled can have a big influence in reaching success or experiencing disappointment. Although a life's work is not created or ruined in the first months, a poor start can take years to overcome. It is not just a matter of giving up student attitudes and behaviors; making the transition also requires taking the time to understand and earn the rights, responsibilities, and credibility of being a sales professional.[4] (See Selling Scenario 18.2.)

Many new hires want to make a great first impression so that they charge ahead, and fail to recognize that the organization was there long before they were and has already developed its own way of doing things. The first thing to do is to learn the organization's culture, its values, and the way things are done there.

THINKING IT THROUGH	During your first year at your school, you became part of the school's culture. How did you learn about the school's culture and values? How can you apply that learning process to your first job?

Another important aspect of the first year is that you are under a microscope. Your activities are watched closely as management and your peers try to decide if you are someone on whom they can depend. Demonstrate a mature willingness to learn, plus respect for those with experience. Part of this mature willingness to learn means that you hold your expectations in check, and that you keep your promotion hopes realistic. Remember, too, that recruiters tend to engage in puffery when presenting the opportunities

S E L L I N G   S C E N A R I O

18.2

Bleepers and Bloopers in Sales

The first year in anyone's career can be exciting, especially in sales, when closing those first big deals is thrilling. On the other hand, the first year is filled with gaffes and bonehead mistakes; things you wish had never happened.

Trent Weaver joined Health Images, a company that provides magnetic resonance imaging services to physicians, after a couple of years of professional baseball. "I had just finished covering my entire territory and had every doctor's name and vital information on cards. Three months' work was represented on 200 index cards in a shoebox. One morning, I put the box on top of my car, got in, and drove away, scattering all of the cards across one of the main roads in the middle of morning rush hour." Trent realized his mistake within a couple of blocks and returned to the scene. "I managed to find every single card, but I lost my beeper. Of course, the beeper was a lot easier to replace!"

Michelle LeBlanc is one of Irwin's rising sales stars (Irwin publishes this textbook). But in her first month, she made her share of mistakes. "I familiarized myself with all of our more current textbooks and then began making sales calls. On each sales call, I try to find out what classes the professor teaches, what book he or she is using, and then try to determine the professor's needs so I can recommend the best book. I asked one professor what book he was using and when he told me, I replied that I was unfamiliar with it. Who published it? He didn't know, but he pulled the book off his shelf and opened it up. All I could do was laugh when he pointed out that it was published by my own company." In Michelle's defense, the book was being replaced by a newer text, but that was one mistake she hasn't made since.

Jeff Ducate was the top rep in 1993 for the San Antonio Convention and Visitor's Bureau, after joining the bureau in 1992. "My job is to bring conventions to San Antonio, and many of my accounts are located in Washington D.C. and Chicago. I planned an entire week of sales calls in Chicago, and flew up on Sunday so I could begin making calls early Monday morning. But in the middle of Monday morning, I realized my lunch appointment was with an account located in DC., so I called and rescheduled. When I visited them in DC, I took them to dinner. But the restaurant would not accept Visa, only American Express, which I did not have. So while they waited, I took a cab back to the hotel, cashed a check, and then returned so I could pay the bill with cash. They are one of my best accounts now, but they won't let me forget those first two mistakes!"

Jim Murray also sells in San Antonio, representing the Hilton Hotel located on the San Antonio River. The famous riverwalk is a popular attraction, especially at night. After a few drinks in the hotel bar, Jim and his customer decided to stroll the walk. Unfortunately, Jim's customer walked straight out of the hotel and into the river. Jim grabbed him by his belt and kept him from taking a complete bath. "It dampened his spirits a little bit, but his company still does business with us," notes Jim.

Each one of these salespeople has achieved significant early success, but not without a mistake or two along the way. "It didn't seem funny at the time," says Jeff, "but when you do something silly and you still win the account, you realize you can relax and not worry about being perfect all of the time. The mark of a true professional is how you overcome mistakes, not whether you never make one."

and benefits of a company. While the recruiter said it may be possible to earn a promotion in six months, the average may be much longer.

Seek a partnership with your manager. While partnership implies a peer-level relationship and you do not have the experience to be a true peer with your manager, use the same partnering skills with him or her that you would use with customers. Find out what your manager needs and wants, and then do it. Keep in mind that every workday is test day, except you sometimes write the questions. Just like your professor, your manager wants the answers, not the problems. Provide your boss with solutions and you will be well on the way to a partnership; keep in mind, however, the need to respect your manager's position and experience, as discussed above.

YOU MANAGE YOUR CAREER

Managing your career wisely will require conscious effort on your part. You are the person in your company to whom your career means the most. Take the time and effort to invest in yourself so that you can grow in your career. Once you have a position within an organization, your objective will be to develop yourself not simply to get a promotion, but to be successful in that promotion. (In order to get the promotion after that, you will need to do well in the job you are seeking.) You should take several significant actions in each position along the way. The first action is to understand the options that you have, because sales can often lead to many different positions.

Dual Career Path

When you start out in sales, many career options are open. Career paths can alternate between sales and marketing, or follow a route entirely within sales or entirely within marketing. You may even wind up as chief executive officer of a major global corporation. To exemplify how you might pursue various positions, Exhibit 18.7 depicts the career path for salespeople at Lanier Voice Products. Note that, in addition to sales management opportunities, they have opportunities in training, marketing, and product development that all begin in sales.

Learn Your Current Job

Learn all you can about the job you now have. Many people want promotions as fast as they can get them, regardless of their readiness. But consider the fact that you will probably be managing people holding the job you now have. To be truly effective as their manager, you should learn all you can about the job while in the best position to do so—while you are one of them.

Learn the Job You Want Next

A manager once said, "In order to become a manager, you must first be a manager." He meant that promoting someone is easier when that person already has the characteristics required by the position—that person already acts like a manager—rather than only having potential. A recent study of Fortune 500 firms and their promotion practices supports his statement.

E X H I B I T   18 . 7   LANIER VOICE PRODUCTS CAREER PATH

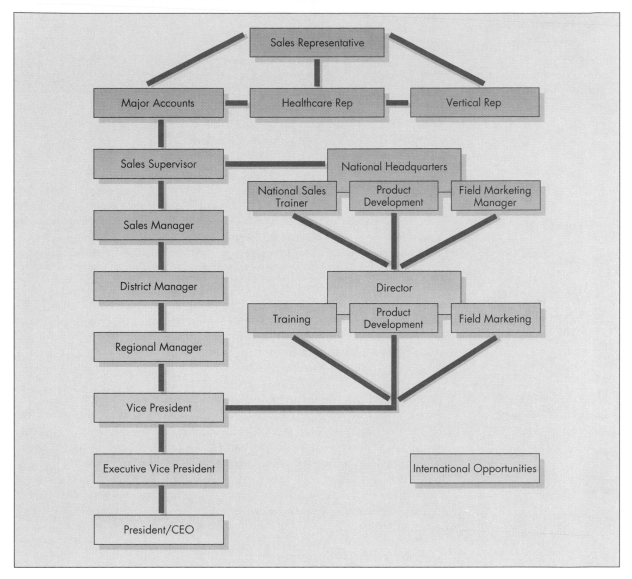

Of the 11 characteristics the firms said were crucial to effective sales management, 10 must exist in order for a promotion to take place (see Exhibit 18.8 for a list of the characteristics).

Several ways exist for you to learn about the job you desire. First, solicit the help of people who hold the job now. Many companies expect managers to develop their people. Take advantage of that; ask for the help of such managers. Find out what they did to prepare themselves and what you should do.

Second, volunteer to take on special projects that will demonstrate your leadership and organizational abilities. Taking projects off the hands of your manager can also give you an opportunity to see what responsibilities he

E X H I B I T   18 . 8

TRAITS CRUCIAL FOR
SALES MANAGEMENT
Ten of the top 11 must have
been demonstrated on the
person prior to promotion.

Trait*	Must Exist prior to Promotion
1. Motivation	X
2. Human relations skills	X
3. Higher than average energy	X
4. Ambition	X
5. Human interaction	X
6. Persuasiveness	X
7. Behavior flexibility	X
8. Perception of threshold social cues	X
9. Intellectual ability	X
10. Personal impact	X
11. Tolerance of uncertainty	

*Listed in order of most frequently agreed as crucial to least frequently agreed.

Source: Based on responses of Fortune 500 companies in a 1989 survey. See Donald Guest and Havva Meric, "The Fortune 500 Companies' Selection Criteria for Promotion to First Level Sales Management: An Empirical Study," *Journal of Personal Selling and Sales Management,* Fall 1989, pp. 47–58.

or she has. Look for ways that you can contribute to the overall sales team to show your commitment to the organization, your ability to lead and develop others, and your management skills.

DEVELOPING YOUR SKILLS

Years of hard work and frustration usually preceded "overnight" successes. Rarely does true overnight success occur. More often, success results from years of practice, of limited success and unlimited failure, and of determination to persevere. That is as true in sales as in any profession.

Salespeople, to improve their selling skills and raise their level of earnings, must constantly seek new ways to perform. But salespeople must also know what they do that already works! They need to evaluate their performance, looking for ways to improve their sales presentations.

Sources of Improvement

Most companies continue to train their salespeople after basic sales training, but most training of experienced salespeople is product related rather than sales skills related. If you want to improve your selling skills, you may have to actively seek assistance.

The first place to start is with the field sales manager. When that person works with you in your territory, solicit feedback after each call. During these curbside conferences, you can learn a great deal about what you are doing from an objective observer. One warning, however. Make sure that your manager only observes during the sales call and does not try to get into the act! As we discussed in the previous chapter, many sales managers are ex-salespeople who get excited in the heat of battle and may try to take over the sales call.

Peers provide another source. Who is successful in the company? When together for a sales meeting, many successful salespeople pick each other's brains for new ideas and strategies. Offer to work with them in their territory for a day or so in order to learn from them. In most situations, they will be flattered and helpful. Noncompeting salespeople in professional organizations such as Sales and Marketing Executives, an international organization of salespeople and marketing managers, will also be flattered to share their tips with you.

Bookstores offer a wealth of material for developing sales skills. Many good books remind salespeople of the basics of selling and present advanced methods of selling and negotiating. Be sure to save this book too, as you will want to refer to it when you are in the field.

Sales seminars and cassette tapes are also available. Seminars, such as those offered by Dale Carnegie, Wilson Learning, and Tom Hopkins, can be very motivating. But many experienced salespeople desire more than just motivation; they look for seminars that also teach new ways of presenting and gaining commitment, as well as other sales skills. When they can't attend the seminar, they purchase cassette tapes. They can listen while driving, using what would have been unproductive time to improve their skills.

In this course, you have begun to develop your interpersonal persuasion, or selling, skills. Whether or not you plan a career in sales, you owe it to yourself to continue to develop these skills.

■ MANAGING STRESS

Selling can be a stressful career. For example, with three days left in the month, Richard Langlotz's (profiled in the chapter opener) sales team once lost $100,000 in business. One sale alone, worth $60,000, would have made the team's quota, but that account delayed their order for a few months. The rest decided to go with competition. Suddenly, it looked as though Richard was going to finish the month at only 50 percent of quota. To top it off, one of his salespeople quit. What did he do? "I took my sales team to a pizza place." He thought about calling a meeting and getting tough with his team, but he realized that they already had enough stress and didn't need any more from him. At the pizza parlor, without any prompting from him, each salesperson examined his or her prospect lists and determined how the team was going to move sales forecasted for the next month into the current month. And while they didn't recover the entire $100,000, they did sell enough to cover the team's quota.

THINKING IT THROUGH	**W**hat stresses you out now? How do you deal with it? What are some of the good ways you handle stress? What are some ways that you respond to stress that may not be so healthy?

Sales can be very rewarding, but also very stressful. Many salespeople liken the job to a roller-coaster ride, with great emotional highs when sales are good but emotional lows when sales are poor. There are two kinds of stress that occur in sales; situational stress and felt stress. Stress can also be caused by factors in a salesperson's personal life, such as divorce, death of a loved one, and other events.

For some, coping with stress results in changing jobs.[5] Changing jobs may be the right thing for some people to do. Others turn to less healthy releases, such as absenteeism, drugs, alcohol, and so forth. All jobs have some stress; managing that stress is important to leading a happy and healthy life.

Managing stress does not always mean removing the cause of stress. Sometimes, as with the loss of a loved one, most people find that they must manage the influence that the causes of stress have over them.

Situational Stress

Situational stress is short-term anxiety caused by a situational factor.[6] You may face situational stress when waiting to make a sales presentation for your class, for example. The best strategy to deal with situational stress is to leave the situation or remove the situational factor causing the stress, but that cannot always be done. You can't, for example, simply tell your instructor that you are too stressed to sell in class today so you are leaving! One technique for managing situational stress is to imagine that the situational factor has been removed. In class, imagine that you have already finished your role play. Mentally consider that feeling of relief you get when you know you have done a job well. Sometimes imaging success can reduce feelings of stress.

In sales, situational stress may be caused by impending presentations, deadlines for closing orders (as in Richard Langlotz's case), and similar situations. Situational stress can cause stage fright in even the most experienced salespeople. One price of success is that situational stress will continue to occur, but successful salespeople learn to control their feelings of situational stress.

Felt Stress

Felt stress is longer term in nature than situational stress, because the causes are more enduring. **Felt stress** is psychological distress brought about by job demands or constraints encountered in the work environment.[7] Perhaps the most common form of felt stress is **role stress,** or feelings of stress caused by a lack of role accuracy. **Role accuracy** refers to the degree to which the salesperson's perceptions of the sales role are accurate.[8]

Role stress is brought about by one (or both) of the following problems: role conflict and role ambiguity. **Role conflict** occurs when two partners demand incompatible actions of the salesperson. For example, a customer wants higher levels of service from the salesperson, whereas the sales manager wants the salesperson to spend time working with new accounts. Conflict occurs because the salesperson does not have time for both.

Role ambiguity occurs when the salesperson is not sure what actions are required. The salesperson may not be sure what is expected, how to achieve it, or how performance will be evaluated and rewarded.

In general, the best way to handle role stress is to increase role accuracy. When the problem is role ambiguity, simply asking for further instruction or reviewing training materials may be helpful. Curbside coaching and other management support can also be requested.

Role conflict and role overload, however, require prioritizing activities. In the example of the salesperson who feels stress due to conflict between the customer's demands and the manager's demands, the salesperson must decide whose needs will be met. Once that decision is made, further stress can be avoided by refusing to dwell on the conflict. Note that the conflict is still there (both parties have conflicting demands), but the effect on the salesperson is minimized.

In either case, a strong partnership with the sales manager can greatly aid in reducing stress. When a partnership is formed between a sales manager and salesperson, the salesperson has a better understanding of the demands of the job, which activities should receive priority, and how the job should be performed. Partners also have access to more resources and more information, which can help remove some of the organizational constraints that could bring about stress.[9]

Summary

A sales career offers many opportunities for growth and personal development, but that career has to start somewhere, which is the purpose of the job search. The objective of a job search is to find a good match between what you need and have to offer and what a company needs and has to offer.

To achieve a good match, which results in mutual satisfaction, you must first understand who you are, specifically what you need and what you have to offer. You can ask yourself a number of questions to stimulate your thinking about the type of person you are and what you will need from a sales position. In addition, as you review your experiences in school, work, and other activities, you can identify the skills and characteristics that you have to offer.

Finding industries and companies with the characteristics you desire will require that you apply your marketing research skills. The library contains many sources of information that will help you. Personal sources can also be useful in providing information as well as leads for interviews.

Sources for job interviews include the campus placement office, personal contacts, and advertisements. Resumes are personal brochures that help sell a candidate. Writing effective cover letters will help you get interviews off campus, while the interview itself is similar to a sales call. Plan questions that demonstrate your knowledge of and interest in the company. Also plan to ask for information that will help you make your decision. Follow up after the interview to demonstrate your desire and perseverance.

You are the person in the company to whom your career means the most. This means that you must actively manage your own career. Set career goals that are compatible with family and personal objectives. Keeping the reasons for these career goals in front of you will enable you to make better decisions.

Learn the job you have now. You may someday manage people who have this job; the better you know it, the better you will be at managing it. "To become a manager, you must first be a manager." Learn the manager's job as well and volunteer for activities and projects that will let you demonstrate your management ability.

Stress can occur in any job. Situational stress is short term, whereas felt stress is longer term.

Sales offers a challenging and exciting career. The opportunities are so varied that virtually every type of person can probably fit into some sales position. Even if you choose a career in another field, take advantage of the material in this chapter. You should find these job search and career management tips helpful in any field. Good luck!

KEY TERMS

application form 566	references 566
assessment centers 567	role accuracy 586
disguised interview 578	role ambiguity 587
FEB 577	role conflict 586
felt stress 586	role stress 586
greeter 578	situational stress 586
group interviews 578	stress interview 578
interviews 567	tests 567
panel interviews 578	

QUESTIONS AND PROBLEMS

1. The chapter text contained questions you should ask yourself in order to understand your needs. Answer those questions now. What else should you consider?

2. Some people recommend signing up for as many interviews as possible, reasoning that the experience will be helpful when you find a company with a job you really want. And who knows? You might find a job you like. Is this ethical? Why or why not? Are companies ethical when they come to campus and interview although a job is not available, just so they maintain a presence on campus?

3. What would you do differently if you were being interviewed by an amiable, a driver, an analytical, or an expressive? What about a panel interview with one driver and one amiable? One analytical and one expressive?

4. Is a resume the only document you should take into an interview? What other things might be helpful in documenting your capabilities?

5. Analyze yourself. List your strengths and weaknesses. Do you belong in sales? Why or why not?

6. What type of sales position would you like? Are you qualified for that job? If not, what do you need, and how would you go about getting it?

7. How would you express your career objective in one sentence? If you are thinking of two or more industries, rewrite the career objective as you would for a resume to be sent to recruiters in each industry.

8. Answer the questions in Exhibit 18.5 as you would in a sales job interview.

9. Your summer internship in a sales job was a very bad experience. Your biggest complaint was that the sales manager put too much pressure on you

and wanted you to hard sell. In spite of this negative experience, you like sales, so you are interviewing for a sales position. What would you say if asked why you do not seek full-time employment with the summer internship firm?

10. "A job interview is simply another sales call, only this time you are selling yourself instead of a product or service." Do you agree with that statement? Why or why not?

11. How does partnering reduce stress? Could multiple partnerships lead to role conflict? What should the salesperson do then?

CASE PROBLEMS

CASE 18 • 1
BECKY MEDLEY'S INTERVIEW

At 8:45 AM, Becky arrived at her campus placement center for her 9:00 interview. She was surprised to be greeted by Dave Spetzer, whom she had known when he was in her marketing class. This conversation followed.

DAVE   "Becky, good to see you! I see that you are interviewing with us today." *[shakes Becky's hand and offers her a chair in the lobby]*

BECKY   "Dave Spetzer! Hi, how are you? I didn't know you were with Mega-Derm. I've got the 9:00 spot."

DAVE   "Great! I started with Mega-Derm right after graduation, and it has been a great six months. Tell me, are you interviewing with many pharmaceutical firms or just Mega-Derm?"

BECKY   "I'm very interested in pharmaceuticals, but I only want to work for one of the best. One of the physicians at the campus medical center recommended Mega-Derm. She said that your company has the best line of dermatological products on the market."

DAVE   "Great! I'm glad to hear that others agree we are one of the best." *[leans a little closer]* "Look, just relax in the interview. Mega-Derm really likes to get people from State, and I'm sure you will do well." *[looks up at the entrance of an older man.]* "Oh, here's Mark McDonald, my sales manager. He'll be interviewing you today. Mark, here's an old friend of mine, Becky Medley."

MARK   *[stepping forward and offering his hand]* "Becky, it's nice to meet you."

BECKY   *[shaking his hand firmly]* "It's nice to meet you, too, Mr. Mc-Donald." *[turning to Dave]* "Dave, it was good to see you again. Perhaps we'll talk some more later."
[Becky and Mark seat themselves in the interviewing room; Mark opens a notebook]

MARK   "Tell me about yourself, Becky."

BECKY   "I'm the oldest of three children, and we were raised in a small town in the eastern part of the state. As a kid, I was very interested in dance and gymnastics and wanted to be an Olympic gymnast. But an ankle injury ended my gymnastics career. Still, I learned a lot about self-discipline and the importance of hard work to achieve success, and I am still involved in gymnastics as a judge for youth meets. I chose State because it offers a strong marketing program. Marketing, and sales especially, seem to me to be a place where your success is directly related to your efforts. And I believe that more strongly now that I have taken the marketing courses here at State."

MARK   [writing furiously in his notebook] "I see." [momentary silence as he finishes his notes, then looks up] "Tell me about a time when you were the leader of a group and things were not going your way. Perhaps it looked as if the group wasn't going to meet your objectives. What did you do?"

BECKY   "Let's see. There was the time when we were working on a group project for my marketing research class. Understand, though, that we had not elected a formal leader or anything. But no one in the group really wanted to do the project; they all thought research was boring. So at a group meeting, I suggested we talk about what we liked to do in marketing. After all, we were all marketing majors. Each person talked about why they had chosen marketing. Then I framed the project around what they wanted out of marketing. When they looked at it as a marketing project instead of a research project, it became something they wanted to do."

MARK   "Did you get an A?"

BECKY   "No, we got a B+. But more important, we were the only group that had fun, and I think we learned more as a result."

The interview went on for nearly 30 minutes. Becky thought she had done fairly well. She stopped in the lobby to write down her impressions and record Mark's answers to her questions about the company. She smiled at Dave, who was talking to another applicant.

QUESTIONS

1. What did Becky do right? Why was that right? What did she do wrong? Why was that wrong?

2. What was Dave's purpose at the interview? What do you think Dave could tell Mark McDonald about Becky?

CASE 18 • 2
THE SUNDAY CLASSIFIEDS

Last Sunday, the following ads appeared in your local paper:

QUESTIONS

1. What characteristics do you have that might work well in these positions? What characteristics do you think are necessary to be successful in these jobs, and why?

2. John Walker called and wants to interview you tomorrow. You never heard of the company until you saw the ad. How will you learn more about it?

3. It turns out that Bellmead is a division of a U.S.-based Fortune 500 company, whereas Delta Telco is a distributor for several Japanese manufacturers. Bellmead employs 535 salespeople; Delta Telco employs 47 salespeople. What are the advantages and disadvantages of working for Bellmead? For Delta Telco?

ADDITIONAL REFERENCES

Boone, Louis, and John Milewicz. "Is Professional Selling the Route to the Top of the Corporate Hierarchy?" *Journal of Personal Selling and Sales Management,* Spring 1989, pp. 42–54.

Bragg, Arthur. "Personal Selling Goes to College." *Sales & Marketing Management,* March 1988, pp. 35–37.

Dalrymple, Douglas J, and William M Strahle. "Career Path Charting: Framework for Sales Force Evaluation." *Journal of Personal Selling and Sales Management,* Summer 1990, pp. 59–72.

Gable, Myron; Charles Hollan; and Frank Dangello. "Increasing the Utility of the Application Blank: Relationship between Job Application Information and Subsequent Performance and Turnover of Salespeople." *Journal of Personal Selling and Sales Management,* Summer 1992, pp. 39–56.

Ganesan, Shankar; Barton A Weitz; and George John. "Hiring and Promotion Policies in Sales Force Management: Some Antecedents and Consequences." *Journal of Personal Selling and Sales Management,* Spring 1993, pp. 15–26.

Guest, Donald, and Havva Meric. "The Fortune 500 Companies' Selection Criteria for Promotion to First Level Sales Management: An Empirical Study," *Journal of Personal Selling and Sales Management,* Fall 1989, pp. 47–58.

Hill, John S, and Meg Birdseye. "Salesperson Selection in Multinational Corporations: An Empirical Study." *Journal of Personal Selling and Sales Management,* Summer 1989, pp. 39–47.

Swenson, Michael J; William R Swinyard; Frederick W Langrehr; and Scott M Smith. "The Appeal of Personal Selling as a Career: A Decade Later." *Journal of Personal Selling and Sales Management,* Winter 1993, pp. 51–64.

Wotruba, Thomas; Edwin Simpson; and Jennifer Reed-Draznick. "The Recruiting Interview as Perceived by College Student Applicants for Sales Positions." *Journal of Personal Selling and Sales Management,* Fall 1989, pp. 13–24.

ROLE PLAY CASES

This section of your textbook provides a practical tool for developing your selling skills. Your professor will probably assign you a selling scenario to role play in class. In this section, you will find information on both the Minute Maid and Pledge role plays.

We have also included some helpful information on how to prepare for role plays, as well as how to make constructive, helpful comments on the role plays you will observe.

Have fun!

How to Prepare for Role Plays

Preparing for role plays will depend somewhat on the topic of the role play. Some of the role plays you are doing will involve only part of the sales call. We will assume, however, that you are preparing for a complete sales call.

The first step is to organize your information. What do you know about this buyer? Do you know anything about his or her social style? What activity has there been in this account? What do you know about this type of customer? For example, if you are calling on a convenience store, what do you know about convenience stores in general as they relate to your product (e.g., do they usually carry your product)?

The next step is to write down your call objectives. Include primary, minimum, and visionary objectives.

Next, write a list of possible needs. Based on what you know about the person on whom you are calling, the account's buying history, and the type of account, what do you think he or she might need? How would he or she go about making the decision, and how would that person make the purchase (would he or she finance, pay cash, order by phone, etc.)?

Based on that information, you can begin to prepare for the content of the sales call. Develop open/closed or SPIN questions designed to develop those needs. Anticipate what about that person's situation would create a problem that would lead to a need.

Examine your product and your promotions. What features will resolve those needs? What promotions

will help him or her buy? Then develop phrases that present benefits; that is, that tie features to needs. Also, gather any materials that you can use; prepare testimonial letters, brochures, contracts, and any other support documents. You may also want to make a business card to have something to hand to the buyer.

Make a list of all of the objections you can think of. Then develop responses to those objections. Plan how you will obtain commitment, based on your call objectives. Then memorize your approach. Many students tell us that they are extremely nervous just before a role play (we'll deal with that some more later). One way to handle this is to memorize your opener, all the way up to SPIN. Once you get that far, you forget about the camera and the class watching you and you can settle down.

Now practice the rest of the role play. You can practice your presentation out loud in front of the mirror or a friend. One word of caution, though: Not all of your presentation will be needed, because you will prepare for needs that may not exist. Don't go through the whole thing for the buyer during the actual sales call; just use the parts that are needed.

Mentally role play, playing a constant "what if?" game. What if the buyer says this, how will you respond? What if the answer to a situation question is that, what will you do then? You won't cover all of the possibilities, but you will be a lot better prepared for what actually does happen.

Now a word on nerves. We've already discussed one technique (memorizing the approach) for handling nerves. Another technique is designed to help you remain calm. One thing that happens is that students worry about the role play, causing stress and nerves to build up. You can minimize this by imagining yourself being finished. Think about how good it will be to walk out of the classroom, done with the sales call. Or think about what you have planned for that evening, weekend, or whenever. Or think about one of your favorite places and what it must be like to be there, right now. These thoughts keep your mind off the role play so that stress won't build up.

Be sure to arrive to class early on the day of your role play, so you won't feel rushed. Also, *remember to take all your visuals and blank videotape (if required) to class!*

Just before you begin the role play, take a deep breath, think about your opener, and smile. Aspiring concert pianists are taught to sit down and place their hands in their lap, then begin. This keeps them from rushing the beginning of the first piece. You don't want to rush, either.

Finally, if you are being videotaped, be sure to watch your tape after you're done and evaluate your performance. An unplayed videotape is of no value at all.

Good luck, and have fun.

How to Make Comments on Role Plays

As a student observer, you may be asked to evaluate your peers' performances, and your evaluations may become part of their grade. Whether your evaluation is averaged into their final grade or not, it is important for their development, and yours, that you do a good job.

As you watch role plays for the purpose of providing feedback, you will find yourself learning more about the art of selling. You will observe and think of ways to phrase ideas better, how to handle different types of customers, and how to develop strategies for persuading others. But this requires that you observe carefully.

Identify what the person actually did. It is best if you can identify the technique used. For example, you recognize an objection-handling method as the feel-felt-found technique. Identifying what you saw serves two purposes: First, you have to learn the techniques (which helps you

on exams and in your own role plays), and second, you can discuss the technique more appropriately after the role play.

Then note if the technique was appropriate or not. How did the buyer respond? How would you have responded if the technique was used on you? Was the technique appropriate for the situation, for the buyer's social style, and for the product?

Finally, think about what you would have done if the technique was not appropriate. During the role play, you won't have time for anything but writing down what the person actually did. But in the moments afterward, you can contemplate alternative approaches.

Your comments to the seller, then, can be phrased in this manner. When the student used a technique or offered a phrase that you don't think was the best one possible, use this formula: First, identify what the person did and discuss why it was inappropriate or less than optimal. Then offer an alternative and present why you think it is better. Finally, end with a comment on something the person did that was good. If you don't observe any problems, you can still do that last step of commenting on what was good.

Keep in mind that immediately after a presentation, the seller's emotions are strongest. The person is usually convinced that the presentation was just awful and there was nothing good about it. Find something positive about which to comment. Everyone does something well in every role play. You can really help someone's confidence if you can find that good thing and hold it up for them to see. Then they will be more receptive to instructional comments.

Role Play Case

Case • 1
Minute Maid

You are a salesperson for the local Coca-Cola bottler in your area, and your main product to sell today is the newly introduced Minute Maid Orange Soda. Coca-Cola soft drinks (*not* including this new product) have 40 percent of the total soft drink market share, which makes it number one in the industry. Annual revenues are nearly $7 billion per year. Revenues in your state alone are around $7.3 million.

There is no sales information on the Minute Maid soda, because we are assuming that it was introduced into the general market only one month ago.

Coca-Cola Foods Division has made Minute Maid orange juice (both frozen and ready to serve) for years. The name Minute Maid connotes nature, purity, vitamin C, and general health. Coca-Cola hopes that people will equate those healthy images with its new soda. The new soda is being positioned as a nutritious and delicious drink for the young, active, health-conscious consumer segment. Features of the product include the following:

- 10 percent real fruit juice (some nutritionists claim that this in no way makes the drink healthy).
- Caffeine free.

- Delicious orange flavor.
- Diet and regular versions available.
- Well-known Minute Maid name.

All products are fully guaranteed to the consumer. (If the consumer is dissatisfied, he or she simply has to return the product to the "store" for a full refund or replacement. The "store" then receives a credit from Minute Maid.) However, the "store" cannot simply return unsold merchandise. There are no guarantees that the "store" will sell the merchandise.

Coca-Cola has a group of salespersons (like yourself) that actually calls on important accounts. It also has route delivery people who actually deliver the product and take routine reorders (you are *not* one of these truck drivers).

Fountain Accounts (like Special Situation 1)

Cost:	$30.00 per canister of concentrate
	$6.50 deposit on each canister
	Free tap handle symbols
Quantity discounts:	7 percent off for 10 to 24 canisters in one order
	15 percent off for 25 or more canisters in one order

Retail Accounts (like Special Situations 2, 3, 4, and 5)

Cost:	$11.16 per case (a case holds 8 six-packs)
Suggested retail:	$1.89/six-pack
Quantity discounts:	7 percent off for 15 to 50 cases
	2 percent off for full pallet sales (50 cases to the pallet)
Special product introduction discount:	$1.75/case rebate for the first-time order
Special product introduction discount:	$6.50 off each canister for the first-time order

---

Special Situation 1

You are a salesperson for the local Coca-Cola Bottling Company distributor. Today you are calling on the corporate headquarters of Consolidated Food Service. Consolidated owns a total of five Hardee's franchises in the area. Consolidated can choose any drinks to serve in its Hardee's Restaurants; the only requirement is that they be of high quality. Consolidated currently sells several products from Coca-Cola (Coke, Diet Coke) and several products from Pepsi (Dr Pepper, 7-Up, Sunkist Orange) in all five of its stores. You have never called on this account before. Your objective is to convince Consolidated to start carrying your drinks in all five restaurants (i.e., replacing Sunkist Orange with your product). Sunkist Orange is priced 5 percent less than your list price for Minute Maid.

Special Situation 2

You are a salesperson for the local Coca-Cola Bottling Company distributor. You are calling on the manager of IGA Grocery Store, a full-service grocery store located in a local, midsized town. This is the main grocery store in the town, but it is very small compared to most supermarkets today. IGA is an independent grocer that you have called on many times in the past. Coca-Cola products have only performed about average in the store, whereas Pepsi brands are much stronger. Today, you are introducing the new product to the store manager for the first time. Your objective is to convince the store manager to stock your product and also to erect an end-of-aisle display that will hold 40 cases of product. You will offer him or her a $1.75/case rebate for this first-time order.

Special Situation 3

You are a salesperson for the Coca-Cola National Accounts Sales Force. You are calling on the senior grocery buyer of Kroger in Cincinnati, Ohio. Kroger has carried your Minute Maid orange juice and Coca-Cola products in the past, but recently has started taking away your shelf space and using it for Kroger brand orange juice and cola products. Your goal is to convince the buyer to approve your new drink for all of the Krogers across the United States. (Each local manager can buy any product approved by the home office.) Your boss has given you approval to discount your normal pricing (including cost, quanity discounts, and the special product introduction discount) up to 10 percent, because Kroger is so large and important.

Special Situation 4

You are a salesperson for the local Coca-Cola Bottling Company distributor. You are calling on the manager of Simpson's Market located in a very small community nearby. Simpson's is an independent grocer that you have never called on before, primarily because it is too small.

(It is similar in size to most convenience stores with which you are familiar.) They do not carry any of your Minute Maid orange juice at this time but do sell various Coca-Cola products. Your objective is to convince the store manager to stock your product and also to erect an end-of-aisle display that will hold 15 cases of product. You will offer him or her a $1.75/case rebate for this first-time offer.

Special Situation 5

You are calling on the head of the county school board. The junior high and senior high schools in the county already sell Coke and diet Coke (from a vending machine located in the lunchroom) in addition to the usual milk/chocolate milk for lunches. Several influential parents in one of the large high schools have been petitioning for the removal of all soft drinks. You have not been able to find out how the head of the school board feels about this issue. Your objective today is to convince the head (whom you have never met before) to suggest that the board allow your products to be sold in the junior and senior high schools in the county.

ROLE PLAY

CASE • 2

You just took over a new territory today, June 1st (remember that date), and you sell Pledge cleaning and dusting products for S.C. Johnson (Johnson Wax). You have two types of products, the aerosol cans and the pump-spray bottles. Both are sold in retail stores, and the pump spray is sold in one-gallon containers for industrial users.

There are four scents of Pledge: lemon, garden, potpourri, and original. (Note: Johnson Wax changes scents regularly. If you find a new scent in your grocery store, feel free to use it.) Retail cans are sold in large and small cans, with 24 large or 36 small cans in a case. There are 24 pumps in a case for retail or six one-gallon containers are in an industrial case, with one pump container sent free with each case. Regular prices are as follows:

Retail Accounts	$24.00 per case, suggested retail $1.99 for large can or pump, $1.49 for small can
	2 percent discount for 10 cases (one size or one scent only)
	5 percent discount for pallet (50 cases, any mixture of size and scent by the case)
Industrial Accounts	$20.00 per case
	5 percent discount for case contract (agreeing to purchase 50 cases over a 12-month period, with minimum shipment of 3 cases per order. (Note: If customer fails to purchase 50 cases over the 12-month period, he or she is rebilled the difference between the discount and the single-case price.)
	7 percent discount for pallet order (50 cases in one shipment)

June 1 Promotions Announcement

RETAIL PROMOTIONS

Pallet pack: An end-of-aisle display of 50 cases, containing a mix of all sizes and scents, with a 7 percent discount.

Advertising: A free-standing insert coupon of 50¢ off large-size cans on Sunday June 14, plus a $1 million TV ad campaign from June 10 to June 28.

Forty percent reimbursement to retailer of ad costs for up to ¼ page of a display ad bought by the retailer featuring Pledge. For example, if the retailer bought a full-page ad and devoted ¼ of that space to Pledge, the retailer would receive 40 percent times ¼ of the page cost. If the retailer devoted ⅛ of the page to Pledge, the retailer would get 40 percent of ⅛ of the page cost back from Pledge.

Preferred Retailer Program: For small retailers with little local competition (rural retailers)—order 10 cases of large-size lemon or wood scent, plus feature the product in a newspaper ad, and the retailer receives a 4 percent discount plus ad reimbursement (see above).

INDUSTRIAL PROMOTIONS

New industrial customers: 10 percent off new case contracts (instead of 5 percent).

Current case contracts: Receive an extra 5 percent off orders of 10 cases received by June 30 (cannot be applied to new case contracts—the most anyone can take off one order is 10 percent).

Preferred industrial customer program: All orders by June 30 of 5 cases or more by customers that are not on case contract receive a 5 percent discount.

COMPETITIVE INFORMATION   Your company has given you the following information about your product versus competitors:

Industrial pricing varies greatly and market share isn't available on a local basis; however, Pledge is the largest national seller. Both Pledge and Endust clean as they wax and repel dust; other brands may not. If an off-brand is used, probe regarding scent, cleaning ability, and protection (waxing). Delivery cost may be extra for other brands, but *delivery is always included for Pledge.*

Customer Situations: Retail

SITUATION 1: AFFILIATED FOODSTORES, WITH 24 STORES IN YOUR TERRITORY

Purchase history: 1/10/9X: One case each size and scent. Drop shipped directly to each store.

3/05/9X: Eight cases mixed scents, part of a spring cleaning promo. Drop shipped directly to each store.

Other information: No co-op advertising with Johnson this year. Also carries Liquid Gold and Endust.

You have an appointment with the HBA (Health and Beauty Aids) buyer set up by the previous rep.

SITUATION 2: SAFEWAY GROCERY STORES, FIVE STORES IN YOUR TERRITORY

Purchase history: 2/15/9X: Five cases Original Scent, large cans only. Shipped to Safeway's warehouse.

Other information: None available.

You have an appointment with the non-grocery items buyer.

Retail Brand	Market Share	Cost per Case	Retail Price	Discounts
Pledge	38%	$24	$1.99 large 1.99 pump 1.49 small	Yes, quantity and advertising
Endust	24	Approx. 22	1.79 large 1.15 small	Yes, quantity and advertising
Liquid Gold	8	27	2.49	No
Others	30 (total)	20 (avg.)	1.50 large .99 small	No

SITUATION 3: CIRCLE K, 24 CONVENIENCE STORES IN YOUR TERRITORY

Purchase history: None.

Other information: The buyer sees reps for new products on Fridays, so you are dropping in Friday morning.

SITUATION 4: HEB, 67 GROCERY STORES ACROSS THE STATE, WITH HEADQUARTERS IN YOUR TERRITORY

Purchase history: 1/10/9X: Three pallets, mixed scents and sizes.
2/05/9X: Five pallets, mixed scents and sizes.
3/10/9X: Four pallets, mixed scents and sizes, for Spring Cleaning promo.
4/29/9X: Two pallets, mixed scents and sizes.

Other information: All shipments to HEB warehouse in your territory.
Carries Endust, which averages two facings per store.
Pledge averages eight facings per store.
You are meeting with the senior buyer.

SITUATION 5: BILL'S GROCERY, IN A SMALL RURAL TOWN

Purchase history: 1/05/9X: One case, original, small cans.

Other information: Order was taken through telemarketing.
Doesn't look like previous rep ever visited this store.

Industrial Situations

SITUATION 1: CARTER MEDICAL SERVICES (LARGE OFFICE BUILDING)

Purchase history: 1/01/9X: Five cases—original.
2/06/9X: Seven cases—original.
3/21/9X: Four cases—original (phone orders).
4/04/9X: Five cases—original.
5/20/9X: Six cases—original (phone orders).

Other information: No case contract.

You have an appointment today for 3:00.

SITUATION 2: MORRIS BUSINESS FORMS (MANUFACTURING FACILITY WITH LARGE OFFICE BUILDING IN FRONT)

Purchase history: None.

Other information: None.

You have no appointment, but have located the purchasing agent's name, and you plan to drop in.

SITUATION 3: COLLINS RADAR (LARGE MANUFACTURING FACILITY)

Purchase history: 1/10/9X: 5 cases—original.
2/27/9X: 4 cases—lemon.

Other information: Case contract established 1/10/9X.
Purchased Endust in March, April, and May.

SITUATION 4: WESTINGCLOCK (SEVERAL BUILDINGS, SOME OFFICE, SOME MANUFACTURING)

Purchase history: 1/08/9X: 1 case—original.
3/14/9X: 3 cases—lemon.
5/12/9X: 1 case—original.

Other information: On case contract since March.

SITUATION 5: WHEELER JANITORIAL SERVICES

Purchase history: None.

Other information: You've heard that they perform cleaning services for two major manufacturers in town; you called to make an appointment and the purchasing agent's secretary said to drop in on Friday because the purchasing agent sees all new salespeople then.

NOTES

CHAPTER 1 *1.* Thayer Taylor, "Selling in the Future," *Sales & Marketing Management,* June 1992, p. 60. See also Arthur Bragg, "Getting Face-to-Face with Customers," *Sales & Marketing Management,* February 1991, pp. 44–48. *2.* Philip Kotler, *Marketing Management: Analysis, Planning, Implementation and Control,* 8th ed. (Englewood Cliffs, NJ: Prentice Hall, 1994), p. 321. *3.* This section draws heavily on Thomas Wotruba, "The Evolution of Personal Selling," *Journal of Personal Selling and Sales Management,* Summer 1991, pp. 1–12. See also Robert Bartels, *The History of Marketing Thought* (Columbus, OH: Publishing Horizon, 1988). *4.* Gerhard Gschwandtner, "Take This Chart and Burn It," *Personal Selling Power,* April 1993, pp. 18–23; Robert Spekman, "Strategic Supplier Selection: Understanding Long-Term Relationships," *Business Horizons,* July–August 1988, pp. 75–81; and Kate Bertrand, "Crafting Win-Win Situations in Buyer-Seller Relationships," *Business Marketing,* June 1986, pp. 42–50. *5.* Thomas Forbes, "Top Guns," *Selling,* October 1993, p. 59. *6.* "How Firms in Mexico Reach Isolated Rural Villages," *Business Latin American,* September 9, 1991, pp. 289–95. *7.* William Keenan, Jr., "America's Best Sales Forces: Six at the Summit," *Sales & Marketing Management,* June 1990, pp. 72–73. *8.* Martin Everett, "Selling's New Breed: Smart and Feisty," *Sales & Marketing Management,* October 1989, pp. 52, 54. *9.* William Keenan, Jr., "The Difference in Selling Services," *Sales & Marketing Management,* March 1989, pp. 48–52. *10.* Barton Weitz, "Effectiveness in Sales Interactions," *Journal of Marketing,* Winter 1981, pp. 85–103. *11.* John Hill and Arthur Allaway, "How U.S.-based Companies Manage Sales in Foreign Countries," *Industrial Marketing Management,* February 1993, pp. 7–41; and Brian Flynn, "The Challenges of Multinational Sales Training," *Training and Development Journal,* November 1987, pp. 54–56. *12.* Barton Weitz, Harish Sujan, and Mita Sujan, "Knowledge, Motivation, and Adaptive Selling: A Framework for Improving Selling Effectiveness," *Journal of Marketing,* October 1986, pp. 174–91; Rosann Spiro and Barton Weitz, "Adaptive Selling: Conceptualization, Measurement, and Nomological Validity," *Journal of Marketing Research,* February 1990, pp. 61–69; and Fred Morgan and Jeffrey Stoltman, "Adaptive Selling—Insights from Social Cognition," *Journal of Personal Selling and Sales Management,* Fall 1990, pp. 43–54. *13.* Gerhard Gschwandtner, "Donald Trump: 13 Blueprints for Achievement," *Personal Selling Power,* November 1993, p. 19. *14.* Arthur Bragg, "Are Good Salespeople Born or Made?" *Sales & Marketing Management,* September 1988, pp. 74–78. *15.* Martha White, "The 1992–83 Job Outlook in Brief," *Occupational Outlook Quarterly,* Spring 1992, pp. 14–37. *16.* Louis Boone and John Milewicz, "Is Professional Selling the Route to the Top of the Corporate Hierarchy?" *Journal of Personal Selling and Sales Management,* Spring 1989, pp. 42–54. *17.* Source unknown. *18.* Bill Kelley, "Who Says You Can't Go Home Again?" *Sales & Marketing Management,* September 1989, p. 39.

CHAPTER 2 *1.* "Taking Aim at Tomorrow's Challenges," *Sales & Marketing Management,* September 1991, p. 68. *2.* Irwin Gross, "Business Marketing," *ISBM Newsletter,* College of Business Administration, The Pennsylvania State University, Spring 1993. *3.* Sandy Jap and Barton Weitz, "A Taxonomy of Long-Term Relationships," working paper, College of Business Administration, University of Florida, 1994; and F. Robert Dwyer, Paul Schurr, and Sejo Oh, "Developing Buyer-Seller Relationships," *Journal of Marketing,* 51 (April 1987), pp. 11–27. *4.* "Building Relationships: Siemens Adds the Personal Touch to Technical Selling," *Business Marketing,* August 1992, pp. 34–35. *5.* BG Yovonvich, "Partnering at Its Best," *Business Marketing,* March 1992, p. 36. *6.* Robert Krapel, Deborah Salmond, and Robert Spekman, "A Strategic Approach to Managing Buyer-Seller Relationships," *European Journal of Marketing,* 25 (1991), pp. 22–37; BG Yovovich, "Do's and Don'ts of Partnering," *Business Marketing,* March 1992, pp. 38–39; and "Smart Selling: How Companies Are Winning Over Today's Tough Customers," *Business Week,* August 3, 1992, pp. 46–52. *7.* See Chapter 13 in Michael Levy and Barton Weitz, *Retailing Management,* 2nd ed. (Burr Ridge, IL: Irwin, 1994). *8.* Company documents. *9.* "Taking Aim at Tomorrow's Challenges," *Sales & Marketing Management,* September 1991, p. 80. *10.* "Pritchett on Quick Response," *Discount Merchandiser,* April 1992, p. 64. *11.* John Swan and Johannah Nolan, "Gaining Customer Trust: A Conceptual Guide for the Salesperson," *Journal of Personal Selling and Sales Management,* November 1985, pp. 39–48; and John Swan, I Fred Trawick, David Rink, and Jenney Roberts, "Measuring Dimensions of Purchaser Trust of Industrial Salespeople," *Journal of Personal Selling and Sales Management,* 8 (May 1988), pp. 1–9. *12.* Erin Anderson and Barton A Weitz, "Determinants of Continuity in Conventional Industrial Channel Dyads," *Marketing Science,* 8 (Fall 1989), pp. 310–23; Dennis Bialeszewski and Michael Giallourakis, "Perceived Communication Skills and Resultant Trust Perceptions within the Channel of Distribution," *Journal of the Academy of Marketing Science,* 13 (Spring 1985), pp. 206–17; and Christine Moorman, Gerald Zaltman, and Rohit Deshpande, "Relationships between Providers and Users of Market Research: The Dynamics of Trust within and between Organizations," *Journal of Marketing Research,* 29 (August 1992), pp. 314–28. *13.* Edmund Lawler, "Building Relationships," *Business Marketing,* August 1992, p. 34. *14.* James Morgan and Susan Zimmerman, "Building World Class Supplier Relationships," *Purchasing,* August 16, 1990, p. 2. *15.* Don McCreary, *Japanese–U.S. Business Negotiations* (New York: Praeger, 1986); Frank Acuff, "Negotiating in the Pacific Rim," *The International Executive,* May 1990, p. 21. *16.* Yovonvich, "Partnering at Its Best," p. 37. *17.* Erin Anderson and Barton Weitz, "The Use of Pledges to Build and Sustain Commitment in Distribution Channels," *Journal of Marketing Research,* 29 (February 1992), pp. 18–34. *18.* Patricia Sellers, "How to Remake Your Sales Force," *Fortune,* May 4, 1992, p. 103. *19.* Ibid., p. 102. *20.* "Should Salespeople's Compensation Be Tied to Customer Satisfaction?" *Sales & Marketing Management,* November 1992, pp. 21–22. *21.* Gerrard Macintosh, Kenneth Anglin, Davis Szymanski, and James Gentry, "Relationship Development in Selling: A Cognitive Analysis," *Journal of Personal Selling and Sales Management,* 12 (Fall 1992), pp. 24–34; and Thomas Leigh and Patrick McGraw, "Mapping the Procedural Knowledge of Industrial Sales Personnel: A Script Theoretic Investigation," *Journal of Marketing,* 53 (January 1989), pp. 16–34. *22.* Lawler, "Building Relationships," p. 34. *23.* William Keenan, Jr., "America's Best Sales Forces: Six at the Summit," *Sales & Marketing Management,* June 1990, pp. 72–73. *24.* Ibid., p. 72. *25.* Tom Eisenhart, "Sales Force Automation," *Business Marketing,* September 1992, pp. 90–98. *26.* Gerhard Gschwandtner, "Sales Trainers Face the Future of Professionalism in Selling," *Personal Selling Power,* March 1993, pp. 28–31.

CHAPTER 3   *1.* Scott Kelley and Michael Dorsch, "Ethical Climate, Organizational Commitment, and Indebtedness among Purchasing Executives," *Journal of Personal Selling and Sales Management* 11 (Fall 1991), pp. 55–65; I Fredrick Trawick, John Swan, Gail McGee, and David Rink, "Influence of Buyer Ethics and Salesperson Behavior on Intention to Choose a Supplier," *Journal of the Academy of Marketing Science* 19 (Winter 1991), pp. 17–23; and Rosemary Lagace, Robert Dahlstrom, and Jule Assenheimer, "The Relevance of Ethical Salesperson Behavior on Relationship Quality: The Pharmaceutical Industry," *Journal of Personal Selling & Sales Management* 11 (Fall 1991), pp. 39–47. *2.* Debra Haley, "Sales Management Students vs. Business Practitioners: Ethical Dilemmas and Perceptual Differences," *Journal of Personal Selling and Sales Management* 11 (Spring 1992), pp. 60–63; and Pratibha and James Kellaris, "Toward Understanding Marketing Students' Judgement of Controversial Personal Selling Practices," *Journal of Business Research* 24 (June 1992), pp. 313–28. *3.* Thomas Wotruba, "A Comprehensive Framework for the Analysis of Ethical Behavior, with a Focus on Sales Organizations," *Journal of Personal Selling and Sales Management* 10 (Spring 1990), pp. 29–42; Anusorn Singhapakdi and Scott Vitell, "Analyzing the Ethical Decision Making of Sales Professionals," *Journal of Personal Selling and Sales Management* 11 (Fall 1991), pp. 2–12; and K. Douglas Hoffman, Vince Howe, and Donald Hardigree, "Ethical Dilemmas Faced in the Selling of Complex Services: Significant Others and Competitive Pressure," *Journal of Personal Selling and Sales Management* 11 (Fall 1991), pp. 13–25. *4.* Richard Belramini, "Exploring the Effectiveness of Business Gifts: A Controlled Field Experiment," *Journal of the Academy of Marketing Science* 20 (Winter 1992), pp. 87–92; and Monroe Bird, "Gift Giving and Gift Taking in Industrial Companies," *Industrial Marketing Management,* May 1989, pp. 91–94. *5.* Bird, pp. 91–94. *6.* Bristol Voss, "Eat, Drink, and Be Wary," *Sales & Marketing Management,* January 1991, pp. 49–57; and David Finn and William Moncrief, "Salesforce Entertainment Activities," *Industrial Marketing Management,* November 1985, p. 230. *7.* Bill Kelley, "When a Key Person Leaves for a Competitor," *Sales & Marketing Management,* February 1988, pp. 48–50. *8.* Kathryn Lewis and Pamela Johnson, "Preventing Sexual Harassment Complaints Based on Hostile Environments," *SAM Advanced Management Journal* 56 (Spring 1991), pp. 21–32; Galen, "Ending Sexual Harassment," *Business Week,* March 18, 1991, pp. 98–100; and Grethen Morgenson, "Watch That Leer," *Forbes,* May 15, 1989, pp. 69–72. *9.* Robert Ford and Frank McLaughlin, "Sexual Harassment at Work," *Business Horizons,* November–December 1988, pp. 14–19. *10.* S J Vitell and L J Grove, "Marketing Ethics and the Technique of Neutralization," *Journal of Business Ethics,* 1987, pp. 433–38. *11.* "Putting the Fear of Crime into Corporations," *Business Week,* March 12,

1990, p. 35; and "Soon, Corporate Crime May Really Not Pay," *Business Week,* February 12, 1990, p. 36. *12.* Joseph Vaccaro, "The Law and Selling," *Journal of Business and Industrial Marketing,* Winter 1987, pp. 45–46. *13.* Steven Sack, "Some Words on Warranties," *Sales & Marketing Management,* December 1986, pp. 52, 54. *14.* Steven Sack, "Legal Puffery: Truth or Consequences," *Sales & Marketing Management,* October 1986, pp. 59–60. *15.* Steven Sack, "Watch the Words," *Sales & Marketing Management,* July 1985, p. 56. *16.* See Steven Sack, "The High Risks of Dirty Tricks," *Sales & Marketing Management,* November 11, 1985, pp. 56–59; and Steven Sack, "Treat the Customer Right—Or Else," *Sales & Marketing Management,* January 13, 1986, pp. 63–64. *17.* Steven Sack, "Price Advice: Keep It Fair," *Sales & Marketing Management,* May 1986, pp. 53–55. *18.* Karl Boedecker, Fred Morgan, and Jeffrey Stoltman, "Legal Dimensions of Salespersons' Statements: A Review and Managerial Suggestions," *Journal of Marketing,* January 1991, pp. 70–80. *19.* This section is based largely on Chapters 5 and 7 in Philip Cateora, *International Marketing,* 8th ed. (Homewood, IL: Irwin, 1993). *20.* Kathleen Getz, "International Codes of Conduct: An Analysis of Ethical Reasoning," *Journal of Business Ethics* 7 (1990), pp. 567–77; and Sak Onkvisit and John Shaw, "International Corporate Bribery: Some Legal, Cultural, Economic, and Ethical-Philosophical and Marketing Considerations," *Journal of Global Marketing* 42 (1991), pp. 5–20.

CHAPTER 4   *1.* Edward Doherty, "How to Steal a Satisfied Customer," *Sales & Marketing Management,* March 1990, pp. 40–41. *2.* Dan Dunn, John Friar, and Claude Thomas, "An Approach to Selling High-Tech Solutions," *Industrial Marketing Management,* May 1991, pp. 149–59; and A. Hamid Noori, "What It Takes to Supply Japanese OEMS," *Industrial Marketing Management,* February 1990, pp. 21–30. *3.* Vithala Rao and Edward McLaughlin, "Modeling the Decision to Add a New Product by Channel Intermediaries," *Journal of Marketing,* January 1989, pp. 80–88; Richard Germain and Cornelia Droge, "Wholesale Operations and Vendor Evaluation," *Journal of Business Research,* September 1990, pp. 119–30; and Janet Wagner, Richard Ettenson, and Jean Parrish, "Vendor Selection among Retail Buyers: An Analysis by Merchandise Division," *Journal of Retailing,* Spring 1989, pp. 58–79. *4.* Leonard Lindenmuth and Philip Burger, "Corporate Buying of Health Care Plans: A Framework for Marketing Theory and Practice," *Journal of Health Care Marketing* 10 (June 1990), pp. 36–41. *5.* John Franke, "Military Makes Its Own Purchasing Rules," *Marketing News,* October 9, 1990, p. 7; Don Hill, "Who Says Uncle Sam's a Tough Sell?" *Sales & Marketing Management,* July 1988, pp. 43–47; and Ronald Still, "Buying Process in the U.S. Department of Defense," *Industrial Marketing Management,* August 1980, pp. 291–98. *6.* "This Will Melt in Your Mouth, Not in the Sands," *USA Today,* December 12, 1990. *7.* "Success with Commercial Product Procurement," *Contract Management,* August 1990, p. 24. *8.* Shirley Cayer, "Low Key, but Savvy," *Purchasing,* October 1989, p. 54. *9.* Daniel Glick, "The Magic of 'Mr. Spud,'" *Newsweek,* November 27, 1989, p. 63. *10.* The classic study of organizational buying is in Patrick Robinson, Charles Faris, and Yoram Wind, *Industrial Buying and Creative Marketing* (Boston: Allyn & Bacon, 1967). For an interesting comparison of organizational buying in other countries, see Johan Roos, Ellen Veie, and Lawrence Welsch, "A Case Study of Equipment Purchasing in Czechoslovakia," *Industrial Marketing Management,* August 1992, pp. 257–63; and Tomasz Domanski and Elizbieta Guzek, "Industrial Buying Behavior: The Case of Poland," *Journal of Business Research,* January 1992, pp. 11–18. *11.* Donald Barclay, "Organizational Buying Outcomes and Their Effects on Subsequent Decisions," *European Journal of Marketing* 4 (1992), pp. 48–64. **12.** For an empirical study of different buying situations, see Erin Anderson, Barton Weitz, and Wujin Chu, "Industrial Purchasing: An Empirical Exploration of the Buy-Class Framework," *Journal of Marketing,* Fall 1987, pp. 71–86. **13.** Robert McWilliams, Earl Naumann, and Stan Scott, "Determining Buying Center Size," *Industrial Marketing Management,* February 1992, pp. 43–50; James Martin, James Daley, and Henry Burdg, "Buying Influences and Perceptions of Transportation Services," *Industrial Marketing Management,* November 1988, pp. 305–14; Robert Tho\mas, "Industrial Market Segmentation on Buying Center Purchase Responsibilities," *Journal of the Academy of Marketing Sciences,* Summer 1989, pp. 243–52; Ajay Kohli, "Determinants of Influence in Organizational Buying: A Contingency Approach," *Journal of Marketing,* July 1989, pp. 50–65; and Melvin Mattson, "How to Determine the Composition and Influence of a Buying Center," *Industrial Marketing Management,* August 1988, pp. 204–14. **14.** I Fredrick Trawick, John Swan, and David Rink, "Back-Door Selling: Violation of Cultural versus Professional Ethics by Salespeople and Purchaser Choice of Supplier," *Journal of Business Research,* Summer 1988, pp. 299–309. **15.** "How to Use Chinese Culture to Your Advantage," *Personal Selling Power,* January–February 1994, p. 19. **16.** Elizabeth Wilson, Gary Lilien, and David Wilson, "Developing and Testing a Contingency Paradigm of Group Choice in Organizational Buying," *Journal of Marketing Research,* November 1991, pp. 452–66; Bixby Cooper, Cornelia Drodge, and Patricia Daughtery, "How Buyers and Operations Personnel Evaluate Service," *Industrial Marketing Management,* February 1991, pp. 81–85; and William Soukup, "Supplier Selection Strategies," *Journal of Purchasing and Materials Management,* August 1987, pp. 7–12. **17.** LaVon Koerner and Jim Holden, "The Political 'Third Dimension' in Selling," *Business Marketing,* March 1988, pp. 92–96; and Paul Anderson and Terry Chambers, "A Reward-Measurement Model of Organizational Buying Behavior," *Journal of Marketing,* Spring 1985, pp. 7–23. **18.** Tony Henthorne, Michael LaTour, and Alvin Williams, "How Organizational Buyers Reduce Risk," *Industrial Marketing Management,* February 1993, pp. 41–48: Robert Settle and Pamela Alreck, "Risky Business," *Sales & Marketing Management,* January 1989, pp. 48–52; and Christopher Puto, Wesley Patton, and Ronald King, "Risk Handling Strategies in Industrial Vendor Selection Strategies," *Journal of Marketing,* Winter 1985, pp. 89–98. **19.** Donald Jackson, Janet Keith, and Richard Burdick, "The Relative Importance of Various Promotional Elements in Different Industrial Purchase Situations," *Journal of Advertising,* Fall 1988, pp. 216–22. **20.** Michael Morris, Ramone Avila, and Alvin Burns, "The Nature of Industrial Source Loyalty: An Attitudinal Perspective," in K D BaBahns (ed.), *Developments in Marketing Science,* vol. II (Miami, FL: Academy of Marketing Sciences, 1988), pp. 333–37. **21.** J William Semich, "How Apple Computer Buys for the 1990s," *Purchasing,* June 22, 1989, pp. 43–47; and David Burt, "Managing Suppliers Up to Speed," *Harvard Business Review,* July–August 1989, pp. 127–35. **22.** Marc Beauchamp, "No More Weekend Stands," *Forbes,* September 17, 1990, pp. 190–91. **23.** John Barrett, "Why Major Account Selling Works," *Industrial Marketing Management,* November 1986, pp. 63–73; and Benson Shaprio and Rowland Moriarity, *National Account Management,* Report No. 82-100 (Cambridge, MA: Marketing Science Institute, 1982). **24.** Kate Bertrand, "Marketers Discover What 'Quality' Means," *Business Marketing,* April 1987, p. 61; John Young, "The Quality Focus at Hewlett-Packard," *Journal of Business Strategy* 5 (Winter 1985), pp. 6–12; and Tom Eisenhart, "'Total Quality' Is the Key to U.S. Competitiveness," *Business Marketing,* June 1990, p. 31–32. **25.** Paul Dion, Peter Banting, Sharon Picard, and V. Kasturi, "JIT Implementation: A Growth Opportunity for Purchasing," *International Journal of Purchasing and Ma-* terials Management 28 (Fall 1992), pp. 32–38; Charles O'Neal, "JIT Procurement and Relationship Marketing," *Industrial Marketing Management,* February 1989, pp. 55–63; Gary Frazier, Robert Spekman, and Charles O'Neal, "Just-in-Time Exchange Systems in Industrial Markets," *Journal of Marketing,* Fall 1989, pp. 321–25; Charles O'Neal, "The Buyer-Seller Linkage in a Just-in-Time Environment," *Journal of Purchasing and Materials Management,* Spring 1987, pp. 7–13; Paul Dion, Peter Banting, and Lorreta Hasey, "The Impact of JIT on Industrial Marketers," *Industrial Marketing Management,* February 1990, pp. 41–47; Anne Porter, "'JIT II' Is Here," *Purchasing,* September 12, 1991, pp. 60–67; and Robert Knorr and John Neuman, "Quick Response Technology: The Key to Outstanding Growth," *Journal of Business Strategy* 13 (September/October 1992), pp. 61–64. **26.** S Joe Puri and Pradeep Korgaonkar, "Couple the Buying and Selling Teams," *Industrial Marketing Management,* November 1991, pp. 311–17; Somerby Dowst and Ernest Raia, "Teaming Up for the '90s," *Purchasing,* February 1990, pp. 54–59. **27.** Daniel Bragg and Chan Hahn, "Material Requirements Planning and Purchasing," *Journal of Purchasing and Materials Management,* Spring 1989, pp. 41–67. **28.** Mohan Reddy and Michael Marvin, "Developing a Manufacturer-Distributor Information Partnership," *Industrial Marketing Management,* May 1986, pp. 157–63. **29.** Louis De Rose, "Meet Today's Buying Influence with Value Analysis," *Industrial Marketing Management,* May 1991, pp. 87–90; "Value Analysis 90: A Special Report," *Purchasing,* June 7, 1990, pp. 62–116; and Jean Graham, "A Simple Idea Saves $8 million a Year," *Purchasing,* May 21, 1992, pp. 47–49. **30.** "PA's Examine the People Who Sell to Them," *Sales & Marketing Management,* November 11, 1985, p. 41. **31.** Robert Reich, "The Myth of 'Made in the U.S.A.'," *The Wall Street Journal,* July 5, 1991, p. A6. **32.** "Are Your Suppliers' Reps Ready to Go to Bat for You," *Purchasing Magazine,* June 3, 1993, pp. 665–66.

Chapter 5

1. See Jacob Weisberg, "Watch Your Language," *Sales & Marketing Management,* September 15, 1980, pp. 58–59, for a discussion of how to avoid sexist language. **2.** John Brenner, "Words for Selling Yourself: Turn Misuse and Abuse into Deft Effective Sparkle," *Marketing Times,* March–April 1981, pp. 40–43. **3.** Camile Schuster and Jeffrey Danes, "Asking Questions: Some Characteristics of Successful Sales Encounters," *Journal of Personal Selling and Sales Management,* May 1986, pp. 17–28. **4.** Stephen Castleberry and C David Sheppard, "Effective Interpersonal Listening and Personal Selling," *Journal of Personal Selling and Sales Management,* 1 (Winter 1993), pp. 35–50; Om Kharbanda and Ernest Stallworthy, "A Vital Negotiating Skill," *Journal of Managerial Psychology,* 6 (1991) pp. 6–9, 49–52; Morey Stettner, "Salespeople Who Listen and What They Find Out," *Management Review,* June 1988, pp. 44–45; Kerry Johnson, "Salespeople: Are You Listening?" *Personal Selling Power,* May–June 1989, pp. 14–15; and Florence Wolff, *Perceptive Listening* (New York: Holt, Rinehart and Winston, 1983). **5.** C Barnum and N Wolniansky, "Taking Cues from Body Language," *Management Review,* June 1989, p. 59; David Stewart, Sid Hecker, and John Graham, "It's More Than What You Say: Assessing the Influence of Nonverbal Communication in Marketing," *Psychology and Marketing,* Winter 1987, pp. 302–22; and Allan Pease, *Signals: How to Use Body Language for Power, Success and Love* (New York: Bantam, 1984). **6.** Paul Ekman, *Telling Lies* (New York: Norton, 1985); and Mark Knapp and Mark Comadena, "Telling It Like It Isn't: A Review of Theory and Research on Deceptive Communications," *Human Communication Research,* April 1979, pp. 270–85. **7.** Paul Ekman and Wallace Friesen, *Unmasking the Face: A Guide to Recognizing Emotions from Facial*

Expressions, 2nd ed. (Englewood Cliffs, NJ: Prentice Hall, 1984). *8.* This section and the following section rely heavily on Gerhard Gschwandtner and Pat Garnett, *Non-Verbal Selling Power* (Englewood Cliffs, NJ: Prentice Hall, 1985). *9.* David Urban, "Neuro-Linguistic Programming Revisited: A Critical Literature Review and Its Implications for Sales," in Terry Childers et al. (eds.), *AMA Winter Educators Conference: Marketing Theory and Practice* (Chicago, IL: American Marketing Association, 1991), pp. 212–19; and Allen Konopacki, "Eye Movements Betray a Prospect's Inner Feelings," *Marketing News,* May 8, 1987, p. 4. *10.* "The Eyes Have It!" in Philip Cateora, *International Marketing,* 8th ed. (Burr Ridge, IL: Irwin, 1993), p. 555. *11.* "Some Gestures Not Necessarily A-OK Abroad," *Houston Post,* February 12, 1989, p. A34. *12.* Michael McCaskey, "The Hidden Messages Managers Send," *Harvard Business Review,* November–December 1979, p. 147. *13.* See James McElroy, Paul Morrow, and Sevo Eroglo, "The Atmospherics of Personal Selling," *Journal of Personal Selling and Sales Management,* Fall 1990, pp. 31–42; and Edward T Hall, *The Hidden Dimension* (Garden City, NY: Doubleday, 1966). *14.* S Worchel, "The Influence of Contextual Variables on Interpersonal Spacing," *Journal of Nonverbal Behavior,* May 1986, pp. 230–54. *15.* Tony Henthorne, Michael LaTour, and Alvin Williams, "Initial Impressions in the Organizational Buyer-Seller Dyad: Sales Management Implications," *Journal of Personal Selling & Sales Management,* 12 (Summer 1992), pp. 57–65; Betsy Wiesendanger, "Do You Need an Image Consultant?" *Sales & Marketing Management,* May 1992, pp. 30–33, 36; John Molloy, *New Dress for Success* (New York: Warner, 1988); and David Stevenson, "When a Sales Pitch Won't Do," *Training and Development Journal,* June 1985, pp. 18–19. *16.* John Hill, Richard Still, and Unal Boya, "Managing the Multinational Salesforce," *International Marketing Review,* 8 (1991), pp. 19–31; and Brian Flynn, "Homing In on Foreign Customer Sales," *Business Marketing,* June 1987, pp. 90–94. *17.* D Riddle and Z Lonham, "Internationalizing Written Business English: Twenty Propositions for Native English Speakers," *Journal of Language for International Business,* Spring 1985, pp. 45–48. *18. Doing Business in the New Europe* (New York: American Express and Lufthansa, 1991).

CHAPTER 6

1. For another view of sales presentations, see Marvin Jolson, "Canned Adaptiveness: A New Direction for Modern Salesmanship," *Business Horizons,* January–February 1989, pp. 7–12. *2.* James Lukaszewski and Paul Ridgeway, "To Put Your Best Foot Forward, Start by Taking These 21 Simple Steps," *Sales and Marketing Management,* June 1992, pp. 84–86. *3.* Barton Weitz, "Effectiveness in Sales Interactions: A Contingency Approach," *Journal of Marketing,* Winter 1981, pp. 83–105. *4.* "What Is the Best Advice on Selling You Have Ever Been Given?" *Sales & Marketing Management,* July 1988, p. 8. *5.* Ibid. *6.* "For Levi's, a Flattering Fit Overseas," *Business Week,* November 5, 1990, p. 76. *7.* Barton Weitz, Harish Sujan, and Mita Sujan, "Knowledge, Motivation, and Adaptive Behavior: A Framework for Improving Selling Effectiveness," *Journal of Marketing,* October 1986, pp. 174–91; Harish Sujan, Mita Sujan, and James Bettman, "Knowledge Structure Differences between Effective and Less Effective Salespeople," *Journal of Marketing Research,* February 1988, pp. 81–86; David Szymanski, "Determinants of Selling Effectiveness: The Importance of Declarative Knowledge to the Personal Selling Concept," *Journal of Marketing,* January 1988, pp. 64–77; and Leslie Fine, "Refining the Concept of Salesperson Adaptability," in Chris Allen et al. (eds.), *Marketing Theory and Applications* (Chicago, IL: American Marketing Association, 1992), pp. 42–49. *8.* Robert Trotter, "The Mystery of Mastery," *Psychology Today,* July 1986, pp. 32–38. *9.* Harish Sujan, Mita

Sujan, and Barton Weitz, "Increasing Sales Productivity by Getting Salespeople to Work Smarter," *Journal of Personal Selling and Sales Management,* August 1988, p. 15. *10.* David Merrill and Roger Reid, *Personal Styles and Effective Performance* (Radnor, PA: Chilton, 1981); and Robert Bolton and Dorothy Bolton, *Social Style/Management Style* (New York: AMACOM, 1984). *11.* A more complete version of this matrix has 16 categories, with each person having a dominant and a secondary social style. For example, President Clinton's dominant style might be analytical, but his secondary style might be amiable. Incorporating a secondary style overcomes some problems with simply classifying a person into one of the four categories. *12.* V R Buzzotta and R E Lefton, "What Makes a Sales Winner?" *Training and Development,* November 1981, pp. 70–73. *13.* Gerald Manning and Barry Reece, *Selling Today: A Personal Approach,* 4th ed. (Boston: Allyn & Bacon, 1990), pp. 100–11. *14.* Howard Stevens, "Matching Sales Skills to Customer Needs," *Management Review,* June 1989, pp. 44–47. *15.* See Paul Petach, "Picking the Pitch for the Prospect, by Computer," *Business Marketing,* October 1988, pp. 78–81; Robert Collins, "Artificial Intelligence in Personal Selling," *Journal of Personal Selling and Sales Management,* May 1984, pp. 58–66; Arlyn Rubash, Rawlie Sullivan, and Paul Herzog, "The Use of an 'Expert' to Train Salespeople," *Journal of Personal Selling and Sales Management,* August 1987, pp. 49–56; and Hubert Hennessey, "Accelerating the Salesperson Learning Curve," *Journal of Personal Selling and Sales Management,* November 1988, pp. 77–82.

CHAPTER 7

1. Office of Management and Budget, "Prompt Payment: 1989 Report to Congress," as reported in *Inc.,* July 1990, p. 95. *2.* Martin Everett, "Systems Integrators: Marketing's New Maestros," *Sales and Marketing Management,* November 1990, pp. 50–60. *3.* Porter Henry, *Secrets of the Master Sellers* (New York: AMACOM, 1978), p. 29. *4.* Neil Baum, "Secrets to Lasting Rapport," *Personal Selling Power,* March 1993, p. 55. *5.* "Response Cards Enter the Electronic Age," *Sales and Marketing Management,* April 1990, p. 27. *6.* Betty Wiesendanger, "Are Your Salespeople Trade Show Duds?" *Sales and Marketing Management,* August 1990, pp. 40–46. See also Susan Greco, "Stretching the Trade Show Budget," *Inc.,* May 1992, p. 83. *7.* See also Tom Richman, "A Seminar of One," *Inc.,* December 1991, p. 153; and Jay Finegan, "Reach Out and Teach Someone," *Inc.,* October 1990, p. 112+. *8.* Richard R. Szathmary, "What's in a List?" *Sales & Marketing Management,* October 1992, p. 114. *9.* Cyndee Miller, "North American Marketers Await Trade Pact: U.S. Companies Eager to Head South," *Marketing News* 27(10), 1993, p. 1+. *10.* For example, see Teri Lammers, "The Pacific Rim on a Shoestring," *Inc.,* June 1991, pp. 122–23. *11.* "Salespeople 'Hate' Making Cold Calls," *American Salesman,* May 1989, pp. 6–7. But not *everyone* hates them. See, for example, the story of Chuck Piola, who has made 15,000 cold calls and loves them: Jay Finegan, "King of Cold Calls," *Inc.,* June 1991, 101–7; and Melissa Campanelli, "The King of Cold Calls Goes On Call," *Sales & Marketing Management,* November 1993, p. 10. *12.* See also Susan Greco, "Using Others to Sell Your Products," *Inc.,* August 1991, p. 81. *13.* Martin Everett, "How Outsiders Can Get You Inside," *Sales & Marketing Management,* February 1990, pp. 56–57. *14.* Kenneth Schneider, "Telemarketing as a Promotional Tool: Its Effects and Side-Effects," *Journal of Consumer Marketing,* Winter 1985, pp. 29–39. *15.* Paul B Brown, "Building Sales: How to Make Every Marketing Dollar Count," *Inc.,* March 1991, pp. 98–99. See also Ernan Roman, "Integrated Direct Marketing: Managing the Mix," *Sales and Marketing Management,* May 1991, pp. 82–87. *16.* Richard Edwards, "Direct Mailing—

Making It More Effective," *American Salesman,* April 1990, pp. 16–19. **17.** Tom Richman, "A Good Name Is Hard to Find," *Inc.,* July 1991, p. 69. **18.** "A Company of Lead Generators," *Inc.,* September 1987, p. 111. See also Susan Greco, "Using Service Reps to Generate Leads," *Inc.,* May 1992, p. 141. **19.** Albert G Holzinger, "Selling in the New Europe," *Nation's Business,* December 1991, pp. 18–24. **20.** William E Gregory, Jr., "Time to Ask Hard-Nosed Questions," *Sales & Marketing Management,* October 1989, pp. 88–93. **21.** See David M Szymanski and Gilbert A Churchill, Jr., "Client Evaluation Cues: A Comparison of Successful and Unsuccessful Salespeople," *Journal of Marketing Research,* May 1990, pp. 163–74. **22.** Dennis Fox, "The Fear Factor: Why Traditional Sales Training Doesn't Always Work," *Sales and Marketing Management,* February 1992, pp. 60–64.

CHAPTER 8 **1.** Edward O Welles, "Quick Study," *Inc.,* April 1992, pp. 67–76. **2.** See Harvey Mackay, *Swim with the Sharks without Being Eaten Alive* (New York: Morrow, 1988), pp. 25–34. **3.** NEXIS is a leading source of national and international news and information for professionals and is provided by Mead Data Central, Inc., Dayton, Ohio, (800) 227-4908. **4.** "Sales Talk," *Sales & Marketing Management,* March 1990, p. 120. **5.** Madelyn R Callahan, "Tending the Sales Relationship," *Training and Development,* December 1992, p. 34. **6.** Harvey B Mackay, "The CEO Hits the Road (and other Sales Tales)," *Harvard Business Review,* March–April 1990, p. 32. **7.** Neil Rackham, *Major Account Sales Strategy* (New York: McGraw-Hill, 1989), p. 39. **8.** Porter Henry, *Secrets of the Master Sellers* (New York: AMACOM, 1987), p. 72. **9.** Jack Falvey, "Without a Goal for Every Call, a Salesperson Is Just a Well-Paid Tourist," *Sales & Marketing Management,* June 1989, p. 92. **10.** John P Kirwan, Jr., "The Precision Selling Payoff," *Sales & Marketing Management,* January 1992, pp. 59–61. **11.** Jim Hersma, personal correspondence, May 2, 1993, used with permission. **12.** I Martin Jacknis, "Multiple Choice: Why Your Salespeople Should Have Not One, but Three Objectives Every Time They Make a Call," *Inc.,* December 1987, p. 184. **13.** "Should Salespeople Go over the Heads of Purchasing Agents?" *Sales & Marketing Management,* May 1992, p. 14. **14.** Terry Booten, "How to Crack a New Account," *Executive Female,* July/August 1992, p. 18. **15.** Rackham, *Major Account Sales Strategy,* p. 39. **16.** Ibid., p. 30. **17.** Nancy J Adler, *International Dimensions of Organizational Behavior* (Boston: Kent Publishing Company, 1986), p. 33.

CHAPTER 9 **1.** Of course, many aspects of first impressions are outside the control of the salesperson. See, for example Tony L Henthorne, Michael S LaTour, and Alvin J Williams, "Initial Impressions in the Organizational Buyer-Seller Dyad: Sales Management Implications," *Journal of Personal Selling and Sales Management,* Summer 1992, pp. 57–65, which found that different first impressions were formed as a function or race and gender. **2.** Ann Marie Sabath, "When Your Salespeople Are Rough around the Edges," *Sales & Marketing Management,* February 1991, p. 88. **3.** See "Serve and Ye Shall Get," *Personal Selling Power,* March 1993, p. 40. **4.** Dale Carnegie, a noted sales training consultant, would disagree with this advice. He suggests that not to offer a handshake shows a lack of assertiveness. **5.** John R Graham, "The 'Good Old Days' Are Gone Forever: Seize the Opportunities for Change," *Personal Selling Power,* March 1993, p. 49. **6.** Ken Delmar, *Winning Moves* (New York: Warner, 1984), p. 4. **7.** Ron Zemke and Kristin Anderson, "Customers from Hell," *Training,* February 1990, pp. 25–33. **8.** Neil Rackham, *SPIN Selling* (New York: McGraw-Hill, 1988). **9.** Arthur Bragg, "Put Your

Program to the Test," *Sales and Marketing Management,* February 1990, p. 10. **10.** See Calman P Phillips, "The Not-so-Sweet Sound of Sales Talk," *Training,* September 1988, pp. 56–62. **11.** Rackham, *SPIN Selling.* **12.** Sergey Frank, "Global Networking: Vivé Les Differences!" *Sales & Marketing Management,* May 1992, p. 66. **13.** Ray Hanson, personal correspondence, used by permission. **14.** See Josh Gordon, "Making a Sales Presentation Work," *Folio,* March 1992, pp. 91–92. **15.** See Daniel A Sauers, "Limber Up Mentally before Big Sales Presentations," *Marketing News,* March 19, 1990, p. 10. **16.** Nancy J Adler, *International Dimensions of Organizational Behavior* (Boston: Kent Publishing Co., 1986), p. 55. **17.** Credibility can be influenced by many factors. For example, see John Tsalikis, Oscar W DeShields, Jr., and Michael S LaTour, "The Role of Accent on the Credibility and Effectiveness of the Salesperson," *Journal of Personal Selling and Sales Management,* Winter 1991, pp. 31–41. They found that, for an American audience, using a standard American accent resulted in more credibility than did Greek-accented English. See also Frank K Sonnenberg, "If I Had Only One Client," *Sales & Marketing Management,* November 1993, pp. 104–7. **18.** Jim Hersma, May 2, 1993, personal correspondence, used with permission. **19.** John E Swan, I Fredrick Trawick, and David W Silva, "How Industrial Salespeople Gain Customer Trust," *Industrial Marketing Management,* 1985, pp. 203–11. **20.** Richard Whiteley, "Do Selling and Quality Mix?" *Sales & Marketing Management,* October 1993, p. 70. **21.** Tracey Brill, personal correspondence, used with permission.

CHAPTER 10 **1.** See Bob Boylan, "Insuring Effective 'Re-Presentation,'" *Business Marketing,* January 1993, p. 59. **2.** See Mauri Edwards, "Now Presenting . . ." *Sales & Marketing Management,* November 1992, pp. 23–26. **3.** Pricilla C Brown, "How to Project the 'Big Picture,'" *Business Marketing,* January 1993, p. 56. **4.** Kate Bertrand, "The Presentation Sensation: Multimedia Technology Provides New Impact," *Business Marketing,* June 1992, p. 32. **5.** See Bristol Voss, "Sales Tools: A Presentation Update," *Sales & Marketing Management,* November 1992, pp. 96–97. **6.** Information from this section was gathered from a number of sources, including Mack Hanan, *Consultative Selling: The Hanan Formula for High-Margin Sales at High Levels* (New York: AMACOM, 1990). **7.** Don Wiley, "What's the Etiquette of the RFP?" *Communication News,* October 1990, p. 20. **8.** This section was developed from several sources: Stewart A Washburn, "Daniel in the Lion's Den: Selling to Groups," *Journal of Management Consulting,* Spring 1992, pp. 9–19; Steve Zurier, "Making Group Presentations Pay Off: The Goal Is to Reach Several Buying Influences at Once," *Industrial Distribution,* June 1989, p. 41; Joseph Conlin, "Teaming Up," *Sales and Marketing Management,* October 1993, pp. 98–104; and Richard G Ensman, Jr., "How To Participate in a Meeting," *Ideas,* October 1992, pp. 11–12. **9.** This section is based on information from Frank K Sonnenberg, "Presentations That Persuade," *Journal of Business Strategy,* September–October 1988, pp. 55–58; Jack Falvey, "Does Your Company Need First Aid for Its Visuals?" *Sales and Marketing Management,* July 1990, pp. 97–99; and Richard Kern, "Making Visual Aids Work for You," *Sales & Marketing Management,* February 1989, pp. 45–48.

CHAPTER 11 **1.** Richard Kern, "The Art of Overcoming Resistance," *Sales & Marketing Management,* March 1990, p. 101. **2.** Saul W Gellerman, "The Tests of a Good Salesperson," *Harvard Business Review,* May–June 1990, p. 68. **3.** See Roger M Pell, "The Road to Success Is Paved with Objections," *Bank Mar-*

keting, February 1990, pp. 16–17. **4.** Ray Schmitz, April 28, 1993, personal correspondence, used with permission. **5.** *Increase Your Selling Power* (Pittsburgh: Westinghouse Electric Corp.), sec. 3, pp. 4–5. **6.** See Paul H Schurr, Louis H Stone, and Lee Ann Beller, "Effective Selling Approaches to Buyers' Objections," *Industrial Marketing Management* 14 (1985), pp. 195–202 for a research-based approach to responding to objections. **7.** See Gordon Bethard, "Clarify the Question before You Answer It," *Agri Marketing,* January 1990, pp. 74–75. **8.** Joseph P Vaccaro and Derek W F Coward, "Managerial and Legal Issues of Price Haggling: A Sales Manager's Dilemma," *Journal of Personal Selling and Sales Management,* Summer 1993, pp. 79–86. **9.** Steve Zurier, "How to Overcome Price Objections: Salespeople Can Fight Back by Selling Value," *Industrial Distribution,* March 1990, p. 55. **10.** See Alan Cimberg, "Overcoming Price Objections," *Small Business Reports,* July 1990, pp. 2–6. **11.** Tracey Brill, personal correspondence, used with permission. **12.** See Sergey Frank, "Global Negotiating: Vivé Les Differences!" *Sales and Marketing Management,* May 1992, p. 64.

CHAPTER 12   **1.** "No More Commando Selling," *Sales & Marketing Management,* May 1986, pp. 29–30. **2.** Jack Falvey, "For the Best Close, Keep an Open Mind," *Sales & Marketing Management,* April 1990, pp. 10, 12. **3.** Tim Conner, "The New Psychology of Closing Sales," *American Salesman,* September 1987, p. 25. **4.** See, for example, Russell H Granger, "Selling, Not Closing, the Key," *National Underwriter,* April 25, 1988, pp. 67–69; and Irving Feldman, "The Pros Don't Close!" *The American Salesman,* July 1986, pp. 3–5. **5.** Neil Rackham, *Spin Selling* (New York: McGraw-Hill, 1988), pp. 19–51. **6.** Marvin A Jolson, "Selling Assertively," *Business Horizons,* September–October 1984, pp. 71–77. **7.** See Sergey Frank, "Global Negotiating: Vivé Les Differences!" *Sales & Marketing Management,* May 1992, p. 67. **8.** See Paul B Brown, "A Bird in the Hand," *Inc.,* August 1989, pp. 114–15. **9.** Harvey B Mackay, "Humanize Your Selling Strategy," *Harvard Business Review,* March–April 1988, p. 47 (emphasis added). **10.** Robert B Miller and Stephen E Heiman, "Risky Business: Knowing When to Hit the Brakes," *Sales & Marketing Management,* March 1992, pp. 44–47. **11.** Richard Kern, "A Follow-Up Program for Lost Sales," *Sales & Marketing Management,* November 1989, pp. 124–25. **12.** Ted Pollock, "Service—More Important Than Ever," *American Salesman,* September 1990, p. 26. **13.** Jay Finegan, "Stand and Deliver," *Inc.,* November 1992, p. 140. **14.** John G. Jones, *Salesmanship and Sales Management* (New York: Alexander Hamilton Institute, 1918), p. 99.

CHAPTER 13   **1.** Christopher Power, Lisa Driscoll, and Earl Bohn, "Smart Selling," *Business Week,* August 3, 1992, pp. 46–48; and Frederick F. Reichheld and Earl Sasser, "Zero Defections: Quality Comes to Services," *Harvard Business Review,* September–October 1990, pp. 105–11. **2.** William O'Connell and William Keenan, Jr., "The Shape of Things to Come," *Sales & Marketing Management,* January 1990, pp. 36–41. **3.** Tony Vavra, *Aftermarketing: How to Keep Customers for Life through Relationship Marketing* (Homewood, IL: Business One-Irwin, 1992). **4.** Jon M. Hawes, Kenneth E Mast, and John E Swan, "Trust Earning Perceptions of Sellers and Buyers," *Journal of Personal Selling and Sales Management,* Spring, 1989, pp. 1–8. **5.** "Eastman Kodak Brings Training into Sharper Focus," *Sales & Marketing Management,* September 1992, p. 62. **6.** Hawes, Mast, and Swan, "Trust Earning Perceptions," pp. 1–8. **7.** "Salespeople's Selling Skills," *American Salesman,* April 1990, pp. 10–11. **8.** "What Qualities Make Sales Representatives Valuable

to Customers? Survey Shows That Being the Customer's Advocate Is Most Important," *Agency Sales Magazine,* June 1987, pp. 34–35. **9.** James P Morgan, "How the Top Ten Measure Up," *Purchasing,* June 4, 1992, pp. 62–63. **10.** Millind Lele and Jagdish Sheth, *The Customer Is Key* (New York: John Wiley & Sons, 1987). **11.** Morgan, "How the Top Ten Measure Up," pp. 62–63. **12.** Dwight D Davis, with Bill Sharp and Mark Schlack, "Can Digital Sustain Alpha's Edge?" *Datamation,* March 1, 1993, pp. 24–31. **13.** Christopher Hoyt and Hunter Hastings, "Re-Connect with the Consumer," PROMO/Progressive Grocer Special Report, *PROMO: The International Magazine for Promotion Marketing,* December 1993, pp. 14–15. **14.** "MasterCard Program to Teach Cross-Selling," *American Banker,* January 26, 1993, p. 2. **15.** "Quality Is Key for Purchasing," *Purchasing,* January 17, 1991, p. 137. **16.** James P Morgan and Shirley Cayer, "Working with World-Class Suppliers: True Believers," *Purchasing,* August 13, 1992, pp. 50–52. **17.** Ibid. **18.** James P Morgan, "Supply Strategy: Buyer-Supplier Alliances," *Purchasing,* pp. 34B13–34B16. **19.** Jean Graham, "A Simple Idea Saves $8 Million a Year," *Purchasing,* May 21, 1992, pp. 47–49. **20.** Lisa M Ellram, "The Supplier Selection Decision in Strategic Partnerships," *Journal of Purchasing and Materials Management,* October 1990, pp. 8–14. **21.** Gilbert A Churchill, Neil M Ford, and Orville C Walker, Jr., *Sales Force Management* (Homewood, IL: Irwin, 1993). **22.** Paul Kelly, *Situational Selling* (New York: AMACOM, 1988). **23.** This section is based on Kelly, *Situational Selling;* see also John F Tanner, Jr., and Stephen B Castleberry, "The Participation Model: Factors Related to Buying Decision Participation," *Journal of Business to Business Marketing,* 1993, pp. 35–61. **24.** Kelly, *Situational Selling.* **25.** Robert Bly, *Keeping Clients Satisfied* (Englewood Cliffs, NJ: Prentice Hall, 1993). **26.** Ron Willingham, *Integrity Selling* (New York: Doubleday, 1987).

CHAPTER 14   **1.** For a complete listing of potential issues to be negotiated, see William F Morrison, *The Prenegotiation Handbook* (New York: Wiley, 1985), pp. 113–74. **2.** Sharon Nelton, "The Womanly Art of the Deal," *Nation's Business,* January 1993, p. 60. **3.** See Nancy J Adler, *International Dimensions of Organizational Behavior* (Boston: Kent Publishing Company, 1986), pp. 157–58. **4.** R J Lewicki and J A Litterer, *Negotiation* (Homewood, IL: Irwin, 1985), p. 47. **5.** See, for example, Peter J D Carnevale and Edward J. Lawler, "Time Pressure and the Development of Integrative Agreements in Bilateral Negotiations," *Journal of Conflict Resolution,* December 1986, pp. 636–59. **6.** See, for example, William A Donohue and Robert Kolt, *Managing Interpersonal Conflict* (Newbury Park, CA: Sage Publications, 1992), pp. 99–111. **7.** Fred Edmund Jandt and Paul Gillette, *Win-Win Negotiating: Turning Conflict into Agreement* (New York: Wiley, 1985). **8.** See Michael E Roloff and Jerry M Jordan, "Achieving Negotiation Goals: The 'Fruits and Foibles' of Planning Ahead," in *Communication and Negotiation,* Linden L Putnam and Michael E Roloff, eds. (Newbury Park, CA: Sage Publications, 1992), p. 35. **9.** Negotiator Pro, Beacon Expert Systems, Inc., Brookline, MA. **10.** Adler, p. 175. **11.** See Alvin L Goldman, *Settling For More: Negotiating Strategies and Techniques* (Washington, DC: BNA Books, 1991), pp. 218–27 for a complete description of bargaining teams. **12.** The information in this section was developed from Kenneth Thomas, "Conflict and Conflict Management," in *The Handbook of Industrial and Organizational Psychology,* Marvin Dunnette, ed. (Skokie, IL: Rand McNally, 1976). **13.** See William A Donohue and Closepet N Ramesh, "Negotiator-Opponent Relationships," in *Communication and Negotiation,* Linda L Putnam and Michael E Roloff, eds. (Newbury Park, CA: Sage Publications, 1992); and Naoko Oikawa and John

F Tanner, Jr., "The Influence of Japanese Culture on Business Relationships and Negotiations," *The Journal of Services Marketing,* Summer 1992, pp. 67–74. *14.* For a more complete discussion of agenda content, agenda sequence, stating the issues, etc., see Goldman, pp. 160–96. *15.* See Donohue and Kolt, p. 56; also see Roderick Macleod, *China Inc.: How to Do Business with the Chinese* (Toronto: Bantam Books, 1988), pp. 75–76. *16.* This section was developed from a number of sources, including Homer B Smith, *Selling through Negotiation: The Handbook of Sales Negotiation* (Chevy Chase, MD: Marketing Education Associates, 1987); and Gerard I Nierenberg, *The Complete Negotiator* (New York: Neirenberg & Zeif Publishers, 1986). *17.* See Roger Fisher and William Ury, *Getting to Yes: Negotiating Agreement without Giving In,* 2nd ed. (Boston: Houghton Mifflin, 1991). *18.* See Smith, *Selling through Negotiation;* and Nierenberg, *The Complete Negotiator.* *19.* Adler, p. 176. *20.* Donohue and Ramesh, "Negotiator-Opponent Relationships."

CHAPTER 15   *1.* Michael Levy and Barton A Weitz, *Retailing Management* (Homewood IL: Irwin, 1992), pp. 248–56. *2.* Janet Wagner, Richard Ettenson, and Jean Parrish, "Vendor Selection among Retail Buyers: An Analysis by Merchandise Division," *Journal of Retailing,* Spring 1989, pp. 58–79. *3.* Statistics from the Trade Show Bureau, Denver, Colorado. *4.* Wendy Hatoum, "Selling Your Soles," *Sporting Goods Dealer,* April 1993, pp. 40–42. *5.* Ibid. *6.* Michael Sansolo, "Partners vs. Profits," *PROMO: The International Magazine for Promotion Marketing,* December 1993, pp. 8–9 of a PROMO/Progressive Grocer Special Report insert. *7.* Kerry E Smith, "No Brand Too Small," *PROMO: The International Magazine for Promotion Marketing,* December 1993, pp. 4–5 of a PROMO/Progressive Grocer Special Report insert. *8.* This example is based on data presented in Christopher Hoyt and Hunter Hastings, "Re-Connect with the Consumer," *PROMO: The International Magazine for Promotion Marketing,* December 1993, pp. 14–15 of a PROMO/Progressive Grocer Special Report insert.

CHAPTER 17   *1.* Lawrence B Chonko, John F Tanner, Jr., and Ellen Reid Smith, "The Sales Force's Role in International

Marketing Research and Marketing Research Information Systems," *Journal of Personal Selling and Sales Management,* Winter 1991, pp. 69–80. *2.* Shelby D Hunt, and Arturo Vasquez-Parraga, "Organizational Consequences, Marketing Ethics, and Salesforce Supervision," *Journal of Marketing Research,* February 1993, pp. 78–90. *3.* Much of this section is based on the work of Richard P Nielsen, "What Can Managers Do about Unethical Management?" *Journal of Business Ethics,* 1987, pp. 309–20, and "Negotiating as an Ethics Action (Praxis) Strategy," *Journal of Business Ethics,* 1989, pp. 383–90. *4.* William Moncrief, Shannon H Shipp, Charles W Lamb, Jr., and David W Cravens, "Examining the Roles of Telemarketing in Sales Strategy," *Journal of Personal Selling and Sales Management,* Fall 1989, pp. 1–12.

CHAPTER 18   *1.* Eugene Johnson, "How Do Sales Managers View College Preparation for Sales?" *Journal of Personal Selling and Sales Management,* Summer 1990, pp. 69–72. *2.* John L Munschauer, "The Resume: How to Speak to Employer's Needs," *CPC Annual,* 1992–1993, pp. 27–41. *3.* Gene Garofalo and Gary Drummond, *Sales Professional's Survival Guide* (Englewood Cliffs, NJ: Prentice Hall, 1987). *4.* Ed Holton, "The Critical First Year on the Job," *CPC Annual,* 1992–1993, pp. 72–75. *5.* Susan M Keaveney and James E Nelson, "Coping with Organizational Role Stress: Intrinsic Motivational Orientation, Perceived Role Benefits, and Psychological Withdrawal," *Journal of the Academy of Marketing Science,* Spring 1993, pp. 113–15. *6.* John F Tanner, Jr., Mark G Dunn, and Lawrence B Chonko, "Vertical Exchange and Salesperson Stress," *Journal of Personal Selling and Sales Management,* Spring 1993, pp. 27–35. *7.* Ibid. *8.* Gilbert A Churchill, Jr., Neil M Ford, and Orville C Walker, Jr., *Sales Force Management,* 4th ed. (Homewood IL: Irwin, 1993). *9.* John F Tanner, Jr. and Stephen B Castleberry, "Vertical Exchange Quality and Performance: Studying the Role of the Sales Manager," *Journal of Personal Selling and Sales Management,* pp. 17–27; and Rosemary Lagace, "Leader-Member Exchange: Antecedents and Consequences of the Cadre and Hired Hand," *Journal of Personal Selling and Sales Management,* February 1990, pp. 11–19.

GLOSSARY

ABC analysis Evaluating the importance of an account; the most important is an A account, the second most important is a B account, and the least important is a C account.

accommodating mode Resolving conflict by being unassertive and highly cooperative; when using this approach, people often neglect their own needs and desires to satisfy the concerns of the other party.

account opportunity Another term for the sales potential dimensions of the sales-call allocation grid.

active listening The listener attempts to draw out as much information as possible by actively processing information received and stimulating the communication of additional information.

activity goals Behavioral objectives, such as the number of calls made in a day.

adaptive planning The development of alternative paths to the same goal in a negotiation session.

adaptive selling Approach to personal selling in which selling behaviors and approaches are altered during a sales interaction or across customer interactions, based on information about the nature of the selling situation.

administrative law Laws established by local, state, or federal regulatory agencies, such as the Federal Trade Commission or the Food and Drug Administration.

adoption process Step or steps that a person or organization goes through when making an initial purchase and then using a new product or service.

after-tax cash flows Used to evaluate a purchase, this measure ensures that the company has enough cash to pay for the purchase.

agenda Listing of what will and will not be discussed, and in what sequence, in a negotiation session.

agent Person who acts in place of his or her company. See also **manufacturers' agents.**

aggressive Sales style that controls the sales interaction but often does not gain commitment because it prejudices the customer's needs and fails to probe for information.

amiable Category in the social style matrix describing people who like cooperation and close relationships. Amiables are low on assertiveness and high on responsiveness.

analytical Category in the social style matrix describing people who emphasize facts and logic. Analyticals are low on assertiveness and responsiveness.

application form Preprinted form completed by a candidate applying for a job.

approach Method designed to get the prospect's attention and interest quickly.

articulation The production of recognizable speech.

assertive Sales manner that stresses responding to customer needs while being self-confident and positive.

assertiveness Dimension of the social style matrix assessing the degree to which people have opinions on issues and make their positions clear to others publicly.

assessment centers Central location for evaluating job candidates.

avoiding mode Resolving conflict in an unassertive and uncooperative manner. In this mode people make no attempt to resolve their own needs or the needs of others.

awareness phase The first phase in the development of buyer-seller relationship in which salespeople locate and qualify prospects, and buyers consider various sources of supply.

backdoor selling Actions by one salesperson that go behind the back of a purchaser to directly contact other members of the buying center.

balanced presentation When the salesperson shows all sides of the situation—that is, to be totally honest.

balance sheet method Attempting to obtain commitment by asking the buyer to think of the pros and cons of the various alternatives—often referred to as the Ben Franklin method.

barriers   Buyer's subordinates who plan and schedule interviews for their superiors—also called screens.

benefit   How a particular feature will help a particular buyer.

benefit approach   Approach method in which the salesperson focuses on the prospect's needs by stating a benefit of the product or service.

benefit summary method   Obtaining commitment by simply reminding the prospect of the agreed-upon benefits of the proposal.

bird dog   Individual who, for a fee, will provide the names of leads for the salesperson. Also called spotters.

blitz   Canvassing method in which a large group of salespeople attempt to make calls on all the prospective businesses in a given geographic territory on a specified day.

body language   Nonverbal signals communicated through facial expressions, arms, hands, and legs.

bonus   Lump sum incentive payment based on performance.

boomerang method   Responding to objections by turning the objection into a reason for acting now.

bottoms-up forecasting   A forecast compiled by adding each salesperson's forecast for total company sales.

bounceback card   Card returned from a lead that requests additional information.

brainstorming session   A meeting in which people are allowed to creatively explore different methods of achieving goals.

bribes   Payments made to buyers to influence their purchase decisions.

browbeating   A negotiation strategy in which buyers attempt to alter the selling team's enthusiasm and self-respect by making unflattering comments.

budget bogey   Negotiation strategy in which one side claims that the budget does not allow for the solution proposed. Also called budget limitation tactic.

budget limitation tactic   See **budget bogey.**

business defamation   Making unfair or untrue statements to customers about a competitor, its products, or its salespeople.

buy forward   Purchasing an entire year's inventory at the low price.

buyer's remorse   The insecurity that a buyer feels about whether the choice was a wise one—also called postpurchase dissonance.

buying center   Informal, cross-department group of people involved in a purchase decision.

buying community   Small, informal group of people in similar positions who communicate regularly, often both socially and professionally.

buying signals   Nonverbal cues given by the buyer that indicates the buyer may be ready to commit. Also called closing cues.

canned presentation   See **standard memorized sales presentation.**

cap   A limit placed on a salespersons earnings.

capital equipment   Major purchases made by business, such as computer systems, that are used by the business for several years in their operations or production.

category management   In selling to retailers, a current trend in the area of full-line selling.

center-of-influence method   A prospecting method where the salesperson cultivates well-known, influential people in the territory who are willing to supply lead information.

champion   Also called advocates or internal salespeople; works for the buying firm in the areas most affected by the proposed change and works with the salesperson for the success of the proposal.

change agent   A person who is a cause of change in an organization.

circular routing   Method of scheduling sales calls that involves circular patterns.

closed questions   Questions that require the prospect to simply answer yes or no or to offer a short fill-in-the-blank type of response.

closing   Common term for obtaining commitment, which usually refers only to asking for the buyer's business.

closing cues   See **buying signals.**

cloverleaf   Method for scheduling sales calls that involves using loops to cover different portions of the territory on different days or weeks; on a map it should resemble a cloverleaf.

cold calls   See **cold canvass method.**

cold canvass method   A prospecting method in which a sales representative tries to generate leads for new business by calling on totally unfamiliar organizations; also called cold calls.

collaborating mode   Resolving conflict by seeking to maximize the satisfaction of both parties and hence truly reach a win-win solution.

collusion   Agreement between competitors, made after contacting customers, concerning their relationships with customers.

combination plan   This plan provides salary and commission, and offers the greatest flexibility for motivating and controlling the activities of salespeople.

commission base   Unit of analysis used to determine commissions; for example, unit sales, dollar sales, or gross margin.

commission rate   Percent of base paid or the amount per base unit paid in a commission compensation plan; for example, a percentage of dollar sales or an amount per unit sold.

commitment phase   The fourth stage in the development of buyer-seller relationship in which the buyer and seller have implicitly or explicitly pledged to continue the relationship for an extended time period.

common law   Legal precedents that arise out of court decisions.

compensation method   Method used to respond helpfully to objections by agreeing that the objection is valid, but then proceeding to show any compensating advantages.

competence   The buyer's perception that the salesperson knows what he or she is talking about.

competing mode   Resolving conflict in an assertive and noncooperative manner.

complacency   Assuming that the business is yours and will always be yours.

compliment approach   Approach in which the salesperson begins the sales call by complimenting the buyer in some fashion.

compromising mode   Resolving conflict by being somewhat cooperative and somewhat assertive. People using this approach attempt to find a quick, mutually acceptable solution that partially satisfies both parties.

concession   When one party in a negotiation meeting agrees to change their position in some fashion.

consequence questions   Questions that illustrate the consequences of a disadvantage in a competitor's product.

conspiracy   An agreement between competitors, made prior to contacting customers, concerning their relationships with customers.

consultative selling philosophy   Form of customized presentation in which salespeople identify the prospect's needs and then recommend the best solution, even when the best solution does not include the salesperson's own products or services.

contract to sell   An offer made by a salesperson that received an unqualified acceptance by a buyer.

conversion goals   Measures of salesperson efficiency.

conversion rate   Similar to a batting average, it is calculated by dividing performance results by activity results; for example, dividing the number of sales by the number of calls.

coop advertising   Advertising paid for by both retailer and manufacturer, often with some assistance in preparing the ad from the manufacturer.

corporate culture   The values and beliefs held by a company and expressed by senior management.

coupon clippers   People who like to send off for product information even though they have no intention of ever buying the product or service.

credibility   The characteristic of being perceived by the buyer as believable and reliable.

credible commitments   Tangible investments in a relationship that indicate commitment to the relationship.

creeping commitment   Purchase decision process that arises when decisions made early in the process have significant influence on decisions made later in the process.

cross-selling   Similar to full-line selling, except that the additional products sold are not directly associated with the initial products.

cumulative discounts   Quantity discounts for purchases over a period of time. The buyer is allowed to add up all the purchases to determine the total quantity and the total quantity discount.

curiosity approach   The salesperson arouses interest by making an unexpected comment that piques the prospect's curiosity.

customer intentions survey   Method of forecasting sales. Customers are asked how much they intend to buy over the forecasting period.

customer orientation   Selling approach based on keeping the customer's interests paramount.

customer service rep   In-bound salespeople that handle customer concerns.

customized presentation   Presentation developed from a detailed and comprehensive analysis or survey of the prospect's needs that is not canned or memorized in any fashion.

deal   Promotional discount offered by a manufacturer to a retailer, often, but not always, in exchange for featuring a product in a newspaper ad and/or a special display.

deception Unethical practice of withholding information or telling "white lies."

deciders Buying center members who make the final selection of the product to purchase.

decoding Communication activity undertaken by a receiver interpreting the meaning of the received message.

deferred dating Scheduling payment of a bill at a later (deferred) date. Often done by the manufacturer to allow a reseller time to sell the product in order to generate the cash needed to pay for it.

dependability The buyer's perception that the salesperson will live up to promises made; is not something a salesperson can demonstrate immediately.

derived demand Situation in which the demand for a producer's goods are based on what its customers sell.

diagnostic feedback Information given to a salesperson indicating how he or she is performing.

direct denial Method of answering objections in which the salesperson makes a relatively strong statement indicating the error the prospect has made.

direct request method Attaining commitment by simply asking for one in a straightforward statement.

disadvantage questions Questions that ask a customer to articulate a specific problem.

disguised interview Discussion between an applicant and an interviewer in which the applicant is unaware that the interviewer is evaluating the applicant for the position.

distribution channel Set of people and organizations responsible for the flow of products and services from the producer to the ultimate user.

dormant accounts Accounts that have not purchased for a specified time.

double-barrelled questions A question that actually asks more than one question at the same time.

draw Advance from the company to a salesperson made against future commissions.

driver Category in the social style matrix describing task-oriented people who are high on assertiveness and low on responsiveness.

efficient customer response (ECR) Distribution systems that drive inventory to the lowest possible levels, increase the frequency of shipping, and automate ordering and inventory control processes without the problems of stockouts and higher costs.

elaboration questions Questions that are positive requests for additional information, rather than simply verbal encouragements.

electronic mail Method of sending correspondence from one computer to another.

emotional outburst tactic A negotiation strategy in which one party attempts to gain concessions by resorting to a display of strong emotion.

encoding Communication activity undertaken by a sender translating his or her thought into a message.

encouragement probes Questions or nonverbal signals that encourage customers to reveal further information.

endless-chain method A prospecting method whereby a sales representative attempts to get at least one additional lead from each person he or she interviews.

end users Businesses that purchase goods and services to support their own production and operations.

ethics Principles governing the behavior of an individual or group.

ethics review boards May consist of experts inside and outside the company who are responsible for reviewing ethics policies, investigating allegations of unethical behavior, and acting as a sounding board for employees.

evaluative feedback Information to a salesperson indicating how he or she is performing.

excuses Concerns expressed by the buyer that are intended to mask the buyer's true objections.

executive summary In a written proposal, this is a one page or less summary that describes the total cost minus total savings, a brief description of the problem to be solved, and a brief description of the proposed solution.

expansion phase The third phase in the development of a relationship in which it makes a significant effort to share information and further investigate the potential relationship benefits.

expense budget An expense budget may be expressed in dollars or as a percentage of sales volume.

expert opinions Method of forecasting sales that involves averaging the estimates of several experts.

expert systems Computer program that mimics a human expert.

exploration phase The second phase in the development of a relationship in which both buyers and sellers explore the potential benefits and costs associated with the relationship.

expressed warranty   Warranty specified through oral or written communications.

expressive   Category in the social style matrix describing people who are both competitive and approachable. They are high on assertiveness and responsiveness.

extrinsic orientation   An orientation of salespeople characterized by viewing their job as a way of achieving rewards, such as compensation given to them by others.

face   A person's desire for a positive identity or self-concept.

factual questions   Questions that ask for factual information and usually start with one of the following five words: who, what, where, how, and why.

fax   Short for facsimile; an electronic document transfer device.

feature   A quality or characteristic of the product or service.

feature   Putting a product on sale, with a special display and featuring the product in advertising.

FEB   Stands for Feature, Evidence, Benefit; technique useful in interviewing.

feedback   See **diagnostic feedback** and **evaluative feedback.**

feel-felt-found method   Method of helpfully responding to objections in which salespersons show how others held similar views before trying the product or service.

field sales manager   First-level manager.

field salespeople   Salespeople who spend considerable time in the customer's place of business, communicating with the customer face-to-face.

field support rep   A telemarketer that works with field salespeople, and does more than prospect for leads.

FOB (free on board)   Term used to designate the point at which responsibility shifts from seller to buyer.

FOB (free on board) destination   Terms of a contract indicating the seller has title until the goods are received at the destination.

FOB (free on board) factory   Terms of a contract indicating the buyer has title when the goods leave the seller's facility.

follow up   What a salesperson does after commitment is achieved.

Foreign Corrupt Practices Act   A law that governs the behavior of US business in foreign countries restricting the bribing of foreign officials.

forestall   When salespeople resolve objections before buyers have a chance to raise them.

FSI (free-standing insert)   Advertisement that is printed separately, then inserted in a newspaper.

full-line selling   Selling the entire line of associated products.

functional relationship   A series of market exchanges between a buyer and seller, linked together over time. These relationships are characterized as win-lose relationships.

gatekeepers   Buying center members who influence the buying process by controlling the flow of information and/or limiting the alternatives considered.

geographic salesperson   Salesperson assigned a specific geographic territory in which to sell all the company's products and services.

global accounts manager   Sales executive responsible for coordinating sales efforts for one account globally.

good guy–bad guy routine   A negotiation strategy in which one team member acts as the good guy while another team member acts as the bad guy. The goal of the strategy is to have the opposing team accept the good guy's proposal to avoid the consequences of the bad guy's proposal.

goodwill   Value of the feelings or attitudes customers or prospects have toward a company and its products.

greeter   Interviewer in a lobby who greets the applicant and may conduct a disguised interview.

gross margin quota   Are minimum levels of acceptable profit or gross margin performance.

guaranteed prices   Prices guaranteed to be the lowest. If prices fall, the buyer is refunded the difference between the original and the new price for any inventory still in stock.

halo effect   How and what you do in one thing changes a person's perceptions about other things you do.

honesty   Both truthfulness and sincerity. Highly related to dependability. Related to how candid a salesperson is.

house accounts   Accounts assigned to a sales executive, not the specific salesperson responsible for the territory containing the account.

implication questions   Questions that logically follow one or more problem questions (in SPIN). These are designed to help the prospect recognize the true ramifications of the problem.

implied warranty   Warranty that is not expressly stated through oral or written communication but is still an obligation defined by law.

impression management   Activities that salespeople engage in to affect and manage the buyer's impression of them.

inbound telemarketing   Use of the telephone, usually with an 800 number, that allows leads and/or customers to call for additional information or to place an order.

incentive pay   Compensation based on performance.

indirect denial   Method used to respond to objections in which the salesperson denies the objection but attempts to soften the response by first agreeing with the prospect that the objection is an important one.

inflection   Tone of voice.

influencers   Buying center members inside or outside an organization who directly or indirectly influence the buying process.

influential adversaries   Individuals in the buyer's organization who carry great influence and are opposed to the salesperson's product or service.

inside salespeople   Salespeople who work at their employer's location and interact with customers by telephone or letter.

internal selling   A communication process by which salespeople influence other employees in their firms to support their sales efforts with customers.

intrinsic motivation   Motivation stimulated by the rewards salespeople get from simply doing their job.

intrinsic orientation   An orientation of salespeople characterized by seeking rewards from simply doing their jobs well.

introduction approach   Approach method in which salespeople simply state their name and the name of their company.

inventory turnover   Measure of how efficiently a retailer manages inventory, calculated by dividing net sales by inventory.

invitation to negotiate   The initiation of an interaction, usually a sales presentation, which results in an offer.

job descriptions   Formal written descriptions of the duties and responsibilities of a job.

just-in-time (JIT) inventory control   A planning systems for reducing inventory by having frequent deliveries planned just in time for the delivered products to be assembled into the final product.

key accounts   Large accounts, usually generating more than a specified amount in revenue per year, that receive special treatment.

kickbacks   Payments made to buyers based on the amount of orders they place for a salesperson's products or services.

lead   A potential prospect; a person or organization that might have the characteristics of a true prospect.

leapfrog routing   Method of scheduling calls that requires the identification of clusters of customers; visiting on these clusters and "leaping" over single sparsely located accounts should minimize travel time from the sales office to customers.

life cycle costing   Method for determining the cost of equipment or supplier over its useful life.

likeability   Behaving in a friendly manner and finding a common ground between the buyer and seller.

list price   Quoted or published price in a manufacturer's catalog or price list, from which buyers may receive discounts.

lowballing   Negotiation strategy in which one party voices agreement and then raises the cost of that agreement in some way.

lubrication   Small sums of money or gifts, typically paid to officials in foreign countries, to get the officials to do their job more rapidly.

magic eraser   See **probing method.**

major sales   Sale that involves a long selling cycle, a large customer commitment, an ongoing relationship, and large risks for the buyer if a bad decision is made.

manufacturers' agents   Independent businesspeople who are paid a commission by a manufacturer for all products and services they sell.

market analysis   Method of developing sales strategies by looking for patterns among customers in their needs and methods of purchasing.

market exchange   A relationship that involves a short-term transaction between a buyer and seller who do not expect to be involved in future transactions with each other.

marketing concept Business philosophy emphasizing that the key to business success is determining the needs and wants of customers and satisfying these needs and wants more effectively than competitors.

marketing era A business era, from 1960 to 1990, in which firms focused on practicing the marketing concept. In this era, salespeople were responsible for employing all the firm's resources to uncover and satisfy their customers' needs.

marketing mix Elements used by firms to market their offering—product, price, place (distribution), and promotion. Personal selling is part of the promotion element.

markets Mall where manufacturers show and sell products to retailers. Also, a short period of time when manufacturers gather to sell products to retailers.

market share Percentage of total market sales that is accounted for by one product or total product category sales divided by brand sales.

material requirement planning (MRP) Planning system for reducing inventory levels by forecasting sales, developing a production schedule, and ordering parts and raw materials with specific delivery dates.

mini-max strategy Approach used to set negotiation objectives that help the sellers understand and prepare for the trade-offs that will occur in the negotiation session.

minimum call objective Minimum that a salesperson hopes to accomplish in an upcoming sales call.

minimum position Negotiation objective that states the absolute minimum level the team is willing to accept.

missionary salespeople Salespeople who work for a manufacturer and promote the manufacturer's products to other firms. But those firms buy products from distributors or other manufacturers, not directly with the salesperson's firms.

modified rebuy Purchase decision process associated with a customer who has purchased the product or service in the past but is interested in obtaining additional information.

MRO supplies Minor purchases made by businesses for maintenance and repairs, such as towels and pencils.

MRP See **material requirement planning.**

multiattribute model Model describing how information about a product's performance on various dimensions is used to make an overall evaluation of the product.

multilevel selling Strategy that involves using multiple levels of company employees to call on similar levels in an account; for example, the VP of sales might call on the VP of purchasing.

multiple-sense appeals Appealing to as many of the senses (hearing, sight, touch, taste, and smell) as possible.

national accounts Prospects or customers that are covered by single, national sales strategy; may be a house account.

national accounts manager Sales executive responsible for managing and coordinating sales efforts on a single account nationwide.

need payoff questions Questions that ask about the usefulness of solving the problem.

needs-satisfaction philosophy Form of customized presentation in which the prospect's unique needs are identified and then the salesperson shows how his product or service can meet those needs.

negotiation Decision-making process through which buyers and sellers resolve areas of conflict and arrive at agreements.

negotiation jujitsu Negotiation response in which the attacked person or team steps away from the opponent's attack and then directs the opponent back to the issues being discussed.

net present value (NPV) The investment minus the net value today of future cash inflow (i.e., discounted back to their present value today at the firm's cost of capital).

net price Price buyers pay after all discounts and allowances are subtracted.

net profit margin The profit on the product, expressed as a percentage of sales.

net sales Total sales minus returns.

new task Purchase decision process associated with the initial purchase of a product or service.

nibbling Negotiation strategy in which the buyer requests a small extra or add-on after the deal has been closed. When compared with lowballing, a nibble is a much smaller request.

niche Small portion of the overall market, preferably one in which the salesperson can be successful.

noise Sounds unrelated to the message being exchanged between a salesperson and a customer.

nonverbal communications Nonspoken forms of expression—body language, space, and appearance—that communicate thoughts and emotions.

objection   Concern or question raised by the buyer.

OEM (original equipment manufacturer)   Business that purchases goods (components, subassemblies, raw and processed materials) to incorporate into products they manufacture.

offer   A specific statement by a seller outlining what the seller will provide and what is expected from the buyer.

office scanning   An activity in which the salesperson looks around the prospect's environment for relevant topics to talk about.

open-door policy   General management technique that allows subordinates to by-pass immediate managers and take concerns straight to upper management when the subordinates feel a lack of support from the immediate manager.

open questions   Questions which require the prospect to go beyond a simple yes/no response.

opinion questions   Questions that ask for a customer's feelings on a subject.

opportunity cost   The return a buyer would have earned from a different use of the same investment capital.

original equipment manufacturer   See **OEM.**

outbound telemarketing   Using the telephone to generate and qualify leads to determine whether they are truly prospects or not. Also used to secure orders and provide customer contact.

outlined presentation   Systematically arranged presentation that outlines the most important sales points. Often includes the necessary steps for determining the prospect's needs and for building goodwill at the close of the sale.

panel interview   Job interview conducted by more than one person.

partnering era   A business era, beginning in 1990, in which firms focus on developing long-term mutually beneficial relationships with their customers. The role of salespeople in this era is to work with customers and their firm to develop solutions to problems that benefit both companies.

partnership   Ongoing, mutually beneficial relationship between a buyer and a seller.

participative leadership   Style of leadership that allows followers to make a contribution to decision making.

pass-up method   Responding to an objection by letting the buyer talk, acknowledging that you heard the

concern, and then moving on to another topic without trying to resolve the concern.

payback period   Length of time it takes for the investment cash outflows to be returned in the form of cash inflows or savings.

performance goals   Goals relating to outcomes, such as revenue.

personal selling   Interpersonal communication process in which a seller uncovers and satisfies the needs of a buyer to the mutual, long-term benefit of both parties.

pioneer selling   Selling a new and different product, service, or idea. In these situations it is usually more difficult for the salesperson to establish a need in the buyer's mind.

PM (push money)   See **push money** and **spiffs.**

portfolio   Collection of visual aids that can be used to enhance communication during a sales call.

postcard pack   Cards that provide targeted information from a number of firms. This pack is mailed to prospective buyers.

postpone method   Objection-response technique in which the salesperson asks permission to answer the question at a later time.

postpurchase dissonance   See **buyer's remorse.**

preferred supplier   The supplier is assured a large percentage of the buyer's business and will get the first opportunity to earn new business.

price discrimination   Situation in which a seller gives unjustified special prices, discounts, or special services to some customers and not to others.

primary call objective   Actual goal that the salesperson hopes to achieve in an upcoming sales call.

prime selling time   Time of day that a salesperson is most likely to be able to see a customer.

probing method   Method to obtain commitment in which the salesperson initially uses the direct request method, and if unsuccessful uses a series of probing questions designed to discover the reason for the hesitation.

problem questions   Questions about specific difficulties, problems, or dissatisfactions that the prospect has.

product approach   Approach in which the salesperson actually demonstrates the product features and benefits as soon as he or she walks up to the prospect.

production era   A business era, prior to 1930, in which firms focused on making products with little concern for buyers' needs and developing products to satisfy those needs. The role of salespeople in this era was taking orders.

productivity goals   Objective concerning how efficiently a salesperson works, such as sales per call. Efficiency measures indicate an output divided by an input.

professional   Someone who engages in an occupation requiring great skill or knowledge and whose capabilities are respected by co-workers.

profit quota   Minimum levels of acceptable profit or gross margin performance.

prospect   A lead that is a good candidate for making a sale.

prospecting   The process of locating potential customers for a product or service.

puffery   Exaggerated statements about the performance of products or services.

pull   Marketing strategy designed to stimulate demand among consumers.

push   Marketing strategy designed to stimulate sales efforts by the manufacturer's salespeople and/or the resellers.

push money (PM)   Money paid directly to the retailer's salespeople by the manufacturer for selling the manufacturer's product.

qualifying a lead   The process of determining if a lead is in fact a prospect.

quantifying the solution   Showing the prospect that the cost of the proposal is offset by added value.

question approach   Beginning the conversation with a question or stating an interesting fact in the form of a question.

quick response   Minimizing order quantities to the lowest level possible while increasing the speed of delivery in order to drive inventory turnover; accomplished by prepackaging certain combinations of products.

quota   Quantitative level of performance for a specific time period.

rapport   A close, harmonious relationship founded on mutual trust.

reciprocity   Special relationship in which two companies agree to buy products from each other.

references   People who know an applicant for a sales position and can provide information about that applicant to the hiring company.

referral approach   Approach in which the name of a satisfied customer or friend of the prospect is used at the beginning of a sales call.

referred lead   Name of a lead provided by either a customer or a prospect of the salesperson.

reflective probes   Neutral statements that reaffirm or repeat a customer's comment or emotion, allowing the salesperson to dig deeper and stimulate customers to continue their thoughts in a logical manner.

relational partnership   Long-term business relationship in which the buyer and seller have a close trusting relationship, but have not made significant investments in the relationship. These relationships are characterized as win-win relationships.

relationship behaviors   Actions taken by a manager to deal with a subordinate's feelings and welfare, to develop support, or build the salesperson's self-confidence or commitment to the job or organization.

relationship manager   The role of salespeople in the partnering era to manage their firms' resources to develop win-win relationships with customers.

request for proposal   See **RFP.**

resale price maintenance   Contractual term in which a producer establishes a minimum price below which distributors or retailers cannot sell their products.

resellers   Businesses, typically distributors and retailers, that purchase products for resale.

responsiveness   The degree to which people react emotionally when they are in social situations. One of the two dimensions in the social style matrix.

retail salespeople   Salespeople who sell to customers who come into a store.

return on investment (ROI)   Net profits (or savings) expected from a given investment, expressed as a percentage of the investment.

revenue quota   The minimum amount of sales revenue necessary for acceptable performance.

RFP (request for proposals)   An RFP is issued by a potential buyer desiring bids from several potential vendors for a product. RFPs often include specifications for the product, desired payment terms, and other information helpful to the bidder. Also called request for bids or request for quotes.

role clarity   Degree to which a salesperson understands the job and what is required to perform it.

routine call patterns   Method of scheduling calls used when the same customers are seen regularly.

routing   Method of scheduling sales calls in order to minimize travel time.

salary   Compensation paid periodically to an employee, independent of performance.

sale   The transfer of title to goods and services by the seller to the buyer in exchange for money.

sales-call allocation grid   Grid used to determine account strategy; the dimensions are the strength of the company's positions with the account and the account's sales potential.

sales era   A business era, from 1930 to 1960, in which firms focused on increasing demand for the products they produced. The role of salespeople in this era was persuading customers to buy products using high-press selling techniques.

sales quota   The minimum number of sales in units.

screens   See **barriers.**

selective perception   When we hear what we want to hear, not necessarily what the other person is saying.

selling   See **personal selling.**

selling history   How well a product or product-line sold during the same season in the previous year.

sexual harassment   Unwelcome sexual advances, requests for sexual favors, and other verbal (jokes and graffiti) and physical contact.

simple cost-benefit analysis   A simple listing of the costs and savings that a buyer can expect from an investment.

situation questions   General data-gathering questions about background and current facts that are very broad in nature.

small talk   Talk about current news, hobbies, and the like that usually breaks the ice for the actual presentation.

social style matrix   Method for classifying customers based on their preferred communication style. The two dimensions used to classify customers are assertiveness and responsiveness.

soft savings   The value of offset costs and productivity gains.

speaking-listening difference   The difference between the 120- to 160-words-per-minute rate of speaking versus the 800-words-per-minute rate of listening.

spiffs   Payments made by a producer to a reseller's salespeople to motivate the salespeople to sell the producer's products or services.

SPIN   Logical sequence of questions in which the needs of a prospect are identified. The sequence is: situation questions, problem questions, implication questions, and need payoff questions.

spotters   See **bird dog.**

standard memorized sales presentation   Carefully prepared sales story that includes all the key selling points arranged in the most effective order; often called a canned sales presentation.

statutory laws   Laws based on legislation passed by either state legislatures or Congress.

straight commission   Pays a certain amount per sale, and the plan includes a base and a rate but does not include a salary.

straight-line routing   Method of scheduling sales calls involving straight-line patterns.

straight rebuy   Purchase decision process involving a customer with considerable knowledge gained from having purchased the product or service a number of times.

strategic partnership   Long-term business relationship in which the buyer and seller have made significant investments to improve the profitability of both parties in the relationship. These relationships are characterized as win-win relationships.

strategic profit model   Mathematical formula used to examine the impact of strategic decisions on profit and return on investment.

strength of position   Dimension of the sales call allocation grid that considers the seller's strength in landing sales at an account.

stress interview   Any interview that subjects an applicant to significant stress; the purpose is to determine how the applicant handles stress.

submissive   Selling style of certain salespeople, often excellent socializers, who like to spend a lot of time talking about nonbusiness activities. These people are usually reluctant to attempt to obtain commitment.

subordination   Payment of large sums of money to officials to get them to do something that is illegal.

suggested retail price   Price for which the manufacturer suggests the store retail the product.

systems integrators   Outside vendors who have been delegated the responsibility for purchasing. These vendors have the authority to buy products and services from others.

target position   Negotiation objective that states what the team hopes to achieve by the time the session is completed.

task behaviors   Actions taken by a manager to enable a subordinate to complete a task.

team selling   Employees with varying areas of expertise within the firm work together to sell to the same account(s).

telemarketing   Systematic and continuous program of communicating with customers and prospects via telephone and/or other person-to-person electronic media.

testimonials   Statements, usually in the form of letters, written by satisfied customers about a product or service.

tests   Personality or skills assessments used in assessing the match between a position's requirements and an applicant's personality or skills.

total quality management (TQM)   A set of programs and policies designed to meet customer needs by delivering defect-free products when customers want them, 100 percent of the time.

TQM   See **total quality management.**

trade   All members of the channel of distribution that resell the product between the manufacturer and the user.

trade discounts   Usually expressed as a percentage, trade discounts are used when the price is quoted to reseller in terms of a percentage off the suggested retail price.

trade fairs   The European term for trade shows.

trade promotions   Promotions aimed at securing retailer support for a product.

trade salespeople   Salespeople selling to firms that resell the products rather than using them within their own firms.

trade shows   Short exhibitions of products by manufacturers and distributors.

trial close   Questions the salesperson asks in order to take the pulse of the situation throughout a presentation.

trust   A firm belief or confidence in the honesty, integrity, and reliability of another person.

turnaround   Amount of time to respond to a customer request or deliver a customer's order.

turn over (TO)   When an account is given to another salesperson because the buyer refuses to deal with the current salesperson.

turnover   How quickly a product sells, calculated by dividing net sales by average inventory.

two-way communication   Interpersonal communications in which both parties act as senders and receivers. Salespeople send messages to customers and receive feedback from them. Customers send messages to salespeople and receive responses.

tying agreement   Agreement between a buyer and a seller in which the buyer is required to purchase one product in order to get another.

Uniform Commercial Code (UCC)   Legal guide to commercial practice in the United States.

upgrading   Convincing the customer to use a higher quality product or the newer product.

users   Members of a buying center that ultimately will use the product purchased.

value analysis   Problem-solving approach for reducing the cost of a product, while still providing the same level of performance.

variable call patterns   These occur when the salesperson must call on different accounts.

variable routing   Method of scheduling sales calls used when customers are not visited on a cyclical or regular basis.

vendor   A supplier.

vendor loyalty   A buyer becomes committed to a specific supplier because of the supplier's superior performance.

verbal communications   Communications involving the transmission of words either in face-to-face communications, over the telephone, or through written messages.

versatility   A characteristic of people, associated with the social style matrix, who increase the productivity of social relationships by adjusting to the needs of the other party.

visionary call objective   The most optimistic goal that the salesperson thinks would be possible to achieve in an upcoming sales call.

voice characteristics   The rate of speech, loudness, pitch, quality, and articulation of a person's voice.

warranty   Assurance by the seller that the goods will perform as represented.

willingness   Salesperson's desire and commitment to accomplish an objective or task.

win-lose negotiating   Negotiating philosophy in which the negotiator attempts to win all the important concessions and thus triumph over his or her opponent.

win-win negotiating   Negotiating philosophy in which the negotiator attempts to secure an agreement that completely satisfies both parties.

word picture   Story or scenario designed to help the buyer visualize a point.

zoning   Method of scheduling calls that divides a territory into areas called zones. Calls are made in a zone for a specified length of time, then made in another zone for the same amount of time.

INDEXES

COMPANY INDEX

Name and Subject Index

Moriarity, Rowland, N3
Morris, Dick, 96
Morris, Michael H., 555
Morrison, William F., 447, N6
Morrow, Paula C., 285, N4
Motivation, sales success and, 23
MRO supplies, 93, 102
Mullich, Joe, 319
Multiattribute model, 106-7
    customer purchase decisions and, 111
Multilevel selling, 547
Multiple-sense appeals, 290
Mulvey, Al, 115
Munn, John, 529
Munschauer, John L., N7
Munson, J. Michael, 286
Murphy, Patrick, 87
Murphy's Law, 303
Murray, Jim, 581
Murray, Tom, 214n, 230
Mutual gain, in relationships, 46-47
Mutual trust
    definition of, 43-44
    developing trust and, 45

NAFTA (North American Free Trade Agreement), 216
Narus, James, 56
National account manager (NAM), 116, 543-44
National accounts, 207
National Association of Purchasing Management, The (NAPM), 115
Naumann, Earl, N3
Need payoff questions, 270
Needs, buying center members', 112-13
Needs, prospect's, 203-4
    asking open/closed questions and, 267-68
    identifying, 266-72
    reiterating needs, 270-71
    strategy for, 272
    using SPIN technique and, 268-70
Negotiation
    areas of, 423-24
    defined, 422
    versus nonnegotiation selling, 422-23
    traits for, 424-25
Negotiation jujitsu, 440
Negotiation meeting
    browbeating, 439-40
    budget limiting tactic, 439
    emotional outbursts and, 438-39
    general guidelines for, 435-36
    good guy-bad guy routine, 437
    lowballing and, 437-38
    making concessions, 440-41
    preliminaries for, 434-35
    successful approach to, 441-42
    win-lose negotiators and, 436-40
Negotiation session, 425-26
    behavior patterns and, 432-34
    information control, 434
    location of, 426
    objectives of, 426-30
    team selection/management of, 430-32
    time allocation for, 426
Negotiation team, 430-31
Neill, Mark, 120
Nelson, James E., N7
Nelton, Sharon, N6

Nerenberg, Gerald, 165
Net present value (NPV), 307
Net price, 464
Net profit margin, 455
Net sales, 454-55
New task, 101
New York State Industrial Directory, 214
Newzell, Bob, 279n
NEXIS, 238
Nibbling, 438
Niches, 501
Nickels, William G., 137n
Nielsen, Richard P., N7
Nielson's Retail Index, 462
Nierenberg, Gerard I., N7
Noise, defined, 132
Nolan, Johannah, N1
Nonverbal communication, 146-47
    appearance and, 155-58
    body language and, 148-50
    space and physical contact, 154-55
Nonverbal cues, 275-76
    buyer's commitment and, 359
Noori, A. Hamid, N2
Notarantonio, Elaine, 165

Objections
    additional objections, 331-32
    to appointment times, 322
    change of established routine, 324-26
    defined, 322
    dislike of company, 326-27
    dislike of salesperson, 327-28
    lack of interest, 326
    lack of money, 328
    lack of sufficient information, 324
    lack of understanding, 326-27
    need for more time, 330-31
    no need for product/services, 323
    to obtaining commitment, 322-23
    post-sale objections, 323
    during presentation, 322
    price objection, 345-48
    product lacks value for cost, 328-30
    quality is low, 344
Objections, responding to
    anticipation and, 334
    applying methods, 344-45
    boomerang method, 341-42
    compensation method, 340
    developing positive attitude, 332-34
    direct denial, 338-39
    effective methods for, 337-38
    evaluating objections, 336
    feel-felt-found method, 340-41
    forestalling known concerns, 335-36
    indirect denial, 339
    pass-up method, 342-43
    postpone method, 343-44
    relaxed, receptive attitude and, 334-35
Obligations and performance (UCC), 74
O'Connell, William, N6
Offer, defined under UCC, 73
Office scanning, 264
Oh, Sejo, N1
O'Hara, Bradley S., 252
Oikawa, Naoko, N6
Olshavsky, Richard, 197
Olson, Eric, 32
O'Neil, Shaquille, 175
One-way information flow, 131-32

Onkvisit, Sak, N2
Open-door policy, 537
Open-ended questions, 138-39
Opening position, 426
Open questions, 267
Opportunity cost, 307-8
Oral versus written agreement, 73-74
Order processing, 390-91
Organizational buying/selling, 95-97
    buying decisions, 100-103
    complexity of buying process, 95-97
    steps in buying process, 97-100
Organizational buying trends, 114
    centralized purchasing, 115-16
    global sourcing, 119
    JIT systems and, 116-18
    life-cycle costing, 118-19
    long-term relationships, 119-20
    purchasing agent's importance and, 115
    total quality management and, 116
    value analysis and, 118
Organizational structure and culture, 47
Original equipment manufacturers (OEM), 92-93
Osborn, Albert, 120
Out-bound, defined, 545
Outbound telemarketing, 217
Outlined presentation, 168-69

Paduch, John, 407
Panel interviews, 578
Paperwork and reports, 509-10
    using computer for, 512-13
Parasuraman, A., 520
Partnering era, 12-14
    selling in, 52-54
Partnerships; *see also* Internal partnerships; Relationships
    avoiding common problems, 411-12
    building trust and, 386
    change agents and, 407-11
    commitment to, 404-7
    competence and, 387
    corporate culture and, 406-7
    cross-selling and, 402-3
    customer orientation and, 388
    customer satisfaction and, 398
    dependability and, 386-87
    expansion of relationship, 399
    exploration stage, 389
    generating repeat orders, 399-401
    handling customer complaints, 392-98
    honesty and, 388
    likability and, 388
    model for building, 1
    monitoring order processing, 390-91
    setting expectations and, 389
    start-up assistance, 391
    TQM and, 403-4
    with the trade, 476-78
    upgrading and, 402
    value of customers and, 384-85
Pass-up method, 342-43
Patterson, Paul, 126
Patton, Wesley, N3
Payback period, 306-7
Pease, Allan, N3
Pell, Roger M., N5
Penney, James Cash, 38
Perdue, Barbara C., 447